THE DENG XIAOPING ERA

THE DENG XIAOPING ERA

AN INQUIRY

INTO THE FATE OF

CHINESE SOCIALISM,

1978-1994

MAURICE MEISNER

HILL AND WANG

NEW YORK

Published simultaneously in Canada by HarperCollins*CanadaLtd*
Printed in the United States of America
Designed by Abby Kagan
First edition, 1996
Library of Congress Cataloging in Publication Data
Meisner, Maurice J.
The Deng Xiaoping era : an inquiry into the fate of Chinese
socialism, 1978–1994 / Maurice Meisner.
p.   cm.
Includes index.
1. China—Politics and government—1976–   2. Teng, Hsiao-p' ing,
1904–   3. Socialism—China. 4. China—Economic conditions—1976–
I. Title.
DS779.26.M45   1996   951.05'7—dc20   95-49995 CIP

FOR LYNN AND MATTHEW

CONTENTS

PREFACE

A society that has conjured up such gigantic means of produc-
tion and exchange is like the sorcerer who is no longer able to
control the powers of the netherworld whom he has called up
by his spells.

Karl Marx and Friedrich Engels,
The Manifesto of the Communist Party

Few recall today that Deng Xiaoping came to power in 1978 on a
platform championing "socialist democracy." The promise to revitalize the socialist goals of the Communist Revolution and democratize
the People's Republic—not simply the promise of a higher standard
of living—won Deng the enthusiastic support of China's urban population, workers and intellectuals alike. For those who envisioned a
democratic socialist future, the last months of 1978 and the first
months of 1979 were a uniquely exciting time, filled with new hope
and great expectations.

The era of Deng Xiaoping has yielded phenomenal economic
growth for the Chinese nation and relative prosperity for the Chinese
people. But neither socialism nor democracy has prospered in the
years since 1978. No sooner was Deng securely in power than "socialist democracy" faded into a ritualized slogan, and, as time went
on, even the slogan was rarely heard. Driven by a nationalist passion

to make China "rich and strong," the new regime's market reforms unleashed a frenzied process of capitalist development that soon made the Chinese economy the world's second largest—and even sooner overwhelmed the socialist goals reformers once proclaimed modern economic development would serve.

For the majority of the Chinese people, material conditions of life have improved far more rapidly (even if far more inequitably) than anyone could have anticipated at the close of the Mao period. But this progress has been accompanied by social devastations on a grand scale and by a spiritual impoverishment of unprecedented depth. By the early 1980s the political apathy and social cynicism that were pervasive in the cities, especially among the youth, were being called a "crisis of faith"; in recent years the phenomenon has been described in much more somber and even pathological terms, with phrases such as "the loss of meaning" and "the death of the spirit" now commonplace. The malady, whose characteristic symptom is an inability to conceive of a future worth striving for, was evident even before the physical and psychic assault launched by the Communist state against the Chinese people in June 1989.

The spiritual decline of Chinese Communism began in the last decade of the Mao era, bound up with the disillusionment that followed from the Cultural Revolution and a growing feeling that the Maoist system had become outmoded and its energies exhausted. But the deep and widespread nihilism that plagues China today is a distinctively post-Mao phenomenon, as the writings and reflections of China's most sensitive social critics, such as Liu Binyan, make clear. Liu, the famed dissident journalist, has been almost unique among Chinese intellectuals in taking the pulse of the common people and attempting to speak on their behalf. In 1988, a year before the great Democracy Movement, he observed:

> The biggest problem we face today in China is not commodity prices or the cost of living . . . the most serious problem is the widespread spiritual malaise among people from all walks of life, a growing mood of depression, even despair, a loss of hope for the future and of any sense of social responsibility, as if China were no longer their country and society owed them

something. I haven't seen this sort of attitude before, at least not in the past forty years. And there is no solution in sight.[1]

The spiritual malaise Liu Binyan detected in 1988, following a decade of market reforms, spread and deepened after the brutal military suppression of the Democracy Movement in 1989.

It is not my purpose, and certainly not my place, to analyze the psychological condition of the Chinese people at the close of the era dominated by Deng Xiaoping. My aims in this volume are far more limited, and they are essentially two. First, as a historical narrative of post-Mao China, this book attempts to tell the story of how the promise of socialist democracy, the platform on which Deng and his reformist colleagues stood in 1978, degenerated into what some observers have termed "market Stalinism"—or what I prefer to call bureaucratic capitalism. Second, interwoven into the narrative of the Deng era is an extended commentary on the fate of socialism in late-twentieth-century China.

The emphasis on socialism in this book will strike some as odd, or at best quixotic. It is, after all, an age when the reigning orthodoxies insist that socialism is passé and capitalism universally and eternally triumphant. It is true, certainly, that this volume reflects an old hope that the Chinese Communist Revolution would eventually yield a socialist society. But by the later years of the Mao regime that hope had become very faint and the history of the Deng era has done little to revive it. Yet a concern with the fate of socialism in China is not a foreigner's ideological preoccupation artificially imposed on the Chinese historical record. One need not nourish socialist hopes (or illusions) to appreciate the significance of socialism in modern Chinese history. From the beginning of the twentieth century, socialist ideas and visions have inspired the revolutionary movements that have molded modern Chinese history. During the first two decades of the century, Chinese intellectuals and political activists were drawn to a great variety of Western socialist doctrines, among which anarchist ideas were at first the most prominent. Under the

[1] Liu Binyan, *China's Crisis, China's Hope* (Cambridge: Harvard University Press, 1990), p. 22.

stimulus of the Russian Bolshevik Revolution of 1917, and especially the May Fourth Movement of 1919, Marxism became the predominant socialist theory in China. For half a century, from the 1920s to the 1970s, socialism in China was largely—although not exclusively— identified with the political history of the Chinese Communist Party.

One of the more significant developments of what now can be called the Deng Xiaoping era is that the old but tenuous tie between socialism and Communism, long eroding, has finally snapped. Those who savor historical irony cannot fail to note that the Communist regime at the close of the Deng era appears, in social reality if not in ideological rhetoric, as the creator and protector of Chinese capitalism. And from this there logically follows the further irony that the main enemy of the Communist state today is not capitalism but socialism, a socialism no longer burdened by an association with political despotism.

As capitalism further develops, and as more recoil from its "icy waters of egotistical calculation," new socialist movements will rise in opposition, drawing support from the democratic strivings of the Chinese people and perhaps from the rudimentary socialist values and traditions inherited from earlier periods of Chinese Communism and other revolutionary movements.

In these and other ways that will be explored in this volume, socialism remains an integral part of contemporary Chinese history, continuing in new forms the century-long quest of Chinese intellectuals to avoid the painful vicissitudes of capitalism. It is the central concern of the following chapters, however unfashionable the concern might now be, to look at the transformation of economy and society during the era of Deng Xiaoping not simply as a case study in a universal process of modernization but to ask what the changes mean for Chinese socialism and its future prospects. That question guides the treatment of the story of Deng Xiaoping's consolidation of power (related in Part II), the analysis of the social consequences of Deng's market reforms (Part III), the political and intellectual history of the late 1980s, culminating in the great Democracy Movement of 1989 and its brutal suppression (Part IV), and the inquiry into the closing years of the Deng era (Part V). The introductory part of the volume (Chapters 1 and 2) sketches the history of the Chinese Communist Revolution (1919–49) and the Mao era in the People's Republic (1949–76), in an attempt to provide some of the essential historical background for understanding China during the reign of Deng Xiaoping.

ACKNOWLEDGMENTS

This book has been long in the making, and over the years that it has taken to make it I have accumulated many more debts than can be discharged in an acknowledgments page. Nonetheless, I must express a word of gratitude to at least a few of those to whom I owe the most.

Much of this volume is based on the labors of a great many scholars, journalists, and other observers who have written on (or spoken about) the recent history of China. Most, probably, will not agree with many of my interpretations of that history, but I trust that they will not feel that I have misused their work. My debt to them is only very inadequately acknowledged in the notes and the bibliography.

In writing the history of very recent decades, one inevitably comes to rely heavily on daily newspapers, weekly or monthly periodicals, and contemporary governmental reports. Most of these, in the fullness of time, will be canonized as primary historical sources. I can only hope that I have chosen wisely in the meantime.

I owe a special debt to the students in my graduate Chinese history seminar, upon whom I have inflicted portions of the manuscript over the past five years and from whose work I have learned a great deal—and sometimes borrowed. For their criticisms, ideas, and assistance, I am grateful to Lisa Brennan, Tina Chen, Mike Farmer, Fu Keh-chang, Han Tie, Diane Jones, Kim Soo-young, Kung

Chi-keung, Lai Ming-yan, Helen Leung, Kira Lillard, Lin Weiran, Thomas Lutze, Daniel Meissner, Dreux Montgomery, Tu Chuande, and Wang Yaan-iee. Life would have been less rich without them and the book would have been poorer.

My colleagues in the History Department at the University of Wisconsin–Madison again provided generous doses of intellectual stimulation and encouragement, particularly Professors William Brown, Theodore Hamerow, Stanley Kutler, Lin Yu-sheng, and Thomas McCormick. The staff of the department was enormously helpful in preparing the manuscript for publication. I am especially grateful to Anita Olson and Danny Struebing.

A number of very special friends read all or parts of the manuscript in its various drafts and made invaluable criticisms and comments. I owe very special thanks to Frederick Vanderbilt Field, Bob Pollin, Lin Chun, Jim Peck, and Arif Dirlik. Patricia Van der Leun and Sara Bershtel were extraordinarily high towers of professional strength and moral encouragement during sometimes trying times. I treasure their friendship.

Lynn Lubkeman is both my most rigorous and most loving critic. To repeat the cliché that the book would not have been completed without her is, in this case, literally true. It is to Lynn, and our young son Matthew, that the volume is affectionately dedicated.

Madison, Wisconsin
January 1996

★

PART ONE

CAPITALISM AND THE MAOIST LEGACY

1

THE CHINESE REVOLUTION
AND THE QUESTION OF
CAPITALISM

IN 1867 KARL MARX rendered his judgment on the historical future of economically backward lands. Observing that "the natural laws of capitalist production [were] working with iron necessity towards inevitable results," he concluded: "the country that is more developed industrially only shows, to the less developed, the image of its own future."[1]

Thus did Marx reply to those of his contemporaries, particularly his Russian Populist admirers, who advocated a noncapitalist road to socialism. Although avoiding the agonies of a capitalist regime was humanly and morally desirable, and although Marx was reluctant to dismiss the hope entirely,[2] in the final analysis he thought it was historically impossible. Marx's conclusion was entirely in keeping with the logic of his historical thought. For what crucially distinguished Marxism from other nineteenth-century Western socialist theories was precisely the proposition that socialism presupposed capitalism. The critiques of the socialist doctrines that Marx and

---

[1] Preface to the first German edition of *Kapital*. Karl Marx, *Capital*, Vol. 1 (Chicago: Kerr, 1906), p. 13.

[2] The hope, if not necessarily the expectation, is ambiguously expressed in Marx's writings on Russia during the last decade of his life. The most persuasive case that Marx seriously entertained the possibility of a noncapitalist path to socialism is made in Teodor Shanin (ed.), *Late Marx and the Russian Road* (New York: Monthly Review Press, 1983).

Engels pejoratively labeled "utopian" rested, in large measure, on the failure of those doctrines to appreciate the historically progressive role of modern capitalism. The utopian socialists, the founding fathers of Marxism charged, recognized neither large-scale capitalist industry as the essential material foundation for the future socialist society nor the modern proletariat as the social agent destined to bring about that future. Marxism, in contrast, presented itself not simply as a critique of capitalism but also as a theory which championed the historical necessity of capitalism, even if not its social desirability.

On the assumption that socialism presupposed capitalism, Marx warned of the futility, and indeed the danger, of "premature" attempts to carry out socialist revolutions in historical situations where, as Marx put it, "the material conditions are not yet created which make necessary the abolition of the bourgeois mode of production." People, he counseled, "do not build themselves a new world out of the fruits of the earth, as vulgar superstition believes, but out of the historical accomplishments of their declining civilization. They must, in the course of their development, begin by themselves producing the material conditions of a new society, and no effort of mind or will can free them from this destiny."[3]

For Marx, then, a genuine socialist reorganization of society could be accomplished only on the basis of the highly developed productive forces and techniques created by capitalism—for only conditions of economic abundance would allow people to free themselves from the tyranny of the division of labor, permit the shortening of the workday, and thereby yield the free time for the emergence of new "all-round" people who would freely, cooperatively, and creatively develop their true human potentialities. Without that capitalist material foundation, a socialist revolution would yield only a "crude social leveling," and that in turn would result in the growth of new social inequalities and the reemergence of what Marx called "the old muck" of the past. Thus Marx insisted that "the successive phases of [a society's] normal development" could not be avoided either by "bold leaps" or by "legal enactment."[4]

[3] Karl Marx, "Die moralisierende Kritik und die kritisierende Moral," in Marx, *Selected Writings in Sociology and Social Philosophy*, T. B. Bottomore and Maximilien Rubel (eds.) (London: Watts, 1956), p. 240.
[4] Marx, Preface to the first German edition of *Kapital*, pp. 14–15.

That Marxist revolutionary movements in the twentieth century have been victorious in economically backward and largely agrarian lands lacking the Marxian-defined material and social prerequisites for socialism is, of course, one of the great ironies of modern history. It is certainly *the* great irony of the history of Marxism in the modern world, although one that contemporary Marxist theories have yet to explain adequately. Intellectually, Marxism has taken root and flourished in most of the modern world, but it was only in relatively backward countries that the modern revolutionary doctrine was translated into successful anticapitalist (if not necessarily socialist) revolutions. The first of these revolutions, heralding an unanticipated twentieth-century historical pattern, took place in Russia in 1917, and the greatest was consummated three decades later in China. Others, of lesser scope and scale, followed until the 1980s, the decade that marks the end of the era of Marxian-led peasant revolutions—due, in no small measure, to the disappearance of traditional peasantries.

Twentieth-century Marxist revolutionaries have been confronted with a cruel historical paradox. They have discovered that in the developed capitalist countries, where the Marxian-defined social and material prerequisites for socialism are present, the road to revolution has been closed. Modern historical experience, thus far, has yielded little to support the Marxist belief that socialism is the logical and necessary historical outcome of industrial capitalism and that the urban proletariat is the truly revolutionary class in the modern world. On the other hand, for a good part of the twentieth century, Marxist-led revolutions did succeed in lands where capitalism was underdeveloped and where bourgeois revolutions had proved abortive. But in the cases where such revolutions have triumphed, politically victorious Marxists have been denied the necessary socioeconomic preconditions for socialism. Having achieved power in largely precapitalist lands, Marxist political parties were confronted with the task of constructing the economic foundations for socialism rather than socialism itself—and with social results that proved less than entirely salutary, and certainly far less than socialist.

The dilemmas and paradoxes confronting Marxists who have come to power in economically backward countries are strikingly apparent in the post-Maoist period in the People's Republic of China. The very conditions of backwardness which permitted the Chinese Communists to win power in the first place are now seen by Mao Zedong's successors as the main barrier to the realization of the socialist goals that Communist political power presumably is intended to serve. In Chinese Marxist attempts to explain this historical paradox and to resolve the consequent theoretical and practical dilemmas, Karl Marx's view of capitalism as a necessary and progressive stage of development in a "normal" process of historical evolution has assumed enormous prominence. Unlike Mao Zedong, who, much in the fashion of the Russian Populists, celebrated the relative absence of capitalism as an advantage for building socialism, Mao's more ideologically orthodox successors regard the failure of China to experience a full and genuine capitalist phase of development as one of the great tragedies of modern Chinese history. The abortiveness of Chinese capitalism, they argue, perpetuated economic backwardness and permitted the "vestiges of feudalism" to persist long after 1949, gravely distorting the new socialist society and producing such evils as the utopianism of the Great Leap, the cult of Mao, and the Cultural Revolution.

This orthodox Marxist argument, supported by copious quotations from classic Marxist texts, serves to justify ideologically the adoption of capitalist economic forms and free market mechanisms—albeit within the framework of what post-Maoist leaders insist is an essentially "socialist system." Nonetheless, by identifying "feudalism" as the primary enemy of progress in China today, and by treating capitalism (feudalism's natural historic antagonist) as a relatively progressive force in China's current stage of development, Chinese Communist theoreticians suggest that "socialism with Chinese characteristics" will incorporate many of the features historically associated with capitalism for many decades to come.

The deradicalizing social and economic policies that have been pursued under this ideological construct, the nature and results of which will be examined in this volume, have been an eclectic and uneasy mixture of "socialist" and "capitalist" elements—which, among other consequences, have hopelessly confused the means and ends of Chinese socialism. At the same time, the course pursued by Mao Zedong's successors has permitted foreign observers to describe the post-Mao order in strikingly different ways—as both "socialist"

and "capitalist," in accordance with their differing ideological proclivities and the political preferences of the moment.

The post-Mao combination of "socialist" and "capitalist" forms of
economic life is perhaps not an illogical outcome of the Chinese
Communist revolution. For the People's Republic was the product of
a revolution undertaken by a political party pursuing socialist aims
in a backward and essentially precapitalist land. It was inevitable
that the socialist aspirations of the revolutionaries would clash with
the bourgeois limitations of the undeveloped historical environment
in which they found themselves, and that the revolution would thus
assume contradictory bourgeois and socialist characteristics. The tension between the two was present at the birth of the Chinese Communist Party early in the century and runs throughout the history of
the Chinese Communist movement.

THE ORIGINS OF CHINESE COMMUNISM

When the Chinese Communist Party was organized in 1921, its
youthful founders anticipated that they would lead a socialist revolutionary movement. Inspired by the messianic message of the Russian October Revolution, which seemed to herald an imminent
worldwide revolutionary upheaval, the early Chinese Communists believed that China had an essential—and essentially socialist—role
to play in an international process of revolutionary transformation. In
the chiliastic revolutionary atmosphere of the times, it was quite natural that they should have ignored Marxist teachings on the capitalist
prerequisites for socialism. By doing so, they echoed the Chinese
intelligentsia's long-standing aversion to experiencing the agonies of
a capitalist regime. China's early revolutionaries, many of whom were
associated with Sun Yat-sen and the Alliance Society during the first
two decades of the century, envisioned a socialist future. However
vague their socialist visions often were, they shared an almost universal desire that China should avoid the social evils and class
conflicts associated with capitalism in Western countries. It was precisely because of that desire, molded in large part by nationalist
considerations, that Marxist theory struck so few responsive chords
among the early revolutionary intelligentsia, for the version of Marx-

ism that initially had arrived in China conveyed the orthodox Marxist assumption that socialism presupposed capitalism. It was an unappealing message for nationalists, as was the accompanying implication that socialist intellectuals in an economically backward land had little to do, save to wait patiently on the sidelines, until modern capitalist productive forces had completed their historical work. Indeed, nothing could have been more distasteful to Chinese intellectuals harboring bitter anti-imperialist resentments than the Communist Manifesto's proclamation that the Western "bourgeoisie creates a world after its own image."

It was not until the May Fourth Movement of 1919, which radically transformed the character of Chinese intellectual and political life, along with the impact of the Russian October Revolution and Leninism, that significant numbers of Chinese intellectuals began to embrace Marxism. Many did so, initially, by ignoring the question of capitalism in favor of chiliastic visions of an imminent world socialist revolution.

But the question of capitalism in a largely precapitalist land could not long be avoided. As hopes for a worldwide socialist revolution waned in the early 1920s, and as the Soviet Union was inexorably driven to Stalin's doctrine of "socialism in one country," the youthful Chinese Communists found themselves junior partners in a Comintern-imposed alliance with the Guomindang, in which the older revolutionary organization led by Sun Yat-sen (and soon by Chiang Kai-shek) was designated as the leading party in China's "national" (or "bourgeois-democratic") revolution. Socialism was now no longer to be seen as the alternative to capitalism but rather as its natural successor. And the time of succession was unpredictable. Chen Duxiu, co-founder and first leader of the Chinese Communist Party, originally had viewed socialism as a way for China to avoid the pains of capitalist development. Observing, in 1920, that capitalism had produced wars and a host of social evils along with modern industry, he optimistically concluded: "Fortunately, in China, where capitalism has not yet developed . . . we can best use socialism to develop education and industry and avoid [capitalism's] mistakes."[5] But a few

5 Chen Duxiu, "Zhi Luosi xiansheng dexin" (Letter to Bertrand Russell), *Shehui zhuyi taolun ji* (Collection of Discussions on Socialism) (Canton, 1922), pp. 44–45.

years later he adopted more orthodox Marxist perspectives. "The economically and culturally backward countries," he wrote in 1923 as the Communist-Guomindang alliance was being fashioned, "are not injured by the development of capitalism but rather by the lack of capitalist development."[6] Emphasizing the workings of objective social and economic laws, Chen argued that capitalist industrialization inevitably would compel the Chinese bourgeoisie to carry out a democratic revolution, insisting that such a bourgeois act was the necessary historical prerequisite for a proletarian socialist revolution.[7]

Chen Duxiu's views on capitalism and on the necessary stages of historical development were not universally shared by China's early Marxists, many of whom were reluctant to entertain the dismal prospect of a lengthy capitalist era, and some of whom were inclined to see China as a "proletarian nation" prepared to follow a uniquely socialist path of development. But it was Chen Duxiu's position that accorded not only with the logic of Marxist theory but also with Chinese historical and political realities. For China, "the sick man of Asia," as it was so long known, remained a largely agrarian land with little modern industry. Eighty-five percent of its 500 million people were peasants, most desperately impoverished and laboring under precapitalist modes of exploitation, whereas there were no more than 2 million industrial workers in the tiny semi-modern sector of the economy. Imperialism, as Karl Marx had anticipated, had indeed battered down "all Chinese walls," breaking apart the old Confucian order. But imperialism did not, as Marx had also predicted, create "a world after its own [Western capitalist] image." Modern capitalism, to be sure, had emerged in China by the turn of the century, but it did so only in weak and distorted form. Largely the product of Western imperialism, Chinese capitalism was inextricably tied to foreign capital and confined mostly to Western-dominated treaty ports. The modern Chinese bourgeoisie, as a consequence, was but a pale reflection of its Western counterparts, its members primarily engaged in commerce and finance rather than industry. It was, in fact, largely a compradore bourgeoisie in the service of foreign capitalists,

[6] Chen Duxiu, *Zhongguo keming wendi lunwenji* (A Collection of Articles on Problems of the Chinese Revolution) (Shanghai, 1927), p. 38.
[7] Ibid., pp. 33–38.

however much its members may have resented their dependence on foreign patrons.

Under such conditions of extreme economic and social backwardness, compounded by the disintegration of the traditional political order into warlord feudatories, hopes for a socialist revolution were, from any Marxist point of view, sheer political fantasy. What China required was not a socialist revolution but rather a capitalist one—a bourgeois-democratic revolution that would serve to politically unify the fragmented country, liberate it from foreign economic and political impingements, do away with ancient precapitalist restraints on trade and production, and thereby create favorable conditions for the flourishing of private property and the development of indigenous capitalist productive forces. Thus the Communist-Guomindang alliance, formally consummated early in 1924, was not simply a product of the immediate national interests of the new Soviet state; it also grew out of the demands of the internal Chinese condition, a condition that resulted from a century-long history of economic stagnation and political failure.

The message that the Chinese revolution was still in its "bourgeois" stage was a disheartening one for most Chinese Communists. Their socialist hopes had to be put aside in favor of a perhaps prolonged period of capitalist development. But it was a message they were forced to accept, for it was demanded of them by both Moscow's political authority and the historical situation in which they found themselves.

The alliance between the Guomindang and the Communists was forged on a most narrow conception of a "bourgeois-democratic" revolution. Despite the fiery revolutionary rhetoric and slogans that flowed so freely during the years 1925–27, the two sides met on narrowly defined nationalist grounds, in common pursuit of the goals of Chinese independence and political unification. But the political ground proved far too narrow to accommodate the great popular revolutionary upsurge of the time. As increasingly militant urban workers and rebellious peasants threatened property, the owners of property were driven into the waiting arms of the more conservative leaders of the Guomindang. The Guomindang-Communist alliance broke apart on the radicalism of the mass revolutionary movement it had stimulated. The threat of social revolution—and of socialism—

was ended by military force in 1927, when Chiang Kai-shek turned his army to the bloody task of suppressing the workers' and peasants' movements, and to destroying the Chinese Communist Party. It was not to be the last time in twentieth-century history that a Soviet-built army was employed to crush a popular revolutionary movement.

The counterrevolution of 1927 was a defeat for both socialism and capitalism in China. Chiang Kai-shek's Guomindang regime was duly recognized as the government of China by governments around the globe, including the one in Moscow. And the Nationalist regime did preserve the property of the propertied classes. But it was a spurious national unity, resting on tenuous alliances with warlord armies and the cooperation of local landlord elites. The Nationalist government of Chiang Kai-shek did little to ease the burden of the imperialist economic impingement. Traditional, and essentially pre-capitalist, socioeconomic relationships in the countryside were untouched. The Guomindang in power accumulated great wealth for its leaders, but provided little impetus for modern capitalist economic development. Indeed, the "Nanking decade" (1927–37) was largely a period of economic stagnation, exacerbating the wretched plight of the Chinese people. Thus the task of completing China's unfinished bourgeois-democratic revolution fell to the Chinese Communist Party, whose remaining members were dispersed in remote rural areas and struggling to survive the wreckage of 1927. And the question of the place of capitalism in China's modern development soon became one of the many problems confronting Mao Zedong.

MAOISM AND CAPITALISM

Mao Zedong's views on capitalism were ambiguous from the outset. If Marxist-Leninist theory taught that capitalism was a universally necessary and progressive stage of historical development, Mao's nationalist and populist impulses militated against embracing that elemental Marxist proposition. Nonetheless, during most of the revolutionary era, and indeed for several years after 1949, official Maoist theory emphasized the essentially "bourgeois" character of the Chinese revolution, an emphasis that received its main ideological expression in the celebrated theory of "New Democracy."[8] It also found expression in the official description of the new Communist state as a "people's democratic dictatorship" rather than a "dictatorship of the proletariat," the latter, of course, being the accepted Marxist formula for a socialist revolutionary outcome. Moreover, during the Yan'an period (1935–45) and after, Maoism not only insisted on the necessity of a bourgeois stage of development but also championed the historically progressive role of indigenous Chinese capitalism. On the eve of the founding of the People's Republic in 1949, Mao declared that "China must utilize all elements of urban and rural capitalism that are beneficial and not harmful to the national economy. . . . Our present policy is to regulate capitalism, not destroy it."[9]

These pronouncements received practical expression in the reformist agrarian policies of the Yan'an era, in the eminently bourgeois character of the Land Reform campaign of the early 1950s (which created a capitalist, not a socialist, rural economy), and in the promotion of "national capitalism" in the cities during the early years of the People's Republic.[10]

Yet modern Chinese historical conditions were not conducive to an acceptance of the Marxist faith in the progressiveness of capitalism. It was not old Confucian biases against commercial activities that made Chinese intellectuals suspicious of capitalist development but rather modern nationalist impulses. For modern capitalism in China was not primarily an indigenous phenomenon, but rather one imported under the aegis of foreign imperialism. Insofar as industrial capitalism grew in twentieth-century China, and it certainly was not very far, it not only re-created all the social evils associated with early industrialism in the West but also developed primarily in the foreign-dominated treaty ports. A perception of capitalism as an alien phenomenon has been a universal response to the social effects of early industrialization. It was a perception that the modern Chinese

---

[8] For an extensive and insightful analysis of this aspect of Maoism, see Thomas Lutze, *The Theory and Practice of New Democracy*, Ph.D. dissertation, Department of History, University of Wisconsin-Madison, 1996.

[9] Mao Tse-tung (Mao Zedong), "On the People's Democratic Dictatorship," *Selected Works of Mao Tse-tung*, Vol. 4 (Peking: Foreign Languages Press, 1961), p. 421.

[10] The era of "national capitalism" and the social results of the Land Reform campaign are briefly discussed in Chapter 2.

historical experience magnified. Although some Western-oriented Chinese Marxists attempted to adhere to orthodox Marxist perspectives, the Chinese situation did not encourage faith in the socialist potential of a capitalism which seemed so alien in origin and so distorted in form. The dominant tendency, which found its most powerful expression in Maoism, was to identify capitalism with imperialism, to see both as external impingements on the Chinese nation, and to look elsewhere for the sources of socialist regeneration.

Chinese Marxist rejections of the conventional Marxist analysis of the historical role of capitalism were facilitated by the absence of a Marxist intellectual tradition in China. For most early Chinese converts to Communism, a political commitment to the Marxist-Leninist program of revolution long preceded any real intellectual commitment to Marxist theory. For many years, the young Chinese Communists had only the most superficial understanding of Marxism, and they were afforded little time and opportunity to correct the deficiency as they were immediately thrust into the frenetic politics of an increasingly complex revolutionary situation in the 1920s. Consequently, they were far less firmly tied to Marxist theoretical concepts than their Russian and Western counterparts, most of whom had spent many years immersed in the study of classical Marxian texts. For Mao Zedong, then, it was intellectually much easier than it had been for Lenin to ignore or revise basic Marxian views. Lenin had spent a good part of his early revolutionary career attempting to refute the Populist argument that Russia could achieve socialism without capitalism. Mao had no desire to retrace Lenin's ideological steps.

Nonetheless, political and ideological considerations dictated retaining orthodox Marxist-Leninist formulas on the question of the "stages" of development. In formal Maoist theory, accordingly, an apparently firm distinction was made between the bourgeois and socialist phases of the revolution. While drawing the distinction seemed to imply acceptance of the Marxist view that socialism presupposed capitalism, theoretical appearances were deceptive. For an elemental hostility to capitalism—in any form and in any revolutionary stage —permeated Maoism from its beginnings in the mid-1920s. For Mao, capitalism in China was perceived as an alien and politically undesirable force. The product of foreign imperialism, Chinese capitalism, in the Maoist view, remained inextricably tied to the external impingement. Thus as early as 1926, Mao not only condemned the compradore "big bourgeoisie" as traitors to the nation but described the presumably progressive indigenous bourgeoisie as a politically unreliable class, one potentially hostile to the revolutionary movement and, ultimately, politically irrelevant. "As to the vacillating middle bourgeoisie," he wrote, "its right wing must be considered our enemy; even if it is not already, it will soon become so. Its left wing may become our friend, but it is not our true friend."[11]

Even at the height of the united-front policy with the Guomindang, which was vigorously pursued to resist the Japanese invaders, Maoist suspicions of indigenous capitalism and the national bourgeoisie remained. As Mao wrote in 1939: "National capitalism has developed to a certain extent and played a considerable part in China's political and cultural life, but it has not become the principal socioeconomic form in China; quite feeble in strength, it is mostly tied in varying degrees to both foreign imperialism and domestic feudalism."[12] With native Chinese capitalism "mostly tied" to foreign imperialism, the oft-repeated Leninist distinction between a reactionary compradore bourgeoisie and a presumably progressive national bourgeoisie largely vanishes.[13]

Mao Zedong's celebrated theory of New Democracy did envision a partly capitalist economy for China over a lengthy historical period. Mao drew a seemingly sharp division between the democratic and socialist stages of the revolution. "In the course of its history," he insisted, "the Chinese revolution must go through two stages, first, the democratic revolution, and second, the socialist revolution, and by their very nature they are two different revolutionary processes."[14]

[11] Mao Tse-tung (Mao Zedong), "Analysis of the Classes in Chinese Society." The official *Selected Works* version of this article is considerably different from the original document, and the quotations reproduced here are from extracts from the original translated in Stuart R. Schram (ed.), *The Political Thought of Mao Tse-tung* (New York: Praeger, 1969), pp. 210–14.
[12] Mao Tse-tung (Mao Zedong), *The Chinese Revolution and the Chinese Communist Party* (1939) (Peking: Foreign Languages Press, 1954), p. 22.
[13] The distinction also has vanished in a number of Western scholarly accounts on the history of modern Chinese capitalism. Marie-Clare Bergère, for example, has concluded: "The real contradiction lies not between a 'national' and a 'compradore' bourgeoisie, but between the economic dependence of the entire bourgeoisie [on foreign imperialism] and its unanimous nationalist aims." Bergère, "The Role of the Bourgeoisie," in Mary C. Wright (ed.), *China in Revolution: The First Phase, 1900–1913* (New Haven: Yale University Press, 1968), p. 253.
[14] Mao, "On New Democracy," *Selected Works of Mao Tse-tung*, Vol. 2 (Peking: Foreign Languages Press, 1967), pp. 341–42.

Moreover, he discovered a necessary historical link between capitalism and socialism, observing that the "objective mission" of China's bourgeois-democratic revolution was "to clear the path for the development of capitalism" and thereby prepare the way for the development of socialism.[15] Further, he criticized as "utopian" the "theory of a single revolution" and the notion of "revolution at one stroke."[16] And he repeatedly emphasized, in the decade prior to the victory of 1949, that China's "new democratic" revolution was directed against feudalism and monopoly capitalism, "not at wiping out capitalism in general." In view of China's backwardness, he wrote in 1947, "it will still be necessary to permit the existence for a long time of a capitalist sector of the economy represented by the extensive petty bourgeoisie and middle bourgeoisie."[17]

Yet Mao attached so many qualifications and modifications to his version of bourgeois-democratic revolution that it seems unlikely he really envisioned a discrete bourgeois stage or a course of development that proceeded somewhere between capitalism and socialism. Even though he sometimes found it politically expedient to point to similarities between his theory of New Democracy and Sun Yat-sen's program,[18] the aim that Mao assigned to what he characterized as "a special, new type" of bourgeois-democratic revolution was, as he candidly put it, "to steer away from a capitalist future and head towards the realization of socialism"[19]—and to do so as quickly as possible under the guidance of a Marxist political party that proclaimed socialist and communist goals. In this novel conception of bourgeois revolution, there was little place for the actual bourgeoisie or even a political party representing capitalist interests. Rather, the leadership of the revolutionary process, Mao emphasized, "rests on the shoulders of the party of the Chinese proletariat, the Chinese Communist Party, for without its leadership no revolution can succeed."[20] Here can be

[15] Ibid., p. 344.
[16] Ibid., p. 360. The bourgeois stage would span a lengthy historical era, Mao often seemed to suggest: "the present task of the revolution in China is to fight imperialism and feudalism, and socialism is out of the question until this task is completed . . . the first step will need quite a long time and cannot be accomplished overnight. We are not utopians and cannot divorce ourselves from the actual conditions confronting us" (p. 358).
[17] Mao, "The Present Situation and Our Tasks," *Selected Works of Mao Tse-tung*, Vol. 4, p. 168.
[18] Mao, "On New Democracy," pp. 352–53.
[19] Mao, *The Chinese Revolution and the Chinese Communist Party*, pp. 53–55.
[20] Ibid.

found not a conception of "revolution by stages" but rather the seeds of Mao's notion of "permanent revolution."

It seems most unlikely that Mao ever was converted, even temporarily, to any genuine Marxist faith in the historical progressiveness of capitalism, much less to the proposition that socialism presupposes the material, social, and cultural products of a developed capitalist economy. He did, of course, make customary ideological bows to prevailing Stalinist orthodoxies on "revolution by stages" and the dogma of a universal and unilinear scheme of historical development. Thus he felt compelled to argue, however feebly, that "China's feudal society . . . carried within itself the embryo of capitalism," and that "China would of herself have developed slowly into a capitalist society even if there had been no influence of foreign capitalism."[21] But he also observed, and with more conviction, that the actual historical case was that China "remained sluggish in her economic, political and cultural development after her transition from slave to feudal society." So sluggish was the movement of Chinese history, in fact, that the feudal system persisted for three thousand years, and "it was not until the middle of the nineteenth century that great internal changes took place in China as a result of the penetration of foreign capitalism." It was imperialism that undermined the old feudal economy and "created certain objective conditions and possibilities for the development of China's capitalist production," resulting in the emergence of "national capitalism . . . in rudimentary forms."[22]

Thus, for Mao, even "national capitalism" was the product of foreign imperialism, and therefore assumed an alien character. Indeed, one cannot escape the impression that Mao viewed capitalism in general as an alien and unnatural phenomenon. The impression is reinforced by Mao's treatment of social classes and class struggles in both traditional and modern Chinese history. The differences between Marxism and Maoism in this realm are striking. In the conventional Marxian analysis of feudalism, the major concern is the struggle between the old feudal aristocracy and the newly arisen bourgeoisie; the peasantry, although the main victim of feudal exploitation, is not

---

[21] Ibid., p. 13.
[22] Ibid., pp. 5, 11–14.

a major historical actor. In Maoist theory, by contrast, the major class struggle throughout China's long feudal history was between peasants and landlords, not between a bourgeoisie and the feudal ruling classes. Moreover, Mao set forth the proposition (which was to remain the Chinese Marxist ideological orthodoxy throughout the Mao era) that the class struggles of the peasantry "alone formed the real motive force of historical development in China's feudal society."[23]

Just as the nature and social composition of class struggles in China differed from those in the West in their premodern histories, so they did in contemporary times. Whereas Marx's conception of modern revolution centered on the activity of the classes involved in capitalist relations of production, the bourgeoisie and the proletariat, Mao was primarily concerned with the relationship between peasants and intellectuals. For the sources of revolutionary activism, and indeed for the sources of socialism, Mao was disposed to look to those classes and strata of Chinese society least influenced by modern capitalist forces of production—to an essentially precapitalist peasantry and to an intelligentsia uncorrupted by bourgeois ideology. For Mao, much like the nineteenth-century Russian Populists, capitalism was seen not as the harbinger of socialism but rather as a barrier to its realization.

Thus, from the beginning, Maoism looked not to the Marxian-defined revolutionary potentialities of modern capitalist forces of production but to "the Chinese people" as the wellspring of revolution —and of socialism. "The people," of course, were the vast peasant masses who constituted the overwhelming majority of that organic entity of the 395 million Chinese whom Mao identified in 1926 as "the true friends" of the revolution.[24] By employing an essentially numerical standard to measure the revolutionary potential of social classes, Mao not only dispensed with the bourgeoisie but ignored the urban proletariat as well. He was exclusively drawn, as he so passionately expressed it in his 1927 "Hunan Report," to the spontaneity of peasant revolt, that elemental "tornado-like" force he predicted would rise in a manner "so extraordinarily swift and violent that no

[23] Ibid., pp. 7, 11.
[24] Mao, "Analysis of the Classes in Chinese Society."

power, however great, will be able to suppress it."[25] The Maoist vision of peasant revolution was set forth in its most pristine form in this seminal document—which, among its many remarkable features, ignored both capitalism and the modern social classes capitalism had produced.

Mao Zedong's belief that the peasantry was the truly revolutionary class in the modern world was to remain one of the enduring features of Maoism, even though Mao's later writings were formulated in more orthodox Marxist-Leninist terms. Mao's early antipathy to capitalism also proved enduring, as did his reluctance to accept Marxist teachings on its universality and historical progressiveness. Although formal Maoist theory, as officially canonized during the Yan'an period, duly repeated conventional Marxist views on "the necessary stages" of social development, for Mao himself it clearly remained the case that capitalism was neither an inevitable nor a desirable stage.

Mao's celebration of the revolutionary creativity of the peasantry and his hostility to capitalism were closely related beliefs; what molded both, and linked the two together, was a broader perception of the socialist advantages of backwardness. While Mao deplored China's material backwardness and was determined to overcome it, he saw in that very condition of backwardness a reservoir of revolutionary energy and a source of moral purity.[26] Much in the fashion of the Russian Populists, Mao found special revolutionary virtues in the fact that China, unlike the West, was relatively uncorrupted by capitalist influences.

Thus as early as 1930 Mao was convinced that "the revolution will certainly move towards an upsurge more quickly in China than

[25] Mao, "Report on an Investigation of the Peasant Movement in Hunan," *Selected Works of Mao Tse-tung*, Vol. 1 (London: Lawrence & Wishart, 1954), p. 22. The "Report," as Benjamin Schwartz once observed, "might just as well have been written by a Russian *narodnik* as by a Marxist-Leninist. Nowhere here do we find those strictures on the independent revolutionary role of the peasantry which run through all Marxist-Leninist literature." Benjamin I. Schwartz, *Chinese Communism and the Rise of Mao* (Cambridge: Harvard University Press, 1951), p. 76.
[26] This is evident in Mao's earliest pre-Marxian writings. Proclaiming in 1919, "Our Chinese people possess great intrinsic energy," he observed that China had been impotent for "thousands of years"—but this historical backwardness augured great political advantages for the future, for, as Mao put it, "that which has accumulated for a long time will surely burst forth quickly." From extracts from articles published in the *Xiangjiang pinglun* in July and August 1919, translated in Schram (ed.), *The Political Thought of Mao Tse-tung*, p. 163.

in Western Europe."[27] For Mao it was not capitalism but rather the absence of capitalist development that held the promise of socialism. As he later argued, the backward countries were more amenable to social revolutionary transformation because their people were less poisoned by bourgeois ideology than in the industrialized countries of the West, where, he charged, the bourgeoisie and their pernicious ideas had penetrated "every nook and cranny," stifling the revolutionary spirit.[28]

Mao Zedong's views on the relationship between socialism and capitalism, his belief that the peasantry was the truly revolutionary class, and his faith in the advantages of backwardness departed fundamentally from the premises of Marxist theory. Further, Maoism was a doctrine that rejected, at least implicitly, the Marxist belief in the workings of objective historical laws, the belief that socialism is immanent in the progressive movement of history itself. In the Maoist view, the consciousness, the moral virtues, and the actions of dedicated people were the decisive factors in determining the course of history.

These Maoist ideas on capitalism, socialism, and economic backwardness recall Marx's warning about that "vulgar superstition" which holds that men can build themselves a new society "out of the fruits of the earth," rather than out of the accomplishments of their predecessors. Whereas Marx insisted that people must, "in the course of their development, begin by themselves producing the material conditions of a new society" and that "no effort of mind or will can free them from this destiny," Mao believed that it was precisely efforts of mind and will that would bring mankind to its socialist destination.

If Mao shared little with Marx on the question of the historical role of capitalism and on the relationship between socialism and economic backwardness, it is interesting to note a curious affinity between Maoism and conservative Western social theorists, such as W. W. Rostow and Adam Ulam, who argue that Marxism is an ideology that finds its natural home in economically backward soci-

[27] Mao, "A Single Spark Can Start a Prairie Fire," *Selected Works of Mao Tse-tung*, Vol. 1, p. 118.

[28] Mao, "Reading Notes on the Soviet Union's 'Political Economy' " (1960), *Mao Zedong sixiang wansui* (Taipei, 1969), p. 333.

eties.[29] Ulam, for example, attributes the appeal of Marxism, to masses and intellectuals alike in economically undeveloped lands, to the social psychology that accompanies the transition from preindustrial to industrial society. Original Marxism, he emphasizes, having been formulated in similar historical circumstances in early- and mid-nineteenth-century Europe, is thus "the natural ideology" for twentieth-century societies striving for industrialization. Whereas for Ulam, Marxism, once having taken root in an economically backward environment, essentially becomes an ideology of modernization that provides a socialist facade for an intensified process of capitalist industrialization,[30] for Mao Zedong, Marxism was taken as a guide for the socialist development of an economically undeveloped land through uninterrupted processes of radical social change.

Mao Zedong's Populist-type refashioning of Marxist-Leninist doctrine took him far from the premises of the Marxist theory that it was claimed he had "creatively developed." Yet it was precisely Mao's departures from orthodox Marxist views that formed the ideological prerequisites for the revolutionary strategy that brought the Chinese Communist Party to power. No orthodox Marxist or Leninist could have foreseen, much less presided over, so unique and strange a revolutionary process which assumed the form of a war of the backward countryside against the advanced cities, one where the forces of peasant revolt were mobilized to "surround and overwhelm" the cities, while a politically inactive urban proletariat passively awaited its liberation by armies of peasants. The strategy that brought the revolution from the countryside to the cities, based on the principles of what came to be celebrated as "people's war," was not simply the result of the "objective imperatives" of the early-twentieth-century Chinese historical situation. Revolutions presuppose revolutionaries

---

[29] W. W. Rostow, *The Stages of Economic Growth: A Non-Communist Manifesto* (Cambridge: Cambridge University Press, 1960); and Adam Ulam, *The Unfinished Revolution: An Essay on the Sources of Influence of Marxism and Communism* (New York: Vintage, 1964).

[30] For Ulam, socialism, "once it assumes power, has as its mission the fullest development of the productive resources of society . . . the [socialist] state will in no wise proceed differently from the capitalist: i.e., it will take the worker's surplus labor in the form of surplus value and will sink it in further investment." Thus, for Ulam, socialism "is simply capitalism without the capitalists . . . Except for the abolition of private property in the means of production (its rationalization), socialism continues and intensifies all the main characteristics of capitalism." Ulam, *The Unfinished Revolution*, p. 45.

—and indeed revolutionaries who are able to appreciate the political opportunities a historical environment offers. The Chinese revolution presupposed revolutionaries who were willing to abandon the cities and the proletariat and look to the revolutionary potentialities latent in the vast and backward Chinese countryside. Such was the essential revolutionary role performed by Maoist ideology, and more particularly by Mao Zedong's ideological peculiarities—which, from conventional Marxist perspectives, were often condemned as heretical "utopian" departures from Marxist-Leninist theory.

SOCIALISM AND CAPITALISM
IN THE CHINESE COMMUNIST REVOLUTION

Isaac Deutscher once characterized the Russian October Revolution of 1917 as "a combination of bourgeois and proletarian revolutions."[31] It was "bourgeois" in the sense that the revolution promoted the growth of capitalist forms of private property in the countryside by breaking up the estates of the aristocracy and giving land to the peasants. It was a socialist revolution in the cities, insofar as it was rooted in the urban working class and aimed to abolish private ownership of modern industry.

The Communist Revolution in China can also be described as a combination of capitalist and socialist elements. But in China the objective forces favoring a capitalist-type revolution were far stronger than they had been in Russia and the socialist content far weaker. At the time of the Communist victory in 1949 China was a much more backward country than Russia had been at the time of the Bolshevik triumph. Czarist Russia, of course, was a backward and undeveloped country in comparison with the industrialized capitalist countries of Western Europe. But it was far in advance of China. In pre-1949 China, with a population of 500 million, there were fewer than 3 million industrial workers (many of whom labored in small shops lacking mechanical power), whereas in prerevolutionary Russia there were 6 million industrial workers among a population of ap-

---

[31] Isaac Deutscher, *The Unfinished Revolution: Russia, 1917–1967* (London: Oxford University Press, 1967), p. 22.

proximately 125 million. On a per capita basis, industrial output in China, even in the best of pre-1949 years, was less than one-eighth of what it was in Russia in 1917.

Chinese agriculture compared even less favorably. Whereas the Russian agrarian economy traditionally produced surpluses for export, China's prerevolutionary farm economy yielded endemic famines which, decade after decade, took a staggering toll of lives. Between 1850 and 1930, an average of 4.5 percent of each generation died from famines.[32] The famine of the late 1920s in the sparsely populated provinces of the Northwest, for example, resulted in some 5 million deaths, killing one-third of the population of Shensi province alone. Even in normal times, observers estimate, per capita agricultural production in pre-1949 China was only about one-fifth of that in czarist Russia. And even after Stalin's assault on the Russian countryside during the First Five Year Plan, as Carl Riskin noted: "Soviet foodgrain production per capita in the disastrous year of 1932 was actually some 45 percent higher than the comparable figure for China in the average year of 1957."[33] Laboring under a primitive technology, and with nearly a quarter of humanity dependent on no more than 6 percent of the world's arable land, Chinese agriculture was a precarious enterprise even in the best of times, capable of providing little more than bare subsistence for the great majority of the Chinese people. Beyond the enormous human costs and suffering this inevitably entailed, it also meant that the potential surplus that could be extracted from the countryside to finance modern industrialization would be far smaller in China than in Russia.

China's backwardness in industry and agriculture, as compared with Russia, was exacerbated by backwardness in a variety of other areas: much less developed railroad, transportation, and communication systems (and ones that had been built primarily to serve foreign imperialist interests); a population burdened by a substantially higher rate of illiteracy and a considerably lower level of education; and a country far more lacking in modern scientific and technological knowledge.

---

[32] Carl Riskin, *China's Political Economy: The Quest for Development Since 1949* (New York: Oxford University Press, 1987), p. 24.
[33] Ibid., p. 6.

The essential precondition for socialism, it always has been assumed, is the dominance of productive processes which have a social character, which is to say, a well-developed industrial economy. With little modern industry and an overwhelming peasant population, China obviously lacked that necessary precondition. If the economic foundations for socialism were inadequate in Russia, as Lenin and the Bolsheviks repeatedly emphasized, they were virtually absent in China. The extreme material backwardness of China dictated, even more strongly than in Russia, a bourgeois revolution (which presumably would be followed by an era of capitalist development), not a socialist one.

It was not only economic and material underdevelopment that appeared to confine the Chinese revolution to bourgeois limits but also the character of the revolution itself and the social composition of the revolutionaries. Whereas in Russia the Bolsheviks came to power primarily on the basis of the active support of the urban proletariat, a class presumably socialist in its aims, the Chinese Communist Party and the Red Army were composed mostly of peasants, a "petty bourgeois" class by Marxist definition. The Chinese proletariat was not only tiny but, after 1927, politically inactive for the most part, having been terrorized into passivity by Chiang Kai-shek's counterrevolution. As the rural-based Maoist revolution neared its climax in the late 1940s, the urban workers, passively awaiting their liberation by peasant armies, could provide no socialist content to the revolutionary cause. In view of the backward agrarian state of China and the mostly peasant composition of the Chinese Communist movement, the Chinese revolution, from any Marxist perspective, could be no more than a bourgeois revolution. Maoist theory, as has been noted, formally recognized this elemental Marxist truth, emphasizing the bourgeois character of the revolutionary process, at least in the Party's official ideological pronouncements, and drew a seemingly firm distinction between the "bourgeois-democratic" and the socialist stages of the revolution.

Yet in China, as in Russia, the bourgeois revolution was presided over by a Marxist political party committed to socialist goals. The leaders of China's Communist Party sought a socialist future no less ardently than their Russian counterparts. Indeed, in some respects, the subjective will to achieve socialism was greater among the Chinese Communists, who were less inhibited by Marxist theoretical strictures on the economic preconditions for socialism. Whereas Russian Bolshevik leaders pinned their socialist hopes on the deus ex machina of world revolution, the leaders of the Chinese party looked to their own revolutionary past, and especially to the principles and traditions of the hallowed Yan'an era, a time when the Party had forged a quasi-socialist tradition of egalitarian values and practices. Economic policies that promoted the combination of industrial and agricultural production, educational measures which integrated learning with productive labor, and requirements that officials and intellectuals regularly participate in manual labor together with the masses—whatever the immediate considerations that may have motivated these practices—were later celebrated as foreshadowing the eventual realization of the Marxist goals of abolishing the distinctions between town and countryside, between workers and peasants, and between mental and manual labor. The ideal (and later idealized) Yan'an cadre—the "red and expert" guerrilla leader capable of performing a variety of economic, political, and military tasks—was to be celebrated as a prophetic pointer to Marx's "all-round" man of the communist future.

It is ironic that in the course of a revolution that took place in so primitive a rural environment, values and institutions were forged, albeit in rudimentary and embryonic forms, that pointed to the goals that Marxist theory attributed to an urban proletarian revolution. If China was almost entirely lacking in the material preconditions for socialism, this condition in no way diminished the socialist vision and will of China's Communist revolutionaries. The Chinese Communist victory was thus accompanied by a tension between the subjective socialist aims of the revolutionaries and the objective conditions of the country over which they had come to rule. This tension would reveal itself soon after the establishment of the People's Republic—with results that Maoists would celebrate and Mao Zedong's successors would come to deplore.

2

THE PERMANENCE OF REVOLUTION: THE MAO ERA, 1949–76

THE VICTORY OF THE CHINESE COMMUNIST PARTY in 1949 brought China its first social revolution since 221 B.C., fundamentally transforming both state and society. What made the Communist triumph socially revolutionary, and not simply another change of political regimes in a long Chinese line of political upheavals, was the destruction of the gentry class. The gentry had been the longest-lived ruling class in world history, a unique social formation whose members had dominated the political, economic, and cultural life of China for some two millennia.[1] By the early decades of the twentieth century the gentry had largely degenerated into a parasitic landlord class. The destruction of the gentry by Communist revolutionaries—during the long revolutionary struggle in the countryside and the nationwide Land Reform campaign (1950–52)—did in fact make "Liberation" meaningfully (if not fully) liberating for the great majority of the Chinese people.

The destruction of the gentry class also removed a crucial barrier to China's modern economic development. It was—in the terminology that came to be favored in post-Mao China—essential to "the lib-

---

[1] For a brief but brilliant discussion of the origins and uniqueness of the Chinese gentry, and the multiplicity of its roles, see Frederic Wakeman, Jr., *The Fall of Imperial China* (New York: The Free Press, 1975), Chapter 2.

eration of the productive forces" as well as to the liberation of the Chinese peasantry. Land Reform not only increased agricultural production, albeit modestly; it also channeled the agrarian surplus to productive uses, primarily to finance state-sponsored industrialization, rather than allowing it to be squandered by a parasitic landed elite.

While the Chinese Communist Revolution was a momentous social revolution, it was not necessarily a socialist one.[2] During the early years of the People's Republic, China's new Communist rulers could claim many accomplishments, but there was little that was socialist about the policies they pursued. The new Beijing regime was quick to accomplish the elusive "bourgeois nationalist" revolution that Sun Yat-sen and the Guomindang had sought since the turn of the century—essentially, national unification and national independence. The Communists not only unified most of the territory ruled under the old empire;[3] they also established a bureaucratic apparatus that actually governed the vast land, extending from the capital in Beijing to the remotest villages. For the first time in Chinese history there existed the political basis for a national market, another eminently bourgeois accomplishment.

National independence was also realized for the first time, at least in China's tragic modern history, an eminently bourgeois goal that had proved beyond the reach of Chiang Kai-shek's Nationalist Party. In proclaiming the People's Republic in 1949, Mao Zedong proudly declared that China had finally "stood up" in the world—after more than a century of being beaten down and humiliated by the imperialist powers of the West and Japan.

Mao's declaration of national independence was soon followed by the freezing of foreign assets, the confiscation and nationalization of foreign properties and businesses, the severance of organizational

[2] The term "social revolution" is used here in the Marxian sense as the coincidence of fundamental social and political change. As Marx put it: "Every revolution breaks up the old society; to this extent it is social. Every revolution overthrows the existing ruling power; to this extent it is political." Art. II (1844), MEGA I/3, p. 22. Karl Marx, *Selected Writings in Sociology and Social Philosophy*, p. 238. Social revolutions have been rare events in world history, as Theda Skocpol has pointed out in *States and Social Revolutions* (Cambridge: Cambridge University Press, 1979), p. 3.

[3] With, of course, the notable exceptions of Taiwan, Hong Kong, and Soviet enclaves in Manchuria.

ties between the small Chinese Christian community and foreign churches, and the expulsion of most foreigners from China. These were not so much acts of "Communist tyranny," as they were loudly denounced by Western commentators at the time, as assertions of Chinese nationalism, providing a measure of emotional compensation for a century of humiliation and suffering under the imperialist yoke.

Chinese military successes in the Korean War provided even greater nationalist satisfaction, although achieved at great human and economic cost. In November 1950, hardly more than a year after the establishment of the People's Republic, Chinese troops intervened to halt General Douglas MacArthur's reckless "march to the Yalu." The initial Chinese victories, and then the ability of the Chinese army to fight the most powerful of Western countries to a military stalemate, signaled the emergence of China as a major world power. It also stimulated great patriotic pride among the Chinese people, expanding and reinforcing the nationalist legitimacy of the new Communist regime.

About these early political achievements—national unification, national independence, and the ability to protect Chinese borders from foreign impingement—there was, of course, nothing socialist. Nor was there anything particularly socialist about the early social and economic policies of the new government. In the cities, where what little there was of a modern economy had been ruined by a decade of war and a predatory Guomindang bureaucracy, social order was reestablished and economic rehabilitation undertaken. The new government brought the most ruinous inflation in modern world history under control; restored basic municipal services and elemental standards of sanitation; rooted out a vast criminal underworld of secret societies and gangster organizations; and largely eradicated chronic social evils such as prostitution, drug addiction, and infanticide. By 1952 China's tiny modern industrial sector, ravaged by decades of foreign invasion and civil war, was restored, and production surpassed its highest prewar levels.

China's Communist regime achieved these accomplishments through policies that any responsible government would have pursued. Indeed, they were policies that the old regime would have pursued had the Guomindang survived and proved capable of implementing its own political platform.

The most socially radical program of the new Communist state—the Land Reform campaign of 1950–52—was also well within the limits of a bourgeois revolution. Land Reform destroyed the precapitalist gentry class, redistributing among poor landless and land-short peasants a portion of the lands (about 30 percent of the total cultivated area) controlled by gentry-landlords and rich peasants.[4] The landlords who survived the sometimes violent class struggles in the villages (and the overwhelming majority did physically survive[5]) were reduced to the economic status of poor peasants and often to the social status of outcasts.

But what emerged from Land Reform was not socialism, nor even a general social leveling in the countryside, for significant and sometimes wide socioeconomic differences remained. The social result was an essentially capitalist system of individual peasant proprietorship, with government-issued title deeds officially confirming the private ownership of family farms. Land, legally alienable, could be bought, sold, and mortgaged. Communist-sponsored Land Reform was revolutionary, but in a capitalist not a socialist sense, creating conditions favorable for the flourishing of bourgeois property in the vast and largely precapitalist Chinese countryside.

Capitalist enterprises also flourished in the cities during the early years of the People's Republic. To be sure, most of the modern sector of the urban economy came under the ownership of the Communist state at the outset. The banks, industries, and large commercial organizations run by the Guomindang state, and those owned by members of the "bureaucratic" and "compradore" bourgeoisie closely tied to the Nationalist regime, were confiscated and nationalized by the Communists in 1949 and 1950. Most members of the "bureaucratic bourgeoisie" had fled the country with the fall of the old regime in

---

[4] Vivienne Shue estimates that in the south-central provinces of China, probably not untypical in this respect, 40 percent of the land was confiscated and approximately 60 percent of the population received some land in the redistribution. The amounts, however, were not great. As Shue observes: "Land reform made a relatively few people poorer, and a great many people somewhat better off. But it made no one rich." Vivienne Shue, *Peasant China in Transition* (Berkeley: University of California Press, 1980), p. 90.

[5] It is estimated that from 1 to 4 percent of landlord family members were killed during the land reform period, 1949–52. Benedict Stavis, *The Politics of Agricultural Mechanization in China* (Ithaca: Cornell University Press, 1978), pp. 29–30. Cited in Shue, *Peasant China in Transition*, p. 80n.

any event, and there was hardly any alternative to state expropriation of their abandoned properties. But most owners of commercial and industrial enterprises who remained on the mainland, and who were willing to cooperate with the new Communist rulers, were designated "national capitalists" and permitted to operate their companies in capitalist fashion. Indeed, they were encouraged to do so, in accordance with Mao Zedong's 1949 dictum that China must "utilize all elements of urban and rural capitalism that are beneficial and not harmful to the national economy."[6]

The number of privately owned industrial firms actually increased during the early years of Communist rule, accounting for nearly 40 percent of total industrial production in 1953.[7] An even greater percentage of commercial firms remained under private ownership, and individual handicraft workers and petty shopkeepers were largely untouched by the new regime for the time being. In the early years of the People's Republic, urban China had, in effect, a mixed economy, albeit one where the private sector operated under strict state regulations on prices, wages, working conditions, and profits.

The encouragement of capitalist enterprises in the cities and the creation of a petty bourgeois rural economy corresponded to the new Communist state's official ideology. That ideology, revolving around the Maoist theory of New Democracy, emphasized the "bourgeois" character of the Chinese revolution and insisted on a capitalist stage of development as the necessary precondition for building socialism.

There was, of course, nothing politically democratic about the theory and practice of New Democracy, the Maoist version of the Marxist concept of "bourgeois-democratic" revolution. Political power was monopolized by the Communist Party from the outset of the People's Republic, and the claim that the new Chinese state was a "people's democratic dictatorship" based on an alliance of four progressive social classes (peasantry, proletariat, petty bourgeoisie, and national bourgeoisie) was ideological disguise. Although few were deceived by the disguise, Communist political power in the early years presided over a mostly capitalist economy. Bourgeois property

---

[6] "On the People's Democratic Dictatorship," *Selected Works of Mao Tse-tung*, Vol. 4 (Peking: Foreign Languages Press, 1961), p. 421.
[7] As calculated by Barry M. Richman, *Industrial Society in Communist China* (New York: Random House, 1969), p. 899.

and social relations were dominant in the rural areas and made up a significant portion of the urban economy. Moreover, in accordance with Marxist perspectives on the relationship between social and economic change, it was anticipated that a long period of capitalist development would precede any attempt at radical social transformation—or so Maoist theory seemed to suggest at the time.

This was not to be the case. At the end of 1952, hardly three years after the founding of the People's Republic, Party leaders decided to embark on a program of rapid industrialization based on the Soviet model of development. It was a fateful decision, with consequences that the Chinese Communists could hardly have foreseen at the time. No less portentous, the Party also decided to bring the "bourgeois" phase of the revolution to a close and begin the socialist reorganization of Chinese society. China's First Five Year Plan, closely modeled after Stalin's plan of 1928–32, was inaugurated on January 1, 1953. And the beginning of China's "transition to socialism" was formally announced just nine months later, on October 1, 1953. It was but the fourth anniversary of the founding of the People's Republic. In retrospect it seems surprising that Mao Zedong was so uncritical in importing the Stalinist model of industrial development and so quick to "skip over" the bourgeois phase of the revolution in favor of a vaguely conceived "transition to socialism," thereby abandoning his much-celebrated theory of New Democracy.

The attractiveness of a Soviet-type "heavy industrial push" is easier to understand than the decision to attempt to build a socialist society in conditions of extreme material scarcity. Immediate considerations of national security as well as long-term nationalist goals of a "wealthy and powerful" country seemed to demand that China undertake a program of rapid industrialization. Long-term socialist hopes also rested on the construction of a modern industrial economy. In the political and ideological context of the times, it was only natural that the Chinese Communists would look to the Soviet historical experience, however much Maoists had come to distrust Moscow over the revolutionary years. The Soviet Union, after all, was the sole historical example of modern industrialization under Communist political auspices, the only actually existing "socialist" alternative to capitalism. And it had been an economically successful model, at least by the standards of the time. The heroic Soviet victory over invading Nazi German armies, still fresh in mind in the early postwar years, seemed to vindicate Stalin's industrial policies, even to those aware of the enormous human and social costs exacted by Stalinism. Moreover, for a China isolated in an international arena dominated by a hostile United States, only the Soviet Union could provide economic aid (however paltry it proved to be) and technological assistance for industrial development.

Thus, despite Mao Zedong's long-standing distrust of Stalin and his frequent warnings against the "mechanical absorption of foreign material," it was Mao who took the lead in borrowing Stalinist methods of industrialization. There is no evidence of serious disagreement among the higher leaders of the Chinese Communist Party about Soviet-modeled industrial development. Even with all the benefits of historical hindsight, and latter-day critiques, including Mao's own,[8] it is difficult to imagine what a viable alternative might have been.

Less comprehensible is the 1953 decision to inaugurate the "transition to socialism," a transformation officially proclaimed "basically completed" by Deng Xiaoping and others only three years later, when Communist leaders gathered at the Eighth Party Congress in September 1956.[9] China in 1953 (or, for that matter, in 1956) possessed virtually none of the material and social preconditions for socialism —without which, Marx had warned, any attempt to construct a socialist society would prove futile, creating fertile grounds for the growth of political despotism and greater social inequalities.

Prior to 1953, Mao Zedong seemed to have reconciled himself to the historical restraints that the lack of capitalist development imposed on China's quest for socialism. As has been noted, he long had emphasized the bourgeois character of the Chinese revolution and encouraged the growth of indigenous capitalism. His theory of New Democracy, calling for a broad coalition of social classes, seemed to suggest that a partially capitalist "mixed economy" would

[8] Mao later attributed the initial Chinese enthusiasm for the Soviet model to inexperience. See Mao Zedong, "Talk at the Chengtu Conference" (March 10, 1958), *Mao Tse-tung Unrehearsed: Talks and Letters, 1956–71*, Stuart R. Schram (ed.) (Middlesex, England: Penguin, 1974), pp. 98–99.
[9] Teng Hsaio-p'ing (Deng Xiaoping), "Report on the Revision of the Constitution of the Communist Party of China," *Eighth National Congress of the Communist Party of China*, Vol. 1: *Documents* (Peking: Foreign Languages Press, 1956), pp. 169–228.

be the most suitable economic system for a country embarking on modern development from such a low level of material culture. China had yet to complete the work of capitalism and it was implied that social relations appropriate to that task would be retained for many decades to come. In the meantime, the material foundations for an eventual socialist future would be laid.

Yet China's "transition to socialism," announced in 1953, was pursued with inordinate haste. Within a few short years, privately owned commercial and industrial firms in the cities, their assets depleted by harsh government political campaigns, were de facto nationalized. By 1956 the urban bourgeoisie had all but ceased to exist as a social class, its members reduced to pensioners collecting paltry dividends on government bonds exchanged for their factories and businesses.

At the same time that the brief era of "national capitalism" was coming to an abrupt end in the cities, private ownership of land was being abolished in the countryside. As originally envisioned by Party leaders, the introduction of cooperative forms of work organization in the rural areas at first proceeded slowly and with the voluntary cooperation of the peasants. Mao Zedong suddenly sped up the process with his July 1955 speech "On the Question of Agricultural Cooperation." The unanticipated result, as Party cadres and poorer peasants took up Mao's call for a more rapid pace of rural social change, was the establishment of collective farms throughout the Chinese countryside. The collectivization of agriculture—"the high tide of socialism," as it was hailed at the time—was accomplished in little more than a year, and without the great disruptions and economic chaos that had marked its brutal Soviet precedent in the early 1930s.

In retrospect, it is puzzling that Chinese Communist leaders pursued the "transition to socialism" with such great haste between 1953 and 1956, abandoning not only Marxian teachings on the social and material prerequisites for socialism but also the relatively cautious socioeconomic policies that had come to be identified with Mao Zedong over the preceding decade. In the post-Mao era the rapidity of the change came under critical scrutiny. The noted economist Xu Dixin recalled:

> We had originally determined that the process of [socialist] transformation should take some fifteen years. However, be-

cause of a subjective desire to speed things up and the adoption of stereotyped methods . . . the transformation was achieved within four years. We were particularly over-hasty in pressing on with agricultural co-operation and the transformation of handicrafts and small businesses. The changes were too fast.[10]

Yet there is no evidence that Mao's senior colleagues—Liu Shaoqi, Deng Xiaoping, and Zhou Enlai—objected to the pace of change at the time. Indeed, Liu and Deng celebrated it in their speeches at the Eighth Party Congress in 1956. Among higher Party leaders, only Chen Yun—known as a "conservative" and a "hard-line Marxist" in the post-Mao era—appeared to have serious reservations about "socialist transformation," apparently favoring the continuation of the policies identified with the period of New Democracy.[11]

Perhaps the easy Chinese acceptance of the Soviet definition of socialism facilitated the hasty quest to build a new society in the mid-1950s. "Socialism," in its simplistic Stalinist rendering, meant little more than the nationalization of productive property, or, more precisely, the ownership or control of the major means of production by a state dominated by a Marxist-Leninist party. Absent from the Stalinist definition, and indeed condemned as an ideological heresy, was the elemental Marxian principle that the immediate producers in a socialist society should control the conditions and the products of their labor.

By the time Chinese Communists began to confront the problem of building a socialist society, the Stalinist equation of socialism with state property had come to be accepted by most Marxists and anti-Marxists alike. It was appealing in its simplicity—making "socialism" seem relatively easy to attain, despite conditions of economic backwardness. Stalinist-style socialism was also appealing because it posed no threat to bureaucratic rule. Indeed, a socialism that was *simply* the nationalization of property reinforced the power of the increasingly autonomous bureaucratic dictatorship that the Communist Revolution had yielded.

[10] Xu Dixin et al., *China's Search for Economic Growth* (Beijing: New World Press, 1982), pp. 14–15.
[11] Chen Yun, Speech, *Eighth National Congress of the Communist Party of China*, Vol. 2, pp. 157–76.

Mao Zedong did not intend to enrich the bureaucracy. He long had harbored a special hostility to bureaucracy—at least in word and sentiment if not always in deed. By the mid-1950s he was already suspicious that the revolutionary Communist cadres he had led to victory were becoming conservative bureaucratic administrators, obstacles to the radical social changes he envisioned. Socialism, for Mao, meant more than the nationalization of property; above all, it meant a continuous process of the revolutionary transformation of social relations and human nature. His haste to inaugurate that process in 1953 and after was accompanied by the reappearance of the more "utopian" strains in his thought, strains which had been temporarily (and perhaps unnaturally) repressed by the theory and practice of New Democracy. His faith in the ability of human beings to mold social reality in accordance with the dictates of their consciousness, regardless of the material circumstances in which they found themselves, reemerged, as did his elemental antipathy to capitalism. Perhaps most important, there was a revival of his youthful nationalist-populist faith in the advantages of backwardness, a belief that backwardness itself was the source of special revolutionary virtues that would soon propel China to the forefront of nations.[12] These notions soon were to find quasi-theoretical expression in the idea of "permanent revolution."

In the post-Mao era it has often been charged that Mao Zedong artificially forced the pace of social change in the mid-1950s, abandoning the bourgeois phase of the revolution before capitalism had completed its historic task of destroying feudalism. As a result, it is argued, a premature Chinese socialism was fatally flawed from the outset not only by a weak material base but also by a lingering "feudal consciousness" which distorted the political and social life of the People's Republic. Patriarchy, political dictatorship, and utopian socioeconomic policies doomed to failure were the consequences of the abortive Maoist rush toward socialism.

[12] For a discussion of Mao's belief in "the advantages of backwardness," see Maurice Meisner, *Marxism, Maoism, and Utopianism* (Madison: University of Wisconsin Press, 1982), esp. chapter 3.

With the knowledge historical hindsight generously affords, one might well arrive at the conclusion that the long-term interests of the Chinese people as well as the interests of Chinese socialism would have been better served had the "bourgeois-democratic" theory and practice of New Democracy survived several more decades than it did, and had China experienced a more gradual process of social change based on firmer economic foundations. But people act on the basis of their experiences and in response to the immediate situations they confront, without benefit of the wisdom of posterity. In the early 1950s, Chinese Communist leaders, inspired and made confident by their extraordinary record of revolutionary and postrevolutionary successes, saw an opportunity to move China forward to what they believed to be the higher realm of socialism, and they seized the opportunity, determined that China would never again be left behind in the progressive march of history.

Mao Zedong may have been the most ardent promoter of what was officially called "the general line for the transition to socialism" announced in 1953, but there is little evidence that other Party leaders disagreed. Not even those praised today as "realistic" and "pragmatic" Communist leaders, such as Liu Shaoqi and Deng Xiaoping, appear to have had reservations about passing over the "bourgeois" phase of the revolution, at least none they were willing to express. Mao's 1955 speech speeding up the collectivization of agriculture, which violated the consensus of Party leaders on the pace of agrarian change, created deep resentments, to be sure. But when agricultural collectivization was accomplished during "the socialist high tide" of 1955–56 without repeating the disasters of its Soviet precedent, virtually all Party leaders hastened to applaud the result.

Thus when the Eighth Congress of the Communist Party of China convened in September 1956, the first such meeting since 1945, Liu Shaoqi hailed "the socialist transformation of agriculture, handicrafts, and capitalist industry and commerce," which he predicted would be completed by the end of 1957.[13] Deng Xiaoping, who delivered the second of the two main reports at the Eighth Congress, similarly

[13] Liu Shao-ch'i (Liu Shaoqi), "The Political Report of the Central Committee of the Communist Party of China to the Eighth National Congress of the Party" (September 15, 1956), *Eighth National Congress of the Communist Party of China*, Vol. 1: *Documents* (Peking, 1956), p. 21.

celebrated what he called the "decisive victories in the work of socialist transformation" achieved since 1953.[14] Only Chen Yun failed to join the consensus.

By "socialist transformation" Liu and Deng essentially meant the abolition of private ownership of the means of production, with state ownership in the cities and "collective" ownership in the rural areas predominant by late 1956. With the exploiting classes of the old society thus eliminated and a "socialist system" established—"socialist" at least according to the prevailing Stalinist definition of the time—Liu and Deng proclaimed the virtual elimination of class divisions in Chinese society and thus the end of class struggles.[15] Most social differences, as Deng Xiaoping put it, had been reduced to "only a matter of division of labor within the same class."[16] It followed that the "main contradiction" in Chinese society was no longer between antagonistic social classes but "between the advanced socialist system and the backward productive forces."[17] The main task confronting the Party was no longer radical social change but rapid economic development: the construction of a modern industrial economy that would raise China's material foundation to a level appropriate to its "advanced socialist system." This, it was estimated at the time, would require three additional five-year plans, with a continuing emphasis on the development of heavy industry.[18] The formulations of the Eighth Congress generally reflected the ideological logic of the Stalinist model of development—to which most Party leaders, especially Liu Shaoqi and Deng Xiaoping, remained wedded.

Mao Zedong was less sanguine about China's socialist accomplishments than the authors of the documents which issued from the Eighth Congress. In late 1956, Mao, virtually alone among Commu-

[14] Deng Xiaoping, "Report on the Revision of the Constitution of the Communist Party of China" (September 16, 1956), ibid., p. 171.
[15] As officially formulated: "A decisive victory has already been won in this socialist transformation. This means that the contradiction between the proletariat and the bourgeoisie in our country has basically been resolved, that the history of the system of class exploitation, which lasted for several thousand years in our country, has on the whole been brought to an end, and that the social system of socialism has, in the main, been established in China." "Resolution of the Eighth National Congress of the Communist Party of China on the Political Report of the Central Committee" (September 27, 1956), ibid., pp. 115–16.
[16] Liu, "Political Report," p. 15, and Deng, "Report on the Revision," p. 213.
[17] "Resolution," p. 116.
[18] Ibid., pp. 116–17.

nist leaders, was concerned with the decidedly nonsocialist consequences of the Soviet model of development. The First Five Year Plan, to be sure, was proving even more economically successful than anticipated. Industrial production was growing at an average annual rate of 18 percent, and China's modern industrial capacity would double in a period of five years. But the social costs of economic growth were heavy, most notably the expansion of a privileged bureaucracy required to operate the rapidly expanding state-managed economy, the growth of professional and technological elites increasingly separated from the masses of workers and peasants, a growing gap between the modernizing cities and the backward (and exploited) countryside, and the decay of the revolutionary spirit. Stalinist-style industrialization was creating new social and economic inequalities at an extraordinarily rapid pace, making the socialist utopia that modern economic development was intended to serve ever more remote. The means and ends of socialism were becoming hopelessly confused.

In addition to a growing concern over the social consequences of industrialization, Mao Zedong's conception of socialism itself began to diverge from the orthodox Marxist-Leninist definition. The meaning of socialism, save as a desirable future ideal, was not a matter to which Mao had devoted a great deal of thought before the mid-1950s. When asked by an English correspondent in 1938 to describe his vision of China's future, he replied, prosaically, more in the fashion of a liberal democratic reformer than a revolutionary socialist: "Every man has food to eat and clothes to wear. Every man understands the rights and duties of citizenship and has a fair chance of education and amusement. The marriage customs are to be reformed, roads built, industry developed, a six-hour day established. There is no foreign aggression. No man oppresses another. There is equality and freedom and universal love. Together all [will] build the peace of the world."[19]

When Mao referred to socialism and Communism in subsequent years, he did so only in vague and general terms. On the occasion of the revolutionary victory in 1949 he reaffirmed the Chinese Communist Party's commitment to the Marxist goal of a classless society—but only to announce its postponement to an indefinite time in

[19] *The Times* (London), July 25, 1938.

the future and to reemphasize that the Chinese revolution remained in its bourgeois phase, thereby also emphasizing that all energies should be turned to the task of economic development.[20] In 1949, Mao conceived of socialism in Stalinist terms, hailing the Soviet Union as "a great and glorious socialist state." And when he suddenly launched China's "transition to socialism" in late 1952, he remained wedded to the Soviet definition of socialism as essentially ownership of productive property by a state under the guidance of a Marxist-Leninist party.

It was only as he became aware of the social and ideological consequences of Soviet-style industrialization, and as he observed the transformation of China's revolutionary cadres into bureaucratic rulers, that Mao began to reconsider the meaning of socialism. It was a process of reconsideration that was to prove ultimately abortive in both theory and practice, as we shall see, contributing greatly to the political turbulence that marked the final two decades of the Maoist era.

By 1956 Mao Zedong began to question the Stalinist orthodoxy that socialism was a discrete stage in historical development, a new mode of production definitively distinguished from the preceding capitalist stage and one which developed in evolutionary fashion in accordance with the growth of the productive forces. Instead, he had begun to conceive of socialism in a way that was both more flexible and more complex—as a dynamic process of change and conflict where the struggle between socialist and capitalist forces continued, where the outcome of the struggle had yet to be decided (and where indeed there might not be any final resolution), as a process of change in which the unpredictable factors of human will and consciousness still had a prominent role to play.

Mao thus rejected the Eighth Party Congress's thesis that the main contradiction in Chinese society was between an advanced "socialist system" and backward productive forces. In Mao's view, socialism required more than economic development; it also presup-

---

[20] For example, "On the People's Democratic Dictatorship," *Selected Works of Mao Tse-tung*, esp. pp. 411–12, 418–22.

posed the transformation of human beings, indeed of human nature. He also soon came to reject the official Party dictum that internal class divisions and struggles had virtually ceased. For Mao, the principal contradiction remained the conflict between the forces of capitalism and socialism, and between the ideas associated with these historic antagonists, whatever new forms the struggle might take. Such struggle, Mao believed, was essential for the vitality of society; it was the necessary motor of change and progress.

Mao's conception of socialism, however vague and amorphous, had the virtue of not being frozen in a Stalinist mold. It thus left open a possible future that might allow for something other than the Soviet-type bureaucratic formations that grotesquely represented themselves as socialist. But Maoist socialism suffered from a fatal flaw, for it was a doctrine that refused to recognize that popular democracy was a necessary means to achieve socialism—and one of its essential ends as well. The Chinese Communist Party had adopted and refined Stalinist political methods during the revolutionary days. Those Soviet-borrowed methods were enormously expanded in scope and scale after 1949, and further reinforced by the demands of the First Five Year Plan. But while Mao Zedong soon attempted to abandon the Stalinist model of industrialization and searched for an alternative road to development, this was not the case with the Stalinist political system, as the episode of the Hundred Flowers reveals.

The Hundred Flowers movement of 1956–57 was largely Mao Zedong's initiative, pursued in opposition to the Party bureaucracy. In a seemingly democratic spirit, Mao called for "a hundred flowers to bloom" and "a hundred schools of thought to contend," urging "the people" to criticize the Communist Party from without to let fresh air into its hermetic Leninist shell.

Intellectuals and then students, if not the people in general, eventually responded to the Maoist call in the great "blooming and contending" of the spring of 1957. They denounced the special privileges of bureaucrats, criticized political injustices and socioeconomic inequalities, and called for socialist democracy and socialist legality to remedy the deficiencies. It was an eminently socialist critique of the Communist regime, for the most part. Yet the democratic and socialist potential of the movement was suddenly aborted in late June when Mao Zedong joined Party leaders in turning on those who had taken up his invitation to "bloom and contend." Intellectuals and others who had participated in the campaign, criticizing not socialism but its absence, were denounced as "counterrevolutionaries" and punished in the ensuing "antirightist" witch-hunt.

In the Hundred Flowers campaign Mao Zedong questioned the Leninist infallibility of the Chinese Communist Party, but only to bolster his own claim as the source of essential political truths. He emerged from the episode as both the leader of the Party and as the spokesman for "the people." In the latter guise, he could stand above the Party and its leaders by representing himself as the incarnation of the popular will. The tension between leader and institution, long in the making, was now apparent. It was a prophetic pointer to the Cultural Revolution.

LATE MAOISM: FROM PERMANENT TO CONTINUOUS REVOLUTION

For almost two decades Maoism proceeded in accordance with the dictates of "permanent revolution," a doctrine demanding unceasing radical social and ideological change that presumably would move China to ever higher stages of social development. "In making revolution, one must strike while the iron is hot, one revolution following another; the revolution must advance without interruption," Mao Zedong declared in January 1958, in presenting himself as an advocate of "permanent revolution." It was, in effect, a repudiation of the Eighth Congress of 1956, that most non-Maoist of Party conclaves.

The theory of permanent revolution was introduced at a time when the political situation in China was particularly repressive, thereby linking social radicalism and political despotism, an association that was to fatally distort the remainder of the Maoist era. The critics Mao had called into being in the Hundred Flowers campaign had been betrayed by the Chairman. The cruel suppression of June 1957 destroyed what little hope there may have been that China's "transition to socialism" might proceed on a democratic basis. Fear was greatly intensified by the ensuing antirightist campaign, which enormously expanded the scale and scope of the repression. Deng Xiaoping was put in charge of the massive witch-hunt, a role he performed with no lack of zeal. By the time the campaign was formally terminated in May 1958, the heresy-hunt had claimed several million victims, many tens of thousands of whom were dispatched to labor in the barren reaches of Xinjiang and northern Manchuria. There they became invisible nonpersons, no longer counted as members of "the people," and largely forgotten until allowed to return to the cities twenty years later. It was a cruel episode, enormously destructive of human life and wasteful of precious talent.[21]

The antirightist campaign was not confined to intellectuals. It soon turned into a vast purge of the Party and the government, striking suspected opponents of Mao's new economic policies. The first victims of the purge were members of the central economic bureaucracies that had implemented the First Five Year Plan; the campaign then extended to regional Party and government organizations. Offices were emptied as millions of cadres were "sent down," ousted, or demoted. Cleansed of "non-Maoists," economic power was decentralized, devolving from central government ministries to provincial governments and especially to local Party organizations.[22] The purge of the Party-state bureaucracy and the decentralization of economic responsibility set the stage for a new socioeconomic strategy that Mao Zedong had been preparing—the Party-led mass mobilization of labor at the local level that was to proceed under the banner of the Great Leap Forward.

A climate of fear pervaded the land, and especially the bureaucracy and the intelligentsia, when the Great Leap Forward campaign was launched in the spring of 1958. And yet the Great Leap inspired great hope among the Chinese people, arousing utopian expectations

[21] Although Deng Xiaoping must be credited with "rehabilitating" the remaining victims of the witch-hunt after 1978, he never publicly expressed any regret over his role as the chief witch-hunter, insisting (after he came to power in 1978) that the antirightist campaign had been "necessary" and acknowledging only that its scope had been broadened unduly.

[22] For a detailed and perceptive analysis of the forms of decentralization that followed from the antirightist campaign, see Franz Schurmann, *Ideology and Organization in Communist China* (Berkeley: University of California Press, 1968), pp. 195–219.

of material abundance in an egalitarian communist society. China would achieve the economic levels of the most advanced capitalist countries in fifteen years, Mao Zedong promised. The masses themselves would master modern science and technology, it was proclaimed, thereby eliminating the necessity for privileged economic and bureaucratic elites. Three years of hard work would usher in a thousand years of communist happiness, the slogan of the day proclaimed.

The curious combination of fear and hope that marked the launching of the Great Leap was to be a fatal combination, fatal not only for the movement but also quite literally deadly for tens of millions of peasants who were to become the unintended victims of the adventure.

The Great Leap had its ideological roots in Mao's belief that the revolution must be made "permanent" if it was to survive, that the "consolidation" of the revolution at any particular stage would serve only to solidify the power of "vested interest groups" embedded in the postrevolutionary sociopolitical order, and that this would result in stagnation and the death of the revolution. Thus the Chinese Communists, presumably having achieved "socialism" in 1956, could not pause to consolidate the system and develop the productive forces, as the Eighth Party Congress had counseled. Rather it was essential to proceed in "uninterrupted" fashion toward the ever higher stages of socialism and communism, despite conditions of economic backwardness.

In the post-Mao years, Mao Zedong has been repeatedly criticized for having attempted to impose ever more radical socialist relations of production that were well beyond the capability of China's weak material base to sustain. The resulting contradictions and economic irrationalities hindered China's development and created a "socialism of poverty," it is said. Had the late Chairman heard the charges, he might have acknowledged that his aim was not to create a state of equilibrium between social relations and productive forces—a prescription for stagnation and regression, he would have maintained.[23]

---

[23] ". . . disequilibrium is normal and absolute, whereas equilibrium is temporary and relative," Mao believed, while "disequilibrium" was the dynamic force propelling social and economic progress. Mao Zedong, "Sixty Points on Working Methods," in Jerome Chen (ed.), *Mao Papers* (London: Oxford University Press, 1970), pp. 65–66.

Socialist forms of social organization, and the development of a popular communist consciousness, did not automatically result from the growth of the productive forces, he would have argued. Instead, they were goals that had to be pursued in the here and now, regardless of the low level of China's material productive forces. For Mao Zedong believed that changes in "the superstructure"—in social relations and consciousness—were more the precondition than the product of economic development.

Mao not only gave primacy to social and ideological factors over economic ones; he also believed that backwardness offered special advantages for social progress and creative development. Nothing better conveys the utopian character of the Maoist mentality during the Great Leap era (and nothing more strikingly indicates the extent of Mao's departures from Marxist theory) than the thesis celebrating the virtues of being "poor and blank" set forth in April 1958, just as the mobilization for the Leap was getting underway:

> Apart from their other characteristics, China's 600 million people have two remarkable peculiarities; they are, first of all, poor, and secondly blank. That may seem like a bad thing, but it is really a good thing. Poor people want change, want to do things, want revolution. A clean sheet of paper has no blotches, and so the newest and most beautiful words can be written on it, the newest and most beautiful pictures can be painted on it.[24]

Two years later, as if to underscore his departures from Soviet Marxism, Mao Zedong corrected Lenin:

> Lenin said: "The more backward the country, the more difficult its transition to socialism." Now it seems that this way of speaking is incorrect. As a matter of fact, the more backward the economy, the easier, not the more difficult, the transition from capitalism to socialism.[25]

[24] *Hongqi* (Red Flag), June 1, 1958. Also *Peking Review*, June 10, 1958.
[25] Mao Zedong, "Reading Notes on the Soviet Union's 'Political Economy' " (1960), *Mao Zedong sixiang wansui* (Taipei, 1969), pp. 333–34.

In the early 1980s, such were some of the "erroneous theses" that Mao Zedong's posthumous critics were to set forth as evidence of the late Chairman's "leftist" deviations from Marxist orthodoxy. In 1958, however, the Great Leap Forward campaign was launched on the basis of such utopian notions—and, initially, with the enthusiastic support of Deng Xiaoping and Liu Shaoqi. If Liu and Deng did not necessarily share Mao's belief in the revolutionary virtues of being "poor and blank," they were inspired by his nationalist vision of a "great leap" to a modern and powerful China.

The economic strategy of the Great Leap radically departed from the Soviet model of centralized economic planning that Chinese Communist leaders so ardently had embraced in the early 1950s. Economic decision making and control were now to be decentralized, transferred to local administrative organs and to basic production units. The emphasis on capital-intensive industries gave way to a more balanced relationship between agriculture, consumer-goods industries, and heavy industry based on the principle of "simultaneous development." But the key to the new economic strategy was the labor power of the masses. This enormous but greatly underutilized resource now was to be fully mobilized, through new forms of social organization and ideological inspiration, in a vast crusade to achieve both communism and modernization simultaneously.

The movement focused on the countryside, where most of China's labor power resided. The rural people's communes, hastily organized over the summer of 1958, were to combine industry with agriculture, education with productive work, and economic with political power. The communes, as celebrated in the utopian literature of the time, were not only to mobilize labor rationally but also to perform all the social revolutionary tasks Marxists traditionally assigned to "the dictatorship of the proletariat"—including the elimination of "the three differences" between town and countryside, between workers and peasants, and between mental and manual labor. The rural commune was to be the agency for China's "leap" to a communist society.

With cadres and masses alike inspired by utopian expectations, the Great Leap began with extraordinary efforts to greatly increase both industrial and agricultural production. The first frenetic phase of the campaign was marked by the general militarization of life and work, which mixed uneasily with social radicalism. By the fall of

1958, the movement was already encountering serious difficulties. The mobilization of tens of millions of peasants to work on large-scale construction and irrigation projects disrupted agricultural production; food shortages and a decline in peasant morale followed. The crisis was exacerbated by growing confusion over the operation of the hastily organized communes, the resistance of better-off peasants to a general economic leveling, the breakdown of the central planning system, and the physical exhaustion of the laboring population. In December 1958, Communist Party leaders began what was to prove a prolonged and tortuous retreat from the radicalism of the Great Leap Forward campaign.

While many factors contributed to the human disaster that was in the making, it is clear that the Great Leap collapsed under the weight of its own extravagant ambitions and inner contradictions. Yet had the retreat announced at the end of 1958 continued unimpeded, the famine that eventually took the lives of 20 million or more people almost certainly would have been avoided.[26] The real culprit in the tragedy was China's Stalinist political system.

The malevolence of the political system revealed itself in two ways. One was in the person of Mao Zedong, who, when faced with a challenge to his authority and prestige in a system that demanded a supreme leader, subordinated the interests of the peasants he had so ardently championed to his personal political interests. At the Lushan plenum in the summer of 1959, Mao demanded the dismissal and political disgrace of Marshal Peng Dehuai, the most outspoken critic of the Great Leap. To justify the purge of the popular PLA general, one of the great heroes of the revolution and the Korean War, Mao further insisted on resuscitating the radical policies Peng had condemned—at a time when economic rationality, and indeed sheer human survival, demanded retreat. For Mao it proved a Pyrrhic victory, gained at the cost of prolonging the suffering of the people.

---

[26] Estimates of famine deaths by Western demographers, ranging from 15 to 30 million victims, are based on mortality and birth rate statistics for the late 1950s and early 1960s. The estimates are essentially calculations of the number of people who were apparently "missing" from the population in the 1960s because of what are assumed to be departures from "normal" levels — i.c., an excess of deaths and a dearth of births. While there is considerable controversy over the methods of calculation and over the reliability of the statistics, there is little doubt that a human catastrophe of enormous magnitude took place.

Equally pernicious was the behavior of millions of high and low Party bureaucrats. Driven by the fears generated by the continuing antirightist purge as well as by the utopian expectations of the time, local cadres and their superiors initially claimed miraculous productive achievements. Accordingly, central state authorities made erroneous calculations about grain production and supplies, from which there followed ruinous policies. Then, as the campaign was collapsing, frightened cadres often concealed famine conditions in their localities, fatally delaying the dispatch of relief supplies to the most gravely afflicted areas in the more remote parts of the countryside. As is true of most famines, China at the end of the Great Leap suffered not so much from an absolute insufficiency of food to feed its population (at least at subsistence levels) as from the maldistribution of what was available. The great human tragedy that ensued must be attributed to China's Stalinist political system presided over by ambitious and frightened bureaucrats.

Yet Mao Zedong must bear the ultimate responsibility for the famine of "the bitter years" that took the lives of millions of peasants, just as he must receive the largest share of the credit for liberating the Chinese peasantry from the condition of chronic famine that afflicted them for generations prior to 1949. Mao's intention in the Great Leap was to modernize the Chinese countryside, not to starve the peasantry. But historical actors, in the end, must be judged by their actions and the results of their actions, not by their intentions. Mao Zedong was the principal author of the Great Leap Forward campaign; he was mainly responsible for initiating the antirightist witch-hunt that so poisoned Chinese political life (and doomed the Great Leap), even if he left it to Deng Xiaoping to actually carry out the purge; and it was Mao who insisted on reviving the radical policies of the Great Leap in the summer of 1959, when it was clear enough that to do so was economically irrational and socially reckless.

Yet if Mao must bear the major portion of the blame for the tragic results of the Great Leap Forward campaign, this does not mean that his intentions (and those of others involved in the adventure) should be ignored. Intentions *do* have a moral significance in history, and the distance between what historical actors plan and what results from the implementation of their plans is one of the things that historians are obliged to measure. Thus, the human tragedy of the Great Leap cannot be equated with the actions of genocidal political despots who quite deliberately wipe out whole populations.

The "Great Proletarian Cultural Revolution," as it was to be officially named, followed the disastrous conclusion of the Great Leap Forward campaign by only half a decade. The suffering brought to the Chinese people by the Great Leap was incomparably greater than that visited upon them by the Cultural Revolution, even if one stretches the latter to a decade-long upheaval (1966–76), as official custom now has it.[27] Yet in post-Mao China, it is the Cultural Revolution that is far more frequently and vociferously condemned than the Great Leap. To be sure, the Great Leap is viewed as an economic disaster, resulting from "leftist errors" that violated "objective" economic laws. About the human costs, little is publicly said. But the Cultural Revolution is officially condemned as responsible for "the most severe setback and the heaviest losses suffered by the Party, the state and the people since the founding of the People's Republic."[28]

The reasons for this historically unbalanced and morally grotesque accounting are not far to seek. Many of the leaders of the post-Mao regime, including Deng Xiaoping, originally supported the Great Leap and played a prominent role in its "antirightist" prelude. Moreover, the victims of the adventure were mostly silent peasants. By contrast, the most prominent victims of the Cultural Revolution were articulate intellectuals and high Party officials—among them Deng Xiaoping.

With the failure of the Great Leap, Mao Zedong retreated from the center of the political stage, only grudgingly accepting responsibility for the debacle. In the early 1960s, control of the state apparatus fell into the hands of veteran Party bureaucrats led by Liu Shaoqi and Deng Xiaoping. By reviving central planning, pursuing

[27] From 20 to 30 million people died as a result of the Great Leap, according to most Western demographic estimates, while estimates of the Cultural Revolution death toll rarely exceed 400,000 people, a good portion of whom were radical Red Guards slaughtered by the Army. The Cultural Revolution, declared concluded in 1969, was in the post-Mao era officially extended to the time of the fall of "the Gang of Four" in the autumn of 1976.

[28] As officially stated in the 1981 "Resolution on Certain Questions in the History of Our Party Since the Founding of the People's Republic of China," *Beijing Review*, July 6, 1981, pp. 10–39.

flexible economic policies,[29] and utilizing a disciplined Leninist Party apparatus, Liu and Deng were remarkably successful in overcoming the economic crisis and bringing about a renewal of economic growth.

But there was a social price to be paid for this economic success—greater bureaucratization, growing social and intellectual elitism, increasing economic inequalities, the erosion of ideological commitment, and a further confusion of the means and ends of socialism. Mao Zedong, already haunted by fears of a "capitalist restoration," was now convinced that China was following the "revisionist" path the Soviet Union had traveled. The stage was set for the Cultural Revolution.

The Great Proletarian Cultural Revolution (1966–69) is usually interpreted as a gigantic power struggle instigated by Mao Zedong in an attempt to regain political supremacy after the debacle of the Great Leap. Yet if power, pure and simple, were his aim, Mao surely could have found simpler and less hazardous ways than to call upon the people to rebel against the authority of the Communist Party and to risk the obvious social and political perils that such a course entailed. In the early 1960s, Mao still enjoyed enormous popular prestige; he could command the support of most of China's military forces, now headed by his protégé Lin Biao; and he retained the loyalty of rank-and-file Communist Party cadres, even if not the undivided allegiance of all higher Party leaders. The ingredients for constructing a personal dictatorship were by no means lacking.

But Mao's aims in launching the Cultural Revolution involved more than a quest for personal power, which he already enjoyed in abundant measure. At the heart of Mao's strange and bizarre effort was a desperate attempt to revive a revolution that seemed to be dying and thus to keep open the possibility of a socialist future. Political decrees issued from above could not achieve this; it was essential, rather, to spiritually revitalize and politically activate the people. "The only method is for the masses to liberate themselves, and any method of doing things in their stead must not be used,"

---

[29] "It doesn't matter whether the cat is black or white; as long as it catches mice, it's a good cat," the maxim that later was to be so often cited as evidence of Deng Xiaoping's celebrated "pragmatism," was first heard in 1962.

was one of the most loudly proclaimed of the original principles of the Cultural Revolution.[30]

In Mao's mind, no doubt, the revolutionary activity of the masses and his own personal power were inseparable. It is one of the more universal and banal features of politics that most leaders are convinced that the general welfare is best served by the successful pursuit of their personal political interests. But the point is not to divine Mao's real motives and unravel the inner workings of his mind. The revolutionary socialist goals Mao proclaimed at the beginning of the Cultural Revolution must be taken seriously today because they were taken seriously by the Chinese people at the time. The failure of the scholar of the Cultural Revolution to take the proclaimed goals into full account makes it impossible to understand why so many millions of people responded with such great enthusiasm and militancy to Maoist ideological appeals during the Cultural Revolution—and why so much disillusionment and despair followed in the tragic wake of the great upheaval.

The ideology of the Cultural Revolution set forth the thesis that China's postrevolutionary order had created a new bureaucratic ruling class, a functional "bourgeoisie" that was exploiting the masses of workers and peasants by virtue of its political power. The origins of this Maoist proposition can be traced to the Hundred Flowers movement of 1957, when Mao insisted that the class struggle between the bourgeoisie and the proletariat persisted in socialist society, albeit in "the ideological field." Mao was also becoming critical of the decline of revolutionary ideals among Communist Party cadres, who, he charged, sought special privileges and personal gain and had grown apart from the masses.[31] In the early and mid 1960s he stressed the gravity of China's class struggle. He warned that the new socialist society was producing "new bourgeois elements" and a new "bureaucratic class." He attributed the origins of this new "bourgeoisie" to the inequalities generated by Communist China's political

---

[30] One of the famous "Sixteen Articles," the charter of the Cultural Revolution, promulgated in August 1966. *Decision of the Central Committee of the Chinese Communist Party Concerning the Great Proletarian Cultural Revolution* (Peking: Foreign Languages Press, 1966).

[31] Both themes appear in the major theoretical treatise of the period, "On the Correct Handling of Contradictions Among the People," initially delivered as a speech in February 1957 and published (in revised form) in June of that year.

system, a Stalinist hierarchy of bureaucratic ranks and status. And, accordingly, he found the leaders of that new exploiting class to be officials in the upper echelons of the Chinese Communist Party— "people in positions of authority within the Party who take the capitalist road," as he charged on the eve of the Cultural Revolution.

These extraordinary propositions—extraordinary at least for the leader of a Communist state—were accompanied by the transformation of the theory of "permanent revolution" *(budan geming)* into the theory of "continuing the revolution" *(jixu geming)*, the latter to be officially enshrined as the essence of Mao Zedong Thought in 1969. It was more than a semantic change that occurred over the decade. Whereas the theory of permanent revolution retained the notion of progressive stages in the achievement of socialism and communism, albeit stages rapidly passed through, in the theory of "continuing the revolution" socialism was seen less as a positive utopia than as a prolonged negation of capitalism, as a period of continuous struggle against the myriad forces of the past and present that threatened a "capitalist restoration."[32] The notion of "continuous revolution" reflected the pessimism that overtook Mao Zedong in the 1960s, when he brooded over the possibility of the restoration of "the reactionary classes" and when he warned that China could turn fascist.

In conceiving the Cultural Revolution, Mao had arrived at a conclusion that no other Communist in power had been willing to entertain. As if in defiant anticipation of what was to become the ultimate heresy of the era that succeeded his own, Mao came to believe that a socialist society, if left to its own devices, would generate a new exploiting class. The new ruling class would be fashioned not from the remnants of the old bourgeoisie that had been destroyed by the revolution but rather from the bureaucrats of the Communist present, the onetime revolutionaries of mostly humble social origins

---

[32] On the two theories, and the distinction between them, see John Bryan Starr, *Continuing the Revolution: The Political Thought of Mao* (Princeton: Princeton University Press, 1979); Stuart R. Schram, "Mao Tse-tung and the Theory of Permanent Revolution," *The China Quarterly*, No. 46 (April–June 1971), pp. 221–44; James Peck, "Revolution Versus Modernization and Revisionism," in Victor Nee and James Peck (eds.), *China's Uninterrupted Revolution* (New York: Pantheon, 1975); and, most extensively, Michael Sullivan, "Mao Zedong's Theory of Continuing the Revolution: Ideological and Policy Disputation During the Transition to the Post-Mao Era, 1974–78," unpublished Ph.D. dissertation, The Flinders University of South Australia, 1993, 3 vols.

who had become rulers after 1949 and who now appropriated an increasing share of what the laboring masses produced. Mao sometimes bluntly referred to them as "the bureaucratic class," whose members, he charged, were becoming "bourgeois elements sucking the blood of the workers."[33]

Mao's views about the social evolution of postrevolutionary China were remarkably similar to those of Milovan Djilas, the Yugoslav theorist whose writings about the metamorphosis of a Communist Party elite into a "new class" earned him a place in one of President Tito's jail cells. But whereas most Western observers hailed Djilas as insightful and courageous, Mao's ideas were widely dismissed as the paranoiac ravings of a fanatic ideologue.

Among the many strands in the ideology of the Cultural Revolution, none struck more responsive chords in Chinese society than the antibureaucratic appeals of the aging Mao. Only a decade and a half after the victory of the revolution, popular resentment against cadre arrogance and bureaucratic privilege was widespread. Although the highest officials of the regime—numbering perhaps 100,000 in the upper echelons of China's *nomenklatura*—enjoyed such perquisites as comfortable homes with servants and chauffeur-driven cars, on the whole the privileges of China's bloated army of bureaucrats were paltry compared to those of their Soviet counterparts (not to speak of luxurious living standards of the ruling classes of most capitalist countries). Yet the hierarchical distinctions cut sharply, and the hypocrisy was glaring in a society whose leaders so loudly professed egalitarian values and constantly proclaimed that it was the sacred duty of cadres to "serve the people." Many citizens were only too eager to take full advantage of the newly proclaimed "right to rebel" against established authority.

The freedom to organize which the urban populace briefly enjoyed during the early phases of the Cultural Revolution led to an orgy of verbal and physical violence directed against Communist bureaucrats and "bourgeois" intellectuals, neither of whom were to forget their torment—or their tormentors. The attack on the Communist Party, sanctioned by a deified Mao Zedong, was a principal aim of the movement. But the method of the attack on the Party—the Cultural

---

[33] "Selections from Chairman Mao," Joint Publication Research Service No. 49826, p. 23.

Revolutionary principle of encouraging "the free mobilization of the masses"—could not be confined to ferreting out Mao's opponents in the political apparatus. It also gave powerful organizational expression to a myriad of socioeconomic grievances and divisions that the new sociopolitical order had generated—and which hitherto had lain half hidden. Indeed, much of what happened during the Cultural Revolution was unintended. As Hong Yung Lee explains: "Although the elite groups initiated the mass mobilization, once the masses were mobilized the movement gained its own momentum. The elite groups endeavored to manipulate the masses, but the masses found numerous ways to express themselves spontaneously. The Cultural Revolution manifested every conceivable type of human problem and every kind of political behavior."[34]

There was a certain social rationality in the spontaneous, if sometimes cruel and bizarre, political behavior of the masses during the tumultuous and violent years 1966–68. The chaotic conflicts between the bewildering variety of organizations that appeared and then suddenly vanished were, as a general rule, struggles between social groups who had a conservative stake in the postrevolutionary order of things and those who did not. But the unaccustomed freedom of organization and expression that briefly reigned also unleashed nihilistic tendencies, senseless brutalities, and frenzies of violence. As conditions became dangerously chaotic in the early months of 1967, and as the country seemed to slide toward civil war, Mao Zedong embarked upon a long, agonizing, and bloodstained retreat from the proclaimed principles and goals of the Cultural Revolution. The much-celebrated "right to rebel," which a godlike Mao had granted to the people, now was withdrawn by Mao—and, to make that point brutally clear, he dispatched the Army to restore order.

What was ultimately restored was essentially the pre-Cultural Revolution order of things. Whereas the Cultural Revolution began with a Maoist-inspired attack on the Chinese Communist Party, it concluded with a Maoist drive to reestablish the authority of the Party—and to eliminate all mass organizations that were not under the control of the Leninist apparatus. The political structure that

---

[34] Hong Yung Lee, *The Politics of the Chinese Cultural Revolution* (Berkeley: University of California Press, 1978), p. 1.

emerged from the fierce battles of the Cultural Revolution was little changed from that which existed prior to the great upheaval, save that it was shorn of some of Mao Zedong's more prominent political opponents. And even most of the "capitalist roaders," who had been so vociferously denounced and then "overthrown" in the late 1960s, were rapidly returned to their bureaucratic positions in the early 1970s, not excluding Deng Xiaoping. Deng, branded "the second leading person in authority taking the capitalist road" during the heyday of the Cultural Revolution, was recalled to high office with Mao's approval in 1973, rapidly rising to become Premier Zhou En-lai's heir apparent by the end of 1975. As we shall see, Deng Xiaoping was very much involved in the byzantine political struggles that marked the closing years of the Mao era.

Although the Cultural Revolution generated much radical rhetoric about a revolutionary transformation of the social division of labor, there were in fact no significant changes in the relations and organization of production in either town or countryside. Such reforms as issued from the upheaval were minor, or quickly reversed in the early 1970s, or (as in cultural and educational policies) simply obscurantist from the outset.

Nonetheless, the Cultural Revolution raised profoundly important questions about the means and ends of socialism in the twentieth century—questions which future socialists (and not only in China) will find they cannot ignore as this most violent of centuries comes to a close. At no time in world history have the consequences of the transformation of revolutionaries into rulers been exposed so clearly. Never in the history of modern socialist movements has the problem of the relationship between rulers and ruled in a society where private ownership of productive property has been abolished been raised so sharply. Rarely has there been so searching an inquiry into the sources of inequality, elitism, hierarchy, and bureaucracy.

The Cultural Revolution also brought to attention a host of questions about the social consequences of economic and technological progress. It raised anew questions about the viability of socialism pursued as a national enterprise in a global capitalist economy, and revealed, in stark images, the banality of evil and the forces of inhumaneness and violence that lurk so near the surface in what is now fashionable to romanticize as "civil society."

Some of these questions were originally posed by Mao Zedong from on high at the beginning of the Cultural Revolution; others were raised by the mass movement from below; and some emerged from the dynamics of the ill-fated movement itself. In the end, all the questions and issues remained unanswered and unresolved. The proclaimed goals of the Cultural Revolution were soon distorted and eventually betrayed by its leaders, including Mao Zedong. The wreckage of the movement left millions of physically and psychologically wounded victims, among them many of the youthful Red Guards whom Mao had called into being and then called upon the People's Liberation Army to dispatch. Never has a revolution so literally consumed its own children.

The tragedy of the Cultural Revolution's tortured and brutal course was compounded by how little some learned from it. For the most part, participants and observers alike searched only for ways to condemn the upheaval, not for new ways to address the real problems that the failures of Maoism left unresolved. Many of the victims of the Cultural Revolution, both cadres and intellectuals, who later emerged as leaders of the post-Mao regime appear to have derived from the experience mainly the lesson that "chaos" (luan) was to be avoided at all costs, an imperative that was to serve as a sanction for the perpetuation of political dictatorship.

But if the Cultural Revolution brought no significant changes in the Communist political system or in the social division of labor that the system enforced, it did stimulate important changes in popular political consciousness, especially in the cities. The brief but intense period of "mass democracy," a quite exceptional time when the Chinese people enjoyed freedom of political expression and organization, wrought profound changes in attitudes toward political authority, especially among those who hastened to take up the initial, if short-lived, Maoist invitation to "dare to rebel" against the holders of bureaucratic power. In the end, the Cultural Revolution, both because of the impact of its original ideals and because of the Maoist betrayal of those ideals, bred political skepticism, a skepticism that often turned to political cynicism and passivity. Yet it also engendered activistic intellectual and political expression among some, especially among members of what Liu Binyan has called "the thinking generation," youths who grew to political maturity in the days of the

Cultural Revolution and whose subsequent political lives were decisively molded by both the positive and the negative lessons they drew from their experiences during the great upheaval. Through the agency of that generation, many of the original ideals and slogans of the Cultural Revolution were to echo in the popular democratic movements that emerged in the post-Mao years.

The failure of the Cultural Revolution left an exhausted Maoism, a doctrine and a regime incapable of carrying out the long-heralded "transition to socialism." In the last dreary years of the Mao era, despite all the fiery revolutionary rhetoric that masked the bureaucratic factional struggles of the time, the social state of China remained essentially what it had been in the mid-1950s—a Soviet-style, bureaucratically dominated social formation, complete with an increasingly inefficient "command economy" and a Leninist party dictatorship.

It would be fruitless to attempt to locate such a society along a conventionally drawn historical line running from capitalism to socialism. To be sure, the Mao regime must be credited with several quasi-socialist achievements. Among them were policies that mitigated the commodification of labor by providing lifetime job security and comprehensive social welfare for a portion of the urban working class; programs and practices, albeit mostly symbolic, to moderate the ravages of the division of labor and occupational specialization; and partially successful efforts to limit the extremes of social and economic inequality modern economic development fosters. But despite the ubiquitous use of the label "socialist" by both the regime's ideologists and its critics, based on a common confusion between the nationalization and the socialization of productive property, Maoist China lacked the essential social and political preconditions for socialism. Most important, it was not a society where the direct producers controlled the conditions and products of their labor, certainly the essence of any meaningful conception of socialism. Rather, labor and the products of labor were commanded by a bureaucratic apparatus that stood high above society, well beyond any form of popular control. And the absence of even the most elemental democratic structures precluded any process of evolution toward a "self-government of the producers," the political form that Karl Marx assumed would be an essential, indeed a defining, feature of a genuinely socialist society.

If Maoist China was not really socialist, was it then essentially capitalist? Like other Soviet-type societies, the Chinese socioeconomic system during the Mao period operated in the fashion of a capitalist economy in several important respects. The members of the working population were denied control of the means of production and thus were forced to sell, or barter, their labor power to bureaucratic agencies. Wage labor was the predominant mode of labor, explicitly in urban factories and enterprises and, in thinly disguised forms, in the "collectivized" countryside. And it was through the exploitation of the laborers that "surplus value" was maximized, and extracted by the bureaucracy to carry out an unceasing and massive process of primitive capital accumulation. In brief, the unpaid labor of the people financed the industrialization program organized by the Communist state. If capitalism is defined, at least in Marxian terms, as "a way of production founded on the exploitation of wage labor for the accumulation of capital" (with exploitation understood in terms of "surplus value"),[35] then one might well conclude that Maoist China was an essentially capitalist social formation.

Was Chinese socialism, then, simply another case of "capitalism without the capitalists," as Adam Ulam once characterized all Communist regimes?[36] However appealing in its simplicity it might be to view the Communist state as some sort of supreme or collective capitalist, it is both theoretically and historically impossible to conceive of "capitalism without capitalists." An economic system presupposes a specific social agent, a class that creates and operates a particular economy—and benefits from doing so. The necessary agent in the

[35] As formulated by Robert C. Tucker in *The Marxian Revolutionary Idea* (New York: Norton, 1969), pp. 42–43. A somewhat more elaborate but compatible definition of capitalism, also derived from original Marxian sources, has been presented by Eric Wolf: "The capitalist mode . . . shows three intertwined characteristics. First, capitalists detain control of the means of production. Second, laborers are denied independent access to means of production and must sell their labor power to the capitalists. Third, the maximization of surplus produced by the laborers with the means of production owned by the capitalists entails ceaseless accumulation accompanied by changes in methods of production." *Europe and the People Without History* (Berkeley: University of California Press, 1982), p. 78.
[36] Ulam, *The Unfinished Revolution*, p. 45.

case of the capitalist mode of production is a bourgeoisie. But the Chinese bourgeoisie had been destroyed by the Communist Revolution, along with the landed gentry, and ceased to exist as a functioning social class by the mid-1950s.

The Maoist regime abolished not only the bourgeoisie as a social class but also private ownership of productive property in general, thereby doing away with another essential element of a capitalist economy. Also lacking was a labor market, for although commodity production in general continued throughout the Mao period, both labor and the major means of production were removed from the sphere of commodities. Moreover, the eminently and uniquely capitalist "law of value" was greatly restricted by the state's central planning apparatus, which set prices and determined rates of investment and consumption in an essentially nonmarket economy.[37]

With many of the essential features of a capitalist economy absent or drastically modified, it would be misleading to call the Maoist regime "capitalist"—just as it is impossible to accept the socialist claims that were made by its rulers and ideologists. Neither really capitalist nor truly socialist, Maoist China was sometimes simply called "postrevolutionary" or "transitional."

Yet if the Mao period was "transitional," it was never entirely clear where that process of transition was leading. What was clear enough was that it was a bureaucratically dominated social formation. With the removal of the old ruling classes of rural landlords and urban bourgeoisie, and the inability of workers and peasants to exercise power on their own, Communist bureaucrats, increasingly removed from their revolutionary origins, came to fill the social void, dominating the political and economic life of the People's Republic. Yet however pervasive and powerful the bureaucracy, its rule rested

---

[37] The "law of value," as explained by Riskin, "refers to the tendency, under competitive market conditions, for goods to exchange with each other at rates proportional to their relative socially necessary labour times." Riskin, *China's Political Economy* (New York: Oxford University Press, 1987), pp. 165–66. For a discussion of use of the "law of value" in the post-Mao reform period, see below, Chapter 8. It might be noted that while Mao Zedong acknowledged that commodity production would continue in a socialist society (although labor would no longer be a commodity), he insisted that the "regulating function" of the law of value would give way to planning. See "Critique of Stalin's 'Economic Problems of Socialism' " in Mao Zedong, *A Critique of Soviet Economics* (New York: Monthly Review Press, 1977), pp. 135–47.

on fragile social foundations—and not because of Maoist hostilities and political uncertainties alone. More important, bureaucrats were unable to root their power in property. They could not convert their sometimes considerable material privileges into capital. And they could pass on neither wealth nor position to their descendants. In these respects, they lacked several of the essential social and material attributes of a ruling class.

They also lacked the means to ideologically legitimate their social and economic privileges. China's bureaucrats perforce posed as the self-sacrificing guardians of the revolution and the bearers of socialism, whether out of genuine belief or as a matter of customary political ritual. In either case, in the need to claim legitimacy in Marxist terms, they reflected the socialist norms that were still dominant in Chinese society during the Mao era, a society where Marxian goals and values still mattered. Indeed, Maoist China was most socialist in its *striving* for a socialist future and in the popularized egalitarian goals and values that such a vision entailed. In social reality, as has been suggested, Mao Zedong's socialist accomplishments were modest, and in some respects grotesque caricatures of elemental socialist principles. But in the sense that Lenin once said that "our system is socialist because it is moving to socialism,"[38] Mao could perhaps claim Chinese progress toward socialism on the basis of the goals that were so ardently sought in his time.

At the end of the Mao period China contained elements of both socialism and capitalism—but without being either essentially socialist or essentially capitalist. The hybrid character of the Mao regime reflected the contradiction between the bourgeois and socialist aspects of the Chinese revolution, a contradiction which Mao Zedong's successors would inherit.

[38] Cited in Seweryn Bialer, *Stalin's Successors: Leadership, Stability and Change in the Soviet Union* (New York: Cambridge University Press, 1980), p. 26.

PART TWO

THE RISE
OF DENG XIAOPING

3

THE TRANSITION
TO THE POST-MAO ERA,
1976–78

MAO ZEDONG DIED ON SEPTEMBER 9, 1976. Six weeks before, in what must have seemed an eerie portent of political upheaval and dynastic change, a devastating earthquake struck North China, leveling the industrial city of Tangshan and leaving 240,000 dead.[1]

Mao left China with more than the rubble of the Tangshan earthquake to clear away. The turmoil of the Cultural Revolution of the late 1960s and the byzantine political struggles which followed in the 1970s had taken their toll, rending the fabric of the postrevolutionary order. Signs of social disintegration and discontent were unmistakable in the fateful summer of 1976. The economy stagnated and staggered for lack of any coherent policy direction from the faction-ridden government, its leaders preoccupied with the struggle to claim Mao's mantle. Popular antipathy toward the regime had been dramatically expressed in the Tiananmen incident of early April, when demonstrators had clashed with militiamen in the square be-

---

[1] The earthquake, which came on July 28 and measured 8.2 on the Richter scale, was one of the greatest natural disasters of modern times. Its epicenter was at Tangshan, a newly industrialized coking coal and steel city with a population of over 1 million, but it wrought damage over wide areas of Hebei province, especially in the city of Tianjin, and to a lesser degree in Beijing itself. Refusing offers of foreign assistance, the government launched a campaign to criticize, as a "feudal superstition," the traditional notion of the Mandate of Heaven, which held that natural disasters foreshadowed political ones. Relief efforts were largely left to the PLA.

neath the Gate of Heavenly Peace. The regime's insensitivity to the hundreds of thousands of citizens who had come to honor the memory of Zhou Enlai (who had died in January 1976) during the Qing Ming festival seemed sacrilegious, deepening popular hostility. What the government condemned as a "counterrevolutionary incident" became enshrined in the political consciousness of the urban populace as the "April Fifth Movement," a powerful symbol of popular resistance to an arbitrary state.

Over the summer months, a wave of strikes, factory slowdowns, and absenteeism—fueled by a combination of economic and political grievances—swept through most major industrial centers. In some areas workers began arming themselves, preparing to resume the unresolved factional battles of the Cultural Revolution. An upsurge in common crime, including bank robberies and the looting of state granaries, added to the social turbulence. The economy suffered from the deteriorating social and political condition. Whereas industrial production had more than doubled over the previous decade (from 1966 to 1975), it stagnated in the year 1976, barely increasing by 1 percent compared to the previous year.[2] While the Chinese economy was hardly "on the brink of collapse," as was repeatedly claimed in the self-serving statements of Mao's successors, it was in serious trouble.

More ominous was the central government's inability to control factional political conflicts in the provinces, which sometimes erupted into armed violence. The Beijing regime could no longer count on the undivided support of the Army to enforce its authority. Indeed, one of the most powerful military leaders, General Xu Shiyu, whose command covered much of South China, openly defied the authorities in the capital by taking Deng Xiaoping under his protection at his Canton headquarters following the Tiananmen incident of April 1976, when Deng had once again been purged as an "unrepentant capitalist roader." Deng's main tormentors now were the members of a bureaucratic clique who claimed to embody the radical spirit of both Mao

[2] The gross value of industrial production (in constant prices) increased from 152.6 billion yuan in 1966 to 321.9 billion yuan in 1975. In 1976 the figure was 326.2 billion, an increase of only 1.3 percent. Robert Michael Field, "The Performance of Industry During the Cultural Revolution," *The China Quarterly*, No. 108 (December 1986), Table 1, p. 627. Agricultural output apparently was little affected by the events of 1976.

and the Cultural Revolution, the most prominent of whom were soon to be branded the "Gang of Four"—Zhang Chunqiao, Maoist theoretician and leader of the abortive Shanghai People's Commune in 1967; Yao Wenyuan, Shanghai polemicist whose celebrated article had announced the opening of the Cultural Revolution; Jiang Qing, Mao's wife and would-be cultural czar; and Wang Hongwen, onetime textile worker who had been elevated to the highest levels of Party leadership during the Cultural Revolution.

From the sanctuary provided by his military allies, Deng Xiaoping prepared to do battle with his leftist foes in Beijing, even contemplating the possibility of civil war. In the summer of 1976, Deng reportedly told his supporters:

> Either we accept the fate of being slaughtered and let the Party and the country degenerate, let the country which was founded with the heart and soul of our proletarian revolutionaries of the old generation be destroyed by these four people, and let history retrogress one hundred years, or we should struggle against them. . . . If we win, everything can be solved. If we lose, we can take to the mountains. . . . At present, we can at least use the strength of the Canton Military Region, the Fuzhou Military Region, and the Nanking Military Region to fight against them.[3]

In mid-1976, China suffered from a dearth of leadership to deal with this perilous situation. Zhou Enlai, who had guided the central state apparatus for over a quarter of a century, had died in January. Mao Zedong, paralyzed by a stroke, lay semi-comatose over the summer. And Deng Xiaoping, once Zhou's heir apparent as Premier if not necessarily his natural successor, had been banished once again.

It was left to the weak and inexperienced Hua Guofeng to manage the affairs of state and to hold the Communist bureaucracy together during this perilous transition to the post-Mao era. The son of a poor peasant from the impoverished northwestern province of Shanxi, Hua had joined the Red Army as a teenager in the late 1930s and had enjoyed a successful if not especially distinguished career in the

---

[3] Quoted in a 1978 speech by Zhang Pinghua, director of the Party's propaganda department. Cited in Roger Garside, *Coming Alive: China After Mao* (New York: Mentor, 1982), p. 130.

postrevolutionary bureaucratic order.[4] He had quietly and slowly risen to national political prominence through a combination of fortuitous events and Mao Zedong's personal patronage. Hua made his initial political mark and favorable impression on Mao by ardently promoting agricultural collectivization in Hunan province in 1955. He remained a loyal supporter of Mao and his policies over the turbulent two decades which followed. It was not so much his experience in agrarian policy as his adroitness in following Mao through the tortuous course of the Cultural Revolution that placed Hua at the center of national political life. At the Ninth Party Congress in 1969, which formally concluded the upheaval, Hua was elected to the Party Central Committee. He was installed in the central government in Beijing shortly after and, in January 1975, the National People's Congress named him Vice-Premier of the State Council and Minister of Public Security. In the latter capacity, Hua's power over China's secret police organization was considerably enhanced when Kang Sheng ("China's Beria," as he was sometimes called) died in December 1975.

Yet Hua lacked the attributes of a strong leader, and he was unable to fill the powerful offices he inherited with real political substance. Beyond his personal loyalty to Mao and Mao's policies of the moment, Hua was a political cipher. His ideology was at best amorphous and his personality bland. He inspired neither love nor hate; indeed, he was totally uninspirational. Of course, it was precisely his political weakness that made Hua temporarily and grudgingly acceptable to the various factions struggling to succeed Mao.

But an amiable personality was insufficient to win the trust of those contending for power in 1976. The fact that Hua had risen to political prominence during the Cultural Revolution when so many others had fallen and that he occupied the premiership that many thought rightfully belonged to Deng Xiaoping did little to endear him to veteran Party and Army leaders determined to restore the pre-

---

[4] Most of what is known (or has been reported) about Hua's political career can be found in Michel Oksenberg and Sai-cheung Yeung, "Hua Kuo-feng's Pre-Cultural Revolution Hunan Years, 1949–66: The Making of a Political Generalist," *The China Quarterly*, No. 69 (March 1977), pp. 3–53. Needless to say, the brevity of Hua's tenure as China's leader cut short scholarly interest in his political career.

Cultural Revolution order of things. And Hua—who lacked ideological zeal and was inclined to take a middle position whenever
possible—had come under attack from the "leftist" Cultural Revolutionary faction in 1975, accused of "revisionism" and "capitula-
tionism." The leftist attacks on Hua resumed in the summer of 1976,
as Mao lay dying.

When Mao died in the early morning hours of September 9 and
the government broadcast the news on radio and television, the state
he had founded twenty-seven years before did not collapse, contrary
to the long-standing predictions of many and the hopes of some.
There was no social disorder. "People did keep calm," a British
diplomat in Beijing at the time observed. "There were many who
wept, but there was not the same stunned grief as there had been for
Zhou [Enlai]. People were anxious for their future but put much time
into decorating shops, markets, cinemas, and other public places with
yellow-and-black drapery and a profusion of white silk-paper flowers."[5] Hua Guofeng declared an eight-day period of mourning and
soon announced plans to construct an enormous mausoleum in the
square beneath the Gate of Heavenly Peace, where the Chairman's
body would permanently reside in a crystal box. On September 18
more than a million people assembled in that square to commemorate
their dead leader. Hua Guofeng, flanked on the rostrum by China's
highest remaining leaders (few of whom owed him political allegiance), delivered the official eulogy, supplementing his tribute to
Mao's revolutionary accomplishments with an exhortation to the populace to "deepen the struggle to criticize Deng Xiaoping."

Much more than mourning was going on in China in the weeks
following the death of Mao Zedong. The leaders of China's political
and military bureaucracies moved quickly to eliminate what remained of the old Cultural Revolution group, seeking to swiftly conclude the debilitating factional struggle that had marked and marred
the last years of the Mao era. The veteran bureaucrats who had survived the Cultural Revolution, or who had been returned to office in
the early 1970s, mostly looked to Deng Xiaoping as their natural
leader. Deng himself had quietly moved from Canton to Beijing
shortly after Mao's death, but he remained politically invisible, for it

[5] Garside, *Coming Alive*, p. 129.

was still a time that required the badge of Mao's personal legitimation. However, there was no lack of Party and PLA leaders who acted in Deng's stead, and some probably according to his instructions. In the meantime, the active veteran bureaucrats, with barely concealed feelings of contempt for the upstart Hua Guofeng, found Hua politically useful. His task was to purge the Party and state leadership of the remaining Cultural Revolutionary radicals, especially those soon to be known as the Gang of Four, and to do so under a Maoist cloak.

Mao's death left the Gang defenseless, for while Mao had afforded them political protection, he had not sufficient confidence in his self-proclaimed disciples to trust them with the real levers of state power. To be sure, the Gang appeared politically formidable in the early autumn of 1976. All stood high in the formal Party and state hierarchies; they and their apparent allies formed a majority of the Party Politburo and they occupied two of the four remaining seats on its Standing Committee.[6] They commanded workers' militias in Shanghai, Beijing, and other major cities. And they dominated the official media and the cultural bureaucracy.

But the power of the Four was largely illusory, mostly a product of the revolutionary rhetoric with which they filled the pages of the official press. While the Gang numbered the Minister of Culture among their supporters, their opponents included the Minister of Defense, most of the generals of the PLA, and the secret police. Aware of the precariousness of their position, the Gang made frenzied efforts to seize state power in the weeks after Mao's death. They alerted their confederates in Shanghai to arm the workers' militia and prepare for a possible insurrection. They attempted, unsuccessfully, to win the cooperation of PLA commanders in Beijing. Their writers launched new and increasingly harsh assaults on Hua Guofeng as a "rightist" molded in the image of Deng Xiaoping. Jiang Qing appeared at Politburo meetings claiming to be her dead husband's chosen successor—by virtue of a probably doctored slip of paper on which the dying Mao purportedly had written: "Act according to the principles laid down," principles allegedly communicated to Jiang

[6] With Mao's death, the members of the Standing Committee of the Politburo had been reduced to four: Hua Guofeng, Ye Jianying, Zhang Chunqiao, and Wang Hongwen.

Qing alone. It was a revised version of one of the instructions Mao presumably had given Hua Guofeng on April 30, which in its original form cryptically read: "Act according to past principles." Another handwritten message Hua claimed to have been handed from Mao's deathbed was composed of six characters which read: "With you in charge, I am at ease." Hua would seem to have had the best of these rather dubious claims to legitimacy, and he was to use them, along with the Army and the secret police, to secure his brief succession to the chairmanship of the Chinese Communist Party.

The brandishing of these varying versions of Mao's deathbed "instructions" gave a macabre cast to the acrimonious Politburo meetings held in late September to settle the succession crisis. But principles, either "past" or "laid down," had little to do with the outcome. The principles which were to govern the political life of the Party so often had been revised, and so long ignored, that the participants in the struggle would have been hard pressed to say what they once might have been. The problem of succession was to be settled neither by principles nor by Politburo meetings but rather by naked military force.

The fall of the Gang was plotted by Hua Guofeng and Minister of Defense Ye Jianying in concert with most of the top commanders of the PLA. Abundant military forces were available to carry out the mission, but it was decided that the task might best be performed under a Maoist facade. To that end, Hua secured the services of Wang Dongxing, who had been Mao's personal bodyguard and who commanded an elite force of 20,000 soldiers known as the 8341 Unit, whose function was to guard high Party leaders in their official compounds in Zhongnanhai in the center of Beijing.

With the remnants of the old Cultural Revolution group politically isolated, it remained only for the armed forces and security police to complete the process of what soon was to be celebrated as "the smashing of the Gang of Four." The "smashing"—or, more precisely, the coup—combined the melodrama of an old imperial palace intrigue with the cold precision of a modern military operation. In accordance with a carefully conceived plan, Hua Guofeng called an emergency meeting of the Politburo's Standing Committee for midnight on October 5. When Zhang Chunqiao and Wang Hongwen arrived at the customary meeting hall at Party headquarters in Zhong-

nanhai, they were seized by armed soldiers of the 8341 Unit, hand-
cuffed, and taken off to jail—with Hua and Ye Jianying observing
the proceedings on closed-circuit television in an adjoining room.
Simultaneously, Jiang Qing and Yao Wenyuan were arrested in their
homes by other soldiers of the 8341 Unit. Within a few hours in the
early morning of October 6, the Gang and dozens of their more prominent followers were placed in solitary confinement in several Beijing
area prisons. Shanghai, supposedly a radical bastion, remained quiet
in the days and weeks which followed as PLA and civilian secret
police agencies were busily engaged in arresting (and sometimes ex-
ecuting) followers of the Gang who held positions in Party and state
bureaucracies.

Few Chinese mourned the demise of the Gang of Four, who had
earned reputations as political schemers, hypocrites, and opportun-
ists. Their ideological dogmatism, cultural vandalism, and xenophobic nationalism had put the intelligentsia into bitterly hostile
opposition. Nor could the Four claim any significant popular following among the urban masses, except for isolated (and what proved
unreliable) pockets of working-class support in Shanghai and elsewhere. The great majority of the urban populace had come to resent
the arbitrary and coercive political methods of the Gang—and longed
for an end to the political strife the purposes of which had long
become incomprehensible, save as a way to further the personal ambitions of political leaders. But if the Gang's fall was well deserved
and popularly applauded, the manner in which it came about was a
sad commentary on how the Cultural Revolution had distorted the
political life of the People's Republic. The Cultural Revolution
had been launched in 1966 on the principle that "the only method
is for the masses to liberate themselves, and any method of doing
things in their stead must not be used." That principle had been
abandoned in practice within a few months of its proclamation, but
by the mid-1970s Chinese politics had degenerated to the point
where political disputes were settled by military force. The Cultural
Revolution began with loud declarations of the virtues of popular
democracy; yet what came to be called "the cultural revolution decade" ended (and the post-Mao era was inaugurated) with an armed
coup d'état.

The Cultural Revolution had further created a situation where leadership claims were based almost solely on what were alleged to have been Mao Zedong's personal benedictions, with hardly even the pretense of adhering to proclaimed Leninist norms of "inner-party democracy." Both the Gang of Four and Hua Guofeng had made their bids for power by invoking Mao's alleged deathbed wishes, ignoring the normal workings of Party organs. The decision to elevate Hua to the chairmanship of the Communist Party was made by a handful of leaders meeting in secret, ad hoc sessions in October 1976. Although they spoke in the name of the Central Committee—which in fact did not convene to formally ratify the decision until almost a year later —they invoked what was said to have been Mao's final request to legitimize the act. The ghost of the dead Mao loomed larger than the collective will of the Party, and certainly larger than the desires of the masses whom the Party claimed to represent.

To bolster his claim as rightful heir, Hua Guofeng took great pains to cultivate a Maoist image. He attempted to imitate Mao not only in political style but in physical appearance, permitting his hair to grow long in the fashion of the late Chairman. His portraits became omnipresent in public places, always hung alongside those of his predecessor. Giant oil paintings were produced depicting Mao and Hua as the closest of comrades at critical points in the history of the revolution. As the self-appointed editor of the long-delayed fifth volume of *The Selected Works of Mao Tse-tung*, a carefully selected and edited version of Mao's writings over the years 1949–57, finally published in March 1977, Hua Guofeng wrote a preface and a bland commentary in a feeble attempt to establish his credentials as a Marxist theoretician. Plans to compile and publish the collected works of Mao were announced, but the project was soon abandoned as post-Mao leaders came to the realization that little could be found in Mao's post-1957 writings to support the policies they were pursuing. In the meantime, much was made in the official press of the scrap of paper the dying Mao presumably had given Hua bearing the six characters which read: "With you in charge, I am at ease." Hua and his associates further and rather rashly pledged, in a highly publicized declaration of February 1977, "to support whatever policy decisions were made by Chairman Mao" and to "unswervingly follow whatever instructions were given by Chairman Mao," a declaration that was to earn them the name "the whatever faction," a pejorative label bestowed by their political opponents. And Hua spared no public expense in hastening the construction of the ornate Mao Memorial Hall in Tiananmen Square, which he formally dedicated in May 1977 and where millions would come on pilgrimages to pay homage to the embalmed corpse of the late Chairman.

But behind this elaborate Maoist facade, Hua Guofeng was taking the first tentative steps in a de-Maoification process that would turn into a torrent of deradicalizing change by the end of the decade. Significant shifts initially came in cultural and educational policies, the areas of Chinese life where the influence of the Gang of Four had been the greatest.

THE NEW "HUNDRED FLOWERS"

Among the myriad accusations made against the Gang of Four, none is more deserved than the charge that they turned China into a cultural desert during the Cultural Revolution. The early years of the People's Republic hardly will be recorded as one of the great eras of cultural and intellectual creativity in Chinese history, burdened as they were by Maoist dogmas on art, literature, and philosophy. But prior to 1966—and within the limits imposed by Maoist political and cultural orthodoxies—China did enjoy a reasonably lively cultural and scholarly life. During the early postrevolutionary years, moreover, the new society benefited from an enormous expansion of education at all levels, a striking rise in literacy, and the rapid assimilation of modern scientific and technological knowledge.

This progress certainly did not continue during the "cultural revolution decade" of 1966–76, which soon came to be called "the ten lost years." In the name of "revolutionary culture," Jiang Qing and her collaborators imposed repressive and culturally obscurantist policies which had a deadening effect on Chinese society. Most pre-Cultural Revolution art, literature, films, and plays were banned— the products of a sinister "antisocialist" dictatorship, according to Jiang Qing. Little new was produced to take their place, as few writers were allowed to write (or publish what they did manage to write in secret) and few artists were permitted to paint. Foreign books and journals were treated as state secrets. Libraries and museums were often closed, or, when open, access to their contents severely restricted. For cultural sustenance, the people were largely reduced to viewing eight officially approved "revolutionary" operas and ballets. Such, in brief, were the cultural results of the Cultural Revolution.

The state of the universities was little better. Closed for three years or longer during the Cultural Revolution, most had reopened by the early 1970s—but with drastically reduced enrollments, demoralized faculties, and students both emotionally and academically ill prepared to resume their studies.[7] The plight of the universities was bluntly described by the Minister of Education, Zhou Rungxin, an official generally sympathetic to the educational reforms Mao had intended, when he lamented in 1975: "In the universities now: no more culture, no more theory, no more scientific research."[8]

Following the purge of the Gang of Four, Hua Guofeng began to do away with the more absurd and obscurantist policies of the old Cultural Revolution group—without, however, denouncing the Cultural Revolution. Faced with the delicate task of condemning the despotic cultural policies of Jiang Qing without criticizing the dogmas on art and literature laid down by her late husband, in January 1977 the government announced a new "hundred flowers" policy, supported by copious if selective quotations from Mao's 1957 speech "On the Correct Handling of Contradictions Among the People" and his Yan'an talks on art and literature. The new hundred flowers policy, like the old, portended something less than the birth of intellectual freedom, but it did stimulate a literary and artistic renaissance of sorts, at least compared with the previous decade's cultural aridity. A multitude of hitherto banned plays, operas, musical productions, and films once again appeared in theaters. Literary and scholarly journals moribund since 1966 resumed publication, supplemented by a growing list of new periodicals. A particularly noteworthy feature of the literary revival was an outpouring of short stories by young writers describing their experiences during the Cultural Revolution,

---

[7] University and college enrollments, which had reached 900,000 during the 1965–66 academic year, were no more than 200,000 in 1971–72 and 500,000 in 1975–76.

[8] Cited in Mark Selden (ed.), *The People's Republic of China: A Documentary History of Revolutionary Change* (New York: Monthly Review Press, 1979), p. 156.

a body of writing that came to be known as "the literature of the wounded generation."[9]

As bookstore shelves were restocked with both Chinese and foreign works, the ranks of writers and artists were fortified as the government undertook the "rehabilitation" of intellectuals purged, arrested, or otherwise rendered silent during the Cultural Revolution or before, a rectification of old wrongs that proceeded at an agonizingly slow pace in 1977 but which gained force throughout 1978. And the xenophobic fear of foreign influence, which had contributed to the stifling of artistic life during the previous decade, gave way to a revival of the Maoist slogan of making "foreign things serve China," in accordance with which the government promoted cultural exchanges with foreign lands and the publication of new translated editions of Western literary classics.

Educational policy proved a far more politically sensitive issue than the cultural thaw. The Maoist reform of the school system had been loudly celebrated as one of the major accomplishments of the Cultural Revolution, not only in China but also abroad. The proclaimed principles were admirable, particularly for a society that aspired to socialism: the ideal of combining education with productive labor; the notion of "open-door schooling," which included sending students to work in the surrounding society and the recruitment of experienced peasants and workers as temporary or part-time teachers to offer instruction on the practical application of technological knowledge; and the general egalitarian restructuring of the educational system to provide equal opportunities for the children of workers and peasants. Yet whatever benefits these measures may have brought to elementary and secondary education, Mao's policies, or at least the manner in which they were implemented, had paralyzed higher education and retarded the development of science and technology.

[9] For a perceptive survey and discussion of the literary revival in the early post-Mao years, see Sylvia Chan, "The Blooming of a 'Hundred Flowers' and the Literature of the 'Wounded Generation,' " in Bill Brugger (ed.), *China Since the Gang of Four* (New York: St. Martin's, 1980), pp. 174–201. Also, for a sampling of the literature, Perry Link (ed.), *Roses and Thorns: The Second Blooming of a Hundred Flowers in Chinese Fiction, 1979–1980* (Berkeley: University of California Press, 1984); and Bennett Lee and Geremie Barmé (eds.), *The Wounded: New Stories of the Cultural Revolution* (Hong Kong: Joint Publishing Co., 1979).

To remove these barriers to modern economic development, the Hua Guofeng regime began to reestablish the elitist educational system of the pre-Cultural Revolution period. The new government began its efforts to revive the universities in the spring of 1977. Under the traditional admonition "respect the teacher," the old system of hierarchical ranks was restored in the colleges and discipline was demanded in the classroom. In the autumn of 1977, school entrance examinations were fully reestablished and the requirement that middle school graduates spend several years engaged in manual labor prior to their college education was abolished. University enrollments were increased and the college curriculum was expanded to four years, replacing the three-year system introduced during the Cultural Revolution. There shortly followed the restoration of the two-track system in elementary and middle schools, which included the reappearance of "key point" schools that channeled a small number of the most academically promising students onto an elite educational route leading from kindergarten to college.[10]

The retreat to familiar educational policies did serve to revive the universities, but not without costs to the socially egalitarian ideals Chinese Communist leaders still proclaimed. Nor did the revitalization of higher education come without cost to the lower levels of the education system, for what was given to the universities and research institutes was partially taken from the elementary and secondary schools, particularly in the countryside. As college enrollment climbed, the number of children enrolled in elementary and secondary schools declined, and various part-time adult education and work-study programs and institutions atrophied.

The elitist character of Hua's educational policies were to be refined and greatly elaborated by Deng Xiaoping in the 1980s, foreshadowing the generally conservative social policies that were to be pursued in the post-Mao era. For both Hua and Deng, the overriding goal was rapid economic development, to which all social and socialist considerations were to be subordinated.

---

[10] For a superb critical analysis of these and other early post-Mao changes, see Suzanne Pepper, "Chinese Education After Mao," *The China Quarterly*, No. 81 (March 1980), pp. 1–65.

THE TEN YEAR PLAN

In the last months of 1976, following the purge of the Gang of Four, Hua Guofeng turned his attention to China's economic problems and cultivated an image as an innovative modernizer. Over the next year he organized dozens of national work conferences on economic problems, personally presiding over several of the more prominent gatherings. In the heated debates on economic policies which had raged during Mao's last years, Hua had characteristically pursued a quiet middle course, hoping to offend neither the right nor the left factions of the Party. Now established as Mao's successor, he emerged as an ardent advocate of the Four Modernizations, a term that was to acquire extraordinary status as official economic policy when it was formally incorporated in the revised Party constitution in August 1977—and, for good measure, in the new state constitution promulgated in March 1978.

The term "Four Modernizations" derived from Zhou Enlai's January 1975 report to the Fourth National People's Congress in which he had made his stirring call for the rapid modernization of agriculture, industry, national defense, and science and technology—so that China would be transformed into a "powerful, modern socialist country" by the end of the century. But with Zhou mortally ill with cancer, having left his hospital bed to deliver his speech to the Fourth Congress, it had been left to then Vice-Premier Deng Xiaoping to formulate concrete plans to realize the goals Zhou had set forth. The three policy documents Deng produced in the autumn of 1975, while paying appropriate lip service to the Maoist orthodoxies of the time, rested on Deng's long-standing (and eminently orthodox Marxist) belief that the level of a country's economic development was ultimately the determining factor in its history. Quoting copiously from the writings of Lenin and Mao, both of whom he interpreted in an economically deterministic fashion, Deng proposed a program for rapid economic development. He called for the full restoration of managerial authority in the factories and greater material rewards for those who labored in them. He advocated the large-scale importation of modern technology from the advanced capitalist countries, to be financed by the export of Chinese coal and oil. And he put special emphasis on the development of modern science, which required revamping the higher education system and regaining the support of the intelligentsia.[11]

Although Deng's policy documents were quickly labeled "the three poisonous weeds" by his leftist opponents, the debate which ensued during the final year of the Maoist regime had not been on the issue of "modernization," which all favored, or even on "the Four Modernizations," but rather on the methods that were to be employed in modernizing China, the pace at which the process should proceed, and especially the question of how the means of modern economic development were to be reconciled with the ends of socialism. For Mao and his leftist disciples, only a "continuous" process of revolutionizing popular consciousness and social relationships would ensure that modernization served socialist goals. Deng Xiaoping, by contrast, was convinced that China had achieved a basically socialist system of ownership by 1956, as he had maintained at the Eighth Party Congress that year, and believed that further social change should follow only from the further development of the country's productive forces. He combined the orthodox Marxist belief that socialism presupposed a high level of economic development with the comforting Stalinist orthodoxy that the growth of the productive forces within the framework of a "socialist system" would automatically guarantee the future transition to communism.

When Hua Guofeng turned his attention to China's economic problems in late 1976, it was more Deng's perspectives than Mao's precepts that informed his policies. Like Deng, he seemed to believe that the rapid development of the economy was all that was needed to make China both powerful *and* socialist. Indeed, the economic policies pursued by the Hua government in the years 1977–78 were largely borrowed from the proposals Deng had set forth in 1975—although, in attempting to implement his program, Hua at first ignored Deng, instead invoking the authority of the dead Zhou Enlai

---

[11] The three documents drafted by the State Council under Deng's guidance in 1975 were entitled: "On the General Program for All Work of the Whole Party and the Whole Country"; "Some Questions on Accelerating the Development of Industry"; and "Report on the Work of the Chinese Academy of Sciences." Although not formally published, all were extensively discussed and debated in the official press at the time. For English translations of the original documents, see Chi Hsin, *The Case of the Gang of Four* (Hong Kong: Cosmos Books, 1977), pp. 203–95.

and the pre-Great Leap writings of Mao Zedong. Special prominence was given to Mao's 1956 speech "On the Ten Great Relationships," a rather enigmatic statement that lent itself to a variety of interpretations, now first officially published some twenty years after Mao had composed it.

Among Hua Guofeng's initial actions in the economic realm, following his triumph over the Gang of Four, was to demand labor discipline in the factories, where factional political disputes had disrupted production in 1976. A continuing purge of alleged supporters of the Gang in industrial enterprises was accompanied by measures to strengthen the authority of factory managers and enforce newly introduced work rules and regulations. Incongruously employing Maoist slogans, the new leader stressed the need for "scientific" managerial techniques and modern business methods, as Deng Xiaoping had advocated in 1975. And borrowing from Deng's proposals of eighteen months before, Hua launched a "socialist labor emulation" campaign in March 1977, quoting Lenin on the efficacy of such forms of competition among the proletariat.

Other proposals made by Deng in 1975 were also championed by Hua Guofeng in 1977. Stressing China's need to learn from "good and advanced foreign experience," an old Maoist slogan, Hua promoted foreign trade and the importation of modern technology from the advanced capitalist countries, doubling China's exports and imports over the following two years.[12] Hua's economic advisors also began to emphasize the importance of the role of profits in the operation of economic enterprises, a policy for which it was more difficult to find an appropriate Maoist slogan. To spur labor productivity (and no doubt to make new factory disciplinary rules less unpalatable to the laborers), most workers in state enterprises, along with teachers and government functionaries, were given a 10 percent wage raise on October 1, 1977, the twenty-eighth anniversary of the founding of the People's Republic. It was the first significant salary increase in

[12] The expansion of foreign trade and technology imports was not entirely innovative. The Maoist policy of self-reliance had proved sufficiently flexible to accommodate a tripling of foreign trade between 1971 and 1975, primarily with non-Communist countries. The sharp drop in foreign trade in 1975, as Carl Riskin has pointed out, was due to economic as well as political factors, particularly the combination of inflation and recession in the international capitalist economy, which at once raised the costs of foreign technology and machinery while depressing China's exports, resulting in unanticipated balance-of-payments deficits. Riskin, *China's Political Economy*, p. 259.

the cities in two decades. These measures, along with others, proved economically salutary. Industrial production, which was virtually stagnant in 1976, increased by 13 percent in 1977.

Changes in agricultural policy were slower to unfold, partly because Hua Guofeng's political credentials owed so much to his support of Mao's agrarian policies. In the agricultural realm, Hua at first confined himself to promoting "learn from Dazhai" (Mao's egalitarian rural model) campaigns and calling for the mechanization of farming, both eminently Maoist themes. But by the end of 1977 there were hints of change, including the encouragement of larger private family plots for subsidiary production, expanded rural markets, and proposals for limiting the autonomy of the communes.

Although still loudly proclaiming fidelity to the Thought of Mao and the principles of the Cultural Revolution, the leaders of the Hua regime made quiet but significant ideological shifts to support their pursuit of the Four Modernizations. On the hoary debate over the relationship between politics and economics, Hua clearly came down on the side of the primacy of economic factors. A major report on the economy issued in September 1977—which called for greater centralized control over the industrial sector, increased borrowing of foreign technology, and a larger role for profits in the operation of economic enterprises—proclaimed that "revolution can never be substituted for production," a statement with which Mao would have agreed if the order were reversed. There was a marked deemphasis on class struggle in favor of slogans exhorting the masses to increase production and productivity, and there were increasingly strident campaigns against the alleged heresy of "egalitarianism." But perhaps more reflective of the tenor of the times than official ideology —where changes were more in tone than in substance—was the reappearance of the economic planners of the 1950s, about whom little had been heard for two decades. Most prominent among them was Chen Yun, one of the main architects of the First Five Year Plan of 1953–57, who long had advocated a supplementary role for market forces in a planned economy and who was reputed to admire Yugoslav experiments in "market socialism." Another of the old economic experts who reemerged was Sun Yefang, a sophisticated Marxist political economist best known for his argument that the "law of value" continued to operate in a socialist economy.

Calls for speeding up the pace of economic development, heard ever more urgently throughout 1977, culminated in the report Hua Guofeng delivered to the Fifth National People's Congress in February 1978. Hua presented, and the assembled delegates duly ratified, a Ten Year Plan for the years 1976–85 which ambitiously set forth the goals of the Four Modernizations. Over the eight remaining years of the belatedly unveiled Ten Year Plan, Hua proposed investment for capital construction in industry surpassing the total investment of the entire twenty-eight-year period since 1949. Although he repeated the long-standing ideological orthodoxy that "agriculture is the foundation of the national economy," the Plan clearly emphasized the modern industrial sector and especially heavy industry. Hua called for the construction of 120 large-scale industrial projects by 1985, including ten major iron and steel complexes, nine nonferrous-metal complexes, eight new coal mines, ten oil and gas fields, six new trunk railways, five large harbors, and thirty major power stations. Coal production was to double over the remaining eight years of the Plan (to more than a billion tons by 1985) and steel output was to more than double, from about 24 million tons in 1977 to a targeted 60 million tons in 1985. By the end of the century, Hua predicted, "the output of major industrial products will approach, equal or outstrip that of the most developed capitalist countries."[13]

The Ten Year Plan demanded enormous increases in the importation of foreign capital and technology, a vast expansion of foreign trade based on the export of Chinese raw materials and agricultural products, and ever larger accumulations of capital. Hua's economic program, presented as an effort to make up for lost years in economic development (due, it usually was said, to "the sabotage of the Gang of Four"), portended further increases in China's already unbearably high accumulation rate.[14]

The capital required to finance the proposed development of large-scale industries and the massive import of modern technology left little for investment in agriculture or consumer goods industries.

[13] Hua Kuo-feng, "Report to the Fifth National People's Congress" (February 26, 1978), *Peking Review*, March 10, 1978, pp. 7–41.

[14] The accumulation rate, the portion of the national product withheld from consumption for investment to expand productive capacity, did in fact rise to a high of 36.7 percent in 1978. It was to be lowered in subsequent years, with the abandonment of the Ten Year Plan in favor of new economic policies.

THE RISE OF DENG XIAOPING ★ 79

Nonetheless, the Ten Year Plan envisioned that the value of agricultural output would grow by 4.5 percent per year—more than twice the average per annum increase during the preceding two decades —with much of the surplus slated for export to raise capital for industrial development. This would be accomplished, it was assumed, through an accelerated program of agricultural mechanization. The Ten Year Plan called for the mechanization of 85 percent of all farm work by 1985. Ambitious targets were set for increases in the production of tractors, drainage and irrigation machinery, and chemical fertilizers. More consumer goods also would be produced, it was said, but the Plan provided only 5 percent of total state industrial investment for light (or consumer goods) industries, an even smaller percentage than during the "heavy industrial push" of the First Five Year Plan of 1953–57.[15] About socialist goals, little was heard from the new government, save for ritualistic utterances which assumed that the desired social changes would follow naturally from the envisioned economic transformation. The assumption was eminently Stalinist, as was the economic development strategy it rationalized.

The Four Modernizations in their 1978 incarnation promised all things (or at least all material things) to all people. Urban workers were promised higher wages and regular promotions in a rapidly developing industrial economy, along with better housing and expanded welfare benefits. Peasants were promised increased state support for agriculture, greater freedom to cultivate larger private plots and to trade in rural markets, and higher incomes. Intellectuals, and especially scientists, were promised salaries and status appropriate to their specialized knowledge and professional talents, greater opportunities to pursue their careers in a revamped system of higher education and an expanded network of research institutes, and more autonomy in their particular areas of expertise in accordance with the revived "hundred flowers" policy. All social groups, both in the cities and in the countryside, were promised stores stocked with consumer products and the means to purchase them. And the armed forces were promised a modernized defense capacity. Although military modernization seemed to rank lowest on the list of the Four

---

[15] Under the First Five Year Plan, 11 percent of state capital investment in the industrial sector went to consumer goods industries.

Modernizations, most PLA generals no doubt welcomed the Ten Year Plan's enormous emphasis on developing basic industries and modern technology, the necessary prerequisites for building a modern military machine.

While the economic goals of the Ten Year Plan were at first widely applauded, the applause soon began to fade when questions were raised about how Hua Guofeng's heady proposals were to be financed. Official planners estimated in 1978 that at least US $630 billion would be required to carry the Plan through 1985, about fourteen times the amount invested to finance China's rapid industrialization during the ten-year period 1949–59.[16] The question of how so enormous a sum could be acquired was to loom large in the ensuing policy deliberations in Beijing.

Hua Guofeng's grandiose version of the Four Modernizations had been borrowed, in large measure, from the proposals set forth by Deng Xiaoping in 1975. The Ten Year Plan drew heavily, if selectively, from the three policy documents Deng had sponsored in the autumn of that year; it was, in fact, a revised and bloated version of an economic plan drafted by the State Council in 1975 when that body had been operating under Deng's direction, shortly before his second fall from power. Having embraced Deng's 1975 policies in 1977, Hua hardly could avoid embracing Deng himself. And there were powerful political and military voices demanding the embrace as early as the autumn of 1976, when Hua Guofeng was conducting public celebrations of "the smashing of the Gang of Four" and even as he was still anachronistically promoting "the campaign to criticize Deng Xiaoping." For Hua Guofeng, it was to prove a necessary but fatal union.

---

[16] Chu-yüan Cheng, "The Modernization of Chinese Industry," in Richard Baum (ed.), *China's Four Modernizations: The New Technological Revolution* (Boulder, Co.: Westview Press, 1980), p. 36.

4

THE TRIUMPH OF DENG XIAOPING

IN THE TURBULENT HISTORY of Chinese Communist politics, the saga of Deng Xiaoping surely makes for one of the most intriguing chapters. Twice purged by Mao Zedong, Deng twice returned to power, once with Mao's consent and once again after Mao's death. In his second political reincarnation, he became the dictator of China for the better part of two decades in an era that the aging—and now reform-minded—Deng was determined to make definitively post-Maoist.

The story of his eventual triumph seems all the more remarkable because the man himself so long seemed unremarkable. A rather drab figure among Chinese Communist leaders, at least in comparison to such men of heroic stature as Mao, Zhou Enlai and Zhu De, Deng made his political mark by operating the day-to-day organizational levers of the Party from behind the scenes, barely known to the Chinese people until he was denounced as "China's second Khrushchev" during the Cultural Revolution. His name was not identified with any great events of the revolution and he could make no claim to credentials as a Marxist theoretician. But Deng's ascendancy came when the times called for a leader with less than heroic qualities and, certainly, with something other than revolutionary qualifications.

Yet Deng was once a revolutionary. Unlike Mikhail Gorbachev,[1]

---

[1] Gorbachev was not born until fourteen years after the Russian October Revolution.

with whom he once was often compared, Deng Xiaoping was a revolutionary activist from the early days of the Chinese Communist movement. Indeed, he was a member of the original May Fourth generation of Communist leaders—although, born in 1904 (from a well-to-do gentry family in Sichuan province), he barely qualified, chronologically, for membership in that most remarkable of generations. Still a young teenager at the time of the May Fourth incident of 1919, he nonetheless was caught up in the radical intellectual and political currents of the period, journeying to France as a work-study student in 1923. There he joined the Paris branch of the Chinese Communist Party then led by Zhou Enlai, whose friendship and patronage Deng was to retain for half a century. Deng returned to China in 1925 by way of Moscow and participated in the great revolutionary upsurge of 1925–27.

Among the survivors of the counterrevolutionary carnage of 1927, he spent two precarious years working in the small Communist underground in Shanghai before retreating to the countryside to become an organizer of peasant armies, a leader of the ill-fated Jiangxi Soviet government in the early 1930s, and a survivor of the Long March of 1934–35. During the Yan'an era and the final years of the Civil War he served in various Red Army units, primarily as a political commissar rather than a military leader. The personal and political relationships he cultivated with Red Army generals over the revolutionary years were to serve him well in the postrevolutionary era.

Deng's not inconsiderable contributions to the Communist victory of 1949 and his demonstrated administrative abilities earned him a politically prominent place in the postrevolutionary order. By the mid-1950s he had risen, "step by step," as he later defined the proper method of bureaucratic promotion, to the higher echelons of the central Party apparatus in Beijing. He was selected for membership in the Politburo in 1955 and, the next year, at the Eighth Party Congress, he joined Liu Shaoqi in delivering one of the two main reports.[2] At the Eighth Congress, he was promoted to the Politburo's Standing Committee, which ranked him sixth among top Party leaders, and he was also appointed to the revived post of Secretary-

[2] Teng Hsiao-p'ing (Deng Xiaoping), "Report on the Revision of the Constitution of the Communist Party of China," *Eighth National Congress of the Communist Party of China: Documents* (Peking, 1956), Vol. 1, pp. 169–228.

General. The latter position provided Deng with considerable control over the Party's organizational apparatus, which he employed to support the policies of Liu Shaoqi in the early 1960s. Thereby earning Mao's ire, he was purged as "the second-leading person in authority taking the capitalist road" during the Cultural Revolution. But unlike Liu, Deng managed to survive the ordeal both politically and physically. He retained his Party membership and spent his days working in a tractor factory and growing vegetables in Nanchang—and his nights, it was claimed, reading the works of Marx and Lenin.

After six years in political exile, Deng, now sixty-nine, returned to power in 1973—with Zhou Enlai's support and Mao's acquiescence. But his tenure as the dying Zhou's putative successor was brief, as has been noted. Under attack by the Gang of Four in 1975 and eventually blamed for the Tiananmen incident of April 1976, he was once again branded "China's Khrushchev" as well as "an unrepentant capitalist roader" and dismissed from all the high offices he had only so recently regained. He was permitted, however, to retain his Party membership, "so as to see how he will behave in the future," the Politburo decided.

Deng's behavior was not what his leftist critics desired, although it was perhaps what they might have expected. Deng was unimpressed with the charges made against him. "If they tell you that you're a capitalist roader, it means you're doing a good job," he remarked.[3] Nor did his second fall from power diminish his political will. During the summer of 1976, with Mao Zedong on his deathbed and the Gang of Four dominating the political stage, Deng plotted his return to power with his PLA allies in South China, even contemplating, if necessary, the possibility of civil war. The necessity did not arise. The death of Mao in September and the subsequent downfall of the Gang opened a new and climactic chapter in the remarkable political history of Deng Xiaoping.

In September 1976, Deng quietly returned to Beijing from his refuge in Canton and probably played a behind-the-scenes role in the October coup that brought down the Gang of Four. But even after the

---

[3] "Sayings of Teng," Appendix 2 in Ross Terrill, *The Future of China After Mao* (New York: Dell, 1978), p. 268.

deed was done, Deng was still officially out of favor. Denunciations
of Deng had become one of the standard political rituals of the year
1976 and performances of the ritual lingered on to the year's end.
Hua Guofeng, much to his later political embarrassment, stubbornly
persisted until December in urging criticism of "Deng Xiaoping's
counterrevolutionary revisionist line." But the campaign against
Deng, which lacked vigor and was greeted with public indifference,
had become politically anachronistic after the fall of the Gang of
Four. As official criticism of Deng faded, a well-orchestrated movement praising him emerged. In December 1976, wallposters appeared
in various cities calling for Deng's return to office. But more than
wallposters were brought out on Deng's behalf, for he had powerful
and increasingly vocal advocates among provincial Party leaders,
PLA generals, and in the Politburo itself, especially Vice-Premier Li
Xiannian.

Hua Guofeng, however fervently he proclaimed his fidelity to
"whatever" policies and instructions Mao Zedong had laid down,
could not long resist the pressure of prominent Party and military
leaders who rallied behind Deng Xiaoping. Nor would it have been
logical for him to do so. Hua could hardly continue to denounce the
crimes of the Gang without offering compensation to the most celebrated victim of their villainies. Nor could he long pursue the policies
originally devised by Deng in 1975 while excluding their author from
the political arena. Thus Hua, whose own accession to the highest
offices in the land resulted from a political compromise, soon agreed
to a compromise proposed by Defense Minister Ye Jianying. Deng,
according to the agreement, would not be installed as Premier (thus
the successor to the increasingly venerated Zhou Enlai), as his supporters wished, but he would be restored to the positions he had
occupied in early 1976. The slanderous charges against him, now
attributed to the Gang of Four alone, were to be officially repudiated.
The decision was formalized at a July 1977 meeting of the Party
Central Committee. Deng again became a member of the Standing
Committee of the Politburo, a Vice-Premier of the State Council, and
Chief of the General Staff of the PLA.

When the Eleventh Congress of the Chinese Communist Party
convened the next month, Deng Xiaoping, who only a year earlier
was being hounded for myriad political and ideological heresies, was

now firmly established as one of China's three top leaders. Ahead of him on the Politburo Standing Committee were only Party Chairman Hua Guofeng and Minister of Defense Ye Jianying. Vice-Premier Li Xiannian and Wang Dongxing (commander of the praetorian 8341 Unit) ranked lower. It was to prove an unstable political alignment.

In his report to the Eleventh Party Congress on August 12, 1977, which took four hours to deliver, Hua Guofeng continued to link his political fortunes to the legacies of Mao Zedong and the Cultural Revolution.[4] Yet his radical rhetoric only thinly masked the deradicalizing social and economic policies that had come to be associated with the term "Four Modernizations," policies largely borrowed from Deng Xiaoping's proposals of 1975. Deng's policy drafts of that year, hitherto officially condemned as "the three poisonous weeds," now were hailed as "fragrant flowers." Deng himself delivered the Congress' closing address, calling for "less empty talk and more hard work."[5]

Part of the "hard work" that followed from the Eleventh Congress was a massive purge of leftists, which Hua Guofeng had demanded in his report. Nearly half of the 35 million Party members, it was revealed, had been recruited since the beginning of the Cultural Revolution in 1966. The influence of these new cadres, generally younger in years and more radical in political orientation than those they had joined or replaced, was drastically reduced. At the higher levels of the Party apparatus the positions of purged leftists were occupied by veteran Party cadres who had risen through the ranks in the years prior to the Cultural Revolution. Of the 201 members of the new Central Committee selected at the Eleventh Congress, 76 were officials who had been purged as "capitalist roaders" during the Cultural Revolution and rehabilitated after 1972. The new Politburo was dominated by senior military and Party leaders who had been prominent in the pre-Cultural Revolution order. It was not a body that could easily be controlled by Hua Guofeng, a relatively youthful newcomer to this higher political realm, despite the high offices he occupied.

---

[4] Hua Kuo-feng, "Political Report to the 11th National Congress of the Communist Party of China" (August 12, 1977), *Peking Review*, August 26, 1977, pp. 23–57.

[5] Teng Hsiao-p'ing, (Deng Xiaoping), "Closing Address at the 11th National Congress of the Communist Party of China" (August 18, 1977), *Peking Review*, September 2, 1977, pp. 38–40.

But it was a group amenable to the leadership of Deng Xiaoping.

In the months following the Eleventh Congress, Deng Xiaoping played an increasingly prominent role in the making of both foreign and domestic policies. As the purge of leftists in the Party and state bureaucracies widened, especially through a major campaign to remove "hidden followers of the Gang of Four," Deng's supporters flocked back to official positions, high and low. In February 1978 Deng must have found ironic satisfaction in Hua Guofeng's enthusiastic embrace of the ten-year program for economic development that had been drafted by the State Council under Deng's direction in early 1975, especially when Hua accused the jailed Gang of "slander and vilification" for having criticized Deng's original document.[6] Deng no doubt also found it satisfying that he rather than Hua delivered the major speech to the highly publicized National Science Conference held in March 1978. Deng seized the opportunity to challenge several old Maoist orthodoxies and enhance his appeal to the intelligentsia. Science and technology, he argued, were part of the productive forces rather than the "relations of production," thus implying social neutrality. He also proclaimed that intellectuals were members of the working class, a proposition he first set forth in 1956, only to be contradicted by Mao. And the Maoist notion of "red and expert," which prized a socialist political consciousness more than technical expertise, was broadly redefined in apolitical and nationalist terms to apply to all scientists and technicians who love "our socialist motherland."[7] To his growing list of active supporters, Deng could now add most of China's intellectuals.

During the first half of 1978 the leaders of the Chinese Communist Party appeared more united than at any time since the early 1950s. Deng Xiaoping's restoration seemed to have resolved the most contentious political issue of the day, and Party leaders seemed firmly joined together under the banner of the Four Modernizations. They refrained from criticizing each other, safely confining themselves to denunciations of the imprisoned Gang and the long-dead Lin Biao. The Eleventh Party Congress' call to "bring about great

[6] Hua Kuo-feng, "Report to the Fifth National People's Congress" (February 26, 1978), *Peking Review*, March 10, 1978, pp. 7–41.

[7] Teng Hsiao-p'ing (Deng Xiaoping), "Opening Speech to the National Science Conference" (March 18, 1978), *Peking Review*, March 24, 1978, pp. 9–19.

order across the land" seemed to have been heeded, at least by those who ruled the land. Hua Guofeng, Ye Jianying, and Deng Xiaoping —China's ruling triumvirate—appeared to be ruling in harmony.

But appearances were deceptive. Deng Xiaoping's second resurrection neither settled the question of Deng's place in the post-Mao order nor resolved the multitude of social and political issues that had come to be associated with his name and fate. Unlike at the time of his first rehabilitation in 1973, when Deng was willing to "let bygones be bygones," as he said at the time, in 1978 he was determined to sweep aside all his former critics and potential foes and assume supreme power himself. With Mao Zedong safely buried and the Gang of Four securely locked in their jail cells, Deng now had the opportunity to do so.

It is hardly surprising that Deng, once restored to the top echelon of Party leadership in mid-1977, would prove unwilling to share power with Hua Guofeng, much less play second fiddle to an upstart who had risen to power during the years Deng was falling. Hua, after all, had achieved political prominence as a result of the Cultural Revolution, when Deng had been purged and humiliated. Hua's succession to the premiership upon Zhou Enlai's death in January 1976 made him little more than a usurper in the eyes of Deng and his supporters, who believed that Deng was the natural successor to the venerated Premier. Moreover, Hua had demonstrated no lack of zeal in pursuing the "campaign to criticize Deng Xiaoping" in the autumn of 1976.

In early 1978, even after Deng once again had risen to the heights of the Party hierarchy, Hua Guofeng's political dominance seemed secure. Hua was not only Chairman of the Chinese Communist Party but also Premier of the State Council, and to these he added the chairmanship of the Central Military Commission—making him simultaneously head of the Party, the government, and the Army. No leader in the history of the People's Republic, not even Mao, had officially held all three posts at once.

But Hua's high political positions could not conceal his political weaknesses. He had no definable power base in China's political and military bureaucracies, nor could he claim the firm support of any group in society at large. To be sure, Hua, having risen to political prominence during the Cultural Revolution, seemed to represent (or,

at least, politically symbolize) a particular sector of the bureaucracy—the cadres who had risen to positions of authority (and new
Party members recruited) after 1966. But this was an amorphous
group of younger and mostly lower-level officials, barely conscious of
their particular interests and certainly incapable of politically articulating them. And even this potential base of political support for
Hua had been eroded by the 1977–78 campaign against "hidden
followers of the Gang of Four," which fell hardest on those who had
risen in the political apparatus during the final decade of the Mao
era. It was thus quite logical politically that while Hua was calling
for an end to the campaign against "hidden followers" in 1978, Deng
and his supporters were urging an intensification of the purge.[8]

Hua Guofeng could do little to add substance to the powerful
official titles he held. Lacking a strong personality and bearing thin
political credentials, he had quietly arrived on the national political
stage during the tumultuous battles of the Cultural Revolution without
creating powerful enemies (save for the Gang) and without cultivating
loyal followers. The fortuitous successor to the greatest heroes of a
heroic generation of revolutionary leaders, Hua Guofeng was what he
appeared to be—a provincial bureaucrat of peasant background. He
laid claim to Mao's legacy and, along with it, the more dubious legacy
of the Cultural Revolution, but he did so at a time when the Cultural
Revolution and, implicitly, Mao himself were coming under public
criticism. The Maoist legacy was at once Hua's sole claim to political
legitimacy and his fatal political albatross, one which he neither
could survive with nor do without.

Precisely where Hua Guofeng suffered from acute political lia-
bilities, Deng Xiaoping possessed enormous political assets. While
Hua lacked a viable base of political support, Deng enjoyed the backing of most senior Party leaders and veteran bureaucrats, many of
whom had been his longtime associates and virtually all of whom
shared his antipathy to the Cultural Revolution. Deng's advocacy of
reviving Leninist Party norms and his oft-stated view that one should
"rise step by step" up the bureaucratic ladder (rather than by "helicopter," as did the Gang of Four and Hua) appealed both to the

---

[8] In February 1978, at the Fifth National People's Congress, Hua announced that the investigation (and purge) of those associated with the Gang had been successfully concluded. Hua,
"Report," *Peking Review*, March 10, 1978, p. 10. The announcement proved premature.

self-interest and to the bureaucratic ideals of veteran officials. The restoration of Leninist Party traditions (and Deng could certainly claim sterling Leninist credentials) and the promise of bureaucratic regularity seemed particularly attractive after the turmoil of the Cultural Revolution, and encouraged veteran officials—longing for political order and social stability—to look to Deng for leadership.

Deng could also count on the support of many military leaders, the fruit of his close association with Red Army officers during the revolutionary years. The PLA did not speak in a monolithic voice, but insofar as the Army made its political presence felt in the early post-Mao years it did so mostly on behalf of Deng Xiaoping. Deng himself had assumed the post of Chief of the General Staff of the PLA, in addition to his other positions, and his close ally, Wei Guoqing, who was notorious for his massacres of radical youth during the Cultural Revolution, was now director of the PLA's General Political Department.

In addition to veteran bureaucrats and PLA generals, Deng could number most Chinese intellectuals among his supporters. Powerless on their own, intellectuals could be an articulate and potent force in Chinese politics when they acquired the patronage of high Party leaders. Deng adroitly cultivated their support by championing their interests and aspirations. Although he could not pretend to have inherited the hallowed place Zhou Enlai occupied in the intelligentsia's political consciousness, Deng rightly could claim to have been a consistent advocate of Zhou's relatively favorable policies toward intellectuals. Since the mid-1950s, Deng, like Zhou, had attempted to soften Maoist political suspicions of intellectuals. In his 1975 policy documents, Deng provided a particularly prominent place for intellectuals in achieving the Four Modernizations. At the same time, he was an early and outspoken critic of the Gang of Four for their persecution of intellectuals, their disregard for modern science, and the devastating effects of their policies on higher education. Although making no intellectual claims for himself (he was far more interested in political claims), Deng frequently voiced his respect for intellectuals. "You have to trust intellectuals before you can employ their services," he pleaded shortly before his second fall from power.[9]

Having returned to high office, Deng elaborated his views on the

[9] "Sayings of Teng," in Terrill, *The Future of China After Mao*, p. 268.

role of intellectuals—and solidified their political support—in his address to the National Science Conference in March 1978. Proclaiming "forever gone" the days when such villains as the Gang of Four could "willfully sabotage the cause of science and persecute the intellectuals," Deng declared that the mastery of modern science and technology was "the crux of the Four Modernizations." The distinction between mental and manual labor was no longer a Marxist (or Maoist) social contradiction to be overcome but rather, according to Deng, a more or less natural and harmonious socioeconomic relationship: "The difference between [the intellectuals] and the manual workers lies only in a different role in the social division of labor. Those who labor, whether by hand or by brain, are all working people in a socialist society." Thus intellectuals, or at least the "overwhelming majority" of them, were to be classified as "part of the proletariat" and therefore no longer politically distrusted.[10] But if intellectuals were "part of the proletariat," they were by no means to be treated as ordinary proletarians. Unusually "talented people" were to be identified and provided with special training and facilities, Deng proposed, while established experts were to have "powers and responsibilities commensurate with their positions."

To the intelligentsia, Deng Xiaoping thus promised the rapid development of science and technology, a wide degree of professional autonomy, greater authority in an expanded educational system constructed on familiar foundations, and far higher material benefits and social status than they had thus far enjoyed. It was a most non-Maoist speech, even though, as the political fashion of the time still demanded, abundantly decorated with references to the "teachings of Chairman Mao."

The combination of veteran Party bureaucrats, PLA leaders, and the intelligentsia constituted a formidable political coalition of elites backing Deng's drive for Party supremacy—especially formidable at a time when the workers and peasants, in whose interests the Party claimed to speak, were politically mute. But it was the issue of the Cultural Revolution or, more precisely, the burning desire of its victims for justice and retribution that provided the real dynamism in Deng's drive for power. That he and members of his family had been

---

[10] Teng Hsiao-p'ing (Deng Xiaoping), "Opening Speech to the National Science Conference."

victimized during the Cultural Revolution won him the sympathy and support of millions who had suffered over the previous decade. Cadres who had been politically purged and publicly humiliated, intellectuals who had been persecuted, some 17 million urban youths who had been shipped off to remote areas of the countryside, and millions of ordinary citizens who had been subjected to physical and psychological abuse and political condemnation looked upon Deng as a fellow sufferer—and saw in Deng's political resurrection the hope for a "reversal of unjust verdicts." Deng's power was to grow, and Hua Guofeng's to decline, in direct proportion to the "reversal of the verdicts" of the Cultural Revolution era.

In launching his drive for total dominance in 1978, Deng took a leaf from Mao's book of political tactics. Effective political action, the late Chairman always had emphasized, required appropriate ideological preparation. Deng, accordingly, undermined the Maoist ideological foundations of the Cultural Revolution by reviving two simple Maoist propositions: the injunction to "seek truth from facts" and the notion that "practice is the sole criterion of truth."

In the summer and autumn months of 1978, the ideologists of what came to be known as Deng Xiaoping's "practice faction" presented the principles of "seeking truth from facts" and making "practice the sole criterion of truth" as the essence of "Marxism-Leninism-Mao Zedong Thought." Although clearly intended to serve an anti-Maoist purpose, the theoretical writings of Deng's supporters were copiously decorated with quotations from the writings of Mao Zedong, especially his celebrated 1939 essay "On Practice." However unremarkable, indeed banal, these two slogans may have appeared, they were of enormous political import. For in 1978 they were used to imply that those aspects of Mao Zedong Thought that no longer corresponded to "the facts" no longer conformed to "truth," and thus could be discarded. This was to prove the opening wedge for the wholesale reinterpretation of Maoist theory. More important, it was suggested that the theories and policies of the Cultural Revolution, tested and found wanting in "practice," should be abandoned.

The results of this ideological campaign were the dismantling of the theoretical structure of the Cultural Revolution, the discrediting of the political symbolism associated with the upheaval, and the reversal of many of the "verdicts" made during the last decade of the Maoist era—all ideologically justified by the "practice" criterion and the injunction to "seek truth from facts." Those who interpreted what the "facts" were and what they meant were, of course, those who held political power, but Deng's ideologists preferred to assume that the "facts" spoke for themselves and to claim that "truth" could be scientifically ascertained through understanding of the workings of "objective laws."

The "reversal of verdicts" gained momentum and received concrete expression throughout 1978 in the restoration of high Party leaders who had been purged during the Cultural Revolution. Prominent among those who returned to positions of authority were Lu Dingyi, the former head of the Party's Propaganda Department, and Peng Zhen, the first of the members of the Politburo felled during the Cultural Revolution, who after a twelve-year political exile in the mountains of Shanxi province was now assigned the task of drafting a new criminal code. Also restored to power, or at least to public prominence, were the economic specialists who designed the First Five Year Plan and formulated the policies Deng had favored in the 1950s and early 1960s, most notably Bo Yibo and Sun Yefang, who rejoined the politically more important Chen Yun as China's chief economic planners.

Along with the return of the living there came well-publicized posthumous "rehabilitations" of many of Mao's old political foes. Among the "rehabilitations" none was more pregnant with political meaning than that of Peng Dehuai. Mao's dismissal of the popular general in 1959 was regarded by surviving Party leaders as one of the gravest injustices of the Maoist era, and pleas to rectify the wrong had been heard from many quarters for nearly two decades. Peng had died in 1974 but the case of Peng Dehuai remained a matter of enormous symbolic significance, both within the Party and in society at large. When Peng was officially and publicly "rehabilitated" on December 25, 1978, Deng Xiaoping delivered the eulogy, honoring the dead marshal as one of the great heroes of the revolution and restoring him to the place in history he had occupied before 1959.

It was, of course, impossible to honor Peng Dehuai without implying that Mao Zedong had been something less than completely honorable. Nor, for that matter, was it possible to avoid implicit criticism of the policies of the Great Leap, which Peng had so vigorously condemned and which led to his purge. But Party leaders were not yet prepared to confront openly the complex and politically explosive issue of Mao's historical role, and they were not to do so publicly for another two and a half years. In the meantime, they found it more politically convenient to selectively invoke Mao's ideological legacy to support their partial reversals of the late Chairman's political deeds and social policies.

Political rehabilitations were not confined to Party luminaries. Throughout 1978 many thousands of low- and middle-level cadres purged during the Cultural Revolution, or during what now was being called the "fascist" reign of the Gang of Four, were restored to their positions. The unheralded release in June 1978 of more than 100,000 political prisoners signaled a more significant break with the Maoist past. Intellectuals and Party cadres who had been branded "counterrevolutionaries" or "rightists" and who had been banished to labor in remote areas of the countryside, as part of a 1957 purge—in which Deng Xiaoping had been a leading witch-hunter[11]—quietly began to return to the cities to resume their work as "brain laborers." Certainly one of the more poignant episodes in the history of the People's Republic was the "return from silence" of many older writers, artists, dramatists, and musicians in 1978 and 1979. Some, such as the renowned writer Ding Ling, had spent as long as two decades in labor camps in the barren reaches of northern Manchuria.[12]

Of all the "verdicts" reversed in late 1978, none had greater immediate political impact than the overturning of the Party's original judgment on the Tiananmen incident of April 5, 1976. The demonstration of that day had been condemned as a "counterrevolutionary act" at the time, and that remained the official verdict for two years after the fall of the Gang of Four. But for the 100,000 or more citizens of Beijing who participated in the events of early April, and the many millions more across the land who shared their longings for freedom,

[11] Deng delivered the main political report on the antirightist movement to the Third Plenary Session of the Eighth Central Committee in the autumn of 1957, reviewing the early stages of the campaign and preparing the later stages. The report was published in *People's Daily* on October 19, 1957.

[12] For a vivid account of the odyssey of Ding Ling, see Jonathan D. Spence, *The Gate of Heavenly Peace* (New York: Viking, 1981), pp. 335–69.

the April 1976 demonstration was viewed as a heroic act of popular resistance to a despotic state. The young activists who participated in the Tiananmen affair and who provided it with continuing political expression and increasing symbolic significance—mostly younger workers and former Red Guards now in their late twenties and early thirties—enshrined the time as the April Fifth Movement. They saw themselves as heirs of the hallowed May Fourth Movement, which originated at the same site beneath the Gate of Heavenly Peace more than half a century before. They wrote poems to commemorate the birth of their own generation's movement for democracy and enlightenment, expressing their sorrows over the oppressions of the past and their determination to bring about a democratic future. The poems were circulated, at first clandestinely, among members of a growing network of young dissidents who were creating what soon was to emerge as the Democracy Movement. Early in 1978 some of the poems appeared on posters pasted on a two-hundred-yard stretch of brick wall in downtown Beijing, within a mile of the Gate of Heavenly Peace. Other posters soon were put up on what came to be known as Democracy Wall, calling on the Party to reverse its verdict on the Tiananmen incident and demanding punishment for Wu De, the mayor of Beijing who had ordered the suppression of the April 1976 demonstrations.

Deng Xiaoping and his allies at first encouraged the burgeoning Democracy Movement, partly because some among the leaders of the "practice faction" truly sympathized with the young activists and partly because they wished to use the movement from below for their own political ends at the top. On September 20, 1978, *China Youth*, the official organ of the Communist Youth League, published a highly favorable account of the April 1976 Tiananmen incident, denouncing the militiamen who had dispersed the demonstrators as a "fascist force." It was the first issue of *China Youth* to appear since 1966, when, at the beginning of the Cultural Revolution, the Youth League had been disbanded along with many other organizational appendages of the Communist Party. Neither the reappearance of the journal nor the revised version of the events of April 5, 1976, could have come about without the support of high Party leaders. The political patron, in this case, was Hu Yaobang, Deng Xiaoping's most favored protégé and new chief of the Party's Organization Department. Hu

Yaobang was also apparently responsible for another politically explosive article in the same issue of *China Youth*—a critique of the cult of Mao Zedong, denounced as a form of "religious superstition."

Three weeks after the publication of *China Youth*, Wu De was dismissed as mayor of Beijing. One of the first acts of his successor was to proclaim the Tiananmen demonstration "a revolutionary event," a judgment endorsed and formally announced by the Party Central Committee on November 15. Nearly four hundred demonstrators who had been arrested and convicted as "counterrevolutionaries" in April 1976 were now exonerated; a play honoring the victims of the time was hastily staged in Beijing; the poems of the Tiananmen activists were collected and some officially published; and newspapers were filled with articles lauding the revolutionary spirit of the people who had gathered at the square beneath the Gate of Heavenly Peace two and a half years before.

Encouraged by what appeared to be official approval, the Democracy Movement grew rapidly in both scope and intensity during the months of November and December 1978. The wallposters expressing the grievances, demands, and hopes of ever wider sectors of the population increased both in number and in political militancy, spreading from the original site of Democracy Wall through adjoining streets in downtown Beijing to the Gate of Heavenly Peace Square itself—the symbolic and physical center of the Chinese Communist state. The posters detailed social and political injustices, past and present, and the sufferings of individuals and groups at the hands of despotic political authorities. They exposed the personal tragedies of individuals caught up in the Cultural Revolution and criticized the leaders of the upheaval, not excluding Mao Zedong. Also attacked were surviving "Maoists" who still sat in the Politburo, especially Wang Dongxing and Wu De. Hua Guofeng was largely ignored whereas Deng Xiaoping was frequently praised, sometimes as "the living Zhou Enlai."

More important, the wallposters called for the democratization of political institutions, the protection of human rights, and the establishment of a modern legal system. The conception of democracy held by most of the activists in the movement, and the specific measures they advocated to institute it, were largely drawn from the Marxian model of the Paris Commune, especially Marx's *The Civil War in*

France and Lenin's *State and Revolution.* Ironically, a movement that was mostly critical of Mao Zedong and the Cultural Revolution quoted the very Marxian texts Mao had set forth as required reading during the Cultural Revolution.

Even as the cold winds of late November heralded the onset of the harsh Beijing winter, ever larger numbers of people gathered in the evenings to read and discuss the posters in what soon came to be known as Democracy Forum. Discussions soon turned into political meetings, rallies, and marches, and the growing number of participants began to spill into the square beneath the Gate of Heavenly Peace. The ex-Red Guards and young workers who spearheaded the movement were joined by other urban dwellers as well as by a small number of peasants who had come to the capital to protest oppression and hunger in the countryside. On a smaller scale, democracy walls and democracy forums appeared in several dozen other cities, including Shanghai, Wuhan, Tianjin, Xi'an, and various provincial centers.

Deng Xiaoping gave his blessings to the Democracy Movement for the time being, remarking to foreign visitors that he considered the wallposter campaign a "good thing," although he discouraged public criticism of Mao. Support also came from the official Party organ, the *People's Daily,* which printed a series of articles advocating "socialist democracy" and "socialist legality." By the beginning of December, the activists in the Democracy Movement were doing more than writing wallposters. They had begun to establish their own organizations and to publish unofficial journals—mimeographed "people's publications," as they were called—which were eagerly purchased and read by the growing number of citizens taking part in the activities near Democracy Wall. The movement from below, a heady time and an exhilarating experience for participants and observers alike,[13] was taking on an increasingly political character.

As the Democracy Movement grew in the streets of downtown Beijing and around the Gate of Heavenly Peace, the leaders of the Chinese Communist Party were gathering for meetings in their official

---

[13] The feelings of exhilaration and hope that marked the time are well captured and conveyed in Roger Garside's eyewitness description of the movement in *Coming Alive: China After Mao* (New York: Mentor, 1982), esp. pp. 195–243.

headquarters located above the square. A month-long central work conference of top Party leaders had been underway since November 10, making preparations for the convening of the Third Plenum of the Party's Eleventh Central Committee. The latter met in formal session from December 18 to December 22, 1978. This Central Committee meeting was to prove crucial in charting the history of post-Mao China.

THE THIRD PLENUM

As is customary with meetings of the higher organs of the Chinese Communist Party, the official communiqué issued by the plenary session of the Central Committee in late December 1978 proclaimed the achievement of "stability and unity." And, as is usually the case, the ritualized phrase served only to mask the political and ideological conflicts among Party leaders that took place behind closed doors. A more accurate picture of the politics of the time was to be found on walls in the streets of Beijing, where poster writers were demanding the ouster of Party leaders identified with Mao Zedong and the policies of the Cultural Revolution while praising Deng Xiaoping. Just as Deng must have been pleased with the public wallposter campaign, so he clearly must have been satisfied with the political results of the third formal meeting of the Central Committee originally elected at the Eleventh Party Congress in 1977. For the decisions of the Third Plenum were a decisive, if not yet complete, triumph for Deng and his allies.

Throughout the year 1978, in direct proportion to the growth of Deng Xiaoping's influence, the political coalition that had overthrown the Gang of Four was increasingly divided into two opposing camps: the self-styled "practice faction" of Deng and his allies, who proceeded under the banal but politically potent slogan "Practice is the sole criterion of truth"; and those whom the eventual victors would label the "whatever faction," the surviving "leftists" led by Hua Guofeng who in early 1977 had somewhat impetuously vowed to follow "whatever policies" Mao had formulated and "whatever instructions" the late Chairman had issued. At the meetings of the Third Plenum, and with the assistance of the Democracy Movement activists who gathered in the square below the halls where the Party leaders met, Deng's "practice faction" proved victorious. Elevated to a Party vice-chairmanship at the Third Plenum was Deng's most powerful ally at the time, Chen Yun, the veteran economic planner and the principal formulator of Liu Shaoqi's policies in the early 1960s. Several other Deng supporters were newly elected to the Politburo, including Hu Yaobang, whom Deng was soon to install as Party chief in place of Hua Guofeng. Deng's dominance over the Central Committee as a whole was fortified by the addition of nine new members.

The surviving "Maoists" on the Politburo, now ridiculed as "what-everists," were not dismissed from their formal Party positions, but they were relieved of most of their responsibilities and rendered largely powerless. One by one, over the next two years, they were removed from their offices in pragmatically efficient fashion. Hua Guofeng, an accomplished political compromiser, attempted to re-main above the factional battles, but he was indelibly stamped with a Maoist imprint in what had become a post-Mao era. As Chairman of the Communist Party, Hua formally presided over the Third Ple-num; he emerged from the meeting with his title intact but not his power. Henceforth, he was to perform little more than ceremonial functions in accordance with Deng's instructions.

While the Third Plenum emphasized "collective leadership" and discouraged "publicity" for individual leaders, the latter admonition did not apply to Deng Xiaoping. Precisely at the time the Party was promoting the principle of "collective leadership," Deng Xiaoping was gathering in his own hands as much actual power as Mao Zedong had ever enjoyed.

No less favorable to Deng than the personnel changes in Party leadership was the Third Plenum's implicit criticism of Mao Zedong, accomplished by the formal "rehabilitations" of many of the late Chairman's political foes. While the official communiqué of the Third Plenum fulsomely invoked the authority and the writings of Mao, as was still the political fashion of the time, and announced that an assessment of the Cultural Revolution was to be put off until an "appropriate time" in the future, the political message was clear: Mao was no longer immune to criticism, at least with respect to the last two decades of his rule. With the door now officially opened (although perhaps not as wide as some assumed at the time) and with the ideological sanction of the now ubiquitous slogan "Practice is the sole criterion of truth," a torrent of criticism of Mao and his policies was to follow.

The most publicized, and in the long run the most significant, decision of the Third Plenum was to "shift the emphasis of the Party's work to socialist modernization." Socialist modernization was hardly a new term, but it was infused with a new meaning. Before, the term had meant the employment of state power to develop a backward economy to serve ultimate socialist goals. Now, it meant the subordination of all considerations, social and otherwise, to the task of rapid national economic development, pure and simple. Politics and political work, accordingly, were no longer primarily seen as the striving to achieve socialism but rather were to be judged mainly by economic criteria.

In accordance with this economic measurement, socialism itself increasingly tended to be defined as little more than modernization. As leading Party officials typically declared after the Third Plenum: "The aim of our Party in leading the whole nation in making revolution and taking over political power is, in the final analysis, to develop the economy."[14] Hitherto, modern economic development had been seen by Chinese Communist leaders as the means to achieve a socialist and communist future. Now, they seemed to suggest that economic development as such was the final goal. Deng Xiaoping was foremost among those who inverted the means and ends of socialism, and he did so in nationalist fashion: "The purpose of socialism is to make the country rich and strong."[15] It was as if Chinese Communist leaders were out to confirm the anti-Communist thesis of the American political scientist Adam Ulam, who had argued (some two decades before the Third Plenum) that Marxism in the modern world is essentially an ideology of modernization, having little to do with socialism but a great deal to do with industrialism.[16]

The immediate practical expression of the Third Plenum's version of socialist modernization was a return to the semi-market-oriented

[14] Han Guang, "On the Development of Modern Industry," *Beijing Review*, March 24, 1979, p. 9.
[15] Deng, in comments to a visiting Romanian delegation in November 1980. *The New York Times*, December 30, 1980, p. 2.
[16] Ulam, *The Unfinished Revolution* (New York: Vintage, 1964), esp. pp. 3–57.

policies that had been pursued by Chen Yun in the early 1960s under Liu Shaoqi's political auspices. That experiment had been aborted by the Cultural Revolution. Now, nearly two decades later, Chen and others had the opportunity to pursue similar policies in expanded and systematic fashion on the basis of the Third Plenum's injunction to combine "market adjustment with adjustment by the plan." The formula was ambiguous, but it proved sufficiently elastic to sanction far-reaching market-oriented changes in the Chinese economy, which were to proceed far beyond what Chen Yun originally envisioned.

At the same time, an enormous emphasis was placed on social and political stability, which Deng and his allies believed to be an essential condition for the successful pursuit of the Four Modern-izations. Thus the December 1978 Central Committee communiqué called for a halt to mass political campaigns and proclaimed that "the large-scale turbulent class struggles of a mass character have in the main come to an end." The phrase was quoted from (and duly attributed to) Mao Zedong. The words do indeed appear in Mao's 1957 speech "On the Correct Handling of Contradictions Among the People," but in another context and for a far different purpose. In 1957, Mao had argued that although class struggles of a "turbulent" character were mainly over, class struggle nonetheless still continued in different forms,[17] reaffirming his belief in the continuance of class struggle under socialism. Twenty-one years later, Mao's successors used the phrase to proclaim the termination of class struggles. It was but one of many instances in post-Mao China where Mao's words and writings were used for purposes incongruous with their original intent.

The Third Plenum's position on the question of class struggle was a major departure from what hitherto had been understood as Mao Zedong Thought. The social and theoretical implications of the issue of class struggle—or what was now said to be its virtual disappear-ance—will be examined in later chapters. Here it need only be noted that several months after the Third Plenum, Deng Xiaoping was to proclaim that class distinctions in Chinese society had been basically eliminated (much as Stalin had decreed the cessation of class strug-

---

[17] Mao Tse-tung, *On the Correct Handling of Contradictions Among the People* (Peking: Foreign Languages Press, 1957), p. 50.

gle in the Soviet Union in 1936), and, accordingly, Chinese Communist ideologists began to treat class struggle as a minor residue of the past.

The shift to "socialist modernization" at the end of 1978 was ideologically rationalized by the prevailing slogan of the time, "Practice is the sole criterion of truth." This phrase, like the statement on "turbulent class struggles," was borrowed from Mao's writings, but it was given a most non-Maoist interpretation. For it was made clear that the ultimate criterion for determining "truth" was success in promoting the development of China's productive forces, pure and simple, regardless of the means employed or their social consequences. To that economic end, all other measurements of "truth" were subordinated.

The Third Plenum also seemed to respond positively, if somewhat vaguely, to the demands for political change coming from the Democracy Movement then underway in the streets of Beijing. "Democracy" and "political reform," Party leaders proclaimed, were essential to the realization of the Four Modernizations. Thus the "constitutional rights of citizens" were to be protected, it was promised, and special emphasis was placed on developing a "socialist legal system." The promise of democratic reforms from above gave new impetus and hope to the popular democratic movement below—and led some observers to celebrate prematurely, in the euphoric atmosphere of the last months of 1978, what some hailed as "Deng Xiaoping's march to socialist democracy."

Deng was indeed on the march at the end of 1978, but not necessarily in a democratic direction. For the Third Plenum's tentative promises to promote democratic rights were accompanied, indeed overshadowed, by a clear insistence on the leading role of the Chinese Communist Party and on the need to restore firm Leninist organizational principles to the Party's work. Deng and his allies strove to strengthen the Party organization, and particularly to ensure that its various branches and members obeyed established rules and procedures in accordance with Leninist tenets of "democratic centralism." Envisioned was a return to the way the Party functioned in the early 1950s, before its proper Leninist character was undermined by Maoist "abnormalities." The restoration of traditional Party norms strengthened the positions and power of veteran Party leaders and thus reinforced the dominance of Deng Xiaoping. The emphasis of the Third Plenum was more on "inner-Party democracy" according to Leninist precepts than on democracy in society at large. The incompatibility between the democratic ideals advocated in the streets of Beijing and the Leninist concept of "the vanguard party" that Deng Xiaoping and Chen Yun were promoting behind the closed doors of the Central Committee meeting room was soon to become apparent.

The Third Plenum appears now as an event of momentous historical significance. It inaugurated the wholesale deradicalization of a revolution that had for so long proved uniquely resistant to institutionalization and to "the universality of the Thermidorean reaction."[18] What came in the wake of the Third Plenum was an astonishingly rapid decline in revolutionary commitment in Chinese society; a halt to radical social change (and indeed the reversal of many progressive social changes previously made); and, most important, the fading of any real vision of a socialist and communist future. The latter is most important because, as Robert Tucker has reminded us, "the radical is not simply a rebel but a visionary." The radical "negation of what exists proceeds from an underlying affirmation, an idealized image of the world as it ought to be."[19] In the years after the Third Plenum, fewer and fewer visionaries were to be found in China. Both official ideology and the popular mood were profoundly anti-utopian.

These deradicalizing tendencies were, of course, long in the making. In large part they were reactions to the failures of the late Maoist era, particularly the Great Leap and, even more, the Cultural Revolution. They were not fabricated out of whole cloth by a meeting of the Central Committee. But the Third Plenum did much to release, promote, and sanctify these tendencies.

At the time of the Third Plenum, there were few hints of the far-reaching economic reforms that would dominate the history of the next decade. Indeed, it is most unlikely that Deng had in mind the capitalist-oriented economic changes that were to follow. On eco-

[18] The widely used term derives from Crane Brinton's influential comparative study of revolutions and their life cycles. Brinton characterizes Thermidor as "a convalescence from the fever of revolution." For a discussion of his concept of the universality of the phenomenon, see *The Anatomy of Revolution*, rev. ed. (New York: Vintage, 1965), pp. 205–35.
[19] Tucker, *The Marxian Revolutionary Idea*, p. 182.

nomic policy, the official communiqué of the Central Committee set forth only the vague and seemingly innocuous formula to combine "market adjustment with adjustment by the plan." Economic revitalization was certainly on almost everyone's agenda. But what really excited imaginations and aroused hopes was the promise of socialist democracy. In the heady days of November and December 1978, many were hailing Deng Xiaoping as the prophet of a truly socialist future, anticipating not the deradicalization of the revolution but its democratic revitalization. The first test of that promise would come with Deng's response to the burgeoning Democracy Movement, which had greatly assisted China's new leader in his rise to power.

5

THE RISE AND FALL
OF THE DEMOCRACY MOVEMENT,
1978–81

AS DENG XIAOPING savored his domestic political victories of November and December 1978, he also sought triumphs abroad. As it happened, the formal establishment of diplomatic relations between the People's Republic and the United States coincided with the victory of Deng's "practice faction" over his "whateverist" opponents. On December 16, 1978, two days before the Third Plenum met to formally ratify Deng's ascendancy, Washington and Beijing simultaneously announced that the two countries had agreed—after several months of secret negotiations—to establish official diplomatic ties on the first day of the new year.

The timing was not entirely coincidental. The long-delayed Sino-American agreement required Chinese concessions on the issue of Taiwan, which Deng was reluctant to make—for fear of undermining his nationalist credentials—until his internal political dominance was secure. For while the United States agreed to terminate official diplomatic relations and abrogate its mutual defense treaty with the Guomindang regime in Taipei, the Beijing government acquiesced in "unofficial" American cultural, economic, and political relations with Taiwan, including a continuing supply of United States armaments to the island, even though Washington acknowledged "the Chinese position that there is but one China and Taiwan is part of China."

That "normalization" was not to be entirely normal was made a matter of American law in March 1979 when Congress passed the Taiwan Relations Act, maintaining the substance of existing United States military and economic ties with Taiwan in ostensibly "official" form. Save for verbal protests, Beijing was forced into a de facto acceptance of a continuing American military protectorate over territory all acknowledged to be part of "one China"—for the sake of such strategic and economic advantages "normalization" promised to bring.

Nonetheless, three decades after the founding of the People's Republic, the United States finally had formally recognized the political result of the Chinese revolution. The normalization of relations had been long in the making, essentially accomplished in the early 1970s by the unlikely quartet of Mao Zedong, Richard Nixon, Zhou Enlai, and Henry Kissinger.[1] It was Deng Xiaoping's political good fortune to preside over the consummation of a diplomatic process initiated by the Mao regime seven years before, and he celebrated the historic event by accepting an invitation from President Carter to visit the United States. During his highly publicized 1979 tour, which included stops in Washington, Atlanta, Houston, and Seattle from January 28 to February 4, Deng was accorded all the honors due a head of state, which he was in fact if not in name. Lest there be any doubt of his newly attained prominence on the world stage, he was also named *Time* magazine's "man of the year," the somewhat dubious honor hitherto bestowed on only two other Chinese political leaders —Chiang Kai-shek and Mao Zedong.

Despite the Taiwan Relations Act, many American politicians were critical, habitually obsessed as they were by menacing images of "Red China." Among the more vocal critics was Ronald Reagan, who condemned the new Beijing-Washington relationship as "based on the betrayal of the Free Chinese on Taiwan" and lamented that an American government had "cold-bloodedly betrayed a friend for political expediency." He complained that from the United States the Chinese wanted only "technology and sophisticated industrial equipment," ominously warning of the peril that an industrialized Com-

---

[1] The famous "Ping-Pong diplomacy" of early 1971 culminated in Kissinger's surprise appearance in Beijing in the summer of that year and President Nixon's celebrated February 1972 visit. The latter, in turn, yielded the "Shanghai Communiqué," which established the essential conditions for the normalization of diplomatic relations.

munist China would pose by the end of the century.[2] Yet two years later, when Ronald Reagan came to occupy the White House, his more primeval anti-Communist ideological impulses were muted, at least as far as China was concerned. The Reagan administration's China policy was to be governed by the same anti-Soviet realpolitik considerations that had inspired Richard Nixon and Henry Kissinger to pursue normalized relations with the People's Republic a decade earlier. Indeed, during the Reagan presidency, the United States was not only to sell China "sophisticated industrial equipment" but also to supply technologically sophisticated weapon systems.

The formal establishment of diplomatic relations between China and the United States came at a time when Beijing was far more active in world affairs than at any time in the history of the People's Republic. Chinese foreign policy objectives were as much economic as strategic, for the Four Modernizations required a vast expansion of foreign trade and the import of modern technology and capital. Japanese government leaders and industrialists were particularly eager to fill the need and reap the profits; rapidly growing economic and cultural ties between the two countries were cemented by a Sino-Japanese treaty of peace and friendship in 1978. In August of that year, Premier and Party Chairman Hua Guofeng embarked on state visits to Romania, Yugoslavia, and Iran, eclectically praising both the "Yugoslav model" of socialism and the Shah's model of "modernization." The choice of Eastern European countries on Hua's tour was dictated by the anti-Soviet considerations that still governed Chinese foreign policy at the time. Tito had broken with Stalin in 1948 and Yugoslavia long had been numbered among the nonaligned countries, and the "national Communist" Romanian regime had pursued an independent foreign policy since the 1960s. In the autumn of 1979, Hua Guofeng became the first Chinese head of government (albeit now a titular head) to visit Western Europe, exhorting his hosts in France, West Germany, Great Britain, and Italy to bolster their military forces to counter Soviet expansionism.

Hua Guofeng's 1978 trip to Yugoslavia had been preceded by visits of various Chinese delegations eager to learn Yugoslav eco-

[2] Cited in Ronnie Dugger, *On Reagan: The Man and His Presidency* (New York: McGraw-Hill, 1983), pp. 371, 527.

nomic policies and managerial systems, at a time when some Chinese economic specialists were intrigued by what was called "the Yugoslav path to socialism." That interest had been stimulated, in part, by President Tito's visit to China in the summer of 1977. Although Tito had been castigated during the Mao era as the prime symbol of capitalist "revisionism," the invitation to the Yugoslav leader had been extended by Mao personally in 1975. But it was not accepted by the Yugoslavs until after Mao's death, when, ironically, Tito became the first foreign leader to visit the Mao mausoleum.

The anti-Soviet obsessions that the leaders of post-Mao China inherited from their Maoist predecessors (but which slowly were to give way to a Sino-Soviet rapprochement during the Deng era) produced embarrassments along with triumphs in Chinese foreign policy. The People's Republic continued to be the world's only country ruled by a Marxist party to carry on full diplomatic relations (and an expanding trade) with the fascist Pinochet dictatorship in Chile. And Chinese leaders managed to lavish praise on the Shah's regime in Iran on the very eve of the collapse of the corrupt Pahlevi dynasty. But most embarrassing of all was China's Vietnam war.

China's relations with Vietnam, strained since the collapse of the American-supported Saigon regime and the Communist unification of Vietnam in 1975, rapidly deteriorated during the course of 1978. The sources of hostility were many: the persecution of ethnic Chinese in Vietnam; a long-simmering dispute over control of the Paracel and Spratly islands in the potentially oil-rich South China Sea; tensions along a disputed eight-hundred-mile border; and Vietnam's increasingly close alignment with the Soviet Union. But what apparently precipitated Beijing's decision to attack its erstwhile ally was the Vietnamese invasion of Kampuchea (Cambodia), the capture of Phnom Penh early in January 1979, and the installation of a Vietnamese-supported Cambodian government in place of the Chinese-backed Pol Pot regime, the latter best-known to the world for its genocidal policies of "revolutionary purification" in 1975–76. Thus during the course of his visit to the United States in late January 1979, Deng Xiaoping swaggeringly spoke of "teaching Vietnam a lesson." The refrain was quickly taken up by the official Chinese press, which labeled Vietnam "the Asian Cuba" (i.e., a Soviet satellite) and blustered about the need to "punish" the Vietnamese for their transgressions. On February 17, several days after Deng returned to Beijing, Chinese troops invaded Vietnam in what was officially called a "defensive counterattack."

What the leaders in Beijing apparently contemplated was a repetition of the brief Sino-Indian border war of 1962, when the PLA demonstrated its military superiority in a quick and relatively bloodless strike across a disputed border. But the Vietnamese, long experienced in dealing with foreign invaders, refused to cooperate. While the best divisions of the Vietnamese Army were deployed to defend Hanoi, far south of the battle zone, regional and second-rank forces successfully resisted the Chinese invaders in the northern border areas. After two weeks of difficult and bloody fighting, Chinese troops had advanced only twenty-five miles into Vietnam and had yet to engage the main forces of the Vietnamese Army. Faced with fighting a far wider war than had been contemplated with an army unprepared for the task, and courting Soviet intervention on behalf of its Vietnamese ally, Chinese leaders decided to abandon the ill-fated adventure in the first week of March, only a month after Deng Xiaoping's return from the United States. Amidst proclamations from Beijing that Vietnam had been taught the proper lesson, Chinese troops withdrew, razing Vietnamese towns and villages in the course of the retreat.[3]

The invasion of Vietnam achieved little for China, save to reveal to its leaders the military inefficiency of the PLA and the antiquated state of its weaponry. The war, of course, made the Vietnamese government more rather than less dependent on the Soviet Union. Beyond the political and military miscalculations, the war exacted tragic human costs: 20,000 Chinese casualties and (according to Chinese reports) 50,000 dead and wounded Vietnamese soldiers. To these must be added the widespread destruction of civilian life and property in the northern border provinces of Vietnam. Further, the war

---

[3] For a perceptive account of the causes and results of the invasion, see Daniel Tretiak, "China's Vietnam War and Its Consequences," *The China Quarterly*, No. 80 (December 1979), pp. 740–67. For a superb analysis of the origins of the Chinese invasion, and the U.S. role in it, see Marilyn B. Young, *The Vietnam Wars 1945–1990* (New York: HarperCollins, 1991), pp. 305–12.

badly tarnished the image of the People's Republic as the world's lone "superpower" that refrained from overt aggression and big-power bullying. The arrogant chauvinism reflected in the claim that China had the right to "teach a lesson" to Vietnam by military force did little to enhance China's international prestige. Even in the United States, its own armies having retreated from Vietnam only four years before, most political leaders (save for a handful of right-wing Republicans and Henry Kissinger) condemned the Chinese invasion, as was the case throughout most of the world. To many it seemed that Vietnam had suffered more than enough foreign invaders. After French, Japanese, and American armies had ravaged the country, China's invasion appeared cruel and the rhetoric of its leaders crude, whatever the initial causes of the hostilities.

China's abortive military adventure in Vietnam was a defeat for Deng Xiaoping politically as it was for China militarily, the first serious setback for China's new leader in what had been an uninterrupted string of political triumphs over a two-year period. It brought Deng internal as well as international criticism. Public domestic criticism of China's foreign policy was virtually unknown in the history of the People's Republic, but it now came from the Democracy Movement, which had aided Deng in his political ascent in the last months of 1978 and which flourished in the early months of 1979, following Deng's victory at the Third Plenum. Shortly after the Chinese invasion in February 1979, antiwar wallposters appeared, one paternalistically critical of "a big country like China" for "striking a little child like Vietnam."[4]

The link between criticism of the war and the Democracy Movement was further revealed on March 29 with the arrest of Wei Jingsheng, the movement's best-known figure. At the time of his arrest, Wei was accused, among other absurd accusations, of having passed "military secrets" on the Vietnam war to foreigners.[5] When Wei was brought to trial later in 1979, he was charged by the state prosecutor with having "willingly become the running dog of Vietnam."

Deng Xiaoping reacted harshly to criticism of the war, defending

---

[4] Cited in Andrew Nathan, *Chinese Democracy* (Berkeley: University of California Press, 1985), p. 14.

[5] See below, p. 118, n. 19.

the Chinese invasion and attacking the Democracy Movement. The attacks came in two bitter speeches, delivered on March 16 and March 30, 1979, in which Deng laid the political-ideological ground-work for the suppression of his erstwhile democratic allies. There were other and more important reasons why Deng was intent on re-moving the youthful Democracy Movement activists from Chinese po-litical life, not the least important of which was his determination to maintain the total political supremacy of the Chinese Communist Party. But the war in Vietnam, and criticism of it, undoubtedly added to the harshness of the repression.

THE DEMOCRACY MOVEMENT

In the early months of 1979, as Deng Xiaoping was preoccupied with his triumphant visit to the United States and his less than triumphant military adventure in Vietnam, the Democracy Movement was grow-ing in size, scope, and militancy. The movement had spread from Beijing to other large cities and provincial centers and to university campuses, its youthful activists encouraged by the results of the Third Plenum and emboldened by official Party promises of "socialist de-mocracy" and "socialist legality." The Democracy Movement was also becoming vaguely identified with popular discontent and social un-rest. Disturbances took place in Shanghai and elsewhere as demo-bilized soldiers and "rusticated youths" returned to the cities demanding jobs, sometimes organizing marches and staging acts of civil disobedience to call attention to their plight. Thousands of peas-ants, defying regulations on unauthorized travel, came to Beijing to petition the government to remedy poverty and injustice in depressed rural areas. It was a time, they had heard, when the government was redressing the wrongs of the past.

The presence of impoverished peasants in the main streets of the capital, the demonstrators clad in ragged clothing in the bitter cold of the Beijing winter and bearing petitions detailing personal histories of misery and oppression was, of course, an embarrassment to the government. Even more embarrassing, and potentially politically dan-gerous, were the efforts of some of the democratic activists to organize the peasant petitioners and speak on their behalf. On January 8,

1979, Fu Yuehua, a thirty-one-year-old Beijing municipal worker, led peasant protesters on a march through the streets of Beijing to the Gate of Heavenly Peace. Ten days later she was arrested, and eventually was tried and convicted on a charge of disturbing public order.

Over the next two months, despite local police harassment, the Democracy Movement grew and flourished in much of urban China, while Party leaders pondered how to deal with the youthful activists. Unofficial organizations, bearing such names as the April Fifth Forum, the Enlightenment Society, and the China Human Rights League, proliferated, each publishing a mimeographed journal or newspaper. In Beijing alone there were no fewer than fifty-five such "people's publications,"[6] and, all told, many times that number in other cities and on university campuses.

Although the arrest of Fu Yuehua in January 1979 signaled that the regime would not tolerate the Democracy Movement becoming a vehicle for broader social protest, it did seem that the new government might be willing to permit some limited expression of heterodox ideas. That impression was reinforced in early February with the official rehabilitation of the "Li Yizhe" group.

Li Yizhe was the acronym used by three young Cantonese dissidents in the early 1970s who were the intellectual and spiritual founders of China's new Democracy Movement. The three, *Li* Zhengtian, Chen *Yi*yang, and Wang Xi*zhe*, had been Red Guards during the Cultural Revolution. Bitterly disillusioned with the tragic results of the upheaval, they undertook to analyze the reasons for the failure of the Cultural Revolution, which had yielded not the popular democratic system they had once envisioned but rather what they called a "feudal fascist autocracy" personified by Lin Biao and the Gang of Four.

The political philosophy of the Li Yizhe was a curious combination of Maoist and post-Maoist ideas. They praised the "revolutionary mass democracy" of the early days of the Cultural Revolution, which long had been out of fashion, and at the same time advocated "socialist legality," which was not yet in fashion. The most celebrated

---

[6] Nathan, *Chinese Democracy*, p. 23.

of their lengthy treatises, "On Socialist Democracy and the Legal System," which won them nationwide renown, originally appeared as a poster in Canton in November 1974, covering a hundred yards of a wall in one of the more prominent streets of the city. The poster called upon the National People's Congress, which was soon scheduled to convene, to guarantee democratic rights by instituting a system of mass supervision over Party leaders, punish officials who were responsible for illegal arrests and torture, and limit the privileges of bureaucrats.[7]

"On Socialist Democracy and the Legal System" was condemned in the waning days of the Maoist regime by both the "conservative" and "radical" wings of the Party, although for different reasons. The harshest attacks came from the "leftist" leaders who were later to be branded as the Gang of Four. Although the Li Yizhe continued to champion many of the original ideas of the Cultural Revolution which the leftist leaders professed, the most trenchant critiques made by the young dissidents were aimed at the Gang faction, whom they characterized as "careerists" pursuing a "feudalistic fascist" course.

This critique of "ultraleftism" did not go unnoticed by the more astute veteran Party leaders, especially Zhao Ziyang, one of Deng Xiaoping's protégés, whom Deng later installed as Premier of the People's Republic and eventually head of the Party. Zhao, who in 1974 was Party Secretary for Guangdong province, attempted to enlist the Li Yizhe group in his own political entourage, ignoring the Cultural Revolution strains in their writings. The attempt proved abortive, however, and the Li Yizhe soon fell victim to the factional Party struggles of the time. Their appeal to the Fourth National People's Congress was ignored when the delegates convened in January 1975 to hear the dying Zhou Enlai's impassioned call for what soon was to be known as the Four Modernizations, even though it was that Congress which, on Mao Zedong's recommendation, added to the new state constitution the "four great freedoms"—the right of the people to "speak out freely, air views freely, hold great debates, and write big character posters." The celebrated clause did not prevent the authorities from punishing the Li Yizhe group for having exercised

---

[7] For English translations of "On Socialist Democracy and the Legal System," see *Issues and Studies* (Taipei), January 1976, and *Chinese Law and Government*, Vol. 10, No. 3 (Fall 1977).

these newly proclaimed freedoms. After being subjected to an official campaign of "criticism and struggle," Li Zhengtian, Chen Yiyang, and Wang Xizhe were arrested in March 1975 and dispatched to labor in a penal colony.

The three Li Yizhe authors were released in February 1979, shortly after the Third Plenum, although Wang Xizhe, the most theoretically sophisticated member of the group, would eventually be sentenced by the Deng regime to a far longer jail term than he had suffered under the Mao regime. Their official "rehabilitation," satisfying one of the demands of the democracy activists, took place with considerable public fanfare on February 6, 1979, and seemed to augur well for the Democracy Movement. But hopes for continued official tolerance soon were dashed. In mid-March, as Chinese troops were retreating from Vietnam, an angry Deng Xiaoping complained that the youthful activists had "gone too far" and warned that an amorphous movement operating beyond the control of the Party threatened to undermine the "stability and unity" necessary to carry out the Four Modernizations. In a March 30 speech to high-level Party officials, Deng clearly laid down measures to be taken to ensure that all political discussion was in accordance with "the four cardinal principles," which demanded "upholding the socialist road, the dictatorship of the proletariat, the leadership of the Communist Party, and Marxism-Leninism-Mao Zedong Thought." Of the four, Deng was to emphasize time and again, the leadership of the Party was the most important. In the course of his March 30 speech, Deng drew an analogy with ominous import for democratic activists who questioned the total political supremacy of the Chinese Communist Party: "Lin Biao and the Gang of Four . . . kicked aside the Party committees to 'make revolution,' and it is clear to all what kind of revolution they made. If today we tried to achieve democracy by kicking aside the Party committees, isn't it equally clear what kind of democracy we would produce?"[8]

The official press followed Deng Xiaoping's lead with virulent condemnations of the "ultrademocracy" and "anarchism" that allegedly was running rampant. The regime did not confine itself to verbal

[8] "Uphold the Four Cardinal Principles," *Selected Works of Deng Xiaoping* (Beijing: Foreign Languages Press, 1984), p. 178.

denunciations. The secret police were enlisted in the campaign against "ultrademocracy." On March 28, municipal authorities in Beijing, in accordance with Deng's instructions, issued regulations severely restricting unofficial political activities, publications, and wallposters. On the following day, agents of the Public Security Bureau arrested Wei Jingsheng, the most outspoken leader of the Democracy Movement, along with several of Wei's associates. Other arrests soon followed. The Agence France-Presse correspondent in Beijing reported on April 4 (in one of a long series of reported incidents and a far greater number that went unreported in the Western press): "Four Chinese human-rights activists were arrested today as they tried to paste up a wallposter attacking 'China's bureaucratic system' and its 'masters.' "[9] The crackdown had begun, and it was to continue over the next two years with hundreds of arrests, jailings, and administrative decrees dispatching young activists to labor camps until the Democracy Movement had been removed from public view.

THE CASE OF WEI JINGSHENG

Wei Jingsheng was by no means typical of participants in the Democracy Movement, but his arrest and trial were of great symbolic significance, marking the end of what some called the "Beijing Spring," a rather misleading analogy to the "Prague Spring" of 1968. The case of Wei aroused international protest, including a telegram to the Chinese government from the Soviet human rights activist Andrei Sakharov, and badly tarnished the democratic image that the new Deng regime was attempting to cultivate. It was of greater importance, however, because the government's persecution of the youthful Chinese dissident drove other young democrats either into silence or to increasingly radical social critiques and political conclusions—and many into jails and labor camps.

Wei Jingsheng, the son of a high-ranking Party and government official, became a Red Guard in 1966, when, as he later recalled, "many of us who joined were dissatisfied with the state of society,

[9] *The New York Times*, April 5, 1979.

disliking the inequalities that existed."[10] Whereas the formative political experiences of most of those who later became leaders in the Democracy Movement were with radical Red Guard organizations opposed to the established Party apparatus during the Cultural Revolution, Wei, as was appropriate for the son of a Party bureaucrat, found himself a member of a conservative group. "The Red Guard organization which I had joined, the United Action Committee, was made up largely of the offspring of senior officials," he recollected. Thus Wei escaped the brutal military repressions inflicted on many of the more radical Red Guards in 1968, and also was able to avoid being sent off to labor in the countryside. Instead, his "revolutionary experiences" culminated in his appointment as an officer in the PLA. Following four years of service as a squad commander in the Northwest, he refused an offer of a low-level position in the bureaucracy and instead took a job as an electrician in the Beijing zoological gardens. On December 5, 1978, the twenty-nine-year-old Wei Jingsheng's celebrated treatise, "The Fifth Modernization—Democracy and Others," was posted on Democracy Wall in the capital.

"The Fifth Modernization" was reprinted in the first issue of the unofficial journal *Explorations (Tansuo)*, which Wei Jingsheng and his compatriots founded on January 9, 1979. Two sequels to "The Fifth Modernization" appeared in subsequent issues of *Explorations* in January and these were followed by an exposé of the barbarous conditions under which political prisoners were incarcerated in Qincheng, the maximum-security prison near Beijing, or the "twentieth-century Bastille" as Wei called it. Most of the prisoners, Wei noted with bitter irony, were Communists who had joined the Party "to fight for the freedom and well-being of China and mankind" and thus had devoted their lives to winning power for the very party which then incarcerated them in Qincheng.[11]

[10] The quotations and information in this paragraph are taken from the brief autobiography Wei Jingsheng related in early 1979, as reported by Roger Garside in *Coming Alive*, pp. 246–56.

[11] English translations of Wei's "The Fifth Modernization—Democracy and Others," and its two "sequels," are printed in *Issues and Studies*, June 1981, pp. 83–92; August 1981, pp. 77–87; and September 1981, pp. 86–92. For an English translation of Wei's article on Qincheng prison, see James Seymour (ed.), *The Fifth Modernization: China's Human Rights Movement, 1978–79* (Stanfordville, N.Y.: Human Rights Publishing Group, 1980), pp. 219–21.

Wei Jingsheng's writings were wholesale condemnations of the Chinese Communist regime. Largely self-educated, Wei wrote with a crude, raw power. If his writings sometimes lacked historical accuracy and theoretical sophistication, they conveyed an uncompromising political honesty and a burning moral fervor that demanded attention and respect, if not necessarily always agreement. They quickly received the attention of the authorities. He attacked not only Mao Zedong but also Deng Xiaoping—and indeed the system that produced them. He undertook critiques of not only the Cultural Revolution and the Great Leap, as was becoming fashionable after the Third Plenum, but also the whole history of the People's Republic, which, in Wei's view, remained a "feudalistic monarchy under a socialist cloak." Although he sometimes quoted Marx in support of his critiques, he regarded Marxism as outdated, and, more frequently, simply a tool employed by bureaucrats to enslave the people. At times, he attributed the evils of Communism to Marxist theory and to "German philosophy" in general. The remedy for the ills which afflicted China and its people was democracy, the "fifth modernization," which Wei argued was not only the essential prerequisite for the realization of the Four Modernizations but also an ultimate end in its own right and one necessary for the achievement of the true goal of modern social development, which he defined as the freedom and happiness of the individual, who was endowed with "heaven-given human rights."[12]

Democracy, for Wei, was not to be achieved through reform from above but rather by the revolutionary transformation of a society he condemned as divided into "officials and slaves."[13] He did little to conceal his distrust of China's post-Maoist leaders and barely disguised his contempt for them. In his initial December 5, 1978, treatise, Wei already suggested that Deng Xiaoping had betrayed the promises most democratic activists still hopefully anticipated China's new leader would bring about. Wei Jingsheng was also uninhibited

---

[12] Wei Jingsheng, *Explorations*, No. 3 (translation in Joint Publication Research Service No. 73421). As Andrew Nathan has pointed out, in arguing for the absolute primacy of the "human rights" of the individual, Wei was virtually unique among Chinese democrats, who (following in the mainstream of modern Chinese democratic thought) tended to view individual rights as a means to strengthen the state and nation. Nathan, *Chinese Democracy*, pp. 104–6.

[13] Wei Jingsheng, "A Sequel to 'The Fifth Modernization—Democracy and Others,' " *Explorations*, January 9, 1979, in *Issues and Studies*, August 1981, p. 78.

in rejecting Deng's most cherished ideological orthodoxies. Whereas Deng believed that rapid economic development would more or less automatically result in a flourishing socialist society, Wei observed that the Soviet Union had achieved industrialization but its economic power was simply an instrument in the hands of a privileged elite.[14] While Deng and his ideologists championed new legal codes as the centerpiece of democratic reform, Wei pointed out that "law is a fixed part of any political system," amenable to both democratic and authoritarian uses. "The rule of law was practiced in ancient times," Wei wrote, referring to China's Legalist tradition. "In practicing it, Qin Shi Huang did not bring any benefit to the people. . . . Neither will the contemporary Qin Shi Huang [i.e., Deng Xiaoping] do anything good with it. Actually, history has told us: autocratic rule plus the rule of law equals tyranny."[15]

Yet however sweeping Wei Jingsheng's condemnations of contemporary Chinese politics and society were, however contemptuous he was of Communist leaders both past and present, what he attacked was not socialism in China but rather its absence in any genuine and meaningfully democratic sense. No theme in his writings appears more forcefully than the charge that the Chinese Communist Party had betrayed its socialist ideals and turned the masses of workers and peasants into servants of the state. Although he had nothing but scorn for Mao Zedong, the iconoclastic Wei praised aspects of the Cultural Revolution at a time when it was no longer fashionable to do so. And the aspects he praised are revealing. In the initial treatise, he wrote: "The Cultural Revolution was the first time the Chinese people displayed their power and made all the reactionary forces shudder." But the mass movement of 1966 was distorted and eventually suppressed by tyrants.[16] For Wei, the Chinese Communist political system was one which inevitably produced tyrants and would continue to do so. In the last issue of *Explorations* he edited, which was published on March 25, 1979, Wei warned that "the people must be [made] aware of Deng Xiaoping's metamorphosis into a dictator."[17]

[14] Wei Jingsheng, "The Second Sequel to 'The Fifth Modernization—Democracy and Others,' " *Explorations*, January 29, 1979, translated in *Issues and Studies*, September 1981, p. 90.
[15] Ibid., p. 90.
[16] "The Fifth Modernization—Democracy and Others," p. 92.
[17] Wei Jingsheng, "Yao minzhu haishi xin de ducai?" (Democracy or New Dictatorship?), Joint Publication Research Service No. 73421, pp. 28–30. See also Kjeld Erik Brodsgaard, "The Democracy Movement in China," *Asian Survey*, July 1981, pp. 747–74.

Wei's article, "Democracy or New Dictatorship?," was written in response to a speech Deng delivered on March 16, when China's new "paramount leader" accused Democracy Movement activists of operating like the Gang of Four, exploiting resentments created by the Cultural Revolution, and establishing secret relations with agents from Taiwan and foreign countries.[18]

On March 29, four days after the publication of his critique of Deng Xiaoping, Wei Jingsheng was arrested along with other members of the *Explorations* group, accused of providing foreigners with "military intelligence" on the Chinese invasion of Vietnam, engaging in counterrevolutionary agitation, and seeking to overthrow the "dictatorship of the proletariat."[19] Wei was brought to trial in Beijing on October 16, 1979. The proceedings were concluded in a single day, in the course of which the state prosecutor, invoking Deng Xiaoping's recently proclaimed "four cardinal principles," denounced Wei as "a running dog of Vietnam" as well as a counterrevolutionary criminal.[20] Wei Jingsheng, speaking eloquently in his own defense, invoked, in turn, Mao's "four great freedoms."[21] This failed to impress the court, which promptly convicted Wei of revealing secret military information to foreigners and publishing counterrevolutionary materials, condemning him as both a national traitor and a class enemy. Amidst worldwide protests, he was sentenced to fifteen years' imprisonment. The official press hailed the semi-public trial as a sterling demonstration of the rule of law brought about by post-Maoist legal reforms. For Wei, no doubt, the proceedings simply confirmed his view that laws were no less useful to autocracies than they are to democracies.

Although the trial of Wei was advertised by the government as a public one, and the proceedings were reported, albeit selectively, in

[18] Deng Xiaoping, speech of March 16, 1979, translated in FBIS 21 (March 1979), pp. L1–L2.
[19] The charge of revealing "military secrets" was apparently based on Wei Jingsheng's discussion of the Sino-Vietnamese war with a Reuters correspondent in Beijing. Details of the incident are discussed in Garside, *Coming Alive*, pp. 258–59. As Wei noted in his statement of defense, his only knowledge of Chinese military operations in Vietnam came from what had been publicly reported in Chinese newspapers and radio broadcasts.
[20] For a perceptive account of the trial, see Spence, *The Gate of Heavenly Peace*, pp. 362–65. Also Garside, *Coming Alive*, pp. 257–63.
[21] For an English translation of Wei's courtroom speech in his defense, see *Issues and Studies*, March 1980, pp. 108–9.

the official press, foreign correspondents and friends of Wei were barred from the courtroom. No official transcript of the trial was published. But an unofficial one, based on a secretly made tape recording of the proceeding, was posted on Democracy Wall in early November by members of another democratic organization, the April Fifth Forum. Those held responsible were promptly arrested.

The Wei Jingsheng affair was one of the very few cases of political persecution in the history of the People's Republic to command serious international attention and protest—due, no doubt, to the partially public character of the trial. Thereafter, the Beijing regime reverted to its customary practice of conducting political trials in secret.

THE SUPPRESSION OF THE DEMOCRACY MOVEMENT

When Wei Jingsheng was arrested in March 1979, the Democracy Movement was no longer confined to isolated wallposter writers. In the early months of the year, the youthful activists, most of whom anticipated a new era of socialist democracy under Deng Xiaoping's auspices, had established a great variety of quasi-political organizations producing dozens of mimeographed literary and political journals in most major cities and many provincial centers.[22] The new organizations were small, usually numbering no more than twenty or thirty active members; the circulation of their journals rarely exceeded several hundred copies;[23] and the groups remained localized, their activities largely uncoordinated. Yet the young democrats, while relatively few in number, clearly expressed the hopes and grievances of many.

[22] For brief descriptions of some of the more prominent organizations and journals, see Brodsgaard, "The Democracy Movement in China," pp. 764–69. Roger Garside has provided an interesting account of the Enlightenment Society and its guiding spirit, the poet Huang Xiang, in *Coming Alive*, pp. 263–77.

[23] There were exceptions to the limited number of copies of unofficial journals printed, especially when the government found a particular issue politically useful—as in the case of one number of the journal *Beijing Spring*, which was published in 10,000 copies at the Foreign Languages Press (Brodsgaard, pp. 765–66). Otherwise, publishers of unofficial magazines were denied access to printing shops (which required governmental approval) and were forced to rely on handwritten stencils and primitive mimeograph machines set up in their homes. Even basic supplies such as ink and paper could be purchased only in small quantities.

What concerned the Deng regime was not only the radical and critical political content of unofficial writings printed outside of Party control, but also the more immediate danger that the embryonic democratic societies might become vehicles for social protest. That Party leaders regarded the problems and grievances of peasants as the Party's business alone was made clear by the January 1979 arrest of Fu Yuehua, who was finally brought to trial and sentenced to two years' imprisonment in December for disrupting public order—and then, when released in 1981, immediately dispatched to a labor camp by administrative decree.[24] The greater fear was the potentially explosive situation created by the return of "rusticated youths." Of the 17 million urban youths sent to the countryside since the Cultural Revolution, more than 7 million had made their way back to the cities (either legally or otherwise) by the end of 1978, swelling the ranks of the urban unemployed. Along with their demands for jobs and education, neither of which the government had the capacity to supply, the frustrations that had built up during what the returned youths bitterly called their "lost years" were expressed in demonstrations and riots, which were particularly widespread in Shanghai in the early months of 1979. The activists of the Democracy Movement, who shared many of their experiences and grievances, were the natural political leaders of the returned youths. The crackdown on the Democracy Movement was as much motivated by the regime's determination to abort that possibility as it was by the authorities' distaste for the ideological heresies of the young democrats.

The arrest of Wei Jingsheng in late March 1979, which signaled the beginning of the repression, was followed by a long series of arrests of leaders of the movement and the banning of unofficial publications. The ideological and political rationale for state repression was set forth by Deng Xiaoping, bristling over his military misadventure in Vietnam, in secret Party speeches delivered at meetings

---

[24] On the arrest and trial of Fu Yuehua, see Arlette Laduguie, "The Human Rights Movement," *Index on Censorship*, February 1980, pp. 18–29, and Seymour (ed.), *The Fifth Modernization*, pp. 102–4, 256–59. During the course of the trial, the presiding judge castigated Fu as a "moral degenerate." On the sexist aspects and implications of the case, see Spence, *The Gate of Heavenly Peace*, pp. 366–68.

of senior officials on March 16 and March 30.[25] More and more activists were judged to be in violation of the "four cardinal principles," and were duly punished. Laws and regulations dating from the early 1950s (promulgated during the Korean War) providing for the "punishment of counterrevolutionaries," the protection of "state secrets," and the restriction of publications were resuscitated and invoked against the members of the Democracy Movement. Also employed was the security act of 1957, which had sanctioned the antirightist campaign and provided for internment in labor camps by administrative decree, incongruously revived at the very time most of the remaining victims of the 1957–58 antirightist witch-hunt were being released from "reeducation through labor" and other forms of political bondage.

The repression was naturally accompanied by a renewed emphasis on the Leninist virtues of discipline and authority. A strikingly grotesque application of the "four cardinal principles" came on the occasion of the third anniversary of the Tiananmen incident. The demonstrations of April 1976, which had taken place in defiance of the authority of the Communist Party and whose spirit animated the Democracy Movement, were now reinterpreted as a "Party-led" movement rather than a spontaneous popular uprising.[26]

The more moderate democratic organizations, especially those with ties to influential Party leaders,[27] survived the initial wave of repression, but the scope of their activities was increasingly restricted by government decrees and police harassment. The unexpectedly harsh sentence meted out to Wei Jingsheng in October 1979, rather than mollifying the Party leadership's thirst for revenge against their critics, seemed only to intensify the witch-hunt. The month after Wei had been sent off to prison, Deng Xiaoping heightened the leadership's paranoia over social and political disorder in a speech to higher-level cadres by fostering the myth that the Democracy

---

[25] On Deng's March 16, 1979, speech, see translation in FBIS 21 (March 1979), pp. L1–L2; and *The New York Times*, March 23, 1979, p. 7. For the March 30 speech, "Uphold the Four Cardinal Principles," *Selected Works of Deng Xiaoping*, pp. 166–91.

[26] "Carry Forward the Revolutionary Tiananmen Spirit," *People's Daily* editorial of April 5, 1979. *Peking Review*, April 13, 1979, pp. 11–12.

[27] On the relationship between Democracy Movement groups and the Party, see Nathan, *Chinese Democracy*, pp. 39–43.

Movement harbored national traitors as well as ideological heretics. Party and state secrets, he complained, were no longer secure when the sons and daughters of high officials were writing posters for Democracy Wall and revealing state and Party secrets to foreigners.[28]

In early December, following Deng's speech, municipal authorities in Beijing closed Democracy Wall, which, the official press shrilly complained, was a threat to "social order and public security." The main link between the democratic activists and Chinese society was now severed. Henceforth, wallposters were to be confined to a remote park in the city's western suburbs, and even at that out-of-the-way site authors were required to officially register their posters, providing the police with their names, addresses, and work units. Other cities and provinces soon adopted similar repressive measures, along with increasingly stringent restrictions on the sale and circulation of the few remaining unofficial journals. On what formerly had been Democracy Wall, commercial advertisements replaced political posters and poetry. It was a telling sign of the times.

Any remaining doubt about who was in charge of the repression was removed when Deng Xiaoping addressed a Party central work conference on January 16, 1980, emphasizing the overriding need for order and firmly laying down the orthodoxy that "Party leadership" was "the core of the four cardinal principles." Linking "democrats" and "dissidents" to anarchists and other saboteurs of social order, Deng called for the abolition of the "four greats," which included the constitutionally guaranteed freedom to write big character posters. Such freedoms, he observed, "have never played a positive role." He added that in dealing with criminals "such as Wei Jingsheng and his ilk," immediate police action was required, as China could not afford to wait until its legal system was perfected.[29]

Throughout the year 1980, state-controlled newspapers and periodicals were filled with articles repeating, and elaborating in extenso the ideological dicta Deng had laid down in his January 16 speech. The purpose of the propaganda campaign was to discredit

---

[28] For a revised version of the original speech, see "Senior Cadres Should Take the Lead in Maintaining and Enriching the Party's Fine Traditions" (November 2, 1979), *Selected Works of Deng Xiaoping*, pp. 208–23.

[29] "The Present Situation and the Tasks Before Us," *Selected Works of Deng Xiaoping*, pp. 224–58.

the views set forth by Democracy Movement writers, and to ideolog-ically rationalize the suppression of the movement, which was then proceeding apace. Following Deng's declaration that Communist Party leadership was "the core" of the "four cardinal principles," the official press attacked the idea of a multiparty system advocated by some of the democratic organizations. The Dengist decree repeated the old Stalinist orthodoxy that with the elimination of antagonistic class interests, there was no social basis for more than a single Com-munist Party, which represented the interests of society as a whole. Nor was there a need for any form of popular supervision over that party, as many democratic writers alternatively suggested. Deng Xiao-ping, though acknowledging that the Party had made "serious mis-takes" in the course of its history, held that such mistakes were always "corrected by the Party itself, not by any extraneous force."[30] Deng and his ideologists were insistent on re-creating the image of an infallible Leninist party—infallible over the long term, in any event.

The Party's ideological assault on the Democracy Movement in 1980 also included lengthy treatises, which angrily denied the pos-sibility that China's "socialist" society could yield a new "bureau-cratic ruling class," as many of the democrats had come to believe. Also produced were analyses suggesting that Marx's Paris Commune model of "the self-government of the producers" was badly flawed, and therefore an inappropriate model for China's "dictatorship of the proletariat." And there were arguments that grotesquely reinterpreted "socialist democracy" in authoritarian fashion, extolling "discipline" and "order" as the features which demonstrated its superiority over "bourgeois democracy."

In his January 16 speech, Deng Xiaoping had demanded the ab-olition of the "four great freedoms," which Mao had insisted be added to the constitution in 1975. The Fifth National People's Congress, convened on August 30, 1980, duly obliged, eliminating the "four greats" from Article 45 of the state constitution—and, for good mea-sure, deleting the clause granting workers the right to strike. It was at this Congress that the now powerless Hua Guofeng formally re-signed his empty premiership in favor of Deng's handpicked succes-

[30] Ibid., p. 252.

sor, Zhao Ziyang, having already been replaced earlier that year as Party head by Hu Yaobang, another of Deng's protégés. Local police now quickly moved to mop up the remnants of the once-flourishing Democracy Movement. Posters were ripped off the walls of Yuedan Park, even though few readers had ventured to visit the secluded area during the time it served as the officially designated location for big character posters; the few remaining unofficial journals, including purely literary magazines, were forced to cease publication; and hundreds of young activists, now truly dissidents, were arrested, and many were sent to labor camps by administrative decree. At the time, the regime's ideologists and supporters were celebrating China's newly promulgated legal codes, evidence, it was said, of the country's progress in "socialist democratization."

In suppressing the Democracy Movement, Deng Xiaoping sent into opposition—and often into prison—many youthful activists who had assisted him in his rise to power during the exciting and hope-filled months of November and December 1978 and who had continued to look to him in the months thereafter as the bearer of democratic reforms. But Deng's alliance with the Democracy Movement had been a brief marriage of political convenience. Once he achieved control of the Party, and especially when he had established himself as China's acknowledged "paramount leader," Deng had little use, and even less tolerance, for his young democratic allies. The final disintegration of that curious alliance is tragically reflected in the story of Wang Xizhe, the main author of the famous 1974 Li Yizhe poster.

WANG XIZHE

Of the three writers collectively known under the pen name Li Yizhe, only Wang Xizhe became an activist in the post-Mao Democracy Movement. Chen Yiyang withdrew from politics to pursue private endeavors following the group's much-publicized "rehabilitation" in early 1979; and Li Zhengtian joined the reformist wing of the Communist Party, expressing the hope that he could more effectively pursue democratic goals by working within the existing Party-state system than as a critic from without. Many young democrats shared

Li's view, whether as a genuine belief or out of an instinct for self-preservation. Party reformers, in turn, cultivated the more talented of the Democracy Movement leaders by offering them positions in official cultural organizations or in the political apparatus.[31]

Wang Xizhe resisted these temptations, turning down an offer of an attractive job at the prestigious Pearl River Film Studio in Canton. Instead, he continued his independent course as a writer and movement activist. Wang wrote prolifically and perceptively from an original Marxist (but decidedly non-Leninist) perspective, producing critical analyses of Mao Zedong and the Cultural Revolution and exploring the forms of political organization best suited to realize his vision of China's transformation into a democratic socialist society.[32] He was critical of Mao, but he also was a trenchant critic of the Party bureaucracy; indeed, his critique of Mao was partly based on the view that Mao did not truly oppose China's bureaucratic system. He condemned the results of the Cultural Revolution and the manipulation of the movement by its leaders for their own political ends, but he praised many of the original ideals and aims of the upheaval. He was especially attracted to the spontaneous democratic radicalism of the early stages of the Cultural Revolution and the goal of reorganizing political power in accordance with the eminently democratic principles of the Paris Commune. In the post-Mao era, he initially supported Deng Xiaoping and the Party reformers but also advocated mass supervision of Party leaders, envisioning a time when the Party would no longer be necessary. Wang's writings found a nationwide readership, and, as many were published or reprinted in Hong Kong, commanded a degree of international attention as well.

It was not until the general repression that came in the wake of

[31] Li Zhengtian, for example, married the daughter of a PLA general and was appointed to the faculty of the Guangzhou Academy of Fine Arts.

[32] Wang Xizhe's writings of this period include: "Party Leadership and People's Supervision"; "Mao Zedong and the Cultural Revolution"; "Strive for the Class Dictatorship of the Proletariat"; and "Proletarian Dictatorship Is a Humanitarian Dictatorship." Several of his essays, along with various speeches and interviews, were collected and published in Hong Kong in 1981 under the title *Wang Xizhe Lunwen Ji* (Collected Essays of Wang Xizhe) (Hong Kong: The Seventies Magazine Press, 1981). For an abridged English translation of "Proletarian Dictatorship Is a Humanitarian Dictatorship," see Helen F. Siu and Zelda Stern (eds.), *Mao's Harvest* (New York: Oxford University Press, 1983), pp. 210–19. Wang's main work, "Mao Zedong and the Cultural Revolution," is translated in *Chinese Law and Government* (Armonk, N.Y.: M. E. Sharpe, 1985), pp. 1–98.

Wei Jingsheng's trial that Wang Xizhe fully lost hope in Deng's promises of "socialist democratization." When Deng demanded the abolition of the "four great freedoms" in early 1980, Wang bitterly
concluded that "Deng Xiaoping does not respect the constitution."[33]
With the repression now having reached Guangdong, hitherto an area
of relative official tolerance for the democratic activists, Wang undertook to edit his own journal—or, more precisely, what he called
a newsletter containing "personal correspondence" to circumvent the
ban on unofficial publications. He grew increasingly outspoken in
protesting the dictatorial character and oppressive acts of the regime,
inexorably moving closer to the fateful conclusion that a "privileged
class" of bureaucrats, represented by the Chinese Communist Party,
was the main obstacle to the realization of democracy and socialism
in China.

In the early months of 1981, a new and final wave of repression
against the remnants of the Democracy Movement swept over the
land. Again, it was Deng Xiaoping who took the lead in launching
the suppression. Addressing a Party central work conference on December 25, 1980, Deng, in a vitriolic outburst that might have given
pause to those who continued to praise his "moderate" and "pragmatic" virtues, lumped together the youthful advocates of democracy
with common criminals, warning that "a minority of fringe youths"
not only were guilty of "anti-Party and anti-socialist statements" but
also were engaged in "murder and arson, the manufacturing of ex-
plosives, robbery and thievery, rape and gang rape . . . [and] organized prostitution." He further charged that the "so-called dissidents"
of the Democracy Movement were "now using the methods of the
Great Cultural Revolution to incite and cause trouble." Deng took
special pains to refute the view, now current among the remaining
members of the movement, that the Party bureaucracy had transformed itself into a new ruling class. "There is absolutely not, or
could there ever be, a so-called bureaucratic class," he decreed.[34]

The official press followed Deng's speech with a savage ideological campaign against "illegal underground activities," denying the
existence of a "bureaucratic class" and linking the young democrats

---

[33] *Qishi Niandai* (The Seventies), June 30, 1980, pp. 54–56.
[34] FBIS Daily Report, May 4, 1981, p. W8, and *Issues and Studies*, July 1981, pp. 115–16.

to the pernicious politics of the Cultural Revolution and to the "remnant forces of Lin Biao and the Gang of Four."[35] The police followed soon thereafter with a nationwide wave of arrests. Wang Xizhe was arrested in Guangzhou on April 20, 1981. A year later, he was convicted of disseminating "counterrevolutionary propaganda to overthrow the dictatorship of the proletariat," and sentenced to fourteen years' imprisonment. Having been betrayed once by Mao's promise of an antibureaucratic revolution, Wang was betrayed a second time by Deng's promise of democracy. The few surviving activists of the Democracy Movement were now indeed relegated to what the regime for some time had been calling "illegal underground activities."

LIBERALIZATION AND REPRESSION

The suppression of the Democracy Movement, paradoxically, was accompanied by a general liberalization of cultural and intellectual life. Throughout 1979, just as Wei Jingsheng and other young activists were being jailed, thousands of older intellectuals, victims of the antirightist campaign and the Cultural Revolution, were released from prisons and labor camps and returned to Beijing and Shanghai to resume their interrupted careers.

It was also a time when many old ideological and cultural orthodoxies were abandoned or ignored. Writers, artists, and scholars who had been silenced for a decade or longer returned to their work, producing an ever-increasing volume of new novels, plays, films, journals, and books. Cultural and intellectual life was further enlivened by the reappearance of many hitherto banned foreign works. It was a particularly poignant moment when Bertolt Brecht's *The Life of Galileo* was staged in Beijing in 1980, marking a new Chinese opening to the world of international culture and holding special symbolic significance for Chinese intellectuals who had suffered through decades of ideological heresy hunts. "Emancipate the mind" was the official slogan of the time, and for a while it was by no means an empty slogan.

[35] *People's Daily* editorial, February 8, 1981, in FBIS Daily Report, February 9, 1981, pp. L5–L8.

The cultural renaissance was part of a broader political emancipation that included a wide-ranging "reversal of incorrect verdicts" for both high Party leaders and ordinary citizens. Among those posthumously rehabilitated were once-disgraced Party luminaries such as the writer Qu Qiubai, an early Communist leader executed by the Guomindang in 1935 but denounced as a renegade during the Cultural Revolution,[36] and, as we have seen, Liu Shaoqi, purged by Mao as China's foremost "capitalist roader" in the late 1960s. Also rehabilitated were some 10 million people who had been branded with pejorative political labels during the Maoist era and deprived of "citizen's rights." The vast majority were the offspring of former bourgeois, landlord, and rich peasant families. These were classes that no longer existed in social reality but rather only in memory, yet this had been sufficient to make many millions victims of the socially archaic and politically pernicious system of "class labels." The abandonment of that system was a major political advance that mitigated arbitrary social and economic discrimination against individuals solely on the basis of distant social background.

Not only were there "reversals of incorrect verdicts" but also promises of democratic political reforms coming from the very highest leaders of the Chinese Communist Party. Speaking to an enlarged session of the Politburo on August 18, 1980, Deng Xiaoping called for "the democratization of the life of society as a whole." He criticized the overcentralization of power in the Chinese political system, the excessive power of individual leaders, their patriarchal habits, the system of lifelong tenure for leaders and cadres, their appetite for privilege, the lack of distinction between Party and state administrations, and bureaucratism in general. Deng attributed these political evils not only to China's long tradition of "feudal despotism," but also, more significantly, to the Stalinist imprint on the Comintern. As a remedy he proposed (and the proposal was seemingly not far different from what the democratic activists had been advocating) that "people's democracy" should be developed into a system "to ensure

[36] On the life and thought of Qu—and his posthumous fate in Party history—see Paul Pickowicz's superb study *Marxist Literary Thought in China: The Influence of Ch'u Chiu-pai* (Berkeley: University of California Press, 1981); the perceptive commentary on Qu in Spence, *The Gate of Heavenly Peace*, passim; and Kung Chi-keung, "Intellectuals and Masses: The Case of Qu Qiubai," Ph.D. dissertation, Department of History, University of Wisconsin-Madison, 1995.

that the people as a whole genuinely enjoy the power to supervise the state in a variety of effective ways, and especially to supervise political power at the basic level, as well as in all enterprises and undertakings."[37] The first step, albeit a small one, in implementing political reform was to come in the autumn of 1980 with the introduction of a degree of competitiveness in scheduled elections to local people's congresses.

The intellectual and political liberalization of 1979–80 and the promises of democratic reforms stand in striking contrast to the harsh repression of the young Democracy Movement. But there was a political logic, however perverse, to this seeming incongruity. For intellectuals, especially members of the established intelligentsia, posed no political threat to the regime. They had no organizations of their own beyond those under the firm control of the Party. They did not join the Democracy Movement, whose demands most intellectuals regarded as premature and whose methods they thought unrealistic. However much some intellectuals may have sympathized with the aims of the young democrats, they kept a respectable political distance. Indeed, they had little taste for political activism of any sort. This distrust of politics was hardly surprising in light of their bitter experiences from the Hundred Flowers campaign through the "Cultural Revolution decade." Most intellectuals thus proved amenable, indeed more than a bit eager, to avail themselves of the new professional opportunities and the social and material privileges the Deng regime now offered. And the government, in turn, was in desperate need of the intelligentsia's expertise to carry out its program of modern economic and technological development—and to ideologically rationalize the way it was to be pursued. China's intellectuals, and especially the vast and rapidly growing technological intelligentsia, were soon to be a crucial component of the social base of the post-Mao regime.

The young activists of the Democracy Movement, by contrast, were quite dispensable, especially after they had served Deng Xiao-

[37] Deng Xiaoping, "On the Reform of the System of Party and State Leadership" (Speech of August 18, 1980, to enlarged session of CCP Politburo), *Selected Works of Deng Xiaoping*, pp. 302–25, and *Beijing Review*, October 3, 1983, and October 10, 1983. Deng's August 1980 speech, and other Party statements on political reform, will be discussed in greater detail in Chapter 8.

ping's political purposes in late 1978. They had little expertise to contribute to the Four Modernizations. Their formal schooling had been cut short by the Cultural Revolution and they remained mostly uneducated, save for the political self-education they had acquired during the Cultural Revolution and after—and in that respect they were perhaps far too educated in the eyes of Deng and other Party leaders. Ultimately, what the Leninist leaders of the post-Mao order could not tolerate was the uncompromising anti-authoritarianism of the youthful democracy advocates, particularly their refusal to accept the political and ideological leadership of the Chinese Communist Party. The non-Leninist proclivities of the movement were not only ideologically heretical but also found practical political expression in organizational activities that were not under Party control—undertaken by groups, however small and embryonic, which seemed to threaten the regime's obsessively held goal of "stability and unity." What proved particularly intolerable, and grated more than a few raw official nerves, were the Maoist strains in the Democracy Movement writings, especially the revived charge that China was ruled by a privileged "bureaucratic class." For Party leaders in Beijing, many of the ideas and activities of the young democrats raised the specter of the Cultural Revolution. It was this fear, along with the closely related challenge to the Leninist "vanguard party," that produced the final rupture between Deng Xiaoping and his onetime allies in the Democracy Movement—and led to the suppression of the true advocates of socialist democratization, amidst a hail of official charges that the ideology and methods of the Cultural Revolution were being resurrected.

The accusations that the democracy activists had revived the politics of the Cultural Revolution were untrue and unfair. But they are revealing. They show, beyond the presence of a degree of political paranoia in Beijing over the danger of "chaos" (*luan*), that the differences between the Dengist leaders and their former supporters in the Democracy Movement extended to differing assessments of the Cultural Revolution. The young democrats condemned the Cultural Revolution as did their elders, most having suffered more from the upheaval than their new persecutors in Beijing, but they did so because Mao and Maoist leaders had betrayed the egalitarian political and social goals they initially had proclaimed. Now the activists came to believe that many post-Mao Party leaders condemned the Cultural Revolution for other reasons—and for the wrong ones. As *Beijing Spring*, one of the more moderate of the unofficial journals, bluntly put the matter in August 1979:

> The privileged few oppose the Cultural Revolution, for it weakened their power and positions. They have come to the understanding that dictatorship in fact runs counter to the interests of the privileged class, consequently desiring an aristocracy in which bureaucrats enjoy privileges as befitting their positions in the hierarchy rather than suffer the gnawing fear of purge under an autocrat.[38]

The article went on to optimistically predict that "the people will not give their approval to a restoration of the old institutions [that existed] prior to the Cultural Revolution. Nor will they sanction a comeback of the privileged classes, who existed before the Cultural Revolution, under the name of 'stability and solidarity.' "

Democracy Movement attacks against "the privileged classes" initially were directed primarily against the "whateverist" faction of the Party and the sector of the bureaucracy it represented, but the term soon came to be applied to Party leaders and cadres in general when it became clear, as Wei Jingsheng had foretold, that Deng Xiaoping would discard "the masquerade of supporting democracy" and assume dictatorial power.[39]

THE END OF THE DEMOCRACY MOVEMENT, 1980–81

The democratic activists of 1978–81 called their endeavors "the April Fifth Movement," commemorating the 1976 incident that had initially moved them to political action. And looking to broader historical precedents, they saw themselves in the hallowed tradition of the May Fourth Movement of 1919. Like the May Fourth Movement,

---

[38] "The Nation Will Remain Chaotic Until the Privileged Class Is Exterminated," *Beijing Spring*, No. 7 (August 10, 1979), translated in *Issues and Studies*, May 1980, pp. 85–86.
[39] Wei Jingsheng, "Democracy or New Dictatorship?"

the April Fifth Movement had begun with a demonstration on the square beneath the Gate of Heavenly Peace. Both movements demanded human rights and democracy in opposition to dictatorial regimes. In both cases, radical young activists anticipated that their actions would herald "the awakening of the Chinese people." "The April Fifth Movement," it was typically proclaimed, "is the successor to the May Fourth Movement, its deepening and development."[40]

But the historical analogy proved faulty. Unlike the May Fourth Movement, the Democracy Movement did not win the active support of other social groups. Few university students joined the self-educated ex-Red Guard activists who initiated and led the embryonic movement. Nor did intellectuals, in striking contrast to the May Fourth era. The popular support that the Democracy Movement acquired was meager, and came mostly from a small number of younger urban workers whose life experiences were similar to those who wrote wallposters and "people's publications," workers in their late twenties and early thirties whose educations had been cut short by the Cultural Revolution.[41] Older workers were mostly indifferent to the movement. Having exhausted their political energies and impulses in the futile battles of the Cultural Revolution, older workers were now willing to voice only economic grievances. The young democracy activists were thus socially isolated—and the government took measures to ensure that they would remain so, preventing the establishment of organizational links between the Democracy Movement and other social groups who harbored grievances.

An opportunity to break out of this isolation from society seemed to present itself in late 1980, when the government announced liberalized provisions for elections to local people's congresses. The elections themselves were of minor political significance, essentially Soviet-style Party-managed exercises that were part of an indirect process of selecting delegates to the largely powerless National Peo-

[40] From a November 30, 1978, poster on Democracy Wall written by the poet Huang Xiang, a leader of the Enlightenment Society. Cited in Garside, *Coming Alive*, p. 223.

[41] As *New York Times* correspondent Fox Butterfield reported from Beijing at the height of activities around Democracy Wall at the end of November 1978: "The actual number of people involved in writing and reading the posters is relatively small, perhaps ten thousand out of Peking's population of eight million. Most of them are young, in their 20's or early 30's, members of the generation that were caught up in the Cultural Revolution, people who were unable to continue with their education." *The New York Times*, December 1, 1978.

ple's Congress, a body which convened on occasion to formally ratify Party-fashioned decisions on government policies and the operation of the state bureaucracy. The ritualistic local elections had been held since the early 1950s, until suspended during the Cultural Revolution. After a hiatus of over a decade, the local elections of 1980 were to be held under new regulations that permitted a small measure of unaccustomed competition. By participating in these local electoral campaigns, however far removed they were from the real levers of power, some Democracy Movement activists hoped to reach wider sectors of society.

Thus in the autumn of 1980, democracy activists entered electoral contests in a number of university and factory precincts, appealing to students and workers for support. In the few instances where the democrats succeeded in stimulating serious political debate and turning ritualized election procedures into genuine political competitions, mostly on university campuses, they inevitably came into conflict with local Party organizations. The Democracy Movement candidate who won the election at Beijing University, after a month-long period of political ferment and controversy, was not permitted to take his post as a deputy. At Hunan Teachers College in Changsha, where the intervention of Party officials in the local elections incited students to demonstrations, boycotts of classes, hunger strikes, and a militant march on the provincial Party headquarters, the election was officially declared null and void—and a promised new election was never held.[42]

The Party responded to these and other disruptive incidents by adding restrictive amendments to the election law, duly adopted by the National People's Congress in 1982, including the deletion of a provision that granted candidates the right to freely conduct election campaigns. Henceforth, as had been customary, electoral campaigning was to be confined to Party-dominated election committees, which would "brief voters" on the candidates at officially convened meetings. But the immediate result of the incidents that marked—and, from the government's point of view, marred—the elections of 1980

---

[42] A description and analysis of the elections of 1980 is to be found in Chapter 10 of Nathan, *Chinese Democracy* (pp. 193–223). On the events in Changsha, see pp. 209–19 and Liang Heng, *Son of the Revolution* (New York: Knopf, 1983).

was to strengthen the regime's determination to eliminate what remained of the Democracy Movement.

Also contributing to the demise of the Democracy Movement in China was the rise of Solidarity in Poland in 1979–80. For many young Chinese democrats, Solidarity inspired hopes for an alliance between intellectuals and workers that would serve as the social basis for a popular political organization independent of Party and state control. Some Democracy Movement activists did in fact attempt to win working-class support, especially during the local elections of 1980, although with little success.[43] For Chinese Party leaders, Solidarity could be viewed only in equivocal and ambivalent ways. The dramatic events in Poland were more or less accurately reported in the Chinese press, but the government took no official position, neither lauding the emergence of Solidarity nor condemning the suppression of the workers' movement. The unspoken belief was that Solidarity was a welcome development insofar as it caused difficulties for Moscow, but certainly not an example to be followed in China, lest it cause difficulties for the regime in Beijing. Official fears that it might be emulated were heightened by scattered workers' strikes in 1980, which in some cases raised demands for independent trade unions, probably inspired by the news from Poland. That possibility, in turn, undoubtedly added urgency to the regime's determination to keep the Democracy Movement separated from society and its discontents.

The policy proved eminently successful. In the end, the youthful democracy advocates remained socially isolated, and social isolation in turn facilitated the crushing of the movement, which was accomplished with remarkably little public protest. The final crackdown was launched by Deng Xiaoping's harsh speech of December 25, 1980, and that was soon followed by the Party Politburo's distribution of a secret directive, the notorious "Document No. 9," which in-

[43] One such effort, that of Fu Shenqi, a worker in a Shanghai generator factory and also the editor of several Democracy Movement journals, is related in Nathan, *Chinese Democracy*, pp. 219–20. Although not selected as a candidate by the Party-controlled election committee in the factory precinct, the twenty-six-year-old Fu nonetheless won 46 percent of the vote on a write-in basis. He was among the democratic activists arrested in April 1981—ironically after participating in a ceremony commemorating the fifth anniversary of the 1976 Tiananmen incident (Nathan, *Chinese Democracy*, p. 221).

structed local officials to suppress all unofficial organizations and publications by June 1, 1981, arrest the leaders of the remaining dissident groups, and expel Party members who had assisted their illegal activities. From this there followed the massive arrests of April 1981, which effectively closed the last chapter in the history of post-Mao China's first Democracy Movement.

But more than state repression was involved in the passing of the democratic movement. Also contributing to its demise was the general depoliticization of social life that accompanied Deng Xiaoping's economic reform program.

In part, depoliticization was one of the many unintended results of the Cultural Revolution. On popular political consciousness, the Cultural Revolution left a dual and contradictory legacy. On the one hand, the Cultural Revolution, or, more precisely, its failure, gave rise to the Democracy Movement, whose members strove to build a socialist democracy by remedying the political defects of the Mao regime. But in larger measure, the legacy of the Cultural Revolution was one that bred political disillusionment, cynicism, and apathy among the urban population. The new regime of Deng Xiaoping did not attempt to fill the void by fostering new social ideals but rather by promising the masses a better material life. As part of its economic reform policies, the government encouraged the production, importation, and purchase of consumer goods, which soon began to appear on department store shelves in ever-increasing quantity and variety, promoted by advertisements patterned after American and Japanese fashions. Billboards displaying Seiko watches and Sony television sets replaced (or were pasted over) those that bore the faded political slogans of the Cultural Revolution and the once-ubiquitous sayings of Chairman Mao. Readers of "people's publications" dwindled as consumerism gained sway, as new officially sanctioned magazines and journals offered more appealing literary fare than had been available in the past, and as Chinese youth were increasingly attracted to Western popular culture. People began to turn more and more to private pursuits, and such political interests that remained were mostly submerged by expectations of an improving material standard of living.

Leaders of what was left of the once-flourishing Democracy Movement were well aware that they lived in a depoliticized social environment unreceptive to their political ideals and visions, as Xu Wenli, editor of the suppressed *April Fifth Forum*, acknowledged in an interview with *Washington Post* correspondent Michael Weisskopf shortly before he was arrested by agents of the Public Security Bureau on April 10, 1981. In summarizing the secretly arranged interview, Weisskopf later wrote: "Xu emphasized . . . that he supported the party and socialism but believed that democratic freedom to elect leaders was necessary to help the nation modernize. Nevertheless, he conceded, most Chinese were more interested in improving their life styles than increasing their democratic rights."[44]

In the end, the Democracy Movement was the victim of both state repression and popular political apathy.

The Third Plenum and the events surrounding it raised hopes that the Revolution would be revitalized and democratized. "Socialist democracy," and not simply economic reform, was the great promise of the time, which was at first personified by Deng Xiaoping, the preeminent figure in the dramatic events of late 1978. But the true carriers of the ideal of socialist democracy were the young radicals of the Democracy Movement. Among the severest critics of the departed Mao regime, they nevertheless had rescued the more rational elements of the radical core of Maoism, which they attempted to use for democratic ends in a heroic and lonely effort to fashion a genuinely socialist society.

Deng Xiaoping, after a brief appearance (and it was perhaps never any more than appearance) as a "socialist democratizer," soon emerged as the champion of order. Surrounded by men who shared his obsessive fear of "chaos," a fear bred in part by memories of the Cultural Revolution, and the representative of groups who had a vested interest in preserving the essentials of China's existing bureaucratic order, Deng became the leader of a classic Thermidorean response, the imposition of "order" on those who seemed to threaten it. The crushing of the Democracy Movement was a conservative reaction to the radical challenge of socialist democracy.

[44] "Arrest of Dissident Editor in China Spurs Fears of a New Clampdown," *The Washington Post*, April 20, 1981, pp. A1, A24.

6

THE PLACE OF MAO ZEDONG
IN POST-MAO CHINA

FROM 1979 TO 1981, while the Democracy Movement was being suppressed, Deng Xiaoping was consolidating his control over the Party and state apparatus, eliminating the left-wing members of the coalition that had brought down the Gang of Four. If Deng was at first reluctant to jail the young activists who had supported his rise to power, his purge of his "leftist" Party opponents was coldly deliberate, methodically carried out, and more than a bit vengeful.

Deng sought more than personal power and political revenge. He also aimed to eliminate all potential opposition to the far-reaching economic reforms he had begun to introduce in 1979. The first task was to remove from positions of authority Party leaders identified with the policies of the late Mao era, especially the "whateverists." Earlier, Deng Xiaoping privately had ridiculed Hua Guofeng and others who rashly had taken that vow early in 1977, observing that "Marx and Engels did not put forward any 'whatever' doctrine, nor did Lenin and Stalin, nor did Comrade Mao Zedong himself."[1] In 1979, Deng publicly moved against the remaining self-proclaimed Mao loyalists, directing the official press to discredit the "whateverists" personally,

---

[1] Deng Xiaoping, "The 'Two Whatever' Policy Does Not Accord with Marxism" (May 24, 1977). See *Beijing Review*, August 15, 1983, for excerpts from comments Deng purportedly made in 1977 in a private discussion with two unidentified members of the Party Central Committee.

while launching a major ideological campaign in preparation for their political excommunication.

The ideological work focused on "ultraleftism," which was to become the major heresy of the early Deng era. Originally directed against the long-dead Lin Biao and the imprisoned Gang of Four, the "ultraleft" deviation soon came to officially characterize most of the final two decades of the Maoist era, as multitudes of scholars and theoreticians were brought forth to expound on the "petty bourgeois" social and ideological roots of the Great Leap Forward campaign and the Cultural Revolution.

The question as to which heretical ideological label was to be stamped on the Gang as they were consigned to political oblivion long had been a source of controversy and confusion. For two years following the arrest of the Four, they were branded as "ultrarightists," having conspired to seize state power with the aim of restoring capitalism, it was charged. By the beginning of 1979, in accordance with the directives of the Third Plenum, the Gang (together with Lin Biao) had been converted into "ultraleftists." As the Deng regime increasingly contemplated social and economic policies condemned as "capitalist" in the Mao era, it became politically convenient to identify "leftism" as the principal ideological and political danger.[2]

Thus, beginning in 1979, a wide-ranging critique of "ultraleftism," both in the Party's history and in the present, was undertaken by the new regime, dominating both the official press and academic journals.[3] The ideological campaign was given considerable political impetus when the venerable Marshal Ye Jianying delivered the main speech commemorating the thirtieth anniversary of the founding of the People's Republic on October 1, 1979. In his address, which had been approved in detail beforehand by the Party Central Committee, Ye not only attributed the disasters of the Great Leap to "leftist errors" which violated presumably "objective" economic laws, but

---

[2] While post-Mao Chinese theoreticians have been reasonably consistent in using the terms "leftism" and "ultraleftism," this has not been the case with foreign journalists and others who use the terms "leftist," "radical," and "conservative" synonymously to describe real or suspected opponents of Deng Xiaoping's policies.

[3] For a detailed and highly perceptive analysis of the various critiques of ultraleftism in the history of the Chinese Communist Party, see William Joseph, *The Critique of Ultra-Leftism in China, 1958–1981* (Stanford: Stanford University Press, 1984).

also described the Cultural Revolution as a "calamity" for the Chinese nation wrought by those leaders who pursued an "ultraleft" line.[4] Save for the abortive Liuist era of the early 1960s, the final eighteen years of Mao's rule were now open to critical scrutiny. Although Ye Jianying placed the blame on Lin Biao and the Gang of Four, as was still the official political custom, it was clear to all that Mao Zedong and many others also bore responsibility for the failures and sufferings of the Great Leap and the Cultural Revolution.

Among the political survivors tainted with the ultraleft heresy were the "whateverists" who still sat on the Politburo. Most were purged at a meeting of the Central Committee held in February 1980 (the Fifth Plenum), including Wang Dongxing, the former head of the elite 8341 Unit who had engineered the arrest of the Gang of Four in 1976. Also purged was Chen Yonggui, the peasant leader of the once-celebrated Dazhai brigade who had been elevated to the Party Politburo and to a vice-premiership during the Cultural Revolution. The places of the departing "leftists," who were political beneficiaries of the Cultural Revolution, were taken by veteran Party leaders, who had been branded "rightists" during the upheaval. Such economic specialists as Chen Yun and Bo Yibo, who were leading policymakers during what now were seen as the only two positive periods in the history of the People's Republic—namely, the Soviet-modeled years through 1957 and the Liuist era of the early 1960s—achieved increasing political prominence and power, as did Peng Zhen, the first of the high Party leaders felled in the Cultural Revolution.

It was not entirely fortuitous that the Fifth Plenum, which cast off remnant "Maoists" and restored Liu Shaoqi to an honorable resting place in Party history, also recommended, on Deng's suggestion, the abolition of the constitutional rights of citizens to "speak out freely, air views freely, hold great debates, and write big character posters." The "four greats" (*sida*) were uncomfortably reminiscent of the attack on the Leninist party organization during the Cultural Revolution, and they fed the post-Mao leaders' almost paranoiac fear

---

[4] "Comrade Ye Jianying's Speech," *Beijing Review*, October 5, 1979, pp. 7–32. Ye spoke on behalf of the Party Central Committee, the Standing Committee of the National People's Congress (which he chaired), and the State Council.

of the ever-present danger of "chaos"—in addition to being a legal inconvenience for a regime that was busy jailing both the remaining Democracy Movement activists and a varied assortment of "leftists." The recommendation was, of course, duly accepted by the National People's Congress when it convened in August 1980, just as the Congress formally ratified various personnel changes in the state administration, also previously decided upon within the inner councils of the Party.

The political burial of Hua Guofeng was performed in a relatively graceful manner. Although he remained the formal head of Party and state for a time, by mid-1979 he had been reduced to a ceremonial role in both positions, awarding medals to model workers, delivering eulogies at state funerals, presiding over banquets for visiting dignitaries, delivering standard speeches on official occasions, and touring foreign lands. Hua's Party chairmanship was converted into little more than a titular position in February 1980, when the Fifth Plenum of the Central Committee reestablished the Soviet-style office of the Party Secretariat and the post of Secretary-General, a position Deng Xiaoping had occupied before Mao abolished it.[5] Named to fill the revived secretary-generalship was Hu Yaobang, one of Deng's closest associates since their service together as political commissars in the Second Field Army in the late 1930s.[6] Hu Yaobang was simultaneously elevated to the Standing Committee of the Politburo and appointed head of the Party's Propaganda Department as well. Through the mechanism of the re-created Secretariat, Hu Yaobang (with Deng Xiaoping standing close behind him) effectively controlled the Party's organizational apparatus.

Hua Guofeng's next demotion came in September 1980, when he was forced to resign his position as Premier of the State Council,

[5] The Secretariat of the Party Central Committee and the post of Secretary-General had been revived by the Eighth Party Congress in 1956, with Deng Xiaoping (then the sixth-highest-ranking member in the Party hierarchy) selected to fill the position. The office was abolished during the Cultural Revolution, before again being revived in 1980. The post of Party Chairman, which Mao so long had occupied, was formally abolished in September 1982.
[6] Hu Yaobang was born in Hunan in 1915 and joined the CCP in 1933. After serving under Deng during the revolutionary years, he also did so in the early years of the People's Republic when Deng was the political-military head in Sichuan province. Following Deng to Beijing in 1952, he was purged along with his patron during the Cultural Revolution, but, like Deng, was twice rehabilitated. Hu's elevation to the Politburo came at the Third Plenum of December 1978.

ostensibly to honor the constitutional myth, now being promoted by Party reformers, that there was a real distinction between Party and state bureaucracies. Deng selected as China's new Premier Zhao Ziyang, who had risen rapidly up the post-1949 bureaucratic ladder (only briefly delayed by the Cultural Revolution) to become Party head of Sichuan province, where his experiments in economic reform had attracted Deng's attention. Summoned to Beijing in January 1980, Zhao had been quickly elevated to the Politburo's Standing Committee prior to assuming the premiership.[7]

Hua Guofeng finally relinquished his now-empty title of Chairman of the Chinese Communist Party in June 1981, when the Central Committee convened its Sixth Plenum, the meeting which also issued the Party's official historical assessment of Mao Zedong. The chairmanship, now a redundant office in any event, fell to Secretary-General Hu Yaobang. A year later, at the Twelfth Congress of the Chinese Communist Party held in September 1982, Hua Guofeng was dropped from membership in the Politburo, thus bringing to a close the last chapter in the political history of Mao Zedong's first successor. Hua faded into obscurity as one of 348 members of the Party Central Committee. The incongruity of having both a Party Chairman and a Party Secretary-General was resolved by abolishing the former office. Hu Yaobang, in his capacity as Secretary-General, was reconfirmed as head of the Party by the delegates at the Twelfth Congress, although Deng Xiaoping remained China's "paramount leader," as Western journalists customarily described him. The Twelfth Congress itself, which Deng called the most important in the Party's history since the Seventh Congress in 1945, when Mao's leadership had been consecrated and celebrated, was largely devoted to ratifying Deng's economic reform policies and the post-Mao political order he had fashioned.

---

[7] Zhao Ziyang, the son of a Hunan landlord, was born in 1919. He joined the Young Communist League as a teenager and the Communist Party in 1938, serving as a political cadre in the Red Army during the last decade of the revolutionary war. By the early 1960s he had ascended to the post of Party Secretary in Guangdong province. Purged during the Cultural Revolution, he was restored (as Mao was restoring many veteran cadres after the fall of Lin Biao) to his Guangdong post in 1972, where he offered limited political patronage to the Li Yizhe group. He headed the provincial government and Party organizations in Deng Xiaoping's native Sichuan from 1975 until his promotion to Beijing early in 1980. In form, if not necessarily entirely in substance, he went to great lengths to pattern himself after Zhou Enlai.

THE QUESTION OF MAO

Deng Xiaoping's consolidation of power, and the implementation of his program of economic reforms, required more than the removal of the "whateverists" and their replacement by men loyal to the new leader. Deng also had to demystify Mao Zedong, whose ghost dominated the political consciousness of the new era almost as much as his person and personality had dominated the turbulent politics of his own time. Maoist policies and precepts could be revised, or abandoned, only by demonstrating the fallibilities of their author.

To do so was a politically delicate and precarious enterprise, and not only because of the semi-magical aura that still surrounded the name of the departed Chairman. In comparable historical significance, Mao was the Lenin as well as the Stalin of the Chinese revolution. Like Lenin, Mao was the acknowledged leader of the revolution and the founder of the new society, and, like Stalin, he had been the supreme ruler of the postrevolutionary state for more than a quarter of a century. To simply denounce Mao as a tyrant and enumerate his tyrannies to explain the evils of the past, as Nikita Khrushchev had denounced Stalin at the Twentieth Soviet Party Congress in 1956, would have risked calling into question not only the political legitimacy of the Chinese Communist state but the moral validity of the revolution that produced it. In condemning Stalin in 1956, Khrushchev had invoked the authority of Lenin and traced a line of political continuity from the October Revolution to the present, however much that line was distorted during the Stalinist era. For Mao's successors, there was no Chinese Lenin to call upon other than Mao himself. It was thus for good reason that in the summer of 1980, shortly after Party theoreticians had begun to prepare the official assessment of Mao that would publicly appear a year later, Deng Xiaoping vowed that "we shall not do to Mao Zedong what Khrushchev did to Stalin at the 20th Soviet Communist Party Congress," observing that "it isn't only [Mao's] portrait which remains in Tiananmen Square; it is the memory of a man who guided us to victory and built a country."[8]

---

[8] Deng Xiaoping, interview with Oriana Fallaci, *The Washington Post*, August 31, 1980, p. D4.

As Deng's comment forcefully suggests, there were not only matters of political legitimacy at stake in the Party's treatment of Mao but also profound patriotic feelings—and, with them, the Chinese Communist Party's claim to the mantle of modern Chinese nationalism, a claim that was to assume ever-increasing importance in the post-Mao era as the Party's revolutionary claims receded. Mao Zedong, as Deng Xiaoping said, had "built a country" and enabled a long-humiliated China to "stand up in the world."

There were also the sentiments of the masses of the Chinese people to consider. The enormous popular prestige Mao had acquired during his lifetime, on both nationalist and revolutionary grounds, lingered on long after his death, especially among the peasants, many of whom continued to venerate their still-deified leader. Nor did the dead Mao lack worshippers among members of the Communist Party, many of whom had joined the Party during the Cultural Revolution decade. And to those must be added the millions of surviving veteran Party cadres who had fought with Mao during the revolutionary era, along with many of the officers of the PLA, among whom Maoist traditions remained deeply embedded.

Thus Mao's official assessors, whatever their personal feelings about their former leader (and feelings were deeply ambivalent even among the late Chairman's severest critics), had reason to tread warily in arriving at an evaluation of the place of Mao Zedong in the history of the People's Republic.

Well before the Party's official assessment of Mao Zedong was unveiled in June 1981, the myth of Mao was undermined by a long series of symbolic political and ideological acts. Rarely was Mao explicitly criticized in official pronouncements. Indeed, the tendency was to invoke the ideological authority of Mao in setting forth a critique of the Maoist past—or, more precisely, the final two decades of the Maoist past came under official attack by drawing on the late Chairman's own pre-1958 doctrines and writings. This was not merely clever politics (although it was certainly that too); it also reflected a genuinely held belief on the part of most of Mao's successors that there was a real distinction to be drawn between an early Mao, a great revolutionary leader who pursued a generally correct political line, and a late Mao (circa 1958–76), who lapsed into "leftist" deviations and utopian errors. It was on the basis of this distinction that Party theoreticians were soon to make the extraordinary claim that the aging Mao Zedong had violated the essential principles of his own thought!

Historians were also enlisted in the task. Encouraged to reinvestigate the history of the Chinese Communist Party, they gave new (and overdue) attention to Party leaders of the 1920s and 1930s who had been neglected in official Maoist historiography lest their appearance in history books serve to dim Mao's luster. The accomplishments of such early Party leaders (and revolutionary martyrs) as Li Dazhao, Cai Hesen, and Qu Qiubai were now lauded in articles and books, and their writings republished. Even Chen Duxiu, the scapegoat for the failures of 1927 and long portrayed as a renegade, was accorded sympathetic treatment. The purpose now was precisely to dim Mao's luster as well as to rectify the historical record.

Just as Party history was broadened and revised to make it more than the story of Mao Zedong, so Mao's Thought was now said to be the accumulated wisdom of the Party as a whole, not the creation of one man alone. Although Mao Zedong Thought was still officially celebrated as the Party's guiding ideology, the doctrine was increasingly shorn of its more radical elements in the post-Mao years. In the meantime, redefining the doctrine as a collective product of the Party, rather than as simply the writings of Mao, served the eminently practical political purpose of providing China's new leaders with considerable flexibility in ideology and policy. The meaning of Mao Zedong Thought was no longer necessarily what Mao had meant but rather now was left to the interpretation of those in power.

The closest China's new leaders came to a direct critique of Mao prior to the June 1981 "Resolution" was in denouncing his "personality cult," which they blamed on the machinations of Lin Biao and the Gang of Four and the persistence of China's feudal traditions. But Chinese Marxist theoreticians were hard pressed to provide a credible historical explanation for the Mao cult. In part this reflected a long-standing (and oft-noted) problem in Marxist theory, and especially in orthodox Marxist-Leninist doctrine. It was no easy task to reconcile the accepted Marxist thesis that the state is an agency of class rule with the phenomenon of personal dictatorships, where the supreme leader seems to stand above society, social classes, and their conflicts. Karl Marx had confronted the problem in his own lifetime, in the person of Louis Bonaparte, who, as Napoleon III, exercised dictatorial authority over France in the mid-nineteenth century. Under the rule of Bonaparte, Marx noted, the French state appeared "to have made itself completely independent" of French society. But Marx felt the need to find a social-class basis for the political phenomenon—and the class he discovered was the peasantry. The power of the French state under Napoleon III, Marx argued, was "not suspended in midair," as it appeared to be, for "Bonaparte represents a class, and the most numerous class of French society at that, the smallholding peasants." A combination of peasant superstitions and historical tradition had led gullible French peasants to believe "in the miracle that a man named Napoleon would bring all the glory back to them," and hence their support for Bonaparte and his cult. "The political influence of the smallholding peasants, therefore, finds its final expression in the executive power subordinating society to itself," Marx concluded.[9]

Marx's attribution of the Bonapartist cult to "the political influence of the smallholding peasants," whatever its utility for understanding mid-nineteenth-century French history, tended to become universalized by later Marxists as an explanation for all "personality cults" in all historical circumstances. Thus the leaders of the Chinese Communist Party, when confronted in 1956 with the problem of explaining Stalin's "cult of personality," after Khrushchev had denounced it, invoked Marx's analysis offered a century earlier. "The cult of the individual is rooted not only in the exploiting classes but also in the small producers," the Chinese commentary of April 1956 read. "As is well known, patriarchism is a product of a small-producer economy."[10]

While finding peasants and their traditions to be the social and ideological source of personality cults has been the politically favored Marxist explanation, the Marxist tradition offered alternative explanations that might have been drawn upon. One was to view person-

[9] Karl Marx, *The Eighteenth Brumaire of Louis Bonaparte*, in Marx and Engels, *Selected Works* (Moscow: Foreign Languages Publishing House, 1950), Vol. 1, pp. 302–3.
[10] "On the Historical Experience of the Dictatorship of the Proletariat," *People's Daily* editorial of April 5, 1956, translated in Robert R. Bowie and John K. Fairbank (eds.), *Communist China 1955–1959: Policy Documents* (Cambridge: Harvard University Press, 1962), p. 147.

ality cults in general, and the Mao cult in particular, as an extreme manifestation of alienated political power—in accordance with Marx's original proposition that all political power is a form of alienated social power. This possibility did not escape the attention of some of the more independent and original Chinese Marxist thinkers, who pursued the line of inquiry in the early 1980s in search of an explanation for the cult of Mao—until the inquiry was aborted by the Deng regime in its 1983–84 campaign against "spiritual pollution," which suppressed all serious discussion of the topic of alienation and especially the notion of "socialist alienation."

Another explanation of the leadership cult which could have been pursued was the potentially dictatorial implications of the Leninist scheme of party organization. Those implications had been set forth by Rosa Luxemburg, among others, in the early years of the century. "Ultra-centralism," the "blind subordination" to the party center, which "alone thinks, guides, and decides for all," a Jacobin-type dictatorship of "a handful of politicians," and the "brutalization of public life" that inevitably would follow—such were some of the consequences Luxemburg prophetically feared.[11]

From Luxemburg's critique, the conclusion that the Leninist form of party organization lent itself to personal dictatorships and leadership cults might well have been drawn. But Party theoreticians were reluctant to entertain so radical a conclusion, especially on the basis of the works of Rosa Luxemburg, a heretic in the world Communist movement since Lenin's time. Nonetheless, among several of the bolder advocates of democratization in the early post-Mao period, there was a new and sympathetic interest in Luxemburg, although the tendency was to attempt to reconcile the differences between Luxemburg and Lenin rather than to emphasize them.[12]

Yet on one notable occasion, Deng Xiaoping himself seemed prepared to embark on a critique of the Leninist heritage of the Chinese Communist Party. In a speech on political reform, delivered to a Politburo meeting in August 1980, Deng took up the problem of the

[11] Rosa Luxemburg, "Organizational Questions of Social Democracy" and "The Russian Revolution," *Rosa Luxemburg Speaks*, in Mary-Alice Waters (ed.), (New York: Pathfinder Press, 1970), pp. 114–30, 367–95.

[12] See, for example, Cheng Renqian, "Some Questions on the Reassessment of Rosa Luxemburg," in Su Shaozhi et al., *Marxism in China* (Nottingham: Spokesman, 1983), pp. 96–123.

concentration of power in the hands of individual leaders—and, obliquely, the question of the personal power and the cult of Mao Zedong. He attributed the problem mainly to China's "tradition of feudal autocracy" and the absence of a tradition of democracy and the rule of law. But he also mentioned, as a contributing factor, the "tradition of concentrating power to a high degree in the hands of individual leaders in the work of parties in various countries in the days of the Communist International."[13] It was the Stalinist-dominated Comintern, rather than Lenin, that Deng had in mind, but several influential Party theoreticians close to Deng at the time did set forth more explicit critiques of the Leninist conception of Party organization, of Lenin's excessive emphasis on centralism and his neglect of democracy.[14]

The critique of Leninism, however, did not proceed very far or for very long, at least not in official circles, as Deng and other high Party leaders soon came to recognize the dangerous implications of anti-Leninist arguments for their own power and positions. "Unity and stability," it was increasingly emphasized, could be guaranteed only under Party leadership, the first of the "four cardinal principles." Henceforth, the Mao cult (or what was sometimes euphemistically called "modern superstition"), insofar as it was not blamed on the machinations of Lin Biao and the Gang of Four, was attributed to China's pernicious feudal legacy. It was the persistence of "feudalistic" ideas and a "petty bourgeois ideology," the products of China's patriarchal "small producers' economy," that was ultimately responsible for the phenomenon of the leadership cult and other manifestations of "ultraleftism." The social carrier of such pernicious ideas and ideologies was, of course, the peasantry, mired in social and cultural backwardness. This was essentially the same argument that Chinese Communist leaders had advanced in 1956 to explain the "personality cult" of Stalin, an argument, in turn, derived from Marx's explanation of the dictatorship of Napoleon III in *The Eighteenth Brumaire of Louis Bonaparte*.

[13] Speech of August 18, 1980, *Selected Works of Deng Xiaoping*, pp. 302–25. Also in *Beijing Review*, October 3, 1983, pp. 14–22, and pp. 18–22.
[14] See, for example, Liao Gailong, "The Party's Historical Experience in the Socialist Stage," translated in *Issues and Studies*, October, November, and December 1981. These are texts of speeches delivered July 22 and October 25, 1980.

Having rediscovered the political convenience of attributing the problems of the Communist present to the lingering influence of dark forces inherited from the distant Chinese past, the Leninist scheme of party organization was not reexamined but reaffirmed. Indeed, it was said that the remedy for the phenomenon of the personality cult was strict adherence to Leninist norms of "inner-party democracy," "democratic centralism," and "collective leadership"—although the proclamation of these principles in no way impeded the increasing concentration of power in the hands of Deng Xiaoping. Presumably to cure the masses' addiction to the personality cult, portraits of Mao disappeared from the Great Hall of the People and elsewhere—and, for good measure, portraits of Marx, Engels, Lenin, and Stalin were removed from Tiananmen Square, henceforth to reappear only on celebratory political occasions.

The critique of the "personality cult," however inadequate in historical terms, was perhaps the most important of the preliminary steps taken in dismantling the Mao myth. But what the regime intended as the crucial act in undermining Mao's popular prestige was the trial of the Gang of Four, which finally opened on November 20, 1980, four years after their arrest.

THE TRIAL OF THE GANG

The trial of those already politically condemned as leaders of "the Lin Biao and Jiang Qing counterrevolutionary clique" was acted out over a period of two months during the winter of 1980–81 in the Ministry of Public Security building in Beijing. The ten defendants brought before the special tribunal of thirty-five judges included Chen Boda, the radical Maoist ideologist purged and imprisoned by Mao Zedong in 1970, who was lumped together with the Gang of Four. Posthumously tried along with Chen and the Gang were two former secret police chiefs, Kang Sheng and Xie Fuzhi. A separate panel simultaneously tried eight onetime PLA generals implicated in Lin Biao's alleged 1971 attempt to seize power. Four of the nine tried as members of the "Lin Biao clique" were dead, including, of course, Lin himself.

The lengthy indictment, which took two and a half hours for the chief prosecutor to read, charged the accused with forty-eight criminal offenses ranging from plots to overthrow the government and attempts to assassinate Mao Zedong to illegal arrests, torture, and the persecution of 700,000 people, resulting in 34,000 deaths.[15] As the *New York Times* correspondent in Beijing observed at the time, the indictment "reads more like a tale of feudal court intrigue than a modern legal document,"[16] even though it supposedly was drawn up in accordance with China's newly modernized criminal code. Although the court paid less attention to China's new legal codes than to the Party Politburo, which was in almost continuous session throughout the course of the trial, dictating the proceedings from the original indictment to the final verdict, the trial did set forth a powerful and bitter condemnation of political life in the People's Republic during the final decade of the Mao period. Nightly television broadcasts featured selected segments of the proceedings, showing the tortured faces of the accused and the angry faces of their accusers, who related, in often grisly detail, some of the more horrifying incidents of torture and death during the Cultural Revolution.

If the trial of the Gang was staged for foreign consumption, to demonstrate the post-Mao government's adherence to internationally accepted legal standards, as some observers suggested at the time, then the courtroom drama was something less than successful. To many Westerners, the proceedings in Beijing were uncomfortably reminiscent of Stalin's infamous Moscow Trials of the 1930s. An editorial in *The Washington Post*, typically, characterized it as "a show trial . . . congenial to totalitarians."[17] The inordinate emphasis that the state prosecutors put on the Gang's 1974–76 campaigns to politically discredit Deng Xiaoping, while perhaps satisfying to Deng, did little to bolster the government's claim that the defendants were being tried for criminal rather than political offenses.

The trial of the Gang was, of course, eminently political in nature and purpose, and served to accelerate the ongoing purge of leftists

---

[15] For the text of the official indictment, see *Beijing Review*, December 1, 1980, pp. 9–28.

[16] *The New York Times*, November 21, 1980, p. 12.

[17] "Show Trial in Peking," *The Washington Post*, December 7, 1980, p. D6.

in Party, state, and military bureaucracies and also served as the model for a long series of less publicized local trials of imprisoned "followers of the Gang of Four," which took place in virtually every province. For Hua Guofeng, indelibly stamped with a Cultural Revolution brand, the trial was the final political blow. He formally surrendered his title of Chairman of the Party at the next Central Committee meeting. For Deng Xiaoping and his associates, who carefully orchestrated the trial and its results, it was also clearly an act of political revenge against their onetime tormentors. The trial further served as an emotional catharsis—a satisfying "settling of accounts," as it was called—for millions of urban intellectuals and workers who had suffered during the Cultural Revolution and who now gathered in the evenings to eagerly watch television screens displaying a manacled Jiang Qing on exhibit in an iron cage. But the most important and sensitive political question raised by the ritualized spectacle was that of the role of Mao Zedong himself in the events for which his widow and his longtime associates stood condemned as criminals.

That Mao Zedong was the unnamed defendant in the trial of the Gang of Four few could doubt but none could publicly say. Yet those who staged the proceedings knew full well that the question of responsibility for the Cultural Revolution could not be openly discussed without implicating the man who had conceived the great upheaval and guided it along its tortuous and unanticipated course. Nor could the leaders of the Deng regime have failed to anticipate that an unrepentant Jiang Qing would certainly do so by invoking the authority of her late husband. Some of Jiang Qing's more inflammatory and embarrassing statements were deleted from the official record of the trial, such as her remark "I was Chairman Mao's dog; whomever he told me to bite, I bit." But other, less vivid assertions that her actions were in accord with Mao's instructions were duly reported in the official press. Nor was Mao's role in the events of the time dependent solely on the testimony of his widow. A front-page commentary in *People's Daily*, the official Party newspaper, on December 22, 1980, charged Mao with "mistakes" in launching the Cultural Revolution in 1966 and pursuing an erroneous political course over the following decade. A week later, the chief prosecutor, reading a statement undoubtedly drafted by the Party Politburo, observed that the Chinese people "are very clear that Chairman Mao was responsible . . . for their plight during the Cultural Revolution . . ."[18]

But the aim was not to consign Mao to the same dustbin of history into which the Gang of Four had been thrust. Rather it was to rescue Mao *for* history by separating him from the Gang of Four—a humanly fallible Mao much diminished in stature, to be sure, and occupying a place in a history written by his successors. This separation of Mao from his erstwhile disciples was accomplished through the device of distinguishing between "political errors" and "criminal offenses." The distinction had already been set forth by Deng Xiaoping in the summer of 1980. It was imperative, Deng then had stressed in an interview with a foreign journalist, to clearly distinguish between Mao's "mistakes" and the "crimes" committed by Lin Biao and the Gang of Four, adding, as if to justify the differentiation, that "I must remind you that Chairman Mao devoted most of his life to China and saved the party and the revolution in the most critical moments."[19]

The distinction was taken up by the official press during and after the trial of the Gang, when it was emphasized time and again that there was a "difference in principle between his [Mao's] mistakes and the crimes of Lin Biao, Jiang Qing, and their cohorts."[20] It was on the basis of this perhaps historically and morally dubious distinction that the Party was to issue its official historical verdict on Mao Zedong, five months after the Party, through the medium of an ostensibly criminal court, had rendered its verdict on the Gang of Four.

THE "RESOLUTION"

On the occasion of the sixtieth anniversary of the founding of the Chinese Communist Party, the post-Maoist leaders of the People's Republic announced their long-awaited assessment of the role of Mao

[18] For a succinct summary of the trial of the Gang of Four, see "Quarterly Chronicle and Documentation," *The China Quarterly*, No. 85 (March 1981), pp. 175–84. On the trial of Jiang Qing, see Ross Terrill, *The White-Boned Demon* (New York: Morrow, 1984), Chapters 1 and 8.

[19] Deng interview with Oriana Fallaci.

[20] For example, *Beijing Review*, January 5, 1981, p. 4.

Zedong in the history of the Chinese revolution. One day after formally accepting the resignation of Hua Guofeng as Party Chairman, the Sixth Plenum of the Eleventh Central Committee adopted on June 27, 1981, the "Resolution on Certain Questions in the History of Our Party Since the Founding of the People's Republic of China."[21] The document reviewed the Party's history in the revolutionary years prior to 1949 and evaluated in greater detail the successes and failures of the postrevolutionary history of the Party in power. However, the main purpose of the lengthy Resolution was not to clarify questions of Party history in general but rather to evaluate the historical role of Mao Zedong in particular, as Deng Xiaoping had made clear when the drafting of the document was undertaken in March 1980. Deng also had insisted from the outset that, whatever else might be said about Mao, it was above all essential to "affirm" the place the late Chairman occupied in the history of the Chinese Communist Party and the revolution.[22]

It was said that over four thousand Party leaders and theoreticians took part in the preparation of the Resolution, which was revised repeatedly over a period of fifteen months. Although the final product has often been described as a compromise between conflicting views on how Mao should be publicly portrayed, the Resolution eventually issued was perhaps less a consensus than a reflection of the personal views of Deng Xiaoping. Throughout the lengthy process of the drafting of the document, Deng made a long series of detailed "suggestions" to the drafters, and the final version closely followed the formulations, and even the wording, Deng had recommended. On one occasion, in June 1980, Deng said: "I have gone over the draft of

[21] The Sixth Plenum met in Beijing from June 27 to June 29, 1981. For the text of the Resolution it produced, see Beijing Review, July 6, 1981, pp. 10–39. Although July 1 is normally celebrated as the official Party birthday, the publication of the assessment of Mao was intended, in part, to commemorate the Party's sixtieth anniversary, albeit a few days early. As Deng Xiaoping said at a May 19, 1981, Politburo meeting: "We envisage releasing [the Resolution] on the occasion of the 60th anniversary of the founding of the Party. I see no need to write anything else to mark the 60th anniversary." Deng Xiaoping, "Suggestions on the Drafting of the 'Resolution on Certain Questions in the History of Our Party Since the Founding of the People's Republic of China' " (March 1980–June 1981), Beijing Review, August 1, 1983, p. 21. The text of Deng's "Suggestions" was published several years after they were written and appears in English translation in Beijing Review in two parts: July 25, 1983, pp. 14–24, and August 1, 1983, pp. 18–25.

[22] Deng Xiaoping, "Suggestions," Beijing Review, July 25, 1983, p. 14.

the resolution. It is no good and needs rewriting. We stressed at the very beginning that the historical role of Comrade Mao Zedong must be affirmed and Mao Zedong Thought adhered to and developed. The draft fails to reflect this idea adequately. . . . It is necessary to give a clear account of Comrade Mao Zedong's contributions to socialist revolution and socialist construction . . . We should restore, persist in and even further develop Mao Zedong Thought. Comrade Mao Zedong laid a foundation for us all in these respects, and the resolution should fully reflect these ideas of his."[23]

The final version of the Resolution did indeed "affirm" Mao's contributions to history, as Deng had insisted, copiously celebrating Mao's leadership in the long revolutionary struggle that gave birth to the People's Republic in 1949 and lauding the "brilliant successes" in economic development and "socialist transformation" achieved under Mao's rule during the first seven years of the Communist regime.[24] Yet while praising Mao as a great revolutionary and modernizer through the year 1957, the Resolution was harsh in criticizing the late Chairman's "mistakes" committed over the last two decades of his life. Although the antirightist campaign of 1957 was judged "necessary" and "correct" (Deng and other high Party leaders having played a prominent role in the witch-hunt), Mao was judged incorrect in later having broadened the scope of the campaign, resulting in the persecution of many innocent intellectuals and cadres. It was further charged that Mao's leftist errors were largely responsible for the economic disasters of the Great Leap, even though other Party leaders (including Liu Shaoqi and Deng Xiaoping himself) initially shared responsibility for the ill-fated venture. Indeed, Deng was refreshingly candid, at least at closed-door Party meetings, in acknowledging his own part in events which now had come under critical scrutiny. "I too made mistakes. We were among the activists in the antirightist struggle of 1957," Deng admitted in a 1980 speech, "and I share responsibility for broadening the scope of the struggle—wasn't I General Secretary of the Central Committee then?"[25] And on responsi-

[23] Deng, "Suggestions," *Beijing Review*, July 25, 1983, pp. 17–18.
[24] The discussion of the Resolution in this section is based on the official English-language text published in *Beijing Review*, July 6, 1981, pp. 10–39.
[25] "Adhere to the Party Line and Improve Work Methods" (February 29, 1980), *Selected Works of Deng Xiaoping*, pp. 262–63.

bility for the Great Leap, Deng commented: "Comrade Mao Zedong was overly enthusiastic at the time of the Great Leap Forward, but the rest of us were overly enthusiastic as well. Comrades Liu Shaoqi and Zhou Enlai and I, too, did not object to it, and Comrade Chen Yun kept silent on the matter. We must be fair on these questions and must not give the impression that only one person made mistakes while everybody else was correct, because such an appraisal does not tally with [the] facts."[26]

The Party's principal critique of Mao Zedong was, of course, reserved for the Cultural Revolution era, when the Party itself had been under attack. The Resolution charged that during his later years Mao ruled with ever-increasing "personal arbitrariness," which undermined "democratic centralism in party life," and that he further distorted the political life of the nation by fostering his "personality cult," which, as time went on, "grew graver and graver." Furthermore, and far more grave, Mao invented "erroneous left theses" which violated the principles of his own thought and culminated in the "catastrophe" of the Cultural Revolution. The latter, now officially dated as a decade-long period from May 1966 to the arrest of the Gang of Four in October 1976, was condemned as "responsible for the most severe setback and the heaviest losses suffered by the party, the state, and the people since the founding of the People's Republic." Although the worst horrors of the time were attributed to others—particularly Jiang Qing, Lin Biao, and Kang Sheng—the Resolution did not spare Mao the ultimate responsibility, bluntly stating at the outset that the Cultural Revolution "was initiated and led by Comrade Mao Zedong" and concluding that "chief responsibility for the grave left error of the Cultural Revolution, an error comprehensive in magnitude and protracted in duration, does indeed lie with Comrade Mao Zedong."

The aging Mao's errors prominently included political and ideological tendencies that Marxists traditionally have labeled "utopian" and therefore "unscientific"—at a time when Mao's political and ideological successors were placing an enormous emphasis on the "scientific" character of Marxist theory. Mao, according to his official assessors, "overestimated the role of man's subjective will and ef-

---

26 Deng, "Suggestions," *Beijing Review*, July 25, 1983, p. 17.

forts," invented theories and pursued political practices "divorced from reality," and raised entirely unrealistic expectations of the imminent advent of a communist utopia. In short, he violated what his more orthodox Marxist successors took to be the "objective laws" of historical and economic development. Yet, however harsh the critique of Mao was in many respects, the Party Resolution concluded that Mao's "contributions to the Chinese revolution far outweigh his mistakes." Because of those contributions over the decades, "the Chinese people have always regarded Comrade Mao Zedong as their respected and beloved great leader and teacher."

Many post-Mao Party leaders privately assessed the departed Chairman in a somewhat different fashion, perhaps best reflected in a statement attributed to the veteran economic planner Chen Yun:

> Had Chairman Mao died in 1956, there would have been no doubt that he was a great leader of the Chinese people. . . . Had he died in 1966, his meritorious achievements would have been somewhat tarnished, but his overall record still very good. Since he actually died in 1976, there is nothing we can do about it.[27]

Of the three periods into which Chen divided the Maoist era, the first, 1949 to the mid-1950s, was seen as something of a golden age in the history of the People's Republic, a time when Mao and his colleagues harmoniously followed the Soviet model of political and economic development. Although that model was now widely viewed as flawed and, in any event, no longer relevant for the present, it nonetheless was regarded as appropriate for its time, or at least the best that could have been reasonably devised at the time. The second period, 1957–65, was blemished by the misadventure of the Great Leap, but still historically salvageable by virtue of Liu Shaoqi's restoration of Leninist Party discipline and economic rationality in the early 1960s. The final period of the Mao era, 1966–76, now called "the Cultural Revolution decade," was viewed as an unmitigated catastrophe by those who had been among the principal political vic-

---

[27] *Ming Bao* (Hong Kong), January 15, 1979, p. 1. Cited in Roger Garside, *Coming Alive*, p. 190.

tims of the time. Now restored to power and honor, after years of humiliation and persecution, veteran Party officials nostalgically longed for an earlier Maoism uncorrupted by the radical utopianism that marked and marred the last two decades of the late Chairman's thought and actions.

Thus the praise for Mao that the Party Resolution intermingled with its indictment of his late years reflected more than a search for a much-needed political legitimacy—although it was certainly intended, in part, as a reaffirmation of the moral validity of the revolution of 1949 and of the rule of the Communist Party which resulted from that victory. The praise also reflected the genuine respect and admiration, if not necessarily affection, surviving Party leaders felt for the earlier Mao—for a Mao who was for so long the acknowledged revolutionary leader, the Mao who was China's national liberator, and the Mao who was primarily an economic modernizer, before he became infected with "erroneous leftist" ideas and theories.

While the Western press generally praised the Sixth Plenum's Resolution, hailing it as a major step in "de-Maoification" (not a term used in China, at least not officially), Soviet commentators were critical of the Chinese Communist Party for having failed to abandon "Mao Zedong Thought" as its guiding ideology. But *Pravda* nonetheless expressed the hope that the new Chinese leaders would eventually renounce Maoism entirely and "rejoin the closely knit ranks of the fighters for communism."[28] Earlier, especially after the Third Plenum, there had been a marked abatement in Sino-Soviet ideological warfare. The new leaders in Beijing no longer called the Soviet Union "capitalist" or even "revisionist," as had been customary over the final fifteen years of the Maoist regime. Indeed, early in 1980, Deng Xiaoping referred to the Soviet Union as a country that had practiced socialism for sixty-three years.[29] The Russians reciprocated by praising Deng Xiaoping's "pragmatism" and his "economic common sense," as well as the Chinese party's restoration of Leninist organizational principles.[30] It marked the beginning of a gradual rap-

[28] Alexsandrov article in *Pravda*, July 1, 1981. Cited in "Chronicle and Documentation," *The China Quarterly*, No. 88 (December 1981), p. 735.

[29] Deng Xiaoping, "The Present Situation and the Tasks Before Us" (Speech of January 16, 1980), *Selected Works of Deng Xiaoping*, p. 235.

[30] Alexsandrov article in *Pravda*, April 7, 1980. *International Herald Tribune*, April 8, 1980. Cited in "Chronicle and Documentation," *The China Quarterly*, No. 83 (September 1980), p. 625.

prochement between the People's Republic and the Soviet Union, ending the bitter ideological quarrels of the Maoist era and reducing the differences between the two countries purely to ordinary matters of conflicting national interest.[31]

During the time that the Chinese Communist Party's appraisal of Mao was being drafted, Deng Xiaoping had promised that the Party would deal with the question of Mao far differently than the way Khrushchev had dealt with Stalin in 1956. It was a promise that was honored, or at least obeyed.

Khrushchev's 1956 speech denouncing Stalin and his "cult of personality" was hastily composed and delivered in an impromptu and highly emotional manner at the closing session of the Twentieth Congress. Warning that "we should not wash our dirty linen" in public, Khrushchev kept his "secret" speech secret, at least from the Soviet people, permitting the U.S. State Department to take credit for its initial publication. In the years that followed, the whole issue of Stalin and the evils of the Stalinist era were officially buried and remained beyond the pale of permissible public discussion or serious historical inquiry for three decades, until the Gorbachev era. By contrast, the Chinese Resolution on Mao's role in Party history, whatever its historical deficiencies, was carefully drafted, discussed, and repeatedly revised over a period of fifteen months. It was then not only made public but highly publicized and widely discussed in Chinese society.

Moreover, Mao's successors, unlike Stalin's, were unwilling to deny their former leader credit for the achievements of his time while blaming him for many of the failures. In Khrushchev's speech, by contrast, all the evils of the Stalinist era were attributed to Stalin alone, whereas all economic, social, and military successes were credited to the Party, to Leninism, and the people. It was an unconvincing apportioning of praise and blame that had drawn critical commentary from Chinese leaders in 1956. The Chinese Communists were then critical of Khrushchev for failing to explain how Stalin's "serious mistakes" could have come about, insisting that it was nec-

---

[31] Principally, at the time, old Sino-Soviet border disputes, the Soviet invasion of Afghanistan, and the Vietnamese occupation of Cambodia.

essary to view Stalin from a proper "historical standpoint" and emphasizing that Stalin's acts, both right and wrong, "bore the imprint of the times."[32]

Twenty-five years later, Deng Xiaoping, echoing many of the themes in the 1956 Chinese commentary on Stalin, cautioned that "[we] must not attribute all our problems to the personal qualities of some individuals." "We owe what we have achieved, [both] to the leadership of the Chinese Communist Party *and* Comrade Mao Zedong."[33] Those admonitions, duly taken into account by the drafters of the Resolution, perhaps simply demonstrate that Deng possessed a better sense of history than did Khrushchev. They also reflect a greater sensitivity to popular feelings and their political implications. As Deng observed in making "suggestions" on the draft Resolution in 1980: "If we do not mention Mao Zedong Thought and make an appropriate evaluation of Comrade Mao Zedong's merits and demerits, the old workers will not feel satisfied, nor will the poor and lower-middle peasants of the period of land reform, nor will a good number of cadres who have close ties with them."[34]

Deng's seemingly balanced sense of historical judgment can be partly attributed to the fact that he lacked the personal hatred of Mao that so animated Khrushchev's attack on Stalin. Deng's personal animosities were largely reserved for the Gang of Four and particularly Jiang Qing. To Mao he attributed his political and physical survival over the years as much as he did his political difficulties, claiming that Mao rescued him from the attacks of the pro-Soviet Wang Ming in the mid-1930s; that Mao attempted to protect him politically during the Cultural Revolution, but when that proved unsuccessful made provisions for his physical security when he was dispatched to do manual labor in Jiangxi province; and that it was Mao, not Zhou Enlai, who was instrumental in his restoration to governmental office in 1973.[35]

The differences between the Soviet handling of the Stalin ques-

[32] *On the Historical Experience of the Dictatorship of the Proletariat* (Peking: Foreign Languages Press, 1961), esp. pp. 14–18. Originally published as a lengthy editorial in *People's Daily* on April 5, 1956.

[33] Deng Xiaoping, "Suggestions," *Beijing Review*, July 25, 1983, pp. 19–20.

[34] Deng, "Suggestions," *Beijing Review*, July 25, 1983, p. 18.

[35] Deng interview with Oriana Fallaci.

tion and the Chinese assessment of Mao are also striking in Marxian theoretical and historical terms. In his 1956 speech Khrushchev made no attempt to explain historically either the tyrannies of Stalin that he detailed or the "cult of personality." He presented Stalin as a *diabolus ex machina* and blamed all the evils of the Stalinist era on what he repeatedly called "the willfulness of one man." Subsequent official Soviet commentaries contributed little more to historical understanding, at least not before the Gorbachev era. The Chinese, on the other hand, felt the need to provide a plausible historical explanation for such phenomena as ultraleftism, the Cultural Revolution, and the Mao cult. The official explanation arrived at, although deliberately omitted from the formal Party Resolution (again at Deng Xiaoping's "suggestion"[36]), was pursued in a voluminous body of historical and theoretical literature that preceded and followed the June 1981 Central Committee meeting. It was argued, to relate the argument in its barest summary form, that the abortiveness of capitalism in modern Chinese history and the incompleteness of the Communist Party's "bourgeois-democratic revolution" permitted the persistence of a "feudal consciousness" and "petty bourgeois ideology," the social carrier of which was a peasantry still ideologically rooted in ancient modes of small-scale production. This persisting feudal ideology was the basis for the pernicious "ultraleftist" current which first manifested itself in the utopianism of the Great Leap, then in the personality cult of Mao and the Cultural Revolution, eventually finding its ultimate political expression in the "feudal-fascist" rule of Lin Biao and the Gang of Four. Implicit in this analysis, and reflective of the long-standing contradiction between the bourgeois and socialist features of the Chinese revolution, was criticism of Mao for failing to complete the "bourgeois" tasks of the revolutionary process in his haste to proceed to a socialist reorganization of society.

---

[36] In a talk to the Party Central Committee on June 22, 1981, just a few days before the final version of the Resolution was formally adopted, Deng remarked: "With regard to such other questions as whether to list the influence of petty bourgeois ideology as one of the causes of the 'cultural revolution,' I think it does no harm to omit any reference to it. If it becomes necessary to oppose petty bourgeois ideology, we can deal with it in some other documents in the future. There is no hurry. We don't have to mention it here." Deng Xiaoping, "Suggestions," *Beijing Review*, August 1, 1983, p. 24.

However unsatisfactory the argument may appear as a historical explanation, the Chinese assessment of Mao was, on the whole, far more serious and forthright than the pre-Gorbachev Soviet treatment of Stalin. There was good reason for Deng Xiaoping to claim at the time that the Chinese Communist Party was "bold enough to face up to, and correct, its mistakes."[37] Yet Mao's immediate successors were no more willing than Khrushchev had been to examine the nature of postrevolutionary society and the authoritarian Leninist party system to understand the sources of the evils they recounted. Instead, Chinese Communist leaders and ideologists invoked the dark forces of China's feudal past to explain the negative features of the Communist present and thereby preserve the legitimacy of the political system over which they presided.

In dealing with the problem of the "personality cult," and the evils of the times associated with the phenomenon, both Nikita Khrushchev and Deng Xiaoping were searching for what they viewed as the golden age of their respective Communist pasts. Just as Khrushchev, in addition to invoking Lenin, sought to revive the "innocent" and "sane" Stalinism of the late 1920s, before Stalin began to murder the members of the Stalinist faction, so Deng sought to recapture the "uncorrupted" Maoism of the years prior to 1958, before Mao had succumbed to pernicious radical and utopian ideas. Deng could undertake the quest with a clearer conscience. Khrushchev had stood near the top of the Stalinist hierarchy for many years, including the years when Stalin was murdering virtually all of the Old Bolsheviks, wiping out an entire generation of revolutionary leaders. By virtue of his very survival, Khrushchev was implicated in Stalin's crimes. Unlike those in Stalinist Russia, most of Mao's political foes among the Communist elite physically survived the Mao era—and a good many prospered politically as well. Deng Xiaoping, an eminent survivor, could fairly present himself more as a victim than a participant in the events of the late Mao era that now had come under criticism.

For almost thirty years following Khrushchev's celebrated 1956 speech, Stalin virtually vanished from the official Soviet historical record. The Chinese Communists, by contrast, prominently retained Mao Zedong as a symbol of revolution, nationalism, and moderniza-

---

[37] Deng Xiaoping, "Suggestions," *Beijing Review*, July 25, 1983, p. 17.

tion. It was, of course, a Mao purged of his more radical and utopian ideas who was preserved for history. In official post-Mao writings, Mao appears as a prudent and realistic revolutionary leader, and as the patriotic and modernizing founder of the new state, not the post-revolutionary advocate of permanent revolution.

Not only was a deradicalized Mao appropriated by the Deng regime, but Mao Zedong Thought remained the official ideology of the Chinese Communist Party. That ideology was redefined as the "collective wisdom" of the Party, the product of the thoughts and actions of many Communists who had participated in the revolutionary struggles, not the creation of one man alone. When Mao lived, Mao Zedong Thought was what Mao said it was. In post-Mao China, akin to the accumulated wisdom of a church, the leaders of the Communist Party became the guardians and interpreters of the doctrine. The Thought of Mao could now be selectively and conservatively utilized, emphasizing, for example, the theory of New Democracy, which stressed the bourgeois character of the Chinese revolution and thus promoted national unity, fostered social harmony, and championed the historical progressiveness of capitalism.

Such was the rather ambivalent way the Deng regime broke with the social radicalism of Maoism while retaining a degree of political and ideological continuity with the leader of the revolution.

7

LENINISM, BUREAUCRACY, AND POLITICAL REFORM

IN 1980, while Deng Xiaoping was instructing Party theoreticians on the appropriate historical resting place for Mao Zedong, he also was turning renewed attention to the economic and political reforms he had proposed in 1979. At the outset Deng made it quite clear that all other concerns and goals were to be subordinated to the needs of rapid economic growth. But "democratization" also occupied a prominent place in Deng's program, and it was repeatedly stressed that political reform was an essential prerequisite for success in economic development and an important goal in its own right. The communiqué of the Third Plenum of December 1978, after all, had promised not only to lead China on the proper road to the Four Modernizations but also to "socialist democracy" and "socialist legality."

Yet "socialist democratization," which had aroused such high hopes during the latter months of 1978, proved abortive. Except for the Democracy Movement of 1979–80, which the regime suppressed with little public protest, no popular movements arose or were permitted to arise during the Deng era—until the student protests of the winter of 1986–87 and the spring of 1989 shattered the political calm. It is ironic and revealing that Deng Xiaoping's major and most far-reaching statement on political reform—a speech delivered to an enlarged session of the Party Politburo on August 18, 1980, in which he called for "the democratization of the life of society as a whole"—

came at a time when Deng was preparing the final act in the suppression of the first Democracy Movement. A month after Deng delivered his speech, which was to remain the boldest official pronouncement on political reform, the "four great freedoms" were formally abolished. Over the following six months, the security police were busily engaged in arresting and shipping off to labor camps the last of the young democracy activists. The actions of the regime, if not always necessarily the words of its leader, revealed that democratization was not to extend to activities not sanctioned by the Communist Party.

Nonetheless, the political changes that followed from the Third Plenum were by no means insignificant, and they resulted in a general relaxation of state control over society and the lives of individuals. In addition to the release of many thousands of political prisoners, new legal codes were promulgated in 1979, promising protection of citizens from arbitrary police and administrative practices. Deng Xiaoping's oft-cited speech of August 1980, and various speeches and reports of other Party leaders that year, which came to be known as the Gengshen Reforms,[1] aimed to rectify what Deng called the evils of "bureaucratism, overcentralization of power, the patriarchal way of doing things, lifelong tenure of leading posts, and various kinds of privileges." To combat these chronic political problems, Deng called for the reinvigoration of the Chinese Communist Party in accordance with its proclaimed Leninist principles of "democratic centralism" and "inner-Party democracy." Moreover, just as democratic methods were to be revived within the Party, democracy was to be fostered in society at large through "a system of mass supervision" over cadres, who were to be subject to popular criticism, impeachment, and recall. At local and provincial administrative levels, people's congresses were to be re-created along with workers' congresses in factories, with delegates selected by free elections. Further, the official press was to be reformed so that newspapers and periodicals could better inform citizens of government policies and actions, and also serve as forums for popular criticism of the government. To prevent the overconcentration of power, the distinction be-

---

[1] According to a traditional Chinese chronological scheme of a sixty-year cycle of year names, 1980 was the Gengshen year.

tween Party and state, which virtually had vanished during the Cultural Revolution (and had been difficult to divine before), was now to be firmly established. Finally, and not least important to Deng and other reform leaders, both the Party and state bureaucracies were to undergo a wholesale revamping, with a smaller number of bureaucrats carrying out their functions more efficiently, more professionally, more honestly, and less oppressively.[2]

These were relatively modest aims, none of which posed any serious threat to the political primacy of the Chinese Communist Party. However, such democratic potential as the proposed reforms may have held were largely vitiated by the regime's principal political goals: first, the enormous emphasis on Leninist organizational principles and methods of discipline in the refashioning of the Communist Party and in defining the Party's relationship to society; and, second, the general rationalization and institutionalization of bureaucratic rule. Bureaucratic rationalization was the essence of what most higher Party leaders meant by political reform, and it was conceived, as was almost everything else in post-Mao China, in the service of China's economic modernization.

LENINISM AND THE PARTY

At no time in the history of the People's Republic was there so great an emphasis on the Leninist character and leadership role of the Chinese Communist Party as during the reign of Deng Xiaoping. At no time was there so rigorous an insistence on the Leninist virtues of a centralized organizational structure and the organizational discipline of its members, the only guarantees of social order in the eyes

---

[2] Deng's speech of August 18, 1980, regarded as the charter of the political reform program, was not publicly published in China until the summer of 1983, in Deng's *Selected Works*, a rather odd hiatus for a document that was presumably intended to foster greater public participation in a more democratic political life. For the official English translation of the speech, see *Beijing Review*, October 3, 1983, pp. 14–22, and October 10, 1983, pp. 18–22. Another key document in the Gengshen Reforms was Liao Gailong's report of October 25, 1980, entitled "Historical Experience and Our Road of Development" and delivered to the central Party school. For an analysis of Liao's report, see Stuart R. Schram, *Ideology and Policy in China Since the Third Plenum, 1978–1984* (London: Contemporary China Institute, 1984), pp. 20–24.

of most post-Mao leaders. These beliefs have been accompanied by a typically Leninist distrust of mass political "spontaneity"—and, no doubt with memories of the Cultural Revolution era still fresh, an almost paranoiac fear of "chaos." The restoration of the Party in its more pristine Leninist form was perhaps the inevitable response to the attack on the Party during the Cultural Revolution, many of whose political victims, now back in power, attributed their plight during that time to Mao's violations of accepted Leninist norms of political conduct.

That Deng Xiaoping, once having gained power, proved an ardent Leninist should have surprised no one except those who mistook him for a "socialist democrat" in 1978.[3] Most of his long political career had been devoted to managing the Party's organizational apparatus. Both his revolutionary and postrevolutionary political experiences had schooled him in Leninist organizational techniques and taught him that political stability and economic progress were dependent on a Party that functioned according to strict Leninist principles. He looked with nostalgia to the "golden age" of the People's Republic —the orderly era of the First Five Year Plan, prior to the time Mao began to violate Leninist Party norms. He also looked back fondly to the early 1960s, the years before the Cultural Revolution, when he collaborated closely with Liu Shaoqi, the Leninist par excellence in the history of the Chinese Communist Party.[4] It was only natural that he now wished to restore the Party to what it had been in those times, especially the triumphant time of the Eighth Party Congress of 1956, when he and Liu administered a Party whose leaders ruled in relatively harmonious fashion over a stable and orderly society. Deng did not require old-line conservative Party bureaucrats to convince him of the virtues of a Leninist party organization. Such virtues he had learned on his own long before.

That the post-Mao Chinese political order would be a Leninist

---

[3] The mistake, fostered by Deng for his own immediate political ends, was made both inside China (by many Democracy Movement activists and some intellectuals in the latter months of 1978) and by a good many foreign observers who hastened to celebrate Deng's democratic proclivities. For examples of the latter, see Garside, *Coming Alive*, pp. 182–312.

[4] On Liu Shaoqi's political methods and ideology, and his differences with Mao, see Lowell Dittmer, *Liu Shao-chi'i and the Chinese Cultural Revolution* (Berkeley: University of California Press, 1974).

order was made clear from the beginning. No sooner had Deng established himself as the country's "paramount leader" than he laid down, in a ringing declaration in March 1979, the "four fundamental principles" to guide Chinese political life: the "upholding" of socialism, the dictatorship of the proletariat, the leadership of the Party, and Marxism-Leninism-Mao Zedong Thought.[5] Of the four, as Deng repeatedly emphasized, the leadership of the Party was the most important. Indeed, it was the only one of the four that conveyed a clear political meaning, the other three principles being hoary ideological orthodoxies that bore only the most tenuous relationship to the social and political realities of postrevolutionary China and whose meaning became increasingly ambiguous as the Deng era proceeded. But there was nothing ambiguous about "the leadership of the Party," which defined the limits of change and which dictated that such political reforms as were undertaken were confined to what could be accommodated within the existing Leninist political system.

The effort to reestablish the Party on firm Leninist foundations demanded more than symbolic political acts and official ideological pronouncements. It also required the reintroduction of conventional Leninist organizational devices, such as the Central Disciplinary Commission, headed by Chen Yun, and the Secretariat, initially presided over by Hu Yaobang. Both of these bodies exercised substantial power over the organizational and ideological life of the Party during the Deng era, and both played major roles in a continuing series of "rectification," "purification," and "consolidation" movements which resulted in the purge of millions of Party members, mostly those of suspected leftist inclinations.

"Socialist democracy" and "socialist legality," the slogans Deng Xiaoping had championed during his rise to power, could not long survive Deng's Leninist refashioning of the Party. The crushing of the Democracy Movement, the abolition of the four great freedoms, and the reaffirmation of the four fundamental principles made clear to all that the Party under Deng would not tolerate independent political activities. Socialist democracy, it was increasingly emphasized in the 1980s, could be realized only "under the leadership of the Party," thus rendering the term meaningless. Socialist legality fared

---

[5] "Uphold the Four Basic Principles" (Speech of March 30, 1979), *Selected Works of Deng Xiaoping*, pp. 166–91.

little better in a Leninist political environment. Although the new legal codes provided a greater degree of predictability and regularity in formal police and judicial procedures, they did not significantly reduce the political dominance of the Party-state bureaucracy over society. As official pronouncements typically put the matter: "To obey socialist law is to obey the leadership of the Party."

Other measures officially hailed as progress toward socialist democracy failed to yield their promised results. The effort to differentiate the state administration from the Party did not meaningfully alter the relationship between the two overlapping bureaucracies. In Deng's China, the formal state bureaucracy remained the obedient servant of the Party, as traditionally had been the case, symbolized by meetings of the National People's Congress, which faithfully ratified policies decided upon beforehand within the inner councils of the Communist Party. A notable but minor exception to this tradition was the September 1980 annual meeting of the National People's Congress, which, coming directly after Deng Xiaoping's Gengshen Reform proposals, was distinguished by a degree of lively discussion and disagreement among the assembled delegates, even if they did not venture into anything resembling independent decision making. But by 1981 the Congress had reverted to its customary passivity.[6] Such new or newly named institutions as people's congresses and workers' congresses have not been any more independent of Party control than the Maoist revolutionary committees they replaced.

To his Leninist refashioning of the Chinese Communist Party, Deng Xiaoping added a Stalinist tinge. In a speech delivered in January 1980, Deng complained that Party members lacked specialized knowledge and modern technical skills.[7] His solution to this old "Red/expert" dilemma was not to bring expertise to current Party cadres, as Mao had attempted to do, but rather to bring experts into the Party. It was the same solution Stalin had devised fifty years before. In the 1920s, the Soviet Communist Party, still animated by revolutionary impulses and values, had recruited its membership primarily among industrial workers and to a lesser degree among people from peasant social backgrounds. In the 1930s, under Stalin's bu-

[6] For a journalistic account of the 1981 session, see Christopher Wren, "For China's Legislature, Back to the Rubber Stamp," *The New York Times*, December 14, 1981, p. 6.
[7] Deng Xiaoping, "The Present Situation and the Tasks Before Us," *Selected Works of Deng Xiaoping*, pp. 224–58.

reaucratic institutionalization of the postrevolutionary order, the new recruits were mostly professionals, technicians, and intellectuals. Stalin, as Benjamin Schwartz once observed in comparing the Soviet dictator with Mao Zedong, emphasized the "social engineering" function of the Party rather than its moral virtues. "If Mao was to find the Party insufficiently Red, Stalin found it insufficiently expert," Schwartz wrote.[8]

Deng, far more like Stalin than Mao, stressed the "social engineering" role of the Party in his pursuit of the Four Modernizations, and also found the Party insufficiently expert. He thus instructed the Party to recruit technically skilled people and to give priority for promotion to members who had graduated from universities and senior middle schools prior to the Cultural Revolution. Indeed, Deng favored not only social engineering but also, quite literally, engineers. By the mid-1980s, some 45 percent of the ministers of the central government held college degrees in engineering, as did 25 percent of provincial Party secretaries and 33 percent of provincial governors.[9] The policy of favoring scientists, technicians, and others with professional skills in Party recruitment and promotion became de facto practice in 1980, following speeches made by Deng Xiaoping and Hu Yaobang on cadre policy.

While Deng Xiaoping found the Party insufficiently expert, he also found it far too Red. In 1979 it was revealed that more than one-third of the then 35 million Party members had been recruited during the Cultural Revolution decade (1966–76), and these cadres (along with a good many older ones) were seen as obstacles to Deng's political and economic goals. Thus the Party's emphasis on the recruitment of experts was accompanied by a massive purge of leftists, mostly relatively recent recruits from worker and peasant families who lacked formal higher education and who were suspected of harboring Maoist sympathies.

Although a purge of alleged leftists had been underway since the

---

[8] Benjamin I. Schwartz, "The Reign of Virtue: Some Broad Perspectives on Leader and Party in the Cultural Revolution," in John W. Lewis (ed.), *Party Leadership and Revolutionary Power in China* (London: Cambridge University Press, 1970), p. 164.

[9] Hong Yung Lee, "Political and Administrative Reforms of 1982–86: The Changing Party Leadership and State Bureaucracy," in Michael Ying-Mao Kau and Susan H. Marsh (eds.), *China in the Era of Deng Xiaoping: A Decade of Reform* (Armonk, N.Y.: M. E. Sharpe, 1993), p. 47.

demise of the Gang of Four in the autumn of 1976, it was greatly accelerated after the Party set forth its official assessment of Mao Zedong in June 1981 and new Party leader Hu Yaobang followed with a speech on "Party building," emphasizing the need to achieve political and ideological purity.[10] Political purity was now to be measured by zeal in supporting the line of the Third Plenum and carrying out the economic tasks this entailed. The purge of leftists gained further momentum with the Twelfth Party Congress in September 1982, where the Deng faction consolidated its power and celebrated its triumph, bringing about wholesale personnel changes in the Party Central Committee and the upper echelons of the state bureaucracy. Of the 348 members and alternates on the new Central Committee, 211 were newly elected; 75 percent of the incumbent provincial Party secretaries were sacked in favor of Deng's followers, as were 90 percent of the ministers and vice-ministers in the central government.[11] The Twelfth Congress established stricter requirements for Party membership, which, it was made clear, were aimed at eradicating the lingering political and ideological influences of the Cultural Revolution. Party leaders also announced plans for a massive three-year "consolidation" movement, to be launched in 1983, to "purify" the Party organization, which now numbered some 40 million members. Although what was called "the corrosion of capitalist ideas" was to be combated—and various repressive campaigns against "spiritual pollution" and "bourgeois liberalization" followed—there was little doubt that "leftists" would bear the brunt of the purge. As Chen Yun, in his capacity as head of the Central Disciplinary Commission, announced in September 1982, those to be "rectified" were mainly "people who rose to prominence during the 'Cultural Revolution' by following Lin Biao, Jiang Qing, and their like in 'rebellion' . . ."[12]

[10] For a summary of Hu's August 1981 speech (which followed Deng Xiaoping's July 17 talk emphasizing Party leadership), see Tang Tsou, *The Cultural Revolution and Post-Mao Reforms* (Chicago: University of Chicago Press, 1986), p. 230.

[11] For a summary and analysis of the proceedings of the Congress, see Lowell Dittmer, "The 12th Congress of the Communist Party of China," *The China Quarterly*, No. 93 (March 1983), pp. 108–24. The Standing Committee of the Politburo that emerged from the Congress was formally ranked as follows: Hu Yaobang, Deng Xiaoping, Li Xiannian, Ye Jianying, Zhao Ziyang, and Chen Yun.

[12] Chen Yun, "Discipline Inspection Commission's Report" (September 11, 1982), FBIS, September 13, 1982, pp. K9–K12. The purge of the Party, although an ongoing process, was not officially launched until October 1983, with the meeting of the second plenary session of the Twelfth Central Committee.

Although Party leaders vowed to prohibit "factionalism," events soon revealed that a good many veteran cadres still yearned to "settle scores" left over from the battles of the Cultural Revolution.

Deng Xiaoping's Leninist refashioning of the Communist Party apparatus, beyond establishing his own followers in key positions of power, marked a major departure from the practices of the Maoist era and a momentous step in the deradicalization of the Chinese revolution. Political criteria, as measured by commitment to socialist values, became less and less important in the selection and promotion of Party members, replaced by a greater emphasis on professional expertise.

THE PARTY AND ITS "PARAMOUNT LEADER"

Of all the political evils of the Mao period, few were denounced more frequently in the Deng era than Mao Zedong's personality cult and his practice of one-man rule, officially attributed to the pernicious influence of China's feudal traditions. The official remedy was collective leadership and the restoration of Leninist norms of inner-Party democracy. The remedy was written into the new Party constitution adopted by the Twelfth Congress in 1982, which prohibited "all forms of personality cult." "No leaders are allowed to practice arbitrary individual rule or place themselves above the Party organization," it was decreed. It was obviously Mao Zedong whom the delegates had in mind, for Mao's gravest sin in the eyes of his more orthodox Leninist successors was not so much the personality cult as such, a phenomenon to which other Party leaders had generously contributed,[13] but rather the fact that he had indeed placed himself above the Party from the time of the collectivization campaign in the mid-1950s to the Cultural Revolution. To reinforce the point, the new constitution abolished the post of Party Chairman, the office that Mao

---

[13] The origin of the official cult is usually traced to the Seventh CCP Congress of 1945, when virtually all Party leaders lavished praise on Mao's leadership and canonized "the Thought of Mao Zedong" as the sole guide for the Party. The most ardent celebrant and cult builder, ironically, was Liu Shaoqi, who proclaimed Mao to be "the greatest revolutionary and statesman in Chinese history" and "China's greatest theoretician and scientist." *Collected Works of Liu Shao-chi'i* (Hong Kong: Union Research Institute, 1968), pp. 30–31.

so long had occupied, in favor of a Secretary-General to head the Party, thus making the formal organizational structure of the Chinese Party more like its Soviet counterpart.

Yet even as the principle of collective leadership was ever more loudly proclaimed, the personal power and prestige of Deng Xiaoping grew apace. From the outset of his reign, Deng eschewed the highest titles of formal power, preferring instead to place his two favored disciples, Hu Yaobang and Zhao Ziyang, as the official heads of Party and government—although neither was to remain in Deng's favor for long. Nevertheless, at the Twelfth Congress in 1982, Deng did retain the chairmanship of the Party's Central Military Commission, which provided de facto control of the Army, along with his seat on the six-member Standing Committee of the Politburo. He also assumed the chairmanship of a newly created 158-member Central Advisory Commission, a prestigious and lucrative retirement haven for elderly Party luminaries. But if Deng posed as a sagely advisor rather than supreme leader, the posture in no way diminished the reality of his personal power. No one doubted, and none questioned, at least not publicly, that Deng was China's "paramount leader." Indeed, by 1983 his more zealous followers had begun to mimic aspects of Mao's personality cult that they had only so recently and so vociferously denounced. Newspapers featured photographs of the seventy-nine-year-old Deng swimming at his vacation resort, images eerily reminiscent of Mao Zedong's celebrated swim in the Yangtze on the eve of the Cultural Revolution. In the summer of 1983 the *Selected Works of Deng Xiaoping*, consisting of forty-seven speeches and letters composed over the years 1975–82, was published with great fanfare. The volume was hailed in the official press for its "revolutionary boldness" and the "brilliance" of its theoretical contributions. Additional collections of Deng's speeches, writings, and comments were accompanied by ever-louder official panegyrics. And Deng's "thoughts" in general were praised over the years in a manner that hitherto had been reserved only for the Thought of Mao Zedong. Deng's ideas were lauded as "a great development of Marxism in China" by his erstwhile disciple Zhao Ziyang in 1987,[14] while other Party leaders

---

[14] Zhao Ziyang, Speech of May 13, 1987, published in *People's Daily*, July 10, 1987, and translated in *Beijing Review*, July 20, 1987, pp. 34–35.

hailed "Deng Xiaoping Thought" as a doctrine that would guide Chinese life for at least a century. Just as Mao's works were required reading during the Maoist era, in the Deng era all were advised to read Deng's books, and portions of them were made mandatory reading for Party members, assigned as texts for political study in various Party purification movements and ideological campaigns. As the Deng era wore on, probably fewer and fewer recalled that Wei Jingsheng, just before his arrest in 1979, had warned that "the people must maintain vigilance against Deng Xiaoping's metamorphosis into a dictator."[15]

Despite Deng's enormous personal power, he did not attempt to set himself above the Party as Mao had done. The "paramount leader" preferred to rule China through the established procedures of a refurbished Communist Party organizational apparatus, and between the leader and the institution there was little of the tension that had made the political history of the Mao era so turbulent. This, of course, was in accord with Deng's Leninist beliefs and his overwhelming passion for "stability and unity." When Deng eventually decided to step away from the center of the political stage (although by no means completely off it)—at the Thirteenth Party Congress held in the autumn of 1987—his partial exit was both a personal triumph and an orderly one, his loyal protégés seemingly well positioned to carry on his policies.[16] The promise of socialist democracy remained unfulfilled, and indeed had been half forgotten. Certainly Deng Xiaoping had forgotten it. Shortly before his semi-retirement, he took special pains to praise the virtues of an authoritarian and monolithic Leninist ruling party: "The greatest advantage of the socialist system is that when the central leadership makes a decision it is promptly implemented without interference from any other quarters. . . . We don't have to go through a lot of repetitive discussion and consultation with one branch holding up another. . . . From this point of view, our system is very efficient."[17]

Yet however much Deng Xiaoping wished to reestablish an efficient Communist Party organization, he did not hesitate to ignore

[15] *Tansuo* (Exploration), March 25, 1979.

[16] On the Thirteenth Party Congress, see Chapter 13.

[17] Deng Xiaoping, "We Shall Speed Up Reform," *Fundamental Issues in Present-Day China* (New York: Pergamon Press, 1987), pp. 192–96.

Leninist norms when it suited his personal political interests. In the late 1980s, Deng increasingly came to rely upon the advice of an informal group of Party elders, members of his own generation who, like him, had formally retired from their high Party posts. The informal advice of the "Gang of Old," as they were sometimes called,[18] was to encourage Deng to bring about the downfall of the two Party leaders he had selected to modernize the Party organization in accordance with Leninist precepts—Hu Yaobang and Zhao Ziyang. And, as shall be seen, in arriving at the crucial decisions that were to result in the tragedy of June 4, 1989, Deng Xiaoping operated above formal Party channels, relying on the support of the Gang of Old along with that of elderly PLA generals with whom he had had close political and personal ties since the revolutionary years.

It was no doubt Deng Xiaoping's intention to restore to the Chinese Communist Party the Leninist principle of "inner-Party democracy." But the experience of the Party in the Deng era offers powerful support for Rosa Luxemburg's prediction, made at the time of the Bolshevik Revolution, that Leninist methods of rule are destined to result in a Jacobin-type "dictatorship of a handful of politicians."[19]

BUREAUCRATIC INSTITUTIONALIZATION

The growth of Deng Xiaoping's personal power was accompanied by the institutionalization of the power of the Communist bureaucracy. The sheer size of the bureaucracy spawned by the Communist Revolution staggers the imagination. In the nineteenth century, under the last Chinese dynasty, about 40,000 imperial officials managed the world's largest empire and staffed the oldest continuously existing bureaucratic system. The short-lived Guomindang regime produced a notoriously bloated and parasitic bureaucracy of 2 million officials.[20] Under the Mao regime, the numbers increased dramatically.

---

[18] The "Gang of Old" included such Party luminaries as Peng Zhen, Li Xiannian, Yang Shangkun, Wang Zhen, Chen Yun, Song Renqiong, and Bo Yibo. All, like Deng, were born in the first decade of the century.

[19] Rosa Luxemburg, *The Russian Revolution and Leninism or Marxism?* (Ann Arbor: University of Michigan Press, 1961), p. 72.

[20] Ying-mau Kau, "Patterns of Recruitment and Mobility of Urban Cadres," in John W. Lewis (ed.), *The City in Communist China* (Stanford: Stanford University Press, 1971), pp. 98–99.

By 1958, only nine years after the establishment of the People's Republic, there were 8 million state cadres—that is, full-time salaried bureaucratic functionaries paid by the central government—a figure that does not include a probably greater number of local rural cadres who performed administrative duties supported by payments from local collectives. It is estimated that when Deng Xiaoping achieved ascendancy at the Third Plenum in 1978, he inherited a governmental apparatus that numbered 21 million state cadres.[21]

China's state bureaucrats are ranked in a formal hierarchy of twenty-six grades, with corresponding differences in power, status, privileges, and salary—a system established in the early years of the People's Republic and patterned on the hierarchical Soviet *nomenklatura* system. Despite Maoist egalitarian pronouncements and anti-bureaucratic campaigns over the decades, the essential structure of that Soviet-type system survived the Mao period—and indeed survives to this day on a mammoth scale. Needless to say, those who occupy official positions in the state apparatus (usually members of the Communist Party who hold similar rankings in that parallel government hierarchy) enjoy status, privileges, and above all power denied to the masses of the Chinese people over whom they rule. Although the material privileges of the great majority of China's cadres traditionally have been rather paltry, at least in comparison to the luxuries enjoyed by ruling groups in most other countries, those at the top of the hierarchy have always commanded such amenities as comfortable homes and apartments supplied by the state, servants, chauffeur-driven automobiles, access to special stores reserved for high-level cadres, banquets, travel, vacations at resorts established for the exclusive use of high officials, a network of doctors and hospitals, and special schools for their children—to mention only a few of the privileges that earned them the title of "China's Red capitalist class" during the Cultural Revolution. But even lower-level cadres, however modest their official salaries and material rewards, could claim some measure of the most coveted privilege in China's postrevolutionary society—namely, power over people.

Those who came to occupy positions in the postrevolutionary bu-

---

[21] Hong Yung Lee, "Political and Administrative Reforms," p. 36. The somewhat lesser official figure of 18 million is given in *People's Daily*, December 6, 1980.

reaucracy soon acquired a strong interest in preserving the new organization and their places in it. Even though most of China's bureaucrats, originally recruited primarily from the ranks of revolutionaries of humble rural origin, may conceive of themselves (and certainly have always presented themselves) as guardians of the revolution and servants of the people, they function, in fact, as masters of the people and have become accustomed to the personal material privileges which that mastery bestows upon them. The postrevolutionary Chinese Communist bureaucracy was at once necessary for the political and economic functioning of the new society and incongruous with the socialist goals that the leaders of the new society professed. Bureaucratic dominance over society was certainly incongruous with the Marxist vision of socialism as "the self-government of the producers," with administrative functions performed by ordinary citizens at workers' wages and without special status or privileges—and subject to immediate recall by the masses. The Chinese case was yet another in a long list of historical cases where the organizational apparatus created to achieve socialist ends tended to become the end itself.

Although Mao Zedong was the creator of the Chinese Communist bureaucracy and presided over its extraordinarily rapid growth, he also was its principal critic. Mao viewed the transformation of revolutionaries into bureaucratic rulers with a mixture of pride and disgust. He was proud of his cadres' accomplishments, both as revolutionaries and as putative builders of socialism, and no doubt had some appreciation of their desire to enjoy the fruits of victory. He himself, after all, tasted those fruits in rather abundant measure. But after 1956 he had become more and more critical of their bureaucratic ways, their lust for privileges, and their separation from the masses, complaining (in early 1957) that "some cadres now scramble for fame and fortune and are interested only in personal gain. . . . They vie with each other . . . for luxuries, rank and status."[22] In the early 1960s Mao recited a litany of the cadres' bureaucratic sins:

---

[22] Mao Zedong, "Talks at a Conference of Secretaries of Provincial, Municipal and Autonomous Region Party Committees. I: The Talk of January 18 (1957)," *Selected Works of Mao Tse-tung* (Peking: Foreign Languages Press, 1977), Vol. V, pp. 350–51. A similar criticism of cadre greed was repeated by Mao in his celebrated February 1957 speech, "On the Correct Handling of Contradictions Among the People."

"They seek pleasure and fear hardship; they engage in back door deals; one person becomes an official and the entire family benefits; one person reaches nirvana and all his close associates rise up to heaven; there are parties and gifts and presents."[23] By the eve of the Cultural Revolution, Mao was entertaining the notion that the new society had produced a "bureaucratic class," although he proved reluctant to pursue that perilous line of thought very far.

The Cultural Revolution ostensibly was undertaken to remedy the bureaucratic evils Mao had so bitterly criticized over the preceding decade. In view of the arbitrary and oppressive political practices of China's officials and the luxuries a good many of them enjoyed amidst conditions of general poverty, it is hardly surprising that the anti-bureaucratic and egalitarian goals proclaimed in 1966 should have elicited an enthusiastic popular response. But the pursuit of those goals was soon distorted, and then betrayed, as we have seen.[24] The Cultural Revolution, far from curing bureaucratic evils, only aggravated the arbitrary and corrupt bureaucratic practices from which the Chinese people suffered. Individual officials were attacked and purged, but the bureaucratic system survived. Even the hierarchical order of cadre ranks, which Mao had been criticizing since the mid-1950s, remained intact.[25] In large measure, the failure was of Mao's own making, or, more precisely, the result of his ambivalent attitude toward the bureaucracy he had created and upon which his rule depended. He was, as Richard Kraus has so aptly put it, at once both "the chief cadre and the leading rebel."[26] The ambiguity remained until the end of the Mao era.

Yet if Mao's political practice failed to match his antibureaucratic rhetoric, his ideology and the mass political movements he promoted were less than conducive to the stabilization of bureaucratic rule.

[23] "Chairman Mao Discusses Twenty Manifestations of Bureaucracy," Joint Publication Research Service No. 49829, February 12, 1970, pp. 40–43.
[24] In Chapter 2.
[25] "This business of grading cadres, have done with it!" Mao demanded in 1957. "Let wages be roughly evened out, with slight differences here and there." *Selected Works of Mao Tse-tung*, Vol. 5, p. 350. Yet, in fact, the cadre ranking system survived the Cultural Revolution and the Maoist era pretty much in the same hierarchical form in which it had originally been established.
[26] Richard Curt Kraus, *Class Conflict in Chinese Socialism* (New York: Columbia University Press, 1981), p. 181.

During the Mao era, the bureaucracy remained in a state of flux, its members insecure and fearful, their privileges hidden or at least disguised. But if Mao's style of rule was inhospitable to bureaucratic institutionalization, it did not inhibit the growth of the number of bureaucrats. Indeed, one of the many ironies of the Mao era was that antibureaucratic political campaigns usually resulted in increasing the size of the bureaucracy. Political activists, after all, had to be rewarded, and the usual reward was elevation to bureaucratic office.

The leaders of post-Mao China inherited a bureaucracy that was bloated, inefficient, ridden with petty corruption, and ill suited to carrying out the Four Modernizations. The overwhelming majority of officials had been selected and promoted on the basis of political criteria—their service to the revolution and their leadership in post-1949 political campaigns—rather than for their administrative abilities and technical expertise. Most, the sons and (in far lesser numbers) the daughters of worker and especially poor peasant families, had little or no formal education. Only 6 percent of those who occupied responsible positions in Party and state organs in 1978 could claim college-level training.[27] Their experience was largely rooted in the traditions of a revolutionary era, uncongenial to new leaders intent on pursuing modern economic and technological development in the most rapid possible fashion.

The political aim of Deng Xiaoping was not to do away with the bureaucracy built during the period of Mao's rule—although he did wish to do away with Maoists in the bureaucracy. Rather his aim was to reform and rationalize the existing bureaucratic structure and refashion it to serve his own political and economic goals, taking care in the process to placate the higher-level bureaucrats whose political support he required. Deng's aims, as he enunciated them in 1980, were to make the bureaucratic corps better educated, professionally more competent, and younger.[28] This program of bureaucratic rationalization, not democratic government, was the essence of what Deng meant by "political reform."

To these aims Deng added the perennial goals of eliminating

---

[27] Hong Yung Lee, "Political and Administrative Reforms," p. 37.

[28] Deng Xiaoping, "On the Reform of the System of Party and State Leadership" (Speech of August 18, 1980), *Selected Works of Deng Xiaoping*, p. 308.

bureaucratic corruption and reducing the number of bureaucrats. Reducing the size of the bureaucracy proved to be as elusive a goal under Deng's rule as it had been under Mao's. Indeed, Deng's first political act in his political reform program—the rehabilitation of cadres dismissed during the Cultural Revolution and earlier political campaigns and purges—however laudatory the intent, greatly exacerbated the problem. To make places for rehabilitated cadres, new and redundant official posts were created, enlarging an already overstaffed state apparatus.[29] Vice-ministerships and deputy-directorships proliferated, and administrative expenses took up an increasing share of the government budget.[30]

Bureaucratic overstaffing, as well as the related problem of elderly bureaucrats often too infirm to perform their duties, partially resulted from the tradition of lifelong tenure for cadres. There was neither a mandatory retirement age for officials nor any regular retirement system. Aged cadres clung to office for fear of losing their status, their material privileges, and their influence. Deng Xiaoping and other reform-minded high Party leaders repeatedly called for the abolition of lifetime tenure. But the bureaucracy was resistant. Complaints were heard that abandoning the traditional tenure system would be a betrayal of the old cadres who had made the revolution and, together with the new emphasis on formal education, would discriminate against cadres of worker and peasant backgrounds, particularly those of the land reform generation.

In the end, the regime compromised. No mandatory retirement age was set, but a variety of generous material and social rewards were offered to encourage elderly officials to retire voluntarily. In accordance with the new retirement system (*li xiu*), veteran cadres who relinquished their posts could continue to collect their official salaries and receive pension payments as well. They retained various official privileges, including, for senior bureaucrats, houses, cars and chauffeurs, and access to special stores and medical services. They also could attend official meetings appropriate to their rank and have

[29] Ronald A. Morse (ed.), *The Limits of Reform in China* (Boulder, Co.: Westview Press, 1983), p. 21.
[30] As a proportion of the total government budget, expense for administration almost doubled between 1978 and 1985, rising from 4.2 percent to 8 percent. *People's Daily*, March 7, 1985. Cited in Hong Yung Lee, "Political and Administrative Reforms," p. 51.

access to their files. And most higher-level officials were named to sit on newly created and formally prestigious advisory commissions.

By 1986 more than a million officials had accepted retirement under these generous conditions. The great majority of the retirees were "old cadres" who had joined the Party prior to 1949. Their places were taken by relatively young and educated officials. The generational and political change that took place in the bureaucracy in the mid-1980s further weakened the tenuous links between the postrevolutionary political order and the Chinese Communist revolutionary tradition. The generational change was, of course, inevitable, but the transformation was greatly accelerated by the policies of the Deng regime. When the Thirteenth Party Congress convened in October 1987, well over half of the old cadres had retired from their offices, symbolizing the beginning of the passing of political power to a younger generation of technocratic leaders.

The retirement of veteran officials and old cadres facilitated Deng Xiaoping's most desired political reform, and indeed the essence of what he meant by "political reform," the professionalization of the bureaucracy. The aim was to create a more modernized bureaucratic corps, its members trained in Western-style administrative procedures and in modern science and technology, thereby fashioning a bureaucracy better suited to carrying out economic development. In the recruitment and promotion of officials, preference was given to college and senior middle school graduates of the 1950s and early 1960s, to more recent graduates of the expanded post-Mao university system, and to those who had studied abroad. In 1985, 80 percent of cadres promoted at the central and provincial administrative levels could claim college educations.[31]

The effort to fashion a modernized professional bureaucracy, the emphasis on technical expertise (rather than political "Redness") in selecting leaders, and the championing of the Weberian virtues of administrative rationality mark major departures from a Maoist legacy that once conveyed an antipathy to professionalism, a hostility to occupational specialization, and a general distrust of bureaucratic organization. However economically efficacious a professionally staffed bureaucratic apparatus may prove to be, in the political his-

---

[31] *People's Daily*, September 8, 1985.

tory of Chinese Communism it marks a momentous step in the de-radicalization of a once-revolutionary movement.

Yet while Deng Xiaoping found virtues in bureaucratic profes-sionalism, he also discovered many of the same vices Mao Zedong had so bitterly condemned. In a speech delivered in 1981, Deng recited a list of bureaucratic sins that might well have been borrowed from Mao's catalogue of the "twenty manifestations of bureaucracy" compiled two decades earlier. "The bureaucratic phenomena," Deng declared, "are the most serious problem for our nation and Party. The major manifestations of bureaucratism are: looking down on peo-ple, abusing political power, departing from reality, being separated from the masses, speaking empty words, having ossified ideology, blindly observing absurd regulations, creating redundant organiza-tions, having more people than needed, avoiding decision making, indifference to efficiency, irresponsibility, betraying trust, multiplying red tape, blocking each other, retaliating against others, suppressing democracy, cheating superiors as well as subordinates, taking bribes, and accumulating personal wealth."[32] Deng was to repeat this familiar litany of bureaucratic evils many times.

If Deng was concerned with many of the same bureaucratic vices that had aroused Mao's ire, he differed in the methods he chose to rectify them. Whereas Mao's tendency was to mobilize the masses in popular antibureaucratic political campaigns, usually accompanied by the fiery rhetoric of class struggle and always with less than sat-isfactory results, Deng preferred a combination of material induce-ments and administrative sanctions—offers of attractive retirement plans for elderly cadres and purges of the ranks of the bureaucracy by decrees issued from the top of the political hierarchy. It was an attempt to reform the bureaucracy through bureaucratic means.

Most significantly, the Deng regime promoted attitudes and pol-icies favorable to the institutionalization of bureaucratic rule. In striking contrast to Mao, Deng accepted a privileged bureaucracy as a necessary feature of modern political life. Deng and his associates were determined to create a socially and politically stable environ-ment in which a modern bureaucracy could smoothly perform its

---

[32] *People's Daily*, November 2, 1981. Cited in Hong Yung Lee, "Deng Xiaoping's Reform of the Chinese Bureaucracy," p. 28.

work, unimpeded by intrusions from below. Thus it was declared—
one might say, bureaucratically decreed—that antagonistic class divisions in Chinese society have ceased to exist, thereby eliminating
the rationale for Maoist-style mass political campaigns which had
been so unsettling for higher-level bureaucrats during the Mao era.
And, in accordance with the new doctrine proclaiming the elimination of social class divisions and the cessation of class struggle, the
theory of a bureaucratic ruling class, heard during the Cultural Revolution and revived by democratic activists in 1979, was condemned
as the gravest of ideological heresies.

In addition to eliminating the more radically populist, antibureaucratic strains from the official doctrine still known as Marxism-
Leninism-Mao Zedong Thought, the Deng regime adopted other
measures conducive to bureaucratic institutionalization. These included the rationalization and codification of rules and regulations
governing political and economic organizations and the promulgation
of comprehensive legal codes. The restoration of the pre-Cultural
Revolution system of education supplies an increasingly professionalized bureaucratic apparatus with an ever-increasing number of
technically proficient recruits. And old symbols of authority have
been revived and refurbished to foster social obedience and
discipline.

Particularly salutary for the institutionalization of bureaucratic
rule has been the cessation of mass political campaigns and the general depoliticization of social life. At the outset of the new era, the
masses were officially advised that their business was production, not
politics. As Deng Xiaoping bluntly put it in 1979: "Extracting more
oil is the politics of the petroleum industry, producing more coal is
the politics of coal miners, growing more grain is the politics of peasants, defending the frontiers is the politics of soldiers, and working
hard in study is the politics of students. The only criterion for
[judging] the results of political education is its utility in improving
the economic situation."[33] Politics per se, Deng might have added,
was the exclusive business of the Communist Party. A politically
apathetic population is a condition favorable to the flourishing of
bureaucracy and the condition most favored by bureaucrats, who can

---

[33] *People's Daily*, April 11, 1979.

carry out their duties in an orderly manner and in ways they see fit, with little interference from below.

At the end of 1982, post-Mao leaders consecrated a new era of "stability and unity" with a new state constitution, the fourth such document in the history of the People's Republic. While the new charter added "freedom from arbitrary arrest" and the right to engage in "legitimate religious activities" to the conventionally proclaimed freedoms citizens presumably enjoyed, it eliminated such irritants to the bureaucracy as the right of workers to strike and the "four great freedoms." The deletion of the latter clause symbolized the bureaucratic ideal of the masses as politically passive and socially well-behaved individuals. Further reflecting the desired return to political normalcy, and no doubt nostalgia for the period before the Cultural Revolution, the new constitution reestablished the office of Chief of State (or "President" of the People's Republic), the position held by Liu Shaoqi—until his purge during the Cultural Revolution—and then abolished in the Maoist-fashioned constitution of 1975. The honorific post was initially occupied by the veteran Red Army commander and economic planner Li Xiannian, who embodied what Deng was most eager to display—the combination of revolutionary continuity with the Maoist past and support for the reformist policies of the post-Mao present.

While Deng's political reform program went far in institutionalizing bureaucratic rule in China, long-standing structural problems have been resistant to reformist remedies. The effort to reduce the size of the bureaucratic apparatus proved futile. Although there was some reduction in the number of offices and officials in the central government in Beijing, there were significant increases in the number of cadres at the provincial and county levels of administration. State administrative expenditures grew dramatically, and the bureaucracy as a whole was even more bloated at the end of the Deng era than it was in the late Mao period. Moreover, from the loud reformist rhetoric of the early 1980s on the need to separate Party and state administrations, little of substance followed. In the post-Mao period, as was the case during the Mao era, the state bureaucracy remains the obedient tool of the Party.

Reflective of the tenor of post-Mao times, and instructive for understanding what Dengists mean by "political reform," the regime's ideology does not attempt to disguise the fact that China's modernized bureaucracy is increasingly composed of professional technocrats rather than socialist political leaders. The phenomenon is instead celebrated. At an April 1986 meeting of the National People's Congress, an official statement proudly described the newly elected state councillors, the leaders of the state bureaucracy, as "a group of technocrats who are younger in age, pragmatic, and enthusiastic [about] reform. . . . China is rejuvenating its leadership, making it professionally more competent as a measure to insure the continuity of its current policies for reform and the opening to the outside world."[34] About the socialist and democratic credentials of the new leaders, nothing was said. It was a sign of the times and a portent of the future.

---

[34] New China News Agency dispatch, reported in *The New York Times*, April 13, 1988, p. 3.

PART THREE

THE SOCIAL RESULTS OF MARKET REFORM

8

THE ECONOMIC LEGACIES
OF THE MAO ERA
AND THE POST-MAO REFORMERS

IT IS A UNIVERSAL PROCLIVITY of new governments to attribute their economic problems to the failings of their predecessors. Thus when Hua Guofeng began his brief tenure in late 1976, it was said that the Chinese economy was "on the brink of collapse" due to the sabotage of the Gang of Four. The collapse was averted, it was claimed, only because of the timely intervention of the new regime.

When Deng Xiaoping and his allies achieved political dominance in December 1978, they extended the critique of past economic errors back to most of the Mao era, and added the blunders of Hua Guofeng for good measure, without mentioning that Deng had been the original author of Hua's abortive Ten Year Plan. As time went on, the economists in Deng's political entourage painted an ever-darker picture of the Maoist past. It soon became accepted doctrine that the People's Republic had enjoyed only two relatively brief progressive periods of economic development: the era of the First Five Year Plan of 1953–57 (which, however flawed, had been necessary in its time, especially since those now in power had been advocates of the Soviet model at the time) and the Liuist era in the early 1960s. For the rest of the Mao era, little good could be said.

It was thus that many of those whom Mao had castigated or ignored avenged themselves on the late Chairman's ghost, attributing most of China's economic problems to ultraleftist "subjectivism," "utopianism," and "egalitarianism." Maoists, the post-Mao critics charged, had failed to heed "objective economic laws," whose workings were now clearly revealed by the light of "scientific Marxism." The economic portrait of the Mao period was drawn more darkly than the facts warranted, even as those facts were revealed in the statistical tables compiled by the official economists of the Deng government. Nonetheless, the economic problems the new regime inherited from the Mao era were very real—and they were of staggering proportions.

THE ECONOMIC SUCCESSES AND FAILURES OF MAOISM

The lid of silence that has fallen over the material accomplishments of the Mao era is perhaps a natural reaction to the exaggerated (and often simply false) claims broadcast from Beijing in earlier years—and often uncritically repeated by foreign observers. Many foreigners, once eager to believe the best about the economic achievements of Maoist China, now are inclined to assume the worst, as if to compensate for their earlier credulity. This proclivity is in accord with the political tenor of the times in both China and the West, where there is now much skepticism about the efficacy of central planning amidst a general celebration of the magic of the market. It is understandable that the current leaders of China should be more concerned with their immediate economic problems and successes than with the achievements of the Maoist past. Less comprehensible is the failure of Western scholars to present a more balanced economic accounting; their omissions contribute to the popular impression that the Mao era was a period of economic stagnation. Conventional portraits now picture Mao Zedong vainly seeking a socialist spiritual utopia amidst conditions of poverty and subordinating development to the demands of ideological purity. The "pragmatic" Deng Xiaoping, it is implied, was the first Chinese Communist leader to discover the virtues of modernization.

Yet it is quite impossible to understand the economic problems that the Maoist era bequeathed to the Deng era without first appreciating the Mao regime's striking successes in transforming China from one of the world's most backward agrarian countries into the sixth-largest industrial power by the mid-1970s. Indeed, most of the major problems and deficiencies of the Maoist developmental strategy were the by-products of rapid industrialization, and the reforms that have dominated the history of the post-Mao period cannot be understood without appreciating that elemental economic fact.

The economic history of the People's Republic began with a tiny Chinese industrial plant that was even smaller than Belgium's; on a per capita basis, Chinese industry produced less than one-fiftieth of what Belgium produced. Yet on the basis of the most meager of material resources and with minimal outside assistance in a hostile international environment, China transformed itself into a major industrial power in a period of a quarter century. Over the course of the Mao era, the gross value of total industrial output increased more than 30-fold (12-fold if measured from 1952) and that of heavy industry (where pre-1949 China was particularly deficient) 90-fold.[1] Between 1952 (when industrial production was restored to its highest prewar levels) and the close of the Mao era, industrial output increased at an average per annum rate of 11.2 percent, despite the disruptions in industrial production that resulted from the Great Leap.[2] The largest percentage increases came during the First Five Year Plan (1953–57), when industrial growth averaged 18 percent per annum, more than doubling China's industrial capacity. High rates of growth continued in subsequent years, albeit unevenly. And despite all the disruptions of the Cultural Revolution decade (1966–76), industrial production continued to increase at an average per annum rate of over 10 percent.[3]

Data on several of the crucial sectors in this extraordinary rapid industrialization process might briefly be noted. Between 1952 and

---

[1] Ma Hong and Sun Shangqing (eds.), *Studies in the Problems of China's Economic Structure* (Beijing, 1981), Vol. 1, Joint Publication Research Service CEA-84-064-1, August 3, 1984, pp. 25–26.
[2] State Statistical Bureau, People's Republic of China, *Main Indicators, Development of the National Economy of the People's Republic of China (1949–1978)* (Beijing, 1979); and Table 5.1 in Victor D. Lippit, *The Economic Development of China* (Armonk, N.Y.: M. E. Sharpe, 1987), pp. 106–7. The growth rates are calculated in comparable prices.
[3] State Statistical Bureau, People's Republic of China, *China's Statistical Yearbook, 1984* (Beijing, 1984). For an analysis of China's economic growth and China's economic problems during the Cultural Revolution period, see Penelope B. Prime, "Socialism and Economic Development: The Politics of Accumulation in China," in Dirlik and Meisner (eds.), *Marxism and the Chinese Experience: Issues in Chinese Socialism* (Armonk, N.Y.: M. E. Sharpe, 1989), pp. 136–51.

the close of the Mao era, steel production increased from 1.4 to 31.8 million tons; coal from 66 to 617 million tons; cement from 3 to 65 million tons; timber from 11 to 51 million tons; electric power from 7 to 256 billion kilowatt-hours; crude oil from virtually nothing to 104 million tons; and chemical fertilizer from 39,000 to 8,693,000 tons.[4] By the mid-1970s, China was also producing substantial numbers of jet airplanes, heavy tractors, railway locomotives, and modern oceangoing vessels. The People's Republic also became a significant nuclear power, complete with intercontinental ballistic missiles. Its first successful atomic bomb test was held in 1964, the first hydrogen bomb was produced in 1967, and a satellite was launched into orbit in 1970.

Industrialization, of course, significantly altered the composition of China's workforce and its social structure. Although the great majority of the Chinese people remained peasants, largely tied to the land, the urban proletariat grew from 3 million in 1952 to over 18 million by the mid-1970s. Furthermore, the Maoist program of industrializing the countryside, one of the few surviving and successful accomplishments of the Great Leap, transformed 28 million peasants (out of a total rural labor force of about 300 million) into workers in rural factories, although many operated on primitive technological levels.[5]

However else one may wish to judge the Mao era, it was the period of China's modern industrial revolution that established, however crudely, the basic foundations for China's modern economic development. It was a period when China was transformed from an overwhelmingly agricultural land into a primarily industrial one. In 1952, industry accounted for 36 percent of the gross value of output

[4] Data compiled from U.S. Central Intelligence Agency, *People's Republic of China: Handbook of Economic Indicators* (Washington, D.C., 1976); U.S. Department of Commerce, *The Chinese Economy and Foreign Trade Perspectives* (Washington, D.C., 1977); and Joint Economic Committee of U.S. Congress, *China: A Reassessment of the Economy* (Washington, D.C., 1975), as summarized in Selden, *The People's Republic of China: A Documentary History*, Tables 13 and 14, pp. 135–36.

[5] On Maoist programs and accomplishments in building industry in the countryside, see Jon Sigurdson, *Rural Industrialization in China* (Cambridge: Harvard East Asian Monographs, 1977), and Dwight H. Perkins et al., *Rural Small-Scale Industry in the People's Republic of China* (Berkeley: University of California Press, 1977). These and other works make for salutary reading today when so many foster the impression that the policy of rural industrialization was an invention of the Deng Xiaoping regime.

and agriculture 64 percent; by 1975, the ratio had been reversed, with industry making up 72 percent of the country's economic product, and agriculture 28 percent.[6] Far from being a time of economic stagnation, as popular lore now has it, the Mao period was one of the great modernizing epochs in world history, comparable to the most intensive periods in the industrialization of Germany, Japan, and Russia—the other major latecomers on the modern industrial scene.[7]

These economic achievements were accomplished by the labor of the Chinese people themselves at a time when Maoism could instill a sense of mission and purpose. Save for very limited Soviet aid in the 1950s, no foreign assistance was received.[8] It was as much a hostile international environment (with Soviet hostility to Maoism added to American hostility to the Chinese revolution) as it was the Maoist principle of "self-reliance" that imposed conditions of virtual economic autarky on the People's Republic until the late 1970s. Mao's policy of national self-reliance brought additional economic disadvantages and hardships. But it also allowed for a proud claim: at the end of the Mao era, China stood virtually alone among developing nations with an economy free from foreign debt and internal inflation.

In the post-Mao era it has become the fashion to dwell on the blots and the crimes that mark the Maoist historical record and pass over in silence the accomplishments of the time—lest any mention of the latter be taken as an apology for the former. Yet one need not lapse into historical apologetics to recognize the elementary fact that the Mao regime made immense progress in promoting China's modern industrial transformation—and did so under extremely adverse in-

[6] Carl Riskin, *China's Political Economy*, Table 11.4, "Changes in Sectoral Composition of Output and Labour Force, 1952–1979," p. 270.

[7] Selecting the crucial decades in the industrialization of these various countries, the comparative record stands as follows: In Germany the decadal rate of economic growth for the period 1880–1914 was 33 percent (or 17 percent per capita); in Japan in the years 1874–1929 the decadal rate was 43 percent (28 percent per capita); for the Soviet Union over the period 1928–58 the decadal rate was 54 percent (44 percent per capita); China over the Maoist years 1952–72 achieved a decadal rate of 64 percent (34 percent per capita). Data drawn from Simon Kuznets, *Economic Growth of Nations: Total Output and Production Structure* (Cambridge: Harvard University Press, 1971), Table 4, pp. 38–39; and Gilbert Rozman (ed.), *The Modernization of China* (New York: The Free Press, 1981), Table 10.2, p. 350.

[8] Soviet economic credits were minimal, amounting to only 3 percent of Chinese state investment during the First Five Year Plan. Lippit, *The Economic Development of China*, p. 160.

ternal and external conditions. Without the industrial revolution that took place during Mao's time, the economic reformers who rose to prominence with Deng Xiaoping would have found little to reform.

Agricultural development during the Mao era was far less impressive than the achievements in industry, despite all the Maoist ideological pronouncements emphasizing the agrarian sector and celebrating peasant creativity. After 1957, food production barely kept pace with a population increase that averaged 2 percent per annum, resulting in nearly a doubling of the Chinese population over the Mao era.[9] Per capita grain production was approximately the same in 1975 as it had been at the beginning of collectivized agriculture in 1957.[10] And rural living standards were virtually stagnant over the final two decades of the Mao era, rising on average by less than 1 percent per annum,[11] and that from a miserably low base. Whereas the gross value of industrial output increased tenfold from 1952 to 1975, agricultural output grew only twofold.[12] Even that gain was attained only by vastly increasing the size of the agricultural workforce.[13] Further, the differences between urban and rural incomes widened, despite constant Maoist exhortations to narrow the gap between town and countryside.[14]

Nonetheless, Chinese agriculture during the Maoist era was by

[9] For a study of population growth in the People's Republic, see Judith Banister, *China's Changing Population* (Stanford: Stanford University Press, 1987).

[10] Grain output was 306 kilograms per capita in 1957 and 312 in 1975. Oil-bearing crops decreased over the period, although there was a small increase in the production of pork, beef, and mutton—from 6.3 kilograms per capita in 1957 to 8.7 in 1975. Lippit, *The Economic Development of China*, Table 7.1, p. 165.

[11] According to official data, actual per capita peasant consumption increased by only 22 percent over the period 1957–75. Xue Muqiao (ed.), *Almanac of China's Economy, 1981* (Hong Kong: Modern Cultural Co., 1982), p. 985.

[12] In the 1952–57 period, per capita grain production grew 1.2 percent per year but only at 0.2 percent per annum over the 1957–78 period. Cotton and edible oil crops declined slightly on a per capita measurement during the latter two decades of the Maoist period, while meat production increased (by 1.7 percent per capita per annum). Riskin, *China's Political Economy*, Table 12.3, p. 293.

[13] Between 1952 and 1975, the agricultural labor force increased from 173 million to 295 million people. Riskin, *China's Political Economy*, Table 11.4, p. 270. Estimates on the decline in labor productivity in agriculture over the 1957–75 period vary from 15 to 36 percent. Lippit, *The Economic Development of China*, p. 179.

[14] In 1975, the income of urban dwellers was about two and a half times that of rural people. Between 1952 and 1975, per capita consumption of the agricultural population increased at an average per annum rate of 1.1 percent while for the nonagricultural population it rose at a per annum rate of 2 percent, the relative advantage for the former increasing by 27 percent over the period. Riskin, *China's Political Economy*, pp. 240–41.

no means the total disaster it is now portrayed to have been. Victor Lippit has pointed out that agricultural growth in Maoist China was significantly higher than in Meiji Japan (1868–1912), the much-celebrated case of successful late modernization. From 1952 to the mid-1970s, net agricultural output in China increased at an average per annum rate of 2.5 percent, whereas the figure for the most intensive period of Japan's industrialization (from 1868 to 1912) was 1.7 percent.[15] The oft-repeated comparison between China's agrarian economy at the close of the Mao era and India's is no less true today than when it was politically more fashionable to note it. As Mark Selden once observed: "In 1977 China grew 30 to 40 percent more food per capita [than India] on 14 percent less arable land and distributed it far more equitably to a population which is 50 percent larger."[16]

Economic statistics do not tell all. It has often been pointed out that conventional measurements of income and consumption are inadequate indicators of the actual standard of living and the quality of life. It is also necessary to take into account public consumption in such elemental and essential realms as education, health care, sanitation, and welfare provisions for the elderly and the destitute—matters not easily quantifiable in standard economic calculations. In all of these areas the Mao regime achieved great social progress, and by most key social and demographic indicators the People's Republic compared favorably not only with other low-income countries such as India and Pakistan but also with "middle-income" countries whose per capita GNP was five times that of China.[17] During the Mao era, a largely illiterate population was transformed into a mostly literate one. Primary school education was nearly universalized in the rural areas and junior middle school education in the cities, and adult education and work-study programs were established in both town and countryside.[18] Elemental social safeguards, such as a prohibition on child labor in industry, were implemented, along with minimal

---

[15] Lippit, *The Economic Development of China*, p. 178.

[16] Selden (ed.), *The People's Republic of China: A Documentary History of Revolutionary Change*, p. 134n.

[17] See, for example, Table 7.4, compiled from World Bank data, in Lippit, *The Economic Development of China*, p. 188.

[18] On primary and secondary school enrollments at the end of the Mao period, see Suzanne Pepper, "Chinese Education After Mao: Two Steps Forward, Two Steps Back and Begin Again?" *The China Quarterly*, No. 81 (March 1980), esp. pp. 5–6.

social welfare programs in the countryside, most notably the Five Guarantees of food, clothing, housing, medical care, and burial expenses for the most impoverished members of the population. Urban workers in state enterprises enjoyed job security and state-funded welfare benefits. At the close of the Mao era, the People's Republic could claim a reasonably comprehensive, if still rudimentary, health care system that made it unique among developing countries. Health care, along with improved nutrition and sanitation, contributed to a dramatic increase in life expectancy—from an average of 35 years in pre-1949 China to 65 years in the mid-1970s.

THE ECONOMIC CONTRADICTIONS OF MAOISM

Mao Zedong was fascinated by the contradictions inherent in all phenomena, the ceaselessness of conflict and struggle, and the inevitability of constant change. "One thing destroys another," he said, "things emerge, develop, and are destroyed; everywhere it is like this. If there was no such thing as death, that would be unbearable."[19]

And so it was with Maoism. The Maoist strategy built the foundations for China's modern industrial revolution, but in doing so it created forces that eventually made that strategy obsolete, generating economic contradictions and social tensions that could not be contained within the existing Maoist system. The successes and the failures were inextricably intertwined, both part of Mao's contradictory legacy.

Many of the problems that emerged during the course of Maoist economic development are ones inherent in the Stalinist-type "command economy" that the Chinese Communists adopted in the early years of the People's Republic. It was a decision that Mao later regretted and regretfully explained: "In economic work [in the early 1950s] dogmatism primarily manifested itself in heavy industry, planning, banking and statistics, especially in heavy industry and planning. Since we didn't understand these things and had absolutely no experience, all we could do in our ignorance was to import foreign

[19] Mao Zedong, "Talk on Questions of Philosophy" (August 18, 1964), in Stuart R. Schram (ed.), p. 227.

methods. Our statistical work was practically a copy of Soviet work. . . . We lacked understanding of the whole economic situation, and understood still less the economic differences between the Soviet Union and China. So all we could do was to follow blindly."[20]

Soviet-style central planning, if vigorously pursued, typically yields rapid economic growth (if not necessarily salutary social consequences) in the early stages of industrialization, but its effectiveness typically declines over time. Such was the case in the People's Republic. As China's industrial plant grew larger and increasingly complex, the state's ability to administer the economy rationally declined. Centrally determined production plans designed by planners in Beijing ignorant of local capabilities and social needs resulted in increasingly inefficient practices in the production and distribution of goods, shortages and hoarding of raw materials, bottlenecks in China's still rudimentary transportation system, and the overproduction of some products and chronic shortages of needed goods. To fulfill their quotas, local enterprises increased production but paid less attention to quality and costs. This was the inevitable consequence of a system that measured economic success quantitatively and gave individual production units little responsibility for the profits or losses resulting from their performance. A further sign of economic trouble was declining per capita productivity. Although labor productivity in industry increased by over 50 percent during the First Five Year Plan, it then stagnated, rising on average by less than 1 percent per annum over the last two decades of the Mao period.[21] After 1957, increases in production were dependent on rising capital investment and a rapidly expanding industrial workforce.

As industrialization proceeded, the administrative apparatus cre-

---

[20] Mao Zedong, "Talks at the Chengtu Conference" (March 10, 1958), *Mao Tse-tung Unrehearsed*, pp. 98–99. On another of the many occasions when Mao was critical of the Stalinist model, he also attributed the Chinese adoption to inexperience: "In the early stages of Liberation we had no experience of managing the economy of the entire nation. So in the period of the first five-year plan we could do no more than copy the Soviet Union's methods, although we never felt altogether satisfied about it." Mao Zedong, *A Critique of Soviet Economics*, p. 122.

[21] Jan S. Prybyla, "Economic Problems of Communism: A Case Study of China," *Asian Survey*, Vol. 22, No. 12 (December 1982), pp. 1209–10. Also see Chu-yuan Cheng, *China's Economic Development: Growth and Structural Change* (Boulder, Co.: Westview Press, 1982), pp. 355–56; and Riskin, *China's Political Economy*, pp. 264–65.

ated to manage the state industrial sector grew more rapidly than industry itself, spawning a multitude of vested bureaucratic interests throughout the vast economic hierarchy. From central planning organs in Beijing to individual factories, China's industry became weighed down by redundant administrative and office personnel.[22] Most administrative cadres contributed little to production, but they did have a strong interest in maintaining the existing system and their privileged positions within it. Periodic Maoist campaigns to reduce bureaucracy and simplify administration were of little avail, and indeed sometimes only compounded the problem of overstaffing. The Cultural Revolution, for example, had the unintended consequence of enlarging the industrial bureaucracy. As Andrew Walder has shown, most factory administrators and office workers "sent down" to do manual work on factory benches or in the countryside were returned to their desks in the early 1970s, not in place of the workers who had taken their positions but rather simply adding to the number of people sitting at desks.[23]

The industrial labor force was also bloated, with most factories employing many more workers than needed. And with guaranteed lifetime employment and social welfare benefits provided by the state, regular workers were intent on holding on to what post-Maoist reformers were disparagingly to call their "iron rice bowls"—as if job security was somehow a trivial and unjustifiably selfish concern. The problem was not the right to employment, which was one of the great social gains of the revolution insofar as the promise was honored, but rather that those who had jobs were offered neither the material incentives nor any other means to improve productivity. Nationally set wage rates had been essentially frozen at their 1956 levels,[24] oppor-

[22] The First Five Year Plan generated an extraordinary number of heavily staffed economic ministries and specialized bureaucratic organs. This was especially the case in the realm of heavy industry, where there were six separate bureaucratic ministries dealing with machine building alone. For a detailed analysis of these economic bureaucracies, see Schurmann, *Ideology and Organization in Communist China*, Chapters 4 and 5.

[23] Andrew Walder, "Some Ironies of the Maoist Legacy in Industry," in Mark Selden and Victor Lippit (eds.), *The Transition to Socialism in China* (Armonk, N.Y.: M. E. Sharpe, 1982), pp. 230–31. For a fuller discussion, see Andrew Walder, *Communist Neo-Traditionalism: Work and Authority in Chinese Industry* (Berkeley: University of California Press, 1986).

[24] Determining income levels in the cities is a rather complex and confusing matter. On the one hand, average wages of workers in state enterprises declined after 1957—by 17 percent in real terms over the following two decades—due to the entry of younger workers at lower

tunities for promotion were severely limited, and remuneration in general had little to do with either enterprise or individual productivity.

During the early years of the People's Republic, workers were inspired by the collectivistic goals of the revolution as well as the promise of an improving material life, but the former declined over time and the latter remained unfulfilled. The Cultural Revolution, which sought to revive the revolutionary spirit, ultimately deadened it. From the fruitless battles of the upheaval, the urban working class emerged politically disillusioned and socially apathetic, no longer easily moved by political appeals or moral exhortations. The problem was not the much-debated issue of moral versus material incentives but rather the absence of both. Workers, or at least state workers, were at once secure in their jobs and dissatisfied with the conditions of their existence. Their incomes stagnated, housing conditions in the cities deteriorated (declining from 4.3 square meters per inhabitant in 1952 to 3.6 meters in 1977[25]), and there was little prospect for a better job or a better life in a system with virtually no labor mobility.

The difficulties under which industry labored were exacerbated by technological backwardness. The numbers of those officially classified as scientists and technicians grew dramatically over the Mao era, from 425,000 in 1952 to 5 million in 1979.[26] But the qualifications of the technological intelligentsia were suspect, especially after the termination of Soviet technical assistance in 1960. Moreover, the policy of national self-reliance, coupled with the Maoist view that technology was not socially neutral, limited Chinese access to advanced foreign technology. But the Cultural Revolution struck the most crippling blows, virtually dismantling the system of higher education, disrupting work in basic research, and gravely undermining the morale of the technological intelligentsia. All of these factors

---

levels of the wage scale. On the other hand, average per capita income in the cities grew by 62 percent (between 1957 and 1980) due to a large increase in the percentage of urban inhabitants who held jobs. (See Riskin, *China's Political Economy*, p. 263.) It is likely that average family income in urban areas increased substantially with the influx of women into the workforce and the consequent rise in the number of two-income families.

[25] Andrew Walder, "The Remaking of the Chinese Working Class, 1949–1981," *Modern China*, Vol. 10, No. 1 (January 1984), p. 24.

[26] Tong Dalin and Ju Ping, "Science and Technology," in Yu Guangyuan (ed.), *China's Socialist Modernization* (Beijing: Foreign Languages Press, 1984), p. 644.

contributed to the industrial plant's growing obsolescence, a grave shortage of qualified scientists and technicians, and a decline in labor productivity during the last years of the Mao regime.

The statistically high rates of industrial growth recorded during the last decade of the Mao regime were not accomplished without sacrificing the quality of what was being produced and not without ever-larger amounts of capital investment. What economists term "the accumulation rate," the proportion of the nation's material product withheld from consumption and invested to expand productive capacity, rose from an already high level of 24 percent during the period of the First Five Year Plan to 33 percent in the early 1970s, reaching 36.5 percent in 1978.[27] These high levels of capital accumulation were attained through various means. The most effective one was state exploitation of the peasantry through taxation and especially compulsory deliveries of grain purchased at artificially low official prices. Consumption was further curtailed by the general neglect of light industry and the consequent scarcity of consumer goods—which, in accordance with state pricing policies, sold dearly. Ideological campaigns, especially during the Cultural Revolution, further discouraged consumption by fostering ascetic values and celebrating the virtues of a spartan style of life.[28]

Save for the promotion of asceticism, these methods of capital accumulation were incongruous with Maoist ideological pronouncements. Of the goals Mao Zedong sought, none was more emphasized in theory than narrowing the gap between town and countryside. On many occasions, Mao criticized the Stalinist model of development for having exploited the peasantry to finance urban industrialization. Stalin's "basic error is [his] mistrust of the peasants," he wrote,[29] and he accused the Soviet dictator, with reference to the latter's draconian

[27] Riskin, *China's Political Economy*, Table 6.6, pp. 142, 271. Under the extraordinary circumstances of the Great Leap, the accumulation rate rose to even higher levels, peaking at 44 percent in 1959.

[28] For a penetrating analysis of the Cultural Revolution attack on consumption, see Penelope B. Prime, "Socialism and Economic Development: The Politics of Accumulation in China," in Dirlik and Meisner, *Marxism and the Chinese Experience*, pp. 136–51. On the place of ascetic values in Maoist ideology, see Maurice Meisner, *Marxism, Maoism, and Utopianism* (Madison: University of Wisconsin Press, 1982), Chapter 4.

[29] Mao Zedong, "Concerning Economic Problems of Socialism in the USSR" (November 1958), in Mao Zedong, *A Critique of Soviet Economics* (New York: Monthly Review Press, 1977), p. 135.

policies in the countryside, of "having drained the pond to catch the fish." Moreover, Mao vowed to avoid the mistakes of "some socialist countries which put undue emphasis on heavy industry and neglected light industry and agriculture."[30] He pledged that Chinese policy would enable "agriculture, light industry, and heavy industry to develop at the same time and at a high rate [so that] we may guarantee that the people's livelihood can be suitably improved together with the development of heavy industry."[31] Mao wished to have the best of all worlds, with the rapid and simultaneous development of all three economic sectors, advising that "if you have a strong desire to develop heavy industry, then you will pay attention to the development of light industry and agriculture."[32]

Yet the advice was not heeded in the actual world of Maoist China. Over the years 1949–78, the gross output of heavy industry increased 90-fold whereas light industry increased 20-fold and agriculture only 2.4-fold. Moreover, the heavy industrial sector developed in a manner that tended to serve the needs of heavy industry itself rather than the needs for the technical transformation of agriculture or the development of light industry.[33] These imbalances were partly the result of state investment policies. During the Mao era, the bulk of state funds went to finance the growth of heavy industry; only 12 percent of total state investment went to agriculture and barely 5 percent to the development of consumer goods industries.[34] As consumption and popular living standards suffered, the accumulation rate rose to maintain the high pace of heavy industrial development. Without real gains in productivity, it is unlikely that these high levels of accumulation and investment could have been sustained much longer without further impoverishing the population.

If Maoist economic practice did not always conform to Mao's theories, this does not warrant the conclusion, so easily and simplistically arrived at by some observers, that the Maoist strategy was a

---

[30] Mao, "On the Ten Great Relationships" (April 1956), *Mao Tse-tung Unrehearsed*, p. 62.

[31] Mao, "Reading Notes," p. 77.

[32] Mao, "On the Ten Great Relationships," p. 63.

[33] Dong Fureng, "Some Problems Concerning Chinese Economy," *The China Quarterly*, No. 84 (December 1980), pp. 727–36.

[34] Nicholas R. Lardy, *Agriculture in China's Modern Economic Development* (Cambridge: Cambridge University Press, 1983), Table 3.7, p. 130.

carbon copy of the Stalinist model of development and that Maoism in general was but a variant of Stalinism. The fact remains, as discussed in Chapter 2, that Mao early diagnosed many of the defects of the Soviet model of central planning and recognized that its social consequences were incongruous with the envisioned socialist society. Yet if in some ways Maoist economic policies mitigated the more elitist and socially inegalitarian consequences of Stalinist-style industrialization, in other respects Maoism exacerbated the problems associated with centrally planned economies. The Great Leap, beyond resulting in an economic and human disaster of catastrophic proportions, also virtually destroyed China's planning system. Despite the emphasis on decentralization, this was contrary to Mao's intentions, and he bitterly complained in his July 1959 speech at the Lushan conference that "the planning organs do not concern themselves with planning," acknowledging that he understood "nothing about industrial planning."[35] In the years after the Great Leap, the system of central planning was never effectively restored; most efforts to do so were undermined by the political instabilities and mass campaigns of the period.

While Maoist policies dismantled some of the Soviet-style economic bureaucracies, Mao in the end was unwilling to abandon the Stalinist priority on heavy industry, to which agriculture, consumer goods production, and popular living standards were inevitably subordinated. Industrialization continued to speed along in the last years of Mao's rule, but without an effective planning system to direct its development and functioning, the imbalances endemic in centrally planned economies were compounded.

Thus, as the Mao era was coming to a close, Chinese industry was beset by most of the troubling problems that were chronic in the Soviet Union and the Eastern European countries—waste, inefficiency, overstaffing, bureaucratic inertia, low productivity, petty corruption, the sacrifice of popular living standards for ever-higher rates of capital accumulation, and an immobile working class that was becoming increasingly demoralized and apathetic. Added to these structural problems was a general neglect of trade, services, trans-

[35] Mao Zedong, "Speech at the Lushan Conference" (July 23, 1959), *Mao Tse-tung Unrehearsed*, p. 142.

portation, and housing. In an overly politicized economic environment, where all economic activity not under direct state auspices was politically suspect, the number of shops, handicraft workers, restaurants, and retail outlets declined over the last years of the Mao period, forcing many people (and usually those who could least afford to do so) to travel long distances to obtain needed goods. Such were some of the economic legacies of the Mao era—along with a substantial industrial base—that were bequeathed to post-Mao China.

While Mao Zedong's successors inherited an inefficient and unbalanced urban industrial economy, the problems of the countryside were far more serious and pressing. In a country inhabited by nearly a quarter of the world's people, but with only 6 percent of its arable land, agriculture was a most precarious enterprise even under the best of political and social circumstances, the production of minimally necessary food supplies more dependent on the vagaries of nature than the wisdom of politicians. Even in years of relatively bountiful harvests, agricultural output was depressingly small by prevailing international standards. The crop yield per agricultural worker in China was 1,040 kilograms in 1978, whereas it was 10,265 kilograms in the Soviet Union and 95,452 kilograms in the United States.[36]

Although agricultural output grew at a slightly more rapid pace than the population during the Mao era,[37] the increase resulted not from greater labor productivity (which, it is estimated, declined at least 15 percent over the last two decades of the Mao period[38]) but rather from the addition of 100 million workers to the agrarian labor force.[39] Per capita peasant consumption increased over the period,

[36] *Xinhua Yuebao* (April 1980). Cited in Prybyla, "Economic Problems of Communism," p. 1209.

[37] According to figures released in 1979, agricultural output increased at an average per annum rate of 3.2 percent over the years 1952–78 while population grew by 2 percent per year. State Statistical Bureau, *Main Indicators*.

[38] Estimates on the decline in productivity over the period 1957–75, based on output per hour of working time, range from 15 to 36 percent. Thomas Rawski, "Economic Growth and Employment in China," *World Development* (August–September 1979), pp. 776–77.

[39] Hu Qiaomu, "Observe Economic Laws, Speed Up the Four Modernizations," *Peking Review*, November 24, 1978, p. 18.

but at an agonizingly slow pace, rising only 22 percent from 1957 to 1975.[40]

Prospects for increasing agricultural production and improving productivity appeared dim at the end of the Mao era. Technological backwardness and ecological limitations severely restricted possibilities for expanding the area under cultivation; double- and triple-cropping had largely exhausted possibilities for further intensifying land utilization; and the prevailing system of collective farming offered peasants few incentives to increase production.

Although agricultural output and rural peasant income increased over most of the Mao era, this growth proceeded so slowly and from so low a starting point that it left the peasantry impoverished—and left unfulfilled all the promises of rural prosperity. Moreover, the gap between city and countryside had become wider, and the agrarian sector yielded only a relatively small surplus that the state could extract to finance the Four Modernizations. It was this latter concern, as much as concern for the welfare of the peasantry, that motivated the post-Mao regime to undertake a wholesale revamping of the rural socioeconomic system.

The county's economic future appeared even more ominous when a new census published in June 1979 revealed that the population had reached 970 million (including 18 million living in Taiwan), a figure that grew to 1.06 billion by 1983. A new awareness of the great burden of China's enormous population, still growing by 15 million persons annually, lent new urgency not only to the task of increasing production and productivity but also to stringent birth-control policies designed to enforce the norm of the one-child family. While birth-control measures in the 1960s and 1970s—belatedly introduced after the Great Leap—had reduced population growth from 2 percent to 1.2 percent per annum, the post-Mao leadership was determined to achieve a zero growth rate before the end of the century. Overpopulation, in any event, was one of the legacies of the Mao era, and it was fraught with dire economic implications.

Another economic legacy of the Mao period was the lingering effect of the Great Leap Forward campaign, especially in some of the more remote areas of the countryside. While the history of the Great

[40] Lippit, *The Economic Development of China*, p. 153.

Leap has yet to be written, and although the magnitude of the famine that resulted from the adventure is likely to remain uncertain, such information that is available suggests that the debacle took an enormous human toll, resulting in as many as 20 to 30 million deaths.[41] Most of the afflicted areas of the countryside had recovered by the early 1960s, and some prospered, but other, more remote rural districts remained disaster areas, their populations suffering from chronic hunger.

Maoist policies were also less than entirely successful in achieving the egalitarian social goals proclaimed in official ideology. Industrialization, particularly in its early stages, typically generates great social inequities. Although Maoist policies mitigated the extremes of inequality that accompanied comparable stages of industrialization in the Soviet Union, Japan, and the Western countries, it is clear that the "three great differences"—between town and countryside, worker and peasant, and mental and manual labor—far from diminishing, increased significantly over the quarter century of Maoist industrialization. The most cherished of Maoist egalitarian goals was the elimination of the gap between town and countryside—and, thereby, between workers and peasants. Yet in the period 1952–75 annual average per capita consumption among the agricultural population increased (in comparable prices) from 62 to 124 yuan, whereas among the nonagricultural population it increased from 148 to 324 yuan.[42] Rural and urban per capita income grew at corresponding rates and with similar disparities.[43] The result, at the close of the Mao period, was that the average income of urban inhabitants was approximately three times greater than the rural average.[44] Moreover, despite significant progress in bringing schools and doctors to the countryside, those living in the cities continued to enjoy far better

[41] The estimates of famine-related deaths are based primarily on official mortality statistics. On the problems involved in interpreting these data, see Thomas Bernstein's exceptionally thoughtful article "Stalinism, Famine, and Chinese Peasants," *Theory and Society*, Vol. 13 (May 1984), pp. 343–44; and Lardy, *Agriculture in China's Modern Economic Development*, pp. 150–52.

[42] Riskin, *China's Political Economy*, Table 10.8, p. 241.

[43] Between 1957 and 1979, average per capita real income increased at an average annual rate of 2.9 percent in the cities and only 1.6 percent in the countryside. Ibid., p. 240.

[44] Ibid., p. 240. Estimates of the urban-rural income gap in the late 1970s range from a low of 2.2 to 1, as calculated by the World Bank, to a high of 5.9 to 1, as measured by some Western economists, the latter taking into account state subsidies to urban dwellers.

educational facilities and medical care. Although Maoist ideology celebrated the virtues of rural life, it is not difficult to understand why many peasants sought to migrate to the cities in search of a better life—and why the Communist state placed strict controls on such migration, especially after the Great Leap.

Another inequality that survived the Mao period was that of vast regional differences in levels of economic development and living standards, even though economic inequalities within localities and production units were relatively small by world standards. Although considerable progress was made in bringing modern industry to the more backward provinces and regions, the greater part of modern industrial growth took place in the coastal areas where industry had been concentrated prior to 1949. In agriculture, absolute growth was greater in traditionally prosperous areas than in the more impoverished ones, even though the relative rates of growth were often higher in the latter.

Thus the economic legacy of the Mao regime was marred by glaring social inequalities as well as by grave structural deficiencies. The leaders of post-Mao China inherited a very substantial modern industrial plant, but one which operated inefficiently. They inherited an economy suffering from what they soon were to diagnose as "irrationalities" and "imbalances"—an overemphasis on heavy industry and capital accumulation, and, most seriously, painfully slow growth in agricultural production accompanied by declining productivity. It was an economy that had yielded only the most modest gains in urban and rural living standards for a population long accustomed to austere material conditions of life.

Mao Zedong's successors were not disposed to remedy China's social inequalities. Indeed, some were inclined to attribute many of the country's economic difficulties to Maoist "egalitarianism." But they were determined to rationalize and restructure the economic system and hasten the process of modern development under the banner of the Four Modernizations. The first attempt to do so came with Hua Guofeng's Ten Year Plan, in large measure an effort to reestablish the bureaucratic system of central planning constructed during the First Five Year Plan. But the Ten Year Plan, unveiled in February 1978, was abandoned within a year of its proclamation, crushed under the weight of its own extravagant ambitions. A radically different economic course was foreshadowed at the meeting of the Third Plenum in December 1978, with what came to be hailed as China's "historic shift to socialist modernization."

CHOICES

Mao Zedong left China with an economy desperately in need of major reforms. Maoism could claim many great accomplishments over its long history, but as the Mao era was drawing to a close Maoism had exhausted its creative energies, no longer capable of serving as an inspirational ideology or yielding a viable strategy for long-term economic development.

The interim regime of Hua Guofeng failed to confront most of the economic problems it inherited. Hua attributed China's economic difficulties to "the sabotage of the Gang of Four" and vowed to make up for the economic losses allegedly caused by the now-jailed "radicals." Abandoning much of what remained distinctively Maoist in the Chinese strategy of development, although under an elaborate facade of radical Maoist rhetoric, the Hua regime sought to refurbish the system of central economic planning and once again pursue a "heavy industrial push," this time with the assistance of foreign-borrowed capital and technology. Hua's Ten Year Plan threatened to greatly exacerbate the problems and contradictions inherent in Stalinist-type systems of central economic planning.

When Deng Xiaoping achieved political dominance at the end of 1978, he was surrounded by advisors who counseled a more balanced mode of development. They saw the rigidities of Soviet-style central planning as the main barrier to modernization. They also believed that Maoist alternatives to, and modifications of, the Stalinist model had served only to compound the problems of the original system. Deng's political triumph marked the ascendancy of a new economic development strategy, the eventual course of which could hardly have been even dimly perceived in December 1978.

Yet the policies that have been pursued over the Deng era were by no means predetermined. China's new leaders were presented with choices during the early years of the new regime—and it is as instructive to know which potential alternatives were rejected or ignored as it is to know the one that eventually was adopted.

When Soviet-type systems of centralized planning have outlived their usefulness and their economies suffer from glaring inefficiencies and declining productivity, Communist rulers have been confronted with three broad alternatives. The first, and most politically palatable, is to modify the system of central planning through economic and administrative decentralization, transferring economic decision-making powers to local managers and officials. It is assumed that the transferring of authority, whether to regional administrative units or to local production units,[45] will result in the more efficient use of productive resources by those familiar with local needs and capabilities, stimulate local initiatives to increase production and productivity, and generally provide greater flexibility and rationality for the economy as a whole.

The second alternative is an increased reliance on the market to guide production and motivate the producers. Various price and profit mechanisms historically associated with capitalist economies replace (to greater or lesser degrees) state planning and control of production to determine what is produced, how products are exchanged, and the manner in which productive processes are performed. The market socialism model, carried to its logical end, implies that individual economic enterprises are related horizontally through the market rather than vertically through a central administrative apparatus. Accordingly, the socialist state ideally reduces its economic functions to those commonly performed by capitalist states—retaining its taxing authority and providing credit and subsidies. Externally, the model demands integration into the world capitalist economy, with economic enterprises competing not only with each other but also with foreign imports and markets.

Neither economic decentralization schemes nor market socialism necessarily threatens the essential power of the Leninist Party-state, certainly not as these forms of economic restructuring have been

---

[45] For a perceptive discussion of the distinction between these two forms of decentralization (respectively termed "decentralization II" and "decentralization I"), their differing political and social implications, and the application of "decentralization II" in China during the Great Leap, see Schurmann, *Ideology and Organization in Communist China*, esp. pp. 196–210. On this matter, more will be said in Chapters 10 and 11.

implemented in the People's Republic. Decentralization of economic life and decision making, depending on the form it takes and the extent to which it is pursued, may, of course, adversely affect the interests of certain sectors of the state and Party bureaucracy while favoring other sectors. It is conceivable that market relationships eventually will generate social forces which might undermine the power and authority of the Communist state. But Communist leaders bold enough to experiment with market reforms calculate that they can preserve their monopoly of political power and control what Lenin called "the commanding heights" of the economy. There is now considerable Chinese historical evidence to support the belief that market forces can be accommodated within the existing bureaucratic system, and indeed can prove profitable to the bureaucracy, as we shall have occasion to observe in the following chapters. While the retreat of the state bureaucracy from direct control over economic life weakens segments of the bureaucratic apparatus, the power of the bureaucracy in general remains intact. Both decentralizing and market-type reforms, it needs to be emphasized, are not "natural" economic processes but rather state-created phenomena, and thus the crucial socioeconomic decisions remain in the domain of the bureaucracy.

A third alternative to a bureaucratized centrally planned economy is movement toward a genuinely socialist system where the producers themselves control the conditions and products of their labor. Socialism, as it was traditionally understood before presenting itself in its distorted Stalinist guise, was defined not as state property but rather what Marx termed "the property of the associated producers." Such a restructuring of the economy implies decentralization, to be sure, but authority moves not simply to lower levels of the administrative apparatus or to professional managers but rather to the immediate producers. As Rudolf Bahro has observed, decentralizing economic reform in Communist countries "will remain an unproductive model of inter-bureaucratic activity, a tug-of-war between the leadership and the middle ranks of the managerial pyramid, as long as there is no autonomy for the social forces at the base that are outside of the administration."[46] The genuine socialist alternative to

[46] Rudolf Bahro, *The Alternative in Eastern Europe* (London: Verso, 1981), p. 379.

"the command economy" demands a system where economic units and productive processes are under the collective and democratic control of the workers and peasants who actually perform the productive labor of society.

When Deng Xiaoping and his allies achieved political ascendancy and began to consider new strategies of economic development, they totally ignored the socialist alternative as a possible remedy for China's economic problems. This dismissal is remarkable considering that socialist democracy was the much-heralded promise of the time. But then, on reflection, it is perhaps not so strange that the socialist option was not on the new leader's agenda. For the socialist alternative presupposed the general democratization of national political life. As Bahro has argued: "Given an overall social organization of labour, *political* democracy becomes the decisive constituting moment which determines whether the goals of the economic process . . . are decided by authentic social interests or rather by the restricted power relations and structures of knowledge within the bureaucracy."[47]

Any real movement toward socialism, toward a society based on the political and economic "self-government of the producers," would have left little place for the Communist Party, and no place for a Leninist single-party system. And it also would have meant a decreasing role for the state bureaucracy and the myriad social interests it had come to incorporate. Thus China's new leaders and their economic advisors considered only various forms of economic and administrative decentralization and the expansion of market relationships. There were heated debates over economic policy, but the proposals that were seriously debated were confined to what could be accommodated within the existing political structure. "Economic reform" thus remained an "inter-bureaucratic" affair, and socialism was precluded from the outset. The socialist alternative could be raised only from below, as soon was to be the dramatic case with the Solidarity movement in Poland. But socialism in any genuine sense was no less distasteful to China's reform leaders than it was to Poland's military rulers.

[47] Ibid., p. 380.

THE IDEOLOGY OF ECONOMIC REFORM

The economic specialists and policymakers who rose to prominence with Deng Xiaoping were not a monolithic entity. Western observers have tended to divide them broadly into two opposing camps, "the conservatives" and "the reformers," with the former embedded in the state planning bureaucracies and therefore opposed to far-reaching change. But in the early years of the Deng era, it was more common, and more accurate, to distinguish between "adjusters" and "marketeers" within Deng's reformist coalition.[48] Both groups favored economic reforms, although of different types and to differing degrees.

The adjusters, the most politically important of whom was Chen Yun,[49] advocated reducing state investment in heavy industry in favor of less costly developmental programs in agriculture and light industry. The accumulation rate thereby would be lowered, consumption and consumer spending would increase, and popular living standards would rise. To further stimulate economic development, the adjusters also favored an increased role for market forces, although such forces were to remain subordinate to central economic planning. Chen Yun had been urging such policies for more than twenty years. In the 1956–57 Party debates, he had been the main advocate of a more balanced and slower pattern of economic growth than envisioned in the policies supported by Mao, Liu Shaoqi, and Deng Xiaoping.[50]

[48] Writing at the time of the early reform period (1979–80), Dorothy Solinger identified three distinct tendencies among the Party leadership: "radicals," who distrusted all forms of commodity production and exchange and placed their faith in ever more advanced "socialist relations of production"; "bureaucrats," who were wedded to the existing state structure of central economic planning; and "marketeers," who believed that productive forces could be most rapidly developed through the relatively free exchange of goods. Dorothy J. Solinger, "Marxism and the Market in Socialist China: The Reforms of 1979–1980 in Context," in Victor Nee and David Mozingo (eds.), State and Society in Contemporary China (Ithaca: Cornell University Press, 1983), pp. 194–219. "Bureaucrats" who favored substantial modifications in the system of central economic planning and more balanced development, with a supplementary role for the market, correspond to the label "adjusters."

[49] Chen Yun was among the three highest-ranking Party leaders during the early Deng era. For the later political and policy clashes between Chen and Deng, see Chapters 9, 10, and 15.

[50] Chen Yun's views in the 1956–57 economic policy debates are discussed in Schurmann, Ideology and Organization in Communist China, esp. pp. 195–206. See also Nicholas Lardy and Kenneth Lieberthal (eds.), Chen Yun's Strategy for China's Development: A Non-Maoist Alternative (Armonk, N.Y.: M. E. Sharpe, 1983).

The marketeers, many of whom were attracted to Eastern European models of market socialism, notably Yugoslavia and Hungary, saw market mechanisms as the panacea for China's economic problems. Primarily concerned with rapid increases in production and productivity, they argued that economic development would best be served if market demands rather than central planners determined production and distribution, at least at China's current level of development.

Yet both adjusters and marketeers, and many others not easily categorized, were convinced that the main barrier to China's economic development was the centralized system of state planning borrowed from the Soviet Union in the 1950s. The Soviet model came under attack for familiar deficiencies—inefficiency and waste, the inability of state planners in the capital to determine real social needs, and the stifling of initiative at the level of the production unit by an overcentralized and highly bureaucratized system.

These criticisms had been made long before and in considerable detail not only by critics in the Soviet Union and the Eastern European countries in the early post-Stalin era but also in China itself in the mid-1950s by such eminent and powerful economists as Xue Muqiao and Sun Yefang as well as Chen Yun.[51] Indeed, Mao Zedong had been among the earliest and severest critics of the Stalinist strategy of development, and his criticisms of its bureaucratic, overcentralized, and "lopsided" features foreshadowed many of the critiques made by the reformers of the early post-Mao era. Mao's remedy, as has been noted in Chapter 2, included not only administrative decentralization but also mass mobilization to achieve ever-higher levels of socialization, accompanied by the ideological and spiritual transformation of the people.[52] But in the view of the reformers of the late 1970s, the Maoist alternative to the Stalinist model had only

[51] Chen Yun and Xue Muqiao were not only economic specialists but also high-ranking Party and government figures. In the mid-1950s, Chen was Minister of Commerce and Xue headed the State Statistical Bureau. Sun Yefang was the most theoretically interesting and the most sophisticated Marxist. Although a trenchant critic of the Stalinist model and a proponent of "the law of value," he nonetheless opposed market-oriented solutions.

[52] Although Mao Zedong's proposed remedies differed, his diagnosis of the defects of the Soviet economic model was remarkably similar to that made by post-Maoist reformers. In his April 1956 speech "On the Ten Great Relationships," for example, Mao criticized the Soviet system for its overcentralization of authority, its bureaucratic features, and its "lopsided stress on heavy industry to the neglect of agriculture and light industry." *Selected Works of Mao Tse-tung*, Vol. V, p. 285.

exacerbated the problems, essentially retaining the rigid "command economy" while adding new economic irrationalities to its functioning. The reformers thus undertook a wholesale critique of Maoist policies as well as the whole Soviet model of centralized economic planning.

The Marxian ideological rationale for the economic reform program was set forth by Hu Qiaomu, the president of the newly created Chinese Academy of Social Sciences, in a lengthy speech delivered to the State Council in July 1978,[53] at a time when Deng Xiaoping was approaching his decisive victory at the Third Plenum. Hu Qiaomu drew upon the more deterministic strands in the Marxist tradition to proclaim the existence of "objective economic laws" in a socialist society. These economic laws, he asserted, were analogous to the laws of nature and thus operated independently of human will and consciousness, an orthodox Marxist notion that soon was to become a pervasive feature of official post-Mao Chinese Marxism. It was an assertion reminiscent of Plekhanov's quintessentially deterministic proclamation that the Marxist "swims with the streams of History" and that the forces of historical progress "have nothing to do with human will and consciousness."[54]

Hu Qiaomu argued that it was the duty of political leaders to understand the workings of such objective laws and act according to their dictates. Those dictates included the promotion of an increasingly specialized division of labor and the free operation of "the law of value," which in Marxian definition means that under normal free market conditions a commodity is sold at a price proportional to the socially necessary labor time required to produce it.[55] In accordance with the law of value, then, production should be regulated by the market, or by price and profit mechanisms, rather than by state administrative decisions.[56]

[53] The text of Hu Qiaomu's speech, first published in *People's Daily* in October 1978, appears in English translation in three installments in *Peking Review*. Hu Qiaomu (Hu Ch'iao-mu), "Observe Economic Laws, Speed Up the Four Modernizations," *Peking Review*, November 10, 1978, pp. 7–12; November 17, 1978, pp. 15–23; and November 24, 1978, pp. 13–21.

[54] G. Plekhanov, *Izbrannye filosofskie proizvendeniya* (Moscow, 1956), Vol. 4, p. 86. Quoted in A. Walicki, *The Controversy Over Capitalism* (Oxford: Clarendon Press, 1969), p. 159.

[55] For an exposition of Marx's writings on the law of value, see Ronald Meek, *Studies in the Labour Theory of Value* (London: Lawrence & Wishhart, 1956).

[56] For a discussion and analysis of earlier Chinese debates on the law of value, in the late 1950s and early 1960s, see Riskin, *China's Political Economy*, pp. 165–69.

Objective economic laws also dictated, at least as Hu Qiaomu and other reformers divined their meaning, that authority in economic enterprises should be strengthened in accordance with the "scientific management" methods developed in the advanced capitalist countries. Furthermore, profit-making criteria should govern the operation of enterprises rather than centrally determined production targets. Success was to be measured by profitability, not gross output. Hu sought to stimulate productivity through wider wage differentials, thus appealing to individual material interests. He also proposed a system of legally enforceable contracts between various enterprises, and between the state and enterprises, in both the urban and rural economies. The proposed contracts would partly replace the existing system of central state planning and control. Echoing proposals made by Liu Shaoqi in the early 1960s, Hu called for the reorganization of industry into "specialized companies," or "trusts," which would preside over the productive process from the extraction of raw materials to the manufacture and sale of the finished products, thereby removing Party and state authorities from direct control of daily economic life.

Such measures, Hu argued, would "bring the law of value into play, promote business accounting, raise labor productivity, and [raise] the rate of profit on investment," thereby resulting in greater overall economic efficiency. State control over the economy would be maintained through an expanded state banking system to finance enterprises through loans rather than by direct state investment and control.

Hu Qiaomu was quite candid in advocating the use of capitalist methods. He called not only for the importation of the "advanced science and technology of the developed capitalist countries" but also for the assimilation of "their advanced managerial experience," a proposal far more directly relevant to the social organization of production. And he approvingly quoted Lenin's dictum that "the only socialism we can imagine is one based on all the lessons learnt through large-scale capitalist culture." Despite the invocation of Lenin's authority, to many in attendance at the State Council meeting, Hu's speech must have seemed more like a program for fashioning a capitalist economy than a prescription derived from what the reformers were advertising as "the objective economic laws of socialism."

But Hu Qiaomu and other economic reformers did not envision a capitalist future for China. They had, after all, spent the better part of their lives striving to create a socialist society. Nor did they champion the intrinsic virtues of a market economy—even though, in their reformist zeal, they sometimes tended "to disseminate a naive view of the wonders of the market," as Carl Riskin has observed.[57] Rather, they saw market mechanisms as the means to eventual socialist ends, a way to break down bureaucratic rigidities and speed the development of China's productive forces. A rapid rate of economic growth, assisted by the stimulus of the market, they argued, was necessary for constructing the essential material base for a genuine socialist society.

In this sense, far from being champions of capitalism as such, China's economic reformers can be characterized as orthodox Marxists. Unlike Mao Zedong, who, in most un-Marxian fashion, believed that the more backward the economy the better the prospects for socialism,[58] the post-Mao reformers were firmly tied to the conventional Marxist proposition that socialism presupposes capitalism and its modern industrial accomplishments. But the abortiveness of capitalism in modern Chinese history not only had retarded modern economic development but also had made the "remnants of feudalism," not capitalism, the major obstacle to China's modern development. Thus the primary task was to develop China's productive forces to a high level as rapidly as possible, and to do so by capitalist means if necessary, wiping out persisting feudal influences in the process. Yet if the reformers were willing, indeed eager, to "take the capitalist road," to borrow the old Maoist accusation, they saw that road as one that eventually would arrive at a socialist destination, albeit through a long evolutionary process of economic and social development. On the question of whether the capitalist means they advocated were consistent with the socialist ends they sought, the reformers were perhaps troubled but silent.

---

[57] Carl Riskin, "Market, Maoism, and Economic Reform in China," in Selden and Lippit, *The Transition to Socialism in China*, p. 318.

[58] As Mao had concluded in his 1961 "Reading Notes on the Soviet Union's 'Political Economy,'" *Mao Zedong sixiang wansui* (Taipei, 1969), pp. 333–34. For a discussion of Mao's views on the alleged socialist advantages of backwardness, see Meisner, *Marxism, Maoism, and Utopianism*, Chapters 2 and 3.

ON OBJECTIVE LAWS

In the massive body of theoretical writings produced by China's post-Mao economic reformers, nothing appears more prominently than invocations of "objective economic laws" to support the historical necessity of one or another market reform policy or proposal. The difficulty with the notion that objective laws govern human affairs is obvious. Save for theologians who believe in eternal truths passed down from on high, it is manifestly clear that all "objective laws" of socioeconomic development are the subjective creations of human minds. Such "laws" may represent observed regularities in specific times and places, but they are still mediated by a historically conditioned human consciousness and are ideologically weighted with particular (if usually unacknowledged) political and social interests. Moreover, objective laws, once proclaimed, are then subjectively interpreted by those who believe in their existence; there are, after all, no external objective criteria by which to judge either the validity of the "laws" or the way in which they allegedly operate in the social world. The whole notion of objective laws, in short, is problematic from the outset.

Nonetheless, Marxist literature—from the original writings of Marx and Engels to Kautsky, Plekhanov, Lenin, Stalin, and Mao—is replete with references to objective laws of social and economic development. This deterministic tendency, with considerable assistance from the later works of Engels, was solidified in the orthodox Marxism of the period of the Second International, which tended to convert human beings from the subjects to the objects of History. "The history of mankind," as Karl Kautsky typically put it, "is determined, not by ideas, but by an economic development which progresses irresistibly, *obedient to certain underlying laws*, and not to anyone's wishes or whims."[59] These deterministic strains were inherited by Lenin, who emphasized "the action of universal social laws," especially in his insistence on the inevitability of capitalism in his controversy with the Populists.[60] Stalin also decreed a variety of ob-

[59] Karl Kautsky, *The Class Struggle* (Chicago: Kerr, 1910), p. 119.
[60] See, for example, Lenin, *The Development of Capitalism in Russia*, "The Economic Content of Narodism," and "A Characterisation of Economic Romanticism," in V. I. Lenin, *Collected Works* (Moscow, 1960), Vols. 1–3.

jective economic laws.[61] Even Mao Zedong, when it suited his purposes, invoked objective laws, despite his enormous emphasis on the
crucial historical role of human will and consciousness.

Yet Karl Marx, unlike most of his disciples, refrained from setting
forth universal historical and economic laws that applied to all times
and places. The only general laws that Marx propounded were derived from his study of the workings of modern capitalism. For these
he claimed no universal validity; they were, he made clear, laws or
tendencies applicable only to capitalism as a historically specific
mode of production.

Nonetheless, most post-Mao Chinese Marxist theoreticians have
embraced a variety of "objective" social, historical, and economic
laws and proclaimed them both scientific and universally valid.
Adopting the notion of objective laws in a most unproblematic fashion, they have emphasized the scientific character of Marxism and
have tended to equate the laws of nature with the laws of history.
"The development of society," it is typically said, "is just like the
development of the material world and is determined by objective
rules."[62]

The appeal of the notion of "objective laws" in the post-Mao era
is not difficult to understand. In the intellectual environment of the
early Deng years, when modern science was celebrated as the panacea for China's problems, there was a special attraction to the more
deterministic aspects of Marxist theory that promised to reveal social
laws with scientific accuracy. This was especially appealing to intellectuals who claim a monopoly of the scientific knowledge necessary
to understand the meaning of such laws and their workings. But the
greatest appeal of "objective laws" at the time was that it seemed
useful as an ideological antidote to the Maoist belief that people
armed with the proper will and values can mold social reality in
accordance with their consciousness. The message that was conveyed
by invoking objective laws is that history is governed by more or less

---

[61] Especially in his *Economic Problems of Socialism in the U.S.S.R.* (Moscow, 1952).
[62] *Zhuxue yanjiu* (Philosophic Research), February 1979, JPRS, No. 73710:13. Or as a leading
post-Mao theoretician told a group of visiting foreign scholars in 1980: "The laws of development of social history are objective laws of the processes of natural history." (Discussion at
the Institute of Philosophic Research, Chinese Academy of Social Sciences, Beijing, June 25,
1980.)

immutable patterns of development which cannot be altered by human will and which impose stringent limits on the possibilities for social change. It was therefore charged that the economic difficulties of the Mao era stemmed from Mao Zedong's failure to recognize the restraints imposed by objective economic laws. This, in turn, led to an exaggerated "idealist" emphasis on the factor of human consciousness and to premature socialist-oriented changes in the social relations of production, resulting in economic chaos. As the noted economist Xue Muqiao proclaimed in the early reform period: "Objective economic laws are inviolable and [those] who violate them will be punished." The most flagrant violators of such laws were Lin Biao and the Gang of Four (and, by implication, Mao Zedong), and the Chinese nation which was subjected to their "nonscientific" policies was therefore "punished by the law of objectivity."[63]

What is particularly striking, and of special social significance, in post-Maoist thought and ideology is the tendency to universalize economic laws that Marxists traditionally regarded as historically specific attributes of capitalism. This is especially the case with the much-debated law of value, which Hu Qiaomu had so greatly emphasized in his July 1978 speech.

The law of value, as set forth by Marx, derives mainly from his discussion of the nature of commodities and their modes of exchange and circulation in the first three chapters of Volume I of *Capital*.[64] The law, simply put, rests on the proposition that the value of an article is determined by "the labour-time socially necessary for its production" under "normal [economic] conditions" and "with the average degree of skill and intensity prevalent at the time."[65] All other things being equal, commodities tend to be exchanged in the market in accordance with this socially necessary labor-time criterion. In discussing the law of value, Marx made clear that he was concerned only with "the natural laws of capitalist production," not with economic laws in general. There is no suggestion that the law of value

[63] Xue Muqiao, "Study and Apply the Objective Laws of Socialist Economic Development," *Jingji Yanjiu* (Economic Research), 1979, No. 6.

[64] Marx, *Capital*, Vol. 1, pp. 41–162. The three chapters in *Capital* are themselves only a summary of the lengthier *A Contribution to the Critique of Political Economy*, first published in 1859.

[65] *Capital*, Vol. 1, p. 46.

or any other "laws" expounded in *Capital* are applicable to precapitalist modes of production, much less to any future socialist mode of production, whose "laws" Marx never ventured to speculate about in *Capital* or elsewhere.[66]

These somewhat abstruse theoretical matters came to have important practical implications for the Chinese pursuit of socialism. In order to comprehend those implications, it might be useful to briefly compare Marx with Mao Zedong and with Mao's successors on the question of objective laws in general and the law of value in particular.

Mao Zedong, however much he may have departed from Marxian premises in other areas, was quite faithful to Marx's methodology in treating economic laws as attributes of historically specific modes of production. In his well-known (but officially unpublished) critique of a Soviet economic text, for example, Mao was critical of the ahistorical character of the "objective economic laws" expounded by Stalin: "Quite without foundation the book offers a series of laws, laws which are not discovered and verified through analysis of concrete historical development. Laws cannot be self-explanatory. If one does not work from the concrete processes, the concrete historical development, laws will not be clearly explained."[67]

Mao, unlike some of his more radical disciples, did not regard commodity production as a historically specific feature of capitalism or as likely to foster capitalist relations of production. Rather, like Marx and Lenin, he saw it as compatible with various modes of production. "Commodity production has existed since ancient times," he observed, and he predicted that "even under completely socialized public ownership, commodity exchange will still have to be operative in some areas."[68] But this was not the case with the law of value, which Mao viewed as uniquely capitalist and which he insisted had to be progressively restricted and eventually eliminated. In a socialist

---

[66] This, of course, was in accord with Marx's early critiques of classical political economists who propounded universal and eternal laws of economics transcending specific modes of production.

[67] Mao, "Reading Notes on the Soviet Text 'Political Economy,'" in Mao, *A Critique of Soviet Economics*, p. 108.

[68] Mao, "Critique of Stalin's *Economic Problems of Socialism in the U.S.S.R.*," in *A Critique of Soviet Economics*, pp. 144, 140.

society, he wrote, "the law of value does not have a regulative function. Planning and politics-in-command play that role."[69]

There were good Marxist reasons for this Maoist rejection of the law of value, at least for those who took socialism as their primary goal. For the law of value presupposed the existence of competitive market conditions, inevitably fostered socioeconomic inequalities, and would logically result in the total transformation of labor into a commodity. For Marx, the buying and selling of labor-power was the most crucial distinguishing feature of a capitalist mode of production.[70]

Thus Hu Qiaomu's 1978 speech which emphasized giving "free play" to the law of value had enormous implications for the future direction of Chinese society, probably greater than Hu or his audience realized at the time. Foreshadowed in that speech was not only an expanded role for the market in the Chinese economy but the growth of essentially capitalist relations of production as well.

The law of value (along with related aspects of the ideology of China's reformers) was to become the subject of wide-ranging debates among Chinese Marxist theoreticians following Hu Qiaomu's speech, as it had been a topic of heated controversy in earlier years. In the course of those debates, it was to be quite clearly revealed that proponents of the law of value (and the market-type reforms the "law" ideologically rationalized) were primarily concerned with production, not socialism. They were, in fact, remarkably oblivious to the dilemma of reconciling the means of modern economic development with the still-proclaimed ends of socialism. And insofar as socialism remained a goal at all, it was simply assumed (but never seriously argued) that there was no contradiction between socialism and the law of value.

In the theoretical debates that preceded and accompanied the reforms undertaken in the 1980s by the Deng Xiaoping regime, the old tension between the capitalist and socialist features of the Chinese revolution again reemerged. The capitalist aspect expressed itself in the

[69] Ibid., p. 147.
[70] As is clear to even the most casual reader of *Capital*.

tendency to take a growing number of historically specific characteristics of capitalism and proclaim them expressions of "objective economic laws" applicable to all modes of production. The People's
Republic was still called socialist, of course, and indeed the adjective
"socialist" was automatically applied to all policies and actions,
whatever their actual content or implications. But in the view of most
of the reformers, albeit a view that usually was only implicitly voiced,
China, given its relative economic backwardness, had become socialist prematurely. The real task was to develop the country's productive forces, and to do so by capitalist means and methods—but
under the ideological cover of what were declared to be universally
valid "objective economic laws."

The proposals for restructuring the Chinese economy, and their
ideological rationale, set forth in Hu Qiaomu's 1978 speech provoked
heated debates among Party leaders searching for an alternative to
Hua Guofeng's unworkable Ten Year Plan. Hu's seminal speech was
not published until October 1978, three months after it was delivered.
By then Deng Xiaoping had become convinced of the economic efficacy of some form of market socialism, perhaps impressed by the
results achieved in Sichuan by provincial Party secretary Zhao Ziyang, his future Premier and Party leader. Or, at the very least, Deng
was now willing to permit national experimentation with some of the
measures proposed by the reformers. The issue of market-type reforms, especially those inspired by János Kádár's "New Economic
Mechanism," underway in Hungary for a decade, was one of the more
controversial matters debated at the lengthy Party work conference
in November and December 1978. Deng's political triumphs at the
time meant a partial victory for the economic reformers as well. Thus
at the Third Plenum in December 1978, the Party Central Committee
prescribed combining "market adjustment" with "adjustment by the
plan."

With market solutions now officially sanctioned, there followed a
flood of speeches and writings lauding the efficiency of capitalist
methods and the virtues of "the market." Many of the reform proposals were in fact to be implemented over the next decade, indeed
more rapidly and extensively than anyone could have anticipated at
the end of 1978.

9

THE COUNTRYSIDE:
THE SOCIAL CONSEQUENCES
OF DECOLLECTIVIZATION

THE TENSIONS GENERATED by the revolution's contradictory capitalist and socialist tendencies—one aiming to promote the growth
of bourgeois property and the other aiming to abolish private
property—are nowhere more apparent than in the state's agrarian
policies. Within the four decades following the establishment of the
People's Republic, the Chinese countryside underwent four major
social transformations—all carried out extraordinarily rapidly and all
essentially determined by Party leaders in Beijing.

The Land Reform campaign of 1950–52, which destroyed China's
archaic and parasitic gentry-landlord class and created a system of
individual family peasant proprietorship, was an eminently bourgeois
social revolution. Hardly more than three years following the com-
pletion of land reform, private landownership in the villages was abolished by the collectivization of agricultural production, which was
officially proclaimed to be socialist. The "socialist high tide," as collectivization was called, was almost immediately followed in 1958 by
the amalgamation of the new collective farms into much larger agrarian communes, which were hailed as the agencies for China's leap
to a communist utopia. The commune system remained, although in
changing and attenuated forms, throughout the Mao period.

The political ascendancy of Deng Xiaoping brought the fourth
transformation—the dismantling of the communes and the abandon-

ment of collectivized agriculture in favor of a system of individual family farming. Initially called the "household responsibility system," it was a return, in fact if not in name, to a form of bourgeois property similar in many respects to what had prevailed in 1952 at the conclusion of the Land Reform campaign. Never in human history had the patterns of life and work of more people been subjected to so frequent and so sweeping changes.

The agrarian policies of the Deng Xiaoping regime proceeded cautiously at first, and did not portend the reintroduction of a capitalist economy in the countryside. Following the guidelines of the Third Plenum of December 1978, the new government's initial economic policies were designed to remedy what the reformers had diagnosed as "imbalances" in the Chinese economy. One imbalance, and the first to be rectified, was the disparity between the prices of agricultural and industrial products. In the early years of the People's Republic, prices for agricultural products had been set artificially low, thus perpetuating the "scissors gap" whereby the cities long had exploited the countryside and whereby the Communist state exploited the peasantry to finance urban industrialization after 1949. The gap had been narrowed over the Mao era, but remained wide in the mid-1970s.[1] The "scissors gap" was dramatically narrowed when the Dengist government announced in the spring of 1979 a 20 percent price increase in the state's payment to peasants for compulsory grain deliveries to government stores, a 50 percent premium for above-quota state purchases, and significant price increases for a wide range of other agricultural products.

The Deng government also slashed investment in capital-intensive heavy industry and construction in favor of agriculture and light industry, an effort to correct the imbalances created by the long-standing Maoist overemphasis on the building of a heavy industrial base. Another economic imbalance to undergo "adjustment" was the ratio between accumulation and consumption. The "accumulation rate"—the rate of investment in fixed and working capital withheld

[1] On the statistical and other difficulties involved in calculating the extent of the "scissors gap," see Riskin, *China's Political Economy*, pp. 242–48.

from consumption—which had risen to an intolerable 36 percent in 1978 under Hua Guofeng's Ten Year Plan, was reduced to about 30 percent by 1980, with the aim of eventually lowering it to the approximately 24 percent rate of the First Five Year Plan period.[2]

These policy changes of the early Deng era, while temporarily decreasing funds available to the government for investment in capital-intensive state industries, had the salutary effects of stimulating agricultural production and increasing the ability of both urban and rural inhabitants to purchase consumer goods, which were now produced and imported in ever-larger quantities and sold at lower prices. The marked improvement in living standards and the boom in consumer goods purchasing so evident in the early 1980s resulted directly from the adjustments made in 1979.

Peasants especially benefited from the new policies. In addition to the payment of higher prices for grains and other products, private peasant marketing activities flourished as state restrictions on rural markets and fairs were progressively eased. Moreover, in accordance with decisions taken at the Third Plenum, legal limits on private plots were expanded from 5 to 15 percent of the cultivated land. The government also strongly reaffirmed the autonomy of rural production teams, prohibiting brigade and commune leaders from dictating production targets and work methods and illegally commandeering the team's labor, materials, and capital.

These and other governmental measures reflected the Deng regime's reluctance to further squeeze the peasantry, as surely would eventually have been demanded by the continued pursuit of Hua Guofeng's Ten Year Plan. The abandonment of that plan in favor of the policies pursued under the name of "adjustment" was both economically wise and socially humane.

But the economic reformers in Deng Xiaoping's entourage were not content to ameliorate the conditions under which peasants lived and worked within the existing system of collective farming. Collectivized agriculture itself was seen as the major barrier to greater productivity and economic growth. They thus undertook, implicitly at first, a wide-ranging critique of collective forms of agriculture in

[2] Dong Furen, "Some Problems Concerning the Chinese Economy," *The China Quarterly*, No. 84 (December 1980), pp. 727–36.

general and particularly the methods of the Maoist-inspired "socialist high tide" of 1955–56, which had so swiftly collectivized the Chinese countryside.

As their theoretical point of departure—and as their Marxian ideological rationale—the reformers took the formula that Deng Xiaoping had championed since the Eighth Party Congress of 1956—namely, that the main contradiction in Chinese society was between the country's "advanced socialist system" and its "backward productive forces."[3] From this proposition there naturally followed the injunction that all energies should be turned to expanding China's productive forces so that economic development could be brought into harmony with the stage of social development, freezing further socialist change in the interim. This, of course, stood in contrast to the Maoist view that a continuous process of radical change in the social relations of production (and in popular consciousness) was not only necessary to achieve a socialist society but also the key to stimulating rapid economic growth. "All revolutionary history shows," Mao Zedong had written, "that the full development of new productive forces is not the prerequisite for the transformation of backward production relations."[4] And he added: "First the production relations have to be changed, then and only then the productive forces can be broadly developed. This rule is universal."[5]

Deng Xiaoping's very non-Maoist formula lent itself to a preoccupation with "developing the productive forces" to the exclusion of most other considerations, and also suggested that it might be wise to reverse socialist-oriented changes in work organization that were deemed to have been prematurely undertaken, thereby bringing the "relations of production" into greater correspondence with the undeveloped "forces of production." The notion that there might be some virtue in partially reverting to presocialist (which is to say capitalist) forms of social relationships was not a suggestion that Com-

---

[3] For the original formula, based on the assumption that "a socialist system has already been established in our country" and repeated verbatim in the post-Mao period, see "Resolution of the Eighth National Congress of the Communist Party of China on the Political Report of the Central Committee" (September 27, 1956), *Eighth National Congress of the Communist Party of China*. Vol. 1: *Documents* (Beijing: Foreign Languages Press, 1956), p. 116.

[4] Mao Zedong, "Reading Notes on the Soviet Text 'Political Economy,' " in Mao, *A Critique of Soviet Economics*, p. 51.

[5] Ibid., p. 93.

munist leaders hitherto had made openly. But in the vastly altered political and ideological climate that followed the Third Plenum, it was a suggestion, albeit one made implicitly, that was not beyond the realm of acceptable political discussion. Indeed, it was precisely this implication of the Dengist formula that soon became the main point in the emerging critique of the Maoist collectivization movement of 1955–56.

That critique centered on the charge that Mao Zedong, in accelerating the campaign for agricultural collectivization, had ignored the necessary material prerequisites for socialist relations of production, with the result that collective rural institutions rested on an economic base far too weak to sustain them. It was further charged that the collectivization campaign had involved massive coercion on the part of rural Party cadres, thereby violating the principle of winning the voluntary cooperation of the peasantry for social change. In the process, the Party had thrown the middle peasants, the most efficient agricultural producers, into sullen opposition and had created needless conflicts between poor and middle peasants. It was further argued that the rapidity and apparent success with which collectivization had been accomplished during the "socialist high tide" had yielded a "great leap" psychology among Communist leaders—a belief that great economic and social miracles could be instantly achieved no matter how formidable the material barriers. These chiliastic expectations, in turn, had led directly to the misadventure of the Great Leap Forward campaign—and to the enormous economic and human disasters that followed.

The result, it was concluded, was nearly a quarter of a century of economic stagnation in the countryside. Per capita peasant income, it was repeatedly pointed out, was little more in the late 1970s than it had been in 1955. Thus peasants came to associate collectivized agriculture with continued poverty rather than prosperity, setting back the prospects for socialism in the long run. What was needed to "liberate the productive forces," the reformers argued, was a wholesale transformation of social relations in the rural areas; in effect, the decollectivization of agricultural production and the introduction of the dynamism of a capitalist market—although neither "decollectivization" nor "capitalism" appeared prominently in the reformers' rhetoric.

That the rural economy at the end of the Mao period was in desperate need of major changes is not a proposition that many would dispute. The Maoist commune system did manage to feed a rapidly growing population at better nutritional levels and more equitably than in most low-income countries.[6] Through a system of basic rations and welfare, the communes provided minimal security for the most impoverished and disadvantaged inhabitants in most rural areas. But while collective farming was reasonably successful in some regions, especially in the early-liberated areas of North China, it clearly failed to bring sustained development in a land where most people were living on the bare margins of subsistence to begin with. Overall, after more than two decades of collectivist social experimentation, agricultural production had fallen far below social needs and popular expectations, productivity was declining, and most peasants remained mired in poverty.

Although the problems of Chinese agriculture may well have more to do with ecological and demographic constraints than with forms of social organization, it nonetheless is clear that collectivization and communization (at least as practiced in most areas) had failed to yield viable remedies. Moreover, the burdens under which the peasantry labored were exacerbated during the last two years of the Mao regime by increasingly coercive state policies pursued in the name of socialism. Ideologically zealous and politically opportunistic Party officials, in a Gang of Four-promoted campaign to cut off "capitalist tails" in the mid-1970s, arbitrarily restricted production on tiny family-tilled plots, curtailed individual household handicrafts production, and sometimes prohibited normal peasant marketing and exchange activities. When added to endemic practices of commandism and corruption among rural Party cadres, the campaign compounded the problems of the rural economy and depressed living standards, leaving an increasingly demoralized peasantry in its wake.

Efforts to alleviate the agrarian crisis began before the ascendancy of Deng Xiaoping. In the immediate post-Mao period, under the caretaker regime of Hua Guofeng, the government relaxed its

---

[6] As Carl Riskin concluded on the basis of data from a comprehensive World Bank study: "China's poor emerged from the Maoist era significantly better off than the poor of most other developing countries." Riskin, *China's Political Economy*, p. 250.

more restrictive policies on peasant production and exchange, thereby contributing to a striking 9 percent increase in agricultural output in the year 1978. But Hua Guofeng contemplated no fundamental changes in agricultural policy or rural social organization. Moreover, his Ten Year Plan, with its inordinate emphasis on the development of capital-intensive heavy industry, would have compelled the state, sooner or later, to exact additional—and perhaps unbearable—tribute from the peasantry. It was not until the Third Plenum of December 1978 that the way was opened for more decisive changes in agrarian policy.

The first phase of Deng's rural reform included extensive propaganda campaigns denouncing leftist errors. The most grievous sin was "egalitarianism," presumably a traditional peasant proclivity, and the official press spared no ink in denouncing the economic absurdity of "eating out of the same pot." Private family plots quickly increased to the new legal limit of 15 percent of the cultivated land—and soon beyond—and rural markets proliferated. The Maoist policy of "taking grain as the key link," which aimed at regional self-sufficiency in basic food production, was ridiculed as economically irrational and replaced by policies encouraging crop diversification and specialization. A major ideological drive was launched to discredit the model Maoist Dazhai commune, whose leaders were accused of falsifying production figures, along with a multitude of other political sins and economic errors. Just as the achievements of Dazhai had been inflated during the Mao years, so now its deficiencies were grossly exaggerated. But Dazhai was the established model of the Maoist ideals of self-sufficiency and social equality, ideals incongruous with new visions of a commercialized rural economy, and thus it now had to be converted into a national symbol of economic failure, no matter what the real history of the commune may have been.[7] It was the first of many instances when the new leaders demonstrated that they were

[7] On the actual history of the Dazhai commune in the Mao and post-Mao eras, see William Hinton, *Shenfan* (New York: Random House, 1983); Tang Tsou, Mark Blecher, and Mitchell Meisner, "Organization, Growth and Equality in Xiyang County," *Modern China*, April 1979, pp. 139–86; Tang Tsou et al., "National Agricultural Policy: The Dazhai Model and Local Change in the Post-Mao Era," in Mark Selden and Victor Lippit (eds.), *The Transition to Socialism in China*, pp. 266–99; Tang Tsou et al., "The Responsibility System in Agriculture: Its Implementation in Xiyang and Dazhai," *Modern China*, Vol. 8, No. 1 (January 1982), pp. 41–103.

as adept as their Maoist predecessors in the instant rewriting of history.

DECOLLECTIVIZATION:
THE HOUSEHOLD RESPONSIBILITY SYSTEM

A new and decisive phase in the decollectivization of agricultural production began in September 1980. The Party Central Committee, moving well beyond the guidelines approved at the Third Plenum, established a national agrarian policy on what was termed "the production responsibility system." It was a policy that was soon to result in the dismantling of the rural people's communes and in the reestablishment of the family household as the basic unit of production. This deradicalizing social change proceeded far more swiftly than the leaders in Beijing originally anticipated or perhaps wanted.

Under the responsibility arrangement, as it soon evolved,[8] individual peasant households contracted with the old production team for the private use of a certain portion of the team's land. In return, the household agreed to pay the team a portion of its output—in effect, a rent—to meet state tax and sales quota obligations, supplemented by small sums to support such rapidly waning collective functions the team still performed. Farm tools and draft animals, formerly collectively used by the team, were divided among individual households for private family farming. Although in theory and law both agricultural equipment and land remained collective property, the peasant household, except for its financial obligations to the team, was now free to do what it wished with the land it had contracted and to dispose of the fruits of the land in any manner it chose.

The responsibility or contract system, it was argued, would serve to stimulate peasant initiative and thereby increase productivity. The reformers were motivated less by new social visions of rural life than by the financial needs of the Chinese state. And that, simply put, was an agrarian economy that yielded a surplus sufficient to extract

---

[8] What became known as "the household responsibility system" was briefly preceded in 1979–80 by a scheme of contracting production to small groups (*baohan daozu*) with essential economic functions and control remaining with the larger team.

capital for industrial and agricultural development. Although it was not publicly stated, state leaders were not averse to the re-creation of a smallholding petty capitalist peasantry, with a conservative stake in their family enterprises, who would provide a massive base of political support for the Deng regime.

Ironically, the government's support of individual family farming coincided with its condemnation of the Mao cult and the Gang of Four's "feudal-fascist" reign. Both evils were attributed to lingering "feudal influences" of China's long tradition of a "small producers' economy."[9] No one noticed the incongruity between ideology and policy, at least not in official print.

The contract system in agriculture was not a Chinese innovation among socialist countries. It had been practiced in Hungary since the 1960s under Kádár's "New Economic Mechanism." In China, experiments with various forms of household contracting had been undertaken in 1978 and 1979, especially in Anhui province, where Deng Xiaoping's close political ally Wan Li was First Party Secretary. And in some areas of the countryside, especially in the more impoverished regions, peasants had taken matters into their own hands, dividing up communal property into de facto family farms.

When the responsibility system was officially recommended as national policy by the Deng regime in the early autumn of 1980, its adoption was to be voluntary. Further, the new system was generally to be applicable only in poorer rural regions where collectivized agriculture clearly had failed and in those scattered places where contracting land to individual households already was being successfully practiced. As matters turned out, the household responsibility arrangement soon became virtually mandatory and was rapidly universalized throughout the Chinese countryside.

Within a period of three years, before the end of 1983, 98 percent

---

[9] For typical examples, see Li Yinjua and Lin Chun, "Tentative Discussion on the Struggle Against the Vestiges of Feudalism in China During the Period of Building Socialism," *Lishiyanjiu* (Historical Research), 1979, No. 9; and "On the Ideology of Feudalism," *Wenhuibao*, September 16, 1979, Joint Publication Research Service No. 74526:11. Deng Xiaoping himself placed great emphasis on the pernicious contemporary political influences of "feudal remnants" at the time. See "On the Reform of the System of Party and State Leadership" (August 18, 1980), *Selected Works of Deng Xiaoping*, pp. 302–25. For a discussion of the "feudal remnants" argument in Chinese Communist ideology, see Maurice Meisner, *Marxism, Maoism, and Utopianism* (Madison: University of Wisconsin Press, 1982), Chapter 8.

of peasant households had converted to the new system, engulfing successful as well as struggling collective farms. Decollectivization was accomplished with "one stroke of the knife," presumably the Maoist error committed in the collectivization and communization movements two decades earlier. It is likely that a majority of peasants were eager to embrace a new social arrangement that promised a better material life. But in many rural areas where efficiently managed collectives were relatively prosperous, the contract system was politically imposed on reluctant peasants.[10] As had been the case with the collectivization movements of the 1950s, what was at first proclaimed to be economically and socially voluntary soon became politically obligatory.

The rapid implementation of the household responsibility system has been variously attributed to a penchant for uniformity embedded in Chinese culture and to the persistence of a "great leap" psychology in Chinese Communist thought. But the reasons probably have more to do with immediate practical political considerations. Many Party members, especially local rural cadres, were opposed to the wholesale abandonment of collective farming. But as the Deng Xiaoping faction consolidated its political dominance, and as the purge of Party leftists intensified in the early 1980s, cadres came under relentless pressure to support the rural reform policies. Zealous promotion of the household responsibility system became the cardinal test of political loyalty to the new regime, a way to ward off the danger of being branded leftist. As one astute student of Chinese Communist rural policies and politics observed: "Even though many of them did

[10] The authors of a superb study of a village in Guangdong province observe that while most of the peasants living in what they have renamed "Chen village" welcomed decollectivization, this was by no means universally the case even in Guangdong. They quote an informant from a nearby village on the adoption of the household contracting system: "The peasants were literally forced to do it. In fact, one peasant [in my team] was so angry he refused to draw lots for the parcels of land he was entitled to. . . . Before, people weren't as worried as they are now . . . they felt sure of having something to eat in the end. But now [1982], with all the land distributed, they feel financially insecure. . . . Everyone I know in Xinhui County dislikes the new policies. People practically go around saying, 'Down with Deng Xiaoping.' " Anita Chan, Richard Madsen, and Jonathan Unger, *Chen Village: The Recent History of a Peasant Community in Mao's China* (Berkeley: University of California Press, 1984), p. 270n. On peasant support for, and peasant opposition to, the household responsibility system in Guangdong province, see Jonathan Unger, "The Decollectivization of the Chinese Countryside: A Survey of Twenty-eight Villages," *Pacific Affairs*, Vol. 58, No. 4 (Winter 1985–86), pp. 585–606.

not like the new system, rural officials and cadres ended up imposing it regardless of peasant preference because of the political pressures to which they were subjected."[11] In the village of Dazhai, for example, no local resident would assume the task of implementing the household responsibility system, so the central government dispatched a salaried state cadre to supervise the breakup of the collective into private family farms.[12]

What replaced collective farming was a system Carl Riskin has described as "tenant farming with the production team and state as landlord."[13] While this description aptly captures the essential socioeconomic relationship that emerged in the immediate aftermath of the introduction of the household responsibility system, it doesn't convey the evolution China's rural economy and society experienced during the 1980s. Decollectivization brought about the rapid growth of essentially capitalist relations of production and the emergence of new social class divisions in the rural areas, developments that were partly spontaneous and partly the result of government policy. Although land theoretically remained collective or public property, in fact land became the private property of those who had contracted for its use. To reinforce the perception of ownership, and to satisfy the needs and ambitions of the more entrepreneurial-minded rural inhabitants, new government regulations promulgated in 1983 and 1984 permitted contracted lands to be rented to tenants and wage laborers to be hired. As those who were physically and mentally better endowed, more motivated, and, above all, better connected politically vigorously pursued Deng Xiaoping's dictum that "some must get rich first," the number of rent-paying tenants and hired agricultural laborers grew rapidly. To allay peasant suspicions that the new system might prove temporary, a 1984 government decree permitted land to be contracted for up to fifteen years, a period that was later extended to half a century. By the end of the reform era's first decade, it was generally understood that lands could be freely

---

[11] Thomas P. Bernstein, "Reforming China's Agriculture," unpublished paper presented at the conference "To Reform the Chinese Political Order," Harwich Port, Mass., June 18–23, 1984, p. 46.

[12] William Hinton, "Dazhai Revisited," *Monthly Review*, Vol. 39, No. 10 (March, 1988), p. 38.

[13] Carl Riskin, *China's Political Economy*, p. 288.

passed on to heirs for several generations. It soon became common practice for contracted lands to be rented, bought, sold, and mortgaged as if they were fully alienable private property. There was thus established a de facto capitalist free market in land, if not in formal ownership then in rights to land use, which encouraged much speculation in real estate by China's new monied elites.

New government policies emphasizing the virtues of specialization in production and a greater division of labor gave further impetus to the growth of rural capitalism.[14] Approximately one-fifth of the rural farms were designated "specialized households," where peasants turned from ordinary farming to more lucrative commercial pursuits such as the cultivation of cash crops—tea and silk, the raising of chickens, pigs, and ducks, the herding of livestock, and the operation of fisheries. Other rural inhabitants took advantage of the responsibility system and the rapidly expanding market economy to establish a wide variety of nonagricultural enterprises, such as trading and transportation companies and a variety of repair and retail shops.

Of special economic and social importance was the rapid expansion of industrial enterprises in the countryside, ranging from coal-mining and food-processing operations to factories that produced ever-increasing and varied consumer goods. Rural industry was not an innovation of the Deng era. The industrialization of the countryside long had been a cornerstone of Maoist agrarian policy, having achieved a special prominence during the Great Leap. "Don't crowd into the cities," Mao had urged. "Vigorously develop industry in the countryside and turn peasants into workers on the spot."[15] But in the post-Mao reform era, with the wide economic latitude provided by the responsibility system, rural industrial undertakings burgeoned under the varied auspices of individual entrepreneurs, loosely orga-

[14] For a discussion of the differences between Maoist and post-Mao attitudes toward the division of labor, see Maurice Meisner, "Marx, Mao and Deng on the Division of Labor in History," in Dirlik and Meisner (eds.), pp. 79–116.

[15] Mao Zedong, "Reading Notes on the Soviet Union's 'Political Economy,'" *Mao Zedong sixiang wansui* (Taipei, 1969), p. 389. By the end of the Mao period in 1976 some 20 million peasants had become full- or part-time workers in industries which had been established in the countryside. On the Maoist program of rural industrialization and its results, see Perkins (ed.), *Rural Small-Scale Industry in the People's Republic of China*; and Sigurdson, *Rural Industrialization in China*.

nized collectives, stock companies, and village and township governments. By the late 1980s, rural industry had come to occupy a crucial place in the national economy, employing some 90 million people (almost 25 percent of the rural workforce) and accounting for more than half of the rural domestic product and more than a quarter of China's total gross industrial output.[16] Output and employment were to grow at an even more rapid pace in the 1990s, as rural industry recorded astonishing output gains of more than 30 percent per annum.

What is most distinctively capitalist about the reformed rural economy is not the contracting of land to households but rather the increasing prevalence of wage labor. With the rapid growth of commodity production in the countryside, many rural laborers have been transformed into commodities—people who chose to or were forced to sell their labor to those who were now in a position to exploit that labor for profit. When the responsibility system was initially introduced, government policies (still inhibited by lingering socialist norms) stringently limited the number of wage laborers that households or private entrepreneurs could employ. But the limits were rapidly raised, or simply ignored, and at the Thirteenth Congress of the Chinese Communist Party in 1987, all limits on the hiring of wage labor were removed. The official decision simply ratified the actual economic practice that naturally followed in the wake of decollectivization. Over the half decade preceding the Thirteenth Party Congress, tens of millions of peasants had hired themselves out as agricultural wage laborers on the expanding farms of the specialized households, and some 68 million additional peasants had left farming to work in factories and in other nonagricultural enterprises. Many millions more followed in the early 1990s. Unlike regular workers in state-owned factories, this rapidly expanding class of wage laborers enjoyed neither welfare benefits nor job security. They were hired and fired in accordance with the needs of their varied employers.

Not all the peasants who left the land found regular employment of any sort. By 1989 it was estimated that there were at least

[16] Robert Delfs, "The Perils of Progress," *Far Eastern Economic Review*, March 2, 1989, p. 48.

50 million *youmin*, former peasants who roamed the country, seeking temporary employment in the cities.[17] And in 1993 the government acknowledged that more than 100 million of China's remaining 379 million rural laborers were "surplus" and that the number of redundant rural workers would rise to 200 million by the end of the century.[18]

The rapid growth of wage labor, both in agriculture and in rural industries, is one of the more prominent features of an increasingly commercialized countryside, and it is glaringly incongruous with the government's continued insistence that the rural economy remains essentially "socialist." Socialism, according to Beijing ideologists, rests on two loosely interpreted principles: first, state or collective ownership of the major means of production; and second, remuneration in accordance with the principle of "payment according to work." But decollectivization turned land and most other productive resources into private property; their official status as collective property was retained only in a formal legal sense. The growth of wage labor, especially after virtually all restrictions on the buying and selling of labor-power were removed, made a mockery of the still officially proclaimed principle of "payment according to work." The old (and now abandoned) collectivist "work-point" system, however imperfect and however much abused, could in theory be reconciled with this socialist principle. But what really counted in the reformed rural economy, what determined who "got rich" and who did not, was not the amount of labor people contributed to social production but rather the ownership (or control) of land, capital, and machinery used to exploit labor.

What finally culminated and symbolized the abandonment of collectivist patterns of work—and socialist ideals—in the countryside was the demise of the rural people's communes. The communes had been conceived as autonomous communities where economic, political, and social life would be integrated in a democratic and egalitarian rural setting. They were to combine industrial with agricultural work, education with productive labor, and thereby narrow "the three

[17] The numbers of those who make up this "floating population" of migrant workers fluctuate greatly, depending on economic conditions. Estimates in recent years have ranged from 20 million to 100 million or more.
[18] *People's Daily*, August 4, 1993.

great differences"—between town and countryside, worker and peasant, and mental and manual labor.

In reality, life on the communes bore little resemblance to these democratic and socialist ideals. But the communes did stand as symbolic reminders of Maoist socialist goals. In the post-Mao reform era, however, as the rural economy operated in an increasingly commercialized and capitalist fashion, there was no longer any place for either the institution or the ideal. In accordance with the new state constitution adopted in December 1982, and the new policy which ostensibly demanded the separation of local economic and governmental authority, the political and administrative powers of the communes were transferred to revived *xiang* (township) and village governments, organs under the jurisdiction of the central state administration. With the emasculation of the commune's political authority, there followed the devolution of their economic and social welfare functions into private hands. The communes, now hollow shells, were soon abolished entirely.

The abolition of the communes was officially hailed as a way to reduce central state control over the countryside and its inhabitants, a claim uncritically accepted by most foreign observers, who are ideologically inclined to equate a market economy with individual freedom. The celebration was premature. As Vivienne Shue, an unusually astute scholar of rural China, has demonstrated, commune cadres tended to identify with local peasants and often defended localities against state demands, sometimes by simply failing to carry out government policies.[19] With that buffer removed, rural inhabitants are now potentially more vulnerable to the power of an increasingly impersonal state bureaucracy. As Shue has warned: "We should remain skeptical of the anti-statist banner under which the Deng group is pressing its reforms of the system of rural local governance. Clearly, the real targets of the Deng coalition's modernizing reforms are not central authority or bureaucratic control, but the unitary political, economic, and social authority of the local cadre elite and the relative self-containment of the economic units over which they presided.

---

[19] For an exceptionally perceptive analysis of the relationship between the state and local rural communities in contemporary China, discussed in broad historical perspective, see Vivienne Shue, *The Reach of the State* (Stanford: Stanford University Press, 1988), Chapter 3.

. . . Without the supporting network of an organized community of peasants and cadres, it will almost certainly be harder to defy real pressure from above, when it comes."[20] Much as Shue predicted, in the early 1990s rapacious local officials began to subject peasants to a plethora of legal and extralegal taxes and fees on every conceivable possession and transaction.[21]

While the relationship between state and society in the newly commercialized countryside is still very much in flux, the abolition of the communes reinforced the new values that the Deng regime so strenuously labored to promote. At the time of the dismantling of the communes in the early 1980s, Shue predicted that decommunization "will change the normative framework for decision-making from the ideals of citizenship and communal welfare to the ideals of efficiency, optimal profitability, and corporation development."[22] These new norms have in fact become dominant and they have proved favorable to the development of capitalism in the Chinese countryside in the years since the demise of the once-celebrated rural people's communes.

ECONOMIC RESULTS OF RURAL REFORM

There were remarkable gains in agricultural production and productivity during the first half decade of the Deng era, perhaps the most economically successful period in the history of Chinese agriculture. Between 1978 and 1984, the gross value of output in the countryside, including that of rural industries, grew at an average annual rate of 9 percent, compared with an approximately 4 percent annual growth rate during the final decade of the Mao era. The highest growth rates were achieved in the rural industrial sector, where the accelerating

[20] Ibid., pp. 120–21. Perhaps foreshadowing the pressure that was to come were measures to expand the Party/state security apparatus in the rural areas which accompanied the dismantling of the communes. Wang Xiaotang, "Why the CCP Wants to Set Up Public Security Stations All Over the Countryside," *Zhonggong Yanjiu* (CCP Research), 1982, No. 7, pp. 46–51. Cited in Vivienne Shue, "The Fate of the Communes," *Modern China*, Vol. 10, No. 3 (July 1984), p. 276.
[21] For an informative report on the problem, see Sheryl WuDunn, "China Is Sowing Discontent with 'Taxes' on the Peasants," *The New York Times*, May 19, 1993, pp. A1, A4.
[22] Shue, "The Fate of the Communes," p. 277.

rate of output increased by an average of 21 percent per annum. But basic food production also grew impressively, at an average annual rate of 6.7 percent,[23] although the figure is somewhat artificially inflated due to the fact that many peasants reduced production of relatively low-priced grains in favor of higher-priced cash crops.[24] While the paucity of data makes calculations difficult, it is generally estimated that per capita rural income doubled over the 1978–84 period and that labor productivity (which had been declining in the late Mao era) increased at a per annum rate of about 5 percent.[25]

The fruits of this economic progress soon became visible in most villages, and the new rural prosperity (however unevenly distributed) has been glowingly described by a variety of foreign observers as well as celebrated by the Chinese government as proof of the success of its decollectivization policies. Particularly visible to observers has been a boom in construction, as many well-to-do peasants, making use of the vast reservoir of surplus labor in the countryside, built new (and sometimes rather elaborate) private houses on land they theoretically held under lease or contract. Markets flourished and new business ventures proliferated, providing a vast array of small consumer goods and services for peasants who now enjoyed sharply higher incomes. It soon became commonplace for peasants to own not only bicycles, watches, and radios but also sewing machines and television sets. Rising peasant incomes also permitted a considerable increase in spending for traditional-style marriages, funerals, and festivals—much to the disappointment of the reformers, who optimistically had assumed that greater incomes would yield greater investment in modern agricultural development. The more fortunate among those who took advantage of the government's new maxim that "some must get rich first" began to visit private doctors and dentists and pay tuition fees to send their children to newly established private schools. In the mid-1980s, owning a telephone, it was observed, was "one of the most prestigious hallmarks of China's new rural bourgeoisie."[26]

---

[23] Riskin, *China's Political Economy*, Table 12.1, p. 291.
[24] Especially vegetables, cotton, tobacco, and peanuts.
[25] On the difficulties in determining increases in income and productivity, see Riskin, *China's Political Economy*, pp. 292–96.
[26] Orville Schell, *To Get Rich Is Glorious* (New York: Pantheon, 1985), p. 61.

The rapid increase in agricultural production and productivity in the early 1980s, and the relative rural prosperity that resulted, cannot solely, or even primarily, be attributed to the household responsibility system, as the reformers claim. To no small degree, the agrarian successes of the Deng era capitalized on the economic foundations laid during the Mao era. As Carl Riskin has observed: "It is very likely that part of the spurt in output was due to incentives catching up with technological and infrastructural improvements of the collective era which were not fully exploited then."[27] Certainly the higher yields obtained on individual family farms during the early Deng era would not have been possible had it not been for the vast irrigation and flood-control projects—dams, irrigation works, and river dikes—constructed by collectivized peasants in the 1950s and 1960s.

Also usually ignored in official accounts (and by most foreign observers) is that an upsurge in agricultural production took place prior to the ascendancy of Deng Xiaoping and the reformers, resulting from general relaxation of state pressure and demands on the peasantry under the Hua Guofeng government in 1977–78. As Riskin has pointed out: "The beginning of the spurt in agricultural growth preceded both the price changes and the more radical decollectivization measures. Total agricultural output surged forward by 8.9 per cent in 1978 and 8.6 per cent in 1979, whereas in early 1980 only about 1 per cent of farm households had adopted any form of HRS [household responsibility system]."[28]

Yet the change in the government's pricing policies—namely, the 20 percent increase in state payments for compulsory grain deliveries and the 50 percent premium for above-quota purchases that took effect with the autumn 1979 harvest—probably was the most important overall factor in the new rural prosperity. The new policies contributed to gains in production for over half a decade and to rising peasant income levels through much of the 1980s. State procurement price increases were, of course, unrelated to decollectivization—and, indeed, were put into effect well over a year before the household contract system was officially sanctioned in late 1980.

---

[27] Riskin, *China's Political Economy*, p. 296.
[28] Ibid., pp. 297–98.

The timely availability of new technological and scientific improvements also contributed to the rise in agricultural output. Advances such as larger quantities of better-quality fertilizers and new types of seed, especially hybrid rice, were, for the most part, the fruits of several decades of effort under the Mao regime, which made their largely fortuitous appearance in the late 1970s. Unusually favorable weather conditions in most parts of the country over the years 1977–84 must also be taken into account.

Nonetheless, the household responsibility system must be given partial credit for increasing production and productivity. This was especially true in poorer villages and in regions where collective farming had failed. One striking example was reported by William Hinton, an early and farsighted critic of Deng Xiaoping's agrarian policies. In Fengyang County in Anhui province, a particularly impoverished area where the new system was experimentally introduced several years earlier than in most of the countryside, total grain production under the prevailing system of collective farming was 180,000 tons in 1977. In the drought year of 1978, the yield fell to 147,500 tons. With the introduction of group contracting in 1979, output rose to 220,000 tons. In 1980, when family contracting was implemented, 251,000 tons were produced and output increased dramatically to 359,000 tons in 1982. Average per capita income in Fengyang County doubled over the four-year period 1979–82. While many factors were responsible for these gains, Hinton, certainly no celebrant of individual family farming, concluded that, at least in the case of impoverished Fengyang County, the family contract system "unleashed the energy and enthusiasm of the peasants and pushed production ahead in striking fashion."[29]

The high rate of growth in agricultural production in the early 1980s, which won almost universal acclaim for Deng Xiaoping and the reformers, proved unsustainable. The first signs of trouble appeared in 1985, when there was a sharp and unanticipated decline in grain production. A record grain harvest of 407 million metric tons had

---

[29] William Hinton, "A Trip to Fengyang County: Investigating China's New Family Contract System," *Monthly Review*, Vol. 35, No. 6 (November 1983), pp. 6, 9.

been recorded in 1984, and China briefly became a net exporter of grain. In 1985, however, grain output fell precipitously to 379 million tons, the largest annual decline since the crisis years of the Great Leap. Strenuous governmental efforts managed to slowly raise production to 405 million tons in 1987, by which time China had resumed its customary role as a net grain importer. But in 1988 the grain harvest again declined, to 394 million tons, the fourth consecutive year of harvests considerably below expectations and needs. Instability in, and uncertainty over, grain production was to continue well into the 1990s.

In China, where the supply and the price of grain are quite literally matters of life and death, grain production is not only economically crucial but also of enormous psychological and political significance. The decline and stagnation in grain output in 1985 and after was alarming, evoking memories and fears of famine. As will be seen in the chapters that follow, the grain crisis both reflected and contributed to the larger crisis into which the national economy was sinking in the latter years of the decade.

The immediate cause of the decline in grain production in the mid-1980s was the marketization of the rural economy. This had made it financially advantageous for many farmers to abandon the growing of grain, most of which had to be sold to the government at state-determined prices, in favor of a variety of cash crops that could be sold at relatively high market prices. Peasants, now free to maximize profits as capitalist-type entrepreneurs, and indeed officially encouraged to do so, discovered that growing grain was a relatively unprofitable enterprise, especially as prices for chemical fertilizers and insecticides soared. Many thus turned to immediately profitable activities. This, in turn, led to a cyclical process of gluts and shortages in agricultural products and wild fluctuations in prices, an increasingly chaotic situation that contributed to inflation in the cities and the need to reimpose rationing on certain basic food products.

Faltering grain production coupled with population growth and a decline in arable land under cultivation threatened to undo the dietary advances of the early years of the reform period. The *Far Eastern Economic Review* noted in 1989 that "China will have great difficulty even maintaining its current per capita level of grain consumption of 400 kg through the end of the century" and that "the anticipated improvement in diet that goes hand-in-hand with overall economic development may have to be forestalled indefinitely unless grain imports are increased significantly."[30] Indeed, it was officially acknowledged in early 1989 that annual per capita grain consumption was 34 kilograms less than it had been four years earlier.[31]

By the autumn of 1988, many rural areas were experiencing acute economic problems, and Minister of Agriculture He Kang admitted that "eighty million rural dwellers . . . are threatened by food short-ages this winter, with 20 million people facing serious difficulties in feeding themselves."[32] It was reported that in some villages peasants had to sell grain intended for their own consumption to meet state purchase quotas, something unknown since the famine years that followed the collapse of the Great Leap in the early 1960s.[33] Guang-dong residents, observers noted, were asking visiting relatives from Hong Kong to bring sacks of rice in lieu of such customary gifts as brandy and cigarettes.[34] Grain-short peasants were increasingly re-luctant to fulfill state purchase quotas, especially after the autumn harvest of 1988, when in many areas of the countryside the deficit-ridden government attempted to pay peasants for requisitioned grain with *bai tiao* (white slips of paper), in effect IOUs which promised future payments to distrustful farmers. As state officials increasingly resorted to coercive methods to enforce grain purchase contracts, already strained relations between peasants and local cadres were aggravated, and growing numbers of incidents officially referred to as "taking revenge upon village cadres by the masses" were reported. With deteriorating conditions in the rural areas, more and more peas-ants left the land entirely, or were forced off it by the vicissitudes of the market, swelling the ranks of the urban lumpen proletariat. By 1989, as noted, at least 50 million *youmin* (wandering people), mostly former peasants, were roaming from city to city seeking employment. Some were to participate in the more violent incidents in the great rebellion against the Deng regime in the spring of 1989—and several

[30] *Far Eastern Economic Review*, March 2, 1989, p. 51.
[31] *China Daily*, March 29, 1989.
[32] New China News Agency report, cited in Jonathan Mirsky, "Starvation Threatens 20 Million in China," *The Independent* (London), November 5, 1988.
[33] *Far Eastern Economic Review*, March 2, 1989, p. 47.
[34] Ibid., p. 51.

among them were the first to be executed in the repression that followed. By 1989, and indeed for some years before, government officials and reform ideologists were no longer ridiculing the old Maoist maxim to "take grain as the key link."

Since 1985, agricultural output has tended to stagnate, barely keeping pace with population growth. What kept the rural economy relatively (if unevenly) prosperous and provided an increasing portion of the income for rural inhabitants was the astonishingly rapid development of local industrial enterprises, variously operated by villages, townships, cooperatives, and private entrepreneurs. Between 1984 and 1987, the output of rural industries grew by an average per annum rate of 37.7 percent; it accounted for more than half of the value of production in the countryside by 1987, and employed more than 85 million people, nearly a quarter of the rural labor force.

The rural industrial boom was temporarily interrupted by the severe austerity measures the government imposed in late 1988, for reasons that will be examined in Chapter 10. Rural industries were especially hard hit by the reimposition of centralized controls over bank credit and the allocation of scarce raw materials. Many local enterprises were forced to close and others could operate only at a fraction of their capacity, throwing tens of millions of workers into the ranks of the rural unemployed. The difficulties in the countryside were compounded by drastic reductions in state spending on construction projects in the cities (cut 30 percent in 1989 and 40 percent in 1990), which employed millions of migrant rural laborers on a temporary contract basis. "What farmers really need are stable, reasonable prices. What they will get this year is the return of their unemployed relatives from the city, in need of work and looking to be fed," one analyst observed in 1989.[35]

In 1991, as government austerity policies were eased and then reversed, rural industrial enterprises boomed once again, achieving growth rates averaging more than 30 percent per annum in the new decade. Township and village industries have in fact sustained the rural economy and rural household income in recent years. Since 1987, income from agriculture has been stagnant at best. Farmers

[35] Robert Delfs, "The Perils of Progress," *Far Eastern Economic Review*, March 2, 1989, p. 48.

have suffered from high taxes and illegal fees levied by corrupt officials, they have paid increasingly high prices for fertilizers and other inputs while receiving relatively low prices for their own products, and they have experienced widening social and regional inequalities. The income gap between town and countryside, which was significantly narrowed during the early years of the Deng regime, is now somewhat greater than it was at the beginning of the reform era.

Yet despite the mounting economic problems and inequities of the late 1980s, many of which persisted into the new decade, the Deng era as a whole must be credited with yielding remarkable gains in rural production, productivity, and above all living standards. The years 1979–86 saw the greatest successes: the gross value output (including rural industries) of the rural economy doubled; agricultural production increased at an average annual rate of 6.6 percent; and the output of local industry increased fivefold, growing at an average per annum rate of 29 percent.[36] Most significantly, average per capita income in the countryside more than doubled within a decade, rising from approximately 180 yuan in 1978 to 463 yuan in 1987.[37] Although the achievements since 1987 are far less impressive, save for rural industry, on the whole the agrarian economic record of the Deng era is, comparatively, a most impressive one. There can be little doubt that the living standards of the great majority of the rural population have risen significantly.

Yet the gains in the rural economy did not come about without creating a host of grave social problems and without erecting new barriers for future progress, especially progress toward the achievement of the socialist goals which the leaders of post-Mao China still professed to seek.

THE SOCIAL CONSEQUENCES OF DECOLLECTIVIZATION

A characteristic feature of the rural reform program has been a proclivity to sacrifice long-term social goals to achieve immediate eco-

[36] Harry Harding, *China's Second Revolution* (Washington, D.C.: Brookings Institution, 1987), Table 5.1, p. 106.
[37] State Statistical Bureau figures, cited in *Far Eastern Economic Review*, October 5, 1989, p. 56.

nomic successes. Nowhere is this tendency more apparent than in the effects of the household responsibility system on China's chronic and long-term population problem.

Among the more formidable barriers to the modern economic development of the impoverished countries of the Third World are large and rapidly increasing populations, a burden which the early industrializing countries did not have to bear. The problem was (and remains) particularly acute in China, a land inhabited by 22 percent of the world's population but possessing only 6 percent of the world's arable land. It is a problem deeply rooted in China's millennial history; by the year 1800, China's population already had reached 300 million. In 1949, the Chinese population numbered 540 million and that figure nearly doubled over the quarter century of Maoist rule. The result was a population of 940 million in 1976, partly due to improvements in diet and medical care, partly due to the failure of the Mao regime to implement adequate birth-control policies. Indeed, there was a marked Maoist antipathy to population control, which found its most extreme expression on the eve of the Great Leap Forward campaign when Mao proclaimed that "the more people there are the greater the ferment of ideas, the greater the enthusiasm and the energy."[38] As a consequence, the annual rate of population increase soared to 2.8 percent in the 1960s, greatly exacerbating chronically grave problems of unemployment and underemployment in both town and countryside. It was not until the early 1970s that stringent birth-control policies were imposed and the rate of population increase slowed.[39]

By 1980 the population of China was approaching 1 billion. It is much to the credit of the Deng Xiaoping regime that the new leadership recognized the gravity of the problem and proved willing to adopt unpopular policies. Alarmed by the calculations of demographers which predicted that even with an average of two children per family the population would exceed 1.5 billion well before the middle of the next century, the Deng government promulgated a policy lim-

---

[38] *Hongqi* (Red Flag), June 1, 1958, p. 3.

[39] Although the birth rate was reduced significantly in the 1970s, dropping from 33.6 per 1,000 population in 1970 to 20.0 in 1976, the population increased substantially over the last decade of the Mao era (1966–76), growing at an average annual rate of 2.4 percent. Riskin, *China's Political Economy*, pp. 184–85 and Table 12.7, p. 303.

iting families to one child, with harsh penalties for violators. The goal was to stabilize the population at 1.2 billion by the end of the century and reduce it thereafter. It was a draconian edict, especially in the still tradition-bound rural areas, but a necessary prerequisite for modernization—and perhaps for national survival.

Yet at the very time the government decreed the one-child limit, it was also promoting (and indeed, in some cases, imposing) the household responsibility system, a policy in glaring contradiction to the population-control measures. For with the return to individual family farming, peasants quite naturally found it desirable to have more rather than fewer children. Under the new responsibility system, the amount of land that could be contracted was partially determined by family size. Moreover, it was assumed by most peasants that the labor-power of their children, especially male children, would be needed to effectively cultivate the newly contracted lands. Furthermore, with the decline of collective welfare services, children (especially male children) were seen as necessary to provide some measure of security for parents in their old age. Such were some of the traditional-type calculations made by peasants that came with the restoration of the individual family farm as the main unit of production and life. The result was a marked rise in the rural birth rate in the early 1980s, after a decade of steady declines. For this the household responsibility system was largely responsible.

The state responded to the increase in births with harsher measures to enforce the norm of the one-child family, including confiscation of contracted lands and forced sterilizations and abortions (sometimes as late as the third trimester) in cases where social persuasion and political threats failed. Peasants, in turn, responded with various stratagems to circumvent official birth-control regulations, sometimes, in extremity, resorting to female infanticide and the abandonment of female infants. The tragic irony of this grim battle is that both the Communist state and the peasantry acted in accordance with the dictates of "economic rationality." From the perspective of state leaders, stringent population control is a national economic necessity. But it is not a peasant necessity, at least not in the short run under a system of individual family farming.

The rural population dilemma, and all the human sorrow it entails, is one of the more obvious contradictions between individual and collective interests, and between short- and long-term goals, wrought by China's reformers. They have belatedly discovered, even if they do not fully appreciate, the truth that what is economically rational is not necessarily socially rational, and that the responsibility system has not always lent itself to socially responsible behavior either on the part of the state or the population.

In 1985 the government retreated a bit, modifying the strict one-child rule and mitigating the more drastic measures employed to enforce it.[40] As a result, the birth rate again began to rise in the late 1980s, making it most unlikely that population will stabilize by the year 2000.[41]

Other long-term and general interests have been ill served by reforms that encourage rural dwellers to pursue their immediate private and individualistic interests. As communes, brigades, and production teams atrophied and eventually all but disappeared, collective farm machines and equipment were distributed, or, more precisely, sold as private property. In many areas, this privatization of formerly collective property was performed in a most inequitable fashion, providing those with political power or influence special opportunities for the private accumulation of wealth. William Hinton was one among few foreign observers of this little-known aspect of decollectivization, which he characterized as a "scandalous rip-off that dominated the liquidation of collective property and helped create those so-called 'specialized families' with the requisite 'money, strength and ability' to get rich first." As Hinton described the process: "When the time came to distribute collective assets, people with influence and connections—cadres, their relatives, friends, and cronies—were able to buy, at massive discounts, the tractors, trucks, wells, pumps, processing equipment, and other productive property that the collectives had accumulated over decades through the hard

---

[40] Official spokespersons observed that the slogan "one child for each couple" was not intended to be universally and mechanically applied, and that different measures were to be applied to urban and rural areas. In practice, this meant that couples living in rural areas were generally permitted two children. Statement by Wan Li, *Xinhua*, January 1986, "Quarterly Chronicle and Documentation," *The China Quarterly*, No. 106 (April–June 1986), p. 390. Also *Beijing Review*, March 10, 1986, p. 6.

[41] China's population reached 1.2 billion in early 1995. On the basis of current trends and policies, both Chinese and foreign demographers estimate that the country's population will grow to 1.3 billion by the year 2000 and will exceed 2 billion by 2030.

labor of all members. Not only did the buyers manage to set low prices for these capital assets (often one-third or less of their true value), but they often bought them with easy credit from state banks and then, in the end, often failed to pay what they had promised. . . . The scale of these transactions and the depth of the injury done to the average coop member boggles the mind."[42]

The vast agricultural infrastructure collectively built during the Mao period also suffered from decollectivization. The access roads to fields, and especially the reservoirs, dams, dikes, and terraces constructed to provide irrigation and control floods, were an impressive achievement by any standard of judgment. But in the post-Mao years, not only has little new construction of this sort taken place but much of what existed has been neglected and has consequently deteriorated. The reforms removed much of the organizational structure and the motivation to build and maintain large-scale public projects. The communes and production brigades which in years past constructed and sustained such projects as irrigation facilities no longer exist. In a new social and ideological environment where each individual family is encouraged to pursue its own pecuniary interests, there is little willingness to participate in cooperative endeavors that do not yield immediate financial gain. The central government, which over the 1980s sharply reduced investment in the agrarian sector,[43] has provided neither the organization nor the finances to enable local governmental authorities to effectively take up the slack left by the disappearance of collective institutions. The result was a decline in the irrigated area throughout the 1980s,[44] approximately 1 percent per annum in the land under cultivation in a country where arable

[42] William H. Hinton, "A Response to Hugh Deane," *Monthly Review*, Vol. 40, No. 10 (March 1989), pp. 20–21. For other examples of how cadres acquired private property during decollectivization, see Chan, Madsen, and Unger, *Chen Village*, pp. 265–84.

[43] The proportion of the state capital construction budget that went to agriculture was a paltry 10 percent during the last decade of the Mao era. This figure, under a reduced budget, fell to 6 percent in the early 1980s and to 4 percent in the late 1980s. Bruce Stone, "The Basis for Chinese Agricultural Growth in the 1980s and 1990s: A Comment on Document No. 1, 1984," *The China Quarterly*, No. 101 (March 1985), pp. 119–20; Hinton, "A Response to Hugh Deane," p. 15; Gordon White, *Riding the Tiger: The Politics of Economic Reform in Post-Mao China* (Stanford: Stanford University Press, 1993), p. 91.

[44] Carl Riskin, *China's Political Economy*, p. 310. The sown acreage of agricultural crops fell from 150.1 million hectares in 1978 to 144.2 million in 1984. Ibid., p. 300. Some observers have estimated that arable land has declined by as much as a third since 1957, and at an accelerating pace in the reform period.

land has always been at a premium, portending dire consequences for the future of Chinese agriculture.

Decollectivization has resulted in other casualties, including the end of the "five guarantees" of food, shelter, clothing, fuel, and burial expenses once provided (albeit often minimally) by communes and brigades. With the demise of these quasi-socialist institutions in favor of family farming, already inadequate collective welfare funds to care for the elderly, the handicapped, and the indigent were depleted or disappeared entirely. As in traditional times, the individual family has again been forced to assume the task of social welfare with little assistance from the community or the state. Many households are ill equipped to take on this new burden. The central government acknowledges the problem but has been slow to organize a new welfare system to take the place of the one that has disintegrated. Rather, the government has been content to sponsor academic symposia on "social relief in the rural areas," exhort the populace to undertake philanthropic efforts, and designate "five-guarantee households," who are to receive charitable assistance from their more prosperous neighbors.[45]

Rural education and health care facilities have also suffered. School enrollments dropped as peasant families kept children at home to assist in farm work, while, simultaneously, collective financing of local schools declined along with the dismantling of the communes and production brigades, forcing many teachers not paid by the state to abandon teaching in favor of tilling the land or seeking other work. Brigade medical clinics in many areas have been closed due to the depletion of collective funds. Some of these insolvent facilities, in turn, have been "contracted" to private doctors, dentists, and paramedics who—in accordance with the social and ideological tenor of the times—charge fees for their services and operate on a profit-making basis. Similarly, some formerly collectively supported teachers have opened private schools which charge tuition and claim to offer better-quality educations than rural public schools. These

---

[45] For a discussion of the inadequacy of welfare provisions for poor households and indigent peasants, see Ch'en Ting-chung, "Agriculture in Mainland China: Reforms and Problems," *Issues and Studies*, June 1984, pp. 58–60. On growing inequality in education, health care, and welfare over the reform period, see Deborah Davis's thoughtful and informative article "Chinese Social Welfare: Policies and Outcomes," *The China Quarterly*, No. 119 (September 1989), pp. 577–97.

new educational and medical facilities are, of course, available mainly to those families who make up China's new rural bourgeoisie.

Decollectivization has further led to adverse long-term effects on the ecology of the countryside as peasants have constructed houses on their newly contracted fields, thereby reducing the land available for tilling. To build houses and to fashion furniture to fill them, trees have been indiscriminately felled, thus compounding chronic problems of deforestation and soil erosion. The family contracting system, with all its inherent ambiguities about to whom the land really belongs, initially fostered the "predatory use of the land by its new occupiers, who, afraid it would be taken away again, treated it as a short-run asset and failed to replace soil nutrients or to invest in improvements."[46] Encouraged by the government to "get rich first," peasants have been more than ever disposed to do whatever is most expedient to increase their incomes in the short term. Thus, as Hinton observed: "Herders have stepped up overgrazing in the grasslands, while farmers have stepped up plowing there; foresters and timber-hungry peasants have recklessly cut timber wherever they can find it. Everywhere, and particularly in the loess highlands of North Shaanxi, the mountainous regions of western Szechuan, and the mountains of North Hubei . . . peasants are opening up mountain slopes that never should be cultivated and doing it on a massive scale. It is doubtful if in history there has ever been such a massive, wholesale attack on the environment as is occurring in China now."[47]

It is not that the peasantry is out to destroy the natural world, or that state leaders sanction their doing so. It is the return to small-scale household farming that brings about these unintended and painful consequences. Even when the state tries to protect the environment, their efforts are often undermined by the imperatives of privatized agricultural production in a country where arable land is in such short supply. Hinton has described a striking example of this contradiction:

> With money from the World Bank, China has recently carried through several large drainage and desalination projects along the lower reaches of the Yellow River. I visited one of these

[46] Riskin, *China's Political Economy*, p. 309.
[47] William H. Hinton, "A Response to Hugh Deane," *Monthly Review*, Vol. 40, No. 10 (March, 1989), p. 27.

less than two years after it was completed. Shortsighted peasants had already filled in many of the tertiary ditches in order
to add a few feet to their pitiful small plots. *By atomizing land-
holding and making each family responsible for its own profits
and losses, the regime has virtually guaranteed such destruction.*
Neither regulations nor exhortations will stop it. There will
never be enough police to post one on every ditch.[48]

The long-cherished long-range goal of mechanizing China's agriculture has been another casualty of the reforms. The old problem
of the fragmentation of farming units, which collectivization was
partly designed to solve and was largely successful in accomplishing,
has reappeared with the return to individual family farming. This is
especially the case where decollectivization was carried out by parceling out proportional lands of different quality to individual households under the contract system. The result has been that in many
areas hundreds of separate, tiny plots are privately farmed by several
dozen peasant households who once made up a unified and collective
production team. This new fragmentation of the land virtually pre-
cludes the mechanization of agriculture, which many agronomists believe is the most promising way to achieve significant and sustained
progress in Chinese agricultural production and productivity in future
years. While tractors are now fairly common in China, they usually
are used for hauling freight on the roads rather than for tilling the
fields.

It is ironic that a regime that so ardently champions the benefits
of modern technology would have fashioned an agrarian system so
inimical to the technological modernization and mechanization of agricultural production. But such has been the case. As Hinton caus-
tically remarked: "The reform confirmed the hoe as the preeminent
farm implement and ensured that it would not soon be superseded
by anything more modern."[49]

Perhaps the most serious long-term consequence of the Deng regime's rural reform policies has been the enormous growth of socioeconomic inequality in the countryside and the creation of new class
divisions which virtually guarantee social conflicts, results certainly

[48] Ibid., p. 27 (emphasis added).
[49] Ibid., p. 22.

not intended or desired by the reformers but ones that hardly could have been unanticipated. The official policies which proceeded under the slogan "some must get rich first" were accompanied by official denunciations of "egalitarianism" as among the more heinous of ultraleftist sins. Obviously the Deng regime anticipated increasing inequality as a necessary cost of economic progress. Necessary or not, the one universal effect of decollectivization and other reforms has in fact been the emergence of glaring economic disparities in the countryside. Prior to 1980 the major income differentials in the rural areas were regional (rooted in long-standing differences in ecological, marketing, and general economic conditions in different parts of the country), while the relatively egalitarian work-point system for collectivized production permitted only a rather narrow range of income differentials within localities.[50] Since 1980, enormous differences in income and status *within* villages and localities have developed. By the mid-1980s, the income ratio between the wealthiest and poorest families within a single village or township is said to have been ten or even twenty to one.[51] By all accounts, this process of economic differentiation has proceeded more rapidly over the past decade. A 1994 survey of 2,260 households in a rural county in relatively prosperous Jiangsu province, for example, revealed that 721 households (whose members were mostly involved in private industries and specialized production) had an average annual income of more than 30,000 yuan. Among the remaining 1,539 households, the average income was 760 yuan.[52]

It is not generally the case that the poor have become poorer in the new commercialized economy. The majority of poor families have

---

[50] The coexistence of great regional (and other) inequalities and a relative egalitarianism within villages during the Mao period is examined in considerable detail in Riskin, *China's Political Economy*, Chapter 10, pp. 223–56. See also E. B. Vermeer, "Income Differentials in Rural China," *The China Quarterly*, No. 89 (March 1982), pp. 1–33, and "Income Differentials in Rural China," Comment by Keith Griffin and Reply by E. B. Vermeer, *The China Quarterly*, No. 92 (December 1982), pp. 706–13. On one aspect of regional inequality, see Kenneth R. Walker, "40 Years On: Provincial Contrasts in China's Rural Economic Development," *The China Quarterly*, No. 119 (September 1989), pp. 448–80.

[51] For a discussion of growing economic inequality and social polarization within village communities in the early 1980s, see Riskin, *China's Political Economy*, pp. 306–8.

[52] The figures are taken from a Ministry of Agriculture investigation reported in *Xinhua Daily*, an organ of the provincial Party committee. Jiang Jing, "How Many Peasants Have Really Become Rich?" *China Focus*, Vol. 3, No. 2 (February 1, 1995), p. 4.

benefited from the reforms, sharing (to greater or lesser degrees) in the general rise in rural incomes and living standards. But the crucial social result of the Deng regime's agrarian policies is that they yielded a new rural bourgeoisie—or, if one prefers, a rural entrepreneurial elite.

This class-in-the-making emerged from the minority (but very substantial number) of rural inhabitants who prospered under a system that favored the aggressive and the ambitious, the entrepreneurially inclined, the physically strong, the skilled, the clever, the families with greatest labor-power, and especially individuals and families with political power or access to it. It was soon discovered that the way to prosper in the post-Mao countryside was not to till the soil but to manage the labor and the products of the labor of others. Thus some arranged to contract relatively large tracts of land in the early reform period, which they then subcontracted to other peasants to farm, thereby partially re-creating the exploitative subtenancy arrangements of the pre-1949 rural economy. Some male peasants early abandoned farming (sometimes leaving the task to their wives and children) in order to engage in trade and commerce, which proved to be among the more lucrative activities in an increasingly commercialized rural economy. Some acquired sufficient funds to purchase tractors, hiring others to actually operate the machines and charging farmers fees for their use. A peasant who owned two or more tractors in the early 1980s could live relatively well without working. Other enterprising rural dwellers purchased trucks and established transportation companies, usually hiring laborers to drive the vehicles. Many small commune industries, such as cement plants and sawmills, were contracted to private individuals (or "collective" entrepreneurial groups) who expanded the enterprises, hiring increasing numbers of wage laborers.

It takes no special sociological expertise to know that these growing differentials in income, function, and status portend new social class divisions in the Chinese countryside. Indeed, a new rural class structure is already discernible. Although the social and occupational lines are still fluid and overlapping, one can identify four reasonably distinct classes in the Chinese countryside. First, at the top of that structure is a rural bourgeoisie made up of private owners and contractors of a growing array of rural-based commercial, service, and industrial enterprises; the more successful specialized households that hire wage laborers and are run on a capitalist basis; professional managers and technical personnel who operate the burgeoning township and village enterprises (TVEs); local government and Party officials, many of whom are involved in the TVEs and other profit-making enterprises; and quasi-landlords who sublease contracted lands to peasant tillers. While hardly a cohesive class, these groups share several key socioeconomic characteristics: their members live, in large measure, through the exploitation of labor, and they refrain from engaging in manual labor, perpetuating an ancient social division in a modern capitalist environment.

Second, still the most numerous rural social class is made up of peasants who till the soil on individual family farms. It is a most economically diverse class, ranging from "new rich peasants" (including most specialized households) to families so poor that they fall below the government's official "poverty line." Third, the most rapidly growing class in the countryside is made up of wage laborers, some working in agriculture on capitalist-organized farms, but the majority employed in the TVEs. This rural-based proletariat now numbers well over a hundred million workers who, although low-paid in comparison to urban workers, earn two-thirds of total rural household income. Finally, there is an impoverished and growing rural lumpen proletariat composed of occasional wage laborers, displaced and wandering migrant workers, and unemployed youth, some of whom roam the countryside in criminal gangs.

The Chinese Communist Party, once the champion of the rural poor, now pursues policies that favor the new rural elite, an embryonic bourgeoisie whose members were officially hailed early in the reform period as "representatives of advanced productive forces in the countryside."[53] The Communist regime continues to support the rural bourgeoisie, both materially and ideologically, extolling the most successful entrepreneurs as popular models to emulate. It is likely to remain the dominant Party view that the emergence of a rural bourgeoisie, however incongruous with the regime's continuing

[53] By Vice-Premier Wan Li in "Developing Rural Commodity Production," *Beijing Review*, February 27, 1984, p. 19. The elite of rural entrepreneurs receive not simply the regime's ideological encouragement but also more tangible support, such as bank credits not available to less successful rural dwellers.

socialist claims, is the best hope for capital accumulation, productive investment, and modernization in China's vast countryside. That being the case, it seems inevitable that the socioeconomic inequalities naturally generated by the market will continue to grow and become solidified into firm class divisions.

Many of the negative results of the rural reforms are unintended consequences which state authorities seek to remedy, or at least mitigate. But since the consequences are largely inherent in the reform program itself, remedial efforts have been less than entirely successful and have been further hampered by another result of decollectivization—a decline in the authority and efficiency of rural Party organizations. At the outset, most rural cadres were opposed to the reforms, partly because the new policies seemed so incongruous with the socialist principles they so long had championed. It was also partly a matter of self-interest, for decollectivization meant a loss of customary cadre power over the organization of production and the distribution of work-points, and in many cases loss of income due to the depletion of collective funds. Many local cadres consequently turned to private endeavors, returning to full-time cultivation of the soil on newly contracted lands and seizing new opportunities for commercial and other capitalist-type activities, sometimes resulting in the paralysis and demoralization of local Party branches. But the rural Party organization by no means collapsed. Once the household responsibility system had been firmly established as the national policy, rural cadres, whatever their personal views, were zealous in implementing the new system.

Indeed, local rural cadres very soon discovered that their political positions and connections were highly beneficial for the pursuit of their own economic interests in an increasingly commercialized rural economy. Utilizing their influence, many cadre families were able to contract larger and more fertile lands than ordinary peasants lacking access to political power, establish a variety of private business ventures, obtain bank loans to finance the enterprises, and acquire goods and materials in short supply for illicit dealings on the rapidly expanding black market. As Vice-Premier Wan Li complained early in 1984: "Some cadres are seizing farmland to build houses, obtaining through special connections chemical fertilizer, diesel oil, and other means of production which are in short supply, taking the lead in obstructing the use of land for key construction projects in order to get something from the state, and openly plundering state property. Some cadres secure 'contracts' and take 'shares' by illegal means."[54] One result of this ability to "secure 'contracts' " was that cadres, or former cadres, a tiny percentage of the rural population in all, made up 43 percent of rural households that were classified as "prosperous" at the end of 1983.[55]

Although it is usually assumed that the growth of a market economy undermines bureaucratic power, the paradoxical case in China has been that the market-oriented rural reforms have served to enrich local officials, their relatives, and their friends. Political power has greatly facilitated the establishment and operation of various business ventures by cadres and their clients, while the newly fashioned commercial economy has opened vast new opportunities for official corruption. Local cadres and officials, most of whom are the descendants of poor peasant revolutionaries, have come to occupy a most prominent place among China's new rural bourgeoisie. It is one aspect of the larger phenomenon of bureaucratic capitalism that the economic reforms of the post-Mao era have wrought. The phenomenon, and its implications for the future of Chinese socialism, will be examined at greater length in Chapter 11.

[54] Wan Li, "Speech at the National Rural Work Conference," *People's Daily*, January 18, 1984, p. 1. Cited in Ch'en Ting-chung, "Agriculture in Mainland China," p. 54.
[55] "Who Are the People That Became Rich First in the Rural Areas?" *People's Daily*, January 5, 1984, p. 2.

10

THE CITIES: STATE, MARKET,
AND THE URBAN WORKING CLASS

IN 1952, WHEN CHINA'S NEW COMMUNIST LEADERS had fully reestablished an industrial plant ravaged by more than a decade of foreign invasion and civil war, industrial output accounted for only one-third of the national product. By 1975, as the Mao era was drawing to a close, the ratio had been reversed. The gross value of industrial output had climbed to 71.5 percent of the national product while agriculture accounted for only 28.5 percent.[1]

Future historians, unburdened by the political orthodoxy that economic growth during the Mao period proceeded at "a snail's pace," undoubtedly will record the extraordinarily rapid transformation of China from a primarily agrarian nation to a primarily industrial one (in terms of gross value of output) as one of the great accomplishments of the Mao regime, and one that established the essential material preconditions for the economic successes of the Deng Xiaoping regime. Rather than the now common dichotomy between a stagnant Mao era and a dynamic Deng one, the modern industrial transformation of China will be seen as a half-century-long process spanning both the Mao and post-Mao eras. Indeed, it is a period that compares favorably with the most successful cases of rapid industrialization in modern world history. As the distinguished economist

---

[1] Riskin, *China's Political Economy*, Table 11.4, p. 270.

Y. Y. Kueh has pointed out, the sharp rise in industry's share of China's national income from 1952 to 1987 far exceeded that experienced by early industrializing Britain (1801–41) and Meiji Japan (1878–1927). "In the postwar experience of newly industrializing countries," Kueh has observed, "probably only Taiwan has demonstrated as impressive a record as China . . ."[2]

Yet Maoist efforts to abandon the Stalinist model of industrialization were abortive, and by the close of the Mao era Chinese industry was beginning to suffer from many of the problems common to Soviet-style centrally planned economies—waste, inefficiency, bureaucratic rigidity, declining productivity, and the sacrifice of popular living standards to an obsessive drive for "primitive socialist accumulation." Such were some of the problems that the reformers of the post-Mao era sought to remedy. But some charge that the remedies they proposed and pursued have undermined the socialist character of China's urban economy and society. It is a charge that assumes that the Mao regime did in fact pursue a socialist path of industrialization. It is not an assumption that can be taken for granted.

MAOIST INDUSTRIALIZATION AND CHINESE SOCIALISM

Industrial development in the People's Republic, in both the Mao and Deng eras, is officially called "socialist industrialization." The term derives from the common assumption that state ownership or control of the means of production is ipso facto socialist. Indeed, it is widely and reflexively taken for granted that every increase of central state control over economy and society automatically advances the movement toward socialism whereas any relaxation of state dominance marks a retreat. That this association of socialism and the state is common among both critics and partisans of socialism seemingly endows the assumption with a more or less universal validity.

While the view that socialism is essentially nationalized property

---

[2] Y. Y. Kueh, "The Maoist Legacy and China's New Industrialization Strategy," *The China Quarterly*, No. 119 (September 1989), p. 421.

suits the ideological needs of both orthodox Marxist-Leninists and their antisocialist critics, the definition is incongruous with original Marxian thought. For Karl Marx, the immediate producers' collective control over the conditions and the products of their labor was the crucial principle of a socialist society. Marx quite clearly distinguished between *nationalization* and *socialization*. It was not the state as the "despotic ruler" of production and consumption that defined socialism but rather when social production became the "property of the associated workers."[3]

The organization of Chinese industry during the Mao era had little in common with Marx's conception of socialism as "the communal property of the associated producers." Industry was not communal property but state property, and it was the centralized Maoist state, not the immediate producers, who determined what was produced, the manner in which production was performed, and the disposition of the industrial product. Indeed, the state controlled not only the conditions of production but the producers themselves. Workers in state factories and enterprises were assigned jobs by state agencies, and, lacking freedom of occupation or job choice, they typically remained tied to those positions for the remainder of their working lives. The state, moreover, established by administrative fiat both wages and the general principles of remuneration. Central economic planning, often so easily taken as the distinguishing feature of a socialist economy, was not the collective expression of the immediate producers, but rather the product of decisions taken by a small group of Party leaders in Beijing. The individual factory or enterprise was no less hierarchically organized than factories in capitalist countries, with workers subordinated to professional factory managers and Party committees who were in turn primarily responsible to a central bureaucratic apparatus. Workers in Chinese factories had no more to say about the conditions under which they labored than their counterparts in capitalist countries. Indeed, they had even less to say since independent trade unions were forbidden. Lacking autonomous organizations, workers not only did not control the conditions and products of their labor but had no effective means to collectively bargain with the dominant bureaucratic apparatus that did exercise

[3] Karl Marx, *Grundrisse*, translated by Martin Nicolaus (New York: Vintage, 1973), p. 833.

that control. And over the state that controlled the economy, there were no institutionalized forms of popular democratic control, much less a system of "the self-government of the producers" that Marxist theory demanded of a socialist society.

While such a mode of industrial organization hardly can be described as socialist, it is important to recognize what might be called the "quasi-socialist" (or at least noncapitalist) features of the Maoist system, in order to understand what has changed in the post-Mao era.

The first and most obvious feature of the industrial economy in the Mao period was the absence of private ownership of the means of production. Save for a tiny collective sector of the urban economy, Chinese urban industry was state-owned property, and state enterprises (both industrial and nonindustrial) employed the overwhelming bulk of the urban workforce.[4] Second, the economy was governed by a system of central state planning, which set detailed production targets for both the national economy as a whole and the individual factory, allocating supplies of materials and labor accordingly. The aim was to maximize economic rationality and the rate of growth. Third, the individual enterprise operated not on the basis of the capitalist principle of profitability but rather according to its assigned role in fulfilling social needs as dictated by the overall national economic plan. What constituted "social needs" was defined not by the collective judgment of society—for which no mechanism of expression existed or was even conceived—but rather was determined by central planners in Beijing.

The two remaining quasi-socialist aspects of the system were essential for maintaining the regime's legitimacy in the eyes of the working population—the state's commitment to full employment and job security. In China, the promise of employment for all who were able and willing to work was far more difficult to fulfill than in the Soviet Union or the Eastern European countries due to China's relative economic backwardness and its huge population. The problem of urban unemployment was disguised through the deliberate over-

[4] In the late 1970s, state enterprises produced more than 80 percent of China's total industrial output; the remainder was largely the output of "collective" rural industries. Harding, *China's Second Revolution*, Table 5.2, p. 129. In the cities, virtually all industrial workers were state employees.

staffing of state enterprises, strict controls on peasant migration to the cities, and various *xia-xiang* campaigns which dispatched millions of urban youth to live and work in the countryside. The promise of job security was fulfilled by simply designating the overwhelming majority of state employees "fixed workers," with guaranteed lifetime tenure. These workers, who could be dismissed only under the most exceptional of circumstances, also enjoyed relatively generous welfare benefits such as health insurance, pensions, housing, and childcare facilities. Benefits were typically provided not by the state directly but by the enterprise, which tended to foster paternalistic relationships between the enterprise and its permanent employees, often guaranteeing jobs for the children of older or retired workers, for example. As Gordon White, one of the more astute observers of industrial relations in the People's Republic, observed: "Large state enterprises tended to turn into 'small societies' with mini 'welfare states' and smaller ones operated like large families regulated by particularistic relationships."[5] The system of job security, however laudable as a general principle and however coveted by those who were excluded from it, sometimes bred humiliating forms of personal dependence as workers vied for favors from factory managers and Party officials, such as bonuses, better jobs within the enterprise, and apartments.[6]

It was this system of job security, later pejoratively labeled the "iron rice bowl," that the economic reformers proposed to dismantle—not so much out of concern over the emerging patterns of paternalistic dependence as because it was deemed to be economically inefficient. Workers guaranteed lifetime tenure, it was argued, had little incentive to work and thus the job security system was a major factor in the low productivity of Chinese industry. To remedy the deficiency, the reformers advocated the creation of a free labor market, giving factory managers the power to hire and fire workers on the basis of rational economic criteria. The aim was to refashion workers into commodities, to be bought and sold like other commodities.

[5] Gordon White, "Restructuring the Working Class: Labor Reform in Post-Mao China," in Dirlik and Meisner (eds.), *Marxism and the Chinese Experience*, pp. 153–54.
[6] For a detailed analysis and discussion, see Walder, *Communist Neo-Traditionalism: Work and Authority in Chinese Industry* (Berkeley: University of California Press, 1986).

POST-MAO INDUSTRIAL REFORMS, 1979–84

The initial attempt to reform urban industry, following immediately from the December 1978 Third Plenum's ambiguous injunction to combine "market adjustment" with "adjustment by the plan," preceded the decollectivization of agricultural production in the early 1980s. The policy of "adjustment," which stressed the need for greater specialization and the intensification of the division of labor, was intended to raise labor productivity in industry. The urban working class was presented with a combination of rewards and threats. The rewards included small formal salary increases and a new variety of bonus and profit-sharing schemes based on individual and collective productivity. In return for rather modest material gains, factory workers were subjected to harsher codes of labor discipline, increasingly stringent enforcement of factory rules and regulations, and a more authoritarian managerial system based on what the reformers hailed as modern "scientific managerial techniques." The latter, borrowed from the advanced capitalist countries, was ideologically rationalized by invoking some of the more authoritarian strains in the Marxist-Leninist tradition. The ideologists of the new Deng regime were particularly fond of quoting Lenin, who, in an expression of his well-known technocratic bias, had lavished praise on American and German "scientific" managerial methods.[7] They also frequently invoked Engels, who once warned that "wanting to abolish authority in large-scale industry is tantamount to wanting to abolish industry itself, to destroy the power loom in order to return to the spinning wheel."[8]

While Lenin and Engels were selectively quoted, Mao Zedong was not. Strikingly absent from the reformers' treatises was any mention of the long-standing policy of "the two participations," the Maoist

[7] In addition to his well-known enthusiasm for American "Taylorism," Lenin advocated the adoption of German managerial techniques: "Yes, learn from the Germans!" he wrote in 1918. "History is moving in zigzags. It also happens that it is the Germans who now personify, besides a brutal imperialism, the principle of discipline, organization, harmonious cooperation on the basis of modern machine industry, and strict accounting and control. And that is just what we are lacking. That is just what we must learn." "The Chief Task of Our Day," V. I. Lenin, *Selected Works*, Vol. 2, Part 1 (Moscow: Foreign Languages Publishing House, 1952), pp. 446–47.

[8] Friedrich Engels, "On Authority," Marx and Engels, *Selected Works*, Vol. 1, p. 576.

formula providing for worker participation in management while managers participated in manual labor. The absence is hardly surprising in a reform program that called for an intensification of the division of labor, increased specialization in work and function, and the introduction of "scientific management."

More ominous for the urban working class, and even less amenable to any Marxian justification, was the threatened loss of job security. Many of Deng Xiaoping's more zealous economic advisors, relatively secure in their own bureaucratic offices, loudly and rather impetuously spoke of the necessity to "smash the iron rice bowl"— that is, to abolish the guarantee of lifetime job security and welfare benefits for regular state workers. The threatened destruction of the iron rice bowl was fraught with potentially explosive social and political consequences, for it would have abolished what urban workers viewed as the major accomplishment of the revolution. The socialist legitimacy of the Communist state rested, in very large measure, on the promise to provide secure jobs for all those able and willing to work.

The proposed termination of employment and welfare guarantees was part of a broader reformist scheme to reorganize China's industry on a quasi-capitalist basis, complete with a market for labor. According to the scheme, economic decision-making powers would be decentralized to individual enterprises, which would operate on a profit-making basis in a market economy. A professional factory manager would determine production schedules, wages, and prices in response to prevailing market conditions, with the aim of achieving profitability, rather than in accordance with centrally determined plans. Profit would be the criterion determining whether factories and their employees would thrive or wither away. Unprofitable enterprises were to be closed or simply allowed to fail.

This essentially capitalist model of industrial organization, albeit lacking private ownership of productive property, demanded a free labor market. The full transformation of labor into a commodity, to be freely bought and sold in the marketplace, demanded the elimination of the iron rice bowl, a measure, the reformers argued, that would have the salutary effect of disciplining a lackadaisical workforce and raising labor productivity. Although the reformers ritualistically acknowledged the need to retain a degree of central economic planning, which remained an official ideological orthodoxy, the logic of the market model they advocated pointed to the wholesale dismantling of the state planning apparatus.

The initial 1979–80 attempt to reform the urban industrial sector, in any event, was restricted in scope and proved limited in duration. Some enterprises, mostly smaller factories, were permitted to produce goods directly for local and sometimes foreign markets after fulfilling quotas demanded by the state plan. Several thousand larger enterprises, generally the more efficient and profitable ones, were granted a wide degree of autonomy in marketing their above-plan outputs and retaining the profits for investment or disbursement under what was known as "the Sichuan experiment," a scheme pioneered by Zhao Ziyang several years earlier when he held the post of Party secretary in Deng Xiaoping's native province. The factories chosen to participate in the 1979–80 nationwide experiment were carefully selected and favored by the state with special access to credit, raw materials, technology, and markets—and thus their experience proved to be of limited relevance to the national economy as a whole.[9]

These limited and tentative reforms in the urban industrial sector, coupled with more far-reaching market-type changes in the rural economy, soon brought unanticipated and undesired consequences. One was inflation, officially calculated at about 6 percent in 1979 and 7 percent in 1980. The inflation rate was considerably higher in the cities, for official government statistics failed to take into account sharply rising prices on the flourishing free and black markets, where growing quantities of food and other consumer products were now being bought and sold. Further, official calculations also ignored various forms of disguised price-raising in state stores, such as the repackaging of old products, which were then sold at higher prices under new names.[10] While the inflation rate was relatively modest by world standards, it came as a shock to a population accustomed to virtually complete price stability for almost three decades. Over the twenty-seven-year Mao era, consumer price increases had been held to an average of less than one-half of 1 percent per annum. The inflation of 1979–80 effectively canceled the recent wage increases.

[9] As observed by Edmund Lee, "Economic Reform in Post-Mao China: An Insider's View," *Bulletin of Concerned Asian Scholars*, Vol. 15, No. 1 (1983).

[10] As pointed out by Jan S. Prybyla, "Economic Problems of Communism: A Case Study of China," *Asian Survey*, Vol. 22, No. 12 (December 1982), pp. 1211–12.

At the end of 1980, the government prohibited price increases on all products still under state control. But price stability in the cities and a market economy growing apace in the countryside were not to be easily reconciled.

To mitigate the effects of inflation on urban inhabitants, the government granted monthly wage subsidies to state employees. This, in turn, contributed to growing deficits in the state budget, soon to be a chronic problem of economic life in post-Mao China. Over the four-year period 1979–82, the officially acknowledged deficit came to 50 billion yuan (about US$25 billion), a very modest sum by recent American standards but a heavy burden for a still-fragile Chinese economy and an alarming development for a government which hitherto had scrupulously adhered to a balanced budget. An immediate consequence was a drastic reduction in capital construction, slashed more than 25 percent in 1981 alone, and the cancellation of contracts for the purchase of modern plants and technology negotiated with Japan and Western European countries. In order to finance the deficit, the state issued bonds in 1981 for the first time since the early 1950s, when low-interest-bearing bonds had been sold to acquire the properties of the remaining members of the urban bourgeoisie.

In addition to producing inflation and budgetary deficits, the new economic policies increased the ranks of the unemployed—and also produced the first official acknowledgments of the existence of unemployment in the cities, which according to Vice-Premier Li Xiannian numbered no fewer than 20 million people in 1979, about 20 percent of the urban labor force.[11] The roots of urban unemployment are to be found in the Mao period, partly due to the failure to institute effective birth-control measures, but the economic policies of the Deng regime exacerbated the problem. The emphasis on enterprise profitability and the closing of inefficient factories resulted in the loss of millions of jobs in the early 1980s. With 6 million urban youth reaching working age each year, and the return of millions of "rusticated youth," unemployment became very visible in the cities. Along with it came an upsurge in crime.

After 1980 government employment bureaus no longer guaranteed

---

[11] Li Xiannian's speech discussing unemployment was published not in China at the time but rather in the Hong Kong newspaper *Ming Bao* on June 14, 1979. The problem of unemployment had been noted in the official press in the post-Mao years, although usually without citing specific figures.

positions in state enterprises for new entrants into the urban labor force. Save for the very few who could claim a university education and the top graduates of the better middle schools, those seeking employment were told to rely on their own devices to find or create jobs.

Nonetheless, the Communist state refused to surrender its *ideological* commitment to full employment. In attempting to fulfill that commitment, and to serve other social and economic needs as well, the Deng regime pursued policies to expand urban "collective" enterprises, encourage private entrepreneurship, and establish new industrial undertakings financed by foreign capital. Whatever the original intention, all three of these policies contributed not to fortifying any kind of socialist legitimacy but rather to the growth of a capitalist labor market. The full commodification and exploitation of labor in factories established by foreign capitalists, whether in special economic zones or elsewhere, is obvious and need not be belabored here. The virtues of "cheap Chinese labor" have been sufficiently expounded upon in foreign business journals and newspapers. What requires brief comment is the place of urban collective and petty private enterprises in the history of China's economic reform.

What are officially called "collective enterprises" in the cities, the small urban counterpart of rural township and village industries, range widely in nature, size, and function. Some are relatively sizable light industrial operations producing small consumer goods; others are loosely structured cooperatives of traditional handicrafts persons; some are simple groupings of people working in their own homes on the putting-out system; others are retail or service companies, employing several to several hundred people. While in theory these enterprises are collectively owned and managed by the workers who labor in them, in reality most collective workers are wage laborers and the collectives themselves are mostly under de facto state control, dependent on the government for credit, raw materials, and retail outlets. Workers in collectives, however, occupy a distinctly inferior position to those employed in state enterprises. Their wages are significantly lower, and since they enjoy neither job security nor welfare benefits, their livelihoods are at the mercy of the market. Wage laborers employed by urban collective enterprises increased rapidly in the early reform period, by some 7 million workers between 1981 and 1984,[12] contributing (albeit marginally) to the reformers' demand to "smash the iron rice bowl."

Private and individual economic undertakings, encouraged by government policies, also contributed to the growth of a labor market as well as to the alleviation of unemployment. By the end of the Mao era, the private sector of the urban economy had been virtually eliminated, the number of self-employed workers reduced to a mere 240,000. With the launching of the Dengist economic reform program, private entrepreneurship was not only promoted but extolled. City streets and alleys were soon filled with peddlers offering small household goods and sundry personal items, others selling fruits and vegetables, and vendors hawking cooked foods and medicinal herbs. Small repair, service, and retail businesses proliferated, ranging from barbershops and shoe-repair shops to private inns and restaurants. By 1984 some 3.4 million people were employed in the private sector of the urban economy,[13] some of them working as wage laborers for the more successful entrepreneurs. In a feeble effort to deflect criticism that exploitation of labor was taking place, the wage workers were at first officially known as "apprentices" and "helpers," while the new businessmen, especially the more successful among them, were hailed as "socialist entrepreneurs." Although such fledgling capitalists were initially limited to hiring no more than eight "apprentices," the rapidly rising legal maximum was rarely enforced and soon abolished altogether.

The burgeoning of collective and private enterprises in the cities, however ideologically embarrassing to the government, was economically attractive. It mitigated unemployment and its social dangers, especially among urban youth. It filled a long-standing void in the service and retail sectors of the economy, thus alleviating the daily burdens of life for the common people. And it contributed to a new liveliness in China's cities, as many foreign observers reported in the early 1980s, often by contrasting the relative bustle of cities in the reform era to the austerity and drabness of urban life in the Mao period. But perhaps what was most attractive to the government was

[12] Riskin, *China's Political Economy*, Table 14.1, p. 355.
[13] Ibid.

candidly stated by one of the prominent early economic reformers, Xue Muqiao, who approvingly said of those employed in the growing collective and private sectors: "The state will not be required to pay them wages."[14]

Nor was the state required to pay wages to the increasing numbers of people who hired themselves out as servants in private homes. Servants were hardly a novelty in the People's Republic. But in the Mao era, most domestic servants were state employees working in the offices and homes of high government officials and, in lesser numbers, in the homes of the dwindling members of the "national bourgeoisie." In the post-Mao era, however, maids, cooks, gardeners, and nannies have become commonplace in the private homes of well-to-do families—the growing number of professionals, higher-level intellectuals, middle-level bureaucrats, the more successful private entrepreneurs, and the rapidly increasing numbers of temporary foreign residents. What was once stigmatized as antisocialist, and therefore avoided or hidden, soon came to be paraded as a mark of high social prestige.

While amazing success stories of entrepreneurs have been widely publicized in both Chinese and Western newspapers, the overwhelming majority of those laboring in the new private sector eke out only a bare existence. And they perform society's most menial and least pleasant work, laboring as servants, peddlers, street vendors, day laborers, janitors, and so forth. There is, of course, nothing uniquely capitalist about these occupations. Peddlers and servants have existed in one form or another since the most ancient times and are to be found in virtually every economic system. But the privately employed servants and the peddlers and other petty entrepreneurs who emerged in China in the early reform period were in fact the products of developing capitalist market relationships, of the economic and social inequalities the market was engendering, and of the spread of a "free market" for wage labor that Chinese capitalism required. The servants and peddlers were members of what was becoming an enormous "functional underclass," to borrow John Kenneth Galbraith's felicitous if depressing term, a class that was soon to include tens of

---

[14] Xue Muqiao in a July 1979 radio interview, cited in Garside, *Coming Alive: China After Mao*, p. 358.

millions of migrant laborers. A market economy, Galbraith points out, requires such an underclass of poor people to do the dreary and painful work that makes life so comfortable for the wealthy. The underclass "is integrally a part of a larger economic process and . . . it serves the living standard and the comfort of the more favored community. Economic progress would be far more uncertain and certainly far less rapid without it. The economically fortunate, not excluding those who speak with greatest regret of the existence of this class, are heavily dependent on its presence."[15] The truth of these observations was soon to strike China with a vengeance.

While the appearance of petty entrepreneurs and the privately employed were the by-products of the growing market economy, post-Mao Chinese capitalism did not spring spontaneously from the petty entrepreneurship that was so highly publicized in the early 1980s. Its true sources, as shall be seen, are to be found in the political and financial power of the Chinese Communist state, in the initiatives of local governments, in the influx of foreign capital, and in the greed of Communist bureaucrats.

In 1980, as the Deng Xiaoping regime struggled to control deficits, inflation, and unemployment, it was confronted with an unanticipated decline in basic industrial production, the backbone of the state economy. While the production of consumer goods increased by 17 percent over the previous year, heavy industry grew by only 1.4, the poorest performance since the Great Leap crisis two decades earlier, and energy output declined 3 percent.[16] Although the government intended to correct the imbalance between heavy and light industry, the sharp decline in basic industrial production was alarming. It portended a crisis in industry as a whole, as the economic statistics for the following year were to confirm. In 1981 total industrial production grew by only 4.1 percent, with the output of heavy industry dropping 4.7 percent. Thus in December 1980, and again early in 1981, Party leaders gathered to formulate new and

[15] John Kenneth Galbraith, *The Culture of Contentment* (Boston: Houghton Mifflin, 1992), p. 31.
[16] Riskin, *China's Political Economy*, Table 14.8, p. 369.

more stringent "readjustment" policies that all but halted further experimentation with market reforms in the urban industrial sector.

Readjustment meant a new austerity in state spending to reduce deficits and control inflation, including additional reductions in capital construction, the closing of unprofitable factories dependent on state subsidies, and a freeze on wages and salaries. The readjustment policies demanded strengthening the system of central planning, especially to ensure state control over prices, wages, investment, and the allocation of raw materials and energy. This return to the essentials of a command economy was announced by Deng Xiaoping at the December 1980 Party work conference. "It is absolutely necessary to enforce a high degree of centralization in readjustment," he emphasized.[17] In this Deng was supported, and probably encouraged, by the veteran economic specialist Chen Yun, a moderate reformer who had become alarmed over the neglect of central planning during the previous two years of market euphoria. Behind Deng's return to the old planning system stood powerful social groups whose interests clashed with the reform program. These included not only sectors of the state bureaucracy embedded in the vast planning apparatus but also most members of the urban working class adversely affected by inflation and fearful over threats to job security. Workers desired changes, but these did not include "smashing the iron rice bowl," that favorite phrase of the more zealous economic reformers.

With the central planning system reestablished in 1981, industrial growth resumed in 1982, but at a modest pace. Gross output increased by 6.8 percent in 1982 and by 10.5 percent in 1983. But now the proportion between heavy and light industry was once again reversed. In 1983 heavy industry grew by 12.4 percent whereas light industrial output increased 8.7 percent. By 1985 a balance had been established, with both industrial sectors growing by the astonishingly rapid rate of about 18 percent.[18] It was the beginning of what came to be called an "overheated" economy, a phenomenon that generated grave fiscal and social problems along with exceptionally rapid growth. Overall, during the first phase of reform (1978–85), the av-

[17] "Deng Xiaoping Analyzes the Domestic Situation," FBIS, January 28, 1981, pp. U2–U6.
[18] The figures in this paragraph are drawn from the calculations made by Carl Riskin. See *China's Political Economy*, Table 14.8, p. 369.

erage annual industrial growth rate was 10.1 percent, approximately the same rate achieved during the late Mao era. But in contrast to the Mao period, the output of light consumer goods increased more rapidly than heavy industry, the former at an average per annum rate of 12.6 percent, the latter averaging 8.4 percent. The availability of consumer goods, whose output more than doubled over the first seven years of the Deng regime, was one of the factors (along with wage increases and a lower accumulation rate) responsible for the impressive average annual 6 percent rise in real incomes enjoyed by urban residents to the mid-1980s.[19]

The recentralization of the urban economy in 1980–81 delayed the more ambitious plans to restructure China's urban industry. A new effort to bring market precepts to the urban industrial sector was not announced until late 1984. In the meantime, the government's attention focused on the countryside, where, as we have seen, the family farm was reestablished as the main productive unit, market relationships proliferated, and tens of millions of peasants were transformed into wage laborers in rural industrial enterprises, the most rapidly expanding sector of the Chinese economy.

While the rural economy was the dominant concern of the reformers in the early 1980s, the cities did not remain frozen in time. The urban labor force expanded with the arrival of increasing numbers of peasant migrants. Unable to find employment in the newly commercialized countryside, they were willing to work in the cities on almost any terms, and many were destined to fill the ranks of the functional underclass. While 70 percent of urban workers were employed in the state sector in the mid-1980s, there was substantial growth of employment in urban private and collective enterprises, as we have seen. Workers in the still-tiny private sector, for example, increased from 1.1 million to 3.4 million between 1981 and 1984.[20]

The growing number of nonstate workers did not smash the iron rice bowl, but it did chip away at the system of lifetime job tenure. Government policy further promoted the process by encouraging state enterprises to hire new workers on a contractual basis for limited

[19] After 1986, real wages in the cities stagnated until 1991.
[20] Riskin, *China's Political Economy*, Table 14.1, p. 355.

periods of time rather than as regular workers with job security and welfare benefits. While contract labor was not a new practice in the People's Republic (the distinction between regular state workers and contract laborers had already found political expression in the conflicts of the Cultural Revolution), the number of such workers now rapidly grew.[21] While the total number of workers in state enterprises expanded, the number of workers with lifetime job tenure gradually declined.

There thus began to emerge in China in the early 1980s a "free" labor market in both town and countryside. Beyond the many tens of millions of agricultural and industrial wage laborers in the rural areas, the urban labor market included workers employed in the rapidly growing private and collective sectors, contract laborers in state and other enterprises, domestic servants and service personnel, and a growing "reserve army of labor" consisting of the unemployed, the semi-employed, and a "floating population" of migrant laborers who began to stream into the cities from the rural areas. Such a free labor market, an essential ingredient of a capitalist economy, was much desired by Deng Xiaoping's advisors on economic reform, and the government was soon to make vigorous efforts to expand and universalize it. But before considering the second phase of industrial reform, inaugurated in the autumn of 1984, we must turn to the Deng Xiaoping regime's international economic policies, the realm of foreign trade and investment, where capitalist relationships early gained ascendancy and where departures from Maoist policies were most pronounced.

CHINA AND THE WORLD CAPITALIST MARKET

One of the most hallowed of Maoist principles was self-reliance. The term had both an internal and an external meaning. As applied to foreign economic relationships in the late Mao era, it expressed the

---

[21] A directive instructing state enterprises to hire contract laborers rather than regular employees was formally issued by the Ministry of Labor in February 1983. Riskin, *China's Political Economy*, p. 355. It already had become a widespead practice; by 1981, permanent or "fixed" state employees made up only 42 percent of the total industrial workforce, down from 50 percent in the late Mao era, and the percentage gradually declined over the remainder of the decade and the early 1990s.

belief that China could best achieve modernization and socialism on the basis of its own resources—without aid, loans, and investments from other countries. With the repayment in 1965 of the final installment of the 1950s loans and credits from the Soviet Union, the People's Republic was debt-free, and the government proclaimed that it would remain so. Self-reliance also precluded the development of export industries built to satisfy foreign markets at the expense of domestic needs, a characteristic feature of the Chinese economy in semi-colonial times. Within these self-proclaimed limitations and constraints, foreign trade could be (and indeed was) conducted, albeit on a modest scale and with the purpose of importing only those products that could not be made in China.

The Maoist principle of self-reliance was in part a matter of making a virtue out of necessity. For over two decades the United States enforced a stringent trade embargo against China which largely precluded Chinese trade with the advanced capitalist countries. The embargo was often carried to absurd lengths, requiring, for example, American tourists returning from East Asia to present to U.S. customs officials "certificates of origin" to prove that goods purchased in Hong Kong were not manufactured in China, to conform with the Trading with the Enemy Act. In light of that lengthy embargo, which was not relaxed until President Nixon's dramatic visit to the People's Republic in 1972, American criticisms of Maoist "autarky" are more than a bit hypocritical.

The principle of self-reliance was also deeply rooted in the Chinese Communist revolutionary tradition. During the long revolutionary era, especially during the wartime years when Communist base areas were threatened by both Japanese and Guomindang blockades, economic self-sufficiency was necessary for sheer survival.[22] Moreover, in a land that had been subjected for a century to foreign economic exploitation and humiliation, it is more than understandable that foreign economic relationships would be approached with considerable suspicion and wariness—and that there would be a strong desire to demonstrate that the Chinese people could build their own

---

[22] For a detailed and perceptive analysis of Communist economic policies during the revolutionary years, focusing on the need for self-sufficiency, see Mark Selden, *The Yenan Way in Revolutionary China* (Cambridge: Harvard University Press, 1971), especially Chapter 6.

independent economic future through their own efforts. Although Maoist China was not nearly as autarkic as it so often has been portrayed, foreign trade and technology imports remained marginal elements in a Maoist economic policy that aimed to create an organic, unified, and largely self-reliant (if not wholly self-sufficient) national market.

The principle of self-reliance did not long survive the passing of Mao Zedong. Indeed, it was abandoned by Mao's initial successor, Hua Guofeng, who briefly paraded across the Chinese political stage in Maoist garb. Hua's Ten Year Plan called for massive imports of foreign technology, necessitating rapidly expanding foreign trade and substantial amounts of foreign aid, credits, and loans. Although Hua's extravagant Ten Year Plan was scrapped early in 1979, shortly following Deng Xiaoping's triumph at the Third Plenum, the Deng regime's new economic policies retained Hua's desire to integrate China with the world capitalist market.

As early as 1975 Deng Xiaoping had criticized what he called a "closed-door attitude" held by many of China's leaders. When he achieved power he proclaimed an "open-door" policy for China's international economic relations. The term "open-door," so long and so intimately associated with the history of Western imperialism in China, was a rather curious choice. One wonders whether the term was revived in a fit of historical absentmindedness or chosen in a deliberate attempt to appeal to Western greed. However that may have been, imports and exports soon began to pass through Deng's open door in ever-greater volume. From 1978 to 1988, the value of China's foreign trade more than quadrupled, growing (in current U.S. dollars) from $20 billion to over $80 billion.[23] It quadrupled once again over the next six years, reaching US$236 billion in 1994.[24]

The rapid growth of China's foreign trade in the Deng era should not be considered an abandonment of self-reliance. Indeed, it might better be viewed as a continuation, albeit at a vastly accelerated pace, of the upsurge in foreign trade during the last years of the Mao

[23] Harding, *China's Second Revoluion*, Table 6-1, p. 139; and CIA, *China: Economic Performance in 1987 and Outlook for 1988* (Washington, D.C.: Directorate of Intelligence, EA88-10018, May 1988), Fig. 4, p. 6.

[24] *China Daily*, January 14, 1995, p. 5. Japan was China's largest trading partner in 1994, closely followed by Hong Kong and the United States.

regime, a development dictated by Chinese economic interests and one permitted by a combination of favorable internal and external circumstances not present before the early 1970s. Autarky is no virtue, revolutionary or otherwise, and is certainly not to be equated with the idea of self-reliance. The People's Republic is no less capable than any other nation of pursuing the "law of comparative advantage" in the conduct of foreign trade. The trade that has developed in the post-Mao years has proceeded, by and large, in accordance with the proclaimed Chinese principle of "equality and mutual benefit."

It is ironic that the Maoist policy of self-reliance enabled China, in the post-Mao era, to join the capitalist world economy on far more favorable terms than would have been the case twenty years earlier. During the period when it largely withdrew from the world market, the Maoist state pursued rapid industrial development accompanied by policies of protectionism for infant industries, the building of new administrative structures, and heavy investment in infrastructure, health, and education. This entailed, among other things, the sacrifice of consumer interests and living standards in the short term to achieve long-term benefits. Those benefits became apparent in the Deng era, when China entered the world market on relatively favorable terms and with highly successful economic results. The People's Republic, albeit unconsciously, had followed the essentials of the economic strategy that Friedrich List had devised for Prussia in the nineteenth century, when the backward German states were confronted with the economic and political dominance of an industrialized England.[25]

What raises eyebrows is not the expansion of foreign trade in the post-Mao era but rather the decision to open China to foreign capitalist investment, the craving for foreign capital (which, the reformers insist, is essential for rapid modernization), and, to satisfy that craving, the seeming re-creation of many of the practices and institutional arrangements historically associated with pre-1949 semi-colonial China. The most striking example of this has been the establishment of "special economic zones."

[25] The parallel between Maoist China and the Listian strategy is insightfully drawn by Wolfgang Deckers in "Mao Zedong and Friedrich List on De-Linking," *Journal of Contemporary Asia*, Vol. 24, No. 2 (1994), pp. 217–26.

Special economic zones (SEZs) are not a Chinese invention. When China's reformers began to promote the idea in 1979, there were nearly a hundred such zones operating in various Third World countries, especially in Asia, the most successful located in Taiwan and South Korea. As the Chinese zones were being planned, the Beijing government sent study teams to investigate the operation of such zones in Sri Lanka and the Philippines. The nature and purposes of these zones are simple and can be briefly summarized. Small and well-defined territories within the host countries, they are designed to attract foreign capital and technology by offering foreign investors favorable conditions for making quick profits, especially an unlimited supply of cheap labor and preferential tax and other fiscal arrangements, and the modern amenities of life that temporary foreign residents desire. It is usually stipulated that goods produced in the zones will be exported so as not to compete with domestic industries. At the same time, by confining foreign operations to defined territorial enclaves, it is assumed that the country as a whole can be insulated from foreign influences, a political and psychological necessity in ex-colonial lands historically exploited by imperialism.

The first four special economic zones were designated in 1979 along the southern coast in the provinces of Guangdong and Fujian.[26] The zones, their proponents argued, would attract foreign capital, assist in introducing advanced technology, create new jobs, and serve as "schools" for learning the principles of the marketplace that could then be applied to the structural reform of the urban economy.[27] The original conception of the special economic zones as "schools" that would offer lessons of general relevance for economic reform imparted to these enclaves more than the marginal place they otherwise might have occupied in the economic history of post-Mao China. As Suzanne Pepper observed: "China SEZs . . . represented in miniature the very essence of the new post-Mao reforms. They were advertised

[26] The original four zones were Shenzhen, located near Hong Kong, the largest and most important of the four; Zhuhai, a tiny enclave established near the Portuguese colony of Macao; Shantou, the old treaty port city of Swatow in northern Guangdong province; and Xiamen, the former treaty port known as Amoy located in Fujian province across the straits from Taiwan. The latter two were selected because of their ties with Chinese communities in Southeast Asia, the Philippines, and Taiwan.

[27] Xu Dixin, "China's Special Economic Zones," Beijing Review, December 14, 1981, pp. 14–17.

and promoted as a casebook example of the principles the reformers hoped to adopt for the economy as a whole."[28]

While the SEZs were indeed advertised and promoted by the Deng regime, they also were an embarrassment from the outset, on both nationalist and socialist grounds. Territorial enclaves dominated by foreign capital, where privileged foreigners were served by Chinese servants on Chinese soil, were uncomfortably reminiscent of the old treaty ports and foreign concessions imposed by imperialist aggressors in the nineteenth century. Moreover, the undisguised capitalist character of the special economic zones, with profit maximization the sole motive and principle of economic life, and indeed all aspects of life, seemed incongruous with a presumably "socialist" Chinese economy.

Party leaders and theoreticians were quick to dismiss the treaty port analogy, emphasizing that China retained full sovereignty and political control over the zones, unlike the imperialist enclaves of China's semi-colonial past. Indeed, the historical analogy was faulty, as official ideology claimed. It was the Communist state that had created the zones and had the power to abolish them. Nonetheless, the zones increasingly grated on still-raw nationalist nerves, especially among older Party officials who had participated in a revolution that had combined a war for national independence with socialist strivings. As Harry Harding noted: "One senior leader who had visited Shenzhen [the model zone] was quoted in the Chinese press as saying: 'Apart from the five-starred red flag, everything in Shenzhen has turned capitalist.' Another is alleged to have burst into tears during his inspection tour, declaring that he would never have joined the Communist revolution had he known that Shenzhen would be the result. . . . And the Chinese press repeatedly acknowledged that high Party leaders were comparing the special economic zones to the treaty ports and foreign concessions of the nineteenth and early twentieth centuries."[29]

The regime had an even more difficult time explaining away the

---

[28] Suzanne Pepper, "China's Special Economic Zones: The Current Rescue Bid for a Faltering Experiment." Originally published as a University Field Staff International Report in September 1986 and reprinted in the *Bulletin of Concerned Asian Scholars*, Vol. 20, No. 3 (1988), p. 4.

[29] Harding, *China's Second Revolution*, p. 168.

zones' obviously capitalist nature. Debates erupted over the proper characterization of their economies, with theoreticians variously concluding that they were capitalist, socialist, semi-socialist, New Democratic, and state capitalist. Eventually it was more or less officially and scholastically agreed that while "the principal contradiction" in the zones was indeed between socialist and capitalist modes of production, it was the former that constituted "the principal aspect" of the contradiction. The zones were essentially "socialist," it was officially concluded, by virtue of the overall political dominance of the Communist state. That state, it was emphasized, "controls all economic lifelines," and the special economic zones in general were "under the supervision of the working class state."[30]

In the end, neither nationalist nor socialist considerations counted for much. Ideological exercises continued to be performed, of course, but state policy on the SEZs was determined by purely economic considerations, a weighing of their successes and failures in fulfilling their assigned financial roles. And since the zones seemed economically promising in the early 1980s, state leaders invested increasing amounts of economic and political capital in their development. In 1984 the territorial areas of the four original zones were expanded. Fourteen coastal cities, from Qinhuangdao and Tianjin in the North to Beihai in the Southwest, along with the island of Hainan, were opened to foreign investment. In early 1985, Premier Zhao Ziyang announced that three large regions had been similarly opened as areas for preferential foreign investment and trade—the Pearl River delta surrounding Canton, the Min River delta in Fujian province, and the Yangtze River delta around Shanghai—with two additional regions in North China, the Jiaodong peninsula in Shandong province and the Liaodong peninsula in Manchuria, soon to follow.

The decision to open virtually the entire Chinese coast to foreign investment was motivated in part by the seemingly spectacular success of Shenzhen, one of the original four special economic zones. In the early 1980s, Shenzhen had become the focus of Beijing's efforts to demonstrate the efficacy of its new international economic

---

[30] Shi Xiulin, "Is the Economy of China's Special Economic Zones State Capitalist in Nature?" in Xu Dixin (ed.), *Jingjitegu Tansuo Wenti* (Exploring Questions Concerning the Economic Zones) (*Fujian renmin chubanshe*, 1981).

policies. Partly because of its proximity to Hong Kong, partly because of special assistance from the central government, the once-obscure border town was rapidly transformed into a major center of modern economic activity. Heavily advertised in the official press as the model for special economic zones and for the "open-door" policy in general, by 1984 Shenzhen was proclaimed "the vanguard of urban reform" for all of China.[31]

The statistical and physical transformation was remarkable. In a period of five years (1980–84) it was claimed that Shenzhen had concluded over 3,000 contracts and agreements with foreign investors from fifty countries valued at US$2.3 billion. Of joint-venture arrangements approved for the whole of China, about half were located in Shenzhen. The number of manufacturing enterprises increased from 26 in 1980 to 500 in 1984 while total output grew 29-fold. The population of the zone mushroomed from 25,000 to 350,000, and was projected to reach a million inhabitants by the end of the century. The value of per capita output reportedly approached US$2,000, nearly twenty times the national average, while personal income was said to average almost five times that of urban residents in China as a whole.

This dizzying rate of economic growth, rushing along at what popularly became known as "Shenzhen speed," was facilitated by the building of a modern infrastructure, largely financed by the central government. Shenzhen, or, more precisely, the once-empty fields that surrounded the old town, began to look like a modern city, with industrial parks, high-rise apartments, modern hotels, an impressive new university, a public library, as well as TV and radio stations—all speedily constructed. Its towering International Trade Center is one of the tallest and most modern buildings in all of China.

The Shenzhen boom brought Deng Xiaoping to the special economic zones for an inspection tour early in 1984. Deng was impressed. "The development and experience of Shenzhen proves that our policy of setting up special economic zones is correct," he proclaimed.[32] The personal blessing of China's paramount leader was shortly followed by the opening of the fourteen coastal cities and

[31] *Hongqi* (Red Flag), No. 20 (October 21, 1984), cited in Pepper, "China's Special Economic Zones," p. 10.
[32] *People's Daily*, February 2, 1984. Cited in Pepper, "China's Special Economic Zones," p. 8.

three regions as economic and technical development zones, as well as the inauguration of a new and ambitious phase in market-oriented urban reform.

Hardly more than a year after Deng Xiaoping had placed his personal stamp of approval on Shenzhen, grave deficiencies in the experiment began to be revealed, first by observers in Hong Kong and then in a swelling stream of official acknowledgments during 1985.

First, Shenzhen's much-celebrated record in attracting foreign capital investment, its raison d'être, was far less than it seemed to be. Most of what local officials reported as foreign investment, it was discovered, were not firm contracts but simply letters of intent, with most of the promised capital failing to materialize. Moreover, two-thirds of Shenzhen's capital came not from foreign sources but rather from within China—invested by Chinese enterprises, banks, and provincial governments on more favorable terms than could be obtained elsewhere in the country. Moreover, such investment naturally tended to flow to where immediate returns were highest, to trade and real estate rather than to industrial development. Also, total investment of all types amounted to considerably less than what the government had spent to build Shenzhen's infrastructure. Between 1979 and 1984, it was calculated, foreign investment amounted to no more than one-third of the city's total capital investment.[33]

Shenzhen's impressive figures on industrial development also proved distorted and misleading. Statistics on industrial output were mostly based on the construction of buildings and the zone's general infrastructure, primarily financed by state funds.[34] Although industrial enterprises were established, few used the advanced technology that China's reform leaders hoped the SEZs would help to introduce. Of the 500 or so industrial concerns in Shenzhen in 1984, only

---

[33] Pepper, "China's Special Economic Zones," p. 11.

[34] The official figures on Shenzhen's 1983 industrial output claimed a value of RMB 720 million, but it was later demonstrated (by a Hong Kong economist in a pro-PRC periodical published in Hong Kong) that building construction and property development accounted for about RMB 600 million of that figure. Chen Wenhong, "Where Do Shenzhen's Problems Lie?" *Guangjiaojing* (Wide Angle), No. 2 (February 1985). Cited in Pepper, p. 1. Chen's wide-ranging critique of the economic performance of the SEZs set off, or at least brought into the open, a lengthy controversy on the topic in China which continued in various forms and forums over the remainder of the year. On the impact of Chen's critique, see Pepper, pp. 10–11.

10 percent were advanced technological operations—the remainder were mostly small, labor-intensive enterprises engaged in assembly, processing, and packaging. The overwhelming majority of investors were Hong Kong businessmen attracted by an unlimited supply of cheap labor, duty-free import privileges for capital goods and raw materials, and the prospect of easy entrée to the China market as a whole. Of all of the profits generated in Shenzhen in 1984, only 25 percent came from industrial operations; most of the remainder were derived from retail trade, real estate development, and tourism.[35]

As Shenzhen's economic practices and performance came under critical scrutiny in 1985, it was further revealed that Shenzhen (as was the case with the other zones) had failed to assume its assigned role as an earner of foreign exchange. Rather than exporting its products, some 70 percent of the goods produced in Shenzhen were sold on the Chinese domestic market, often illegally for foreign currencies. Moreover, most of what Shenzhen imported, either from abroad or from other parts of China, wasn't consumed within the zone itself but rather resold for illegal profits to buyers in the interior of China. In short, Shenzhen, in Suzanne Pepper's words, had become "an entrepôt trading center for reduced-duty and duty-free (and smuggled) foreign-made consumer goods,"[36] thereby contributing to the decline in China's foreign exchange reserves and to the alarming 1985 trade deficit.[37]

By the summer of 1985 it had become clear to even the most ardent market reformers that the special economic zones had failed to fulfill their primary goals. Rather than enlarging the pool of capital available for productive investment, they had consumed capital. Instead of models of modern industrial development, the zones had developed into trade and transshipment centers, flooding the domestic market with duty-free consumer goods manufactured abroad, often

[35] Pepper, p. 11.
[36] Ibid.
[37] After enjoying foreign trade surpluses through the early 1980s, China suffered a $12.1 billion deficit in 1985 and a deficit of $8.7 billion in 1986, resulting in a sharp decline in the foreign reserves painstakingly built up over several decades. The government's foreign exchange reserves fell precipitously from $16.7 billion in 1984 to $10.2 billion in 1986. Harding, *China's Second Revolution*, p. 151. The freewheeling SEZs were only a small part of the larger problem of the consequences of market-oriented decentralization undertaken in the second wave of urban reform, beginning in the autumn of 1984.

conveyed through illegal or quasi-legal channels, with a varied assortment of entrepreneurs and officials skimming the profits in the process. Rather than serving as conduits for modern technology, the zones attracted labor-intensive enterprises engaged in assembly and processing.

While the special economic zones failed to yield most of their anticipated economic benefits, they did generate a good many unanticipated problems. In addition to draining the state treasury, the zones re-created many of the features associated with the treaty ports of "old China"—patterns of servitude to foreigners, oppressive forms of labor recruitment and exploitation, and a host of social vices, including prostitution. The zones became places where shady entrepreneurs struck deals with greedy officials, where black markets in foreign currencies flourished, and where myriad forms of corruption were generated. Symbolic of the shadowy character of economic life in the special economic zones was the fact that among the first foreign banks awarded a license to open a branch in Shenzhen was the Bank of Credit & Commerce International—international bankers for the world's most corrupt politicians, spies, narcotics dealers, arms merchants, and terrorists. It was revealed in 1991—when the scandal-ridden BCCI was forced to close its offices in more than seventy countries—that some of China's largest state banks were among the depositors at the BCCI's Shenzhen branch.[38]

Many of the corrupt practices common in the zones—such as padding of construction contracts and bribing officials—were relatively inconsequential, and by the mid-1980s were standard practice throughout China. But some were conducted on a grand scale and could not be ignored. The grandest of all originated on the island of Hainan in 1984.

When Premier Zhao Ziyang visited Hainan in 1983 he had declared that the island's developmental goal was to reach the economic levels of Taiwan within twenty years through the use of market mechanisms. To that end, Hainan was granted a wide degree of autonomy in conducting its own foreign trade, including the right to import a variety of goods duty-free and to retain most of the foreign exchange

---

[38] Julia Leung, "Beijing's Reserves Are Among Funds Frozen at BCCI," *The Wall Street Journal*, August 5, 1991, p. A4.

earned from exports. The officials who governed the island were quick to take advantage of the opportunity, obtaining quasi-legal loans in foreign currency, which eventually amounted to over half a billion U.S. dollars. They imported 89,000 automobiles and trucks, 122,000 motorcycles, nearly 3 million television sets, and 250,000 VCRs, which were then sold on the mainland at three or four times their purchase prices. Party and government officials profited, as well as some 800 Hainan enterprises and their personnel and innumerable bureaucrats on the mainland who served as middlemen in what became a "web of corruption" extending to twenty-seven provinces and cities.[39]

The Hainan operation, which ran uninterrupted from January 1984 through March 1985, was only one example, albeit a rather spectacular one, of the kinds of corruption that were becoming pervasive in China under market-type reforms and the open-door policy. They were modes of economic activity that required not simply entrepreneurial skill but also access to political power. The larger implications of this marriage between bureaucratic power and private profit unintentionally wrought by the post-Mao reforms will be examined in Chapter 11.

The public exposure of the Hainan scheme in the summer of 1985 lent urgency to the critical reexamination of the special economic zones that was already underway—and emboldened critics of Deng's foreign economic policies. The focus was Shenzhen, advertised as the most successful of the experiments. As early as April 1985, Vice-Premier Yao Yilin, an economic specialist associated with the moderate reformer Chen Yun, remarked during the course of an inspection tour of Shenzhen that the enclave survived only through "blood transfusions" from Beijing. It was time, he suggested, to cut off the economic lifeline and prevent the further draining of funds from the state treasury.[40] By the summer of 1985, Deng Xiaoping,

---

[39] For accounts of the Hainan scandal, see Pepper, "China's Special Economic Zones," pp. 14–15; and Lau Shinghou and Louise de Rosario, "Anatomy of a Scam," *China Trade Report*, October 1985, pp. 8–10. It is noteworthy that the Hainan operation proceeded for over a year with central government knowledge and authorization—on the dubious grounds that it was a means to accumulate developmental capital—before political pressure forced Beijing to curtail the more glaringly corrupt practices.

[40] Cited in Harding, *China's Second Revolution*, p. 169.

who a little more than a year before had proclaimed that the history of Shenzhen proved the correctness of current policy on the special economic zones, now relegated Shenzhen to the status of an "experiment"—and indeed an experiment that might fail. In the latter eventuality, he sagely advised, appropriate "lessons" should be drawn.

The debate on Shenzhen continued for the remainder of the year, with promoters of the SEZ policy attempting to fend off a growing torrent of criticism. Shenzhen and the other zones, it was charged, were economic failures as well as social embarrassments. The controversy over the zones came to a head (and was brought to an official end) at a national work conference convened at the end of the year. From December 15, 1985, to January 5, 1986, top Party leaders and their economic advisors met to deliberate the fate and future of the zones. Since Deng Xiaoping and other market-oriented Party reformers had lent so much of their prestige to lauding Shenzhen as a model, it was decided that the political costs of abandoning the experiment were greater than the economic costs of prolonging the city's life. Thus the official verdict was that the original policy on the SEZs was correct and would remain unaltered, although officials in Shenzhen and the other zones were enjoined to improve the style and substance of their work in order to achieve more salutary economic results.[41]

The official slogan was: "The whole country supports the SEZs, and the SEZs serve the whole country," but actual state policy was to deemphasize the SEZs for a time and reduce support for their operations. Government funds going to Shenzhen were cut by nearly 50 percent, severe limits were placed on bank credits and loans, it was ordered that old loans be repaid by 1989, and central state controls were imposed on trading activities to prevent the lucrative practice of selling imported duty-free goods in other parts of China. As a consequence, Shenzhen experienced a severe economic depression in 1986. Construction was brought to a virtual halt with half-finished buildings on deserted construction sites standing as grim reminders of Shenzhen's boomtown past; tourism declined as plans to turn the enclave into "the Hawaii of the East" were abandoned;

[41] Pepper, "China's Special Economic Zones," pp. 16–20.

and many factories closed. Tens of thousands of migrant laborers—
especially young rural women employed in factories or in menial
service jobs—found themselves unemployed and were told to return
to their village homes.[42] While Shenzhen and the other SEZs were
permitted to linger on, no new zones were established and increasingly little was heard or written about the once much-heralded old
ones for half a decade. It was a dramatic demonstration that ultimate
economic authority still resided in the central Chinese state, which
had the power to extinguish free markets as rapidly as it could create
them.

The deemphasis on the original special economic zones was not
a rejection of foreign investment. Foreign capital was simply redi-
rected to the established coastal cities, mostly the former treaty ports,
which were better prepared to receive capital investment and where
the larger share of it naturally had gone in any event.[43] In particular,
the Chinese government attempted to direct foreign capital to Canton,
Shanghai, Tianjin, and Dalian. By 1986 foreign investment in
China—which now included wholly foreign-owned enterprises as
well as joint-venture arrangements[44]—came to approximately US$8
billion. New and less restrictive regulations promulgated in 1986
were designed to encourage the investment of foreign capital at a
more rapid pace—by lowering taxes and other costs of doing business
in China, by removing a variety of bureaucratic bottlenecks, by making explicit the right of foreign firms to hire and fire Chinese workers
at will, and by easing restrictions on the acquisition of foreign
exchange. While these measures did not fully satisfy the demands of
foreign capitalists, who desired direct access to the domestic Chinese

[42] On labor conditions in Shenzhen, especially gender segregation in the workforce and its
broader implications for workers in post-Mao China, see Phyllis Andors' detailed and perceptive investigation "Women and Work in Shenzhen," *Bulletin of Concerned Asian Scholars*,
Vol. 20, No. 3 (July–September 1988), pp. 22–41.

[43] As of mid-1985, Carl Riskin observed: "The bulk of foreign investments, especially the
larger projects, have . . . located outside the SEZs, which have tended to attract mostly overseas
Chinese investment in relatively small undertakings." Riskin, *China's Political Economy*,
p. 331.

[44] Deng's "open-door" policy initially limited foreign ownership to 49 percent of enterprises
in which the Chinese state was the senior partner in "joint ventures." In 1983, however, it
was decided to permit fully foreign-owned and foreign-operated Chinese plants and other economic enterprises to be established on Chinese soil. This facilitated rapid growth of direct
foreign investment.

market as well as unrestricted rights to repatriate their profits in foreign currencies, they did facilitate a greater inflow of capital. By the early spring of 1989, on the eve of the Tiananmen massacre, foreign investment in China, including capital contractually pledged, had grown to US$28 billion,[45] a very substantial sum, although far less than the economic reformers had anticipated a decade earlier. In the 1990s, however, foreign capital began to flow into China at astonishingly high, and accelerating, rates, US$26 billion in 1993 alone and $34 billion in 1994.[46]

China's integration into the world capitalist market has perforce made the economy of the People's Republic increasingly subject to international economic vicissitudes, and the world market dominated by the advanced capitalist countries has not always been kind to developing countries, especially those laboring under the burden of foreign debt. China's burgeoning foreign trade has made its economy subject to both the benefits and the costs of changing world patterns of trade, which are beyond the power of any nation to control. Foreign capital investment has become a significant, although hardly a dominant, factor in the Chinese industrial economy, with enterprises financed by foreign investment growing far more rapidly than those in the state and collective sectors.[47] And China, during the Deng reform period, has been transformed from a debt-free into a major debtor nation. Beginning in 1979, Beijing began to seek large loans from foreign banks and governments and international lending organizations. China's debt grew rapidly in the 1980s, totaling US$28 billion by 1986[48] and reaching at least US$35 billion in 1988.[49] The largest share was owed to private Japanese banks, and much of this consisted of relatively short-term loans at high rates of interest. Considerable

---

[45] *China Daily*, April 21, 1989, p. 1.

[46] *China Daily*, January 19, 1995, p. 1.

[47] In 1988, for example, the output of the foreign-funded sector of Chinese industry—although accounting for less than 2 percent of total industrial output—doubled, whereas state-sector output increased by about 13 percent and the collective sector grew by approximately 29 percent. U.S. Central Intelligence Agency, *The Chinese Economy in 1988 and 1989* (Washington, D.C.: August 1989), Appendix A.

[48] Harding, *China's Second Revolution*, Table 6-7, p. 153.

[49] The actual amount was greater, since the $35 billion figure does not include debt contracted by provincial governments, which by virtue of reformist decentralizing measures were granted considerable autonomy to arrange foreign loans on their own. For the latter, no reliable data is available.

sums were also borrowed on more favorable terms from international financial organizations, traditionally dominated by American capital and interests, especially the World Bank, which over the 1980s arranged loans to China in the amount of $8.5 billion.

While it can be taken for granted that private bank loans to China are made (usually only with the blessings of their respective governments) for the purpose of making profits, both through the collection of interest and by facilitating the opening of markets, it should be noted that what are benignly called "international lending organizations" are by no means purely charitable institutions impartially assisting impoverished Third World countries. Loans from the World Bank, whose largest borrowers are China and India, generally finance worthy projects on highly favorable terms, often at annual interest rates of 1 percent or less, repayable over periods of up to forty years. But along with the generous loans come generous doses of "advice" on the virtues of capitalism and free markets. On the World Bank's role in China during the 1980s, for example, a *New York Times* correspondent in Beijing observed: "During China's economic change, when Chinese economists debated vigorously about stock markets and privatization, the World Bank was there, its data-sheet wizards and worldly economists offering strategy tips and lectures on how to create economic progress. And the bankers were always ready to back up the ideas with money. . . . The Bank had a direct line to China's research organizations, even to some of the nation's top leaders, who were willing and eager to absorb advice on how to make China economically strong."[50] The World Bank's president in the late 1980s, the conservative Republican politician Barber B. Conable, was unusually vigorous in promoting the virtues of a market economy and in pursuing American political and economic interests.[51] It is the unstated assumption on both sides that the World Bank's continued generosity presupposes the continuation of market-oriented policies in China.[52] A striking illustration of this was the resumption in February 1990 of World Bank loans to China which had been suspended

---

[50] Sheryl WuDunn, "World Bank's Lesser Role in China," *The New York Times*, March 5, 1990, p. D8.
[51] See, for example, Clyde H. Farnsworth, "Conable's World Bank," *The New York Times*, February 18, 1990, p. F5.
[52] CIA, *The Chinese Economy in 1988 and 1989*, p. 10.

in June 1989 following the massacre in Tiananmen Square. What changed in China between June and February were not the political policies of the Chinese government, which remained no less repressive than during the preceding half year, but rather assurances on the part of an apparently stable Chinese state leadership that they had no intention of abandoning market reforms. In this, the World Bank, as was customary, followed closely the policies of the U.S. government.

Yet China's growing foreign debt and its thirst for foreign investment, constraining as they may be, do not portend a new era of dependency, much less a reversion to its old semi-colonial status. The Deng regime's policies on foreign investment and borrowing have been, on the whole, comparatively cautious and conservative—a source of considerable frustration for potential foreign investors and bankers. Moreover, the volume of foreign investment and debt, while large in absolute terms, is comparatively small relative to the size of China's economy and even smaller relative to the size of its population. China's foreign debt is less than US$40 per capita—as compared, for example, to approximately $2,000 in Hungary, once the model of market socialism that Chinese reformers were eager to emulate. Most important, the existence of a strong and highly nationalistic Chinese state stands as guarantor that foreign loans and investments will not threaten Chinese national sovereignty. That state, however mixed a blessing it might be in other respects, also stands as testimony to the failure of all historical analogies with earlier eras—when weak, divided, and politically fragmented China was easy prey to the economic and political ambitions of foreign powers. This clearly is no longer the case. The special economic zones, however superficially similar to the old treaty ports, are, after all, creations of the Chinese state, not impositions of foreign imperialism. Such national embarrassments that have accompanied China's entrance into the world of international trade and finance, the leaders of China have mostly brought upon themselves.

What the People's Republic has lost through Deng Xiaoping's open-door policies is not its national autonomy but rather a certain degree of national self-confidence. The Maoist policy of self-reliance, whatever its economic and other deficiencies, did help to convince the Chinese people, so long the psychological as well as economic victims of foreign dominance and humiliations, that they themselves could build a new and modern China through their own efforts and in their own fashion, avoiding in the process what Mao Zedong called "the mechanical absorption of foreign materials." That newly won sense of national self-confidence was quickly undermined by the Deng regime's euphoric promotion of Western capitalist models and techniques. Yet the effects of foreign borrowing are more psychological than political and economic. An independent China, although not necessarily a socialist or self-confident one, will remain one of the enduring achievements of the Communist Revolution.

What needs to be pondered more seriously than misplaced analogies with China's semi-colonial past are the implications of post-Mao international economic policies from the perspective of "world systems" theory. According to most exponents of that view of the modern world economy, all societies, on pain of extinction, must adapt themselves to a global capitalist system. From this it follows that the Deng regime's effort to integrate China into the world capitalist economy is more or less necessary for the country's survival, dictated by the larger economic forces at work in the world in which China finds itself. For Immanuel Wallerstein, the best known of the world-systems theorists, a genuine socialist movement or society would have to seek to "transform the [capitalist] world system as a whole, rather than profit by it."[53] That the post-Mao regime has definitely opted for the latter course is quite obvious, and from Wallerstein's perspective, perhaps quite inevitable.

No less inevitable are the ultimate effects of the capitalist world system on the internal organization of "socialist" countries. As Edward Friedman once put it: "The imperatives of the world market force state power-holders to act in a capitalist manner, that is, to organize their society for competition in world exchange."[54] This is not the place to discuss the validity of the proposition. What is note-

---

[53] Immanuel Wallerstein, *The Capitalist World-Economy* (Cambridge: Cambridge University Press, 1979), p. 101.

[54] Edward Friedman, "Maoist Conceptualizations of the Capitalist World Economy," in Terrence K. Hopkins and Immanuel Wallerstein (eds.), *Processes of the World-System* (Beverly Hills, Calif.: Sage Publications, 1980), p. 181. This, of course, means "the impossibility of building socialism" in individual nation-states whose policies and actions are perforce severely limited by the world capitalist order.

worthy is that the view is shared by many of China's leading economic reformers, who have looked to capitalist experiments in China's international economic policy, such as the special economic zones, as models for the reorganization of China's urban industrial economy as a whole. We must now turn to that urban reform effort, which was resumed in late 1984 and which culminated in the tragedy of 1989.

INDUSTRIAL REFORM: PHASE II, 1984–88

A renewed attempt to transform the urban economy was inaugurated in the autumn of 1984 when the Party Central Committee convened to formally ratify the reform measures proposed by Party Secretary-General Hu Yaobang, Premier Zhao Ziyang, and China's paramount leader, Deng Xiaoping.[55] The new urban reform program did not differ greatly from what had been attempted in 1979 and then largely abandoned late in 1980, save that the 1984 program was more comprehensive and detailed and was implemented with greater vigor and determination. Brimming with confidence from their success in having so rapidly transformed the countryside in accordance with market precepts, the leaders in Beijing undertook to transform the urban economy with a renewed sense of hope, even while recognizing that reforming the economic structure of the cities was a far more difficult task than decollectivizing the countryside.

The guiding principle of urban reform was to remove direct government control over most economic activities in favor of the "free play" of market forces, which it was assumed could more efficiently and rationally determine what was produced and how the products were sold. To that end, greater autonomy was granted to state industrial and other urban enterprises, which were to operate increasingly according to the criterion of profitability and under the supreme control of a director trained in the most advanced managerial methods. Accordingly, the role of the enterprise Party committee, traditionally

---

[55] "Decision of the Central Committee of the Communist Party of China on Reform of the Economic Structure" (October 20, 1984) FBIS Daily Report: China, October 22, 1984, pp. K1–K19.

one of the major instruments of central economic control, was drastically reduced. Central economic controls were further to be reduced by eliminating automatic state capital allocations to enterprises, which were to be replaced by bank loans. Since the loans bore interest and were repayable, it was assumed that they would encourage factory directors to utilize scarce capital with greater prudence and in a more economically rational fashion, thereby mitigating the chronic problem of the overproduction of some goods while there were persistent shortages of other products.

The state also deregulated various commodities whose production and pricing hitherto had been determined by central planners. It was concluded that the extraordinarily complex problem of "price reform"—the creation of a "rational" pricing structure in which the prices of commodities reflected the true costs of their production as well as the demand for them—was well beyond the technical capabilities of state economic planners to resolve. It was thus decided to rely more on market forces to perform this function. Accordingly, the number of goods subject to state-determined prices was reduced in late 1984, and price controls were removed on a variety of key food products (including meat, fish, vegetables, and eggs) in early 1985. Moreover, with the adoption of the "procurement contract system" in early 1985, all agricultural products were freed from mandatory state planning and state price controls. Finally, a new round of administrative decentralization was decreed—an exercise performed several times in the Mao era—allowing provincial and local governments a considerable degree of authority over governmental revenues and expenditures.

The new reform program also emphasized the virtues of specialization and a greater division of labor in industrial organization. Increasing numbers of young and middle-aged managerial personnel were selected for advanced study in modern technology and capitalist managerial methods at universities and business schools in the United States and other advanced capitalist countries, and several foreign-modeled managerial training and industrial relations institutes were established in China.

For the workers who actually performed industrial labor—and who were still on occasion ritualistically referred to as "the masters of the enterprise"—the reformers demanded greater discipline in the workplace and also offered greater material incentives with wider wage and bonus differentials. To such incentives, most workers had proved stubbornly resistant over the preceding years, leading reform ideologists to lament that urban workers (as well as peasants) were still under the influence of such "feudal" ideas as "egalitarianism." However incongruous the identification of egalitarian strivings with feudalism, it had become standard practice in post-Mao China to attribute virtually anything deemed undesirable to the lingering influences of China's feudal past.

The most eminently capitalist of the reform proposals was the principle of enterprise profitability, the notion that factories and other workplaces should thrive or fail in accordance with the criterion of whether they showed profits or losses. Capitalism, after all, is a mode of production that is based on profit maximization, not one in which production is undertaken primarily to meet social needs. Enterprises which are not sufficiently profitable are doomed to failure, whatever their social utility. Profits in a system driven by what Marx called a "werewolf hunger" for surplus value and capital accumulation is precisely what is called "the bottom line" in contemporary popular discourse in the United States. This simple phrase, it would seem, is approximately what China's reformers had in mind when they proposed the principle of enterprise profitability. For many, the proposal conjured up images of closed factories and unemployed workers, fears that were not alleviated by the announcement of plans for a national bankruptcy law, which, after considerable and heated debate, was adopted in December 1986 by the National People's Congress.[56]

A second eminently capitalist feature of the reform program was the effort to universalize a market in labor. Wage labor as such is not uniquely capitalist. It is compatible with a variety of modes of production, and indeed has been the predominant form of remuneration in the urban economic sector throughout the history of the People's Republic. What distinguishes wage labor in a capitalist economy is that human labor-power is a commodity, to be freely bought and sold much in the fashion that the products laborers create are bought and sold on the market. This commodity character of

[56] Experiments in bankruptcy laws and proceedings had been undertaken in several cities for several years prior to the passage of the national law. On the debate over the validity of the concept of bankruptcy in a presumably socialist society, see Harding, *China's Second Revolution*, pp. 116–17.

labor, certainly among the more dehumanizing features of capitalism, had been greatly modified in post-1949 China by the new government's promise of full employment and job security. But that "socialist" commitment, never fully implemented even in the cities, had already been undermined by the initial wave of reforms in 1979–80, as noted earlier. By 1984 regular state employees enjoying job tenure and welfare benefits made up only 40 percent of the total industrial labor force, including workers in rural industries. Invoking "objective economic laws," the reformers intended to do away entirely with the iron rice bowl, substituting the authority of managers to hire and fire workers in accordance with fluctuating market conditions and the financial conditions of their enterprises.

However, opposition to labor reform was intense, not only among the state industrial workers who would have been directly affected but also among other members of the laboring population who aspired to their relatively privileged status and who regarded the state's traditional guarantee of job security as a moral obligation that the Communist government owed to all citizens. Opposition also came from within the Party, not simply from selfish officials who wished to preserve bureaucratic control over labor, as reform ideologists usually dismissed it, but from many cadres who were genuinely concerned with the workers' welfare and the fate of socialism. Such opposition rarely found public expression, for Deng Xiaoping unambiguously had placed his power and prestige behind the reform program. But at least one article, which appeared in a Canton newspaper in early 1986, expressed a moral imperative "to cry out for the iron rice-bowl system with a heavy heart" since "many of our revolutionary comrades struggled all their lives so that the people of the whole country could each have an iron rice-bowl."[57] The author, as Gordon White has observed, "probably spoke for many, particularly state and party cadres and state industrial workers, when he argued that job security was part of 'the superiority of socialism' while attempts to undermine it, such as the labor contract system, were comparable to a capitalist 'wage labor' system."[58]

---

[57] Yi Duming, "In Defence of the 'Iron Rice-Bowl' System," *Yangcheng wanbao* (Canton Evening News), February 23, 1986, in Joint Publication Research Service, China Report: Economic Affairs 347 (1986). Cited in Gordon White, "Restructuring the Working Class: Labor Reform in Post-Mao China," in Dirlik and Meisner, *Marxism and the Chinese Experience*, p. 157.
[58] Ibid.

In the end, a compromise of sorts was reached. Workers already employed in state enterprises as of October 1985 retained their job tenure and welfare benefits, while newly hired state workers were to be employed under a contract system for specified periods of time for specific duties. They could be fired by managers who deemed their work unsatisfactory or dismissed for disciplinary reasons, and they could be laid off if the enterprise went bankrupt. Together with the increasing percentage of workers employed in the expanding private and collective sectors of the urban economy, the new employment contract system in state enterprises meant the withering away, if not necessarily the smashing, of the iron rice bowl. It was a victory for the reformers. But, by all accounts, few workers joined in to applaud the triumph.

The third essentially capitalist feature of the economic plan was price reform, which aimed to free a wide variety of commodities from state-determined prices and instead permit them to fluctuate in accordance with the dictates of the market. The reformers took Hungary's three-tiered price system as their model—on the assumption that Hungary was the most advanced model of "market socialism," blissfully ignorant at the time of Hungary's rapidly deteriorating economy. According to this scheme, the prices of essential industrial products such as steel, coal, and oil would remain fixed by the state; other industrial products would be allowed to float between upper and lower ranges set by the state, with the exact price determined by negotiations between buyer and seller; and most consumer goods, along with agricultural products and most foods, would be allowed to fluctuate freely. Price reform, partially introduced in bits and pieces over the early 1980s, was formalized by the Party Central Committee's October 1984 decision.[59]

To the extent that these three planks of the reform program— enterprise profitability, the creation of a free labor market, and price reform—were actually implemented, China was moving rapidly to-

---

[59] "The Decision on Reform of the Economic Structure" was filled with ambiguities and contradictions. As Carl Riskin has observed, it "called for floating prices on the one hand, and 'absolutely' ruled out raising prices 'at will' on the other; it rather confusingly distinguished competition among enterprises which allows 'only the best to survive,' from the capitalist 'law of the jungle,' which means nothing if not survival of the fittest." *China's Political Economy*, p. 352.

ward an essentially capitalist urban economy in the mid-1980s, albeit under the guidance of a strong state that still claimed to be socialist. Implementation, however, was greatly impeded by the negative socioeconomic consequences that almost immediately resulted from the new reform effort. Inflation was the first and most obvious consequence of price reform. The official inflation rate in 1985 was 9 percent, and almost 7 percent in 1986; the actual rates were considerably higher, according to the calculations of most outside observers. It was certainly higher for goods purchased by urban residents, especially food, whose prices increased at alarming double-digit rates. Early in 1985, consumer prices in Beijing shot up by an average of 30 percent, forcing the municipal government to provide new subsidies for residents, one of the main causes of continuing budget deficits. Similar inflationary outbursts were reported in other major urban areas.

Accompanying inflation, and in large part responsible for it, was the phenomenon benignly called an "overheated economy," a term introduced by foreign economists and eagerly adopted by their Chinese counterparts. This euphemism for the "boom" part of the familiar capitalist "boom and bust" cycle denotes a chaotic flurry of financial and productive activity that yields spectacular immediate results (and spectacular profits for well-placed entrepreneurs and officials) but contributes relatively little to long-term economic growth. China experienced such a boom in late 1984 and early 1985. What went into the making of it were the market-oriented measures that again had begun to be introduced in 1982–83 and which were officially sanctioned—and speeded up—by the Party decision of October 1984. These measures included the general relaxation of state controls over the economy; the decentralization of economic authority from Beijing to provincial and local governments; and the considerable leeway given to a great variety of partially autonomous enterprises whose managers—armed with greatly expanded powers over investment, wages, and spending—had been instructed to demonstrate their worth by generating profits. What set off the boom, and ensured that a bust would follow in its wake, was the removal of price controls over many commodities and especially a mid-1984 monetary decision to expand the financial resources and autonomy of the banking system. Individual enterprises and local governments borrowed freely and with great abandon to expand production, especially the production of those consumer goods whose sale would bring immediate profits. Investment soared, as did expenditures for the import of foreign equipment and products, the latter made possible by wider access to foreign exchange. There was also a surge in wage increases and bonus payments, which further fueled consumer buying.

By early 1985 industrial production was growing at an annual rate of 23 percent. However, it was not a pace either desirable or sustainable, as shortages of raw materials, energy, and transportation soon demonstrated—but not before a good many officials with access to scarce materials and supplies had garnered enormous profits.

The problems generated by the chaotic economy, disciplined by neither state nor market, were aggravated by the 1985 drop in grain production, which, along with galloping inflation, growing corruption, budgetary deficits, and grave shortages of raw materials and energy, brought an end to the boom and an end to the reformist euphoria that had reached its zenith in late 1984 and early 1985. It also brought the return of central state economic controls over credit, prices, investment, and foreign trade. A new period of "consolidation," retrenchment, and austerity was announced at the beginning of 1986 amidst a growing number of closed factories and unemployed workers.

Over the remainder of the decade and into the early 1990s, the urban population experienced the vicissitudes typical of an early capitalist industrial regime as the economy passed in cyclical fashion through relatively brief periods of overheating and consolidation. Industrial growth rates remained high, fluctuating between 8 and 21 percent per annum. Government budget deficits also grew in the late 1980s, reaching record highs of US$5.9 billion in 1986, over $6 billion in 1987, and $9.2 billion in 1988.[60] Deficits, in turn, contributed to inflation, which threatened to spiral completely out of control at the end of the decade. Official data on inflation, which considerably underestimates the actual rate, shows inflation proceeding at an annual rate of about 8 percent over the years 1985–87.

[60] CIA estimates based on Chinese statistics. See CIA, *The Chinese Economy in 1988 and 1989*, p. 16.

That rate nearly tripled in 1988, according to official figures, rising to about 20 percent, and rising further to 25 percent in early 1989 —but galloping to even higher levels in Beijing and other large cities, and resulting in what the government acknowledged to be a declining standard of living for much of the urban population in the months leading up to the Beijing uprising of May–June 1989.[61]

Market-oriented reforms continued through the boom and bust cycles, but in fitful and unsystematic fashion. Deng Xiaoping pushed ahead with reformist remedies when political and economic conditions were favorable, retreating when necessary. The more ardent reform ideologists argued that the unanticipated negative consequences of the reforms were due to the failure to implement market principles (and political reforms) in a timely and thoroughgoing fashion. In 1986 they proposed the fuller creation of markets in labor and land, whereby land could be freely bought and sold. They advocated the partial "privatization" of industrial and other state enterprises, which would be leased to individual entrepreneurs, groups of workers, or run by stockholders. Stocks in these enterprises would be sold to government agencies and collective organizations as well as individuals. By the late 1980s, the majority of state enterprises were operating on some sort of modified leasing or contract arrangement. And experimental stock markets also were established, compelling reform theoreticians to make tortuous ideological arguments to reconcile stock exchanges with socialist principles.

The program of the "radical reformers," as the advocates of more or less wholesale marketization and privatization were sometimes misleadingly called, had by now encountered intense bureaucratic opposition. Their most formidable opponent was Chen Yun, perhaps China's first important advocate of market reform[62] and one of the earliest and most politically potent supporters of Deng Xiaoping. In 1985, Chen Yun clashed with Deng. Chen insisted on preserving the

---

[61] Official statistics for the first six months of 1989, for example, show a 19 percent increase in nominal wages and subsidies for state workers, but this was more than offset by an inflation rate of more than 30 percent in Beijing and other large cities.

[62] In 1956–57, Chen Yun had advocated decentralization to the level of producing units (while strengthening the power of central state economic ministries) and a greater reliance on the market. His proposals were opposed not only by Mao Zedong and Liu Shaoqi but Deng Xiaoping as well. See Schurmann, *Ideology and Organization in Communist China*, pp. 195–206.

primacy of central state planning, supported only a relatively narrow range of market-type measures, and envisioned structural changes in the economy as a process spanning many decades rather than a few years.[63] By now the entire reform program had become inextricably intertwined with the increasingly bitter internal Party political struggles that marked the latter years of the Deng era—struggles that were to result in the political demise of Deng's most prominent disciples, Hu Yaobang, Party head from 1981 to early 1987, and Zhao Ziyang, Party leader from early 1987 until June 1989. The political intrigues, along with the social and economic consequences of the reforms, were to contribute to the crisis that would engulf China in 1989.

Despite the frenetic reformist activity, the seemingly sweeping changes in industrial organization and policy, and the grandiose rhetoric that accompanied the urban reform program both in Beijing and abroad, the Deng regime did not produce a significantly higher rate of industrial growth in the 1980s than had been achieved in the Mao era. Between 1978 and 1987, the average rate of growth in the gross value of industrial output was 12 percent[64] and the rate remained approximately the same through the mid-1990s. Over the Mao period—from 1952 to 1978—the industrial growth rate was 11.2 percent, according to official statistics.[65] More surprisingly, and save for a more balanced ratio between heavy and light industry,[66] the reforms yielded little improvement in the areas where Maoist industrialization had been most deficient. As Harry Harding observed in 1987: "China's industrial problem has been a shortage of efficiency and quality, not any lack of speed or quantity. And on these dimensions, the urban reforms have, as yet, had little beneficial effect."[67]

---

[63] Chen Yun, "Speech Delivered at the National Conference" (September 1, 1985), FBIS, September 23, 1985, pp. K13–K16.

[64] Y. Y. Kueh, "The Maoist Legacy and China's New Industrialization Strategy," p. 446, n. 29.

[65] State Statistical Bureau, *Main Indicators, Development of the National Economy of the People's Republic of China (1949–78)*. Many foreign observers calculate the industrial growth rate (1952–78) at about 10 percent.

[66] Although a more salutary balance between the two industrial sectors was achieved during the early reform period, as Y. Y. Kueh has demonstrated, overall the Deng regime retained a Maoist-type emphasis on the development of heavy industry. Heavy industry's share of the GVIO (gross value of industrial output) was 58 percent at the beginning of the reform period; it remained at about 52 percent from the early 1980s through 1987. "The Maoist Legacy and China's New Industrialization Strategy," pp. 439–40.

[67] Harding, *China's Second Revolution*, pp. 120–21.

What, then, accounts for the striking gains in urban incomes and living standards, at least until 1987? By all statistical measurements, as well as from the reports of most observers, the people of the cities enjoyed substantial improvements in their material standards of life under the Deng regime, albeit in unequal measure. Over the period 1979–87, there were gains in both real wages and labor productivity in urban state enterprises in all years except 1981, with wages averaging a per annum increase of about 5 percent and productivity increasing at approximately the same average per annum rate.[68] Foreigners who visited China during both the Mao and Deng eras unanimously have reported marked improvements in diet, the quality of clothing, and the ownership of personal and household goods such as bicycles, refrigerators, and television sets. Official statistics on living standards, usually taken as generally reliable, amply support these observations. For example, per capita pork consumption (in both town and countryside) nearly doubled between 1978 and 1986, from 7.7 kilograms to 14.3 kilograms, while per capita grain consumption increased from 195 kilograms to 256 kilograms. The ownership of bicycles increased from 74 to 258 million, television sets from 3 to 92 million, and sewing machines from 34 to 109 million. The average income of urban workers (calculated in 1980 constant prices) more than doubled between 1978 and 1986, from 614 yuan to 1,329 yuan per annum. And over the same period per capita living space in the cities grew from 4.2 to 8 square meters.[69]

While there is no doubt that the urban population enjoyed a substantial improvement in living standards through the mid-1980s, that rise cannot primarily be attributed to the market-oriented reforms, which, by all accounts (and even official Chinese government accounts), did little to improve either the quantity or the quality of urban industrial output or the performance of urban industry in general. The availability of a wider variety of consumer goods at lower prices, resulting from the new emphasis on light industries and the increasing volume of imports, was one necessary factor in the improvement in urban living standards. But this itself does not explain

[68] State Statistical Bureau data. See CIA, *China: Economic Performance in 1987 and Outlook for 1988*, Fig. 8, p. 16.
[69] CIA, *China: Economic Performance in 1987 and Outlook for 1988*, Fig. 9, "China: Selected Economic Indicators," p. 22.

the ability of urban residents to purchase such goods, even taking into account a relatively high savings rate during the Mao era, much less does it explain the doubling of average incomes over an eight-year period in the post-Mao era. Some individuals and families, to be sure, were able to achieve a higher material standard of living by seizing upon the new entrepreneurial opportunities. However, only a tiny fraction of the urban population were able to take advantage of such opportunities, and an even smaller percentage were successful in doing so over any sustained period of time. The fact of the matter is that the great majority of urban residents owed their *relative* prosperity not to the urban reforms but rather to the changes in the rural economy in the early 1980s. Writing in 1986, Carl Riskin aptly summed up the essence of the matter: "China's planners and economists agree that there had been no substantial improvement in efficiency of industrial performance through 1984 under the reform regime. Spectacular agricultural progress shielded the economy from the most serious ramifications of its inefficiency, keeping wage goods and materials of agricultural origin cheap and permitting consumer goods industries to advance and living standards to rise."[70]

The truth of this conclusion was to become apparent in the latter years of the decade. The startling decline in grain output in 1985 heralded a general stagnation in agricultural production that was to become the primary economic concern of the Beijing regime before the end of the decade.[71] The close of the period of "spectacular agricultural progress" soon had an impact on the cities. Inflation and other urban economic problems began to mount in 1985. By 1988 the government acknowledged that real urban incomes increased only 1 percent, a figure that was generally taken to mean that most urban

---

[70] Riskin, *China's Political Economy*, p. 372.

[71] After four consecutive years of disappointing harvests, Premier Li Peng, in his report to the Second Session of the Seventh National People's Congress in March 1989, referred to agriculture as the "weak link" in the Chinese economy. Remedial measures undertaken by the government included raising prices for state-contracted agricultural products, recentralizing and increasing the distribution of fertilizers and selling it at low prices to peasants (especially those who grew grain), and increasing state investment in agriculture (which had steadily declined through most of the 1980s). For a summary of Li Peng's government work report, see "Quarterly Chronicle and Documentation," *The China Quarterly*, No. 118 (June 1989), pp. 393–94.

incomes declined.[72] The decline greatly accelerated in the early months of 1989 as agricultural production continued to lag[73] and as the urban population was buffeted by soaring inflation and stagnating wages.

The deteriorating economic situation in the cities in the late 1980s was one factor involved in what the Deng regime found it expedient to call the "counterrevolutionary rebellion" of the spring of 1989. But it was not immediate economic problems alone that created mass discontent. To understand the unrest, and the political movement to which it gave rise, it is necessary to inquire into the peculiar nature of the capitalist system that the reformers unwittingly created.

[72] For the great majority of the urban population, living standards undoubtedly declined greatly in 1988 as wages for state employees remained fixed whereas the inflation rate in the cities was at least 30 percent. Those who profited from the situation were entrepreneurs, including bureaucratic entrepreneurs, who sold goods at market prices. On the latter practice, see Chapter 11.

[73] Grain production, according to official statistics, fell 2 percent in 1988 and overall agricultural output increased in value by only 3 percent, a figure reminiscent of some of the less salutary years of the Mao era. But now, with a partial market economy, stagnation in agricultural production contributed greatly to inflationary pressures. Grain harvests increased significantly in 1989 and 1990.

11

BUREAUCRATIC CAPITALISM

IT IS ONE OF THE MANY IRONIES of contemporary Chinese history that the market reforms that were intended to break down a bureaucratically controlled command economy have served to enrich China's Communist bureaucrats. Yet it is perhaps logical that the marriage of "the market" to an entrenched bureaucratic apparatus would yield not a "socialist market economy," as official ideology labels the result, but rather a form of bureaucratic capitalism.

"Bureaucratic capitalism," a term that refers to the use of political power and official influence for private pecuniary gain through capitalist or quasi-capitalist methods of economic activity, is hardly a novelty in world history. But nowhere has it been more prominent than in the history of China, in both traditional and modern times.

Bureaucratic capitalism was practiced on a grand scale by imperial China's scholar-officials, members of the gentry ruling class who dominated Chinese society for two millennia. In their capacity as officials, and despite their presumed Confucian bias against mercantile activities, China's traditional bureaucrats profited from a vast variety of industrial and commercial undertakings. They did so in numerous ways: state monopolies on the more lucrative items of production and trade; a bewildering variety of official leasing and licensing arrangements under which private merchants and craftsmen were compelled to work; legal and extralegal powers of taxation; and simple (but customarily sanctioned) forms of bribery.

The ancient state monopoly on the production and sale of salt, a huge and highly sophisticated operation, perhaps best exemplifies the workings of bureaucratic capitalism in traditional China. Originally managed by state bureaucrats, by the late imperial era the salt industry was organized, in Frederic Wakeman's description, as a combination of "top-level bureaucratic supervision with merchant management of production and distribution." Under this arrangement, both bureaucratically favored merchants and individual bureaucrats garnered enormous private profits from an enterprise originally designed to provide a stable source of government revenue.[1]

The traditional imperial order tended to convert members of both the bureaucracy and the bourgeoisie into bureaucratic capitalists, with the officials enjoying the clear advantage in this symbiotic relationship. As Etienne Balazs has described it, the equilibrium between the bureaucracy and the commercial-industrial classes was "continuously maintained in the interests of the scholar-officials and the state . . . the scholar-officials and the merchants formed two hostile but interdependent classes . . . the scholar-official became 'bourgeoisified,' while the merchant's ambition turned to becoming a scholar-official and investing his profits in land."[2] This bureaucratically dominated economy thus tended to absorb private merchants, industrialists, and bankers—and despite comparatively high levels of premodern economic development at various periods in Chinese history, an independent bourgeoisie never emerged to seriously challenge the traditional Confucian order.

The decline of the imperial regime under the nineteenth-century imperialist onslaught created vast new opportunities for the growth of bureaucratic capitalism. Under the "self-strengthening" movement, the abortive attempt at conservative modernization made by leaders of the gentry ruling class during the last three decades of the century, powerful provincial viceroys used their positions to promote a great

[1] For a superb summary of the organization and operation of the salt industry, see Wakeman, Jr., *The Fall of Imperial China*, pp. 47–50. By the Qing period, Wakeman observes, the salt monopoly was an enormous enterprise, comprising eleven huge salt yards throughout the country. The largest was the Lianghuai salt-producing zone near Yangzhou, where the Grand Canal joined the Yangzi River. That single yard contained thirty factories, employed 672,000 workers, and annually supplied 4 million taels to the government, or 6 percent of its total revenue (p. 47).

[2] Etienne Balazs, *Chinese Civilization and Bureaucracy* (New Haven: Yale University Press, 1964), p. 32.

variety of capitalist or quasi-capitalist undertakings from which they amassed vast private fortunes. Li Hongzhang, who became China's largest private capitalist at the same time as he occupied the highest political offices in the empire, personified Chinese bureaucratic capitalism at the close of the imperial era.

The revolution of 1911, which brought about the fall of the monarchy, coincided with a relatively vigorous period of capitalist development. The early decades of the century have been called "the golden age of the Chinese bourgeoisie."[3] The golden age was brief. The establishment of the Nationalist government of Chiang Kai-shek in 1927–28 inaugurated a two-decade reign that is perhaps the archetypical case of bureaucratic capitalism in modern world history. Beginning in 1927, Chiang Kai-shek's armies not only crushed the popular movement of workers and peasants that threatened bourgeois property but also terrorized the bourgeoisie itself, in a massive campaign of extortion.[4] State coercion to guarantee the financial support and political cooperation of China's capitalists did not end in 1927. It became a permanent feature of Guomindang (Nationalist Party) rule and a permanent source of enrichment for the regime's bureaucrats. Another better-known form of bureaucratic capitalism was symbolized by the notorious "four big families" (sida), who dominated the Nationalist Party-state apparatus, by virtue of which they privately controlled much of the modern sector of the Chinese economy in the 1930s and 1940s.

The Communist victory of 1949 ended the Guomindang system of bureaucratic capitalism. But it did not eliminate the essential condition that permits a bureaucratic capitalist regime to flourish—the general weakness of social classes and thus the dominance of state over society. While the Communist revolution destroyed the social classes dominant under the old regime—the traditional gentry and the modern bourgeoisie—it did not yield a new class to take their

---

[3] The words are derived from the title of Marie-Claire Bergère's excellent study *The Golden Age of the Chinese Bourgeoisie, 1911–1937* (Cambridge: Cambridge University Press, 1989). The title is somewhat misleading. By Bergère's own evidence, the "golden age" ended in 1927 with the establishment of the Chiang Kai-shek regime, as we shall observe momentarily.

[4] For examples of Guomindang terror against the bourgeoisie in 1927, see Bergère, *The Golden Age*, pp. 280ff.; and Harold Isaacs, *The Tragedy of the Chinese Revolution* (New York: Atheneum, 1966), p. 181.

place, save for the new and rapidly growing Communist bureaucracy itself. The Maoist restraints that had kept the bureaucracy from evolving into what Bergère has termed a "state bourgeoisie"[5] were largely discarded at the close of the Mao era. Deng Xiaoping's institutionalization of bureaucratic power and his introduction of a market economy soon combined to produce a bureaucratic capitalist regime that seemed to hark back to economic practices common during the imperial and Guomindang eras. But, as we shall soon see, it differed in many essential respects.

ECONOMIC REFORMS, OFFICIAL CORRUPTION, AND BUREAUCRATIC CAPITALISM

When the Deng regime first embarked on its economic reform program, it was almost universally assumed that market-oriented changes gravely threatened the material and political interests of the Chinese Communist bureaucracy. A sharp dichotomy between "market" and "bureaucracy" was immediately drawn, especially in the minds of Western observers and China's reformist intelligentsia. As Carl Riskin observed in 1980: "*With the exception of the bureaucracy,* all sections of Chinese society are promised improvements by the reformers."[6] It was argued that the Chinese bureaucratic establishment had been constructed around the Soviet-modeled First Five Year Plan in the 1950s and was thus wedded to centralized economic planning. "For the most part," as Harry Harding argued, "the Chinese bureaucracy is oriented more toward the perpetuation and 'perfection' of the traditional model of state ownership and central planning than toward its fundamental restructuring. In addition, bureaucratic officials have some important personal interests that have been negatively affected by the reform program."[7] It thus became commonplace to attribute such delays and failures that the reform program experienced to the resistance of conservative bureaucrats.

The Chinese bureaucratic establishment, like all established bu-

[5] Bergère, *The Golden Age*, p. 295.
[6] Carl Riskin, "Market, Maoism, and Economic Reform in China," in Selden and Lippit (eds.), *The Transition to Socialism in China*, p. 319 (emphasis added).
[7] Harding, *China's Second Revolution: Reform After Mao*, p. 291.

reaucracies, is, of course, profoundly conservative. Just as most Communist bureaucrats opposed Mao's radical policies, most at first were also suspicious of Deng's market-oriented reforms—if only because of an instinctive distrust of anything unknown and innovative.[8] Their desire to preserve their positions and privileges, reinforced by a preference for the bureaucratic virtues of predictability and stability as well as by simple habit and inertia, was sometimes ideologically disguised as a defense of "socialist principles." But if there were initial suspicions of the reform program, it soon became apparent to China's bureaucrats that they were in a uniquely favorable position to personally profit from the new market mechanisms. Many hastened to do so. In light of the absence of an existing bourgeoisie, the opportunities were great indeed, and Party and state officials were quick to fill the socioeconomic void.

The relationship between the bureaucracy and the market, and the consequent evolution of a system of bureaucratic capitalism in the decade following the Third Plenum of 1978, is abundantly recorded in the official Chinese press—not under the forbidden term "bureaucratic capitalism" but as "corruption" or "official profiteering" (*quandao*). In the 1980s, Chinese newspapers printed ever-increasing numbers of reports about the myriad forms of corruption spreading throughout China's vast bureaucracy. Official corruption, on a scope and scale that shocked even the most hardened of political cynics, was one of the "unintended consequences" of Deng Xiaoping's economic reform program.

The post-Mao regime generally tolerated and, indeed, initially encouraged press exposure of corruption—though it shielded the upper echelons of the Party hierarchy (and especially members of the Deng faction) from the gaze of overzealous reporters. But what the regime refused to tolerate was any discussion of bureaucratic capitalism or any suggestion that there might be a link between the ac-

---

[8] Most of the bureaucratic opposition to the reforms came not from "leftist" or "hard-line Maoist" officials, as popular and popularized lore has it, for most "Maoists" had been quickly purged from the bureaucratic apparatus by the Deng regime after 1978 and the few who remained were rendered powerless. Most opposition, rather, came from established bureaucrats, many of whom had been the targets of earlier Maoist attacks. As Harry Harding reminds us, "it is important to recognize that revolutionary Maoism had little support within the principal [bureaucratic] institutions that govern contemporary China." Ibid., p. 291.

knowledged problem of cadre corruption and the formation of a "bureaucratic bourgeoisie," the existence of which was vigorously denied. Such discussion had long been well beyond the boundaries of acceptable political discourse, much less newspaper speculation. While suppressing the initial post-Mao Democracy Movement in 1980, Deng Xiaoping had condemned the notion of a "bureaucratic class" as a heresy derived from the pernicious ideology of the Cultural Revolution.[9] Instead, it had been officially decreed, China had achieved a "socialist system" (albeit one still at a "lower" or "primary" stage of development),[10] and that problems such as corruption were to be treated as imperfections in that system, amenable to correction by the appropriate legal and ideological therapies.

This was not the conclusion arrived at by Liu Binyan, the most renowned of China's investigative journalists, who specialized in the ways of the bureaucracy. Liu, a victim of the antirightist witch-hunt of 1957, had spent twenty years in political disgrace before he was "rehabilitated" by the post-Mao government in the late 1970s, readmitted to the Communist Party, and appointed special correspondent for the *People's Daily* in 1979. His detailed reports on official corruption and violations of citizens' rights by Party cadres won him great popular acclaim but also the hostility of the Deng regime. In 1987, shortly after the fall of his patron, Communist Party Secretary-General Hu Yaobang,[11] Liu was dismissed from the *People's Daily* and expelled from the Party for a second time. Two years later, in 1989, Liu set forth his assessment of the social results of the corrupt practices he had spent a decade investigating:

> After the economic reform was implemented in 1979, the market economy and open [door] policy created even more opportunities for officials to use their power for private ends. In foreign trade alone, these people make shockingly illegal profits from sales commissions provided by foreign businessmen. . . . Many of the foreign-trade projects were monopolized by children of high-ranking officials. Within a few years' time, China

[9] See Chapter 5.
[10] On the notion of "the primary stage of socialism," see Chapter 13.
[11] See Chapter 12.

has produced *a new bureaucratic bourgeois stratum*. Compared with the old one—one of the "Three Great Mountains" (imperialism, feudalism, and bureaucratic bourgeoisie) of the Kuomintang—it is much more harmful, because the earlier bourgeoisie had fewer assets at its disposal, and it had some fear for law and order as well as for public opinion.[12]

Liu Binyan's conclusion that Deng's market reform policies had produced a "new bureaucratic bourgeois stratum" was not far different from Mao's accusations in the 1960s that the postrevolutionary order had yielded a "new bureaucratic class" and a new "bourgeoisie" rooted in the upper echelons of the Chinese Communist Party, charges elaborated upon by Democracy Movement activists in 1979–80.

When Liu Binyan's reports began to appear in the *People's Daily* in 1979, the Chinese press was already filled with articles about official corruption. Newspapers and radio broadcasts not only increasingly reported on such familiar matters as bureaucratic nepotism and various "backdoor" dealings but also began to broach the far more politically sensitive topic of the special privileges enjoyed by cadres and officials, articulating the resentments of ordinary citizens.

It was not that these were entirely new phenomena in the People's Republic, unknown prior to 1979. The system of bureaucratic hierarchy and privilege can be traced back to the Yan'an period, a time prized for its egalitarianism and its spirit of "plain living and hard work." The system of official privilege expanded enormously in both scope and scale after 1949, as revolutionaries were transformed into rulers. Many of the triumphant revolutionaries wished to enjoy the fruits of their victory and thought it only just that they should be compensated for the sacrifices they had made. These claims were accompanied by the inevitable transformation of the victorious Communist Party from the leader of a revolutionary movement into a state establishment which now attracted careerists as well as revolutionary idealists. Joining the Party after 1949 was no longer a heroic act; it was a step up the ladder of success in the new society.

---

[12] Liu Binyan, with Ruan Ming and Xu Gang, *Tell the World* (New York: Pantheon, 1989), p. 164.

These common postrevolutionary phenomena contributed to the gradual moral decline of the Party, the increasing use of political power for private ends, the abandonment of the revolutionary ideals of "plain living and hard work," and ever-greater inequalities in material goods and social status determined by one's place in the political hierarchy.

Yet the Mao era was still a time when the egalitarian and ascetic values of the revolutionary years, if not necessarily usually practiced, were still remembered, serving to at least restrain bureaucratic greed. Corruption was endemic by the early 1960s, but for the most part petty. In the countryside, local cadre corruption commonly took the form of small-scale embezzlement of collective funds, nepotism, vendettas against personal enemies, and sexual harassment of women.[13] In the cities, corruption was more clear-cut and less traditional, largely centered in the bureaucratically dominated and state-owned economy. Corruption in the urban sector involved backdoor deals among those responsible for making the industrial economy run, especially enterprise managers who required scarce materials and economic bureaucrats who had access to them. Bribery and kickbacks were not uncommon, but still the sums involved were relatively small. It was not so much money that changed hands as favors and payments in kind. In the Mao era, there were few ways to privately accumulate large sums of money—and even fewer ways to spend it—without arousing political suspicions in an economy of scarcity and a moral universe which prized frugality and austerity.

Bureaucrats, of course, enjoyed special privileges, material as well as social, legally and illegally obtained. And the higher bureaucrats were accorded substantial privileges, not so much in salaries as in the perquisites of office—banquets, free travel, housing, access to better medical care and hospitals, special schools for their children, and vacations at exclusive mountain and seaside resorts— among other such amenities well known to those familiar with a Stalinist-style *nomenklatura* system. But the material privileges of even high-level Chinese bureaucrats in the Mao era, while grand in an economy of extreme scarcity, were rather paltry compared to those enjoyed by their counterparts in the Soviet Union and the Eastern

---

[13] Shue, *The Reach of the State*, p. 113.

European countries, as well as in most "developing countries" in Asia, Africa, and Latin America. In a socio-ideological environment that celebrated the virtues of plain living, egalitarianism, and self-denial—and frowned on consumption—bureaucratic privileges had to be hidden and disguised. Even when special privileges were formally legal, they were often seen as morally corrupt, a violation of the egalitarian values the regime preached. In Maoist China, "to get rich" was sinful, not glorious.

Although stories about cadre corruption and bureaucratic privilege already were commonplace in the press by 1979, it is unlikely that corruption in the Communist bureaucracy was substantially greater in the *early* Deng era than it had been during the latter years of the Mao regime. The difference was that now the problem was partially open to exposure in the media and to a degree of public criticism. For Deng Xiaoping's reform regime had significantly relaxed state control over newspapers and broadcasting—and also, for a time, tolerated unofficial publications. Journalists, as a result, hastened to report cases of official corruption and cadre abuses of power. Bureaucratic corruption suddenly became far more visible, and a matter of much greater public concern and condemnation.

What also became more visible at the time were the special material privileges cadres long had enjoyed but hitherto had kept half hidden from the people. As ascetic and egalitarian Maoist values faded from popular consciousness, cadres no longer felt inhibited about displaying their material wealth, meager though it was in most cases, despite condemnations that appeared under such newspaper headlines as "Cadres Live It Up."[14] As a visitor from Hong Kong observed in the summer of 1979:

> While it had formerly kept a low profile, today in this post-Cultural Revolution period the privileged class on the mainland is finally coming out in all its finery. . . . In all I travelled for a month and a half visiting family and friends. Our after-dinner discussions more often than not centered on the various extrav-

[14] The heading of a New China News Agency dispatch from Beijing, December 28, 1979.

agances of the privileged class here. Though the majority of PRC officials live a very stringent and simple life . . . another small group has too often displayed the flagrant habits of capitalists, which has created a bad impression among the masses.[15]

While the official press was relatively free to expose bureaucratic corruption and report on cadre abuses of official positions, at least below the highest levels of the Party leadership, the regime did not permit the use of such terms as "bureaucratic capitalism" or "bureaucratic class" to describe these phenomena. Deng Xiaoping had linked the theory of a "bureaucratic class" to the legacy of the Cultural Revolution and those who promoted the theory were accused by official ideologists of wishing to launch "a second Cultural Revolution," thereby creating the social and political chaos that would facilitate their evil designs to seize power.[16]

Although a "bureaucratic class" and "bureaucratic capitalism" were officially declared nonexistent, the regime did acknowledge that it suffered from the affliction of "bureaucratism," a term that vaguely encompassed official corruption, cadre greed, and "commandism." The label "bureaucratism" (a deficient work style) was attractive because it carried no social class implications and could be cured in due course through appropriate economic, institutional, and ideological remedies. The proposed solution raised no dreaded Maoist specter of class struggle.

It is ironic that just as China's leaders were most vigorously denying the existence of a bureaucratic ruling class in the People's Republic, they were introducing policies that were to generate—in an extraordinarily short period of time—a capitalist economy and a bureaucratic bourgeoisie to preside over it. The rapid expansion of market relationships, the enormous growth in foreign trade, the influx of foreign capital, the decollectivization of agriculture, the encouragement of private enterprise of all sorts, and the various forms of decentralization that loosened central control over the economy com-

---

[15] *Seventies Monthly* (Hong Kong), September 1979 (in *Inside China Mainland*, October 1979, pp. 4–5).

[16] Lin Boye and Zhing Zhe, "A Criticism of the So-Called Opposition to the 'Bureaucratic Class,' " *Hongqi* (Red Flag), No. 5 (March 1981).

bined to breed corruption in epidemic proportions and to transform many Communist bureaucrats into quasi-capitalist entrepreneurs, or, to recall Liu Binyan's characterization, into "a new bureaucratic bourgeois stratum."

THE RURAL PETTY BOURGEOISIE

When Deng Xiaoping decollectivized farming in the early 1980s, he was not out to re-create a rural economy of "small producers," each cultivating their own family plot. His aim was not simply to undo what Mao had done, but rather to modernize and commercialize the Chinese countryside—in effect, to initiate a process of modern capitalist development in the rural areas. Thus, the agrarian policies the regime pursued presupposed the emergence of a new and dynamic rural bourgeoisie who would acquire relatively large landholdings, operate their farms in a modern commercial manner on a high technological level and with a specialized division of labor, accumulate capital, and invest that capital in new industrial, commercial, and service enterprises in the rural areas as well as in more modern farms. It was a prophetic pointer to the future evolution of the new Chinese capitalism that rural cadres and officials formed the backbone of the rural bourgeoisie generated by the reformist policies of the Communist state.

Local rural officials at first viewed the unfolding of Deng's agrarian policies with ambivalence and hostility. The breakup of collective institutions meant a loss of power and income for local cadres. Many also objected on more principled grounds to the destruction of what they believed to be a socialist ordering of rural society that offered peasants security and relative equality. Self-interest and ideological principle were, no doubt, mutually reinforcing. Yet despite that powerful combination, and despite the vaunted ability of local bureaucrats to frustrate central state policies,[17] the rapidity with which

---

[17] As Vivienne Shue has pointed out, by the late Mao period most local officials in the rural areas "had acquired such considerable leverage and such skill at evading or distorting central policy, that top leaders from whatever faction were greatly handicapped in getting *any* policy —even one that was generally beneficial—implemented widely *as it was intended to be implemented.* The lower levels of the state apparatus, reflecting the parcelized or honeycomb

decollectivization was accomplished suggests that most local rural cadres did their bureaucratic duty. In many cases they were perhaps forced to do so by peasant pressure for change, but there was no lack of instances where the household contracting system was imposed upon reluctant peasants.

Whatever their initial reactions to Beijing's decollectivization policies, local officials very soon discovered the virtues of rural reform. They now had power to contract land, to approve contracts for the operation of various private businesses and industries, and to privatize collective property. It became commonplace for local officials to acquire the largest and best parcels of land for themselves, their relatives, and their friends. When not contracting land or enterprises to their own families, cadres often forced peasants to accept them as "power partners" in specialized households or small commercial and industrial enterprises. The officials contributed neither labor nor capital in these "partnerships." Instead, by virtue of their political positions, they offered their power to sign contracts with communes or brigades, or their ability to acquire scarce materials such as fertilizers and gasoline, in exchange for a portion of the profits.[18] Local officials also acquired land for new houses. As a Fuzhou newspaper typically complained in 1982:

> Certain local leading cadres have resorted to various disgusting tactics to seize land for building houses. Some have paid nothing, or just a little token, for the land they have occupied. Some have seized 1 mu of land for every fen [one-tenth of 1 mu] of land they have "approved." Some have not only seized land for building their own houses, but have given cropland to their relatives, friends and "people of special relations" for building houses.
>
> Some have used their public office for private gain. For example, while planning the budget for collective housing con-

---

socioeconomic structure over which it presided, had, in fact, become a maze of power pockets and vested interests manned by people who were constrained to mouth the rhetoric of revolution but who often had everything to gain by protecting and elaborating on the status quo." Shue, *The Reach of the State*, pp. 130–31 (emphasis in original).

[18] See, for example, *Xinhua* Commentator, "It Is Grabbing Unfair Gains, Not 'Entering into Partnership,' " *Xinhua* Domestic Service, October 13, 1983. FBIS, October 14, 1983, p. K5.

struction, they have included the budget for building their own houses into the plan. . . .

Some have sought private gain at public expense. These people, while contracting a construction project to the contractor, allow the contractor to profit from increasing the construction price. After the project is completed, they have accepted the contractor's "thanks" by building for him a house "free of charge."[19]

The secretary of the Party committee of the local commune proved particularly adept in learning capitalist ways of maximizing profits. After appropriating land to build houses, he then proceeded to sell the houses at high prices and augmented his profits by selling the land itself (or, more precisely, by selling the rights to use the land, which technically remained "collective property").[20]

In the course of decollectivization in the early 1980s, these abuses of political power for private enrichment were considered illegal and often denounced in the official press, even though little was actually done to remedy the malady. But "embourgeoisement" through bureaucratic profiteering and corruption soon became so pervasive in the countryside that it came to be accepted by the government as an inevitable part of the reform process, although no doubt resented by ordinary peasants. As Liu Binyan observed in the late 1980s:

If you travel to any county in China, even in the poorest [regions] you will be struck by the splendor of the government buildings, with their assembly halls and guest houses. Not only are the county committee and county government housed in imposing edifices, but every bureau has a building of its own, not to mention spacious compounds and living quarters. Every bureau also has a separate guest house. Even the family-planning offices are located in separate buildings. State funds are sent to these impoverished counties every year to help increase production, buy grain, and build homes: allowances for

19 Editorial in Fuzhou *Fujian Ribao*, March 6, 1982, p. 1. FBIS, March 19, 1982, p. 1.
20 Ibid.

the poor, they are called. The money gets skimmed off at the county level, and then again at the district and village levels. Go to one of the villages and ask a peasant what he gets. He'll tell you that he signed a paper a couple of years ago for 500 yuan, which he never got, then signed a paper last year for 300 yuan, which he never got. In places like this, the party branch secretary and the village chief have fine houses. Some of the district chiefs take the state subsidies—the peasants' money— and buy land in the county seat to build two-story villas, many with large enclosed courtyards. Some live there themselves, others rent them out. The bureaucrats have become unbelievably rapacious.[21]

Petty corruption and rapaciousness had plagued many rural Party organizations in the Mao era. But with land and houses now turned into commodities, the long-standing petty vices of cadres became vehicles for significant private accumulation of capital. Since the Chinese people had long suffered from a dearth of consumer goods, much of that capital initially went into conspicuous consumption, as did rising peasant incomes in general. But increasingly large portions of the capital that cadres accumulated, however obtained, was invested in commercial farming, in large tracts of contracted lands worked by hired laborers or subcontractors (tenant farmers, in effect), in private or "collective" village and township industries, and in a vast variety of private businesses, especially transportation companies and commercial establishments generated by the enormous growth of marketing activities.

In business ventures, rural officials, of course, enjoyed the advantage over ordinary peasants, in fact a twofold advantage. First, by virtue of their political influence, they were more likely to secure contracts and licenses and to do so on more favorable terms. Second, once their enterprises were established, cadre-run farming and business operations were more likely to flourish since the bureaucratic connections of their owners gave them favored access to scarce materials, markets, and bank loans.

In the early 1980s the advantages enjoyed by rural officials in

---

[21] Liu Binyan, *China's Crisis, China's Hope*, pp. 15–16.

their new capacity as private capitalists were frequently noted in the press, and duly denounced as abuses of power. For example, a *Xinhua* report broadcast on Beijing radio in February 1984 charged that "state functionaries in many localities are abusing power by seeking personal gain at public expense through businesses run by their families. This unhealthy tendency has infringed on the interests of the state and the masses, and has seriously corrupted the Party style and social values." *Xinhua* quoted the report of a Party rectification unit which investigated several villages in Jiangsu province. The report read in part:

> Some people abuse their power to get "licenses," issue "personal relations licenses" or receive "special favor licenses." As a result, a phenomenon has appeared in which the families of cadres, staff members, leading cadres and the personnel of responsible departments have many licenses. The masses, who have great difficulty in obtaining a license for individual business, have many complaints about this. Some other people, "taking advantage of being in a favored position," abuse their power to purchase commodities in short supply, or even privately divide up and sell commodities subject to planned supply.[22]

While the official press was filled with exposés of local officials who used political influence to profit from decollectivization, one searches in vain for evidence that the government made serious efforts to curb corruption. Indeed, such efforts would have run counter to the reformers' plans to foster the growth of a new rural elite who would bring about a dynamic capitalist economy in the countryside. Local officials, by virtue of experience and personality, were uniquely well prepared to become members of that envisioned bourgeois elite. By the late 1980s it was clearly government practice (though not acknowledged policy) to encourage the entrepreneurial ambitions of rural cadres. In some cases preferential credits were offered to persuade state cadres to give up their official posts in favor of new

[22] Beijing *Xinhua* Domestic Service, February 8, 1984. FBIS, PRC Regional Affairs (East Region), February 10, 1984, pp. 1–2.

careers in business and real estate.[23] And by the early 1990s, Party and government officials, in both town and countryside, were being publicly and officially exhorted to go into private business, or to *xiahai*, as the popular phrase had it, to "plunge into the sea."[24]

It is not surprising that officials and former officials make up a significant portion of China's new rural bourgeoisie. An even larger proportion are friends or relatives of officials. There are no precise figures, to be sure. The State Statistical Bureau is silent on the composition of post-Mao China's new social strata. But a variety of local reports and studies clearly point to the conclusion that local bureaucracies have partly reproduced themselves in the form of "local rural elites." For example, a 1984 survey of 21,000 households classified as "prosperous" in a county in the northern province of Shanxi revealed that 43 percent were headed by cadres or former cadres,[25] a figure that does not include friends of cadres or others who might be in a patron-client relationship with local bureaucrats.

A more concrete example is related in *Chen Village*, a highly praised study of a community in Guangdong province.[26] Chen Qingfa, a poor young peasant at the time of land reform in the early 1950s, had worked his way up the political hierarchy in "Chen village"[27] during the Mao years. In the 1950s he had been an activist in the collectivization campaign. In the 1970s he was appointed Party sec-

---

[23] Even in the process of leaving government service, the hierarchy of bureaucratic rankings was not forgotten. For example, in the Inner Mongolian county of Zhuozi, it was reported in 1989, the county auditorium was auctioned off to six cadres who bid RMB 220,000 to develop a shopping center on the site. The sale price was then discounted by RMB 90,000, the final preferential sum arrived at according to the rank of the buyers—RMB 15,000 for an ordinary cadre, 20,000 for a section-level cadre, and 25,000 for a county-level cadre. Robert Delfs, "County Capitalism," *Far Eastern Economic Review*, April 27, 1989, p. 27.

[24] The term "plunge into the sea" came into widespread currency in the PRC in 1992, apparently borrowed from Taiwan, where it had pejoratively referred to young women who turned to prostitution. Nicholas Kristof, "China Applauds Officials Who Plunge into Profit," *The New York Times*, April 6, 1993, p. A6.

[25] Lu Yun, "Specialized Households Emerge," *Beijing Review*, December 3, 1984. Cited in Carl Riskin, *China's Political Economy*, p. 308.

[26] Anita Chan, Richard Madsen, and Jonathan Unger, *Chen Village: The Recent History of a Peasant Community in Mao's China* (Berkeley: University of California Press, 1984). This volume has been quite rightly praised as the best of many excellent Chinese village studies.

[27] The names of the village and its inhabitants have been changed to protect the privacy of villagers and interviewees.

retary of the production brigade into which the entire village had
been organized. Described as "cynical and self-serving,"[28] he was
certainly adept at accommodating himself to changing Party policies.
In 1980, Qingfa received orders to decollectivize the village under
the household responsibility system. He proceeded to do so with dispatch, distributing land and selling farm tools, carts, and tractors to
the highest bidders. Even the village's fruit trees and fishponds were
contracted out to private operators, as were the village store and
health clinic.[29] But it was not just a matter of carrying out Party
orders.

> As Party secretary, Qingfa got the lion's share. There was a
> large grove of giant bamboo along the river; and rather than put
> it up for bidding, the [Party] committee agreed to let Qingfa
> take it for ten yuan. The grove was worth more than a hundred
> times that amount. He allocated to himself, free of charge, a
> hillock of honeysuckle (a Chinese medicinal herb) planted in
> earlier years for the health clinic. He had the brigade rent bull-
> dozers to relevel the land occupied by [an] unfinished dike.
> Awarding himself the major portion of this land, he hired field
> hands to till it for him.[30]

Qingfa also appealed for financial assistance from young villagers
who had migrated to Hong Kong, where they had found relatively
well-paying jobs. They hastened to contribute US$10,000, along with
a used two-and-a-half-ton truck and a fifty-foot boat, to help their
ancestral village. "But Qingfa disposed of the new gifts in ways beneficial to old friends from his lineage branch and to relatives of fellow
cadres." In the lucrative transportation businesses that mushroomed
with the rapid spread of marketing, Qingfa arranged for the son of
his deputy Party secretary to operate the truck as a private business,
with a portion of the profits going to the brigade that Qingfa headed.
"The seven villagers who were appointed to operate the boat, again

28 Chan et al., *Chen Village*, p. 276.
29 Ibid., pp. 269–73.
30 Ibid., pp. 276–77. The authors of *Chen Village* note that "connivance by cadres in parceling
out brigade property to them occurred in a lot of villages during the decollectivization drive,"
according to Chinese newspaper reports (p. 277, n. 7).

as a profit-sharing endeavor, were all relatives of people close to or important to Qingfa."[31]

The privatization of the brigade's assets left the Party secretary with fewer economic responsibilities but with his political power intact. Qingfa retained local judicial authority as well as control over the granting of contracts and the issuance of official licenses required for most commercial activities. Villagers, therefore, further enriched the Party secretary by plying him with gifts, in the expectation that he would return the favors. These abuses of power for private economic gain soon became acceptable practice. As the authors of *Chen Village* observe, "a lot of the villagers were not particularly perturbed either by Qingfa's appropriations of property or his gift taking," for the behavior of the Party secretary "seemed in keeping with a widely shared mood of cynical privatism and advantage seeking."[32]

It was thus that a new petty bourgeoisie emerged in the Chinese countryside, at first on a modest scale and in modest ways. It is a class made up of small landlords, commercial farmers, and small businessmen variously involved in commerce, in the operation of service companies, and in village and township industrial enterprises. Communist Party cadres not only served as midwives for the birth of the new class but also make up (along with their relatives and friends)

---

[31] Ibid., p. 277.

[32] Ibid., pp. 277–78. In the early 1980s, when material conditions were rapidly improving for most rural inhabitants, ordinary peasants seemingly accommodated themselves to the phenomenon of cadre self-enrichment. But by the late 1980s the special privileges enjoyed by cadres, and the property they had appropriated, bred resentment and anger among a peasant population facing growing economic hardships and diminishing opportunities. District and provincial party organs, belatedly alarmed over the corruption that pervaded local Party organizations and the deterioration of relationships between cadres and peasants, organized meetings to hear the complaints of villagers. The results of some of the meetings were published in the official Beijing *Peasants' Daily* (*Nongmin Ribao*) and they reveal how deeply peasants felt alienated from the Communist Party, which they once had looked to for spiritual and material sustenance. See, for example, Beijing *Nongmin Ribao*, September 12, 1988, p. 1. FBIS-CHI-88-189, September 29, 1988, pp. 47–49. Peasant antagonism toward the Party was aggravated by the astonishing growth of extralegal taxes cadres exacted from peasants. In some localities there were as many as eighty separate taxes and fees, one or more for every conceivable transaction, not excluding such innovations as a surtax for the repair of the Great Wall. In 1991 the central government issued a regulation limiting the total amount of such taxes and fees to 5 percent of the previous year's income, but the decree was widely ignored, according to all accounts. See *Nongmin Ribao*, September 23, 1988, p. 2 (in *Inside China Mainland*, February 1989, pp. 22–24); and Sheryl WuDunn, "China Is Sowing Discontent with 'Taxes' on the Peasants," *The New York Times*, May 19, 1993, p. 1.

a substantial portion of its membership. As has been the general rule in the history of the People's Republic, this was clearly a case where economic power flowed directly from the possession of political power.

BUREAUCRATIC-COMPRADORE CAPITALISM

In late January 1992, Deng Xiaoping embarked on a month-long tour of southern China in an effort to speed up the pace of capitalist economic development. Featured on Deng's itinerary was the special economic zone of Shenzhen, where China's "senior leader" laid down the principle that "as long as it makes money it's good for China."[33] Having equated patriotism with the making of money, Deng logically followed by once again defining socialism solely in terms of economic development. "Socialism's real nature," he declared, "is to liberate productive forces and the ultimate goal of socialism is to achieve common prosperity."[34] Deng no longer occupied any formal state or Party offices, but his remarks were still treated as "directives" which carried the force of law.[35] His comment that anything that made money was "good for China" definitively sanctified, and stamped with a patriotic seal, the processes of bureaucratic enrichment that had been underway for well over a decade.

The bureaucratic capitalist economy yielded by Deng's market reforms operates on a vastly larger scale in the cities than in the countryside. Several essential ingredients of that system were inherited from the Mao period. One was a huge and relatively autonomous bureaucracy that controlled economic life, but was itself beyond any

[33] Uli Schmetzer, "A Brave New World," *Chicago Tribune*, September 28, 1992, p. 3. On Deng's "southern tour" see Chapter 15.

[34] "Central Document No. 2 (1992)," FBIS-CHI-91-063-S.

[35] Deng's comments and speeches during his southern tour were summarized in a hastily released Party Central Committee circular, "Central Document No. 2 (1992)" on "Transmitting and Studying Comrade Deng Xiaoping's Important Remarks" (see FBIS-CHI-91-063-S). His "remarks" also served as the guiding principles for policies adopted by a Plenary Session of the Politburo in early March 1994, which were duly ratified by the National People's Congress later that month.

form of social control. A second was the moral decline of China's onetime revolutionaries turned rulers. To this rudimentary mixture, Deng Xiaoping's reforms added the crucial elements. One was the introduction of quasi-capitalist market relationships which in effect legalized and greatly expanded China's restricted "second economy," without abolishing the state-operated economy. Second, Deng provided the essential ideological rationale for bureaucratic capitalism by proclaiming that "to get rich is glorious," thereby negating ascetic Maoist norms which hitherto had inhibited bureaucratic greed. Finally, the economic reforms provided the capital that made bureaucratic capitalism profitable. Initially, capital was acquired primarily through foreign trade, foreign investment, and government borrowing from foreign banks and other lending institutions. Indeed, enormous sums of capital flowed through Deng's "open door," with the government's foreign debt alone increasing from zero in 1978 to over US$50 billion by 1990.

All that was wanted for a flourishing capitalist economy was the appropriate social agent—a bourgeoisie. Just as the Communist state had created a quasi-market economy, it also created a quasi-bourgeoisie. It is symbolic of the nature of Chinese capitalism in the post-Mao era that the most prominent early members of that new "bourgeoisie" were the sons and daughters of high Communist officials, soon to be known as the "crown princes and princesses."

In the first year of Deng Xiaoping's reign, it was observed that though changing jobs remained virtually impossible for most Chinese, it had become commonplace among the now mostly middle-aged children of high officials.[36] The offspring of high-level cadres, given their family's influence in the bureaucracy, were well placed to arrange deals between foreign companies and state trading organizations during the 1979–80 "foreign imports craze." The lucrative "commissions" they earned in this compradore role was the first important source of substantial capital accumulation by private individuals in the history of the People's Republic. Later, the crown princes derived additional profits from selling expensive foreign goods (such as automobiles and color television sets) whose importation by others was restricted or forbidden. Less common but even more lucrative were

[36] *Seventies Monthly* (Hong Kong), September 1979 (in *Inside China Mainland*, October 1979).

arrangements made for the illegal export of scarce raw materials which fetched high prices on the world market.

In using political influence for private gain, the children and relatives of the Party elite, including those of Deng Xiaoping and Zhao Ziyang, were in the vanguard. But they were by no means alone in discovering the magic of the market. By the early 1980s money-making had become a pervasive preoccupation of the bureaucracy. Official newspapers were filled with examples and condemnations of official profiteering and corruption. As in the countryside, many forms of bureaucratic corruption in the cities were familiar to observers of the Mao regime—petty bribery, payoffs, the misappropriation of government funds, backdoor deals, and the sale of state property for private profit. What changed as the Deng era went on was not so much the means and methods of corruption as its scope and scale. With the growth of market relationships, especially foreign trade, money became far more plentiful and corruption, correspondingly, far more profitable. As a result, many bureaucrats were able to accumulate significant amounts of capital. Much of this initially went into immediate, often conspicuous consumption, such as the purchase of imported luxury goods and the ostentatious furnishing of private homes located on what in some cities became known as "high official streets."[37] But much of the money was set aside, and eventually went into various business ventures (both speculative and productive) as the state progressively expanded the private economic sphere.

Also contributing to bureaucratic corruption was a new moral climate that prized material riches. This attitude and the behavior it fostered often evoked a romanticized nostalgia for the early Mao years. A commentator in the official *Beijing Daily* lamented in September 1981: "During the fifties our material resources were not very plentiful. Why was it that our social atmosphere was so good then, whereas now, when our material resources are so much more rich, this 'connectionology' is so widespread?"[38] "Connectionology" referred to the study of how best to cultivate bureaucratic ties that

[37] As they were called in cities in Guangdong province. See Jean-Louis Rocca, "Corruption and Its Shadow: An Anthropological View of Corruption in China," *The China Quarterly*, No. 130 (June 1992), p. 415.
[38] *Beijing Daily*, September 29, 1981. Cited in *Cheng Ming* (Hong Kong), December 1981 (in *Inside China Mainland*, February 1982, p. 18).

would yield material benefits. *Guanxi* ("connections" or "influence") was hardly new, but there was a heightened consciousness of its importance—for the rewards of power were now so much greater.

Among the new rewards in the early 1980s was "the private car fad," whereby officials confiscated illegally imported automobiles, treated them as their private property, and used them for pleasure driving. And as in the countryside, high officials appropriated public funds and state materials to build lavish private homes in urban areas. In the city of Wuhan, "a highrise apartment building was constructed especially for the mayor's and vice-mayor's children, and was promptly dubbed 'the young masters' residence.' "[39] Newspapers abounded with stories about how high officials took vacations abroad under the guise of fact-finding missions and used their political influence to send their children to foreign universities. These and other forms of official profiteering, corruption, and abuse of power grew apace as market reforms "deepened" in the 1980s. At the same time, reports of corruption appeared ever less frequently in newspapers, in part because of growing political restraints on the press, in part because bureaucratic corruption had become so commonplace that it was no longer newsworthy.

The Deng regime's response to the growth of official corruption was confused, contradictory, and, above all, ambiguous. The ambiguity derived from the blurring of distinctions between legal and illegal economic activities, for much that was regarded as corrupt and criminal during the Mao period was quite natural, and indeed essential, in a market economy. In that misty realm of transition from pseudo-socialism to bureaucratic capitalism, there were no firm guidelines to distinguish between "economic crimes" and "socialist entrepreneurship," for capitalism had the effect of legalizing many practices that the old regime had condemned as corrupt. Leaders only dimly aware of the transition over which they were presiding, with one foot still planted in the old system and the other groping for a place in the uncharted reformed order, naturally acted with hesitation and inconsistency. Laws and regulations were applied arbitrarily or often simply ignored. Only one principle remained consistent: the higher the bureaucratic rank, the less there was to fear. One observer

---

[39] *Cheng Ming*, December 1981 (in *Inside China Mainland*, February 1982, p. 19).

remarked in 1981: "As to children of high ranking cadres violating the law with impunity, this sort of thing is too common to even bother citing examples."[40]

The Communist Party, to be sure, periodically issued loud declarations condemning bureaucratic corruption and vowed to eradicate economic crime.[41] These were followed by highly publicized anticorruption campaigns which included public executions (mostly of common criminals) and imprisonments. The campaigns were sporadic and short-lived, and rarely extended very far up the bureaucratic hierarchy. Among Party members, Communist leaders were inclined to treat corruption as a problem of "Party style," a matter upon which both Deng Xiaoping and Chen Yun repeatedly expounded in the early 1980s. It was an "individual phenomenon" confined to a small number of people, they emphasized, and should be treated as an "internal contradiction among the people." That being the case, ideological education and moral rejuvenation, not judicial punishment, were the appropriate remedies. Indeed, for a time, the effort to combat corruption was linked to an ill-fated campaign to build a "socialist spiritual civilization."[42]

The inclination to relegate official corruption to the realm of individual behavior, amenable to spiritual therapy, reflected the Party's reluctance to confront the problem seriously. In part this was a matter of bureaucratic self-protection, since many of even the highest Party leaders were involved in business activities that were popularly regarded as corrupt. Reformist leaders also feared that a real crackdown on economic crimes would stifle entrepreneurial initiative and hinder economic development, certainly not an irrational fear since the economy was in fact dependent on a good degree of state tolerance of corruption. On the other hand, Party leaders knew that bureaucratic corruption was weakening the political effectiveness of the

[40] Ibid., p. 20.

[41] See, for example, "Decision of the CCP Central Committee and the State Council on Cracking Down on Serious Crime in the Economic Sphere" (April 13, 1982). Translated in *Issues and Studies*, Vol. 20, No. 2 (February 1984), pp. 102–15.

[42] The first sentence of the April 1982 Central Committee "Decision," for example, reads: "This year, in order to effectively promote socialist material and spiritual civilization, the Party Central Committee has paid special attention to two important tasks, namely, carrying out organizational restructuring which is a component part of the reform of systems, and cracking down on serious crime in the economic sphere." Ibid., p. 102.

Party machine and lowering its already badly tarnished reputation among the people. Thus the bureaucracy was periodically mobilized for anticorruption campaigns; from 1982 to 1988 an annual average of 22,000 economic crime cases reached the courts.[43] But, on the whole, the weight of inertia and self-interest prevailed, and, in the end, as little as possible was done. Official corruption consequently grew, facilitating the growth of bureaucratic capitalism.

The year 1985 was crucial in the de facto legalization of corruption and the establishment of a bureaucratic capitalist regime. In the autumn of 1984, the government had resumed in comprehensive fashion the effort to bring market reforms to urban industry and commerce. The results of that frenetic effort were felt principally in 1985.

The urban reform policies were highly favorable to the private pecuniary interests of the bureaucracy, although they certainly were not consciously intended to serve that end. Of special importance was limited price reform, which removed mandatory state price controls on many agricultural and other commodities—allowing them to fluctuate according to market conditions—while retaining a parallel set of state prices. This created a dual price system (or, more precisely, a three-tiered price system[44]) which provided a quasi-legal sanction for strategically situated officials to buy goods and materials at low state prices and sell them at double or more the purchase price on the free market. This rather simple form of official profiteering (*guandao*) was not new, but it expanded enormously by virtue of "price reform." The government's sanctioning of coexisting state and market prices in effect legalized much of the black market. It was the most common and perhaps the most lucrative method of bureaucratic enrichment.

By 1985 the government was also encouraging the establishment of private businesses operated by individuals or households (*getihu*), creating fresh opportunities for the growth of bureaucratic capitalism.

[43] Rocca, "Corruption and Its Shadow," p. 407.

[44] As Carl Riskin has pointed out, what was adopted in late 1984 was a three-tiered price system based on the Hungarian "market socialism" model: fixed state prices for essential industrial goods such as steel and oil; free market prices for most consumer goods; and an intermediate range of goods subject to state "guidance"—that is, allowed to float between state-determined upper and lower ranges. Riskin, *China's Political Economy*, p. 352. For the purpose of the present discussion, it needs only to be noted that the coexistence of state and market prices was legalized.

324 ★ THE DENG XIAOPING ERA

Simultaneously, with the virtual removal of restrictions on hiring workers and the establishment of a labor market, the opportunities were more profitable as well. Although it was not yet considered legitimate for officials themselves to become private capitalists, as was to become the custom in the 1990s, it was common for friends and relatives of officials to set up businesses funded by bureaucratic capital accumulated through various forms of official profiteering and corruption. In many cases these businesses were "briefcase companies," founded on little capital but enjoying a great deal in the way of official connections. Some were officially licensed as collective enterprises to disguise their ties to officials. Such bureaucratic patronage—in effect, de facto ownership by silent official partners —not only facilitated the establishment of private enterprises but gave such businesses advantages over their competition. Bureaucrats, after all, had ways of avoiding burdensome regulations, and they had easier access to credit and material resources controlled by the government.

Reform policies also greatly enlarged the degree of financial autonomy enjoyed by local governments, individual enterprises, and local branches of banks. The loosening of central government controls over budgets, investment decisions, and economic operations in general provided local officials with far greater sums of capital and greater leeway to use it. Premier Zhao Ziyang's coastal strategy augmented the amount of capital in the hands of local officials. Well underway by 1985, Zhao's policy opened fourteen coastal cities along with the Yangzi and Pearl River deltas to direct foreign investment, allowing local bureaucrats to play a lucrative compradore role, well beyond the effective reach of central government authorities.

Finally, at the end of 1985, the government's indulgent handling of the Hainan Island scandal legitimized the acquisitive instincts of officials and gave impetus to the spread of bureaucratic capitalist activities. Hainan, it will be recalled,[45] had been promoted by Premier Zhao Ziyang as a model market economy whose development was eventually to rival Taiwan's. The island was granted considerable autonomy in foreign trade and various other special economic privi-

---

[45] See Chapter 10. Also Lau Shinghou and Louise de Rosario, "Anatomy of a Scam," *China Trade Report*, October 1985, pp. 8–10.

leges. These were promptly utilized by local Communist officials to obtain quasi-legal bank loans which in turn were used to import nearly 100,000 cars and trucks and millions of television sets, among other goods, which then were sold on the mainland at two or three times the purchase price. When the scandal (the most spectacular of several at the time) was revealed in the summer of 1985, the government was slow to act. When finally moved to action by public outrage, it acted gently. The "punishment" for the chief Communist official involved in the scandal, Lei Yu, was a temporary demotion from his post as secretary of the regional Party committee, although at the same time he was praised by Zhao Ziyang as a man of "ability and energy." The two other officials primarily responsible for the scam were subject only to internal Party reprimands. Moreover, both Zhao and Party head Hu Yaobang visited Hainan over the New Year holidays in early 1986 to bolster the morale of local officials. "Just make amends and everything will be all right," Hu reportedly advised senior cadres on the island. "There's no need to let the affair become a millstone around your necks."[46] And Zhao Ziyang, in the course of his visit, announced a substantial reduction in the taxes Hainan owed the central government.[47] Beyond the political capital that the Deng faction had invested in the Hainan experiment, it was feared that any serious punishment would inhibit the entrepreneurial spirit of cadres in general and dampen their enthusiasm for market reforms.

CROWN PRINCES

The spirit of entrepreneurship certainly remained vigorous among the offspring of top Party leaders. The urban economic reforms of 1984–85 stimulated a period of frenetic economic activity. In 1985 industrial production increased by an astonishing 23 percent. The chaotic and inflationary times saw the virtual disappearance of centralized economic controls and a huge influx of foreign capital, a bonanza for what had become a pervasively corrupt bureaucracy. Graft, bribes, speculation in foreign currencies and commodities, and super-profits

---

[46] *Cheng Ming*, 1986, No. 3 (in *Inside China Mainland*, May 1986, p. 9).
[47] *Wenhuibao*, January 13, 1986. Cited in *ibid.*

made from the sale of scarce state materials to booming industrial plants became common economic practices. In this orgy of official profiteering, the middle-aged children of the very highest leaders of the Chinese Communist Party were the most conspicuous participants, and they occupied an especially prominent place in public perceptions of bureaucratic corruption. The business activities of the sons of Deng Xiaoping and Premier Zhao Ziyang aroused special interest.

Deng Pufang, the son of China's paramount leader, was paralyzed during the Cultural Revolution.[48] A little more than a decade later, when his father came to power, Deng Pufang established the China Welfare Fund for the Handicapped. It is for his leadership of this charitable organization that Deng Pufang is known abroad. In China, however, he is best known as the founder of the Kanghua Development Corporation, a private investment bank and international trading company. Established on the basis of the Deng family's political influence (and, it is suspected, with state funds as well), the Kanghua Corporation soon became a huge, multibillion-dollar conglomerate specializing in international trade. Through political connections, Kanghua won billion-dollar Japanese bank loans, special export permits in Hong Kong, control over enormous amounts of rationed raw materials, and exemption from all taxation, the latter presumably because of Kanghua's contributions to the Fund for the Handicapped. Within a few years the Kanghua Corporation had spawned some two hundred subsidiary companies throughout China and in Hong Kong, and had substantial investments in Europe and the United States.[49] In 1988, to mollify growing public criticism, the operations of the Kanghua Corporation were scaled back, and the tie to the Fund for the Handicapped was severed. But Deng Pufang remained an important actor in China's new financial world. In 1991 Deng Pufang, acting as an investment consultant, led a Chinese business delegation to South Korea.[50] As is characteristic of the ambiguities of bureaucratic capitalism, it was difficult to say whether it was a public or a private mission.

[48] Red Guards allegedly locked Deng Pufang in a Beijing University laboratory contaminated by radioactivity. Pufang escaped by leaping through a fourth-floor window, shattering his spine.
[49] On Deng Pufang's entrepreneurial exploits, see Edward A. Gargan, *China's Fate: A People's Turbulent Struggle with Reform and Repression* (New York: Doubleday, 1991), pp. 16–61.
[50] *The Wall Street Journal*, January 6, 1992, p. A10.

Shortly after Deng Pufang's Korean venture, a second of Deng Xiaoping's sons, Deng Zhifang, entered the international capitalist arena. Having served for some years as an official with the China International Trust and Investment Corporation (CITIC), a huge quasi-governmental financial conglomerate founded by his father in 1979, he appeared in the spring of 1993 as a private financier specializing in property development and formed a partnership with one of Hong Kong's richest capitalists, Li Kashing, the owner of a large real estate concern. Together the two purchased a controlling share of the stock of a major Hong Kong property investment company, Kadar Investments.[51] It was seen as a way for China to gain entry to the Hong Kong stock market through the back door—that is, by buying up a company already listed on the exchange. But it was not clear whether Deng Zhifang acted as a private businessman or on behalf of the Chinese state—or as both, as is more likely the case. Such, again, are the ambiguities of a bureaucratic capitalist regime.

The sons of Premier (and later Party chief) Zhao Ziyang also became adept in using their father's political influence in private business ventures. The Zhao brothers were attracted to the somewhat shadowy business world of the special economic zones. The eldest, Zhao Dajun, with the cooperation of the mayor of Shenzhen, established, and became the managing director of, the Shenzhen City New Technology Development Company in the spring of 1985. An uncommonly large operation for a presumably new business, the offices of the company took up an entire floor, some 8,000 square feet, of one of the larger buildings in the most successful of the zones.[52] A second son, Zhao Sanjun, became head of the Huai Hai Trading Company on Hainan Island, where he specialized in the illegal importation of color television sets.[53]

Virtually all Communist leaders (or ex-leaders) of any significance were patrons of children, spouses, and all manner of other relatives who joined the "business craze," as capitalist ventures were popularly known. As one close observer wrote in the mid-1980s:

---

[51] *The Wall Street Journal*, May 20, 1993.
[52] On Zhao Dajun's business career, see *Cheng Ming*, February 1986 (in *Inside China Mainland* under the title "Cadres' Children and Commercial Connections," April 1986, pp. 1–4).
[53] As Lee Feigon has pointed out, the distrust of Zhao Ziyang by Chinese students derived, in part, from his patronage of his corrupt sons. See Lee Feigon, *China Rising* (Chicago: Ivan R. Dee, 1990), pp. 132–33.

There are innumerable Party Central-level and provincial-level "crown princes" who are involved in the craze for running businesses. In the past few years all kinds of trading companies and exploitation companies have surged forward. In Beijing alone there are more than 3,000, and many of these are run by crown princes or have internal connections with government departments. They are generally known as *yanei* companies. Employing naval vessels or air force planes to transport automobiles and other goods from Qionghui to other places was the masterstroke of the *yanei* companies which enjoy special privileges. Of course quite a few children of senior cadres are also engaged in commercial activities or work in state-run enterprises. It is believed that these people are not necessarily all cashing in on their positions, but judging from what has already been revealed, there is no lack of people among them who are using public office for private gain.[54]

Every faction of the Party became involved in "using public office for private gain." The crown princes and princesses who turned to capitalist activities and around whom popular rumors swirled in the mid-1980s included the son of such luminaries as Bo Yibo (an architect of the First Five Year Plan), the grandson of Marshal Ye Jianying (former President of the People's Republic), a son of Party chief Hu Yaobang, the son of Politburo member and longtime Deng ally Wang Zhen, the daughter and son-in-law of Deng Xiaoping, and the son of onetime ideological czar Hu Qiaomu, among many others. It is not only the businesses of the crown princes that have been favored by Party patrons; so too have those of the spouses of senior cadres—for example, Xue Ming, the widow of the legendary Marshal He Long.[55]

Even the relatives of deceased Communist leaders have been favored by the state in ostensibly private business ventures. Wang Guanying, the brother-in-law of Liu Shaoqi, is a notable case in point. Wang, designated a "national capitalist" and a "democratic personality," had occupied a variety of bureaucratic posts in the People's Republic since 1949. In 1983 he was appointed head of the newly

[54] *Cheng Ming*, February 1986 (in *Inside China Mainland*, April 1986, p. 1).
[55] *Cheng Ming*, February 1986.

founded Everbright Industrial Company, headquartered in Hong Kong. Established and funded by the Chinese state for the purpose of importing advanced industrial technology, it was nonetheless officially insisted that the Everbright organization was a "nongovernmental" enterprise headed by a private capitalist. Its ambiguous status—quasi-official and pseudo-private—is again typical of China's bureaucratic capitalist economy.[56]

By the mid-1980s Deng Xiaoping's much-celebrated market reforms had produced a capitalist economy that revolved around the use of political power for private profit. That it was an economic system based on official corruption was hardly a secret in Chinese society. In the summer of 1985, a Communist Party journal complained of "malpractices [that] mar the reputation of reform. . . . When Party and government organs and cadres use their influence to set up enterprises, most of them make use of common funds and property and sell off commodities which are in short supply or great demand. This is an easy way to make a lot of money and all the profits are siphoned off into the pockets of individuals or small groups."[57] And another Party periodical lamented "pathological changes within the party organism."[58]

At the same time an academic journal noted that "Party and government cadres or their friends and relatives that engage in business would have difficulty getting by if they did not have a network of connections whose mainstay is power." The worst effect of such malpractices, it was charged, has been "to undermine the positive attitudes of the workers. One often hears scathing remarks like 'the workers do the work, and the cadres take the money,' 'the "masters" [that is, the workers, hailed as "the masters of the country" in official ideology] supply the labor while the "public servants" fill their pockets.' If this situation is allowed to continue, social relations will deteriorate, and people will lose faith in the cadres. It will also

[56] For a brief account, see "The 'Everbright Organization' and Its Chairman Wang Kuang-ying," *Issues and Studies*, Vol. 21, No. 3, pp. 142–47.

[57] *Zhibu Shenghuo* (Life in Party Branches), 1985, No. 5 (in *Inside China Mainland*, August 1985, p. 16).

[58] *Xuexi yu yanjiu* (Study and Research), 1986, No. 4 (in *Inside China Mainland*, October 1986, p. 7).

[undermine] faith not only in reform but also in socialism and communism." Although the writer safely attributed "malpractices" to the influence of capitalist ideology, the article came to a depressing conclusion about the whole process of economic reform: "initially designed to be a method of stimulating economic activity [the reform] has become an instrument by which private people and groups can pursue their own selfish interests."[59]

The expansionary market policies of Zhao Ziyang—first in his capacity as Premier of the State Council and then as Communist Party chief—greatly increased the scale of bureaucratic capitalism in the late 1980s and exacerbated the negative social and political consequences of rapid economic growth. The Chinese press responded with increasingly critical and pessimistic accounts of official involvement in economic life. In the summer of 1988, for example, the following condemnation appeared:

> The second business fad [the first was in 1985] took place between 1987 and June 1988 and the number of corporations of every description increased to 400,000 (from 170,000 in 1986), most of which were run by the government and ministries. . . . In Chinese history, "being an official and making a fortune" have always been linked together. The current phenomenon of "profiteering in an official way" in society has gone even further than past cases. Government office-backed, profiteering-oriented corporations have reached their hands into the circulation field, making prices fluctuate as they please. Using the power in their hands, with a telephone call and an approval notice, they can trade short supplies of sought-after commodities without taking them out of depositories. In Guangdong, the combination of officialdom and the market is summarized this way: Notices (all sorts of approval notices and documents) plus money (used as bribes) plus considerations of face (human relationship and connections) equals the secret of business success.
>
> Official profiteering has corrupted society. Ministries and

---

[59] *Shanxi Shifan Daxue* (Shanxi Normal University Journal), 1985, No. 4 (in *Inside China Mainland*, April 1986, p. 5).

commissions under the State Council let their subordinate departments, bureaus, sections, and offices operate under the name of corporations to "engage in profiteering" and thus provinces, prefectures, cities, and counties followed suit.[60]

"The limousines stayed right in the warehouse all the time when they were 'traveling' over half of China, and their price doubled in the process." So began another penetrating summary of the workings of bureaucratic capitalism in an article in *People's Daily* vainly calling for a crackdown on government officials who speculated in the market:

> Goods in short supply are speculated on by the companies with which government officials are closely involved. The masses have a name for them—"official speculators" or "big brother speculators"—a breed much more harmful than numerous "unofficial" small speculators. The nodal point of the "official speculators" lies in the coordination of officials and entrepreneurs, *with administration and business blending into one, the same personnel under supposedly two different organizations, straddling administrative rights and business operations.* Cases where government officials are mixed up with companies take many forms. Some officials, with the titles of "board directors" or "advisors," make powerful connections for their companies, give favorable recommendations, pull strings, and generally serve as their backers. And some retired cadres, without office, set up their own companies and continue to exercise their "residual power" while shouting about making use of their "residual energy." These *administrative-business complexes,* exploiting the powers they have in their hands, speculate and profiteer on goods in tight supply and reap fast fortunes. And in the process, naturally many abuses take place: graft and bribery, misappropriation and embezzlement.[61]

---

[60] Beijing *Zhongguo Xinwen She,* August 24, 1988. FBIS-CHI-88-166 (August 26, 1988), p. 20.
[61] Commentator, "Crack Down on Government-Related Speculators," *People's Daily,* July 14, 1988, p. 1. FBIS-CHI-88-143 (July 26, 1988), pp. 25–26 (emphasis added).

The nature of the "reformed" post-Mao economy thus has been no great mystery to those who experienced and observed the process of its maturation over the 1980s. The ambiguous relationship between the "public" and the "private" spheres—and the complex interrelations between bureaucracy, market, and corruption—were candidly described in detail and with extraordinary perception by Chinese journalists, academics, and others. Even within the limitations of what could be printed officially, many of the accounts were scathing.

Nor was there any mystery about why periodic "anticorruption" campaigns were so utterly futile. As a *Xinhua* commentator gently observed: "It has been reported that the number of cases involving government-owned companies illegally selling and buying supplies has markedly increased over the past several years. However, those who handle such cases have encountered strong resistance and the percentage of cases concluded is fairly low. The reason is these companies are often backed by people with power and authority. Investigators encounter a great deal of resistance when behind-the-scenes backers interfere." The only solution, it was concluded, was to "sever the connection between government officials and businessmen and between official circles and the market."[62]

Needless to say, the tie between the bureaucracy and "the market" forged in the 1980s was not severed. Instead, it was to be strengthened in the 1990s, as we shall see.

To be sure, not all entrepreneurs of the post-Mao era are officials or the relatives and friends of officials. But in the cities the overwhelming majority of those who come from nonbureaucratic backgrounds participate in the market as peddlers, street vendors, hawkers, and small shopkeepers. Those who have truly become rich, in some cases ostentatious millionaires, have been widely publicized but are, of course, rather few in number. All, in any event, whether millionaires or peddlers, are dependent on the bureaucracy for a plethora of licenses and permits, and this invariably requires participation in a well-oiled system of bribes and kickbacks. Similar requirements, although levied in more sophisticated fashion, apply to the enterprises of foreign capitalists and especially to overseas Chinese investors. The latter, seeking that capitalist utopia which com-

---

[62] Beijing *Xinhua* Domestic Service, September 9, 1988. FBIS-CHI-88-177 (September 13, 1988), p. 30.

bines cheap labor with political order, have come to the People's Republic in great numbers and with large sums of capital from Taiwan, Singapore, Hong Kong, and elsewhere. Without bureaucratic partners, in any event, private enterprises of any size are at a grave disadvantage in China's "free market."

There are no official statistics on the number or size of private enterprises directly owned or controlled by officials. It will be many decades before reliable figures are revealed by sociological investigations—or historical excavations. But, by all accounts, the number is very substantial indeed, particularly in the lucrative realm of foreign trade and capital investment. One investigator has estimated that "the proportion of officials' sons in trading companies approaches 90 per cent in the special economic areas and 70 per cent in Shanghai."[63]

The corrupt sons of the highest leaders of the Communist Party have been in the vanguard of China's pioneering transition from "socialism" to bureaucratic capitalism. The crown princes, or the *taizidang* (the "prince's party"), as they have become known, are important not only because they control vast sums of capital but also because they provide the "models" of political-moral behavior which the entire hierarchy of state and Party officials emulates. It is hardly surprising that one of the original demands of the student leaders of the Democracy Movement of 1989 was the publication of a list of the assets of senior Party leaders and their offspring.[64] That demand was, of course, ignored. In the 1990s, after a brief hiatus, official corruption and bureaucratic profiteering once again grew together with "the deepening of reform." By 1993 Communist Party leaders were again openly encouraging officials to *xiahai*, to "plunge into the sea," or to go into business.[65] The regime had surrendered to the imperatives of the bureaucratic capitalist system it had created.

One of the more curious features of China's market economy is that not only have individual officials or groups of officials transformed

[63] Rocca, "Corruption and Its Shadow," p. 415.
[64] See Chapter 14.
[65] See Nicholas D. Kristof, "China Applauds Officials Who Plunge into Profit," *The New York Times*, April 6, 1993, p. A6—where it is also noted that a recent survey found the top job preference of young people was to be an entrepreneur.

themselves into capitalist entrepreneurs but whole bureaucracies, large and small, have been forced to seek profits in the marketplace. State allotments have been frozen or cut, and governmental agencies, from the People's Liberation Army to elementary schools, have been told to make up their budgetary shortfalls by going into business. The Ministry of Public Security owns the Kunlun and other luxury hotels in joint ventures with foreign capitalists; the State Security Ministry[66] operates an import-export company, an employment agency serving foreign companies, and several domestic businesses; and various police and secret police agencies manufacture, and sell on the international market, riot- and crowd-control devices such as electric cattle prods and walkie-talkies.

By far the largest of such bureaucratic entrepreneurs is the People's Liberation Army, which owns the ultraluxurious five-star Palace Hotel in Beijing and the Dongfang Hotel in Canton, as well as a host of manufacturing and commercial enterprises, more than a thousand in Guangdong province alone, it is said.[67] The PLA also has converted some of its weapon-manufacturing facilities into factories which produce such consumer goods as refrigerators and bicycles. Army officers operate lucrative transportation companies, using military trucks and trains to haul lumber, coal, and other materials from the interior to the coastal provinces, where booming factories pay premium prices.[68] In all, it is estimated, the PLA operates more than 20,000 industrial, commercial, and service enterprises. In recent years, the PLA, through its various subsidiaries, has emerged as a major actor in the international capitalist world of finance and investment.

But the export of arms is the PLA's biggest business. Among the various PLA agencies engaged in the international arms trade, the most active is an enterprise known as Polytechnologies Incorporated. The company sells intermediate-range ballistic missiles as well as

---

[66] The State Security Ministry is in charge of foreign intelligence and counterintelligence (spying), and is more or less analogous to the CIA, whereas the Public Security Ministry operates most internal secret police agencies.

[67] Eric Hyer, "China's Arms Merchants: Profits in Command," *The China Quarterly*, No. 132 (December 1992), p. 1111.

[68] In the late 1980s, according to Liu Binyan, the price of coal transported by Army trucks jumped from 30 or 40 yuan at the mine site to 200 or 300 yuan at its destination.

short-range Silkworm missiles, jet planes, and a wide variety of conventional weapons taken directly from PLA stockpiles. Ostensibly a civilian corporation, officially registered as a subsidiary of the China International Trust and Investment Corporation, Polytechnologies is in fact operated by the Armaments Department of the PLA General Staff. The Armaments Department, a bastion of nepotism characteristic of bureaucratic capitalism, is staffed by generals and colonels who are close relatives of the Communist ruling elite. These include the sons-in-law of Deng Xiaoping (He Ping), of former Party chief Zhao Ziyang (Wang Zhihua), and of former President Yang Shangkun (Wang Xiaochao). The department's general director is Major General He Pengfei, the son of the legendary Red Army marshal He Long.[69] Polytechnologies, an eminently capitalist enterprise, its sole aim being the pursuit of profit, operates with a reckless independence, controlled neither by the Ministry of Defense nor the Ministry of Foreign Affairs. It sometimes finds itself working at cross-purposes with official government policy, having, for example, sold arms to the Nicaraguan Contras in 1986 at the very time the Beijing government was negotiating the normalization of diplomatic relations with the Sandinista government in Managua.[70]

Virtually every bureaucratic agency and unit is perforce engaged in one sort of business or another. Even the Central Party School in Beijing, an institution that trains higher-level Communist Party cadres, reportedly has supplemented its budget by selling videotapes of Politburo members delivering presumably secret speeches.[71] Academic departments in universities, their budgets slashed, commonly rely on such profits that can be made from operating restaurants and other small businesses. More lamentable are grade school teachers, victims of the privatization fad and government irresponsibility, who are forced to sell notebooks and candy in the classroom to support themselves and their schools.

The strange phenomenon of bureaucracies turned profit-maximizing enterprises has yielded more than a few oddities. One of the more bizarre cases involved the All-China Federation of Women, an or-

[69] Hyer, "China's Arms Merchants," p. 1113.

[70] Ibid., pp. 1114–15.

[71] Nicholas D. Kristof, "Chinese Aides Speeding Down the Capitalist Road," *The New York Times*, August 14, 1992, p. A6.

ganization originally founded to combat sexual inequality and oppression. In 1992 it was revealed that the federation had imported
young Russian women to work as prostitutes to boost the profits of
the Deng Yue Hotel in Canton, an establishment owned by the federation in a joint venture with a group of Hong Kong capitalists.[72]

It hardly needs to be noted that bureaucratic agencies do not
enter the marketplace in a totally collectivist spirit. Bureaucracies
are, of course, hierarchically organized, and it is safe to assume that
the proceeds from their business activities are distributed according
to rank and power. The enormous profits garnered by the PLA, for
example, insofar as they do not go to the central coffers of the organization, have ended up mostly in the pockets of the generals and
colonels.

THE COMMUNIST STATE BREEDS A BOURGEOISIE

By the late 1980s, China's "reformed" economy was evoking memories of the Guomindang's bureaucratic capitalist regime,[73] which the
Communists had so long and so vociferously denounced. Yet, however striking the similarities, there are several fundamental differences between the bureaucratic capitalist system that Communist
market reforms have wrought and the system of the Guomindang era.
One of the more crucial differences resides in the murky realm of
the relationship between political power and social class, and especially in the nature of "the bourgeoisie" in the two cases.

Capitalism of whatever variety requires a bourgeoisie of some
sort. In the 1920s, the Guomindang bureaucracy established itself in
a society with an existing bourgeoisie, a social class that had been
developing in more or less modern form since the mid-nineteenth
century. The Nationalist regime variously merged with, attached itself
to, imposed itself upon, or simply blackmailed the bourgeoisie. But
it was a class that remained a distinct entity in Chinese society—
and, properly tamed by the state, a class that was utilized by mem-

---

[72] Schmetzer, "A Brave New World."
[73] As with Liu Binyan, who concluded that China's "new bureaucratic bourgeois stratum" was
more harmful than its counterpart of the Guomindang era. Liu Binyan et al., *Tell the World*,
p. 164.

bers of the ruling Nationalist bureaucracy to link themselves to the Chinese and world markets for their own enrichment.

The Chinese Communist state, by contrast, having eliminated the Chinese bourgeoisie as a functioning social group by 1956, had no capitalist class to contend with, nor one to utilize. With the decision to pursue market-type reforms, a class of capitalist entrepreneurs *had to be created* to permit a market economy to function. That task, ironically, could be performed only by the "socialist" state itself.

While the Chinese Communist fabrication of a new social class has been novel in many respects, a state-created bourgeoisie is not entirely without historical precedent. It was attempted with a degree of success in nineteenth-century czarist Russia. Karl Marx and Friedrich Engels were among the first to comment on the phenomenon. In 1881, Marx observed that the Russian state had "hothouse-forced the growth of branches of the Western capitalist system. . . . A certain kind of capitalism, nourished at the expense of the peasants through the intermediary of the state, has been erected," he wrote.[74] Engels supplied the social component some years later, noting that, recognizing the need for modern industry following the Crimean War, "the government set about breeding a Russian capitalist class."[75]

Other historical examples include (with some reservations) the enormous role of the early Meiji state in the building of Japanese capitalism and the subservience of the Japanese bourgeoisie to the imperial bureaucracy; the central role of the state bureaucracy (as part of "the triple alliance") in the development of Brazilian capitalism;[76] and the centrality of the state in capitalist development in South Korea.[77]

In countries that have been latecomers on the industrial scene, pursuing some variant of capitalist modernization in the effort to catch up with the forerunners, the state often has been more the creator than the instrument of the bourgeoisie. Post-Mao China is the

[74] Karl Marx, Letter to V. Zasulich (March 8, 1881), cited in Hal Draper, *Karl Marx's Theory of Revolution*. Vol. 1: *State and Bureaucracy* (New York: Monthly Review Press, 1977), p. 580.
[75] F. Engels, Letter to Bebel (October 1, 1891), cited in Draper, *Karl Marx's Theory of Revolution*, Vol. 1, p. 579.
[76] See Peter Evans, *Dependent Development: The Alliance of Multinational, State and Local Capital in Brazil* (Princeton: Princeton University Press, 1979).
[77] See Jung-en Woo, *Race to the Swift: State and Finance in Korea's Industrialization* (New York: Columbia University Press, 1991).

latest—and the most extreme—version of this phenomenon. The new Chinese bourgeoisie (or rural and urban "entrepreneurial elites," if one prefers) not only is a creature of the state but is actually very largely composed of Party-state officials, their relatives, and their friends, as we have observed. Insofar as a portion of the bourgeoisie is private, not having sprung directly from the bureaucracy, it is nonetheless dependent on the bureaucracy for its existence and economic functioning. As is typically concluded in recent studies, the "private economy is still under the control of officials—everything must be done through them . . ."[78] This dependence is reinforced by the eagerness of the most successful private businessmen to join the Communist Party, where the principal qualifications for membership now appear to be wealth (a sign of appropriate zeal in the pursuit of the Four Modernizations) and loyalty to the Communist regime (evidence of proper patriotic fervor). And further fortifying this dependence is the incorporation of newly organized business guilds and associations (officially "nonofficial" groups, formed in accordance with state policy) into the government-run All-China Federation of Industry and Commerce.

Etienne Balazs, in describing the bureaucratically dominated economy of imperial China, spoke of officials and merchants as forming "two hostile but interdependent classes."[79] The relationship between the Guomindang political elite and the modern Chinese bourgeoisie might be characterized in similar terms. But it is impossible to extend the description to Communist China, where one would be hard pressed to find an equivalent contest between "two hostile" classes. Indeed, in light of the bureaucratic origins of the contemporary Chinese bourgeoisie, it might well be that the reforms of the post-Mao regime have yielded a "purer" bureaucratic capitalism than under its imperial and Guomindang predecessors.

The bureaucratic and dependent character of the new urban and rural entrepreneurial classes does not augur well for political democracy in China. While for many it no doubt is comforting to assume that a capitalist market economy will eventually yield political democracy, there is in fact little twentieth-century historical evidence

---

[78] Rocca, "Corruption and Its Shadow," p. 416.
[79] Balazs, *Chinese Civilization and Bureaucracy*, p. 32.

to support this habitual belief. Capitalism in the modern world has proved compatible with a great variety of political regimes, including fascism.

Modern political democracies have resulted from the complex interplay of a great variety of social, economic, and cultural factors that can only be studied in concrete historical circumstances.[80] There is no universal formula, economic or otherwise, which explains why political democracy is present or absent. There is widespread agreement, however, that an indispensable ingredient in the growth of parliamentary democracy has been a vigorous and *independent* bourgeoisie.[81] That being the historical case, it seems most unlikely that a democratic political role will be played by a contemporary Chinese bourgeoisie that is so dependent upon the state, and indeed so intimately a part of the state bureaucracy. It is improbable, to say the least, that a bourgeoisie whose economic fortunes are so dependent on the political fortunes of the Communist state is likely to mount a serious challenge to the authority of that state. The challenges will come from the victims, not the beneficiaries, of state-sponsored capitalism.

It is, of course, conceivable that over a period of time China's new entrepreneurs will shed their bureaucratic roots, evolve into a genuinely independent bourgeoisie, and assert their interests (which may or may not be conducive to political democracy) against the state. That, at best, is a matter of speculation and the time involved must be measured in generations, perhaps over a century or more. It is speculation, if indulged in, that might be tempered by the knowledge that few twentieth-century capitalist classes have been ardent agents of democratic change—whereas many have been partners in oligarchies, or all too willing to compromise with autocratic regimes.

For the time being, the members of China's new bourgeoisie emerge more as agents of the state than as potential antagonists, providing the bureaucracy with an economic base and the Communist state with a new social base. In playing this dual role, they do not contribute to pluralism, as often is reflexively assumed, but rather

---

[80] By far the most enlightening study on this complex question—and many other questions as well—is Barrington Moore's classic *Social Origins of Dictatorship and Democracy* (Boston: Beacon Press, 1966).

[81] "No bourgeoisie, no democracy," as Moore sums it up. Ibid., p. 418.

tend to further integrate state and society. The history of China's new moneyed elites thus far provides precious little support for the recent faddish notion of an emergent "civil society" that strives to free itself from the clutches of the state. Indeed, the new capitalists, having largely sprung from the bureaucracy, are psychologically as well as economically dependent on the Communist state—and ultimately rely on that state for political protection as well.

While a vigorous and growing entrepreneurial class is essential for national economic development in a market economy, the new Chinese bourgeoisie leads a rather precarious existence. It is a capitalist class, perhaps unique in world history, which is not firmly rooted in private property. This, indeed, is another major difference between the bureaucratic capitalisms of the Communist and Guomindang periods. In republican China the Guomindang spawned a bureaucratic capitalist regime in a society with a fully developed system of private property, as had largely been the case in imperial China as well. Bureaucratic capitalism in the People's Republic, by contrast, emerged in a society which had largely abolished private property.

A de facto system of private property has indeed developed in China over the Deng era. This has primarily taken the legal form of land or enterprises that are leased or contracted by individuals or corporate entities from collective or state organizations. Such leased properties increasingly have been treated as alienable private property—freely bought, sold, and mortgaged. Most important, these "leased" or "contracted" properties are considered sufficiently secure to attract very considerable capital investment, both domestic and foreign. Some movement toward de jure private property has occurred in other areas—in housing, in the establishment of stock markets, and in real estate—although these have been largely experimental. Not surprisingly, the main beneficiaries of "privatization" appear to be enterprising bureaucrats, although thus far the phenomenon has been very limited in China, not nearly as widespread or as chaotically rapacious as "nomenklatura privatization" in parts of Eastern Europe and Russia.[82]

[82] In the early 1990s when the government began selling public lands to private entrepreneurs for urban development, it was reported from the capital of Hainan that "an economics official from Beijing came down to this southern city and used his connections, or quanxi, to go into

Bureaucratic capitalism in Communist China has been associated with extraordinarily high rates of economic growth. By the early 1990s the Chinese economy had become the world's third largest (in terms of gross domestic product measured in terms of purchasing-power parity), propelling the People's Republic ahead of Russia, Germany, and possibly Japan.[83] In world-historical perspectives, the combination of bureaucratic economic dominance and rapid growth over a sustained period is hardly unprecedented. Meiji Japan (where the impulse to promote modern development came from the state) and, more recently, South Korea are two obvious East Asian examples. But it is unprecedented in China. In Chinese history, bureaucratic capitalism has always been an impediment to modern economic development. This was the case in traditional Chinese history (where the "nondevelopment of capitalism" is often attributed to bureaucratic intervention in the economy[84]), in the failure of "conservative modernization" in the late nineteenth century,[85] and in economic stagnation under the Guomindang regime.[86]

In view of these lessons of Chinese history, how is it that a Com-

---

the real estate business. He did not have any capital or experience, but he did O.K. anyway; now he runs a company worth more than $50 million." Sheryl WuDunn, "China Sells Off Public Land to the Well-Connected," *The New York Times*, May 8, 1993, p. 3. It was also reported that "the son of one central Government leader . . . said he had been able to earn $350,000 in a property deal without putting out a cent of his own money. He had never bought or sold real estate before, but he used his name and influence to convince a powerful middle-level official to approve a contract to obtain the land. Then once again through connections, he lined up financing and turned around and resold the land." Ibid.

[83] Steven Greenhouse, "New Tally of World's Economies Catapults China into Third Place," *The New York Times*, May 20, 1993, pp. A1 and A8.

[84] As Balazs has typically put it, ". . . the supreme inhibiting factor [in the development of capitalism] was the overwhelming prestige of the state bureaucracy, which maimed from the start any attempt of the bourgeoisie to be different, to become aware of themselves as a class and fight for an autonomous position in society." *Chinese Civilization and Bureaucracy*, p. 53.

[85] As Feuerwerker concluded: "In the last analysis, instead of furthering economic expansion, the monopoly rights granted to *kuan-tu shang-pan* (official supervision and merchant management) industries acted as a prop for 'bureaucratic capital.'" Albert Feuerwerker, *China's Early Industrialization* (Cambridge: Harvard University Press, 1958), p. 251.

[86] In scholarship on Nationalist China, it is common to treat economic development and bureaucratic capitalism as opposites. For example, Suzanne Pepper writes: "The KMT government was vulnerable to the charge that instead of promoting economic development it encouraged bureaucratic capitalism, meaning the use of public office for personal enterprise and profit." "The KMT-CCP Conflict, 1945–1949," *The Cambridge History of China*, Denis Twitchett and John K. Fairbank (eds.) (New York: Cambridge University Press, 1986), Vol. 13, p. 743.

Bureaucratic capitalism has been indicted as an impediment to modern development in

munist bureaucratic capitalist regime, seemingly so similar to its parasitic Guomindang counterpart, can generate such great economic dynamism? An explanation must begin with the results of the revolution of 1949. The Maoist victory destroyed the major precapitalist social groups and institutional structures that traditionally had inhibited economic development, especially parasitic landlordism. This, in turn, freed the agrarian surplus, which was duly appropriated by a powerful centralized state to finance its ambitious plans for industrialization. The creation of that central state apparatus, out of a chronically ruinous condition of political fragmentation, was the second most important accomplishment of the revolution. These, in brief, were the major bourgeois revolutionary achievements of Chinese Communism.

The Maoist attempt to construct a socialist society on these fragile bourgeois foundations failed, as we have seen, but in the process a very significant degree of industrialization was achieved. That Maoist failure, coupled with the relative material success, opened the way for the full realization of the capitalist and nationalist potential of the Chinese Communist Revolution, as Deng Xiaoping was quick to recognize. That Chinese capitalism would take a predominantly bureaucratic form was perhaps inevitable. Bureaucratic capitalism in one form or another is probably the only viable kind of capitalism in the contemporary age, free market capitalism having retreated long ago to the realm of nostalgic ideology. It certainly was the only capitalist option available to China, which began the market reform era with a huge (and growing) bureaucracy but no bourgeoisie.

It has been suggested that bureaucratic capital in Communist China is rarely used for productive ends.[87] To be sure, China's entrepreneurial elites are busily engaged in such nonproductive activities as speculation in real estate and commodities as well as ostentatious consumption. But such economic and social behavior is

---

other countries as well. A study of Thailand, for example, argues: "The evolution of the Thai economy was rather slow because of, in part, the influence of the bureaucratic capitalists. The existence of the bureaucratic capitalists obstructed the independence of the Thai capitalists and also hampered the growth of Thai capitalism." Sungsidh Piriyarangsan, *Thai Bureaucratic Capitalism, 1932–1960* (Bangkok: Chulalongkorn University Social Research Institute, 1983).
[87] For example, Rocca, "Corruption and Its Shadow," p. 415. Rocca also distinguishes between "predatory" and "creative" corruption, and concludes that China suffers from the former (p. 416).

characteristic of most contemporary capitalist regimes, to greater or lesser degrees, and it ill behooves Americans sitting amidst the moral and socioeconomic wreckage left by the Reagan-Bush years to moralize about the nonproductive practices of the Chinese bourgeoisie. However that may be, there can be little doubt that very considerable sums of bureaucratic capital, whether obtained through corruption or legal business activities, are finding their way into productive investments, especially in the booming rural and township industrial sector. There is no statistical evidence, to be sure, but it would be difficult to explain the extraordinarily high rate of growth in an economy the size of China's on the basis of foreign investment and limited internal private capital investment alone. It is perhaps the paradoxical case that the absence of a well-developed system of private property, universally regarded as an essential prerequisite for a capitalist economy, may well be an advantage for the development of Chinese capitalism in the short term in that it limits opportunities for speculation and thus compels more productive investment than might otherwise take place.

In broader historical perspectives, the process of development that proceeds under the ideological veneer of a "socialist market economy" is perhaps a late-twentieth-century variant of what Barrington Moore termed "conservative modernization."[88] That model of belated capitalist development, for which Bismarckian Germany and Meiji Japan are the major historical prototypes, involves a bourgeois "revolution from above" that sweeps away feudal social and institutional barriers to rapid capitalist modernization. The "revolution from above" is carried out by a strong, relatively autonomous, and highly authoritarian state. The social base on which that state rests consists of an alliance between landed aristocrats who have turned to commercial entrepreneurship and an emergent bourgeoisie; the latter is a vigorous but not yet sufficiently developed class to exercise power on its own. The state, largely independent of particular social classes, sets itself the task of modernizing the nation in an effort to catch up with the advanced capitalist countries. To that end it creates conditions favorable for the rural and urban capitalist classes; it supports a labor-repressive economic system to extract an ever-larger surplus

[88] Moore, *Social Origins of Dictatorship and Democracy*, esp. Chapters 5 and 7.

from the working population, especially in the countryside; and it sets itself the task of directing that surplus in ways that will serve the eminently nationalist goal of building modern industrial and military power.

Post-Mao China appears to be following something resembling this conservative route to capitalist modernization. The Mao era supplied the strong and autonomous state, complete with a powerful apparatus of repression. In its post-Mao metamorphosis, the Communist state, now somewhat "rationalized" according to Weberian precepts, has swept away all social, ideological, and institutional barriers to rapid capitalist development, whether barriers left over from "feudal" China or "socialist" ones erected during the Mao period. In the countryside, collectivist institutions—condemned as "feudal remnants"— have been destroyed in favor of a commercialized rural economy. In the cities, job security and a comprehensive welfare system for the working class,[89] once heralded as a "socialist" accomplishment, are now denounced not only for being economically inefficient but also for fostering "feudal bondage."

What conservative modernization has meant for the working populations of both town and countryside is subjection to ever more intensive modes of labor exploitation, introduced and enforced by the state. A greater portion of a larger surplus is extracted by new bourgeois elites as well as by old bureaucratic ones. It is the peasantry who (it is now clear) is the principal victim of the new bureaucratic capitalist mode of exploitation, as it was under the old "socialist" one. It is from the countryside that the major part of the economic surplus is extracted by the state and by a state-dependent bourgeoisie to finance rapid industrialization. In China, as in all cases of late modernization, it is the peasants who are the main victims of "development."

Such, in brief outline, is the contemporary Chinese version of conservative modernization. It is most decidedly a "revolution from above," for the state not only promotes capitalist economic development but also quite literally created the urban and rural bourgeois classes which capitalism presupposes. In performing this function of

---

[89] Or, more precisely, for a portion of the working class, the state workers under the Mao regime.

breeding a capitalist class, the Chinese process of conservative modernization differs from its German and Japanese predecessors. In both Germany and Japan commercially oriented landed elites and urban bourgeois classes had developed before the drive for rapid modernization. Their absence in China has made the Dengist "revolution from above" an even more profoundly statist affair than its German and Japanese counterparts, and it lends a particularly bureaucratic character to Chinese capitalism and to the new Chinese bourgeoisie.

The capitalist "revolution from above" in post-Mao China (as was the case in Bismarckian Germany and Meiji Japan) not only has conservative social class and political implications but is logically accompanied by conservative social policies, as for example in the Dengist re-creation of a highly elitist school system. It is a pattern of development, moreover, that lends itself to a highly chauvinistic nationalism, which, together with bureaucratic self-interest, appears to be the driving motivation of the leaders of the Chinese Communist Party. It is not a form of development that is likely to favor political democracy. Indeed, as Moore has argued, a conservative capitalist revolution from above has considerable fascist potential,[90] as the histories of Germany and Japan have revealed in abundant measure.

It would be foolish to predict a fascist future for China on the basis of historical precedents that perhaps belong to a unique period in world history. All that can be said is that neither China's bureaucratic capitalist system nor the Dengist revolution from above that created that system is conducive to the socioeconomic pluralism and political democratization that some observers confidently assume will result from a market economy.

---

[90] Moore, *Social Origins of Dictatorship and Democracy*, esp. Chapter 8 (pp. 433–52).

★

PART FOUR

THE DEMOCRACY MOVEMENT (1986—89)

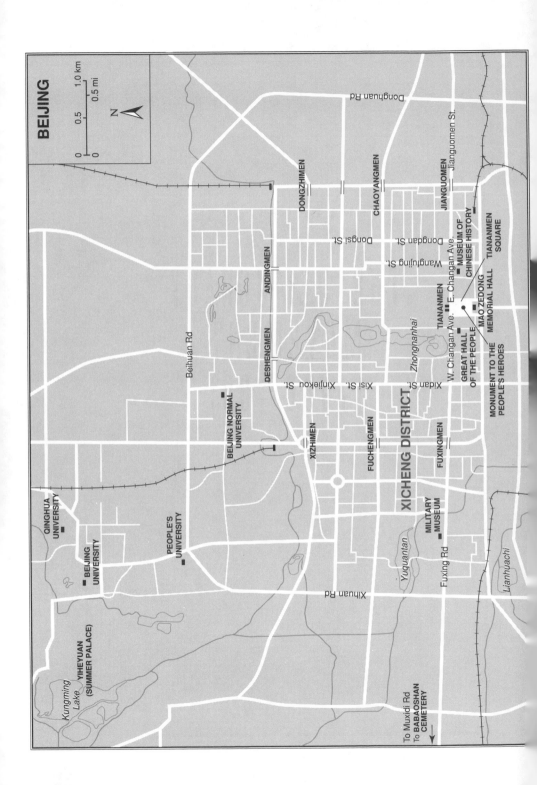

BEIJING

N

0   0.5   1.0 km
0   0.5 mi

Dongzhimen

CHAOYANGMEN

JIANGUOMEN

Jianguomen St.

MUSEUM OF
CHINESE HISTORY

TIANANMEN
SQUARE

MAO ZEDONG
MEMORIAL HALL

MONUMENT TO THE
PEOPLE'S HEROES

GREAT HALL
OF THE PEOPLE

TIANANMEN

E. Changan Ave.

W. Changan Ave.

Wangfujing St.

Dongan St.

Dongsi St.

ANDINGMEN

DESHENGMEN

Beihuan Rd

XIZHIMEN

Xinjiekou St.

Xisi St.

Xidan St.

Zhongnanhai

FUCHENGMEN

XICHENG DISTRICT

FUXINGMEN

MILITARY
MUSEUM

Fuxing Rd

Yuquantan

Lianhuachi

Xihuan Rd

PEOPLE'S
UNIVERSITY

BEIJING NORMAL
UNIVERSITY

QINGHUA
UNIVERSITY

BEIJING
UNIVERSITY

Kungming
Lake YIHEYUAN
(SUMMER PALACE)

To Muxidi Rd
To BABAOSHAN
CEMETERY

Donghuan Rd

12

THE FALL OF HU YAOBANG
AND THE ORIGINS OF
THE DEMOCRACY MOVEMENT

HU YAOBANG WOULD HAVE BEEN a rather minor figure in the history of Chinese Communism had not his death in April 1989 proved the occasion for the student demonstrations that heralded the tragic Beijing Spring. Installed by Deng Xiaoping as Secretary-General of the Communist Party in 1980, Hu Yaobang faithfully carried out the reform policies of the post-Mao regime. And he did so as China's "paramount leader" dictated, even (uncharacteristically for the democratically inclined Hu) denouncing freedom of the press along the way at Deng's insistence. Ousted as Secretary-General of the Party in January 1987, allegedly for being soft on demonstrating students and "bourgeois-liberal" intellectuals, he was sufficiently nonthreatening to be allowed to retain his place as one of five members of the Politburo's Standing Committee. In that capacity, during the final two years of his life, he continued to follow Deng's instructions, offering no public criticism of the policies and practices that were leading to a national disaster.

Although Hu Yaobang lacked Marxian theoretical pretensions, and was ultimately a failure as a Party politician, he could claim a long and courageous record of service to the Communist Revolution. He had joined the Red Army (and the Communist Youth League) in 1930, at the age of fifteen, was admitted to the Party in 1933, during the last year of the ill-fated Jiangxi Soviet, and was a survivor of the

Long March. Hu's political fortunes soon became tied to Deng Xiaoping's. He served as a political commissar under Deng's command
in the Second Field Army during the final decade of the long revolutionary struggle. After the establishment of the People's Republic,
he was an official in Sichuan province until, in 1952, he followed
Deng to Beijing. In the capital, Hu Yaobang's main responsibility
was to head the Communist Youth League, no longer the heroic band
of young rebels he had joined as a teenager but now an established
state-Party organization that grew to a membership of some 30 million
by the early 1960s.

    With the outbreak of the Cultural Revolution, Hu Yaobang was
purged along with Deng, and the Communist Youth League was abolished. Dispatched to a cadre reeducation school in the countryside,
like many veteran Party officials Hu was returned to office in the
early 1970s as Party secretary of the Academy of Sciences, where he
began to build a reputation as a defender of intellectual freedom. In
1977, after the fall of the Gang of Four, Hu was appointed vice
president of the Central Party School for the training of higher-level
cadres and also head of the Party's Organization Department. It was
from these lofty positions that Hu ideologically and politically assisted his old friend Deng Xiaoping in his drive for supreme power.
Hu Yaobang was rewarded for his efforts by being elevated to the
Politburo at the Third Plenum in 1978. Two years later, Deng selected him to fill the newly created office of Party Secretary-General.

    As head of the Chinese Communist Party for nearly seven years,
Hu Yaobang was known as Deng Xiaoping's disciple. Hu had no
power base of his own, no distinctive ideology, and he offered no
political program save for the one Deng instructed him to carry out.
Yet Hu, very much on his own, won the genuine respect and affection
of broad sectors of Chinese society, especially as Deng's popularity
began to fade in the mid-1980s. He was, according to China's famed
and now dissident journalist Liu Binyan, "the only party leader who
enjoyed prestige among the people."[1] Hu Yaobang owed much of his
popularity (albeit far greater after his death than in life) to his close
identification with the more progressive and democratic policies of
the early Deng regime. He was the most prominent Party leader in

----

[1] Liu Binyan, *China's Crisis, China's Hope*, p. xiv.

bringing about the rehabilitation of officials and intellectuals who had been victimized by the antirightist witch-hunt of 1957 and the Cultural Revolution. Among higher Party leaders, Hu was the most ardent and consistent advocate of democratic reforms. He had little taste for Deng's periodic campaigns against "spiritual pollution" and "bourgeois liberalization," and while refraining from any direct confrontations with his mentor, he quietly did what he could to shield intellectuals. He was also the main, if silent, patron of the *People's Daily* during the days when the staff of the official Party organ included such independent-minded critics as the Marxist humanist Wang Ruoshui and the investigative journalist Liu Binyan, the scourge of corrupt Party bureaucrats.[2]

In addition to gaining the respect of intellectuals and students, Hu Yaobang attempted to win the support of the common people. During his tenure as Party leader, he claimed to have visited 1,600 of China's 2,000 counties, occasions which permitted him to indulge a passion for giving lengthy speeches. Hu's personality and personal integrity, if not necessarily his speeches, were well received by the Chinese people. A Party colleague, Ruan Ming, described him as open-minded and humane, a "visionary" and an "idealist" who was "remarkably free of the ruthlessness of character so much a part of the exercise of power in China."[3] Among Party leaders who were increasingly seen (especially after 1985) as venal, corrupt, and arrogant, Hu Yaobang stood out as an honest and kindly man, if not necessarily a great leader.

Hu Yaobang was never the "liberal" some Western observers posthumously make him out to have been.[4] A revolutionary and a Communist since his teens, he devoted his life to the goal of building a socialist China. Unlike the Communist leaders who know virtually nothing of Marxism but whom Western commentators nonetheless call "hard-line Marxists," Hu was actually fond of reading the classic works of Marx and Engels. He wanted for the Chinese what Marx had wanted for the Germans, frequently quoting from the passage where Marx exclaimed: "Once the lightning of thought touches the

---

[2] Ibid., p. 88.
[3] Ruan Ming, Part 2 of Liu Binyan et al., *Tell the World*, p. 77.
[4] See, for example, Perry Link, "The Intellectuals and the Revolt," *The New York Review of Books*, June 29, 1989, p. 41.

garden of people that has never been touched before, Germans will be liberated to become human beings."[5] Hu Yaobang, more than any other recent Chinese Communist leader, was drawn to the democratic and libertarian strains in the Marxist tradition. Hardly a "liberal" or a representative of "liberal thought," Hu Yaobang was in fact a democratic Marxist and a dedicated Communist who devoted his life to realizing his vision of socialism.

Early in April 1989, Hu Yaobang suffered a heart attack while attending a meeting of the Party Politburo. He died a week later, on April 15. When the death of Hu was publicly announced on national television that evening, students gathered at a plaza on the Beijing University campus to exchange ideas and to post their hastily written poems of mourning and commemoration. One couplet spread quickly through the capital: "The one who should not die, died. Those who should die, live!" "Those who should die" referred to Premier Li Peng and Deng Xiaoping.

On April 16, students organized meetings commemorating Hu at several leading universities in Beijing—People's University, Beijing Normal University, and Qinghua University, among others. Joined by some of their teachers, the students soon turned to criticizing corruption and bureaucracy in the Communist Party. The next night campus meetings and demonstrations spilled onto the streets of Beijing, where students were joined by workers and ordinary citizens, culminating in a late evening march to Tiananmen Square in the heart of the capital. No one could have imagined, least of all the student activists, that on the morning of April 18 more than 100,000 people would be gathered in the square, the symbolic center of state power in China, demanding democratic rights for the people. The great Democracy Movement of 1989, sparked by Hu Yaobang's death, was underway even before the official burial of the dead Party leader on April 22. The course of that extraordinary movement, at once one of the most glorious and one of the most tragic chapters in modern Chinese history, will be related shortly. Before attempting to do so, it is necessary to inquire into the conditions which brought together

---

[5] Ruan Ming, in *Tell the World*, p. 73. Mao Zedong had been unimpressed with Hu Yaobang's Marxism. Of Hu, Mao is reported to have said: "Fond of reading, he does not strive for thorough understanding; fond of making speeches, he chatters on forever." Ibid., p. 75.

students, intellectuals, workers, and ordinary citizens into so massive and courageous a defiance of the Communist state, conditions prepared during the years that Hu Yaobang was Secretary-General of the Chinese Communist Party.

In seeking to explain the emergence of the Democracy Movement, most Western observers (and many Chinese participants as well) take it for granted that the fundamental cause of the clash between the Chinese people and the Chinese state was the failure of the Deng Xiaoping regime to carry out timely democratic political reforms corresponding to its program of market-oriented economic reforms. In arguments which would be dismissed as a species of economic determinism were they set forth by Marxists, it is said that Deng's economic reform program created social pressures which could not be contained within the old Communist political structure—and that Deng's failure to bring about meaningful political reforms resulted in insoluble contradictions which found expression in the Democracy Movement and its bloody suppression. Thus it is typically argued that, after a promising beginning, Deng's economic reforms "had stalled in the face of the leadership's unwillingness to accept the loss of political control that was implicit in pressing those reforms further."[6]

There is indeed a good measure of truth in the proposition that modern economic development in postrevolutionary China clashed with an archaic and repressive Communist political structure. But the pursuit of that explanation sometimes obscures an essential truth. Democracy *qua* democracy is valued by the Chinese people; it is not simply a value necessitated by modern economic progress in the post-Mao years. Nor is it a value carried only by students and intellectuals. Chinese demands for democratic rights arose around the turn of the century and soon spread from revolutionary intellectuals and students to the urban masses. Democracy was one of the main demands of the May Fourth Movement, at a time when China had experienced precious little modern economic development. Demands for such elemental democratic rights as the freedom to demonstrate

---

[6] Link, "The Chinese Intellectuals and the Revolt," p. 38.

and organize were militantly pursued by both the urban working class and the peasantry in the great revolutionary upsurge of the mid-1920s. The brutal suppression of that extraordinary movement by Chiang Kai-shek's armies in 1927 did not end the quest for democracy. Demands for democratic freedoms, on the part of both masses and intellectuals alike, found continuing and often militant expression over the next half century during both the Guomindang and Mao regimes. To reduce the question of democracy in China to some arbitrary formula on the relationship between economic and political development, suggesting that democratic reforms were necessitated by the post-Mao regime's market-oriented economic reforms, risks ignoring a nearly century-long history of struggle for democratic freedoms among Chinese who took democracy as something to be valued and striven for in and of itself. Democracy was as much a "necessity" in China in the 1920s as in the 1980s.

The year 1985 appears as a watershed, marking the time when the hope and optimism of the early reform period gave way to increasing doubts about the course the Deng regime was pursuing, to growing pessimism about the future, and eventually to the almost pervasive feeling of hopelessness that overwhelmed urban China in the spring of 1989. It is remarkable how many Chinese, in reflecting on their recent past, mention 1985 as the time when they first felt that things were beginning to go wrong. Liu Binyan expressed the feelings of many when he wrote in 1988: "How could there not be hope for a major country like China? But this is a real issue, for since 1985 many Chinese have begun to have doubts and it is becoming a hotter and hotter topic of conversation. . . . China is unquestionably beset with crises, with more and more dangers cropping up all the time. I have had this feeling too since 1985 and as a result have grown most troubled over China's fate. It is a natural and reasonable reaction."[7]

Remembered as the beginning of China's time of troubles, 1985 was the year when some of the more painful effects of capitalist development began to manifest themselves. The market, whose wonders the post-Mao reformers had so ardently celebrated and which

[7] Liu Binyan, *China's Crisis, China's Hope*, p. 103.

hitherto had yielded mostly salutary results, now began to manifest its unruliness, bringing hardship to much of the urban population and a widespread loss of confidence in the reform program. The fetish of the market began to give way to a fear of the market as an uncontrollable mechanism beyond the power of even the Communist state to regulate.

The developments that made 1985 seem so crucial a year have been discussed in several of the preceding chapters and need be only briefly recalled here. There was, to begin with, the sharp and unanticipated drop in grain production in 1985 that resulted, in part, from the state-sponsored commercialization of the rural economy. Following four successive years of large increases in grain production, the 1985 shortfall sent shock waves through Chinese society, raising doubts about the longevity of the recent agricultural successes. If the Mao regime had overly stressed the importance of grain as "the key link" in the Chinese economy, the Deng regime had gravely underestimated both the economic and the psychological significance of the grain harvest.

Bureaucratic corruption also became a major issue in 1985. It was not necessarily the case that corruption grew that much more rapidly in 1985 than in previous years. But public consciousness of official profiteering certainly increased enormously, partly the result of press revelations of the spectacular Hainan Island scandals.

Of more immediate concern, especially to urban inhabitants, was "price reform." The initial result of the abortive effort, particularly the partial decontrol of prices of agricultural products, was an unaccustomed burst of inflation, sending the cost of basic necessities soaring by over 30 percent in Beijing and other large cities in the early months of 1985. Other economic difficulties followed, including a sharp increase in China's foreign debt (which grew by 50 percent in 1985 alone) and soaring trade and budget deficits, which ensured that the economy would generate strong inflationary pressures for years to come.

These deleterious economic consequences of market reform found social expression in 1985 in reports, for the first time in the Deng era, of armed peasant resistance to tax collectors as well as unrest among urban workers and students. They found immediate political expression in growing conflicts among the higher leaders of the Chinese Communist Party. The main clash was between the "radical" reform faction who favored continued marketization and privatization in accordance with the program set forth in the autumn of 1984, and those wedded to the primacy of central planning who advocated a slower pace of reform. The principal leader of the latter group was Chen Yun. Deng Xiaoping uneasily positioned himself between—and above—the two loosely grouped factions.

As the economic situation became increasingly chaotic in 1985, the political influence of veteran Party bureaucrats grew, reflected in the appointment of Chen Yun to head the Party's Central Disciplinary Commission. From that powerful position, Chen, with the support of Deng Xiaoping, demonstrated considerable zeal in purging radical reformers in provincial Party organizations under the guise of combating corruption. The influence of Secretary-General Hu Yaobang was progressively undermined. As inflation, budgetary problems, and trade deficits grew more serious in the latter months of 1985, the government once again imposed centralized controls over the economy and adopted a variety of austerity measures that resulted in closed factories and unemployed workers. The Chinese people had suffered yet another boom and bust cycle, or, as official terminology put it, a cycle of "overheating" and "consolidation."

The events of the fateful year 1985 led to the beginning of a loss of popular confidence in the government, the reform program, and Deng Xiaoping personally, especially among urban people. It was a loss of confidence that bred disillusionment and then anger during the last years of the decade as economic problems multiplied, bureaucratic corruption clogged the pores of society, and inflation began to lower the living standards of much of the urban population. The relatively painless economic progress of the early 1980s was not to return—and the sense of hope and optimism that marked those years could not be restored.

It is ironic, indeed astonishing, that the West's celebration of Deng Xiaoping and his reforms reached its apogee precisely at the time when Chinese disillusionment with their paramount leader began to grow. *Time* magazine, in its September 23, 1985, issue (which exhibited a most flattering portrait of Deng Xiaoping on the cover), reported that "Deng's personal popularity appears on the increase."

Praising "Deng's great undertaking" and "Deng's innovations," *Time* concluded that "Deng and his reformist allies have displayed an impressive blend of self-criticism and self-confidence in their attempts to balance a measure of freedom with control, unity with diversity, [and] experimentation with tradition."[8] At year's end, *Time* named Deng its "Man of the Year" for a second time, an honor hitherto reserved, at least as far as Chinese were concerned, for Chiang Kai-shek, in the days when the Nationalist dictator had been Henry Luce's favorite world leader. William Buckley's *National Review* also selected Deng as its "Man of the Year" in 1985 and Western politicians, especially of conservative bent, joined in the celebration, often finding in Deng's reforms evidence of the superiority of capitalism and a portent of its universal triumph.[9] The Western celebration of Deng, both popular and scholarly, continued until the very eve of the June 4, 1989, massacre.

If 1985 was a crucial turning point in the history of the Deng regime, this was by no means apparent to the principal historical actors at the time. Consciousness lags behind reality, often far behind. As the year 1986 opened, the reform project continued to be pursued much in the same fashion as before. The economic contradictions, social tensions, and political resentments that Dengist policies had generated, which had briefly revealed themselves in 1985, were largely ignored. Doubts had grown, but they were overshadowed by high economic and social expectations.

At the end of 1985, Deng Xiaoping declared that the Chinese historical experience had demonstrated the need to borrow "some effective capitalist methods" to break down the economically inhibiting effects of an overreliance on central planning.[10] Deng's advice found generous public expression in Premier Zhao Ziyang's speech

[8] "The Second Revolution," *Time*, September 23, 1985, pp. 42–56.
[9] For example, Maurice Stans, writing in the *National Review* in December 1984, expressed the utopian hope: "Perhaps China may, by showing how much a free economy can do for its people, point the way to the demise of rigid Marxism and the ultimate reconciliation of differences among the political systems of the world." Cited in Andrew Nathan, *China's Crisis* (New York: Columbia University Press, 1990), p. 71.
[10] "Quarterly Chronicle and Documentation," *The China Quarterly*, No. 105 (March 1986), p. 183.

to the National People's Congress in March 1986, in which he unveiled China's Seventh Five Year Plan for the years 1986–90. Although the new plan called for more modest rates of growth than
those claimed for the Sixth Five Year Plan of 1981–85—an annual
increase of 6.7 percent in the value of industrial and agricultural
production as opposed to an annual rate of 11 percent for the 1981–
85 period—the capitalist thrust of the new plan was more far-
reaching and explicit than in any previous official document. Zhao
Ziyang emphasized the need to accelerate the transformation of factories and other large-scale enterprises into independent units responsible for their own profits and losses. They were, bluntly put
(although Zhao was not quite so blunt), to operate in accordance with
the eminently capitalist principle of profit-maximization. This would
require as yet unspecified changes in ownership and management
since continued state ownership and management was clearly incompatible with enterprise autonomy. Zhao, of course, did not mention
the "leftist" heresy of workers' self-management as a possible alternative to the old command economy.

Liberally employing the official euphemism of the day, a "socialist commodity economy," Zhao Ziyang also called for a general
expansion of market relationships. The state's role in allocating materials would be drastically reduced and the state would only "guide"
rather than "mandate" economic policy. He further advocated a vast
expansion of foreign trade and investment and, to these ends, called
for a greater emphasis on developing the special economic zones,
despite the 1985 revelations that the zones were more adept in generating corruption than foreign exchange.[11]

A capitalist labor market was critical for the economic plan Zhao
Ziyang outlined. The reformers, therefore, now placed an even greater
emphasis on abolishing the system of job security enjoyed by
many urban workers. Although this was an issue of extreme political
sensitivity, many of the more ardent reformers allied with Zhao argued that "socialist" China, no less than capitalist economies, required a large "reserve army of labor"—that is, masses of
unemployed people who could be hired quickly and cheaply as re-

---

[11] Zhao Ziyang, Speech to the National People's Congress, March 25, 1986. For an English-
language summary of Zhao's speech, see *Beijing Review*, March 31, 1986, pp. 5–6.

quired and fired when no longer needed. For China's urban workers, needless to say, joining the ranks of a "reserve army" of unemployed was hardly an attractive prospect, however much it may have appealed to the growing number of World Bank advisors who had been invited to the People's Republic.

Thus, despite the unsettling events of 1985, the market reform program continued to be advocated and partially implemented in 1986, proceeding in a relatively open political environment. In the spring and summer of 1986, Deng Xiaoping encouraged discussion of political reform, which, he long had promised, would accompany economic reform. In response to Deng's seemingly hopeful words, much was made in the official press of the thirtieth anniversary of the "double-hundred" policy of 1956–57, Mao Zedong's abortive effort to "let a hundred flowers blossom and a hundred schools of thought contend." Prominent intellectuals suggested that the "double-hundred" slogan be given the force of law in order to guarantee that it not become the victim of arbitrary policy changes. It was further suggested that the "double-hundred" formula apply to political as well as academic and intellectual matters, so that it would contribute to the goal of "socialist democracy."[12] Leading Marxist theoreticians such as Su Shaozhi, and even the establishment historian Hu Sheng, emphasized that Marxism was not an unchanging dogma but rather a theory that was in a constant process of transformation in accordance with changing historical conditions, continually shedding ideas that practical experience proved to be incorrect or outmoded in favor of new understandings of social reality. Marxism, it was further argued, was sufficiently flexible to inherit the positive aspects of capitalism and bourgeois civilization.[13] These, of course, were time-honored Marxian propositions, but not ones normally heard in China.

Even more reflective of the intellectual temper of the time was the reappearance in official print of the writings of Wang Ruoshui, the best-known representative of the "alienation school," who had

[12] *People's Daily*, May 16 and May 30, 1986; *Guangming Ribao*, April 30 and May 7, 1986. Cited in "Quarterly Chronicle and Documentation," *The China Quarterly*, No. 107 (September 1986), p. 576.

[13] Hu Sheng in *Hongqi* (Red Flag), May 1, 1986. "Quarterly Chronicle and Documentation," *The China Quarterly*, No. 107 (September 1986), p. 575.

been dismissed from his position as deputy managing editor of the *People's Daily* during the 1983–84 campaign against "spiritual pollution." In the summer of 1986 the Shanghai *Wen Hui Bao* published Wang's "On the Marxist Philosophy of Man," which emphasized the democratic and humanist strains in the Marxist tradition. Marx's vision of communist society, Wang stressed, was that of "a community of free people."[14]

Concrete measures for implementing Deng's promise of political reform were vigorously advocated and openly debated in the summer and fall of 1986, including plans for the separation of the Party from the government, the establishment of a civil service examination system for the selection of officials, and an independent judiciary. The actual implementation and institutionalization of these modest but not insignificant moves toward democratization seemed to be at hand in November 1986 when the Standing Committee of the National People's Congress finally approved an electoral law governing the selection of delegates to local people's congresses. But irregularities in the preparations for the elections to these politically powerless but symbolically important "congresses" proved the occasion for popular protests—and a new wave of state repression finally extinguished what faint hopes still existed for democratization.

On December 5, 1986, on the campus of the University of Science and Technology in the city of Hefei in Anhui province, 3,000 students peacefully gathered to protest the lack of any real choice in upcoming local and university elections. They called for democratic electoral procedures, and demanded improvements in teaching and living conditions. "No democracy, no modernization" soon became the slogan of student demonstrators, who found a staunch ally in Fang Lizhi, the renowned astrophysicist who was also the university's vice president. Fang not only supported the student demands; he postponed scheduled elections at the university to allow students to put forward their own candidates in place of those the authorities had

[14] Wang Ruoshui's treatise "On the Marxist Philosophy of Man" was a rewritten version of several lectures he had delivered in 1985. It was published in two parts, the first part in Shanghai *Wen Hui Bao*, July 17, 1986, p. 2, and the concluding part in *Wen Hui Bao*, July 18, 1986, p. 2.

nominated. The central government was also encouraging. An official of the State Education Commission in Beijing declared that the students had a constitutional right to demonstrate, although he questioned the wisdom of writing large character posters. Wallposters, after all, were uncomfortably reminiscent of the Cultural Revolution and had been officially banned six years before, when the regime suppressed an earlier and now half-forgotten Democracy Movement.[15]

Emboldened by the support of Fang Lizhi and other prominent intellectuals, and by the apparent absence of official disapproval, students from several schools in Hefei organized a larger and more militant demonstration on December 9, the anniversary of the hallowed "resist Japan" movement of 1935, when an earlier generation of student protesters had helped to undermine the nationalist credentials of the Chiang Kai-shek regime.[16] As had been the case with the celebrated December Ninth Movement, the 1986 demonstrations rapidly spread to more than a dozen urban centers, first to Wuhan and other cities along the Yangtze and then to Shanghai.

Hefei, a small and provincial backwater among Chinese cities, seems a most unlikely site for stimulating a nationwide movement that ultimately was to reach to the highest levels of power in Beijing. Yet the University of Science and Technology, although little known beyond Chinese academic circles, is one of the most important and prestigious of China's institutions of higher education. Originally located in Beijing, the university was moved to Hefei during the Cultural Revolution to shield scientific research from the political storms of those turbulent times. The University of Science and Technology remained in the relative tranquillity of Hefei after the Cultural Revolution, and in the 1980s enrolled students selected almost entirely from the families of prominent intellectuals and high-ranking bureaucrats. Thus the students who organized the demonstrations in December 1986 were not without ties to the upper echelons of the Chinese Communist Party, particularly to the democratic reformist faction of the Party whose members were associated with Hu Yao-

---

[15] See Chapter 5.
[16] See John Israel and Donald W. Klein, *Rebels and Bureaucrats: China's December 9ers* (Berkeley: University of California Press, 1976).

bang. The original protests in Hefei may well have been spontaneous, but the student organizers had good reason to believe that they had supporters in high places in Beijing, perhaps including Party chief Hu Yaobang, but certainly members of Hu's extensive intellectual "network."[17]

It was in Shanghai in the latter half of December that the movement came to a head, threatening to become more than a student protest. Initial demonstrations on December 18 quickly escalated. On December 19 more than 10,000 students from various universities in the city marched to the municipal building in the city center, forcing Shanghai mayor Jiang Zemin to acknowledge the students' right to protest even as he sought to convince the demonstrators to abide by the rules and regulations laid down by the Party. Early the next morning the confrontation between students and Communist authorities was inflamed when police arrested and allegedly beat several students who had participated in an all-night vigil at city hall. The incident provoked a much larger and far more militant demonstration the next day, when more than 50,000 protesters crowded into People's Park in the center of Shanghai, disrupting the business of the great metropolis. What frightened Communist leaders was not what the official media condemned as "hooliganism involving smashing cars and insulting women," but rather that the students had been joined by workers and other citizens, albeit in small numbers. This raised "the Polish fear"—the specter of a Solidarity-type alliance between workers and intellectuals against the government, which had haunted the Deng regime since 1980. That fear, combined with the spread of student protests to more than a dozen cities, including Beijing, convinced Deng Xiaoping and other Party elders that the movement should be quashed without further delay. The Party counterattack began the last week of the year.

On December 25 an article in *People's Daily* raised the specter of the Cultural Revolution, observing that the upheaval of the 1960s had also begun with unruly student demonstrators and the use of "big character posters." It was emphasized that the notion of "great de-

---

[17] For a detailed and perceptive account of Hu Yaobang as "the protector of intellectuals," and of the intellectuals politically associated with him, see Merle Goldman, *Sowing the Seeds of Democracy in China: Political Reform in the Deng Xiaoping Era* (Cambridge: Harvard University Press, 1994), esp. Chapters 2 and 8.

mocracy" (that is, the free expression of ideas through channels not under the organizational control of the Party) derived from the Cultural Revolution and led inevitably to anarchy. Just as the Deng regime had played upon public fears of the Cultural Revolution in suppressing an earlier Democracy Movement in 1979–80, so now again images of the "chaos" of "the ten lost years" were invoked to discredit the democratic strivings of a new generation of Chinese youth. For Deng Xiaoping, obsessed as he continued to be with the attack Maoists had made on the Party and the purge of veteran revolutionaries, not least of all himself, the fear of chaos was no doubt very real, and spontaneous student protests were seen as grave threats to the Leninist "unity and stability" he demanded.

Ideological condemnations of the student movement were quickly followed by concrete measures. The Party center ordered municipal authorities in Shanghai and Beijing to demand that demonstrators submit written requests for official approval. In the political atmosphere at the close of 1986, no one dared to make such a request. Participants in such demonstrations that continued were subject to arrest, as were the writers of wallposters, which, it was reiterated, were illegal and possibly a form of "counterrevolutionary" activity. By the first week in January, the demonstrations were petering out under government repression and the commencement of semester examinations.

With the waning of the movement, the government attempted to portray the student demonstrators as relatively blameless, misled, it was suggested, by older intellectuals and unspecified counterrevolutionaries. Students who had been arrested during the course of the protests were released from jail, but this was not always the case with workers, some of whom remained imprisoned, charged with crimes ranging from hooliganism to counterrevolution.

As the student demonstrations were being suppressed, a new campaign against bourgeois liberalization was launched, directed against intellectuals who were leading advocates of democratization. Among the first victims was Fang Lizhi, who was dismissed from his position as vice president of the University of Science and Technology and expelled from the Communist Party. Also removed from official posts and expelled from the Party were Liu Binyan and the philosopher Wang Ruowang. All three, ironically, had been politi-

cally rehabilitated by the Deng regime in 1979 after languishing for
more than two decades as political outcasts in the Mao era, branded
as "rightists" in the sweepingly indiscriminate purge of 1957, in
which Deng Xiaoping was the chief witch-hunter.[18]

The winter of student protests had yet another and more startling
political result—the removal of Hu Yaobang as Party chief in January 1987. Hu was accused by conservative Party elders of having
prematurely terminated the campaign against "spiritual pollution" in
1984, thus permitting "bourgeois liberalization" to flourish and eventually to find political expression in student rebelliousness. Forced
to accept responsibility for the student demonstrations, Hu Yaobang
was nonetheless permitted to remain a member of the Party's Politburo and its six-member Standing Committee. His place as Party
Secretary-General was taken by Premier Zhao Ziyang, another Deng
protégé and an ardent advocate of market reform. To balance the
political ledger, the now vacant premiership was occupied by Li
Peng, a Soviet-trained technocrat and a favorite of conservative Party
bureaucrats.

The abortive student movement was the pretext not the cause of
Hu Yaobang's ouster. Hu's efforts to democratize the Communist
Party (even though he harbored no thoughts of a multiparty system),
his support for democratically oriented intellectuals, and his efforts
to curb the corruption rampant among the children of high Party
leaders[19] had frightened senior bureaucrats, who appealed to Deng
Xiaoping for protection. Deng, whose relationship with Hu Yaobang
had grown tense as Hu pressed for Deng's full retirement, especially
from the chairmanship of the Party's Central Military Commission,
was more than receptive to the appeals of his old comrades. By the
autumn of 1986, it had been informally decided by Party elders that
Hu Yaobang would be replaced as Secretary-General at the Thirteenth Congress, scheduled for the following August.

The student protests hastened Hu's removal. And the process
itself became quite irregular, violating the Leninist Party norms that
Deng had been so insistent on reestablishing during the early years

---

[18] Liu Binyan was granted a passport in 1988 and went into political exile in the United States.

[19] An especially notable case was Hu Yaobang's order to begin arrest proceedings against the
son of orthodox Party ideologist Hu Qiaomu, who was accused of embezzling 3 million yuan.
Liu Binyan et al., *Tell the World*, p. 97.

of his reign. The crucial decision was made by a group of conservative Party elders—Yang Shangkun, Wang Zhen, Peng Zhen, and Bo Yibo—whom Deng informally brought together during the first week in January 1987. Joining this rather conspiratorial gathering of those who soon would be dubbed the "Gang of Old"[20] was the politically ambitious Zhao Ziyang, who craved the highest position in the land, convinced of his special talents as an economic reformer and modernizer. The ouster of Hu Yaobang was announced as a decision of the Standing Committee of the Politburo, which in fact was not convened to discuss the matter.

Neither the fall of Hu Yaobang nor the student demonstrations that precipitated the fall seemed as important at the time (at least not to foreign observers) as they appear in retrospect. Hu, after all, was succeeded as Party Secretary-General by his erstwhile reformist ally Zhao Ziyang, an even more ardent advocate of the virtues of a market economy than the man Zhao had conspired to replace. Moreover, Hu Yaobang remained a member of the Politburo and its Standing Committee, retaining the balance between "radical" and "conservative" reformers over which Deng Xiaoping hovered in Stalin-like fashion, playing off one faction against the other to preserve his status as "paramount leader." Zhao Ziyang, in the meantime, demonstrated great reformist zeal as an economic policymaker, earning the applause of foreign audiences. And acting Secretary-General Zhao quickly moved to moderate the Party's campaign against "bourgeois liberalization" launched in January 1987, lest it disrupt his ambitious plans for economic modernization. After a winter of varied discontents, Chinese life seemed to return to normal by the spring of 1987.

Yet among the more politically astute, the fall of Hu Yaobang was not so easily passed over. An American scholar who was in China in 1987 noted that many intellectuals with Party connections saw the ouster of Hu as an ominous political omen, and hastened to make arrangements for their children to study abroad.[21] Liu Binyan de-

---

[20] The term was apparently coined by Liu Binyan and appears prominently in Liu Binyan et al., *Tell the World*. Members of the "Gang of Old," in Liu's reckoning, included Chen Yun, Li Xiannian, and Song Renqiong in addition to those who plotted Hu Yaobang's downfall in January 1987—Deng Xiaoping, Bo Yibo, Peng Zhen, Wang Zhen, and Yang Shangkun.
[21] Lee Feigon, *China Rising*, pp. 71–72.

scribed the effects in dramatic terms. The fall of Hu Yaobang, Liu recalled:

> . . . sent shock waves throughout the party and society at large, causing Deng Xiaoping's stock to plummet and shattering the people's confidence in the party. Dissension and discord within the party and Deng's clique grew more pronounced, as pessimism and despair throughout society intensified. None of this was posted or written about or made headlines, but the party sensed what was going on through its various sources. In Beijing the people had expressed discontent over the two earlier campaigns [against "bourgeois liberalization"] by their silence, but in this latest campaign, many complained at meetings over the punishment meted out to [Hu Yaobang, Fang Lizhi, Liu Binyan, and Wang Ruowang]. This had never happened before, and even in conservative provincial places like Yantai, Hangzhou, and Taiyuan large posters and handbills appeared.[22]

Twice purged, once under Mao and then under Deng, Liu Binyan reflected upon how much attitudes toward the Communist Party had changed between the Mao and Deng eras:

> On a sweltering night in July 1957, at a general meeting of China Youth Daily workers, I was publicly labeled an antiparty, antisocialist rightist, after which everyone stopped speaking to me. But on the afternoon of January 24, 1987, as news of my expulsion from the party was broadcast on radio and television, no fewer than twenty-seven people, most of whom I barely knew, came to my home to comfort and encourage me. Even before the official announcement, I had received sympathetic telephone calls, telegrams, letters, and visitors, some of whom invited me to take refuge in their homes. Kindhearted readers began sending me food, medicine, cash, and health products. It was an interesting development, for these people all felt that I had suffered from being kicked out of the party, not realizing

[22] Liu Binyan, China's Crisis, China's Hope, p. xv.

that their good wishes were gains that far outweighed my losses, if indeed I had lost anything.[23]

It would be difficult to say if what had changed between 1957 and 1987 was more a loss of fear of the Party or a loss of respect for a once-revered institution. In either case, the public stock of the Chinese Communist Party had plummeted.

The fall of Hu Yaobang overshadowed the significance of the student demonstrations that served as the pretext for Hu's removal. The student protests received considerable political and media attention in December 1986 and early January, when the protesters were actually marching in the streets. But the apparent ease with which the authorities contained the movement, and then quickly snuffed it out, without resort to significant violence, left the impression that it had all been a rather superficial and transient affair. With the installation of Zhao Ziyang as Party chief and the punishment of intellectuals who allegedly promoted "bourgeois liberalization," the student protests were soon forgotten.

Yet it is unlikely that the meaning of the demonstrations, however short-lived, was completely lost on Deng Xiaoping. For nearly a decade Deng had placed an enormous emphasis on building a highly elitist educational system designed to train future professional and political leaders who would carry out a socially harmonious process of rapid modernization. To that end, he had denounced Maoist notions of egalitarianism, decreed the termination of class struggle, demanded "unity and stability" under the guidance of the Communist Party, and emphasized the virtues of occupational specialization in a depoliticized society. As soon as he came to power, Deng had advised the Chinese people that their business was production, not politics. For the youth in particular, Deng decreed in 1979, "working hard in study is the politics of students."[24]

The student protests of the winter of 1986–87 rudely challenged this vision of a harmonious modernization process benignly presided over by the Chinese Communist Party. Students at many of China's most prestigious universities—mostly the sons and daughters of China's political and intellectual elites—made clear that they were not content to study and then simply take their places in society, however comfortable those places might be. The young elite that Deng had so carefully cultivated had proved rebellious, reluctant to follow the easy path of orderly careerism that the regime had laid out for them.

At the beginning of 1987 the Communist leaders of China might have recognized a more ominous portent—had they been more familiar with modern history. As Crane Brinton, among many others, long ago observed, the existence of rebellious young radicals in a ruling class is the first sign of a developing revolutionary situation.[25] In the Deng era that symptom of class desertion first manifested itself in the 1986–87 winter of student protest. It would take another two years for that revolutionary situation to mature.

The ouster of Hu Yaobang and the suppression of the student protest movement was yet another betrayal by Deng Xiaoping, in a long series of betrayals, of his original promise of socialist democracy. By 1987 few Chinese any longer believed that Deng's program would yield either socialism or democracy. Western observers, many of whom had invested so much in their decade-long celebration of Deng Xiaoping, nevertheless continued to portray him as a political and economic reformer. They preferred to believe, as the *New York Times* correspondent in Beijing explained, that in removing Hu Yaobang in January 1987, Deng had been forced to capitulate to "a coalition of hardline Marxists" who had temporarily gained ascendancy, until later that year Deng and Zhao Ziyang were able to "turn back the polemical tide of the hardliners and reassert their authority."[26] Yet politically informed Chinese were well aware at the time that Deng was driven less by hard-liners than by his own Leninist precepts. Well before students had taken to the streets Deng had come to view Hu Yaobang more as a political rival than as a faithful disciple, increasingly distrustful of Hu's democratic inclinations and even more suspicious that Hu lacked the will and ability to properly utilize the authority that rightfully belonged to the Communist Party. The decision to remove Hu was made by Deng himself in the fall of 1986,

[25] Brinton, *The Anatomy of Revolution*, rev. ed., pp. 39–49.
[26] Edward A. Gargan, "China's New Style and Substance," *The New York Times*, November 4, 1987, pp. 1, 5.

after a year of growing tensions between China's still "paramount leader" and his formerly favorite disciple.

The events of January 1987 clearly revealed that Deng Xiaoping had not wavered from "the four cardinal principles" that he laid down in 1980, especially the principle of "the leadership of the Party." However amenable he had been to change and experimentation in the economic realm, he had been consistent and unyielding in his refusal to tolerate any intellectual or political movement outside the organizational control of the Chinese Communist Party. To be sure, Deng often said that economic reform demanded political reform. But what Deng meant by political reform had little to do with the democratic yearnings of intellectuals and students. What Deng meant was once again clearly set forth in a speech he delivered to the Politburo in the spring of 1986 when he observed that "it might even take ten years to restore the Party style and social atmosphere to that of the 1950s, when it was at its best."[27]

What is noteworthy about this comment is that Deng tended to think of "political reform" in terms of the *restoration* of the Communist Party to what it had been in the early years of the People's Republic, when Chinese political and economic life had been most Stalinist. For Deng the political golden age of postrevolutionary China was the period of the Soviet-modeled First Five Year Plan (1953–57), when a more or less united and smoothly functioning Communist Party presided over an orderly and disciplined society. If he was now willing to abandon outmoded Stalinist methods of central economic planning and control, he held fast to his romanticized image of the political order that prevailed during those early postrevolutionary years. That those were also years of his own political successes, culminating in his triumphantly prominent role in the Eighth Party Congress of 1956, no doubt contributed to the attractiveness of the era. Deng Xiaoping's vision of the future thus centered on a harmonious marriage between a "reformed" market economy and an essentially Stalinist political system, albeit a Stalinism in a relatively benign and rational form.

It was from these political perspectives that Deng looked at the

[27] Hong Kong *Ta Kung Pao*, May 16, 1986. "Quarterly Chronicle and Documentation," *The China Quarterly*, No. 107 (September 1986), p. 574.

intellectuals and students who strayed from the path of orderly careerism. While Deng did not demand ideological zealotry from China's intellectuals and students—indeed, he seemed to prefer simple apolitical loyalty—he was unwilling to tolerate the expression of ideas that seemed to foster social and political disorder. Thus when students took to the streets demanding democracy in December 1986, older intellectuals were held responsible for the disturbance and a repressive campaign against "bourgeois liberalization" was launched against them, with several of the more prominent advocates of democratic reforms made scapegoats and singled out for exemplary punishment. While the suppression of the student movement was accomplished by the first week in January, the drive against "bourgeois liberalization" lingered on, the third such repressive campaign directed against intellectuals during the Deng era.

Deng Xiaoping's attitudes toward intellectuals and students were ambivalent and his policies contradictory. While he enjoined intellectuals to learn Western capitalist economic methods (and abundantly provided them with the conditions and incentives to do so), he was increasingly distrustful of their ideological and political proclivities. While it was Deng who long had insisted that China's intellectuals were to be classified as "members of the working class," thereby freeing them from bourgeois class associations, he nonetheless was increasingly suspicious of intellectuals as carriers of democratic ideologies, which he saw as a Western bourgeois threat to Chinese socialism. China's presumably socialist character, in turn, was defined by Deng as the unity and stability guaranteed by the Communist state. And while Deng saw students as the future agents of China's modernization, and had revamped and reinvigorated the system of higher education in elitist fashion to achieve that end, he exhibited a typically Leninist distrust of any expression of political spontaneity. This distrust was greatly magnified by Deng's obsessive memories of the Cultural Revolution, in which spontaneous student actions were identified with the "chaos" wrought by the Maoist upheaval of the 1960s. These attitudes, and the policies which followed from them, were turning China's intellectuals and students—who had done so much to bring Deng to power in 1978 and provided him with such great political support in the early 1980s—into sullen and increasingly hostile opposition. Most of those who had come to oppose the regime in 1987 viewed Deng not as the guardian of socialist orthodoxy but as the defender of a conservative and privileged bureaucracy—and some began to conceive of themselves as members of an embryonic radical opposition. One result of the abortive protests of the winter of 1986–87 and the fall of Hu Yaobang was to radicalize a good many intellectuals and students.

13

ZHAO ZIYANG AND THE IDEOLOGY
OF CHINESE CAPITALISM

ZHAO ZIYANG WAS INSTALLED as Secretary-General of the Chinese Communist Party in late January 1987, a position he long had coveted and indeed had conspired to attain.[1] He moved quickly to demonstrate that the demotion of Hu Yaobang did not signal a retreat from the policies of capitalist restructuring pursued since 1980. Zhao announced that market reforms not only would be continued but "deepened," and he proceeded to move the economy in a capitalist direction with special vigor and enthusiasm. Taking pains to proclaim his fidelity to Deng's Four Cardinal Principles, and insisting that the ongoing campaign against "bourgeois liberalization" was entirely consistent with economic reform, Zhao put his personal stamp on the reform program by proposing a far more prominent role for foreign capital in China's development than most Party leaders had hitherto been willing to contemplate.

The first hint of Zhao's coastal development strategy came in his March 1987 "Report" to the National People's Congress, in which he called for expanding preferential conditions for foreign investors.[2]

[1] Zhao was "acting" Secretary-General of the Party until his position was formalized at the Thirteenth Party Congress in October 1987. He simultaneously retained the premiership of the State Council until Li Peng was named to that position by the National People's Congress in November.

[2] Zhao Ziyang, "Report" to the Fifth Session of the Sixth NPC. For a summary of Zhao's report, see "Quarterly Chronicle and Documentation," *The China Quarterly*, No. 111 (September 1987), pp. 509–12. The full text is translated in *Beijing Review*, April 20, 1987, Supplement, pp. I–XX.

This was soon followed by a proposal that Hainan be granted provincial status to enable the scandal-ridden island to develop a market economy even less regulated than the special economic zones, thereby facilitating the capitalist development of the South and East China coast. The coastal economic strategy was formally approved by the Thirteenth Party Congress in October 1987. In his lengthy "Report" to the Congress, Zhao declared that China "should enter the world economic arena more boldly" with the aim of developing an "export-oriented economy," initially along the coast.[3] Zhao did not pause to note that his proposed policies would exacerbate the already enormous inequalities between the developed coastal areas and the backward interior. He felt no need to address a potential problem that already had been explained away by the now well-established Dengist orthodoxy that some areas, as well as some people, must "get rich first."

China's coastal regions were not only to become more fully integrated into the world capitalist market; they also were to be experimental laboratories for the capitalist restructuring of the entire national economy. Although Zhao Ziyang preferred to label the reformed economy a "socialist market system," he left little doubt as to the capitalist character of his economic blueprint when he proposed "a commodity market for consumer goods" and "markets for other essential factors of production such as funds, labor, technology, information and real estate."[4]

That Zhao assumed, as did most reformers, that economic development required the creation of markets in land and labor illuminates the broader social implications of the post-Mao reform program. For the transformation of land (i.e., nature) and labor (i.e., human beings) into commodities is the most socially destructive consequence of modern industrial capitalism. As Karl Polyani observed: "Labor and land are no other than the human beings themselves of which every society consists and the natural surroundings in which it exists. To include them in the market mechanism means to subordinate the substance of society itself to the laws of the market."[5]

[3] Zhao Ziyang, "Advance Along the Road of Socialism with Chinese Characteristics," Report delivered at the Thirteenth National Congress of the Communist Party of China on October 25, 1987, *Documents of the Thirteenth National Congress of the Communist Party of China (1987)* (Beijing: Foreign Languages Press, 1987), pp. 27–29.

[4] Ibid., p. 36.

[5] Karl Polanyi, *The Great Transformation* (Boston: Beacon Press, 1957), p. 71.

In addition to the commodification of land and labor, Zhao proposed that most prices be set by market forces, with state prices retained for only "a few vital commodities"; he called for the expansion of a capitalist-modeled managerial stratum in economic enterprises; and he suggested sanctioning "unearned income" by owners of private enterprises.[6] Such were some of the more explicitly capitalist features of what Zhao called "socialism with Chinese characteristics."

MARXISM, CAPITALISM, AND THE "PRIMARY STAGE OF SOCIALISM"

In setting forth a long-term plan for economic development in which capitalist methods occupied so prominent a place, it was necessary to offer a socialist theoretical rationale. This was partly accomplished by the notion of the "primary stage of socialism." Zhao suggested that the capitalist reforms he proposed had been derived from this presumably scientific Marxian insight.[7] The ideological groundwork for the capitalist borrowing already had been prepared in the early 1980s by reformist theoreticians. Deng's ideologists did not have to search far in the Marxist theoretical tradition for ideological support. Marxism, after all, distinguished itself from other socialist theories by the proposition that socialism presupposes capitalism. Original Marxist theory, as we have seen, was not only a critique of capitalism but also a doctrine that recognized its historical necessity.[8]

It is hardly surprising that many Chinese Marxists, eager for the modernization of their land, would seize upon those strands in Marxism that celebrate the material accomplishments of capitalism, and there find an ideological sanction for adopting capitalist methods of development. One such ideological formula was already well established in the official canon of the Deng regime—the proposition that the "principal contradiction" in Chinese society is between the country's "advanced socialist relations of production" and its "backward

---

[6] Zhao Ziyang, "Report" to the Thirteenth Party Congress, pp. 36–39.
[7] See Part II of the "Report," entitled "The Primary Stage of Socialism and the Basic Line of the Party," ibid., pp. 9–18.
[8] See Chapter 1.

productive forces." This economically deterministic notion originally had been set forth by Liu Shaoqi and Deng Xiaoping at the Eighth Party Congress in 1956, only to be rejected by Mao Zedong. But with the political ascendancy of Deng in 1978, the 1956 thesis was reestablished as an official ideological orthodoxy and reappeared as a central premise in Deng's writings and speeches.[9]

The Dengist formula demands primacy for rapid economic development (to which all other considerations are to be subordinated) in order to resolve the contradiction between the forces and relations of production, and suggests that a partial retreat to "presocialist" forms of social organization might alleviate the contradiction in the meantime—and speed up the rate of economic growth as well. The use of capitalist methods is justified by the need to bring the social relations of production into harmony with China's still relatively backward productive forces.

This Dengist rationale for a capitalist market economy—a process of capitalist borrowing that is to take place *within* the framework of China's existing Communist political structure—was fortified and refined by Zhao Ziyang's theory of the "primary stage of socialism," formally expounded at the Thirteenth Party Congress in October 1987.

When Zhao Ziyang set forth the idea of the "primary stage of socialism," he was searching for a way to pursue economic development by essentially capitalist means while retaining some sort of socialist claim for China's present and future. He began his discussion of the "primary stage" by insisting that China was "already a socialist society,"[10] presumably defining socialism by the vague criteria Deng Xiaoping had laid down.[11] While rejecting the orthodox Marxist view that a socialist society could be established only on the basis of a

---

[9] As Party ideologists emphasized in their celebratory commentaries on the publication of Deng's *Selected Works* in 1983. See, for example, Zhong Kun, "Study Comrade Deng Xiaoping's Strategic Thought on Socialist Modern Economic Construction," *Jingji yanjiu* (Economic Research), July 20, 1983, pp. 11–16.

[10] "Report" to the Thirteenth Party Congress, p. 10.

[11] Socialism, Deng long had held, was to be defined by two essential principles: first, "public ownership" of the major means of production and, second, "payment according to work." Both were interpreted with great flexibility.

mature capitalist economy, the acceptance of which would have cast doubt on the socialist legitimacy of the People's Republic and the revolution that produced it, Zhao nonetheless retained the standard Marxian assumption that history develops by discrete stages which cannot be "jumped over," with each stage basically determined by the level of the development of the productive forces.

The claim that China was "already socialist" and the simultaneous call for a process of capitalist development to construct the material preconditions for socialism is an incongruity that appears throughout Zhao's speech:

> Precisely because our socialism has emerged from the womb of a semi-colonial, semi-feudal society, with the productive forces lagging far behind those of the developed capitalist countries, we are destined to go through a very long primary stage. During this stage we shall accomplish industrialization and the commercialization, socialization, and modernization of production, which many other countries have achieved under capitalist conditions.[12]

During the "very long primary stage," Zhao envisioned a process of modern economic development that Marxists traditionally have seen following from a bourgeois revolution, but one that Zhao wished to have without surrendering the Chinese claim to socialism. That claim, however tenuous, was intended to legitimize the continued political dominance of the Chinese Communist Party, presumably the institutional guarantor of China's socialist future. Thus Zhao Ziyang repeatedly proclaimed his fidelity to Deng's Four Cardinal Principles, the essence of which was of course "the leading role" of the Party.[13] It was not surprising then that Zhao's discussion of political reform was quite unexceptional. He confined himself to Deng's familiar proposals for improving the existing political system, such as fostering specialization and professionalism in the bureaucracy, clarifying the distinction between the functions of Party and government, and delegating more power to lower administrative levels. None of these

[12] "Report," pp. 10–11.
[13] Ibid., p. 71.

posed any serious threat to the dictatorship of the Communist Party or the privileges of most of its members.[14] While Zhao proclaimed the building of a "socialist democracy" as the eventual goal, he acknowledged that "the immediate objective for the reform of the political structure is limited."[15] That indeed was the case, and it conformed to Deng Xiaoping's determination to maintain "stability and unity" at all costs.

Although the concept of the "primary stage of socialism" was hailed as a creative contribution to Marxist theory by the official press, the notion was by no means novel. Essentially the same conception of China's development had been set forth in 1979 by the Marxist theoretician Su Shaozhi under the title of "undeveloped socialism."[16] Presumably because of the pejorative connotations of the word "undeveloped," official ideologists soon changed the name to the "initial" or the "primary" stage of socialism.[17] The theory had receded into the ideological background after 1981, until Zhao Ziyang resurrected the notion at the Thirteenth Congress.

More than a change in terminology was involved in the transformation of "undeveloped socialism" into the "primary stage of socialism." Su Shaozhi originally conceived of "undeveloped socialism" during the heady days of the early Deng era, when hopes for socialist democracy ran high and when the realization of that vision seemed realistic. His theory was firmly tied to the goal of a genuinely socialist society, the achievement of which was dependent on a lengthy process of modern economic development that was to be combined with the democratization of the Party and the political life of the nation. By contrast, when Zhao Ziyang expounded the "primary stage of socialism" nearly a decade later, neither socialist nor democratic ends were easily discernible in a theory that now had been incorporated into the official ideological canon of the Communist state.

To be sure, Su's notion of "undeveloped socialism" and Zhao's

---

[14] Ibid., pp. 42–60.

[15] Ibid., p. 60.

[16] Su Shaozhi and Feng Lanrui, "Wuchanjieji qude zhengquan hou de shehui fazhan jieduan wenti," *Jingji yanjiu*, 1979, No. 5 (May 1979), pp. 14–19.

[17] The term *primary* stage of socialism" was officially laid down in the Party Central Committee's formal reevaluation of Mao Zedong in June 1981. See "Resolution on Certain Questions in the History of Our Party Since the Founding of the People's Republic of China" (June 27, 1981), *Beijing Review*, July 6, 1981, pp. 10–39.

"primary stage" seemed similar in that both envisioned a lengthy evolutionary process of development, both were based on the economically deterministic assumption that the growth of the productive forces would prove historically decisive in the end, and both sanctioned the employment of capitalist methods operating within a vaguely defined "socialist system." But in Zhao Ziyang's version the democratic content of the original theory had been lost, subordinated to the Leninist imperatives of Deng's Four Cardinal Principles. And socialist ends had been postponed to a future so distant they were rendered meaningless. In April 1987, Deng Xiaoping had announced that "only in the middle of the next century" would it be possible to say that "we are really building socialism."[18] In his "Report" to the Thirteenth Congress, Zhao Ziyang repeated his mentor's prediction, declaring: "It will be at least one hundred years from the 1950s, when the socialist transformation of private ownership of the means of production was basically completed, to the time when socialist modernization will have been in the main accomplished, and all these years belong to the primary stage of socialism."[19] To a population that over the 1980s had grown cynical and despondent about the prospects for both socialism and democracy, Zhao's speech offered little comfort.

What then was socialist about the "primary stage of socialism"? Zhao Ziyang did not explicitly pose the question in his "Report," but he did attempt to answer it. With reference to a Chinese economic system that seemed to be functioning increasingly in a capitalist fashion, Zhao maintained that "the essential difference between the socialist and capitalist commodity economies lies in the form of ownership on which they are based." Thus what made the Chinese economy "socialist," according to Zhao, was "public ownership" of the means of production, or what he also referred to as "ownership by the whole people."[20] Even though it was government policy to encourage the expansion of the cooperative, individual, and private

---

[18] *People's Daily*, May 17, 1987. For the official English version, see Deng Xiaoping, "We Must Continue to Build Socialism and Eliminate Poverty" (remarks of April 26, 1987 to [the Czechoslovak Premier] Lubomir Strougal), *Fundamental Issues in Present-Day China*, pp. 176–78.

[19] "Report," p. 13.

[20] "Report," pp. 32–33.

sectors of the economy, Zhao declared that "public ownership should predominate in the primary stage of socialist society."[21]

The terms "public ownership" and "ownership by the whole people" were, of course, euphemisms for state ownership or control of the economy. And the euphemisms were misleading. State ownership of the means of production has little to do with socialism, and indeed may well be antithetical to socialist goals, particularly when the state is not subject to popular democratic control. Nonetheless, it was on the legalistic fiction of public ownership that Zhao's socialist claims for China rested.

What Zhao really meant by "socialism" was the political dictatorship of the Chinese Communist Party, the institutional repository of ultimate socialist goals. It was the Party and its leaders who presumably would hold those goals firmly in mind during the long evolutionary process that would establish the necessary material conditions for the passage from an ill-defined primary stage to an even more vague notion of the "developed stage of socialism." Yet while a century-long process of economic modernization was presented as the means to ultimate socialist ends, it was also Zhao Ziyang's tendency to define socialism itself simply as the economic modernization of the Chinese nation. "The fundamental task of a socialist society is to expand the productive forces," he informed the delegates to the Thirteenth Congress.[22] In this confusion of the means and ends of socialism, Zhao followed in the ideological footsteps of his mentor, Deng Xiaoping, who earlier in the decade had declared: "The purpose of socialism is to make the country rich and strong."[23] National economic development, traditionally seen by Marxists as the historic function of capitalist regimes produced by bourgeois revolutions, was now taken by China's Communist leaders as the "fundamental task" of socialism.

---

[21] Ibid., p. 38.

[22] Ibid., p. 14. The tendency to equate socialism with economic modernization runs throughout Zhao's speech. See, for example, pp. 70–73.

[23] Deng Xiaoping, Remarks to a visiting Romanian delegation in November 1980. *The New York Times*, December 30, 1980, p. 1.

THE THIRTEENTH PARTY CONGRESS

The Thirteenth Congress was a triumph not only for Zhao Ziyang, whose position as Secretary-General of the Communist Party was formalized, but also for Deng Xiaoping. Indeed, in good measure, the Congress was a celebration of Deng—a celebration of the policies and the ideology as well as the person of China's paramount leader. It was hardly surprising that this was the case since Party congresses invariably celebrate the real or alleged accomplishments of those who prepare them—and the Thirteenth Congress had long been in preparation under Deng's guidance. Thus Deng, beyond positioning his protégés to carry on his reform policies and repeat his ideological formulas, enjoyed the kind of extravagant praise hitherto lavished only on Mao Zedong. Some months before the opening of the Congress, Zhao Ziyang hailed Deng's thought in the fashion that Mao's thought had once been celebrated, as "a model in the integration of the universal truth of Marxism with Chinese reality," and as "a great development of Marxism in China."[24] Zhao elaborated on the "great development" in his "Report" to the Thirteenth Congress, implicitly equating the theoretical and practical contributions of Deng with those of Mao. Zhao declared that there had been "two major historic leaps" in Marxist practice in China since the 1920s. The first was the Communist Revolution itself, a victory led by Mao Zedong. The second took place after the Third Plenum of 1978, when "having analyzed both the positive and the negative experience of more than thirty years since the founding of the People's Republic and studied the experience of other countries and the world situation, the Chinese Communists found a way to build socialism with Chinese characteristics, thus ushering in a new period of socialist development in the country."[25] The Third Plenum of 1978 and the building of "socialism with Chinese characteristics" were, of course, principally the accomplishments of Deng Xiaoping. Thus Deng, the initiator of the second of the "two major historic leaps" in the adaptation of Marxism to Chinese conditions, stood on an equal historical and theoretical plane

[24] Zhao Ziyang speech of May 13, 1987. See *People's Daily*, July 10, 1987, for full text; summary translation in *Beijing Review*, July 20, 1987, pp. 34–35.
[25] "Report," p. 70.

with Mao, the initiator of the first. Indeed, Deng, as the latest comer, implicitly stood higher. Whereas Mao was the acknowledged leader of what Zhao called "the new-democratic revolution," a still-bourgeois stage in Marxist perspectives, Deng pioneered the true way to build socialism under Chinese conditions.

It was not only Deng's thought and policies that were celebrated but also his extraordinary personal attributes. "He is a great man," the *People's Daily* concluded at the conclusion of the Thirteenth Congress. The diminutive Deng, the official Party newspaper proclaimed, "stands taller and sees farther than any of us."[26] In the months preceding and following the Congress a veritable "personality cult" was constructed around Deng, taking forms reminiscent of the now-discredited Mao cult. A new play, *The Decisive Huai-Hai Campaign*, depicted Deng as the principal military strategist of the most momentous of Communist victories over the armies of Chiang Kai-shek, the battle in the central China plains north of the river Huai in November and December 1948. In a prophetic pointer to the future, the play was produced by a drama troupe of the People's Liberation Army. Official newspapers and periodicals lauded Deng's leadership and his thought in increasingly extravagant fashion, and a luxuriantly illustrated biography of Deng was published in both Chinese and English in early 1988.

At the time of the Thirteenth Congress it seemed that the praise lavished on the eighty-three-year-old Deng was for the purpose of marking his triumphant and voluntary exit from the center of the political stage. Well before the Congress convened, Deng had hinted that the forthcoming Party meeting would be the occasion for his retirement, along with that of other Party elders, thus opening the way for a younger generation of leaders. It would have been the first truly voluntary change of leadership in the history of the Chinese Communist Party, a process hitherto dictated by death or political purge. Deng removed himself from consideration for election to the new Politburo, as did such veteran leaders as Chen Yun, Li Xiannian, Peng Zhen, and Hu Qiaomu. The five-member Politburo Standing Committee that emerged from the Thirteenth Congress was made up of Secretary-General Zhao Ziyang, Li Peng, Qiao Shi, Hu Qili, and

[26] *People's Daily*, November 3, 1987.

Yao Yilin. Zhao was the only holdover from the previous Standing Committee, and the average age of the body dropped from seventy-seven to sixty-three.[27] All five members of the new Standing Committee appeared in public in Western-style suits and ties—presumably signs of modernity and "vitality," according to Western observers—rather than in the "Mao jackets" favored by many of Deng Xiaoping's generation of old revolutionaries.[28]

But things were not quite as they appeared. While elderly Communist leaders surrendered their formal positions of power, this by no means rendered them powerless. In the aftermath of the Thirteenth Congress, Deng Xiaoping, who had so ardently championed the need for a younger and more professionally competent generation of leaders, surrounded himself with the "retired" old revolutionaries of his own generation. These veteran bureaucrats—all of whom were born in the first decade of the century and all of whom counted themselves victims of the Cultural Revolution—proceeded to influence affairs of state from behind the scenes through complex informal networks of power and patronage. The Gang of Old functioned much like the oligarchic Genro of Meiji Japan, although with even less formal authority. Moreover, no major Party or state policy decisions were taken without Deng's personal approval. Sometimes he intervened with policy and political initiatives of his own. But Deng's continuing power rested on more than his own personal prestige and influence. At the Thirteenth Congress he had retired from all of his formal Party offices save one—the chairmanship of the Party's Military Affairs Commission—a post he retained, it was claimed at the time, at the insistence of veteran PLA generals. The Party constitution was duly revised to permit Deng to remain head of the Military Affairs Commission even though he was no longer a member of the Politburo, hitherto a requirement for serving as a member of the Party's chief military organ. As long as "the Party controlled the gun," Deng Xiaoping controlled the Army. The significance of Deng's hold on his last formal Party office was not to be fully appreciated until nearly two years after the close of the Thirteenth Party Congress.

[27] The deposed Party head Hu Yaobang remained on the Politburo but was no longer on its Standing Committee.

[28] Chinese Communist leaders attired in Western suits signaled "vitality," according to Western correspondents. AP dispatch from Beijing, November 2, 1987.

★ ★ ★

On November 2, 1987, Zhao Ziyang's position as Secretary-General was ratified by the new Central Committee. Since the fall of Hu Yaobang in January, Zhao had held the Party's leading post in an "acting" capacity, concurrently retaining his position as Premier of the State Council, the head of the civilian government. He now resigned the latter post in favor of Li Peng, the orphaned son of a revolutionary martyr who had been adopted by Zhou Enlai.

From the outset of his appearance at the highest levels of power, Li Peng, in part because he had been educated at an engineering school in the Soviet Union, was cast by Western commentators as a "Marxist hard-liner" and a "conservative," a member of that amorphous and ill-defined group of Communist leaders who allegedly opposed Deng Xiaoping's "liberal" reform program. Yet the assumed divisions between "Marxists" and "liberals," between "conservatives" and "reformers," and between "leftists" and "rightists"—which some find convenient to categorize Chinese Communist leaders—do more to obscure than enlighten political and social conflicts in the Deng era. The real differences have less to do with the substance of the policies that are moving China toward a capitalist economy than with the pace and timing of the movement, the proper mix between plan and market, and the question of political change. Correlations and categorizations are not always easy to come by, and attempts to make them often yield glaring contradictions. Deng Xiaoping, to take a paramount example, is the architect of the capitalist restructuring of China, and thus has been described by many foreign observers as a "liberal reformer"—while at the same time he is the principal advocate of the totalistic authority of the Communist Party, and thus a "conservative Leninist."

Such categories, in any event, are quite irrelevant in the case of Li Peng, who appeared on the political stage lacking strong ideological convictions of any sort. He might best be understood, as Stuart Schram characterized him early in 1988, as "a disciplined executor of the line laid down by the Party [who] will do what Deng Xiaoping and Zhao Ziyang tell him to do . . ."[29]

---

[29] Stuart R. Schram, "China After the 13th Congress," *The China Quarterly*, No. 114 (June 1988), p. 189.

BOOM AND BUST

Zhao Ziyang emerged from the Thirteenth Congress with enormous influence and prestige—and, most important, with the full support of Deng Xiaoping. Zhao wasted no time in moving toward the creation of a more fully capitalist economy, albeit under the thinning ideological veneer of building "socialism with Chinese characteristics." One of those peculiarly "socialist" characteristics was the opening of the entire Chinese coast to foreign capital, the first major policy initiative of the new regime. Early in 1988, Zhao won Deng Xiaoping's approval for the "coastal development strategy" that he had been advocating since his days as Premier. It was a policy that provided not simply an "open door" for foreign capital but an open coast, stretching from Manchuria in the North to Guangdong province in the South. Whereas the creation of the special economic zones had been originally defended—in light of China's long and bitter experience with foreign-dominated treaty ports—by the argument that the SEZs were isolated enclaves from whose influences the country as a whole would be insulated, Zhao's "coastal" scheme encompassed areas with a population of over 200 million. Moreover, the new policy no longer required joint ventures but rather gave free rein to foreign capital and management, holding out to foreign investors the lure of low-paid Chinese workers for labor-intensive factories whose goods would be produced for export.

Zhao's coastal development strategy had the easily anticipated (but officially unmentioned) consequence of accelerating the growth of economic inequalities between the coastal areas and the interior, while at the same time weakening central government control over the coastal provinces, especially in the South. It made the Chinese economy increasingly dependent on the world capitalist market and all its vicissitudes and contributed to the growth of China's trade deficit, which swelled to US$4 billion in 1988 (and $4.5 billion in 1989), even while exports were increasing. Moreover, Zhao's policies facilitated official profiteering, which became pervasive in the late 1980s. Many factors were responsible for the corruption that overwhelmed the Deng regime, but the influx of foreign capital (which accelerated rapidly throughout 1988) was one of the essential factors.

Bureaucratic corruption, and especially public consciousness of corruption, grew dramatically during Zhao Ziyang's reign as Communist Party chief. Liu Binyan recalls 1988 as a year when "members of the bureaucratic stratum, high and low, who had a firm grasp on their special privileges, initiated an unprecedented plundering of the Chinese economy, arrogating billions in public assets to themselves."[30] Yet even as corruption was threatening to engulf the regime, Deng Xiaoping and Zhao Ziyang plunged ahead with their plans for a market economy, demanding ever-greater "speed" and "boldness" in implementing reform measures that were to greatly exacerbate the social and economic burdens of the Chinese people, and especially the 400 million people—more than a third of the population—who now lived in the rapidly growing cities. The most acute of those burdens were galloping inflation and chronic food shortages, the latter resulting from faltering agricultural production. Nonetheless, in March 1988, Zhao Ziyang, ignoring the economic problems as well as the political ones, exhorted the population to learn to "swim in the ocean of the commodity economy."[31]

Beyond the coastal development policy, sporadically implemented where and when it served the interests of local bureaucrats to do so, two other items headed the agenda of the reformers. One was price reform, or the removal of state control over the prices of most goods, which, it was argued, properly should be regulated by the workings of the market. The second was "enterprise reform," or the abolition of government authority over the operation and management of state-owned factories and other enterprises. There was no longer any serious controversy over the substance of these proposals. The debate among Zhao Ziyang's economic advisors centered on which of the two should come first and the pace at which they should be implemented.

Deng Xiaoping intervened in Mao-like fashion to settle the debate in June 1988. In a talk with the visiting President of Ethiopia, Deng remarked that conditions were favorable for wage and price reform. "We are in the process of storming this pass right now," he reportedly said, employing the military imagery he so favored. "We expect it will take us five or six years."[32] Accordingly, Zhao Ziyang immedi-

---

[30] Liu Binyan, *China's Crisis*, p. 79.
[31] Zhao Ziyang, Report to the Second Plenum of the CCP Central Committee (March 15, 1988), *Beijing Review*, March 28–April 3, 1988.
[32] *People's Daily*, June 23, 1988, p. 1. Cited in Nathan, *China's Crisis*, p. 105.

ately called a Politburo meeting to formalize the decision. A plan emerged from the July–August Politburo session at the seaside resort of Beidaihe to raise prices on state-controlled goods and raw materials so that they would approximate market prices by the end of a five-year transition period. The aim, it was said, was to create an economy in which the state would regulate the market while the market would guide the operation of enterprises.

But well before the Politburo formalized Deng's decision, public anticipation of price decontrol created financial chaos. Throughout the summer, in an economy already buffeted by spiraling inflation, fears that money would become worthless fueled massive withdrawals of funds from banks, panic buying and the hoarding of goods, speculation in commodities, and a whirlwind of price-raising by industrial and other enterprises. With the economy careening out of control, Zhao Ziyang had no choice but to abandon price reform. The Politburo decision was reversed even before it had been publicly announced. And when the Party Central Committee convened in late September, it somberly imposed a new round of retrenchment and recentralization, once again bringing the urban reform program to a halt. It was announced that market reform in the cities would be postponed for two years.[33]

The official national inflation rate for 1988 was 19 percent, triple the disturbingly high rate of the previous year and by far the worst since 1949. The actual inflation was probably in the range of 25–30 percent, and considerably higher in the cities. The burden fell hardest on those dependent on state salaries—workers in state enterprises, teachers, intellectuals, and minor governmental functionaries. Although the government provided food subsidies in an effort to compensate for price increases, real income declined for a very substantial portion of the urban population. The government had already acknowledged that living standards fell for 20 percent of urban families in 1987. While no further such official acknowledgments were forthcoming, the 1988 figure undoubtedly was much larger, and the deterioration persisted into 1989, as inflation continued to race along at a 25 percent per annum pace during the first half of the year.

---

[33] Zhao Ziyang, "Report to the Third Plenary Session of the 13th CCP Central Committee," *Beijing Review*, November 14–20, 1988, Supplement, pp. i–viii.

It is one of the peculiarities of the hybrid economy of the Deng era that ruinous inflationary episodes have gone hand in hand with extraordinarily rapid periods of economic growth. And so it was in 1988, when industrial production increased by an astonishing 21 percent. The still-tiny private sector (including both indigenous and foreign-capitalized enterprises, together accounting for 3 percent of Chinese industry) doubled its industrial output; the production of rural and urban "collective" industrial enterprises (about 35 percent of the total) grew by 29 percent; and the still-dominant state industrial sector (the remaining 62 percent) increased its output by 13 percent.[34]

The industrial boom had been fueled by a combination of Zhao Ziyang's expansionary monetary policies and the state's surrender of control over large sections of the economy. Early in 1988 the government had eased credit controls, setting off reckless borrowing from both the central state bank and a variety of new lending institutions such as local governments and credit cooperatives. By year's end, the money supply had increased 50 percent. The borrowers were state and collective industrial and commercial firms, both urban and rural, which were now operating as profit-making capitalist enterprises. In part, this was the intended result of reforms pursued sporadically since 1984, which included measures designed to make enterprises responsible for their own profits and losses. In part, it was a matter of de facto autonomy assumed by new private enterprises and by old provincial and local authorities, especially in the southern coastal regions, who ignored state regulations and decrees—and over whom the central government temporarily had lost effective control. The result was cutthroat competition for scarce raw materials and supplies, pervasive graft by officials who had access to supplies at low state-regulated prices (and who, of course, sold them at soaring market prices), the overproduction of profitable consumer goods, and shortages of necessities for the common people. The economy was out of alignment, and indeed out of control, regulated neither by state nor by market.

The frenzied industrial growth of 1988, which generated unbear-

---

[34] State Statistical Bureau figures, cited in CIA, *The Chinese Economy in 1988 and 1989*, pp. 10–11.

able economic and social strains, was pushing the economy toward a disastrous crash. Shortages of energy and raw materials grew increasingly severe over the year, threatening to close factories and idle workers. Production of coal, oil, and electricity could not satisfy the increasingly voracious appetites of the booming industries. The imbalance between industrial growth and supplies of energy and raw materials was compounded by China's fragile transportation system, which delayed deliveries of coal and raw materials from the Northeast to power plants and factories in the southern and eastern provinces. The looming economic crisis was aggravated by continued stagnation in agriculture. In striking contrast to the impressive gains of the early 1980s, agricultural output in 1988 grew by an anemic 3 percent— and most of this increase came from cash crops and specialized sideline operations. Grain production declined by 2 percent, falling to 394 million tons, 16 million tons below what was anticipated, necessitating wheat purchases from the United States and Canada. Peasants, especially those still engaged in basic food production, suffered from a lack of fertilizers as chemical plants cut output due to energy shortages. And many peasants were enraged when officials in financially strained localities gave out promissory notes in lieu of cash payments for grain. This only compounded food shortages in the cities as angry peasants sometimes responded by withholding grain deliveries to state purchasing agencies.

Many prospered during the short-lived industrial boom: the managers and employees of the rapidly expanding private and collective industries whose products were in high demand; those involved with state and private trading companies who hastened to export commodities and raw materials acquired at low state prices; rural entrepreneurs and urban street vendors who fetched ever-higher market prices for their wares; and, not least of all, local officials and high bureaucrats who enriched themselves by virtue of access to state-priced goods and raw materials. While a good many profited, the boom in industrial production brought hardship to the majority of the people. Most ordinary peasants were forced to sell grain and other commodities at low government-determined prices. Especially adversely affected were the majority of urban inhabitants who were dependent on state salaries and whose living standards were eroding due to inflation.

The suffering was not only material but also social and psychological. Economic hardships were made all the more intolerable by the gross inequalities that so marked Chinese society in 1988. Inequalities had been growing throughout the reform period, but they were greatly exacerbated by the policies of Zhao Ziyang and had suddenly become far more visible. Those who experienced an unaccustomed decline in their living conditions in 1988 saw others who were enriching themselves at the same time—and often flaunting their newly gained wealth. Particularly galling was that much of that enrichment came from official corruption and profiteering, which now was universal.

Under such conditions of unruly market-driven economic growth and the unjust distribution of the fruits of that growth, it is hardly surprising that observers noted a marked decline in social morality in 1988, a growing loss of public confidence in the Deng regime and its policies, and ominous signs of popular unrest. Many of the social vices so indelibly stamped on images of Guomindang China—prostitution, drug addiction, gambling, criminal gangs, and child labor—which had grown almost imperceptibly over the Deng era reappeared with a vengeance in 1988. The social problems were particularly acute in the coastal cities. Reports of a rising dropout rate in primary and middle schools were officially confirmed when the government reported at year's end that 7 million children had left school in 1988, as did many underpaid teachers.[35] The crime rate, already alarmingly high by postrevolutionary Chinese standards, increased by almost 50 percent in 1988 over the 1987 level, according to official figures, and youth gangs proliferated.[36] And by 1988 the bribery of officials had become routine, almost quasi-legal, not only in business arrangements but in the everyday life of common people who had to pay off officials to carry out even the most mundane tasks of their lives.

The social deterioration did not escape official notice, even if it eluded all official remedies. In mid-1988, Hu Qili, a member of the Politburo's Standing Committee, complained of "unhealthy tendencies" in Chinese society and "intolerable corruption" among Chinese

[35] "Quarterly Chronicle and Documentation," *The China Quarterly*, No. 118 (June 1989), pp. 405–6.
[36] Nathan, *China's Crisis*, p. 109.

officials,[37] maladies that the official press elaborated on over the remainder of the year. But the Party's response to corruption was feeble, largely confined to the expulsion of lower-level cadres charged
with smuggling, bribery, and embezzlement. Despite the threat of
public execution (the draconian punishment having been expanded
to include economic as well as violent crimes), the scale and scope
of both official and nonofficial corruption continued to grow.

The combination of deteriorating economic conditions and flourishing corruption served to heighten public consciousness of the
growing gap between the majority of urban inhabitants whose living
standards were falling due to inflation and a minority of high bureaucrats and private entrepreneurs who were waxing rich. A
pervasive feeling of injustice thus compounded growing material
hardships. It was a potentially explosive combination. Social discontent began to give rise to popular protest. A Guangdong police report
in the summer of 1988 warned of an "alarming increase" in workers'
strikes, public protest meetings, and the appearance of illegal big-
character posters.[38] There was a long stream of reports of student
unrest and demonstrations. More worrisome, at least as far as the
government was concerned, was discontent among the urban working
class. And discontent was growing. In the autumn an official of the
state-controlled trade unions, whose membership numbered 100 million workers, revealed that sporadic strikes had occurred throughout
the year in various parts of the country. At a textile mill in Zhejiang
province, for example, 1,500 workers had struck for two days. And
1,100 workers at a medical appliance factory had conducted a three-
month-long strike. Other workers' strikes and slowdowns were reported in the northern provinces, when factory directors in Shenyang,
Beijing, Qingdao, and elsewhere attempted to cut payrolls.[39] Workers
were further angered by the closure or sale of unprofitable smaller
industrial enterprises, sometimes auctioned off to foreign investors
who then installed new managers and leaner workforces.[40]

The economic hardships of the working population were aggra-

---

[37] "Quarterly Chronicle and Documentation," *The China Quarterly*, No. 116 (December 1988),
p. 860.
[38] Ibid., p. 862.
[39] Ibid., p. 866.
[40] Ibid.

vated by the retrenchment policies the government adopted in the latter months of 1988 to control runaway inflation and "cool" the "overheated" economy. Those policies included abandoning price reform, huge reductions in capital investment, strict controls over credit, and other fiscal measures designed to reduce consumption. Most severely affected by the government's austerity measures were the booming township and village industries, the most dynamic sector of the Chinese economy and the one most dependent on easy credit and high levels of consumption. Some of the more marginal of these enterprises were forced to close and others reduced output, leaving millions of young workers unemployed. The jobless workers, most of whom came from peasant families, joined farmers who had been forced off the land and other dispossessed rural people in what soon became a massive migration to the cities in search of jobs. By the early months of 1989 it was estimated that there were some 50 million *youmin*, or "wandering people," moving from city to city desperately seeking work. Their plight and their presence compounded the social and economic problems of the urban areas.

In traditional Chinese history the term *youmin* referred to bands of dispossessed peasants who roamed the countryside in times of economic distress and dynastic decline, often turning to banditry. Sometimes these roving bands united to carry out the large-scale peasant revolts against landlords and officials that occupy so prominent a place in the millennial Chinese historical record. That the traditional term *youmin* was commonly used in 1988–89 by urban intellectuals and others to characterize the wandering population of the unemployed and dispossessed, the victims of the workings of the market, suggests an anticipation of political disorder. Most intellectuals looked upon the "wandering people" as a lumpen proletariat, amenable to reactionary political uses.

The government was by no means oblivious to the potential political dangers of the time. In June 1988, even before austerity policies provoked popular unrest, a national conference was called to devise measures to control social disorder. The participants recommended the establishment of mobile armed police units in the major cities. At a meeting of the Standing Committee of the National People's Congress in early September, the question of social order was the dominant concern, and the Minister of Public Security was called upon to report on the growth of criminal and subversive political activities.[41] Chinese police officials were reportedly dispatched to Chile (then under the fascist military rule of General Pinochet) and Poland (still under the martial-law regime of General Jaruzelski) to learn the latest anti-riot techniques. While these reports were not officially confirmed, the mere circulation of such rumors was symptomatic of the tense political temper of the time.

THE NEW AUTHORITARIANISM

The concern over social unrest gave rise to official interest in a doctrine called the "new authoritarianism." Promoted by "reformist" intellectuals associated with Zhao Ziyang in 1988 and the early months of 1989, the notion of "new authoritarianism" was not entirely new, explicitly derived as it was from the recent historical experiences of Taiwan, South Korea, and Singapore—and, more distantly, Meiji Japan. The lesson that these East Asian histories collectively teach, it was argued, is that the key to economic success in the modern world is to combine political dictatorship with a capitalist market economy. The need for an enlightened autocratic state was all the greater in China in view of the magnitude of the problem of economic development and the tenacity of resistance to market reform. A democratic government, it was stressed, would lack the will and power to overcome these formidable barriers, especially since the "new authoritarians" saw the main obstacles not so much as conservative elements in the bureaucracy as workers and peasants who were suffering the adverse economic effects and social disruptions of Deng's reforms—and who, it was anticipated, would suffer all the more severely as China's transition to capitalism proceeded. It was a time, of course, when inflation and unemployment were giving rise to widespread popular opposition to Deng Xiaoping's policies. And it was a reflection of the political confusion of the times that the "new authoritarians" saw nothing incongruous in a free market economy being presided over by an autocratic Communist state.[42]

[41] Ibid., p. 859.

[42] The leading advocate of the new authoritarianism was Wu Jiaxiang, a researcher attached to the Central Committee of the Chinese Communist Party, who identified Deng Xiaoping with

The incongruity, if indeed it was recognized at all, was resolved by a faith in an enlightened ruler. Indeed, one of the more striking features of new authoritarian ideology is its emphasis on the central importance of a great leader, a farsighted "strongman"—such as, presumably, Chiang Kai-shek in Taiwan, Lee Kuan Yew in Singapore, or the Meiji Emperor in Japan. The contemporary Chinese equivalent was obviously Deng Xiaoping, but the concern was over whether the aging Deng's successors would be as politically powerful and, at the same time, equally committed to market reform.

Even more striking than the attractions of an enlightened autocrat was the importance attached to the intellectuals who would advise the autocrat. The doctrine, as one leading new authoritarian theorist put it, stresses not only the leader but also "the decision-making group closely associated with the leader, [their] brilliant analysis and resolute and decisive actions, the strength to eliminate any and all obstacles, and [their] superior ability to adapt to change."[43] There is no need to belabor the appeal of this notion to elitist intellectuals, especially those who anticipated being part of "the decision-making group" (a term, among a good many others, that the new authoritarians freely borrowed from American political science theory). As one establishment intellectual candidly remarked: "The current crisis is a cauldron out of which a new leader will arise by showing the people that he is capable. *Intellectuals like me design the future.*"[44]

Although the intellectuals who styled themselves new authoritarians clearly enjoyed the support and patronage of Zhao Ziyang, their views did not go unchallenged. Their main critics were democratic Marxists who originally had been among Deng Xiaoping's most ardent supporters. Most had been removed from official positions of influence over the years, and especially since Hu Yaobang's ouster in early 1987. But they still enjoyed a measure of freedom to write and publish in what was a period of relative ideological diversity per-

the doctrine in a work published in late 1988 entitled *Deng Xiaoping: Theory and Practice*. Many of the more important writings promoting (and criticizing) new authoritarianism appeared in the Shanghai *World Economic Herald* in the last months of 1988 and early 1989. For a detailed analysis, see Stanley Rosen and Gary Zou (eds.), "The Chinese Debate on the New Authoritarianism," *Chinese Sociology and Anthropology* (Winter, Spring, and Summer 1991).
[43] Wu Jiaxiang, "Xin quanweizhuyi shuping," *Shijie Jingji daobao*, January 16, 1989. Cited in *Far Eastern Economic Review* (March 9, 1989), p. 12.
[44] Quoted in *Far Eastern Economic Review* (March 9, 1989), p. 12 (emphasis added).

mitted by Party Secretary-General Zhao Ziyang. In a lively debate that took place over the last months of 1988 and early 1989, critics such as the Marxist theoretician Su Shaozhi, who had recently been removed as the head of the Marx-Lenin-Mao Institute in Beijing, charged that the new authoritarians had abandoned such democratic principles as institutional pluralism and the rule of law, which reformist intellectuals had regarded as essential for economic modernization. Other critics observed that the experience of "the three little dragons" (Taiwan, Singapore, and South Korea) was quite irrelevant to the problems confronting so large a dragon as China and charged, moreover, that the whole thrust of new authoritarian thought pointed backward to feudalism.[45]

Although Zhao Ziyang clearly encouraged the dissemination of new authoritarian ideas, he did not participate directly in the debate. In a speech delivered in late January 1989 reaffirming the "leading role" of the Communist Party, however, Zhao denounced the political pluralism advocated by the democratic critics of the new authoritarianism, insisting that political reform in China would not include a multiparty system.[46] The new authoritarians heartily agreed with Zhao, viewing the "chaos" of party politics as incompatible with the strong state and the strong leaders China required to create a stable and growing capitalist economy. There was, in fact, nothing incompatible between the new authoritarianism and the "vanguard" role of a Leninist party—so long as the Party pursued "free market" policies under the guidance of a strong leader and a properly constituted "decision-making group." Such, after all, was the lesson imparted by the historical experience of Taiwan, which had so successfully combined a Leninist-type party with capitalist economic development.

The new authoritarians did promise an eventual transition to democracy. But that transition was not to accompany the arduous process of modern economic development; rather it was to be one of its end products, postponed to an unspecified time in the future, after the creation of a viable capitalist class. They also spoke of the need

[45] For a discussion and analysis of the 1988–89 debate on the new authoritarianism (or "neo-authoritarianism," as it is sometimes called), see Goldman, *Sowing the Seeds of Democracy*, pp. 257–82.

[46] Zhao Ziyang, "Guanyu dang de jianshe de jige wenti" (Speech of January 28, 1989), *People's Daily*, Overseas edition, March 17, 1989, pp. 1–2.

to safeguard "individual freedom," but by this they meant, at least for the foreseeable future, not so much the democratic political rights of the people as the economic rights of the individual in the capitalist marketplace; what they had in mind was the fabled "economic individual" free from undue state interference.

The short-lived debate between the quasi-official new authoritarians and their democratic critics had little effect on Chinese politics. But it did reveal how much the grounds of political controversy had shifted over ten years of "reform." Socialism was rarely mentioned by either side. Both accepted capitalist-oriented "reform" as the goal; the debate centered on whether reform could or should be pursued under a democratic or an autocratic political regime. Marxism had faded into virtual irrelevancy, a quote from classic Marxian texts occasionally injected to support a democratic point. The new authoritarians, mostly young establishment academics and intellectuals closely associated with the Zhao Ziyang regime, drew their ideological inspiration (and most of their quotations) from conservative Western social and political theorists.

Those who assume some necessary link between a capitalist market economy and political democracy might ponder the intellectual change. The Deng era in the history of the People's Republic began in late 1978 with the new regime broadly supported by intellectuals who rallied around the promise of "socialist democracy." A decade later the most vocal intellectual partisans of the regime were advocates of a capitalist autocracy. By 1989 neither socialist nor democratic goals had survived Deng Xiaoping's reform program, at least not in official circles.

14

THE DEMOCRACY MOVEMENT OF 1989

DURING THE FIRST DEMOCRACY MOVEMENT of 1978–80, China's intellectuals kept a safe political distance. Indeed, many disparaged the activities of those extraordinarily brave and creative souls who established embryonic democratic organizations and unofficial journals which published bold political commentary and poignant poetry. And when Deng Xiaoping suppressed the movement and jailed many of the youthful activists in 1980, the intellectuals remained silent. Attracted to Deng's reform program, and seduced by promises that the intelligentsia would occupy a prominent place in the Four Modernizations, intellectuals were reluctant to abandon their hopes and jeopardize their careers. Beyond self-interest, there were hints of snobbishness. The democratic activists of the time, it was whispered, were not even students but rather mostly self-educated workers, members of the "lost generation," who had been schooled in the trials of the Cultural Revolution. They were banished and imprisoned by the state with little notice and no significant public protest.

Some intellectuals no doubt harbored more than a bit of guilt over their failure to support the democratic activists. But it took nearly a decade of Party campaigns against "bourgeois liberalization," the dismissal of democratic Marxist intellectuals from academic and publishing posts, and the painfully slow recognition that there was little democratic substance in Deng's program of political reform before even a small number of intellectuals expressed public criticism of the repression and arrests of 1979–80. Fang Lizhi was the first to attempt to compensate for what many now recognized as the intelligentsia's political and moral failure. On January 6, 1989, Fang wrote a personal letter (which soon became an open letter) to Deng Xiaoping urging freedom for all political prisoners, including Wei Jingsheng, the best known of the Democracy Movement activists who languished in jail. Fang suggested that the release of Wei, whose imprisonment had become symbolic of the violation of elemental human rights in China, domestically as well as internationally, would be an appropriate way to celebrate the forthcoming fortieth anniversary of the founding of the People's Republic.[1]

Fang Lizhi's initiative was supported in February by an open letter—addressed to the National People's Congress—signed by thirty-three well-known intellectuals and artists, including such prominent Marxist theoreticians as Wang Ruoshui and Su Shaozhi and the renowned philosopher Li Zehou, which repeated the call for the release of all political prisoners and added that such a general amnesty would be a fitting way to commemorate the seventieth anniversary of the May Fourth Movement as well as the fortieth birthday of the People's Republic.[2] Forty-two eminent writers and scientists soon followed with an open letter addressed to Party head Zhao Ziyang and Premier Li Peng calling for the release of all youths sentenced to labor reform for political reasons.[3]

In addition to publicly confronting the government with the embarrassing question of political prisoners, Marxist intellectuals challenged the Communist Party's long-standing claim to be the sole interpreter of Marxist doctrine. The lead was taken by Su Shaozhi, dismissed two years earlier as director of the Marxism-Leninism-Mao Zedong Thought Institute, partly because of his sympathy for the student protesters of the winter of 1986–87. Su, in a public speech,

[1] On the trial and imprisonment of Wei Jingsheng, see Chapter 5. For the text of Fang's brief letter to Deng Xiaoping, see Fang Lizhi, *Bringing Down the Great Wall* (New York: Norton, 1992), pp. 242–43.
[2] For the text of the February 16, 1989, letter, see Fang Lizhi, *Bringing Down the Great Wall*, Appendix, p. 305.
[3] For the text, see ibid., pp. 306–8.

was blunt in characterizing the Party's official Marxist canon as a collection of "ossified dogmas" that failed to take into account changes in either world capitalism or Chinese socialism. Official doctrine was denounced for ignoring the cardinal Marxian principle of the unity of theory and practice. Further, Su held that there were many schools of Marxist thought, all of which should be heard, and he was bitterly critical of the Party for punishing such eminent democratic Marxist theorists as Wang Ruoshui and Yu Guangyuan for their failure to adhere to a dogmatized Marxist state canon.[4]

Su Shaozhi had been a key figure in formulating the democratic socialist reform program that had brought Deng Xiaoping to power in 1978. He had occupied a prominent place as an ideologist and economic theorist in the new regime through the mid-1980s. His bitter December 1988 speech was reflective of the disillusionment with the Deng regime that had overtaken many democratic Marxists, especially after the fall of Hu Yaobang in 1987. It was an ominous sign that went unheeded by Party leaders.

After June 4, 1989, Communist leaders were to charge that students had been incited to rebellion by "bourgeois" intellectuals, although the accused were in fact mostly Marxists. All those who had signed open letters and petitions were arrested, forced to flee the country, or otherwise punished. Although it took great personal courage to defy the regime as they did—indeed, only a tiny minority of intellectuals were willing to do so—the dissent was expressed at a time when it appeared that the Communist Party had lost the will, even if not the power, to control society in the Stalinist fashion that had been customary for forty years. Beset by grave economic problems and widespread social unrest, riddled by corruption, torn by internal factional conflicts, and staffed by cadres often more concerned with their private entrepreneurial ventures than with their public political duties, the Party seemed paralyzed in the early months of 1989.

In view of the gravity of the social and economic problems they confronted, Party leaders were relatively unconcerned with intellectual heretics and ideological heresies. The campaign against "bourgeois liberalization," begun again in 1987, was still officially

---

[4] For a summary of Su's speech, see "Quarterly Chronicle and Documentation," *The China Quarterly*, No. 118 (June 1989), pp. 398–99.

underway in 1989—but hardly anyone noticed. Dissident political literature flourished, openly sold (alongside pornography imported from Hong Kong) on book carts in the streets of Beijing and other large cities, with little interference from the authorities. Independent publications, such as the weekly Shanghai *World Economic Herald* (which courageously published Su Shaozhi's December 1988 speech on Marxism, among other heretical documents), managed to elude state suppression and became increasingly influential. Sometimes official publications defied higher authorities and achieved de facto independence. Such was the case with *China Youth Daily*, the organ of the Communist Youth League, which, according to Liu Binyan, had become "one of the most objective newspapers in China." In 1988, Liu recalls, "more than two hundred [of its] reporters and editors were so united that not one of them informed on anyone else. . . . This is a case of a government-run newspaper evolving into a popular one."[5] Not only did some official newspapers transform themselves into independent publications critical of the regime; various Party institutions and organs were becoming centers of opposition and dissent, including sections of the Central Party School in Beijing. Indeed, most of the democratic opposition to the Deng regime came not from "liberals," as Western correspondents reflexively assumed, but rather from members of the Chinese Communist Party who considered themselves true Marxists and socialists.

Deng Xiaoping himself, still lionized in those pre-Tiananmen days as a great reformer in the Western media, did not fare nearly as well in China. His once-great popularity in the urban areas had largely evaporated by 1988. He was openly criticized—and often with a singular lack of respect—in private conversation. And he was sometimes the object of personal attacks, as were members of his family, some of whom were accused of corruption. Party chief Zhao Ziyang, Deng's principal disciple, was seen in the same dim light as his mentor. As a popular rhyme on nepotism and corruption in the post-Mao era went:

> Mao Zedong's son went to the front [where he was killed during the Korean War]. Zhao Ziyang's son speculates in color TVs. Deng Xiaoping's son demands money from everyone.

[5] Liu Binyan, *China's Crisis, China's Hope*, pp. 29–30.

First seen on a wall in Xi'an in the fall of 1988, "by the spring of 1989, this little ditty—or variations upon it—could be seen and heard across China," a visiting American scholar observed.[6]

Disillusioned with Deng Xiaoping and emboldened by the Communist Party's apparent paralysis, prominent intellectuals took the lead in calling for political democratization. But they were also concerned about economic hardships, not least of all their own. One of Deng Xiaoping's great and inexplicable political blunders was that he had allowed the living standards of intellectuals to decline after 1985. Deng, after all, long had championed the interests of intellectuals, advocating that they should enjoy better pay and higher status as well as considerable professional autonomy. This, along with his reform program, had won for Deng the nearly universal support of intellectuals in his drive for power in the late 1970s. And in the early years of the new regime intellectuals prospered materially as well as spiritually, providing Deng with his most reliable base of support. Yet Deng squandered much of this political capital by doing nothing—where relatively little would have sufficed—when inflationary outbursts eroded living standards of intellectuals, their state-set salaries lagging far behind the sharply rising cost of urban living. The issue of low pay for teachers and researchers, and the meager educational budget, had been raised time and again since the early 1980s. But Deng Xiaoping was silent and the government pleaded poverty. The problem reached critical proportions with the galloping inflation of 1988. Intellectuals did not challenge the Communist state simply because of low pay and high prices, but rapidly deteriorating living standards in the cities undoubtedly sharpened their animosity toward the Deng regime and swelled the ranks of dissidents.

In the early months of 1989, a significant number of China's intellectuals were transforming themselves into an intelligentsia, a group alienated from existing state and society, and one whose members were willing to bear the consequences of political action against the existing regime. For a brief time they did in fact play the role of a genuine intelligentsia. Their open letters, petitions, speeches, and writings of the latter months of 1988 and early 1989 found a re-

---

[6] Joseph W. Esherick, "Xi'an Spring," in Jonathan Unger (ed.), *The Pro-Democracy Protests in China: Reports from the Provinces* (Armonk, N.Y.: M. E. Sharpe, 1991), p. 79.

sponsive student audience and thus proved to be the prelude to the student movement that was to begin in April. That movement, which came to include workers as well as students, was essentially spontaneous, self-organized, and independent. But one need not embrace Deng Xiaoping's spurious ex post facto explanation that older "bourgeois" intellectuals led gullible young students to create "turmoil" and "rebellion" to recognize that a relatively small number of democratic intellectuals (most of whom considered themselves to be Marxists) played a most significant role in the origins of what became a massive popular movement. The writings of the intelligentsia introduced and reinforced democratic ideas and ideals among students, and conveyed the message that democracy was not only compatible with socialism but an essential prerequisite for its genuine emergence. Their bold criticisms of the dictatorial political practices and authoritarian values of the Communist Party helped to undermine the legitimacy of the regime, and their open defiance of the Communist state, and the latter's feeble responses, emboldened students and others to speak and act. At the least, intellectuals were catalytic agents in the birth of the Democracy Movement of 1989. It would be historically inaccurate, and unfair to the courageous intellectuals who acted, to minimize the crucial role they played in inspiring the hopes of the Beijing Spring. Others bear the responsibility for the tragedy that resulted.

STUDENT ACTIVISM

Students have played a most revolutionary role in the history of modern China. In the 1890s a portion of the young student-scholar Confucian elite, the sons of the gentry ruling class, lost their faith in traditional values and institutions and refused to take the place of their fathers as the rulers of the old regime. It was the first clear sign of "the defection of the intellectuals," always a symptom of an emerging revolutionary situation. And indeed it did portend the rise of the reformist and revolutionary movements that brought down China's two-thousand-year-old imperial regime, movements in which students and ex-students occupied an especially prominent place.

On May 4, 1919, students demonstrating at the Gate of Heavenly

Peace in Beijing sparked a massive revolutionary anti-imperialist movement that was joined by urban workers, merchants, and the common people of the cities of China. Out of the great political, intellectual, and cultural ferment of the May Fourth Movement emerged the radical social movements and the modern political parties that have molded the history of twentieth-century China. Students often became the leaders of these movements and parties, and especially of the Chinese Communist Party, which was founded in the crucible of May Fourth political activism and cultural revolution. Three decades later, when Mao Zedong stood high atop the Gate of Heavenly Peace to proclaim the establishment of the People's Republic, he, along with most of the other new leaders of China, could claim membership in that hallowed "May Fourth generation." And again, in their rise to power, the Chinese Communists were assisted by new generations of student activists who formed the core of radical nationalist movements in the cities during the 1930s and 1940s. Student activism continued after 1949, although mostly in political movements called forth by the Communist Party or factions of the Party—the Hundred Flowers campaign of 1957, the Cultural Revolution, and the April Fifth Movement of 1976.

Chinese students in 1989 looked upon themselves as the heirs to this long tradition of student activism, and especially to the legacy of the May Fourth Movement, whose seventieth anniversary they were preparing to celebrate. As was the case in the May Fourth era, college and university students in the late 1980s were a tiny elite in Chinese society. Although college enrollments grew rapidly after 1949, and especially after 1978, only about 1 percent of high school graduates were admitted to colleges in the late Deng era, and even this paltry fraction is less than it seems since only a minority of Chinese youth graduated from high school in the late 1980s. College students were not only a small elite numerically but also socially, most of them having enjoyed relatively privileged lives as the sons and daughters of higher-level Party officials, managerial personnel, and intellectuals.

Yet university students, although relatively few in numbers and socially atypical, could be politically potent when they articulated the grievances of other social groups. Such had been the case in the May Fourth Movement of 1919, when student demonstrations were not simply symptomatic of rebelliousness in the ruling classes but catalysts for the politicization of other social groups, eventually providing much of the leadership for a mass revolutionary movement.

The 1989 student demonstrators followed in the footsteps of their May Fourth predecessors, but in moderate fashion and only up to a self-imposed nonrevolutionary point. They did raise issues—such as demands for democratic freedoms and an end to official corruption —that won them the sympathy and support of much of the urban population. It was in fact the political activation of other social groups, especially the urban working class, that made the Democracy Movement more than another incident in a long series of instances of student unrest. But the movement did not proceed in a revolutionary direction (save in the paranoiac minds of elderly Party leaders with long memories of the Cultural Revolution); much less did it produce a mass revolutionary movement. This in part was due to the limited and very moderate aims of most student leaders, who sought not to overthrow the government or even to form an opposition party, but only to win some measure of autonomy for themselves—and perhaps to encourage a long-term process of democratization within the ruling Communist Party in accordance with the Party's own proclaimed Marxian principles. In part it was due to the simple fact, well recognized by most student leaders, that however widespread popular dissatisfaction was with the government, a truly revolutionary situation did not exist. The Deng regime still commanded the loyalty of the Army and the police, and probably the majority of the population, the bulk of whom still lived in the countryside.

The student movement of 1989 was not the product of any grand design. Most of what happened that spring was spontaneous, unanticipated, and unplanned—or, if planned, more often than not planned the night before. The essentially spontaneous character of the movement should not be taken to mean that it took place in an organizational and ideological vacuum. Students were intellectually and politically influenced by the democratic ideas of dissident intellectuals. Sometimes this influence was conveyed in a quasi-organizational form, most notably in the "democracy salons" that were established by leading intellectuals in the summer of 1988, where students came to hear and discuss unorthodox ideas. One such salon met outdoors every Wednesday on the Beijing University campus in the summer and early fall of 1988, and was revived in the spring of 1989 by Wang Dan, an undergraduate history major. Other future leaders of the student movement organized similar discussion groups under a variety of politically innocuous names, such as Wuer Kaixi's Confucius Study Society at Beijing Normal University and Shen Tong's Olympic Science Academy at Beijing University, the latter promoting the writings of the anti-Marxist theorist Karl Popper.[7] "Democracy salons" spread from Beijing to other cities.

In addition to these semi-public salons, student activists, some of them survivors of the suppressed protests of the winter of 1986–87, formed small quasi-political discussion groups that met secretly on university campuses. Early in 1989 many of these student groups were planning political demonstrations to commemorate the seventieth anniversary of the May Fourth Movement, independent of the official commemorative ceremonies being planned by governmental organizations—and, very much in the May Fourth spirit, in defiance of the Party's continuing refusal to permit freedom of organization and expression.

The student political timetable was moved up—and students were galvanized for action—by the news of the death of former Party head Hu Yaobang on April 15. In a mixture of genuine grief and cool political calculation, couplets mourning Hu and wallposters praising his unfinished achievements appeared the night of his death on the campuses of Beijing University, Qinghua University, and other colleges in the capital. The students were consciously following a long tradition of "mourning the dead to criticize the living."

The first explicitly political act began at 3 a.m. when graduate students in the Department of Party History at People's University bicycled to Tiananmen Square to lay wreaths at the Monument to the Heroes of the Revolution.[8] It was the same site where wreaths hon-

---

[7] On the "salons" and similar organizations, see Tony Saich, "The Rise and Fall of the Beijing People's Movement," in Unger, *The Pro-Democracy Protests in China*, pp. 15–16; Lee Feigon, *China Rising*, pp. 113–14. On the Beijing University "democracy salon," Feigon observes: "Much of the discussion was inane, but it fostered an atmosphere of dissent and daring" (p. 113).

[8] On the pioneering role in the Democracy Movement of the politically sophisticated Party History Department students at People's University, see Lee Feigon's important work, *China Rising*, esp. pp. 126–34 and passim.

oring Zhou Enlai had been placed thirteen years before, igniting the much-celebrated April Fifth Movement. The students knew that the death of a Party leader was one of the rare occasions when the regime would tolerate symbolic political actions and spontaneous gatherings of people.

Following in the footsteps of preceding generations of Communist revolutionaries, the student activists embarked on "long marches" to Tiananmen Square—both the center of state power and the symbolic center of protest against established authority. The first of the marches began on the evening of April 17, two days after Hu Yao-bang's death. Five hundred students from Beijing University were joined by students from other universities as well as by nonstudent youth as they made their way through the streets of the sprawling capital city, singing the Communist "Internationale" and other revolutionary songs. In the early hours of the morning about 4,000 orderly marchers, sometimes assisted by police, arrived in Tiananmen Square. On April 18, 1,000 of their number staged a sit-in before the Great Hall of the People, refusing to leave until representatives of the National People's Congress received their petition. During the day on April 18 the number of people in the square swelled to over 10,000 as the original demonstrators were joined by other students, workers, unemployed youth, and curious bystanders. The first physical confrontation occurred that evening when several thousand demonstrators left the square to march on nearby Zhongnanhai, the walled compound where top Party and government leaders live and work. Most of the demonstrators were content to chant political slogans, but some—probably unemployed street-hardened youths—repeatedly attempted to storm the gate that led to the homes of Deng Xiaoping and Li Peng. The skirmishes with guards and police that ensued were minor, but the incident (as it was reported at the time) was sufficient to heighten public sympathy for the student movement at the same time as the frontal assault on the most visible symbol of Communist authority enormously raised the political stakes. Even more politically threatening to Party leaders was the news that an Autonomous Student Union had been established at several universities in Beijing to replace the official government-controlled student organizations. While only a handful of students initially were involved, the very idea of an organization neither controlled nor sanctioned by the Communist Party posed a direct challenge to the regime—and to Deng Xiaoping's Four Cardinal Principles.

Thus even before Hu Yaobang's funeral, which was scheduled for April 22, the movement that had been sparked by his death had moved well beyond mourning for the former Party head. The couplets commemorating Hu that appeared on university walls on the night of April 15 were, within a day or two after Hu's death, overshadowed by wallposters extolling the virtues of democracy and condemning government repression and corruption. Student demonstrators in the streets of Beijing and in other cities no longer confined themselves to requests that the Party offer a fair assessment of Hu Yaobang's political career and a credible explanation for his 1987 political disgrace. They now carried posters, bore petitions, and made speeches demanding the right to freely organize; they called for freedom of the press; they insisted that the cases of those who had been treated unjustly during various campaigns against "bourgeois liberalization" be redressed; they appealed for increases in the education budget; and they demanded the publication of a list of the salaries and other sources of income of Party and government leaders and their children. It was this last demand, the opening salvo in the assault against official profiteering and bureaucratic corruption, that struck a particularly responsive chord among the people of the city, bringing to the student movement the support of growing numbers of workers and other citizens.

As demonstrations in Tiananmen Square grew larger and more chaotic, the government announced that the public would be barred from the square on April 22, the day set aside for Hu Yaobang's memorial services. Student leaders responded with a defiant display of organizational brilliance, funneling thousands of students into the square during the night of April 21–22. When soldiers and police arrived at 6 a.m. to seal off the square, they found more than 10,000 students camped before the Gate of Heavenly Peace. The government had been outwitted—and embarrassed. An American observer summed up the effect of the student maneuver:

> The action captured the imagination of the city. As word spread of what the students had done, thousands of others poured into

the square. By morning, an estimated 100,000 people had joined them in Tiananmen, perhaps seventy thousand of them students. It was the first time that great numbers of masses had joined the student demonstrations—and they had done so in direct defiance of both a municipal regulation against unauthorized demonstrations and a specific directive issued the day before by the public security department.[9]

Communist leaders had planned to keep the services for Hu Yaobang an internal Party affair, with carefully selected segments broadcast on national television. The students forced them to perform the ritual in the presence of a massive public audience. Zhao Ziyang delivered the memorial speech to an invited official audience gathered in the Great Hall of the People, while over 100,000 uninvited mourners patiently waited outdoors in Tiananmen Square. Zhao spoke of Hu Yaobang's life and political accomplishments at some length and in highly laudatory terms. But he failed to mention Hu's ouster as Party Secretary-General in early 1987, the position that Zhao had inherited. An explanation of Hu's fall and disgrace had been one of the demands of demonstrating students. Zhao ignored the demand.

With the conclusion of the memorial meeting, Deng, Zhao, and other high Communist officials left the Great Hall of the People to join the funeral procession. They observed 100,000 people standing quietly in the square, orderly but in silent defiance of the directives of the Public Security Bureau. Beyond the square, more than 1 million citizens lined the route of the motorcade that carried Hu Yaobang's body to Baobaoshan, the cemetery for revolutionary martyrs and high Communist officials, located in the Western suburbs of the capital.

On April 22 the people of Beijing demonstrated an extraordinary combination of organizational potency and self-discipline. The day of Hu Yaobang's funeral did not pass as peacefully in several provincial centers. In the northwestern city of Xi'an student demonstrators were brutally attacked by police in what one observer described as a "classic police riot," provoking attacks on government buildings, rock throwing, and the burning of vehicles. In Changsha, the capital of Hunan province, unemployed youths broke off from an orderly stu-

[9] Lee Feigon, *China Rising*, p. 145.

dent march to embark on a night of rioting and looting.[10] Over most of China, however, the day of Hu Yaobang's funeral passed uneventfully.

In Beijing the contest between student activists and Communist leaders reached an impasse. For a week following Hu Yaobang's death the authorities had tolerated unauthorized demonstrations and overlooked the students' refusal to heed the directives of the Public Security Bureau. But the government had disregarded the students' request for a reassessment of Hu's political career, and continued to ignore broader demands for democratization and for measures to curb official corruption. With the burial of Hu Yaobang, the student movement seemed to have reached a dead end, faced with the intransigence of a powerful Communist state. The movement probably would have faded away in the normal course of events—had dramatic and provocative actions not immediately followed.

On April 23 student leaders announced the establishment of a loosely organized Provisional Autonomous Federation of Beijing University Students to coordinate student activities. On the next day, representatives from twenty-one universities and colleges in Beijing declared a student strike in support of the seven demands they had put forth on April 18, formalizing and publicizing the boycott of classes that had begun the week before. In a far more daring challenge to the Communist regime, the students urged workers and other citizens throughout China to join them, in effect calling for a general strike against the state. Some students launched a "go to the people" movement, fashioned after their May Fourth Movement predecessors. Student activists in Beijing ventured outside their campus gates, so that workers and other citizens could see their banners and hear their speeches. Soon the students began to fan out through the city, distributing leaflets and giving brief street-corner talks. As one foreign observer reported:

> On their propaganda tours the students always left the campuses in groups, fifteen or twenty bicyclists riding together, one in the lead carrying a red banner with the name of the school

[10] See Esherick, "Xi'an Spring," esp. pp. 83–89; and Andrea Worden, "Despair and Hope: A Changsha Chronicle," in ibid., esp. pp. 131–32.

and the department. For a time, one could see them everywhere throughout the city with small crowds gathered around. On street corners they shouted out the message of democracy, emphasizing, at least in their discussions with the public, their opposition to official corruption. And always they repeated that they did "not oppose the government or the party."[11]

Deng Xiaoping responded with rage. No doubt his anger was exacerbated by the personal ridicule students and others had begun to heap upon the once-popular paramount leader. In street demonstrations it became fashionable to call for Deng's real retirement from politics by comparing him with Cixi (Tzu Hsi), the reactionary Empress Dowager who lingered over the decay of the last of China's dynasties, stubbornly clinging to power until her death in 1908. An even more popular sport was the symbolic destruction of Deng through the breaking of small glass bottles in the streets—the name Xiaoping being a homonym for the Chinese word for bottle.

But there were more substantive reasons for Deng's anger. Deng was obsessed by memories of Mao's Cultural Revolution and saw in every instance of student political activism an ominous reflection of the upheaval of the 1960s. Especially foreboding were the proclamations announcing the establishment of *autonomous* student organizations, eerily reminiscent, in Deng's mind, of the disastrous attack on the Communist Party by "rebel" organizations during the Maoist upheaval. "This is not an ordinary student movement; it is turmoil," an enraged Deng Xiaoping declared on April 25, at an informal but fateful Party meeting. "What they are doing now is altogether the same stuff as what the rebels did during the Cultural Revolution. All they want is to create chaos under the heavens."[12]

Deng's paranoia about a new Cultural Revolution was also fed by the "Polish fear," the prospect of workers joining intellectuals and students in a Solidarity-type movement to challenge the authority of

[11] Lee Feigon, *China Rising*, pp. 148–49.
[12] For a perceptive discussion of Deng's angry reaction to the student movement, see Lee Feigon, *China Rising*, pp. 152–55. Also, Han Minzhu (ed.), *Cries for Democracy: Writings and Speeches from the 1989 Chinese Democracy Movement* (Princeton: Princeton University Press, 1990), p. 83. For an English translation of Deng's April 25 remarks, see FBIS, May 31, 1989, pp. 35–36.

the Communist state. It was a fear that had haunted China's leaders since 1980, and apprehensions were raised anew when student activists began to openly seek the support of the people—in Beijing and elsewhere—on April 24. Thus Deng demanded stern action to end the student movement and reportedly said that "we are not afraid to shed blood" to do so. To reinforce the point he ordered two Army divisions to take up positions near the capital and directed the *People's Daily* to make clear that no further disturbances would be tolerated.

The Party's newspaper followed Deng's instructions—and indeed his words—with an editorial that appeared in its April 26 edition. The editorial charged that "abnormal phenomena" had occurred during the period of mourning for Hu Yaobang, including attacks on "Party and state leaders by name." The abnormalities were attributed not directly to the students but rather to an "extremely small number of people" who took advantage of "the young students' feelings of grief for Comrade Hu Yaobang to spread all kinds of rumors and confuse people's minds. . . . Their purpose was to sow dissension among the people, plunge the whole country into chaos, and sabotage the political situation of stability and unity. This is a planned conspiracy and a disturbance. Its essence is to once and for all negate the leadership of the Chinese Communist Party and the socialist system." Deng's remedy was to enforce the prohibition on "illegal organizations" and demonstrations, and to prevent students from "going to factories, rural areas and [other] schools to establish ties."[13]

The warning conveyed by the *People's Daily* editorial was reinforced by the Beijing Public Security Bureau, which issued a circular reiterating that all demonstrations and marches not officially authorized by municipal authorities were illegal, and that the long-standing ban would be strictly enforced now that the mourning period for Hu Yaobang had passed. For good measure the authorities also banned making speeches and passing out leaflets on the streets of Beijing.

The April 26 editorial did not have the effect Deng intended. While some students withdrew from the movement, fearful of the

---

[13] "It is necessary to take a clear stand against disturbances," *People's Daily* editorial, April 26, 1989. For an English translation, see "Quarterly Chronicle and Documentation," *The China Quarterly* No. 119 (September 1989), Appendix A, pp. 717–19.

consequences of participating in what now had been condemned as a "conspiracy," many more students were politically activated by the harsh tone and the outrageous charges.[14] The editorial invited defiance, politically reenergizing and unifying rebellious students.

On the evening of April 26 students on college campuses throughout Beijing, in contact with each other through loosely structured organizations established after April 15, frenetically worked through the night to organize marches and demonstrations for the next day, amidst the din of ubiquitous loudspeakers warning of dire consequences if they did not return to classes. The atmosphere was tense but exhilarating. The decisive historical hour was at hand, it was felt, calling for heroic and self-sacrificing acts. Some students wrote their wills, loudly announcing the fact to relatives and newspaper reporters. Mostly the sons and daughters of China's political and intellectual elite, students phoned their homes to proclaim that they were prepared to die to defend their democratic and patriotic ideals. The parents and grandparents who received the calls were often high Communist bureaucrats and military officers.

During the early morning hours of April 27 students marched out of their campus gates, pushing aside the police and militia who had been sent to enforce the ban on demonstrations. The police offered little more than token resistance, they used neither guns nor clubs, and it was reported that they had been instructed not to use force by Minister of Public Security Qiao Shi. By late morning some 80,000 students from several dozen colleges in Beijing had joined together in a four-mile-long column, marching through the streets of the capital. Tens of thousands of other citizens marched alongside the arm-linked student column. When they reached Tiananmen Square, the students broke into smaller groups, marching throughout the city the rest of the day and well into the evening. Some sought popular support—and won it in full measure. Everywhere the student demonstrators went, carrying high their banners and flags and singing revolutionary songs, they were greeted as returning heroes of a victorious army. The people of Beijing often joined the student marchers, sometimes providing them with food and even money. It was a time of spontaneous expressions of solidarity and affection. When the

---

[14] On student reactions to the April 26 editorial, see Lee Feigon, *China Rising*, pp. 156–57.

students of People's University returned to their campus after midnight, the cooks and workers took it upon themselves to reopen the dining hall to serve the students a late dinner.[15] It was as if the events of the day had repealed all official rules and regulations.

April 27 was a day of momentous importance in the history of the People's Republic. University students, the sons and daughters of the ruling elite, had successfully defied the authority of the Chinese Communist Party, and had done so very publicly and in massive numbers. Even more significantly, it was the day when a substantial number of the citizens of Beijing, in entirely spontaneous displays of support for the students, had declared their opposition to the existing Communist regime. The government, quick to recognize a potentially revolutionary situation, sought to defuse it. By the evening of April 27, even before most students had returned to their campuses, the government announced acceptance of the student demand for meetings with high officials. The students were euphoric. The government had retreated, seemingly in disarray. For the next few weeks, Communist leaders, divided over tactics on how best to pacify student rebelliousness, assumed a relatively conciliatory posture.

On April 28 the government conceded another student demand, informing newspaper editors that they were free to cover the student movement in the manner they best saw fit, ostensibly to permit the masses to make up their own minds on the issues involved. On that same day student leaders announced the establishment of the Autonomous Federation of Beijing University Students as a permanent organization, and dropped Provisional from its title. Led by Wuer Kaixi, a student at Beijing Normal University who soon was to gain fame in a televised debate with Prime Minister Li Peng, the Autonomous Federation appeared far more formidable than it actually was. During its brief month-long history, the Federation was at best a loosely organized coordinating body, vainly attempting to unite the aims and activities of diverse student groups at several dozen universities who produced a bewildering variety of self-proclaimed leaders.

The first public meeting between student representatives and the government was held on April 29. More than forty students from

---

[15] Lee Feigon, *China Rising*, p. 161. For a detailed and insightful firsthand description of the events of April 27, see ibid., Chapter 7.

sixteen colleges in Beijing engaged in the long-awaited "dialogue" with mid-level officials. In another concession to student demands, a videotape recording of the discussion was broadcast on state television, treating many millions of citizens to the rare spectacle of their leaders being publicly questioned—and in accusatory terms—about such matters as official corruption and bureaucratic privilege, the suppression of news by state-controlled media, and the isolation of Party leaders from the people. Although they declined to discuss the reasons for the dismissal of Hu Yaobang, on the whole the government officials appeared conciliatory. They promised that student opinions would be taken seriously, acknowledged that mistakes had been made in educational policy, and promised that more funds would go to universities. Moreover, they claimed to share student demands for stronger measures to deal with corruption and official profiteering. As evidence of that concern, it was announced that the government would suspend the conduct of official business at Beidaihe, a seaside resort reserved for higher state and Party leaders, and that the import of foreign luxury limousines for official use would be forbidden. Imported luxury vehicles had become symbolic of the special privileges that Communist bureaucrats enjoyed. One student suggested, and only half jokingly, that the government's budget deficit, over which there had been much official hand-wringing, could be eliminated if the state sold its fleets of Mercedes.

A second meeting between student representatives and government officials was held on April 30. While there appeared to be some measure of agreement over issues such as official profiteering and the need to increase expenditures for education, the discussions reached a stalemate over the refusal of Party authorities to recognize the legitimacy of the new student organizations. The young students were driven less by specific grievances or grand visions of democracy than by a desire to exert some degree of control over their own lives. It was for this reason that the adjective "autonomous" (*zizhi*) almost invariably appeared in the names of the new student organizations. Students did not aim to overthrow the Chinese Communist Party or even to deny its "leading role," but only to gain a degree of autonomy within the all-pervasive structure of Party authority and some measure of freedom to express their own views and desires through their own organizations.

In pursuing this elemental need for a degree of social and political independence, the young students expressed the unarticulated grievances of most citizens who labored under the weight of a cumbersome, arbitrary, and increasingly corrupt bureaucracy that impinged upon virtually every aspect of their daily lives. But it was this need, however politically innocent, that clashed with the Leninist concept of the Party held by most Communist leaders. Their insistence on the sacrosanct place of the Party found one of its principal expressions in obsessive fears of another Cultural Revolution— among two generations of Party leaders who had been the victims of the Maoist upheaval and who remained traumatized by the experience two decades later. They were convinced that undermining the authority of the Chinese Communist Party would again result in chaos. It was a conviction based on the coincidence of personal experience, ideological habit, and political self-interest.

It is hardly surprising then that Deng Xiaoping was enraged when he learned of the establishment of the Autonomous Federation of Beijing University Students on April 28. He immediately condemned it as a throwback to the "rebel" organizations spawned during the Cultural Revolution and demanded that the secret police disband the new organization.[16] On April 29, the very day that talks between government officials and student representatives began, a *People's Daily* editorial drew ominous parallels between the use of wallposters and boycotts by the 1989 student activists and the methods employed during the Cultural Revolution.

While Deng Xiaoping was prepared from the outset to use force —the security police in the first instance and the Army if necessary—other Party leaders favored compromise to bring about a peaceful resolution of the crisis. They eagerly awaited the return of Party Secretary-General Zhao Ziyang, who had been on an official visit to North Korea since April 23, and thus could disclaim any responsibility for the April 26 *People's Daily* editorial and the events that followed. Zhao's train arrived in Beijing on the evening of April 30, and so began a bitter leadership struggle which pitted Zhao against his longtime mentor and patron, Deng Xiaoping. The conflict was to virtually paralyze the Party apparatus for more than two weeks, allowing the popular democratic movement to grow.

---

[16] "Quarterly Chronicle and Documentation," *The China Quarterly*, No. 119 (September 1989), p. 672.

ZHAO ZIYANG AND THE DEMOCRACY MOVEMENT

Shortly after his return from North Korea, Zhao Ziyang, as widely anticipated, threw his still-considerable political weight behind the Party leaders who favored conciliation. His first public pronouncement, a speech commemorating the seventieth anniversary of the May Fourth Movement delivered on the evening of May 3, was unexceptional, although it later was to be officially criticized for failing to condemn "bourgeois liberalization." Zhao, searching for common ground, reemphasized that the government shared the students' desire to end corruption and increase educational expenditures. But he also stressed the need for "stability" to carry out modernization and economic reform, raising (as Deng repeatedly did) the specter of sliding back to the chaos of the Cultural Revolution. Far more significant were his comments in a May 4 speech delivered to the governors of the Asian Development Bank meeting in Beijing. Zhao Ziyang described the student demands as "reasonable" and said that they should be met through democratic and legal means, urging discussions and dialogue between the government and the students.[17] Although Zhao failed to address the question of the "autonomous" status which the new student organizations claimed, both the content and the tone of his speech seemed intended to distance the formal head of the Communist Party from the "retired" Party elders who still exercised informal power. Among the latter was Deng Xiaoping, still the final arbiter of all important Party and government decisions. The text of the May 4 speech was widely disseminated in Beijing, making clear that the Party was divided over how to deal with the student movement.[18]

What were Zhao's motives in so obviously defying China's paramount leader? Deng Xiaoping, after all, had been Zhao's longtime patron, and together they had conspired only two years before to oust Hu Yaobang as Party chief, a position that Zhao then assumed with Deng's decisive support. No doubt a peaceful resolution of the crisis in which China's intellectual (and student) elite would be permitted

---

[17] "Remarks by Secretary-General Zhao Ziyang to Delegates at the Asian Development Bank Annual Meeting," in Han Minzhu (ed.), *Cries for Democracy*, pp. 132–34.

[18] Bao Tong, Zhao Ziyang's secretary and one of his principal advisors, was presumably responsible for disseminating the text of the speech, or so it was officially charged when Bao was arrested and jailed after the June 4 massacre.

a greater degree of autonomy would have been Zhao's natural inclination and certainly that of the intellectuals who advised him. But
there were also other, more practical political considerations. Zhao
Ziyang's political standing, both in the Communist Party and in society at large, had been eroding well before the Democracy Movement. In the early months of 1989, Deng Xiaoping and other Party
elders had become suspicious of Zhao for not being sufficiently vig-
ilant in combating "bourgeois liberalization," just as had been the
case with Hu Yaobang several years before. At the same time, such
personal popularity as Zhao enjoyed largely evaporated as his ex-
pansive "free market" policies brought inflation and other economic
hardships. Moreover, with his sons prominent in the lucrative import-
export business, Zhao was seen as the personification of the bureaucratic corruption and nepotism that had overtaken the Communist
Party. No doubt Zhao believed, and probably with good reason, that
Deng Xiaoping was preparing to make him the scapegoat for the
economic and other difficulties of the time. Clearly, Zhao saw in the
student movement an opportunity to revive his declining political
fortunes. By vaguely supporting the student demands as "reasonable," Zhao Ziyang appealed both to popular opinion in the cities
and to Party officials who desired a peaceful resolution of the crisis,
probably a majority of Party leaders at the time. Zhao's natural political inclinations and his immediate political self-interest coincided.

As the internal Party conflict raged behind closed doors, the Democracy Movement spread in city streets and squares. Intellectuals,
emboldened by Zhao Ziyang's return and his apparent sympathy for
the student movement, made public statements of support for the
students, which were openly critical of the orthodoxies laid down by
Deng Xiaoping. One of the first such manifestos, written by intellectuals associated with Zhao, was issued on May 4 and had little but
scorn for Deng's views on political reform. It read, in part: "We
cannot accept the absurd view that democracy must be delayed because the quality of the Chinese nation is too low. . . . Democracy,
freedom, human rights and rule by law are the prerequisites for building socialism. We are opposed to taking 'Chinese national conditions'
as a pretext for refusing to accept them."[19] A torrent of statements

---

[19] Cited in "Quarterly Chronicle and Documentation," *The China Quarterly*, No. 119 (September 1989), p. 675.

and petitions demanding democratization, signed by increasingly broad groups of intellectuals and others, followed over the next few weeks. Some intellectuals, including such prominent establishment figures as Dai Qing and the Marxist theoretician Su Shaozhi, embarked on organized lecture tours of university campuses to rally support behind Zhao Ziyang.

Others soon joined, expanding the scope of the Democracy Movement. Prominent among them were journalists, the first professional group to publicly identify themselves as supporters of the students and their demands. In early May, hundreds of journalists employed by Party-controlled newspapers and periodicals marched in street demonstrations, some bearing placards pleading for the right to "tell the truth." On May 9 a petition signed by 1,000 journalists was presented to the All-China Journalists' Association calling for a meeting with members of the Party Central Committee to discuss freedom of the press. It was indicative of the defensive posture of the Party that such a meeting was in fact convened between May 11 and May 13, attended by such Party luminaries as Hu Qili and Wang Renzhi.[20] Zhao Ziyang, still ascendant in the inner councils of the Party, followed with statements promising "press reform" and suggested that there should be unlimited press coverage of the student demonstrations.[21]

The Democracy Movement also expanded geographically. Student marches and demonstrations marking the seventieth anniversary of the May Fourth Movement and supporting the students in Beijing, took place in scores of cities, including Shanghai, Nanjing, Xi'an, Wuhan, Changsha, Fuzhou, Chongqing, and Hangzhou as well as the Manchurian industrial centers of Shenyang, Changchun, and Dalian.[22] The demonstrations in the provincial centers were far smaller than those in Beijing. Even in Shanghai, China's largest city and long the center of political radicalism, only about 10,000 students participated in a peaceful protest in People's Park and a march to the

---

[20] Ibid., pp. 675–76.

[21] Ibid., p. 676.

[22] For a superb collection of essays on the movement outside of Beijing, mostly eyewitness accounts, see Unger, *The Pro-Democracy Protests in China.* For a detailed and perceptive account of the course of the movement in Nanjing, see Richard Lufrano, "Nanjing Spring: The 1989 Student Movement in a Provincial Capital," *Bulletin of Concerned Asian Scholars,* Vol. 24, No. 1 (1992), pp. 19–42.

Municipal Building. Nonetheless, the fact that the movement had become nationwide by early May and that demonstrations everywhere took place in violation of official regulations, and in defiance of the Communist Party, must have brought home to the leaders in Beijing some sense of the seriousness of the situation they confronted.

The long-awaited May 4 demonstration in Beijing was a massive affair. Some 60,000 students from over thirty universities in the capital, joined by representatives from universities throughout the country, and from Hong Kong, marched up Changan Avenue through downtown Beijing. Police lines parted as the columns of arm-linked and banner-waving students approached, facilitating their peaceful passage into Tiananmen Square. Observers marveled at the organizational skills of the marchers and their extraordinary self-discipline. But what was really important about the May 4 march was that it became more than a student demonstration. A group of 500 journalists, clearly identifying themselves by their banners and slogans, marched together with the students, the first of the many organized groups that were soon to join the movement.[23] Most significantly, May 4 was the day when the students won the active support of the workers and citizens of Beijing, so that the number of people assembled in Tiananmen Square swelled to 300,000. There they heard speeches at a rally sponsored by the Autonomous Student Union. Young student leaders emphasized the patriotic aims of the movement, once again stressing that they did not stand in opposition to the government. As had been the case in previous demonstrations, the banners proclaimed support for socialism and the Chinese Communist Party as well for democracy and human rights.

The students' declarations of patriotism are noteworthy on this occasion in light of the regime's none too subtle effort to redefine the meaning of the May Fourth Movement. For the better part of a century the spirit of "May Fourth" had been symbolized by the almost sacred

---

[23] The role of journalists was particularly important. After publicly marching with the students on May 4, they wrote sympathetic articles about the student movement in the days that followed. The appearance of such articles in the official press no doubt influenced public opinion, and appeared to many citizens as a quasi-official sanction for their own participation in the demonstrations.

watchwords "Science" and "Democracy." On the eve of the seventieth anniversary celebrations, however, official statements sometimes substituted the slogan "Science and Patriotism." The student movement retained the traditional "Science and Democracy" slogan. But the students were unwilling to cede to the government a monopoly on patriotism. They thus made a special point of proclaiming their devotion to the nation, which in truth they deeply felt, maintaining that there was no contradiction between patriotism and democracy. In this, as in much else, the student protesters were truer to the original May Fourth spirit than the elderly leaders of the Chinese Communist Party, many of whom could claim membership in the celebrated "May Fourth generation."

The huge demonstration of May 4, 1989, was another victory for the student movement. Yet it seemed somehow anticlimactic, even unexciting. Perhaps it was because the demonstration, so long anticipated, had proven too successful, too peaceful—and, in the end, had changed nothing. In the days that followed, a calm seemed to descend over the capital. There were no large demonstrations or marches. Classes resumed at several colleges and some striking students returned to their studies. It appeared to many that there was a return to normalcy in Beijing.

Yet appearances were deceptive. The grievances, both political and economic, which had given rise to the Democracy Movement remained unresolved. And the extraordinary events since April 15, which had demonstrated that the Chinese Communist Party was by no means an invincible Leninist monolith, had inspired hope and activism among ever-wider sectors of society. The post-May 4 calm stemmed not from a popular movement that had spent its energies, but rather from the paralyzing effect of internal political divisions within both the Communist Party and the Democracy Movement. It was the internal divisions within the Party, mostly hidden from public view at the time, that were the most important. During the first three weeks of May, the fate of a vast social movement was being decided by a small group of men meeting behind closed doors.

Although it was not entirely clear at first, the power struggle in the Party pitted Zhao Ziyang against Deng Xiaoping. During the first two weeks of May, Zhao, Deng's disciple but now also the official head of the Communist Party, seemed to hold the stronger hand,

buoyed by the student movement which he both politically sympathized with and found politically useful. His May 4 speech declaring
the students' demands "reasonable" put him in direct opposition to
Deng, the real author of the now-notorious April 26 *People's Daily*
editorial, which condemned those demands as the product of a sinister anti-Party conspiracy. The speech served to activate politically
many of the intellectuals associated with Zhao, who began organizing
lecture tours of university campuses, encouraging students to press
for democratic reforms. Some of the lectures were not without ideological curiosities. The well-known investigative journalist Dai Qing,
closely associated with Zhao and a recent advocate of the "new authoritarianism," compared the significance of April 27, 1989, with
that of June 6, 1966, the day when Mao Zedong launched the Cultural
Revolution. Both marked the beginning of antiauthoritarian movements, she suggested, and both were directed against Deng Xiaoping.[24] The comparison, however bizarre, no doubt was appealing to
young students who had cultivated a certain superficial nostalgia for
the Cultural Revolution and for Mao, whom they sometimes vaguely
imagined to have been in combat against a conservative Party bureaucracy now personified by Deng Xiaoping. But it is unlikely that
Zhao Ziyang would have applauded if he had heard the speech. Zhao,
however, kept a safe distance from the campuses—and from the
students.

Zhao Ziyang was consistent in his words, if not necessarily in his
actions. In speeches and statements during the first half of May, he
reiterated his support for the student movement and the legitimacy
of the movement's demands. He repeatedly praised the patriotism of
the students. He declared himself in favor of freedom of the press
and an independent judiciary, although he did not go so far as to
advocate popular democracy to replace the rule of the Leninist Party
over which he presided. Zhao called for a retraction of the April 26
People's Daily editorial, one of the principal student demands, and
on May 10 he convened an emergency meeting of the Party Politburo,

[24] In a speech delivered at People's University on May 5, 1989, as reported by Lee Feigon,
China Rising, pp. 189–90. The other dates of antiauthoritarian significance in the history of
the People's Republic listed by Dai Qing were October 1, 1949, marking the official founding
of the PRC, and April 5, 1976, the canonized April Fifth Movement directed against the Gang
of Four.

which backed his proposal for talks with student leaders conducted on a democratic basis. On May 12 a *People's Daily* editorial advocating democracy, human rights, and a system of government based on the principle of "a balance of power" was widely attributed to Zhao.

Zhao Ziyang also pleaded with students to cooperate with the government during Soviet President Mikhail Gorbachev's forthcoming three-day visit to China. Gorbachev, a towering figure in world affairs at the time, was scheduled to arrive on May 15 and to be officially welcomed in Tiananmen Square. It was for that event that hundreds of television and newspaper reporters from around the world had converged on Beijing, directing their cameras to Tiananmen Square. They were, of course, to record a far different—and far greater—drama than the one for which they had journeyed to Beijing.

However much Zhao Ziyang might have sympathized with the students, however "reasonable" he may have judged their demands, he refused to meet personally with student leaders. To do so, he feared, risked a full rupture with Deng Xiaoping and an open split in the Party. Deng, for his part, would brook no compromise with what he had branded the students' "illegal organizations." He retreated not one iota from the harsh judgments he had made in the April 26 *People's Daily* editorial. "Our country will have no peace if this disturbance is not resolutely checked," he then had warned. With the government thus divided between its "senior leader" and his chief disciple, Party and government officials could do little but continue to delay responding to student demands for a "dialogue."

Zhao Ziyang's efforts to resolve the crisis peacefully, somehow in a manner satisfactory to Deng and other Party leaders, on the one hand, and also to increasingly radical student activists, on the other, were complicated by growing factionalism within the student movement. As might have been expected with a movement that was spontaneous, youthful, and massive, the organizational lines were fluid and the ideology was amorphous. New leaders emerged from day to day, speaking with a plethora of voices and announcing a multitude of grievances and demands. To Party bureaucrats, even such relatively sympathetic ones as Zhao, who were accustomed to observing strict organizational rules and following established lines of authority, the student movement was bewildering. Zhao was inhibited not only by a reluctance to break completely with Deng but also by the prospect of negotiating with twenty-year-old students whose claims to leadership were dubious and whose authority was transient. Zhao, after all, was a Leninist, and spontaneity is not a Leninist virtue. Nor, for that matter, does youthful spontaneity appeal to anyone in authority, as the history of student movements around the world abundantly testifies.

Still, as ideologically amorphous and diverse as the student movement was, it was not the case that the students spoke in such a babble of voices as to make negotiations with the government impossible, as some have claimed. What the students wanted was easy enough to divine. Their demands were essentially three, as frequently noted by observers at the time.[25] First, they insisted on direct talks with Party and state leaders, which they termed "dialogue." Second, they wanted the freedom to establish their own organizations, or, more precisely, they wanted government recognition of the "autonomous" organizations that had already been established. Finally, they demanded a retraction of the April 26 *People's Daily* editorial, a demand Zhao Ziyang had already publicly supported. This was hardly a revolutionary (much less a "counterrevolutionary") program that portended permanent chaos and the "negation" of the "socialist system" and the leadership of the Communist Party. Had the government made meaningful concessions on any of the three demands, it likely would have averted the tragic events that were to follow. Had Zhao Ziyang, the formal head of the Communist Party, simply talked with student representatives, it would have at once satisfied both the first and the second of the demands. But Deng Xiaoping was adamant in opposing any sort of compromise. And Zhao Ziyang hesitated during the crucial two weeks when he seemingly held the upper hand in the Party, from approximately May 4 to May 17. The opportunity was lost and it was to have disastrous consequences.

In the student Democracy Movement there was no lack of rival groups and leaders who vied with each other for position and publicity. What was remarkable, however, was the extraordinary unity of aim, spirit, and organization that was achieved by politically inex-

---

[25] For example, by Orville Schell in an article written on June 1, 1989, entitled "China's Spring," *The New York Review of Books*, June 29, 1989, pp. 3–8.

perienced youths in a movement that was entirely spontaneous, assumed massive proportions within a very short period of time, and took place in a land where for most of the previous four decades the "organization of the masses" had been the monopoly of a Leninist party. The inevitable petty factional bickering and conflicts pale into insignificance when set beside the extraordinary camaraderie that the movement generated and maintained, what one Chinese participant movingly described in her diary as "the purity, idealism, courage and sacrifice of these young people that have aroused the nation's conscience and mobilized people in Beijing at every level."[26]

Yet there was one division within the student movement that must be noted in order to understand the events of the Beijing Spring. By the first week in May a split had emerged, one that was indistinct and ambiguous but nonetheless very real and portentous, between those who saw their role as influencing the internal politics of the Chinese Communist Party and those who strove to establish their autonomy from the Party. The former tended to be older and more politically sophisticated students, often with personal or family ties to high-level officials, who believed that the democratization of the Party was the essential prerequisite for moving toward a more democratic society in general. The pioneers in the movement to mourn Hu Yaobang in mid-April, they interpreted Zhao Ziyang's apparent political triumph within the Party organization early in May as a triumph for the Democracy Movement as a whole, or at least as the most that realistically could be accomplished for the time being. Consequently they mostly withdrew from active political participation after the May 4 demonstration, fearful of provoking a conservative reaction that might jeopardize Zhao Ziyang's tenuous ascendancy.

The second and more numerous group of students, mostly young undergraduates, were more radical and iconoclastic, both politically and culturally. Distrustful of all authority, they distrusted Zhao Ziyang as well, lumping him together with Deng Xiaoping and Li Peng as but another conservative Party bureaucrat, an impression reinforced by Zhao's failure to meet with them in the days following May 4. They were not out to overthrow the existing regime, but they were intent on establishing a place in society free of the organiza-

[26] Lu Yuan, "Beijing Diary," *New Left Review*, No. 177 (September–October 1989), p. 6.

tional control of the Party. Yet, while demanding autonomy, they also at the same time yearned for the authorities' approval of that demand. Several observers noted this striking difference between the radical Chinese students of 1989 and radical student protesters elsewhere in the world. As Orville Schell wrote:

> . . . talking to these student protesters at the time, one had little sense of them as revolutionaries bent on deposing the government or Party, or even of their having inappeasable resentments toward the leadership. What was most noticeable about them was not their iconoclasm but their yearning to be listened to and taken seriously by the government and the leaders they were criticizing. Their demand that the Party retract its hard-line editorial reflected the prevailing sentiment among many students: far from wishing to be seen as unpatriotic trouble-makers, they just wanted the government to acknowledge that they too were constructive citizens, albeit critical ones, with something to contribute.[27]

Lee Feigon, observing the euphoria that followed the dramatic April 27 demonstration, made a similar point: "It was not the first time in this century that Chinese students had broken with authority figures, but then or now they were unable to offer a substitute for this authoritarian structure. Ultimately, they still wanted the government to say that what they did was right."[28]

Whatever the deep-seated psychological needs of Chinese students are, or may have been in 1989, younger and more radical leaders moved to the forefront of the movement after the May 4 march. Among them were undergraduates such as Wuer Kaixi of Beijing Normal University and Wang Dan, a history major at Beijing University. The young leaders, seemingly oblivious to the internal political struggles raging within the Communist Party, were quickly frustrated by the government's repeated delays in responding to their demands for a "dialogue." But the divided government was paralyzed, capable of little more than delaying tactics. Impatient student leaders, their frustration with the government turning to anger, were in-

---

[27] Schell, "China's Spring," p. 3.
[28] Lee Feigon, China Rising, p. 178.

creasingly drawn to the tactic of staging a hunger strike as a way to break the stalemate.

THE HUNGER STRIKE

A hunger strike originally was proposed by Chai Ling, a graduate student in psychology and a member of a group of radical students attracted to the philosophy of Mahatma Gandhi. After some hesitation, leaders of the Autonomous Student Union embraced the idea of a hunger strike as a dramatic tactic to force the government into the long-delayed dialogue and as a way to revive a movement that had lost much of its dynamism following the successful May 4 march while remaining true to its commitment to nonviolence. A hunger strike was also seen as a way to dramatize the contrast between the moral virtuousness of the students and the greed of the bureaucrats who despotically ruled the land. Late in the afternoon of Saturday, May 13, after the authorities failed to respond to an ultimatum issued the previous day, some 500 students marched into Tiananmen Square and, with considerable fanfare and publicity, began a sit-in and hunger strike in front of the Monument to the Heroes of the Revolution, located in the center of the square. Other students soon joined the original hunger strikers and many thousands of supporters, students, and citizens gathered around them in ever-greater numbers to offer moral support and material aid.

The hunger strikers camped at the very spot in Tiananmen Square where the official welcoming ceremony for Mikhail Gorbachev was scheduled to take place two days later and where the Soviet leader planned to lay a wreath in honor of Chinese revolutionary martyrs. Gorbachev was then at the height of his popularity, at least on the international stage if not necessarily within the Soviet Union. His visit to China was regarded as a major diplomatic event, and, accordingly, thousands of newspaper and television journalists from around the world descended on Beijing. Gorbachev was the first Soviet leader to visit China in three decades,[29] and for the Chinese

[29] The first since Nikita Khrushchev's stormy meeting with Mao Zedong and other Chinese leaders in Beijing in 1959.

government it was to mark the definitive close of the bitter Sino-Soviet quarrel that had been raging since the late 1950s.

Among the people of Beijing, and especially among students, Gorbachev enjoyed an even greater popularity than he did in other parts of the world at the time. His policy of *glasnost*, openness and democratization, seemed to be precisely what Chinese demonstrators were demanding from their own leaders. Students attempted to appropriate Gorbachev for themselves, inviting him to their campuses to discuss the democratic socialist society he championed and to forgo official ceremonies. His open and ebullient personality presented a striking contrast to the secretiveness and remoteness of China's paramount leader, as was the case with his vigorous promotion of democratic political reforms and freedom of the press. If only China had a Gorbachev, it was commonplace to hear in conversations in Beijing at the time, all would go well.

The combination of the hunger strike in Tiananmen Square and the Gorbachev visit—although the timing was not entirely coincidental—made for high drama. Tension gripped the city as the hour of the Soviet leader's arrival approached and as the hunger strikers time and again refused to leave the square, rejecting the appeals and promises of Zhao Ziyang. The students also rebuffed appeals by intellectuals associated with Zhao and numerous high officials representing the Party Central Committee and the State Council, some of whom actually came to the square to hold discussions with the students on May 14. Further, the students ignored an order from the Public Security Bureau to evacuate the square by the morning of May 15, the day that Gorbachev was scheduled to visit Tiananmen Square. The order went unenforced. The government remained paralyzed, neither able to grant concessions to the striking protesters nor willing to risk bloodshed on the eve of the visit by the man who symbolized the democratization of repressive Leninist states.

The welcoming ceremonies for Gorbachev were rather unostentatiously held at the airport and the Soviet leader was kept out of public sight, confined to official indoor meetings and banquets until his departure for Shanghai on May 18. It was a grand embarrassment for the highly nationalistic leaders of the Chinese government, and especially for Deng Xiaoping, who so greatly prized stability and order. It no doubt fortified Deng's determination to crush the "disturbance" and to teach the students a lesson in the process. In the meantime, the television cameras that had been transported to Beijing to record Gorbachev's appearance were now fixed on the student hunger strikers and their supporters. Satellite television transmission allowed people around the globe to follow the events that were unfolding in the vast expanse beneath China's ancient Gate of Heavenly Peace.

The hunger strike was a stroke of tactical political genius. The drama of courageous young students willing to sacrifice their health and lives for the greater good of the nation captured the imagination of the city. It activated popular support for the students (hitherto widespread but mostly latent) and politicized increasing numbers of Beijing's 10 million people, most importantly portions of the industrial working class. Citizens came to Tiananmen Square in ever-larger groups to demonstrate their support for the hunger strikers and their demands for democratic government and an end to corruption and bureaucratic privilege. On Monday, May 15, the day of Gorbachev's arrival, more than a half million people came to the square. By May 17, the fifth day of the hunger strike, the number of demonstrators who crowded in and around Tiananmen Square was overwhelming. The events of that remarkable day were recorded by Lee Feigon:

> The demonstration on May 17 turned out to be the largest mass rally since the Cultural Revolution and possibly since the founding of the People's Republic of China. More than a million people, by some estimates more than two million, came to Tiananmen Square, most of them marching with their work units. Outside the gates of People's University, eight miles away, the entire wide avenue that passed by the front of the school was clogged from early morning until late at night with marchers heading downtown. Throughout the city, marchers from different directions met at every street corner. One parade would sometimes have to wait for hours until another passed.
>
> The vast, hundred-acre Tiananmen Square was not large enough to accommodate all the protesters. One demonstration would march in and immediately march back out as another

took its place. The road running next to the square, Changan Avenue, reputedly the widest street in the world, was clogged its entire length with marchers going to and from Tiananmen. In the midst of this mass of humanity, one lane remained open for ambulances needed to take hunger-strikers to hospitals. Students joined hands to monitor the traffic. In spite of the mass of these surging throngs, there were no traffic accidents involving the ambulances that sped by throughout the day.[30]

The significance of the massive demonstrations of mid-May was not simply the enormous numbers of participants but their social composition. Students, along with intellectuals and journalists, now had been joined by groups of Party cadres, government office workers, schoolteachers, peasants who had marched in from Beijing's rural suburbs, and, most significantly, hundreds of thousands of factory workers. Editors and staff members of the government's Central Television and Broadcasting stations were represented among the demonstrators, along with staff members of Party newspapers and theoretical journals. Teachers from the Central Party School marched in support of the students, as did lower-level officials and clerks who worked in central government ministries. Uniformed police joined the marchers and even a thousand People's Liberation Army cadets were observed among the demonstrators.[31]

A month after the first student protests, virtually all urban social and occupational groups were represented among those who marched in opposition to the government. All proudly hoisted their own banners identifying their institutions and work units. "These were not masses of anonymous demonstrators," a foreign visitor observed, "but well-labelled groups acting in an orderly (although not regimented) fashion."[32]

It was as if the entire city had spontaneously risen up in defiance of the regime of Deng Xiaoping. The student movement had become a mass movement, a genuine movement of the people of Beijing. Since 1949 China had been a land where "mass movements" and

[30] Lee Feigon, *China Rising*, p. 205.
[31] "Quarterly Chronicle and Documentation," *The China Quarterly*, No. 119 (September 1989), p. 678; Feigon, *China Rising*, p. 206.
[32] Geremie Barmé, "Beijing Days, Beijing Nights," in Unger, *The Pro-Democracy Protest in China*, p. 49.

"campaigns" of all sorts had become a permanent feature of life. Most had been sponsored and organized by the state; a few, such as the April Fifth Movement of 1976, were in protest against the state, as had sometimes been the case in the Cultural Revolution a decade earlier. But none were as massive and spontaneous as the Beijing people's movement of May 1989.

By the middle of May, Tiananmen Square had become a vast stage where a deadly political drama was symbolically being played out amidst a gigantic and joyous cultural festival—or, more accurately, a countercultural festival. The people of Beijing were drawn irresistibly to the square by the hundreds of thousands to offer their political testimonials and at the same time participate in what some Western observers were calling a "Chinese Woodstock." For many it was a profoundly liberating experience as people spoke more freely and acted with fewer inhibitions than at any time since the May Fourth era.

The public political drama revolved around the hunger strikers, whose encampment before the Monument to the Heroes of the Revolution grew into a small municipality, even generating its own waste-disposal and garbage-removal systems as well as rudimentary political offices. As hunger strikers began to faint from dehydration and lack of food, a medical system was also created, complete with volunteer doctors and ambulances which conveyed stricken students to nearby hospitals. The wailing sirens of ambulances, racing through crowded streets along special routes cleared by student marshals, heightened the sense of drama and served as a constant reminder of the political crisis, as did continuous reports of troop movements in and around the capital.

Incongruously, the hunger strike took place in a carnival-like setting. Young people danced and sang folk songs and ballads, sometimes joined by popular cultural idols such as the Taiwanese-born songwriter and singer Hou Dejian and the rock star Cui Jian. Autograph collectors sought out celebrities—well-known intellectuals as well as pop singers—who visited the square. Vendors cooked dumplings and pushcart dealers sold soft drinks and a varied assortment of snacks. Obscure individuals rose to give speeches, saying what was on their minds, and then quickly disappeared into the anonymity of the crowd when their audiences evaporated.

Cosmopolitanism and iconoclasm reigned unchallenged in the

square. Students and others banded their longish hair with colored headbands, emulating radical Japanese and South Korean student demonstrators. In the irreverent fashion of Western student demonstrations of the 1960s, the Chinese protesters sang songs and chanted slogans ridiculing the country's politicians, especially Deng Xiaoping and Li Peng. Exhilarated by their iconoclastic defiance of authority, protesters vied with each other to produce ever more sarcastic and humorous political slogans. One was inspired by the dictum long attributed to Deng Xiaoping which presumably conveyed the essence of his celebrated pragmatism: "I don't care whether the cat is black or white so long as it catches mice." The popular 1989 version was: "We don't care if the cat is black or white so long as it resigns."[33] Intellectuals associated with Party head Zhao Ziyang, emboldened by the events in Tiananmen Square, abandoned their customary caution and issued a statement that referred to Deng as a "senile autocrat."[34]

For a brief time in mid-May it seemed that the Communist government had vanished, its fleets of limousines stored away in garages for the duration. Save for orderly lines of soldiers who stood or sat quietly on the steps of the Great Hall of the People, there was little evidence of state authority in downtown Beijing. Even many of the essential functions of municipal administration had been taken over by the demonstrators. As rebellious journalists joined what came to be called "the press revolt," newspapers, formerly obedient to Party and state organs, openly sided with the students, swelling the numbers of citizens who participated in the Democracy Movement. It was one of those rare moments in world history when genuine feelings of solidarity spontaneously triumph among the people of a huge city. Even the pickpockets of Beijing, it was said, went on a holiday out of sympathy for the hunger strikers.

But the Communist state had not vanished, as everyone knew, despite the euphoria of the moment. The hunger strike had raised the political stakes to dangerous new heights. Tiananmen Square was now *occupied*, no longer simply the destination of marchers and the site of periodic demonstrations. The students now virtually invited

---

[33] Cited in Feigon, *China Rising*, p. 204.
[34] Yan Jiaqi et al., "Declaration of May 17, 1989," in Mok Chiu Yu and J. Frank Harrison (eds.), *Voices from Tiananmen Square* (Montreal: Black Rose Books, 1990), p. 134.

the government, if its leaders were not willing to make concessions, to remove them by force—and thereby further reveal the moral bankruptcy of the regime.

Moral considerations were not uppermost in all minds, however. One of the twentieth century's grand masters of realpolitik, Henry Kissinger, ever respectful of the authority of the state, intoned at the time that no government could possibly allow student rebels to occupy the heart of its capital.[35] So too thought Deng Xiaoping. He and other "retired" Party elders, the self-appointed guardians of the Chinese nation and its "socialist system," were alarmed. Their fears heightened as the hunger strike revived the Democracy Movement in provincial cities and towns in mid-May, and they were terrified by the open participation of Party and government cadres in the marches to Tiananmen Square.

But most alarming was the massive participation of factory workers in the demonstration of May 17 and subsequent protests. Apprehensions grew with the establishment of a new and nonofficial citywide working-class organization, the Capital Workers' Autonomous Federation, whose leaders established their headquarters in Tiananmen Square along with "autonomous" federations of students and intellectuals. This raised, in far more threatening and concrete fashion than ever before, the "Polish fear," which had haunted Chinese Communist leaders for almost a decade.

It was the participation of nonstudent groups, especially workers, that enabled Deng Xiaoping to convince Party leaders that the movement was a "rebellion" that had to be crushed. Deng had been secretly meeting with Party elders since early May, plotting to suppress the "turmoil." He also had been mobilizing military forces to carry out the task, calling upon his old friendships with PLA generals as well as utilizing his power as head of the Party's Central Military Commission, his one remaining formal position. Among the Gang of Old, Deng's inner circle, were such veteran Party leaders as Peng Zhen, Li Xiannian, Chen Yun, Wang Zhen, and Deng Yingchao, the widow of Zhou Enlai. None occupied any official Party or government

[35] In an article originally written for the *Los Angeles Times*, Kissinger said that "no government in the world would have tolerated having the main square of its capital occupied for eight weeks by tens of thousands of demonstrators." For a critical commentary, see Anthony Lewis, "Kissinger and China," *The New York Times*, August 20, 1989, Section D, p. 23.

office, and all were presumably retired. Yet it was this informal group of elders, under Deng's tutelage, who made the critical decisions that were to result in the dispatch of the Army to crush the Democracy Movement.

Their first decision, at Deng Xiaoping's suggestion, was to declare martial law. The decision was conveyed to Zhao Ziyang and other Party leaders when Deng summoned them to his home on May 18, after Gorbachev had departed Beijing for Shanghai. Zhao voiced opposition, but to no avail. A meeting of the Politburo's Standing Committee was convened that evening to formally ratify the decision. Although several others of the five members of that body, reportedly Qiao Shi and Hu Qili, harbored reservations, Zhao cast the only negative vote, after which he submitted his resignation as Party Secretary-General. But Deng ordered that it not be accepted. The paramount leader was more accustomed to purges than to resignations.

After having cast the lone dissenting vote against martial law, Zhao Ziyang embarked on a lonely pilgrimage to the hunger strikers in Tiananmen Square. The day before the fateful May 18 meeting, he had issued a statement in the name of the Party Politburo pleading with the students to end the hunger strike, promising that there would be no reprisals, and praising the students for their patriotic ideals. But he had not gone to see the students. Nor had he talked directly with their leaders, preferring instead to work through formal Party channels. Now, at 4 a.m. on May 19, knowing that his days as leader of the Chinese Communist Party were over, he wandered almost aimlessly among the exhausted students in the square. Tearfully and apologetically he acknowledged, "I have come too late." Although once again pleading with the students to end the hunger strike, he expressed full support for their demands, adding, "We were once young too, and we all had such bursts of energy. We also staged demonstrations . . . [and] we also did not think of the consequences."[36] It is said that he broke down and wept before the students. This, the most human act of his long political career, was one

---

[36] Cited in Feigon, *China Rising*, pp. 209–10.

of the charges to be brought against him during the proceedings that resulted in his formal dismissal as Secretary-General of the Chinese Communist Party.

Zhao Ziyang's role in the Democracy Movement remains enigmatic. Although it is said that he had initially approved the April 26 *People's Daily* editorial,[37] he had changed his position by the time he delivered his May 3 speech. Many observers attribute Zhao's change of heart and his subsequent actions less to sympathy for the students than to political opportunism. Zhao feared that he had lost the confidence of Deng Xiaoping and would soon suffer the same fate as Hu Yaobang. Thus his words and actions of May, as characterized by Geremie Barmé, were little more than "desperate attempts to use the [student] movement to save his own political career."[38]

How Zhao Ziyang might have used the students for his own political ends is not entirely clear. Nor is it clear that the students would have been willing to support Zhao even if he had proved bold enough to call upon them to do so. Popular perceptions of Zhao were little more favorable than those of Deng Xiaoping and Li Peng. Indeed, Zhao, even more than Deng and Li, was seen as the personification of the corruption and nepotism that pervaded the post-Mao regime. Adding to his burdens was the fact that he was the principal author of the economic policies that had brought such great hardships to the people. It was not until his pathetic appearance in Tiananmen Square in the early morning hours of May 19 that his popular image was transformed—and subsequently beatified.

Yet whatever Zhao's original political motives may have been, he was the only major Communist leader who consistently advocated settling the crisis through dialogue and compromise. And he was one of the few higher Party officials who remained steadfast in his opposition to Deng's insistence on declaring martial law and employing military force. Even though many Communist leaders had little taste for Deng's methods, few had the courage to express their doubts and reservations.

But Zhao was incapable of organizing any real political challenge

---

[37] According to articles of late May in *Ming Bao* (Hong Kong). Summary in "Quarterly Chronicle and Documentation," *The China Quarterly*, No. 119 (September 1989), pp. 697–99.
[38] Geremie Barmé, "Beijing Days, Beijing Nights," pp. 48–49.

to Deng, and not just because Deng had the support of the Army. Accustomed to operating within the rules and confines of a Leninist Party organization behind closed doors, Zhao could not seriously entertain the idea of enlisting the support of the non-Party masses, or even masses of students, in an intra-Party political struggle. And it was no doubt difficult emotionally, indeed probably psychologically impossible, for Zhao openly to confront his longtime mentor and patron. It was thus that Zhao had publicly revealed, in his televised meeting with Gorbachev on May 16, that Chinese Party leaders had secretly agreed that all important decisions were to be made by the presumably retired Deng Xiaoping. "Since the Thirteenth Party Congress [1987], we have always reported to Comrade Deng Xiaoping and asked for his advice while dealing with the most important issues," Zhao informed the Soviet leader.[39]

Zhao's comment was to be added to the charges the Party brought against him. It was to be cited as an example of how he had "supported the turmoil and split the Party."[40] For he had implied on May 16 that it was Deng Xiaoping who was ultimately responsible for the regime's refusal to negotiate with the students to bring a peaceful end to the crisis, thus "deliberately directing the fire of criticism" at Deng. But there was yet another implication in Zhao's revelation of this not too well-hidden Party secret. In publicly stating that Deng was the ultimate source of authority in China, Zhao was also acknowledging that this was a fact of Chinese political life to which he had resigned himself. It was more an admission (or at least a premonition) of defeat than a challenge.

Zhao Ziyang was last seen in public during the early morning hours of May 19 wandering among the students in Tiananmen Square, making apologies and apparently seeking forgiveness. He did not attend the meeting convened late that night by the Party Central Committee and the State Council which authorized martial law. Ap-

---

[39] For a discussion of the impact of Zhao's comment, see Feigon, p. 203. For contemporary accounts of Gorbachev's visit, see Bill Keller, "Soviets and China Resuming Normal Ties After 30 Years," *The New York Times*, May 17, 1989, pp. A1, A8; and Bill Keller, "Gorbachev Praises The Students," *NYT*, May 18, 1989, pp. A1, A10.

[40] "Communiqué of the Fourth Plenary Session of the 13th CCP Central Committee" (June 24, 1989), text in "Quarterly Chronicle and Documentation," *The China Quarterly*, No. 119 (September 1989), pp. 729–31.

parently placed under house arrest on May 19 or shortly thereafter, Zhao was formally dismissed as Secretary-General of the Party in late June when the Central Committee approved a Politburo report prepared by Li Peng detailing Zhao's "mistakes" during "the anti-Party, antisocialism turmoil," as the Democracy Movement came to be officially branded.[41] Zhao Ziyang was a victim of both his political ambitions and his comparative lack of political ruthlessness.

MARTIAL LAW

Deng Xiaoping's demand that martial law be declared, which Zhao Ziyang refused to endorse, was taken up with relish by Premier Li Peng on May 19. The day before, on May 18, Li Peng had held a "dialogue" with student leaders in a vain attempt to demonstrate that the government was willing to go to all reasonable lengths to settle the crisis. The fruitless session, portions of which were televised that evening, had been acrimonious and Li Peng had appeared awkward. Now, at the late night meeting of Party and state bureaucrats on May 19, Li found himself in more comfortable and familiar surroundings. Taking the place of the absent Zhao Ziyang, he warned the assembled officials that the "anarchic state" in the capital was "going from bad to worse." He vowed to "take resolute and decisive measures to put an end to the turmoil."[42] Those measures included a declaration of martial law in Beijing, effective at 10 a.m. on May 20, as late night television viewers learned. They also learned—from President Yang Shangkun, one of the members of the Gang of Old who followed Li Peng on the TV screen—that PLA troops would soon arrive in the capital.

In accordance with Li Peng's State Council directive, the formal martial law orders, covering key districts of Beijing, were issued by Mayor Chen Xitong on May 20.[43] Prohibited, among other things,

[41] Ibid., p. 729.

[42] "Speech by Li Peng, delivered on behalf of the CCP Central Committee and the State Council," text in "Quarterly Chronicle and Documentation," *The China Quarterly*, No. 119 (September 1989), pp. 719–23.

[43] There were three martial law orders, the second and third applying to foreigners and journalists, respectively. For the texts, see "Quarterly Chronicle and Documentation," *The China Quarterly*, No. 119 (September 1989), pp. 723–24.

were marches and demonstrations, speeches, student strikes, worker strikes, the distribution of leaflets, and any incitement to "social unrest." To enforce these prohibitions, it was stated that "public security personnel, armed police units, and PLA personnel" were authorized "to adopt any means to forcefully handle matters." Within a few days more than 100,000 PLA soldiers had surrounded Beijing.

The first reaction of the people of Beijing to martial law was to defy the authorities angrily. Students, who had suspended the hunger strike shortly before Li Peng's speech on the night of May 19, now resumed fasting. Hundreds of thousands of workers and other citizens poured into the streets, many marching toward Tiananmen Square in defiance of martial law regulations. Factories were closed and public transportation came to a halt as many citizens began to erect barricades at key intersections to protect the students from the anticipated military assault. Stones, bricks, and concrete blocks, along with trucks and overturned buses, were brought to the suburbs to block the access roads to the city. All over the city, neighborhood groups spontaneously organized in opposition to the martial law regime. More than 300 motorcycles, mostly belonging to youthful small entrepreneurs, were employed in a "Flying Tiger Brigade" to report on troop movements and to coordinate activities of students and citizens. Pedicab drivers organized an ambulance system to convey the wounded to hospitals.

On Sunday, May 21, more than a million people gathered in Tiananmen Square to protest martial law and reaffirm their support for the students. On May 22 it was noted that journalists and well-known literary figures were prominent among the 100,000 people who marched through the streets of the capital in defiance of the government. And on May 23, four days after the declaration of martial law, it was estimated that a million people again demonstrated in the center of Beijing. Elsewhere in the city, citizens were blocking military vehicles and erecting barricades.

If the people of Beijing were united, China's Communist leaders were not. The National People's Congress, theoretically the highest organ of state power, customarily was a docile instrument of the Communist Party. Now its Standing Committee declared its support for the student movement and its opposition to martial law. A telegram was sent to Wan Li, Chairman of the NPC and a high-ranking Party leader, then on an official visit to Canada and the United States. Wan Li, who had issued a statement praising "the patriotic enthusiasm of the young people in China," was asked to return to China immediately, hopefully to convene a meeting of the Congress that would rescind martial law and remove Li Peng as Premier of the State Council, a body formally elected by the Congress.

There was also dissent in the military. On May 21 seven prestigious retired PLA leaders, including former Minister of Defense Zhang Aiping and Navy commander Ye Fei, wrote an open letter to Deng Xiaoping, addressing Deng in his capacity as Chairman of the Party's Central Military Commission. "The People's Army belongs to the people," they reminded China's paramount leader. "It cannot stand in opposition to the people, much less oppress the people, and it absolutely cannot open fire on the people and create a blood-shedding incident. In order to prevent further worsening of the situation, troops should not enter the city."[44] The letter was suggestive of the PLA's old revolutionary traditions, and when it was read over the loudspeakers in Tiananmen Square on May 22, it brought forth tearful cheers from the youthful demonstrators. Elsewhere in the city, students and other activists who encountered PLA units in the streets lectured young soldiers on the responsibilities of membership in a "people's army," brought water to fill their canteens, and invited them to join in singing revolutionary songs. The bewildered soldiers who first entered the city were clearly unprepared to use force against civilians; there was, in fact, considerable fraternization between the soldiers and the people of Beijing. In the early morning hours of May 24, four days after the declaration of martial law, most troops were ordered to withdraw from the capital.

During the last two weeks of May, the people of Beijing were in a virtual state of insurrection, although a uniquely nonviolent one. Martial law was first defied by many citizens and then ignored by all. The government, having long before squandered its moral authority, appeared to be losing control over its apparatus of physical

---

[44] The other five signatories were Yang Dezhi, former head of the PLA General Staff; Song Shilun, a celebrated hero of the Korean War and former president of the PLA Military Academy; Xiao Ke, former Deputy Minister of Defense; Chen Zaido, a former PLA commander; and Li Jukui, former political commissar of the PLA Logistics Department. For the main portion of the text, see *Far Eastern Economic Review*, June 1, 1989, p. 14.

force as well. PLA commanders and soldiers clearly were reluctant to use military force against unarmed civilians. And even members of the secret police and Beijing's elite security organs had openly participated in antigovernment demonstrations.

The Democracy Movement not only was seemingly triumphant in Beijing but was also rapidly spreading through much of the country (if not necessarily the countryside), from cities in Manchuria in the Northeast to the Southwest. In Canton more than a half million people marched in support of the Beijing students on May 24, stimulated in part by a gigantic demonstration of a million people in once politically apathetic Hong Kong. On May 25 demonstrations and marches took place in cities all across the land. It was widely assumed by political observers at the time that Deng Xiaoping would be forced to oust Premier Li Peng, whose martial law decree had been rendered null and void by the citizens of Beijing. It was also widely assumed that Deng would be compelled to recall Zhao Ziyang, the only political leader capable of peacefully resolving the deepening crisis, a move which, in turn, would finally have removed Deng from any position of real influence.[45]

Such was not to be the case. While the people of Beijing were valiantly defying martial law, Deng Xiaoping was gathering the military and political forces to suppress the popular insurrection. Shortly after the declaration of martial law, Deng summoned key PLA generals to a meeting in Wuhan to plan the repression. On May 24, the young soldiers of the 38th Army were replaced by the older and more professionalized soldiers of the 27th Army. The troops of the 27th Army, kept isolated from news reports and told that hooligans and counterrevolutionaries were assaulting soldiers in Beijing, were not to prove hesitant to fire on civilians to put down what they were told was a "counterrevolutionary rebellion."

As PLA armies obedient to Deng's commands were being positioned near the capital, Deng also demanded that each of the seven military regions into which China was divided declare support for Li Peng and for martial law. The last to do so, and with apparent reluctance, was the Beijing Military Region, on May 26. Although deemed a matter of lesser importance, similar oaths of loyalty to the

---

[45] For example, Robert Delfs in the *Far Eastern Economic Review*, June 1, 1989, p. 14.

Li Peng regime and its policies were demanded of—and received from—civilian administrations in each of China's provinces.

The last faint hope for a viable political alternative to the Dengist dictatorship rested with National People's Congress Chairman Wan Li, a longtime political ally of both Deng Xiaoping and Zhao Ziyang. While visiting Canada and the United States, Wan Li had expressed sympathy for the student movement and opposition to martial law. He had cut short his stay in the United States and returned to China on May 24, his plane landing in Shanghai rather than Beijing. On May 27, Wan Li capitulated before Deng's politico-military onslaught, issuing a statement supporting the May 20 martial law speeches of Li Peng and Yang Shangkun and delaying until June 20 a meeting of the NPC Standing Committee. This ensured that the NPC would remain what it always had been— a "parliament" that formalized the decisions of Communist Party leaders. The forty members of the NPC Standing Committee who had bravely taken the unprecedented step of petitioning for an emergency meeting of the body were left to the mercies of Li Peng and Deng Xiaoping.

By the last days of May, Deng Xiaoping had consolidated dictatorial control over China's key political and military organs, a hold which had seemed tenuous only a week before. More than 200,000 troops loyal to the paramount leader now surrounded Beijing. It was the first time since 1949 that PLA main force units had been dispatched to the capital, previously the exclusive domain of the Beijing garrison and elite military units designated to protect top Communist leaders.[46]

THE LAST DAYS OF THE STUDENT MOVEMENT

The Beijing student groups, the organizational heart of the Democracy Movement, rapidly disintegrated in the days following the declaration of martial law on May 20. The decision to resume the hunger strike was soon reversed. To be sure, Beijing students participated in the massive popular protests of May 20–23, when millions of cit-

[46] The purpose, of course, was to ensure that "the Party controlled the gun," which is to say, to minimize the possibility of any military coup.

izens marched and demonstrated in defiance of the martial law regime. The municipal police having disappeared from the scene, students directed traffic and generally helped to keep order. But the leaders of the student movement, having placed their faith in non-violent methods and in the force of moral example, were psychologically as well as physically unprepared for a bloody confrontation with Communist authorities. From the beginning of the movement, they had held out the hope that the existing regime could be democratized, and they felt a moral responsibility to protect their fellow students from state violence. That the government would employ military force against students who were not only fiercely patriotic to the nation but also mostly loyal to the Communist Party had once seemed inconceivable. But it now appeared imminent.

Thus most student leaders, and especially the eloquent Wuer Kaixi, chairman of the Beijing Students' Federation, advised leaving the square. Some spoke of the need for time to reassess theory and tactics, perhaps to educate and organize the people for a long-term democratic struggle. Other leaders felt that abandoning Tiananmen Square, and all the symbolism the departure would entail, would be to condemn the entire Democracy Movement to historical irrelevance—and to condemn China to many more decades of dictatorship. Such was the view of Chai Ling, who had inspired the hunger strike and who now declared that "our presence here and now at the Square is our last and only truth." She awaited "the spilling of blood," for "only when the government descends to the depths of depravity and decides to deal with us by slaughtering us, only when rivers of blood flow in the Square, will the eyes of our country's people truly be opened, and only then will they unite."[47]

Few students shared such apocalyptic visions. The occupants of the square rapidly dwindled during the last week in May as students returned to their campuses, many to participate in the broader citizens' movement that was developing throughout the city. The debate among the student leaders was short-lived. On May 27, Chai Ling joined Wuer Kaixi and Wang Dan in publicly announcing that the students would evacuate the square on May 30.

[47] "Excerpt from Interview with Chai Ling in late May (1989)," in Han Minzhu, *Cries for Democracy*, p. 327.

More to mark the end of the movement than as an attempt to revive it, students at the Central Academy of Fine Arts in Beijing hastily constructed a commemorative statue out of plaster and Styrofoam. The twenty-seven-foot "Goddess of Democracy" was fashioned in three days and three nights, and its various segments were transported by bicycle carts to Tiananmen Square on the night of May 29. It was assembled opposite the giant portrait of Mao Zedong in the early morning hours of May 30, in time for the ceremonies that were to mark the close of the student occupation of the square. For a moment, it briefly revived the movement as tens of thousands of people came to the square to see the statue. The moment was movingly described by a participant:

> Clearly following the image of the American Statue of Liberty, she is nevertheless definitely Chinese—not only her face and hair but even her expression and features. She looks young, brave, heroic and, inevitably, tragic. The ceremony was magnificent. There were about 100,000 people, and everything went off in good order. The police had again simply disappeared. Small pieces performed by students from the Central Drama Institute won thunderous applause, and the sound from official loudspeakers was drowned out by cheering and singing. It was an unforgettable experience to hear the immortal *Internationale* sung in unison by a sea of people including oneself—something quite different from shouting *The East Is Red* in the same place during the Cultural Revolution. Two decades ago it was all about "the great liberator, Chairman Mao"; today it is "No saviour from on high delivers!"[48]

By the end of May virtually all students from Beijing's universities had returned to their campuses. But thousands of students from universities outside of the capital remained in the square. It is estimated that some 200,000 students from some 400 colleges throughout the country had come to Beijing between May 16 and May 27 to demonstrate their support for the Democracy Movement.[49] Most had

[48] Lu Yuan, "Beijing Diary," pp. 7–8.
[49] *Ming Bao* (Hong Kong), May 29, 1989, in FBIS-CHI-89-102, p. 14.

returned to their homes before the end of May, very often with free train tickets the government was only too happy to provide. But some of the more politically committed were determined to stay long enough to record their contribution to the movement. Since they had no housing in the capital, they lived in Tiananmen Square, even though living conditions by late May had become less than inviting. As one participant recalled: "The Square, which even during the days of tightest student organization had resembled a makeshift encampment, now had degenerated into a shantytown, strewn with litter and permeated by the stench of garbage and overflowing portable toilets."[50]

The students from outside of Beijing had formed their own organizations, separate from the Beijing Students' Federation, whose leaders had decided it was premature to establish a national student union.[51] The non-Beijing students rejected the decision to evacuate the square on May 30 and instead, on May 29, conducted a vote on the issue of withdrawal. It was decided to remain in the square until June 20, when the Standing Committee of the National People's Congress was scheduled to meet. To preserve a facade of unity, the Beijing Students' Federation reluctantly agreed to support the decision, although very few of its members remained in the square after May 30.[52]

In the first days of June, Beijing was encircled by more than 200,000 PLA soldiers deployed in two rings around the capital. Other troops, outfitted "in full gear," the New China News Agency ominously reported, were stationed at the airport, the central railway station, and the telegraph building. In Tiananmen Square, only about 5,000 people remained, mostly students from colleges outside of Beijing. Unarmed and aimless, they awaited the arrival of Deng Xiaoping's armies. But the vital force of the Democracy Movement had now spread from the square in the center of the capital to the working-class neighborhoods located in the outskirts of the city.

[50] Han Minzhu, *Cries for Democracy*, p. 342.
[51] On the relations between Beijing and non-Beijing student groups in Tiananmen Square, see Josephine M. T. Khu, "Student Organization in the 1989 Chinese Democracy Movement," *Bulletin of Concerned Asian Scholars*, Vol. 22, No. 3 (July–September 1990), pp. 3–12.
[52] Ibid., pp. 9–10.

THE WORKING CLASS AND COMMUNE OF BEIJING

The solidarity of the people of Beijing during the last weeks of May and the early days of June 1989 has been compared by William Hinton to the heroic actions of the working people of Paris at the time of the Commune of 1871, immortalized in Karl Marx's *Civil War in France*.[53] Orville Schell, another eyewitness, was also moved to draw an analogy with the Paris Commune:

> The atmosphere [in the square] recalled Woodstock in its non-violence and sense of giddy liberation, and the Paris Commune in the conviction among the demonstrators that the "people" had finally risen up to secure the country's heartland from the forces of reaction.[54]

The analogy with the Paris Commune, while hardly exact, is not misleading and by no means undeserved. Rarely in modern history have the people of a large metropolis achieved so great a unity of spirit and action in time of crisis, organized themselves and their municipal affairs so spontaneously and effectively, and displayed such great heroism and self-sacrifice in defense of a besieged city. And the people of Beijing did so entirely on their own, without the assistance of a party, a government, or an army. Indeed, they did so in defiance of established political and military authority. The people of Beijing had no organization to direct them; they relied entirely on their own talent for self-organization.

Overt popular resistance to the Communist state that followed the martial law decree of May 20 marked a new and final phase in the Democracy Movement. The center of the political stage was now no longer occupied by students but rather by Beijing's ordinary "citizens" (*shimin*), as they had come to refer to themselves, especially the urban working class. The leaders of the Chinese Communist Party, who on occasion ritualistically claimed to represent the proletariat, feared workers far more than they did students. Workers could disrupt production—and profits; they numbered several hun-

---

[53] William Hinton, "Tiananmen Massacre," Goldberg Center lecture delivered at the University of Wisconsin-Madison, September 20, 1989.
[54] Schell, "China's Spring," p. 6.

dred million in contrast to the small elite of approximately 4 million college students; and once politically activated, they might not be inclined to adhere to nonviolent methods. Unlike students acting alone, the working class was a potentially revolutionary threat to the Communist regime. It did not go unnoticed, moreover, that many workers had been schooled in the trials of the Cultural Revolution, and possessed organizational skills and political values that clashed with the Deng regime's efforts to depoliticize society.

Unrest among the urban working class, which found expression in strikes and especially slowdowns, had been growing since 1987 as inflation began to erode the gains in wages and living standards made earlier in the decade. For workers in the late 1980s, Deng Xiaoping's economic reforms had come to mean inflation, tighter labor discipline and stricter factory work rules, growing job insecurity, and sometimes unemployment as workforces were reduced, especially as some smaller state enterprises began to be contracted out to private entrepreneurs. State workers, members of China's "labor aristocracy," were angered by increasingly shrill demands of the reformers to "smash the iron rice bowl." And all workers, in factories and offices, both state and nonstate employees, were adversely affected by the government's austerity policies adopted in the autumn of 1988.

Workers thus joined the Democracy Movement not as champions of market reforms but rather more in protest against the consequences of those reforms. In this they differed from democratic intellectuals who called for a more rapid pace of market reform—and probably from most student activists, who generally followed the lead of older intellectuals, vaguely linking economic reform with democratic political change.

What brought workers and students together, however, was a common desire for democracy. To workers, "democracy" meant less a particular form of government than freedom from the bureaucratic tentacles that enveloped their daily lives. The Australian scholar Anita Chan, noting the demeaning oppressiveness of the work-unit (*danwei*) system, has insightfully described what the word "democracy" signified to most citizens in 1989:

In April and May, when the residents of Beijing and other cities throughout China overcame their fears and poured into the streets in a vast sea that swept aside the forces of authority, they experienced an exhilaration of release, what they called *jiefang*, liberation. Some years ago, when I conducted interviews for a book on the Cultural Revolution, again and again people remembered having felt that same heady sense of "liberation" in 1966–67 when they had first joined colleagues in casting free from subservience to their work-unit leadership.[55]

Even more potent than the yearning for democracy that brought workers to the student-initiated movement was a moral revulsion against the pervasive corruption of the Deng regime. "Corruption," as the term was used at the time, meant something more than the usual bribes, backdoor dealings, and other customary kinds of bureaucratic malfeasance. "Corruption" now conveyed a moral condemnation of the whole system of bureaucratic privilege and power. It was a system that essentially had been inherited from the Mao period. But now that Communist leaders, high and low, were so deeply enmeshed in profiteering in the presumably "free" marketplace, they had gone well beyond the bounds of politico-ethical legitimacy in popular perceptions. The use of political power for private gain was viewed as unfair and unjust, and it inflamed slumbering resentments against bureaucratic privilege. Symbolic of bureaucratic immorality, in the eyes of workers, were the lucrative capitalist activities of the offspring and relatives of high Party officials who, as it happened, were indulging in ostentatious consumption at the very time that living standards for many workers and other ordinary citizens were falling.

These popular resentments against bureaucratic profiteering and privilege found expression in the leaflets and short manifestos produced by workers during the Democracy Movement. As early as April 20, five days after the death of Hu Yaobang, a handbill distributed in the streets of Beijing by an embryonic workers' group requested that the Party Central Committee respond to ten questions. Among them:

How much money has Deng Pufang [Deng Xiaoping's son] spent placing bets at the horse races in Hong Kong? Where did this

---

[55] Anita Chan, "China's Long Winter," *Monthly Review*, Vol. 41, No. 8 (January 1990), p. 11.

money come from? Do Mr. and Mrs. Zhao Ziyang pay the golfing fees when they play every week [at an expensive Japanese-managed course near Beijing]? Where does the money for the fees come from? How many houses and palatial retreats do Central Committee leaders have scattered across the country? What are the rates of their material consumption and expenditure? May these figures be made public?[56]

Typical of radical workers' literature of the time, and reflective of growing popular anger and militancy, was a treatise that appeared in mid-May. It read, in part:

The tyranny of the corrupt officials is nothing short of extreme! . . . There is no reactionary force, however, that can stem the tide of the Chinese people's rage. The people will no longer believe the lies of the authorities, for on our banners appear the words: science, democracy, freedom, human rights, and rule by law. . . . We have conscientiously documented the exploitation of the workers. The method of [understanding] exploitation is based on the method for analysis given in Marx's *Das Kapital*. . . . We were astonished to find that the "people's public servants" have devoured all surplus value created by the people's blood and sweat. The total value of this exploitation comes to an amount unmatched in history! Such ruthlessness and replete with "Chinese characteristics"![57] These "people's public servants" have used the blood and sweat of the people to build palatial retreats all over China (guarded by soldiers and labelled as "restricted military zones"); to buy foreign luxury vehicles; and to go abroad on pleasure trips with their children, and even with the children's nannies! . . . The first group to be investigated with regard to their material consumption and use of palatial retreats should include: Deng Xiaoping, Zhao Ziyang, Li Peng, Chen Yun, Li Xiannian, Yang Shangkun, Peng Zhen, Wan Li, Jiang Zemin, Ye Xuanping, and their family

56 Beijing Workers' Union, "Ten Questions," in Han Minzhu, *Cries for Democracy*, pp. 277–78.
57 A bitterly satirical reference to the official ideological formula of "socialism with Chinese characteristics."

members. Their assets should immediately be frozen and subjected to the scrutiny of a National People's Investigative Committee. . . . The people have acquired [political] consciousness!
They have recognized [that] there are only two classes: the rulers and the ruled . . . [and that] the political movements of the
last forty years have served simply as [a] political means of
oppressing the people."[58]

Most workers were sympathetic to the students and their democratic strivings from the beginning of the movement, but what struck
particularly responsive chords among workers and other citizens were
the condemnations of official corruption, especially the demand that
Party leaders and their children make public their incomes and
assets.

The popular determination to root out official profiteering was
intimately related to the demand for democracy. For democratization
was the only real antidote to bureaucratic corruption. But it was not
the case, as Western admirers of China's market reforms never tire
of repeating, that a profound contradiction exists between Deng Xiaoping's "progressive" (i.e., capitalist) economic reforms and China's
retrogressive Stalinist political regime. Indeed, the bureaucratic capitalist regime that emerged from Deng's reforms not only was compatible with a Stalinist-type regime but required it, or at least an
authoritarian political structure very much like it. The Democracy
Movement threatened the economic as well as the political power of
the bureaucracy, especially when the working class became part of
the movement.

Workers had expressed moral support for the students earlier, but
it was only on May 17 that they physically joined the movement en
masse. On that extraordinary day more than a million citizens
marched in downtown Beijing toward the Gate of Heavenly Peace in
support of the hunger strikers. Workers stood out among the demonstrators, as reporters from the *People's Daily* observed:

[58] Beijing Workers' Union, "Notice to All Chinese Compatriots" (May 17, 1989), in Han Minzhu, *Cries for Democracy*, pp. 274–77. For a sampling of workers' letters and declarations
during the Democracy Movement, see also Yu and Harrison, *Voices from Tiananmen Square*,
pp. 107–20.

As of 6:30 in the evening, group after group of workers continued to march along eastern Changan Avenue toward Tiananmen
Square. "Beijing Automobile Manufacturing Company," "Beijing Printing and Dyeing Factory," "Beijing Crane Factory,"
"Beijing Internal Combustion Engine Main Factory," "Capital
Iron and Steel Company" . . . the workers prominently displayed their factories' names and shouted out their heartfelt
feelings: "We Workers Have Come!" "Salute the Students!" The
workers had just come off their shifts; without time to change
their clothes, they rushed to join the demonstrators marching
in support of the students.

Along North Chongwenmen Avenue, workers from the Beijing Coking Factory got out of their factory buses, unfurled their
banners, and set out their placards, quickly forming a contin-
gent of marchers. They had returned to the city from their factory, some fifteen kilometers away in the suburbs, and without
first going home or having dinner, they marched, shouting slogans, toward Tiananmen Square.[59]

Thus students could justly claim, as they did in their fruitless
dialogue with Prime Minister Li Peng on May 18, that the student
movement had become a "people's movement," which the government
could no longer ignore. Yet over the preceding month, student leaders
had not always sought the participation of "the people," and especially not of the urban working class. In demonstrations in Beijing
and elsewhere, student groups typically marched with arms linked to
form perimeters, literally keeping workers and other citizens at arm's
length.

This partial self-isolation reflected the romantic desire of some
students to preserve the moral "purity" of a self-sacrificing and nonviolent student movement.[60] In larger part, it was a calculated tactical
decision on the part of student leaders who hoped to influence the
factional struggles within the Communist Party—and who hoped, ultimately, to win the approval of the Party. The participation of work-

[59] "History Will Remember This Day" (collective report of *People's Daily* reporters, May 17,
1989), in Han Minzhu, *Cries for Democracy*, p. 228.
[60] Such is said to have been the view of Chai Ling, who was known as "Commander-in-
Chief" of the student occupation of the square during the hunger strike. Ibid., p. 280.

ers, the students knew, would be seen by the government as an intolerable political threat, and would quash such possibilities as there were for a peaceful compromise. Students believed that workers were less disciplined than themselves, and the government played on this prejudice, repeatedly warning that the participation of nonstudents in the movement would bring social disorder and increase the likelihood of violence.

Social class biases which students learned from their intellectual mentors also no doubt played a part. China's contemporary intellectuals, with some notable exceptions, have been notorious for their elitism, one expression of which in the 1980s was a lack of interest in the plight of social groups other than their own. As one observer wrote at the close of the decade: "If one sifts carefully through the writings of Chinese intellectuals of all persuasions of the past few years, one is hard pressed to find any mention of working-class grievances." Instead, most of what intellectuals had to say about the urban working class was a loud "chorus of complaints that workers were making more money than themselves."[61] There was thus little reason for the leaders of the Beijing regime to fear a Chinese variant of Poland's Solidarity movement, at least as far as intellectuals were concerned.

Students did not necessarily share all the biases of older intellectuals. But their ambivalent attitudes toward the working class yielded policies and tactics that made the Democracy Movement far less of a popular movement than it might otherwise have become. Workers were not unaware of the class prejudice, and it inhibited their actions. One participant in the Democracy Movement in the industrial city of Chongqing recalled:

> The workers could see that participation was being strictly restricted by the students themselves, as if the workers were not qualified to participate. And from the news on television, accusing workers of spreading rumors, etc., it seemed that workers were being specifically targeted by the authorities. They could see that the sentences imposed against working-class people

---

[61] Chan, "China's Long Winter," p. 5. Earlier in the decade there had been a similar chorus of complaints about the assumed enrichment of the peasantry.

were particularly heavy. Moreover, in Beijing the issues that the students raised had nothing to do with the workers. For example, Wuer Kaixi in his speeches only talked about the students. If he had mentioned the workers as well, appealed to the workers, appealed to them in a sincere manner, the workers might really have come out in a major way.[62]

Despite the proclivity of some youthful student leaders to ignore "the lower classes," workers and other ordinary citizens did in fact come forth in substantial (if not necessarily overwhelming) numbers to support the students—and then to protect them. And from mid-May on, most students enthusiastically welcomed their support.

Workers not only marched by the hundreds of thousands in the massive demonstrations in the capital on May 17–18; they also established their own organizations. The Beijing Workers' Union was organized in April, and the Beijing Workers' Autonomous Union was founded in mid-May, followed shortly by the Capital Workers' Autonomous Union. The latter set up its headquarters in a tent pitched in the northeastern corner of Tiananmen Square, from whose peak flew their own banner. All of these hastily organized groups issued fiery manifestos, vowing to protect the students by preventing the Army from entering the city, and at the same time pledged to advance the class interests of the workers in opposition to a despotic state.

The new workers' unions were established by small groups of activist workers, some of whom were veterans of the battles of the Cultural Revolution. They could not claim a broad base of mass support, although support may well have been forthcoming in time. But the mere existence of illegal worker organizations distributing leaflets calling for a general strike was enough to alarm the government. Indeed, it was more alarming than any student movement could ever be. The organization of independent unions, however tiny their memberships, and the spontaneous outpouring of workers in the May 17–

---

[62] The statement was made by "Hou," an activist in the Democracy Movement in Chongqing who fled to Hong Kong after June 4, in an interview with two well-known Australian scholars. "Hou" was the son of a poor working-class family who had become a successful private entrepreneur. Anita Chan and Jonathan Unger, "Voices from the Protest Movement in Chongqing: Class Accents and Class Tensions," in Unger, *The Pro-Democracy Protests in China*, p. 120.

18 demonstrations were the crucial factors in the Party's fateful decision to impose martial law.

The effect of the martial law decree was precisely the opposite of what the regime anticipated. Instead of cowing demonstrators into submission and establishing "order" in the capital, the government's resort to military force angered and politically activated the citizens of Beijing, generating outrage more than fear. The people's response to Premier Li Peng's martial law proclamation on the night of May 19 was described by one participant as follows:

> Residents young and old swarmed onto the streets to block army trucks, tanks, and armored personnel carriers. Surrounded by thousands of peaceful but determined citizens, the convoys full of armed soldiers stalled, unable to move forward or turn back. In some cases, they were able to advance to within the city's perimeters before running into the human blockades; in others, they were stopped far away from Tiananmen in outlying counties. As news that the army had ground to a halt filtered back to Tiananmen in the deep hours of the night, students there breathed sighs of relief; Tiananmen was evidently safe for the time being.[63]

A handbill distributed in the capital on May 20 by the newly organized Beijing Workers' Autonomous Union called for all workers to strike and also "to block troops from entering the city."[64] Although there were numerous work stoppages, there was no general strike. Nonetheless, many workers and other citizens came forth to block the advance of the Army. A cadre working in the Communist Party's Central Committee office passionately recorded the "May 20 Incident":

> The army's trucks, tanks, and armored personnel carriers have been kept in the suburbs by public buses and garbage cans, and other objects used as roadblocks, and by people who are

[63] Han Minzhu, *Cries for Democracy*, p. 258.
[64] "Beijing Workers' Autonomous Union Preparatory Office Public Notice (No. 1)" (May 20, 1989), in ibid., p. 273.

willing to let their bodies—bodies made of flesh and blood—
be crushed by the tanks. The martial law that Li Peng and his
gang has issued has thus far been rendered as useless as a
blank sheet of paper. The soldiers are being persuaded by excited people and students; some of the persuaders are choking
with sobs, while some soldiers shed tears in return. Quite a
number of soldiers have driven their trucks away.[65]

Massive popular demonstrations, defiantly protesting martial law,
continued for three days. By Tuesday, May 23, most Army units had
retreated from Beijing, some taking up positions on the outskirts of
the city. They were soon to be replaced, as we have noted, by troops
less reluctant to fire on unarmed civilians.

In the days that followed, workers remained determined to defend
the students in Tiananmen Square—and to defend the city. Indeed,
their efforts intensified and became increasingly well organized in
anticipation of new government orders to the PLA to enforce martial
law. Many of the students who had left the square to return to their
campuses joined workers in mobilizing citizens throughout the city.
Millions of leaflets were distributed, big character posters covered
walls, and passionate speeches were delivered on street corners urging citizens to defend the routes into the city. Buses and heavy trucks
were parked across key intersections (usually with the cooperation of
their drivers) to barricade the roadways the PLA would have to take
to reach the center of the capital, and similar barriers were erected
along streets surrounding Tiananmen Square.

It was believed that the Army would strike after dark, probably
between midnight and 5 a.m. Thus workers and students organized
bicycle brigades to quietly patrol the streets at night, ready to alert
sleeping citizens to danger, and to summon them to come to the
defense of the city. Their daytime and early evening equivalent was
the "Flying Tiger Brigade," who roared through the city streets on
motorcycles, reporting suspicious troop movements and conveying
messages from neighborhood to neighborhood.

Over much of Beijing, governmental authority had vanished. City
police were nowhere to be seen, and so workers and students directed

[65] "The Heroic People" (May 21, 1989), in ibid., pp. 267–68.

traffic and assumed general responsibility for maintaining public order. Public transportation came to a halt, many of the city's buses having been pressed into service as street barriers against the anticipated advance of the Army. Workers cut off the power supply of Beijing's subway, for fear that it might be used by troops for a surprise assault on the square through the Qianmen station, located at the southeast corner of Tiananmen Square. Workers' unions vowed to guarantee the transportation of food and other daily necessities to and around the city, although the existing system of distribution continued to function without serious disruption.

More nebulous, but perhaps more important, were the eminently *political* feelings of solidarity, camaraderie, and independence that grew among several million people involved in the resistance movement in Beijing. During the last weeks and days of the Democracy Movement, the streets were filled with ordinary people engaged in animated discussion, exchanging news, freely expressing opinions, and candidly arguing about politics in public places. It was as if the state and its police forces did not exist, as almost seemed to be the case in Beijing in late May. People, in the capital and elsewhere, began to reject their state-designated status as members of "the masses" and began to refer to themselves as *shimin*, literally "city people," a term that was beginning to take on the meaning of a free citizen who existed independently of, and indeed prior to, the state.[66] Just as students, and then worker activists, had established organizations during the Democracy Movement that claimed an "autonomous" (*zizhi*, literally "self-ruling") status in relationship to the state, so now ordinary people who became involved in the movement yearned for an autonomous society, freed from the oppressions of the bureaucratic state.

During those heroic last days of May and the first days of June, the unarmed working people of besieged Beijing demonstrated that their organizational skills, their sense of social discipline, and their extraordinary physical and moral courage more than matched the qualities of the students in the early phases of the Democracy Move-

[66] For a most insightful discussion of the social and political implications of the term *shimin* as it entered the common vocabulary during this time, see Jonathan Unger's "Introduction" to his *The Pro-Democracy Protests in China*, esp. pp. 4–7.

ment. One can only speculate what social and political fruits this entirely spontaneous and self-organized movement might have yielded had it not been strangled in embryo by military forces under the command of Deng Xiaoping.

THE MASSACRE

In the last days of May it appeared that the Communist state had virtually ceased to function, at least in Beijing. But the appearance was deceptive. The regime's organs of repression, especially its myriad secret police agencies, remained intact and performed their intended role, albeit quietly. As Liu Binyan observed:

> The people's government used all the means available to watch over and investigate its own people. There were often a few thousand plainclothes police working in Tiananmen Square. In Beijing hotels, on Changan Avenue, or in the square, countless undercover agents used disguises as well as video cameras to record people's activities. All the active members of the movement were followed. Officials secretly searched their residences, stole their means of transportation, and used all available means to threaten them. . . . In late May, just when the army troops were going to use tear gas to disperse students and people in Beijing, the Beijing Department Store was ordered not to sell towels and gauze masks to anyone who looked like a student.[67]

On May 30 the secret police made their public reappearance, arresting three leaders of the Capital Workers' Autonomous Union, the embryonic labor organization that had established its headquarters in Tiananmen Square. The incident, which resembled a kidnapping more than an arrest, was a harbinger of the general repression that was soon to come, and it foretold that the weight of state repression would fall even more heavily on workers than on students.

It is remarkable that it took the Communist regime a full two weeks to enforce the martial law decree that formally had gone into effect on May 20. Over those weeks the regime seemed like a helpless

[67] Liu Binyan et al., *Tell the World*, pp. 55–56.

giant, ponderously stumbling from one blunder to another, allowing the popular movement to grow and become semi-organized.

It was not that the authorities were unprepared for rebelliousness among the masses. Fearful that market reforms in cities might generate social unrest, in 1983 Deng Xiaoping ordered the creation of a 400,000-man People's Armed Police to strengthen internal security. The new force was trained in the latest anti-riot and crowd-control techniques, eclectically borrowing equipment and tactics from the United States, Poland, South Africa, and Germany. Several units were sent to Poland for anti-riot training, and the People's Armed Police kept American helicopters and electric cattle prods in its arsenal. Some of these imported instruments and techniques had been tested in China—against peasant demonstrators in several northern provinces in 1988 and in the brutal suppression of Tibetan dissenters in March 1989.[68]

The semi-paralysis of the regime during the last days in May was not due to any lack of organized forces of violence prepared to carry out the regime's orders. The problem, rather, stemmed from divisions over power and tactics among China's ruling elites.

Deng Xiaoping, increasingly the target of popular ridicule and scorn, was convinced that only a massive display of force could end the "chaos" in the capital. In this he had the firm support of only the Gang of Old and the always-compliant Li Peng. The opposition to Deng was not confined to his erstwhile disciple, Party chief Zhao Ziyang, whose unforgivable sin was to publicly reveal that there was a split among Party leaders. While Zhao was the only member of the Politburo's Standing Committee to vote formally against martial law, most other members (while preserving a façade of unity and Leninist discipline) were less than enthusiastic about the resort to military force.

It was more than a generational difference, as we have seen. On May 21, a group of retired PLA luminaries had written an open letter to Deng opposing the dispatch of troops to Beijing.[69] And ninety-year-old Nie Rongzhen, the last survivor of the ten marshals of the

---

[68] For additional information on the post-Mao regime's interest in Western state-of-the-art methods of crowd control, see Chan, "China's Long Winter," pp. 6–7; and Roderick Mac-Farquhar, "The End of the Chinese Revolution," *The New York Review of Books*, July 20, 1989, p. 10.

[69] See p. 437 above.

once-revolutionary Red Army, also opposed the use of the PLA, assuring the students in Tiananmen Square that violence would never be used against them.[70]

For most Chinese, Party leaders and ordinary citizens alike, it seemed inconceivable that the People's Liberation Army would ever be ordered to fire on the people. This confidence seemed justified by the behavior of the troops of the 38th Army, the first to enter Beijing after the imposition of martial law on May 20. Blocked by masses of people and barricades, the soldiers retreated or simply sat in place. Some fraternized with students. The 38th Army was ordered to withdraw from the capital on May 23–24, its commanders dismissed by Deng Xiaoping, presumably for failing to order their troops to shoot their way into the city.

Deng now turned to the 27th Army, long commanded by Deng's old political ally, Yang Shangkun, prior to his reincarnation as a civilian leader and his ascension to the presidency of the People's Republic in 1987. In warlord-like fashion, the command then had been turned over to Yang's nephew. Largely composed of veteran soldiers from Sichuan, many of whom had taken part in the Chinese invasion of Vietnam in 1979, there was no doubt that the 27th Army would follow Deng's orders. However, the soldiers and their equipment had to be moved from their bases in Shijiazhuang and elsewhere, and this took the better part of two weeks. It was thus that the PLA attack on Beijing was delayed until the night of June 3.

It was as if foreign invaders were threatening China's capital. With the city surrounded by nearly 200,000 troops at the beginning of June, the unarmed citizens of Beijing had constructed barriers on the roads leading into the huge metropolis and at intersections near Tiananmen Square, where all major roads ultimately converged. Shortly after 6 p.m. on June 3, government radio and television stations broadcast emergency announcements warning residents to keep off

---

[70] Nie Rongzhen (1899–1992) had joined the Communist Party while a student in France in 1923, a year prior to Deng Xiaoping. A survivor of the Long March, he commanded the Communist armies that liberated Beijing and Tianjin in 1948. After 1949 he held various high military and civil posts, and after 1957 headed the commission that oversaw the development of China's atomic bomb.

the streets; the Army, it was said, could no longer tolerate disorder and would crush all resistance to martial law. In response, workers and other citizens, by the tens of thousands, rushed to fortify the barricades in the suburbs; others bicycled to the streets around the Gate of Heavenly Peace to defend the students who remained in the square. It was a collective and spontaneous act of enormous courage, perhaps facilitated by a lingering faith that in the end the "People's Army" would not fire on the people.

As dusk fell, some 40,000 troops, spearheaded by the tanks and armored personnel carriers, launched the invasion of the city, moving from both the eastern and western suburbs along the avenues that led to Tiananmen Square. In the densely populated residential districts in the eastern part of Beijing, huge crowds spilled into the streets, temporarily blocking the Army's advance. From the west, however, the PLA broke through one barricade after another along Fuxing Road, moving toward Tiananmen Square. In a valiant attempt to halt the Army, residents and students from all over the city rushed to the area around the Military Museum of the Chinese People's Revolution and the Muxidi district, about two miles west of the square. It was observed that the civilian reinforcements were "headed by a daredevil team of workers with clubs in hand."[71]

It was in the neighborhoods to the west of the square that the bloodiest battles of the night were fought and where the greatest number of the victims of the Beijing Massacre fell. They were mostly workers and other ordinary Beijing citizens (nameless in the historical records) who had come to the defense of the students—and to the defense of their city.

Around 10:30 p.m. troops of the 27th Army, backed by tanks and armored personnel carriers, opened fire on the unarmed civilians who had formed human barricades in the Muxidi and Xidan districts, less than two miles west of Tiananmen Square.[72] Shortly afterward, according to eyewitness accounts:

[71] Liu Binyan and Xu Gang, "Beijing's Unforgettable Spring," in Liu Binyan et al., *Tell the World*, p. 59.

[72] In the months and years since the Massacre, PLA officers have taken great pains to deny that they were involved in the affair or that they were responsible for the decision to open fire on the civilian defenders. According to the official PLA account, the decision was taken by an Army officer who was directing military operations from a helicopter flying above Fuxing and Fuxingmenwai streets. The officer remains unidentified. *China News Digest*, July 21, 1991, p. 3.

Blood was flowing and bodies were lying in the streets. Soldiers of the Twenty-seventh [Army] used light machine guns and semiautomatic weapons to shoot people in the street and in buildings on either side. Workers and residents coming to help saw a long line of armored vehicles coming from the west at full speed, and hurriedly retreated to the Xidan district. They used everything they could find, from bricks to trucks, to build roadblocks. A worker set fire to the four buses and two trucks that were lying in the middle of the road, shouting, "The People's Liberation Army does not kill the people!" and "Whoever suppresses the student movement will come to no good end!" The armed vehicles stopped. Soldiers jumped out. Suddenly the shouting of slogans stopped. For a few minutes there was dead silence. The people still hoped that the soldiers would use only tear gas or rubber bullets. But at one command, the soldiers raised their guns and fired one round at the residents and students, who fell to the ground. As soon as the gunshots stopped, other people rushed forward to rescue the wounded. The steps of a clinic near Xidan were already covered with blood. But the struggles at the intersections did not stop. Armored vehicles ran over roadblocks, knocked over cars and buses. The unarmed people had only bricks. . . . What they got back in return was bullets, a hail of bullets from machine guns and semiautomatics. People dispersed and ran for their lives. Soldiers ran after them, guns blazing. Even when residents ran into a courtyard or into the shrubbery, the soldiers would catch up with them and kill them.[73]

Similar indiscriminate killings were carried out by the troops invading from the east, as they eventually smashed through the barricades in the heavily populated residential districts near Jianguomen Street. The fighting was particularly intense on East Changan Avenue and adjacent streets, where students, workers, and other citizens were attempting to block the way to Tiananmen Square.

Once the shooting started, rage against the Army sometimes erupted in spontaneous acts of popular violence. Eyewitness accounts

[73] Liu Binyan and Xu Gang, "Beijing's Unforgettable Spring," pp. 59–60.

typically described incidents such as the following: "When after more than an hour the last truck of the convoy had passed by the Minzu Hotel, many hundreds of people (not only students) appeared on the street. They ran after the trucks and shouted protest slogans. A few stones were thrown. The soldiers opened fire with live ammunition. The crowd threw themselves on the ground, but quickly followed the convoy again. The more shots were fired, the more the crowd got determined and outraged. Suddenly they started singing the 'Internationale'; they armed themselves with stones and threw them towards the soldiers. There were also a few Molotov cocktails and the last truck was set on fire."[74]

After particularly cold-blooded killings of unarmed civilians, there were several incidents of soldiers pulled from vehicles and tanks and beaten to death by angry crowds. On the outskirts of Beijing, near Desheng Gate, troops abandoned their blocked vehicles and walked into the city. The entire convoy was then set afire by local residents. "Eighteen trucks and command cars were burning," William Hinton observed, "with flames forty or fifty feet in the air, fuel tanks exploding, and tires melting." The same fate soon befell a second convoy and, in the end, there were thirty-three burned-out vehicles at that one site.[75] The government was later to point to such episodes (distorting the context and chronology of events) as evidence that PLA gunfire was provoked by hooligans and violent counterrevolutionaries.

Even after PLA troops surrounded Tiananmen Square, many people continued to resist, no matter how dangerous and hopeless. A young scholar who vainly attempted to join the students in the square wandered in the streets around the Gate of Heavenly Peace in the early hours of June 4. She later recalled:

When I reached Xidan crossroads, the buses we had seen during the day were raging with flames. I abandoned my bicycle and joined the crowd that was still trying to stop the troops' advance. Thick smoke and tear gas were bringing tears to ev-

---

[74] Report of Amnesty International, August 30, 1989. Cited in John Gittings, *China Changes Face* (New York: Oxford University Press, 1990), pp. 283–84.

[75] William Hinton, *The Great Reversal* (New York: Monthly Review Press, 1990), p. 181.

eryone's eyes. I met F. who told me how the first tanks had crushed the barricades, knocking people off the tops of buses that soon caught fire. By now the way was clear for trucks to move east one by one, the slowness of their advance suggesting that there must be battles somewhere ahead. The whole city of Peking seemed in a state of outrage and extreme agitation. On the side-streets off Changan Avenue, thousands of us rhythmically shouted in the intervals between gunfire: "You animals!" "Li Peng—fascist!" and "Go on strike!" But the troops shot back, killing those who were not swift enough to squat down or move away or who simply took no heed of bullets. People were constantly falling to the ground and being taken to a nearby hospital, but the mood of indignation completely overwhelmed any feelings of fear.[76]

Popular resistance to the Army was heroic but futile in the absence of a military mutiny, about which there were many rumors at the time, but ones based more on hope than on fact. The soldiers had tanks, armored personnel carriers, and AK-47s; the workers were armed only with sticks, steel bars, stones, and Molotov cocktails; the students, for the most part, eschewed weapons of any sort, remaining true to their original vow of nonviolent protest.

The main PLA forces arrived at the Gate of Heavenly Peace shortly after midnight, leaving behind thousands of dead and wounded civilians along the now-bloodstained streets of the capital. Fewer than 5,000 students and others remained in the square, which the Army surrounded and sealed off by 1:30 a.m. Troops in tanks and armored personnel carriers established control over the northern part of the square, setting up loudspeakers that barked out military commands; all civilians were ordered to evacuate the square immediately, under threat of death. The students' own loudspeakers, in reply, played the "Internationale," a cry for liberation and freedom. The contrast between what was heard over the two loudspeaker systems summed up the difference between the two sides.

As soldiers poured into the northern part of the square, the students retreated to the steps around the Monument to the Heroes of

---

[76] Lu Yuan, "Beijing Diary," p. 16.

the Revolution, not far from the Mao Memorial Hall, which anchors the southern end of the square. Having composed their last wills, which they carried in their pockets, they vowed to retreat no further. Chai Ling, according to her later account, told the students that "only the sacrifice of our lives will suffice for the life of the republic." The students responded to her call for martyrdom by singing the "Internationale," "over and over again they sang it, hands clasped tightly together."[77]

The impending bloodbath was averted by the intervention of several highly respected celebrities who had begun a hunger strike in the square on June 2 in solidarity with the student vigil. They included the popular rock singer and composer Hou Dejian, a Taiwanese who had emigrated to the People's Republic in 1983, the literary critic Liu Xiaobo, and a leader of the Workers' Autonomous Union. After apparently having convinced most of the hungry and exhausted students that further sacrifices would be in vain, they negotiated with military commanders to allow for a peaceful student withdrawal from the square.[78] At 5 a.m. on Sunday, June 4, several thousand students, their tents burned or crushed, slowly began to file out of Tiananmen Square. PLA tanks menacingly followed. Chai Ling described the end of the student movement:

> As we went around Mao's mausoleum hand in hand, heading west from the south end of the Square, we saw a dark mass of some 10,000 helmeted soldiers seated at the southern side of the Monument. The students screamed at them, "Dogs!" "Fascists!" . . . We wanted to stick out our chests and march back to the Square. But all the residents stopped us. They said, "Children, do you know, they've set up machine guns, don't make any more sacrifices." So we could only continue heading toward the Xicheng district from Xidan. . . . The further north we went, the closer we got to our schools, the more citizens' eyes were filled with tears.[79]

[77] "I Am Chai Ling . . . I Am Still Alive" (tape of June 8, 1989), in Han Minzhu, *Cries for Democracy*, p. 364.
[78] Ibid.
[79] Ibid., pp. 364, 366. For a fuller, but less accurate, translation of Chai Ling's June 8 tape, see Yu and Harrison, *Voices from Tiananmen Square*, pp. 194–200.

There remains considerable controversy over what actually happened in Tiananmen Square in the early hours of June 4. The government claimed that no one was killed in the square proper. Chai Ling, among others, observed Army tanks flattening the tent headquarters of the Workers' Autonomous Union, killing twenty or more people.[80] A group of about a hundred students refused to leave the square at the negotiated time. Bursts of gunfire were heard shortly after the main body had departed around 5 a.m., and it is presumed that an undetermined number of those who chose to remain were killed. There are also various eyewitness accounts of brutal PLA killings of students in Tiananmen Square—although it must be noted that these mostly anonymous accounts are fragmentary and often contradictory, and even they do not support the greatly exaggerated reports of student exiles which tell of thousands slain by tanks and machine guns in the square.[81]

Whatever the actual number of deaths within the formal boundaries of the square (a perhaps morbidly scholastic but symbolically important matter), the number was relatively small in comparison with those killed in the streets around the square, where the casualties included workers and other citizens as well as students. And student casualties were far outnumbered by those suffered by workers and other Beijing residents, especially in the outlying working-class neighborhoods through which the Army had to pass to reach the city center. It was in these residential areas, far from the cameras and the minds of foreign news correspondents, that the greatest slaughters took place.

After the night of June 3–4, Beijing resembled a city occupied by a conquering army. Armed soldiers patrolled streets strewn with rubble, helicopter gunships hovered overhead, food and medicine were in short supply, most shops and offices were closed, and many buildings bore the marks of gunfire.

On my way home I couldn't believe my eyes. The streets were occupied with roadblocks and hundreds of burned-out vehicles.

[80] "I Am Chai Ling . . . ," p. 364.
[81] For a sampling of such accounts, see Yu and Harrison, *Voices from Tiananmen Square*, pp. 176–203.

Beijing, an ancient city of great cultural value, a city even the Kuomintang preferred to hand over in 1949 rather than see damaged, had become the ugly remains of a battleground.[82]

Scattered resistance to the PLA continued for several days. Military vehicles were set afire. New barricades were hastily erected by civilians and quickly torn down by soldiers. Demonstrations protesting the Massacre in Beijing erupted in dozens of cities across the land. From Tianjin in the North to Canton in the South, there were strikes, marches, and angry rallies; roads and bridges were blocked in some cities and railroad traffic disrupted. In Chengdu, students and workers once again clashed with armed police in several nights of violent rioting and looting; 300 civilians were reportedly killed. In Shanghai, a train killed six student demonstrators, provoking an outburst of violence that included the burning of the train. But in China's largest city, regional Party chief Jiang Zemin and especially Shanghai mayor Zhu Rongji managed to pacify striking workers and demonstrating students without resort to military force—although they did make use of monetary bribes. In Shanghai, as elsewhere, large-scale arrests of workers continued for weeks; most were accused of being common criminals and hooligans.[83]

In Beijing, resistance largely had ceased by June 7, in the face of the overwhelming military presence in the capital and mounting civilian casualties. The activities of the secret police became all-pervasive and mass arrests commenced. PLA troops and security agents took over government and Communist Party offices that had become politically suspect as centers of democratic activity, including the Central Party School and the Chinese Academy of Social Sciences.

It is estimated that some 40,000 people were arrested nationwide in the repression during the months of June and July. Thousands were jailed and probably hundreds were executed for participating in what was officially condemned as a "counterrevolutionary rebellion." Most of those arrested, and virtually all who were executed,

[82] Lu Yuan, "Beijing Diary," p. 18.
[83] Although the protests were nationwide, they varied enormously from place to place in form, scope, and intensity. For a sampling from different regions of the country, see Unger, *The Pro-Democracy Protests in China.*

were workers. With the obvious aim of terrorizing the population, it became a well-publicized policy to systematically subject arrested individuals to beatings and torture.

Students were treated with comparative leniency. Except for the main leaders of the movement, whose twenty-one names appeared on a widely circulated "most wanted" list and who either fled the country or were hunted down, few students were jailed or subjected to physical abuse. One suspects that it was not so much any lingering traditional "respect for the scholar" that accounted for the difference between the treatment of students and workers as the fact that many students had relatives in high bureaucratic places. It was perhaps a certain instinctive feeling of class affinity that was involved, even though many students had proven themselves to be class defectors. Nonetheless, as punishment, the student body of Beijing University was temporarily cut by two-thirds and the 1989–90 entering class was required to labor in the countryside for a year before beginning their studies.

All Beijing citizens—in factories, offices, and other workplaces —were required to write lengthy "self-criticisms," explaining what they had done and thought during the time of the "rebellion." It was a requirement that bred a new kind of solidarity against the regime, this time in the form of tacit agreements to "lie collectively," as John Gittings has put it.[84]

On June 9, Deng Xiaoping, who had observed the military operations in the capital from a retreat in the Western Hills, appeared on national television to congratulate the military and police forces who had quelled the "counterrevolutionary rebellion."[85] He offered assurances that the economic reform and "open-door" policies would continue, perhaps proceeding at an even "faster pace." Otherwise the speech was quite unremarkable, save for the curious way Deng extended self-congratulations to Party leaders of his own generation:

> The storm was bound to happen sooner or later. As determined by the international and domestic climate it . . . was indepen-

[84] Gittings, *China Changes Face*, p. 285.

[85] "Speech of Deng Xiaoping, Chairman of the Central Military Commission, delivered in Beijing to commanders above corps level of the martial law enforcement troops on 9 June 1989," "Quarterly Chronicle and Documentation," *The China Quarterly*, No. 119 (September 1989), Appendix 4, pp. 725–29.

dent of man's will. It was just a matter of time and scale. It has turned out in our favor, for we still have a large group of veterans who have experienced many storms and have a thorough understanding of things. They were on the side of taking resolute action to counter the turmoil. Although some comrades may not understand this now, they will understand eventually and will support the decision of the Central Committee.

Deng Xiaoping opened his June 9 speech by expressing condolences to the Army and police personnel who had died in the suppression of the Democracy Movement, a total of "several dozen" killed and hundreds wounded, the government claimed. But Deng did not mourn the civilian victims, whom he dismissed as "a rebellious clique" and "the dregs of society," the same terms Guomindang rulers once used to describe Communists and their followers during the revolutionary years. The number of civilian deaths, according to the government, was less than 300. The absurdity of the figure was graphically pointed out by William Hinton, an eyewitness to the Massacre: "People [wounded by PLA gunfire] were afraid to stay in the hospital. They thought the troops might come and arrest them, so they got a little first aid and then went home. So many people died at home. By Wednesday [June 7] of that first week there were close to a hundred unclaimed bodies in the PUMC [Peking Union Medical College] hospital and sixty-seven unclaimed bodies in the Fuxing Hospital and similar high numbers in other hospitals around. So just the number of unclaimed bodies in the morgues of the hospitals outnumbered the total number of people the government claimed had been killed, and of course those numbers include only the ones who died in the hospital after coming for treatment. Many people were killed on the street and other people went through the hospital and died at home."[86]

There is no accurate count of civilian casualties, nor will there ever be one. At the time, estimates by independent observers ranged from 2,000 to 7,000 dead, with several times those numbers wounded. By the horrific and numbing standards of the twentieth century, these will not seem especially shocking figures. Yet there was something about the Beijing Massacre that was unusually chill-

[86] Hinton, *The Great Reversal*, p. 183.

ing. No doubt this was partly due to the fortuitous circumstances which brought the world's television cameras to Beijing to broadcast the unfolding of the tragedy. To watch the progression of a tragedy is quite a different experience than to be told afterward that a tragedy took place, however grisly the details in the telling.

Yet quite apart from the fact that the crushing of the Democracy Movement was the first televised political massacre in world history (much as Vietnam was the first televised war), there was something unusually and inhumanly cruel about the way Deng Xiaoping and the Gang of Old were intent on employing deadly force against the Chinese people. The decision to impose martial law and to call in an army that would bloodily enforce the law was not arrived at in the heat of battle or on the spur of the moment—and it was, seemingly, quite unnecessary by any rational measure of even the most crass of political power considerations. Rather, it was a coldly deliberate decision that Deng and his "old comrades" were determined to carry out no matter what the political circumstances and costs. They thus ignored one opportunity after another to peacefully resolve the crisis. They were intent on terrorizing the population, they wanted to punish the people for their transgressions and take revenge upon them for their lack of gratitude, and they were determined to do so by a massive demonstration of the military power they commanded. Thus a ruling clique of old men cold-bloodedly visited death on young students and workers in whose interests they pretended to rule. It was a particularly odious example of the savagery of the modern state that will not easily fade from the memories of those who witnessed the tragedy from afar, much less those who experienced it in China.

Yet military repression of the Democracy Movement was not an entirely irrational response to the threat it posed to China's reformed socioeconomic order. Foreign observers who are so puzzled by how a dictatorial political regime can preside over a flourishing market economy misunderstand the nature of the capitalist system that Deng Xiaoping's economic reforms created in China. It is a capitalist system (as we have seen in Chapter 11) that presupposes bureaucratic hierarchy, massive corruption, political dictatorship (officially known as "stability and unity"), growing inequality and competitiveness, ideological and cultural conservatism, and a socioeconomic system (enforced by the power of the state) that facilitates the most intensive possible exploitation of the working population.

By contrast, the dominant strains in the Democracy Movement, among students and workers alike, were an egalitarian reaction against bureaucratic corruption and privilege, a liberating cultural radicalism, and a demand for political democracy. These features of the popular movement were entirely incongruous with the imperatives of the bureaucratic capitalist system that the post-Mao reforms had created and in hostile opposition to the mentality of those who presided over and profited from that system. Any serious process of democratization posed a mortal threat to the new order, and this was universally recognized by the leaders of the regime, whose differences (insofar as they did not involve personal power rivalries) were more over the tactics of containing the democratic upsurge than over matters of substance or principle.

There was thus nothing inconsistent between the kind of capitalist economy that the post-Mao reforms had created and the fascist-like actions of China's Stalinist political regime in 1989. Indeed, as difficult as it is to acknowledge, there was a certain cruel social rationality in Deng Xiaoping's seemingly irrational response to the Democracy Movement. The events of the Beijing Spring should give pause to those who embrace the easy but problematic equation between capitalism and democracy.

★

PART FIVE

THE CLOSE
OF THE DENG ERA

15

CHINA IN THE 1990S

IN THE GRIM DAYS following June 4, 1989, foreign observers were nearly unanimous in predicting that dire economic consequences would result from the political folly of the Deng regime. The Communist Party's "hard-liners" had triumphed and thus market reforms would end. Coming on top of the austerity measures already imposed to control inflation, the economic effects of the brutal military suppression of the Democracy Movement would inevitably plunge China into a deep and prolonged recession, it was widely predicted.[1] Four months after Tiananmen, the *Wall Street Journal*'s Beijing correspondent summed up the opinion of most foreign observers when he wrote that "it's apparent that the hard-line stance that brought in tanks and troops to clear Tiananmen Square also has swept away plans to let market forces play a greater role in the economy."[2] Comparing China unfavorably with Mikhail Gorbachev's seemingly promising policies of *glasnost* and *perestroika* in the Soviet Union, a comparison that seems quite incongruous today but a natural one to make at the time, it was assumed in late 1989 that China's fate

---

[1] For example, Louise de Rosario, "Peking to Pay the Price," *Far Eastern Economic Review* (June 22, 1989), pp. 44–46.

[2] Adi Ignatius, "China's Economic Reform Program Stalls," *The Wall Street Journal*, September 26, 1989, p. A20.

under Deng Xiaoping's conservative bureaucratic regime would be "Brezhnev-style stagnation."[3]

The predictions proved faulty. In the early and mid-1990s China was to enjoy its greatest economic boom, with astonishingly high rates of growth that exceeded even those recorded during the 1980s. Between economic success and political virtue, it was once again demonstrated, there is no correlation.

Although China suffered a recession in 1989 primarily due to the monetary restraints imposed by the Zhao Ziyang government in the autumn of 1988,[4] the austerity measures were eased in the summer of 1990 as inflation subsided and high rates of growth resumed. Market reforms, far from being abandoned, were "deepened," especially after Deng Xiaoping's dramatic tour of the southern provinces in January 1992. China's GDP expanded by 7.5 percent in 1991, by 13 percent in 1992, and by an extraordinary 14 percent in 1993, with industrial production growing at incredibly high per annum rates exceeding 20 percent.[5] The Chinese economy, it was revealed to the astonishment of many, had become the third largest in the world, measured according to the new International Monetary Fund and World Bank standard of "purchasing power parity," almost the size of the Japanese economy and perhaps only a generation's time away from surpassing the American economy in absolute scale. For more than a century the United States could claim the world's largest economy; now, it was widely if vaguely sensed, a great historic transformation was in the making. In the age of "global capitalism," multinational corporations, and "flexible production," nation-states and national economies still matter, as the recent histories of the East Asian "miracle" economies—in South Korea, Taiwan, and Sin-

[3] Lee Feigon, *China Rising*, p. 249.

[4] China's GNP declined to a growth rate of 3.9 percent in 1989 from 11.2 percent in 1988. State Statistical Bureau, "Communiqué on National Social and Economic Development During 1989," *Beijing Review*, February 19–25, 1990, and March 12–18, 1990.

[5] Ajit Singh, "The Plan, the Market and Evolutionary Economic Reform in China," *UNCTAD Discussion Papers*, No. 76 (December 1993), p. 3; CIA, Annual Report to the U.S. Congress, July 1993, *The New York Times*, August 1, 1993. In striking contrast to China's high rates of growth noted in the text, the GDP of Eastern Europe and the former Soviet Union *fell* drastically by approximately 10 percent in 1991 and 16 percent in 1992, while the advanced industrialized economies stagnated, their collective GDP increasing only 0.5 percent in 1991 and 1.5 percent in 1992. *Financial Times*, April 17–18, 1993, cited in Singh, "The Plan . . . ," pp. 3–4.

gapore—demonstrate, a lesson that Japan first taught and one that China is now reinforcing on a massive scale.

From 1991 to 1994, China's GDP increased even more rapidly than it had in the frenetic 1980s, a decade when China (along with South Korea) led the world in average annual rates of growth.[6] Over the five year period 1990–94, China's GDP grew at an average annual rate of more than 11 percent, whereas it had averaged 9.7 percent over the preceding decade. Western forecasts of economic stagnation made in the wake of the Beijing massacre of 1989 were in part based on a naive belief (or, perhaps, hope) that political evil somehow begets economic punishment. In larger part, foreign predictions reflected a general misunderstanding of the bureaucratic capitalist economy that Deng Xiaoping's reforms created. It is a system that requires political dictatorship, and indeed a state that is prepared to act in a brutally repressive fashion to enforce the intensive exploitation of the working population that yields the capital accumulations necessary for rapid economic growth.

Improving economic conditions in late 1990 muffled the anger of the millions of citizens who had actively participated in the Democracy Movement and the many millions more who had sympathized with them. For those who benefited from the subsequent economic boom, memories of the massacre were submerged under government-promoted waves of consumerism. So Deng Xiaoping had calculated. In a secret speech delivered on June 28, 1989, Deng reportedly had advised that the question of political responsibility for the May–June events be set aside for several years to enable Party leaders to concentrate on improving economic conditions.[7]

But the regime did not rely on economic means alone to control a discontented urban population. In the weeks and months following the PLA assault, secret police agencies carried out a massive wave of arrests throughout China, detaining tens of thousands of leaders

[6] Over the decade 1980–89, China's GDP grew at an average annual rate of 9.7 percent. South Korea's was also 9.7 percent. The median for Asian countries, by far the world's most rapidly growing region, was 5.3 percent. For Latin American countries, it was 1.0 percent; for Africa, 1.5 percent; for Western Europe, 2.3 percent; for North America, 2.8 percent; for Eastern Europe, 1.6 percent. Figures derived from Table 2, "Growth of Production," in World Bank, *World Development Report 1991* (New York: Oxford University Press, 1991), pp. 206–7.

[7] *Far Eastern Economic Review*, August 10, 1989, p. 13.

and activists in what was officially branded "the turmoil and counterrevolutionary rebellion."[8] Most of the arrested were released from custody, but several dozen—mostly workers—were executed and several thousand sentenced to prison terms. "Counterrevolutionary cliques," the government reported, were broken up in cities across the land, from Shanghai to Chengdu to Lhasa in Tibet in a strikingly swift demonstration that administrative and economic decentralization had not undermined the power of the state's agencies of repression. In June 1990, on the first anniversary of the massacre, the government acknowledged that 432 people, including 43 students, remained imprisoned for their participation in the Democracy Movement.[9] The real numbers undoubtedly were greater.

Symbolizing the repression was a highly publicized "most wanted" list of several dozen prominent student leaders and intellectuals. Those who had not fled into exile were hunted down and jailed after summary trials. Since it was officially reported that nearly 3 million students attending over 600 colleges in 84 cities had in some way been involved in the "turmoil,"[10] the regime felt compelled to announce punishments: university enrollments were reduced for the 1989–90 academic year; entering students at some universities were required to complete a year's military training before beginning their studies; and compulsory "political education" was reintroduced into the college curriculum. All of these measures proved transient.

Also transient and ritualistic was an ideological campaign forcing urban inhabitants to gather together in their work units and neighborhood groups to praise the heroic PLA for having put down a "counterrevolutionary rebellion." The political exercises were performed with a notable lack of zeal and were soon abandoned.

In Beijing alone, some 10,000 cadres suspected of having supported the Democracy Movement were purged from the 50-million-member Communist Party, although it was soon discovered that sympathizers in Party organs were far too numerous to allow Deng Xiaoping and new Party Secretary-General Jiang Zemin to control the

---

[8] According to Liu Binyan, from June 4 to early August 1989, 120,000 people were imprisoned, 20,000 in Beijing alone. Liu Binyan et al., *Tell the World*, p. 63. The figures cannot be verified. The estimates of most other observers are considerably lower.

[9] Bob Deans, Cox News Service, from Beijing, June 3, 1990. *Wisconsin State Journal*, June 3, 1990, p. 1H.

[10] *People's Daily*, September 6, 1989.

huge organization as tightly as they wished. More effective was a very limited purge of officials directly associated with Zhao Ziyang, especially members of the former Party head's "brain trust."[11] Zhao himself was permitted to retain his Party membership, but, banished to a villa in central Beijing guarded by the security police, he was neither seen nor heard in public over the remainder of the Deng era.[12]

Purges also struck intellectuals. Several semi-autonomous social and economic research organizations which had cautiously emerged during the 1980s were banned. Government repression was directed especially at the official Chinese Academy of Social Sciences in Beijing, where entire institutes were suspended or reorganized. The regime paid special attention to the Academy's Marxism-Leninism-Mao Zedong Thought Institute in reimposing the regime's ideological authority, particularly over the interpretation and uses of Marxism. Many of the intellectuals who had been prominent in the Democracy Movement fled the country at the time of the military crackdown. Others who were by no means hostile to the Communist state, much less to the revolution that produced it, became arbitrary targets of official criticism and found themselves the victims of Kafka-like inquisitions. Journalists, the professional group that had played the most prominent public role in the Democracy Movement, bore the brunt of the purge. As a result, the limited degree of press freedom that had been painstakingly gained since 1978 was wiped out overnight, and virtually all newspapers and other publications were once again reduced to government organs.

It was during this time of harsh political and intellectual repression that China's greatest economic advance took place.

Deng Xiaoping dominated China's political life in the years immediately following Tiananmen as fully as he had during the previous

---

[11] Zhao Ziyang's main intellectual advisors, the most important of whom was Bao Tong, who was arrested in 1989 and sentenced to prison for nine years, headed various economic research institutes. As Merle Goldman points out, the members of Zhao's "think tanks" were primarily interested in economic, not political, reform. See Goldman, *Sowing the Seeds of Democracy in China: Political Reform in the Deng Xiaoping Era*, pp. 320–25 and passim.

[12] Zhao, reportedly, refused Deng Xiaoping's offer of an honorary Party post and a return to public life in exchange for a confession of guilt for his political errors.

decade. His reputation had been tarnished by the Beijing massacre, which he had ordered and directed (and over which he never was to express any hint of regret publicly), but his power remained intact. Indeed, his power increased, for he had demonstrated that he was the one Party leader who could command the loyalty of the Army. And this remained the case even after he formally resigned the chairmanship of the Communist Party's Central Military Commission in the fall of 1989.

Deng Xiaoping's continuing political dominance was facilitated by the seeming mediocrity of those he selected to preside over affairs of Party and state. Over the course of his first decade as China's paramount leader, Deng had purged both men he had placed at the head of the Communist Party—his erstwhile protégés Hu Yaobang and Zhao Ziyang. Zhao, a man of considerable political skill and even greater ambition, had acquired a following of his own, earning Deng's displeasure even before he was accused of attempting to split the Communist Party during the 1989 student movement. This was not the case with Zhao's successor, the colorless former mayor of Shanghai, Jiang Zemin, who in addition to occupying the position of Secretary-General of the Communist Party was also selected by Deng to be President of the Republic and chairman of the Central Military Commission as well. Jiang Zemin thus simultaneously headed the Party, the government, and the military, leaving little doubt that he was Deng's designated successor.[13] The always obedient Li Peng was retained as Prime Minister, handling the routine affairs of the state bureaucracy.

In the last years of his reign, Deng Xiaoping ruled China much in the manner that Mao had once ruled the land. Like Mao, Deng imposed his will not so much by working within the Party but rather above it—even though, unlike the former Chairman, he occupied no formal Party office. Nonetheless, no Party or state policy of any significance was decided upon without the approval of the paramount leader, even if this involved only a nod of the head in "informal" discussions with the nominal leaders of the Party. A casual talk, an

---

[13] In deciding on Jiang Zemin as Party leader in 1989, Deng apparently sought, and received, the agreement of Chen Yun. Nicholas D. Kristof, "Using Protégés as Pawns," *The New York Times*, February 4, 1990.

"instruction," or even a brief comment in a discussion with colleagues or visiting foreign dignitaries, were treated as commands from on high and were quickly translated into official policy and ideology.

The modest personality cult that had been built around Deng during the 1980s became decidedly less modest after 1989. His writings and speeches, especially those condemning "bourgeois liberalism," were mandatory reading for the post-Tiananmen study sessions required of Party members and others in the months following the Beijing massacre. A two-volume collection, *Deng Xiaoping on Art and Literature*, a topic about which the paramount leader hitherto had not been known to have any special interest, was published in the autumn of 1989, fortifying the Dengist claim to an all-embracing ideological authority. A highly laudatory biography of China's leader, written by his daughter, Deng Rong, appeared with great fanfare in the summer of 1993. A selection of 119 of Deng's "private speeches," mostly edited versions of recorded conversations with other Party leaders and foreign visitors, was published in October 1993, shortly after he celebrated his eighty-ninth birthday. Jiang Zemin and others ever more extravagantly praised "Deng Xiaoping Thought," which it was claimed would guide China's domestic and foreign policies well into the twenty-first century. Deng himself had rather majestically decreed that his basic policies—market reform, the open door, and the Four Cardinal Principles—should remain unchanged for at least a century.[14]

In the fashion of Mao Zedong, Deng would disappear from public view for many months at a time, inevitably sparking rumors of his death. That, in turn, made his reappearances—whether on television screens or in newspaper photographs—all the more dramatic. Like Mao, the more remote Deng became, the more mysteriously dominant he seemed to be; the more physically enfeebled he was, the more politically powerful he appeared. And in his last years, Deng Xiaoping increasingly used the image and writings of Mao Zedong, albeit highly selectively, to promote policies that the late Chairman surely would have condemned as evidence of "the restoration of capitalism."

Deng Xiaoping's most Mao-like political intervention was his re-

---

[14] "Central Document No. 2 (1992): On Transmitting and Studying Comrade Deng Xiaoping's Important Remarks," FBIS-CHI-91-063-S.

markable southern tour. Over a five-week period from January 18 to February 21, 1992, the eighty-seven-year-old Deng visited the cities of Canton, Shanghai, and Wuchang as well as the Shenzhen and Zhuhai special economic zones. Although Deng no longer held any official political positions, the speeches and comments he made during the tour immediately became official policy—and his comments were treated with biblical authority, collected in "Central Document No. 2" and duly made required reading for all Party members.

Deng's purpose in his southern tour was to accelerate the pace of market reform and speed up the rate of economic growth, thereby abandoning the relatively cautious economic policies that the Li Peng government had pursued since the autumn of 1988.[15] "Low-speed development is equal to stagnation or even retrogression," Deng warned. Accordingly, he placed his stamp of approval on the free-wheeling capitalism of Guangdong province, "a leading force for economic development," and he praised the special economic zones, regretting only that Shanghai had not been included among them from the outset. These views flowed from Deng's renewed insistence that the worth of all policies be judged entirely by their economic results—whether they were "conducive to the development of the socialist productive forces, to the growth of the comprehensive national strength of the socialist state, and to the enhancement of people's living standards." Fears that market reforms might have a capitalist outcome were to be allayed by the existence of the Communist state. "Political power is in our hands," Deng reassuringly proclaimed.[16]

In the course of his southern tour, Deng emphasized that the main danger China faced in the post-Tiananmen era was no longer bourgeois liberalization, presumably a rightist phenomenon, but rather leftism. Leftism, in turn, was redefined to meet the needs of the day. The label now was applied to anyone who opposed the rapid pace of marketization and economic growth Deng advocated. The renewed campaign against leftism silenced a variety of old-line Party theoreticians who had demonstrated greater ideological zeal in opposing

[15] Prior to Deng's southern tour, Li Peng sought to limit economic growth to an average 6 percent per annum rate in order to avoid repeating the inflationary and other adverse consequences that contributed to the 1989 crisis.

[16] "Central Document No. 2 (1992)."

bourgeois liberalization than in embracing Deng's economic reform program. It also set the stage for the final inner-Party battle between the Deng faction and senior leaders who wished to retain a dominant place for central planning and who feared that excessively rapid market reforms would bring economic chaos and social turmoil, perhaps even the collapse of the Communist regime itself as had recently occurred throughout Eastern Europe. The most prominent of the skeptics was the venerable Chen Yun, who in March 1992 sarcastically commented:

> Now some people are asking if we are going "fast" and "wide" and "deep" enough and want us to lean towards it in a bolder fashion. Which direction do we go further in? Have Yugoslavia, Eastern Europe and the Soviet Union gone sufficiently far? . . . Our national situation is different from theirs; but our economic foundation is even weaker. . . . We simply cannot afford such painful lessons.[17]

But by late spring the comments that Deng Xiaoping had made during his southern tour had been translated into official Party policies. Deng's prescriptions for "enlivening the economy," as the terminology of the day had it, had been formally adopted (and with great enthusiasm, it was said) by all Party and state organs. Even Chen Yun reluctantly climbed aboard the bandwagon, exhorting local officials in Shanghai to "emancipate" their minds and act in accordance "with the Party's basic line."[18]

In May 1992, the speeches and comments Deng made during his southern tour were formulated as concrete policy proposals in "Central Document No. 4," issued to provincial civilian and military officials. The document called for opening nine border cities in Manchuria and the Northwest to foreign trade and investment as well as the acceleration of economic reform in the interior through the establishment of five open cities along the Yangzi, with Shanghai as the "dragon head." Although Deng Xiaoping complained that the

---

[17] *Cheng Ming* (Hong Kong), April 1, 1992. Cited in "Quarterly Chronicle and Documentation," *The China Quarterly*, No. 131 (September 1992), p. 847.
[18] *Beijing Review*, Vol. 35, No. 19, p. 5.

Communist Party was slow to implement his proposals for a more rapid pace of economic reform and growth, there was in fact marked movement toward a more fully capitalist economy in the spring and summer of 1992. New experiments in stock markets and private homeownership were undertaken. Plans were drawn up to allow some state-owned enterprises to alter their ownership patterns by issuing stocks, which could be purchased by individuals and institutions. Premier Li Peng announced that state enterprises would be granted "full business autonomy," including the right to engage in foreign trade on their own. And fresh opportunities were created for foreign investors and banks, even including the sale of several unprofitable state enterprises to foreign capitalists.

While many of these undertakings foundered, or remained rudimentary and experimental, the political and psychological atmosphere created by Deng's southern tour encouraged expansionary economic and monetary policies that did in fact speed up the pace of economic development. Whereas prior to Deng's tour the Party and the State Council had concluded that an average annual GDP growth rate of 6 percent over the remainder of the decade was as rapid a pace as the Chinese social and natural environment could sustain, in 1992 the GDP actually grew 12 percent, and increased by 14 percent in 1993. In 1994 the GDP surged another 12 percent, making for three successive years of extraordinarily rapid growth.

Deng Xiaoping's proposals for achieving a more rapid pace of development through the adoption of capitalist methods were canonized at the Fourteenth Congress of the Communist Party of China, which met in Beijing from October 12 to October 18, 1992. Deng did not attend the Congress but he dominated the entire proceedings—so much so that the Party constitution was revised to incorporate the remarks made by the senior leader during his tour of southern China earlier that year. What was hailed as Deng's "great theoretical breakthrough" in the development of Marxism-Leninism-Mao Zedong Thought was the concept of a "socialist market economic system," which replaced what had been known as a "socialist planned market economy." What the new term meant, simply put, was a greater role for market competition and free prices in the Chinese economy.

The documents of the Fourteenth Congress emphasized, as Deng long had emphasized, that economic development was the Party's central task and that therefore (although it did not necessarily follow) class struggle was no longer a "principal contradiction." The projected GNP growth rate for the remainder of the century was revised upward from an average 6 percent increase per annum to 9 percent. This would result in significantly exceeding the goal set forth at the beginning of the reform period of quadrupling China's GNP over the years 1980–2000. And, as Deng had counseled, efforts were to be undertaken to make Shanghai one of the world's largest trade and financial centers.[19]

The Fourteenth Congress not only ratified and celebrated Deng Xiaoping's economic policies; it also marked his greatest and most definitive political triumph. There was a wholesale revamping of the personnel in the Party's leading organs. Nearly half of the 189 members of the new Central Committee were newly elected, and there, as in other higher Party organs, the Deng faction was almost totally dominant. Symbolically completing the Dengist political victory was the Congress' decision to abolish the Central Advisory Commission, chaired by Chen Yun.

The Fourteenth Congress also marked the triumph of Deng's proposals for political reform. By "political reform" Deng had never meant democracy, but primarily the modernization and professionalization of the bureaucracy. His aim, as he had put it in 1980, was to make Communist officials "better educated, professionally more competent, and younger." By those criteria, the Fourteenth Congress was eminently successful. The new Central Committee was dominated by middle-aged technocrats, averaging a relatively youthful fifty-six years of age, 84 percent of whom were college graduates, just as the paramount leader had advised at the beginning of his reign.

Deng Xiaoping could claim political successes abroad as well as at home. His ardent promotion of capitalism during his southern tour, combined with the policies enunciated at the Fourteenth Party Congress, led many Western commentators to rechristen him an enlightened free market reformer—barely three years after being universally condemned as "the butcher of Beijing."

[19] On the documents of the Fourteenth Congress, see *Beijing Review*, October 26–November 1, 1992.

★ ★ ★

Ominously hovering in the background of China's economic successes of the early 1990s was the collapse of Communism in Eastern Europe and the disintegration of the Soviet Union. The leaders of the Chinese Communist Party drew two lessons from these events. The first was the need to "deepen" the policies of market reform, which would continue to stimulate rapid economic growth, steadily improve living standards, and thus avoid the popular discontent over economic conditions that had so greatly contributed to the demise of Communist regimes in Europe. Second, and now most important, the fate of the Soviet Union reinforced the Chinese Communist belief in the need to maintain a powerful Leninist party dictatorship, to reject all schemes for a Western-style multiparty system, and—in view of the apparent results of *glasnost*—to intensify efforts to combat bourgeois liberalization.[20] No one clung to these views more tenaciously than Deng Xiaoping, who, in an uncharacteristic but revealing comment on "socialism" in political rather than solely economic terms, declared in 1992 that "our socialist state apparatus is strong and powerful. In case of deviation from the socialist orientation, the state apparatus will . . . intervene and redress the situation."[21] In the spring of 1992, in referring to the 1989 Democracy Movement, Deng had vowed that "if necessary, every possible means will be adopted to eliminate any turmoil in the future as soon as it has appeared. Martial law, or even more severe methods, may be introduced."[22] One result of the collapse of Communism in Europe was to reinforce the conviction of Chinese Communist leaders that Deng Xiaoping had been both just and wise in ordering the massive use of military force in June 1989.

★ ★ ★

[20] For an example, probably quite typical and certainly quite fascinating, of the way in which Chinese leaders assessed events in the Soviet Union in 1991, see the verbatim transcript of a talk by Gao Di, editor of *People's Daily*, delivered on August 30, 1991. Gao claimed to express "the intent of the [CCP] Central Committee, but in my own words." The text is printed in "Quarterly Chronicle and Documentation," *The China Quarterly*, No 130 (June 1992), pp. 482–91.

[21] *People's Daily*, June 22, 1992.

[22] *People's Daily*, April 28, 1992.

The frenzied expansion of industry and trade in the early 1990s again produced an "overheated" economy, with symptoms similar to those that characterized the expansionary phases of the boom and bust cycles of the 1980s. By mid-1993, inflation in the cities was approaching 25 percent per annum; reckless borrowing from unregulated government banks fueled wild speculation in real estate and stocks, especially by local governments and state enterprises; expansionary monetary policies and an influx of foreign capital sparked a new upsurge in official corruption and unofficial crime; there was growing social unrest, both among urban workers whose living standards were threatened by inflation and among farmers, many of whom were receiving "white slips" (IOUs) from officials in exchange for their products; and central authorities were losing control over the fiscal affairs of increasingly autonomous provincial and local governments.

Vice-Premier Zhu Rongji was called upon to deal with this chaotic situation, reminiscent in some respects of the autumn 1988 prelude to the 1989 Beijing Spring. As mayor of Shanghai in June 1989, Zhu had managed to keep relative order in China's largest city without imposing martial law—and without unduly antagonizing either the government in Beijing or the citizens of Shanghai. He did so, in part, by demonstrating a gift for ambiguous comment, such as one he made in a celebrated Shanghai television speech on June 8, 1989, when he vowed that "the truth of what occurred [in Beijing] will eventually be made clear to the whole world."[23] His political reputation grew in an accordingly ambivalent fashion. He came to be misleadingly called "China's Gorbachev" in the Western press at the same time as he became Deng Xiaoping's newest disciple.[24]

Elevated to the Standing Committee of the Party Politburo at the Fourteenth Congress in October 1992, Zhu Rongji was appointed governor of the central People's Bank of China at the beginning of July 1993. Zhu's control of financial policy, combined with his already dominant role in formulating industrial and agricultural poli-

---

[23] Cited in *China Focus*, Vol. 1, No. 6 (July 30, 1993), p. 5.

[24] Zhu Rongji was born in Hunan province in 1928. He joined the Communist Party in 1949 and graduated from Qinghua University in 1951, with a degree in engineering. He was expelled from the Party in 1957 during the antirightist campaign, ironically directed by Deng Xiaoping, who rehabilitated Zhu twenty years later and then became his patron.

cies as Vice-Premier, made him, in the term favored by the popular press, China's "economic czar," eclipsing Premier Li Peng in actual authority even if not in official status. Zhu did not rise to that position without the personal blessings of Deng Xiaoping, who had said that "there are very few people who really understand economics, and Zhu Rongji is one of them; however, his capacity to run the economy has not been fully utilized."[25]

Now, in the summer of 1993, when Zhu's ability to "run the economy" was being fully tested, he faced the daunting task of reducing the rate of economic growth and controlling inflation without provoking a general recession and exacerbating unemployment and social unrest. He also confronted the task of reasserting the central government's financial authority over the provinces without stifling the economic initiatives and dynamism that decentralization had fostered.

Much in the fashion of central bankers in the advanced capitalist countries, Zhu was inclined to rely on monetary and fiscal measures to discipline the economy and achieve what Western economists call a soft landing and what their Chinese counterparts generally refer to as cooling an overheated economy. Zhu proposed to convert the People's Bank into a genuine central bank while leaving other, mostly state-owned banks as commercial banks whose operations would be guided by market forces. This, together with a convertible currency, he believed, would avoid the boom and bust cycles that had marred the earlier reform era. His goal was to reduce China's growth from an unsustainable 12–14 percent annual rise in the GDP to a hopefully stable but still very high 8 or 9 percent.[26] He also wished to ensure that the central government received at least 50 percent of the taxes collected by provincial authorities, rather than a share that had shrunk to an estimated 30 percent in 1992.

The semi-austerity measures Zhu Rongji announced to achieve

---

25 Cited in *China Focus*, Vol. 1, No. 6 (July 30, 1993), p. 5. Deng's well-known comment was made in May 1992.

26 Whether this conformed with Deng Xiaoping's wishes is unclear. In late 1993 the Chinese press reported that Deng had decreed that "slow growth isn't socialism," after having criticized officials who warned of inflationary dangers earlier in the year. Karen Elliott House, "Beijing Vice Premier Vows to Press Reform of Nation's Economy," *The Wall Street Journal*, December 10, 1993, p. 1; Julia Leung, "China Says Zhu Oversees Effort to Cut Inflation," *The Wall Street Journal*, July 6, 1993.

these aims in the summer of 1993 included the recentralization of the banking system; tightening the money supply through higher interest rates and other restrictions on lending; slashing government spending, investment, and consumption, including a ban on the import of automobiles by government agencies; curbing speculation in property and stocks; and efforts to increase savings, which included the forced purchase of low-interest government bonds.[27]

But Deng Xiaoping did not share Zhu Rongji's preference for a more moderate pace of development. In October 1993 the paramount leader's one-sentence pronouncement that "slow growth is not socialism"[28] was enough to quash the austerity program proposed by Zhu Rongji and Premier Li Peng. Deng's point was reinforced when the increasingly frail eighty-nine-year-old patriarch made a brief appearance on national television in the winter of 1994. Deng's voice was not heard, but the announcer quoted him as calling for even faster economic growth, especially in Shanghai, which was rapidly eclipsing Canton as the financial center of Chinese capitalism.

The October 1993 statement and the February 1994 visit to Shanghai together marked Deng Xiaoping's final policy intervention, which had much the same effect as his southern tour of 1992. Austerity plans were scrapped and a period of frenzied economic growth followed. In 1994 China's GDP increased by 12 percent, virtually matching the hectic pace of the previous year. Industrial production grew by more than 20 percent, the greatest gains again made by rural township and village enterprises.

The continuing economic boom brought familiar consequences. The nationwide inflation rate in 1994 rose to 22 percent, according to official calculations, and more than 30 percent in the major cities. While industry forged ahead, grain production declined (by about 3 percent), forcing up the price of basic foodstuffs and placing most of the burden of inflation on the common people of the cities. Frenetic

---

[27] This, of course, was unpopular, and reflected again the economic advantages of bureaucratic office. As an unidentified manual laborer complained to a foreign journalist: "Nobody wants the bonds. In the last couple of years, they paid a high interest rate, and so the leaders bought all the bonds for themselves. But now they hardly pay anything, and the leaders don't want them. So we have to buy them." Nicholas D. Kristof, "China, Barreling Along the Capitalist Road, Now Posts Strict Speed Limits," *The New York Times*, July 23, 1993, p. A3.

[28] *The Wall Street Journal*, December 10, 1993, p. 1.

and chaotic industrialization continued to poison the air and water, and further shrunk the acreage of land under cultivation. Industrial accidents reached frightening proportions, killing an estimated 20,000 workers annually in the early 1990s, and injuring many more.[29]

While *average* living standards probably continued to rise gradually through the mid-1990s, the fruits of economic progress were distributed in an increasingly inequitable fashion, leaving masses of impoverished people in both the cities and the countryside living alongside the not inconsiderable numbers of those who heeded Deng Xiaoping's injunction to "get rich." The gap between rich and poor, growing since 1985, became more and more visible in the 1990s, evoking memories of the extreme social inequalities of Guomindang China. In the cities, China's nouveaux riche—a varied assortment of private entrepreneurs, compradores, managers and technicians, small industrialists, and profiteering bureaucrats—flaunt their wealth at expensive nightclubs and restaurants, wear $2,500 Rolex watches and $500 Pierre Cardin suits (each approximately equal to the average annual per capita urban income), drive imported automobiles—and often complain that there is not enough to do with their money. One of their number, multimillionaire Cheng Chunbo, owner of eighteen private enterprises and delegate to the National People's Congress, attempted, in a novel fashion, to resolve the dilemma of excessive accumulation by investing US$10 million in the Beijing Horse Race Course, located twenty-five miles north of the capital.[30]

There are no official figures on the number of newly rich. Independent observers estimate there are as many as 10 million millionaires (in Chinese *yuan*) in China today. That the number is substantial is suggested by the emergence of the People's Republic as the world's most rapidly growing market for luxury goods. Pierre Cardin, for example, which opened its first boutique in China in late 1989, several months after the Beijing massacre, had expanded to

[29] According to Chinese labor activists. *The Wall Street Journal*, May 19, 1994.
[30] Mr. Cheng, also board chairman of the Beijing Country and Golf Club, acknowledges that his entrepreneurial successes were facilitated by friends in high bureaucratic places. Uli Schmetzer, "In China, a Day at the Races," *Chicago Tribune*, November 7, 1993, Section 1, p. 14.

fifty stores by the end of 1992 and planned to add another fifty in 1993.[31] Whatever the significance of such indicators of wealth, it is clear enough that China's socialist market economy has quickly yielded an upper bourgeoisie. Its members, engaged in gluttonous consumption, are highly visible in the cities, and they no doubt have a powerful stake in the existing Communist order, even if they still lack a cohesive consciousness of their interests as a class.

Also visible and far more numerous are the 50 to 150 million peasants from depressed rural areas who have migrated to the cities in search of work. Living in shantytowns or on the streets, the more fortunate among them work as low-paid contract laborers on round-the-clock construction sites and, in the case of young peasant women, labor in sweatshops under oppressive conditions that hark back to the early decades of the century. Some are employed as servants, nannies, and housecleaners in the homes of urban professionals. But most are day laborers—"one-day mules," as they are called—who gather at street corners early in the morning to compete for jobs. The migrant workers are a functional underclass who do the work that permanent residents of the cities wish to avoid, and who, like their counterparts in other capitalist countries, serve to make life comfortable for the well-to-do. It is the limitless supply of cheap labor provided by the rural migrants that is partly responsible for the rapid development of the cities. But in return for their services, they earn only the contempt of their exploiters. As a candid private entrepreneur cynically explained to a Western reporter: "We think the floating population is terrific. . . . Why? Because we can exploit them. They're willing to work hard in exchange for just enough money to buy some food. We need them and they need us. It's a great partnership."[32]

The Chinese Communist Party, once the champion of the poor, discourages discussion of the plight of the migrant laborers, as a noted Tianjin writer discovered: "I've told several friends that I'd like to write a piece about modern poverty, and some reject the idea out of hand. They tell me that nowadays people write about being

---

[31] *The Wall Street Journal*, January 13, 1993, p. A10.
[32] Nicholas D. Kristof, "China's 50 Million Migrants Slip the Short Leash," *The New York Times*, May 14, 1990, p. A4.

rich, not poor. The newspapers are full of stories about how many millionaires there are in China and how they spend money like water. In a society like today's, full of luxury boutiques and fancy private schools, talk of poverty is so unfashionable that it can actually get you in trouble, in exactly the same way talk of 'wealth' could back in the days of the Cultural Revolution."[33]

The distance between urban China's newly rich and its impoverished migrant laborers makes for as wide a social gap as is likely to be found in any capitalist country, whether among developed or developing nations. Foreigners traveling in Mao's China often commented on the drabness of life in Chinese cities, habitually noting the apparent uniformity of a population clad in blue Mao jackets—evidence of either equality or conformity, depending on the political proclivities of the observer. Visitors at the close of the Deng era are likely to comment on the terrible extremes of wealth and poverty. The rapidity of the social change is no less astonishing than the rapidity of the economic transformation.

Between the nouveaux riche and the new lumpenproletariat are the vast majority of the urban population—workers in state and private factories, employees of commercial and financial enterprises, lower-level government workers, and petty entrepreneurs (*getihu*). While many aspire to membership in the new elite, especially younger entrepreneurs, many more fear falling into the ranks of the lumpenproletariat. Their fears are hardly groundless. The gains that have been made in living standards and income over the reform period are threatened by inflation, the loss of job security resulting from capitalist-type restructuring of state enterprises, and the decay of a comprehensive welfare system that once provided secure pensions, medical care, and income guarantees. In a new partially marketized environment, where individual enterprises are responsible for profits and losses, the first bankruptcies have already thrown millions of workers into the growing ranks of the unemployed, while inefficient or faltering enterprises are sometimes many months behind in wage payments. Workers have responded with slowdowns, demonstrations,

[33] Jiang Zilong, "Workers Struggling with Poverty," *China Focus*, Vol. 2, No. 5 (May 1, 1994), p. 5 (emphasis in original).

and sometimes brief strikes—all of which are illegal—in increasingly militant efforts to preserve job security and welfare benefits.[34]

Urban unrest has been accompanied by a rising tide of peasant discontent. In many rural areas in the 1990s corrupt local officials have enriched themselves by levying extralegal taxes on peasant possessions and inventing fees for every conceivable transaction.[35] Peasants also have been angered by soaring prices for chemical fertilizers and farm machinery, one of the many factors responsible for the stagnation of agricultural production. The central government, especially sensitive to unrest in a vast countryside over which it has only tenuous control, has decreed a 40 percent increase in grain procurement prices and promised to raise state capital investment in agriculture, which had become a vanishing item in the state budget in the late Deng era. More significantly, the government has sanctioned, and haltingly encouraged, a growing movement in Shandong, Jiangsu, and the central provinces in general to abandon the household responsibility system in favor of the partial recollectivization of village property and production.[36] These measures aim to mitigate distress among peasants who find family farming on tiny plots of land an increasingly unprofitable enterprise. But what really has kept peasant discontent from finding rebellious political expression has been the employment and income opportunities afforded by the still-growing rural industrial sector, coupled with the demand for peasant laborers to perform menial work in the cities. Should an economic recession curtail the urban construction boom and arrest the growth of the

[34] For a useful summary of growing worker resistance to restructuring as of mid-1994, see Lincoln Kaye, "Labour Pains," *Far Eastern Economic Review*, June 16, 1994, pp. 32–33. More detailed information can be found in Han Dongfan's *China Labour Bulletin* (Hong Kong), which reports over 10,000 "incidents" of worker unrest in 1993.

[35] In many villages, especially in the interior, soldiers from the local Public Security Bureau, at the direction of the local Party secretary, appear at the doors of peasant households demanding fees for education, road construction, land improvement, and the operation of television sets and other appliances. Taxes commonly collected include a head tax, a grain tax, a tax for families of soldiers, and even a tax for collecting taxes, among a multitude of other forms of extortion. The inhabitants of a village in Sichuan province estimate that such "local fees" consume 40 percent of their income, most of which goes to enriching local Party officials. See Andrew B. Brick, "The Emperor of Heilongcun," *The Wall Street Journal*, July 16, 1993, p A8.

[36] On "recollectivization," see Joseph Kahn in *The Wall Street Journal*, March 10, 1995, pp. A1, A4.

village and township industries, it can be anticipated that the Chinese countryside will be seething with discontent.

Faced with the specter of a rebellious peasantry and the fear of further antagonizing the urban working class, Party leaders, in the name of maintaining social stability, called a virtual halt to capitalist economic restructuring in the summer of 1994. The contrast between the regime's rhetoric and proclaimed policies at the end of 1993 and the mood that prevailed in early 1995 is striking. In the autumn of 1993, spurred by Deng Xiaoping's cryptic statement that "slow growth is not socialism," and amidst much talk about the magic of the market and Adam Smith's "invisible hand," the Party Central Committee met in November to speed the transition to a market economy. Scrapping the austerity program that had been imposed by Vice-Premier Zhu Rongji in the spring, the Central Committee called for the reform of the banking system and the establishment of commercial banks, new tax and currency systems designed to facilitate the growth of private enterprise, and the privatization of smaller state enterprises. Most significantly, 100 large state factories were to be converted, on an initially experimental basis, into private corporations fully responsible for their own profits and losses, with a view to privatizing virtually all 11,000 of China's medium-size and large state industries before the year 2000. "Chinese Factories Greet Capitalism" was the heading *The New York Times* used in reporting the story.[37]

Yet the reformist zeal that was so evident in the autumn of 1993 dissipated over 1994 as workers' protests, especially in the interior cities, made Party leaders fearful of the consequences of massive unemployment that would surely result from the wholesale capitalist restructuring of state enterprises, especially in a land lacking an adequate social welfare system. Thus little was done to reform the urban state sector in 1994, and by the early months of 1995 Party leaders had grown silent on the matter of economic reform, instead stressing the need for social and political stability. The growing caution in economic policy was reinforced by the Mexican financial debacle. Although China's situation was hardly similar, the crisis in Mexico gave rise to new concerns over China's rapidly rising foreign

---

[37] *The New York Times*, November 25, 1993, p. A7.

debt.[38] But perhaps the main reason for the virtual cessation of the urban reform program was the absence on the political stage of Deng Xiaoping, who alone among post-Mao Communist leaders had the power and the prestige to force bold economic initiatives. Neither Deng's putative successor, Jiang Zemin, nor Jiang's potential rivals possessed the risk-taking spirit of the last of China's old revolutionaries.

Deng Xiaoping was last seen in public in February 1994, in a five-minute television segment showing him greeting Communist officials in Shanghai on the occasion of the Lunar New Year. He did not speak, at least not audibly, and his obvious frailty and feebleness signaled to the nation the imminence of his departure. Yet, during his fifteen-year reign, Deng could have fairly claimed that gigantic strides had been made in realizing the long-sought nationalist goals of making China wealthy and powerful in the modern world. But what had become of the socialist goals that Chinese Communist leaders still proclaimed?

[38] At the end of 1994 China's foreign debt had grown to US$100 billion, making China the world's fifth-largest debtor nation, well behind the United States, the world's leader in this dubious category. Although China's debt has become substantial, it is still modest on a per capita basis when compared with most other developing countries. Nonetheless, China's external debt/GNP ratio rose from 15 percent in 1990 to 25 percent in 1994. *The Wall Street Journal*, April 7, 1995, p. A6.

16

THE FATE AND FUTURE
OF CHINESE SOCIALISM

"EVERY ADVANCE IS LIKEWISE a relative regression," Friedrich Engels once wrote as he pondered the costs of economic and technological progress.[1] So it has been with China during the reform era. The economic gains have been spectacular. The social results are calamitous.

China, of course, is hardly unique in suffering the incongruous coincidence of economic progress and social deterioration. Such has been the price of capitalist development everywhere, beginning two centuries ago with the social and cultural degradation of the common people of England, the homeland of capitalist industrialization. China today is experiencing, on a massive scale and in extreme forms, all the social evils of Western capitalism that modern Chinese intellectuals and political leaders sought for over a century to avoid. In endeavoring to build a modern and independent nation, five generations of Chinese intellectuals believed that the technological accomplishments of the West could be appropriated without condemning China to the social chaos and moral corruptions of capitalism. It was a search that led many of them to embrace Western socialism and to the "sinicization" of socialism. That century-long quest now ap-

---

[1] Friedrich Engels, "The Origin of the Family, Private Property and the State," in Marx and Engels, *Selected Works*, Vol. 2, p. 205.

pears to have been all but abandoned. In the 1980s, China's leaders gradually reconciled themselves to enduring the vicissitudes of a capitalist regime—that "social anarchy which turns every economic progress into a social calamity," as Marx so acutely and forebodingly described the workings of capitalism.[2]

Of the sociocultural calamities wrought by capitalism, none is more chilling than the conversion of human beings into commodities to create a labor market, an essential prerequisite for the functioning of a capitalist economy. There is something most unnatural, indeed fictitious, about turning human labor into a product to be bought and sold—for, as Karl Polanyi reminds us,[3] unlike real commodities, human beings are not created for the purpose of being sold in the marketplace. Nonetheless, it was only by borrowing this modern Western capitalist fiction—a task that fell to reformist economists at the Chinese Academy of Social Sciences—that a capitalist labor market was actually created in China, forcing the majority of the working people to barter their labor-power to survive in an increasingly marketized society.

In contrast to the familiar claims of free market doctrine, that most eminently internationalist of all contemporary ideologies, there has been nothing at all natural about the creation of a so-called free labor market in China. As has been true of the histories of all capitalist economies, the power of the state was very much involved in establishing China's labor market. Indeed, in China a highly repressive state apparatus played a particularly direct and coercive role in the commodification of labor, a process that has proceeded with a rapidity and on a scale that is historically unprecedented.

In the early developing capitalist countries the creation of labor markets spanned an agonizing century or more as feudal social relations and traditional rights to subsistence were gradually dissolved. In China, by contrast, it was the quasi-socialist institutions and practices of the Mao period that had to be destroyed in order to create a capitalist labor market, a task that was performed by the Communist state in only a few years. The most important act was the dissolution of the rural communes in the early 1980s. Hitherto, the communes,

[2] Marx, *Capital*, Vol. 1, p. 533.
[3] Polanyi, *The Great Transformation*, esp. pp. 72–73.

whatever their deficiencies in other areas of life and work, had provided at least basic subsistence and security for most of the rural population. With the abolition of the commune system and the commercialization of agriculture, nearly 200 million rural dwellers, about half the total rural workforce, were rendered redundant, unable to subsist on the land. Many have found employment as wage laborers in village and township industries (TVEs) and (in far lesser numbers) in the special economic zones. Others, some 50 million to as many as 100 million at times (depending on the vicissitudes of the market), have become wandering people who migrate from one city to another in search of temporary work, usually at construction sites, and live in shantytowns or on the streets. It was thus that there took place in China that "fearful and painful expropriation of the mass of the people" from the soil, the universal prelude to the dominion of capital.[4]

In the urban economy, dominated by state-owned industry, the full commodification of labor was signaled by the reformers' assault on what they coldly disparaged as the iron rice bowl, the system of lifetime job tenure and welfare benefits enjoyed by regular workers employed in state enterprises. With the expansion of private and collective businesses in the cities, and government policies that encourage hiring temporary and contract workers in state factories, workers with job security are becoming a vanishing minority of the urban working class.

Post-Mao China and the early-developing capitalist countries in Europe began the work of creating a labor market in far different historical circumstances and proceeded from very different social starting points. But the results have been similar: the creation of a propertyless mass of people who are compelled to sell their labor-power in accordance with the demands of the market. Indeed, in terms of the numbers of people affected in a relatively short period of time, China in the reform period has undergone the most massive and intensive process of proletarianization in world history.

In addition to the creation of a labor market, China is beginning to experience another form of commodification typically wrought by capitalist development, the buying and selling of land. Although most land in China legally remains state or collective property, much of

[4] Marx, *Capital*, Vol. 1, p. 835.

the leased land, along with houses and commercial buildings, has come to be treated as private property, with rights to the use of land freely bought, sold, and mortgaged. This, in turn, has stimulated wild speculation in real estate among the monied classes and various bureaucratic agencies. As Polanyi has observed, land, like labor, is a "fictitious commodity," in the sense that it is part of nature and not something produced for sale.[5] But, as Polanyi has also pointed out, turning land into a real commodity is an essential prerequisite for a market economy. As land use in China becomes more subject to market imperatives, it is likely that the de facto privatization of land eventually will be followed by the creation of a de jure system of private property—however much this may further fray the socialist facade of what is still officially called a socialist market economy.

The commodification of land and labor has been facilitated by a radical transformation of social values. What has been officially propagated in China during the reform era is an ethic that champions the individual pursuit of private interest not only as a good in itself but also as patriotic, the best way to achieve the national goal of modernization. It is the successful entrepreneur, no longer the peasant or worker, who is portrayed as the hero of the new age. The new business ethic has replaced old Maoist values that were so antithetical to a commercialized economy, to commodity production, and to the pursuit of profit—such now-vanished and apparently vanquished values as egalitarianism, collectivism, self-sacrifice, and solidarity. Solidarity, to be sure, remains valued in the post-Mao age, but now only in the form of a nationalist solidarity, organized under the guidance of the Communist state.

In addition to the transformation of land and labor into commodities, the market policies of the Deng regime have also commodified culture. This has taken many forms: the emergence of a commercialized—and mostly foreign-borrowed—popular culture in the cities; the pervasiveness of an officially encouraged consumer culture which, in China as elsewhere in the world, fosters popular political indifference and apathy, much to the relief of the government; and new sociocultural values, such as consumerism, which are favorable to the workings of a market economy. Chinese history too has been

[5] Polanyi, *The Great Transformation*, Chapter 6.

commodified, in the form of Disney-like "theme parks." Indeed, everything that is conceivably profitable has been seized upon by enterprising entrepreneurs and bureaucrats, not excluding Mao Zedong, whose posthumously manufactured images are turned into profits.

But it is the commodification of labor that is crucial in the development of Chinese capitalism, the matter of the greatest social and economic significance in the entire reform era, and the secret of China's economic successes.

The creation of a labor market is perhaps the most unnatural and the most inhumane feature of a capitalist economy. Few people of any political persuasion are inclined to celebrate the transformation of human beings into commodities, a mass of propertyless men and women forced to sell their labor at whatever price it will fetch on the market. It is no less a degrading process in China today than it was in its infamous English precedent of two hundred years ago, a major social calamity by almost any standard of judgment. One need not be a Marxist, or a socialist, to appreciate Karl Marx's chilling description of work under the capitalist mode of production:

> . . . the worker sinks to the level of a commodity and becomes indeed the most wretched of commodities. . . . The worker becomes an ever cheaper commodity the more commodities he creates . . . the increasing value of the world of things proceeds in direct proportion [to] the devaluation of the world of men.[6]

This social regression, and the profits of those who benefit from it, are justified on the familiar ideological grounds that a free labor market is an economic imperative in the modern world, that the profits of the owners of capital are just rewards for their special entrepreneurial and managerial skills and the economic risks they take, and that, in any event, the process will benefit society as a whole in the end, whatever the immediate motives and methods might be. It is the latter justification—the promise of improvements in the general material standard of life—that is most stressed by Chinese Communist political leaders and ideologists. The Dengist rationale is in

---

[6] Karl Marx, *Economic and Philosophic Manuscripts of 1844* (Moscow: Foreign Languages Publishing House, 1956), pp. 67–69.

fact not far different from the proposition that Adam Smith set forth more than two centuries ago—that private greed (however morally despicable) generates social wealth. And this has remained a cardinal belief in the ideology of capitalism ever since.

It is true, of course, that there have been dramatic improvements in the living standards of the Chinese people during the reign of Deng Xiaoping. However unequally distributed the gains and whatever the attendant social costs, virtually all sectors of society and all regions of the country enjoy significantly greater incomes and higher material standards of life than they did at the beginning of the reform period. This itself is an achievement of enormous human and economic significance. It is also true, however, that the great majority of the laboring population are victims of more intensive forms of economic exploitation than was the case in the pre-Deng era.

That the working people in both city and countryside generally enjoy greater per capita incomes and improved material conditions of life, on the one hand, and suffer greater exploitation at the same time, may seem contradictory. But the paradox is easily unraveled. For what China's quasi-capitalist regime has done, as capitalism in general is adept at doing, is to enormously expand production and productivity.[7] It has done so in several interrelated ways in both the urban and rural industrial sectors: by the concentration and infusion of capital (both domestic and foreign) seeking high returns on investments; by technological borrowing and innovation; by the introduction of "scientific" managerial methods borrowed from capitalist countries; and, most important, by purchasing at very low cost (by international standards) the labor-power of workers who are relatively well educated, and who are now subject to the discipline of *both* the market and the Communist state. Indeed, it is the Communist state that created the market and enforces its dictates, including the banning of free trade unions.

The result has been the sprouting of all manner of enterprises— state, "collective," private, and bureaucratic—which generate enor-

---

[7] The discussion here is confined to the industrial sector, both rural and urban, which accounts for over 80 percent of China's national income, measured in gross value of production. Agriculture is quite a different matter and the problems in the agrarian sector will be discussed separately below, including the problems of stagnating incomes (since 1985) for most peasants engaged in agricultural production.

mous profits. This, in turn, has led to the rapid expansion of the workforce, providing jobs for tens of millions of people who otherwise would lack significant earnings. Per capita income and family purchasing power have increased accordingly. Nonetheless, the wages paid to most new entrants into the industrial workforce are shockingly low. And it is cheap labor that primarily accounts for the enormous gap between the relatively low costs of production and the relatively high value of what is produced. The width of this gap is roughly indicative of the intensity of labor exploitation that is the hallmark of China's "socialist market economy," however much this process of exploitation may benefit society at large. But to say that a worker laboring in a rural factory is economically better off than she or he would have been without that factory job does not diminish the degree of exploitation.

Needless to say, it is also this wide gap between the costs and the value of production that yields the enormous surplus which the owners (or the controllers) of capital extract in the form of profits. Most of those profits are then reinvested, as capital, to further expand the productive forces in a ceaseless process of profit maximization and capital accumulation that is the driving force of any capitalist regime.

The secret of China's phenomenal economic growth in the post-Mao era is not to be discovered in the values of a moribund Confucian culture or in some special Chinese entrepreneurial genius. Rather it is to be found in the existence of social, economic, and political conditions highly favorable to the extraction of surplus value and the accumulation of capital, eminently universal features of successful processes of capitalist development. Not the least important of those favorable conditions is the presence of a huge mass of economically redundant farmers and urban youths who, subject to the dictates of both state and market, are transformed into low-paid wage laborers.

A market economy is notorious for generating inequality, a truth that has struck China with a vengeance. From presenting itself during the Mao era as the most socially and economically egalitarian of developing countries, China today is widely regarded as one of the most inequitable, often unfavorably compared with Taiwan and South

Korea—and sometimes even with India, known from Mogul times to the present as a land of "magnificence rooted in squalor."[8] Wrenching images (eerily reminiscent of Guomindang China) of great wealth and abject poverty have become commonplace in the reports of journalists and travelers in the 1990s. The great cities, from Canton to Shanghai to Beijing, are home to exclusive boutiques and expensive nightclubs where the nouveaux riche ostentatiously display themselves—and where, at the same time, growing armies of beggars and prostitutes walk the streets. In export zones, owners and managers park imported luxury cars outside their sweatshop factories where young women labor thirteen-hour days fashioning garments for a monthly wage of US$30. In relatively prosperous Guangdong province, migrant workers imported from poorer provinces form an underclass who do the low-paid agricultural work that the Cantonese have abandoned for more lucrative pursuits. And as is so commonly the case in developing and developed capitalist countries the world over, the rich have little but contempt for the poor. Thus the prosperous director of a thriving state-owned but market-restructured shoe company in Shandong was not reluctant to loudly proclaim to an American journalist: "If you want to work hard and use your head, anybody can be rich. If you are lazy, you cannot." Nor was he reluctant to reveal, indeed he was proud to say, that he pays new workers only the minimum salary of approximately US$210 per year, whereas his best managers earn as much as US$17,000 annually.[9]

Growing inequality, although certainly not to the extremes that have come to pass, was anticipated by the Deng regime. From the beginning of the reform program in 1979, "egalitarianism" was denounced as one of the most heinous of "ultraleftist" sins. In the virulence of the attacks on Maoist egalitarian values, ridiculed as "everyone eating out of the same big pot," one detects a primitive capitalist belief that wealth is a stimulant to—and a just reward for—the productive efforts of the rich, whereas poverty is a spur to the poor. Thus the Dengist regime boasts of the number of entrepreneurs who have become millionaires in the reform period, while it

[8] The phrase and characterization are borrowed from Barrington Moore, *Social Origins of Dictatorship and Democracy*, p. 320.

[9] Marcus W. Brauchli, "As the Rich in China Grow Richer, the Poor Are Growing Resentful," *The Wall Street Journal*, October 19, 1993, pp. A1, A17.

has made only the most rudimentary efforts to compensate for the collapse of Mao era public welfare and social security systems, which has left many tens of millions of peasants and others largely dependent on private philanthropy.

Inequality in China today is no longer simply a matter of income differentials or special access to material privileges by virtue of political rank or influence. While old forms of inequality inherited from the Mao era—differences between provinces and regions, between urban and rural areas, and between the rulers and the ruled—have increased in the Deng era, what is really novel is that capitalist development has generated new social groups who enjoy many of the social and economic attributes of a ruling class. Among the newly privileged, both in wealth and in status, are a rural elite of commercial farmers and landholders who employ wage laborers on an increasingly large scale; well-to-do private—but usually politically well-connected—entrepreneurs engaged in a great variety of financial, commercial, and industrial undertakings; a new managerial and professional elite who are the greatest beneficiaries of profit-making enterprises, both industrial and commercial, and both state and "collective"; and, by no means the least important, bureaucrats involved in the market, ranging from the petty capitalism of rural Party cadres to the myriad enterprises and investments of China's largest capitalist entrepreneur, the People's Liberation Army.

There is no reliable data on the incomes of the members of these classes, and thus they have been largely ignored in studies of income distribution.[10] But any serious attempt to comprehend the meaning of inequality in the Deng era, or to understand the social direction of post-Deng China, clearly cannot ignore the newly emergent social groups who derive the greatest benefits from China's socialist market economy. Nor can they be ignored in considering the gap between rich and poor in China. The poor may not necessarily be getting poorer, at least by conventional economic measurements, but the rich are getting richer and the gulf between them is clearly widening. It is likely that powerful resentments are being bred among an urban

---

[10] As is the case, for example, in the most sophisticated of such studies: Aizur Rahman Khan, Keith Griffin, Carl Riskin, and Zhao Renwei, "Household Income and Its Distribution in China," *The China Quarterly*, No. 132 (December 1992), pp. 1029–61.

populace schooled in egalitarian norms and accustomed to relatively small differences in living standards and visible consumption.

Beyond new class differentiations, inequalities inherited from the Mao period have been greatly exacerbated under the reform regime. Regional differences in income, especially between coastal provinces and the interior, wide enough during the Maoist era, have become wider over the post-Mao years.[11] This is largely the result of the government's emphasis on foreign trade and investment and the priority given to developing the already advanced coastal areas.

Of greater social and political import is the widening gap between the cities and the countryside. Through several millennia of Chinese history, cities have prospered through the exploitation of peasants— by means of taxes, rents, corvée labor, and unfair terms of trade.[12] The Communist Revolution, based on organizing the forces of peasant revolt in the countryside to "surround and overwhelm" the cities, promised to eliminate the gap between urban and rural areas. The Land Reform of the early 1950s, and subsequent Maoist efforts to develop the rural areas, certainly mitigated the exploitation of the countryside. But, in the end, the Maoist industrialization of the cities was financed by extracting the surplus from the peasantry.

The reforms of the Deng Xiaoping era promised once again to bring about a more equitable relationship between town and countryside. The reform program initially focused on the rural areas, and rural incomes and living standards soared in the early 1980s, temporarily narrowing the urban-rural gap. This, however, proved to be a one-time gain for the peasants. Since 1985, agricultural production and farm income have stagnated. The breakup of the communes and the commercialization of agriculture revealed an enormous reservoir of redundant labor. Almost half of a rural workforce that numbered more than 400 million at the end of the Mao era have become non-agricultural wage laborers, many employed in rural industries, others working at mostly menial jobs in the cities.

Among those who have remained on the land, a dominant class of commercial farmers has emerged, and they are closely intertwined

[11] For data on the increase in regional inequality in the post-Mao period, as of 1988, see ibid.

[12] On the exploitative relationship between town and countryside in both traditional and modern Chinese history, see the classic study by Fei Hsiao-tung (Fei Xiaotong), *China's Gentry: Essays in Urban-Rural Relations* (Chicago: University of Chicago Press, 1953).

with private entrepreneurs operating trading, trucking, and various service and commercial companies. Together they make up a new rural bourgeoisie who usually can count on—or buy—the support of local Party cadres and county-level officials and judges. The majority of peasants have remained peasants, some working as hired agricultural laborers on relatively large capitalist-type farms, others struggling to maintain their own farms. They suffer from an absence of government welfare assistance and state investment, the decay of rural educational and health-care systems, low prices for their products, the deterioration of much of the water-control and other infrastructures inherited from the collective era, and a plethora of extralegal taxes and fees exacted by corrupt bureaucrats. Due to exhausted and probably pilfered local government coffers, peasants in many areas suffer not only from underpayment for their products but underpayment in "white slips" in lieu of cash.[13]

The deteriorating conditions in agriculture and the plight of the peasantry belatedly became a matter of government concern in 1993. Official newspapers were suddenly filled with editorials lamenting the peasants' burdens, echoing old fears that agricultural production would be insufficient to sustain rapid industrial growth.[14] Nor were Communist leaders oblivious to the political dangers of the farm crisis. Amidst a rash of reports of growing peasant protests, riots, and violent clashes with the authorities, Wan Li, Chairman of the National People's Congress, warned in June 1993 that the problems in agriculture have "severely undermined the interests of the peasants, damaged their enthusiasm, and soured relations between themselves and the Party. Should the state neglect to find solutions to these problems, conditions will go from bad to worse, with the peasants turning against the state and letting agriculture slide into chaos."[15]

---

[13] William Hinton, in a series of articles written in the mid-1980s, was one of very few observers to diagnose the making of what is now known as "the farm crisis"; most scholars continued to celebrate the economic miracle in agriculture years after the miracle abruptly ended in 1985. See "Reform in Stride: Rural Change 1984," "Reform Unravels: Rural Change 1986," and "Dazhai Revisited: 1987." These are reprinted in Hinton, *The Great Reversal* (New York: Monthly Review Press, 1990).

[14] *People's Daily*, and *Guangming ribao*, April 1993. Cited in "Quarterly Chronicle and Documentation," *The China Quarterly*, No. 135 (September 1993), pp. 635–36.

[15] Cited in "Quarterly Chronicle and Documentation," *The China Quarterly*, No. 136 (December 1993), p. 1046.

Remedial measures were announced, including a prohibition on paying peasants with white slips, a probably unenforceable ban on illegal fees and taxes exacted by local bureaucrats, and promises of increased state investment in agriculture.

The plight of the majority of China's farmers during a period of exceptionally rapid industrial growth testifies to the truth of the observation, most forcefully presented by Barrington Moore, that the peasants are the first victims of modernization and, in the end, pay most of the costs, whatever the political character of the regime that presides over the process.[16] The hope that Mao's regime and then the hope that Deng's regime would prove exceptions to the rule have now both been defeated.

Household income studies reinforce the conclusion that the peasants have been the principal victims of Dengist modernization. On the basis of 1988 data, a group of distinguished economists concluded that of all the conventionally measured inequalities, the gap between town and countryside is the widest and has grown the most rapidly in the reform era, and that China's urban-rural disparity in incomes is "very high by the standards of contemporary Asia."[17] There can be little doubt that the disparity has increased since 1988.

Yet to focus on such broad categories as "urban" and "rural" risks obscuring the more important processes of social class differentiation that are taking place within both cities and countryside. What is of long-term historical significance in the rural areas is the emergence of a dominant elite of prosperous commercial farmers and private entrepreneurs, who are now socially and economically distinct from the mass of ordinary peasants and rural industrial workers, and who can count on the political support of the Communist political apparatus in the countryside. It is, of course, ironic that the dominant rural class has the backing of a party that came to power by championing the interests of the poorest and most oppressed peasants. But it is hardly surprising. For the new rural bourgeoisie was created by the Chinese Communist Party in accordance with Deng Xiaoping's

---

[16] Moore, *Social Origins of Dictatorship and Democracy*, esp. Chapter 9.

[17] Khan, Griffin, Riskin, and Zhao, "Household Income and Its Distribution in China," p. 1059.

policies of commercializing the countryside. Indeed, it is a class that in no small measure is composed of rural Party cadres and ex-cadres, and their relatives, friends, and associates.

Accompanying the rise of the new rural bourgeoisie is the proletarianization of much of the peasantry. In the new rural industries, the most rapidly expanding sector of the Chinese economy, young peasants turned workers encounter the harsh conditions of early industrialization, and they do so on the most massive scale in world history. In many areas, twelve- to fifteen-hour workdays are common and low wages are universal; living conditions are primitive, often in unhygienic factory dormitories; overtime work is usually mandatory; many workers are young teenagers and, along with female laborers, are pitilessly victimized by owners and managers; workers are typically fired on the spot at the arbitrary will of managers; working conditions are hazardous, resulting in many thousands of deaths annually in industrial accidents and fires; and workers are often preyed upon by greedy bureaucrats demanding payment of newly invented fees.

While there are national and local laws limiting the length of the workday and prohibiting abuses such as child labor, the laws are rarely enforced. As a Western lawyer representing foreign businesses in Shanghai remarked: "They [the government] threaten every once in a while to tighten up on labor standards and protect workers [but] in reality, the Chinese [authorities] consistently back the managers."[18]

It is true, as champions of Deng Xiaoping's market reforms hasten to note, that even the most miserably paid of the new industrial workers earn more than they would have if they had attempted to remain on the land. And these earnings explain why average rural household income has not declined in recent years, despite the farm crisis. But the social, physical, and psychological costs have been enormous.

The miseries inflicted by proletarianization are made all the more unmerciful by the absence of job security and social benefits for workers in town and village enterprises. The plight of workers who are laid off or injured is compounded by the virtual absence of public

[18] *The Wall Street Journal*, May 19, 1994, p. A4.

welfare in the countryside. With the abolition of the communes, the rural social security and health-care systems largely disappeared, and the government has done little to replace them. The problem is also beginning to affect the cities, as "industrial restructuring," resulting in layoffs and the conversion of regular workers to a contractual status, erodes the highly developed system of social welfare benefits once enjoyed by state workers.

The government is well aware of these problems and promises a social safety net, including unemployment compensation. It is likely that a welfare system deemed sufficient to preserve social and political order eventually will be established. But it is not likely to be an especially benevolent system. A Communist regime that took such great pains to "smash the iron rice bowl," and one that is determined to expand the labor market, will not adopt generous social welfare policies, even within the limited financial means available to it. As English history long ago demonstrated, and contemporary Chinese history confirms, the threat of hunger is the most effective way to provide a marketable supply of "free" labor. Chinese peasants, like their English predecessors, do not willingly leave their homes to entomb themselves in factories. They do so, for the most part, only out of extreme necessity, a necessity now ensured by the coercion of the market, as policymakers in Beijing no doubt coolly calculate.

The natural environment has been another casualty of rapid economic development, as has been the case to greater or lesser degrees in every industrializing country ever since English factory owners began to poison the air and the water early in the nineteenth century.[19] The environmental destruction that was underway during the years of Maoist industrialization has accelerated in the post-Mao era, not only in the pollution of air and water but in the depletion of natural resources, especially forests. But the most perilous problem is the decline in arable land, due to the conversion of farmland into fisheries and other commercial undertakings, industrial development, and the building of houses. Between 1949 and 1992, according to official statistics, arable land declined by 15 percent, while the rural

---

[19] A recognition of the dangers of environmental destruction is not a late-twentieth-century insight. The degradation of the English environment in the early stages of the industrial revolution was condemned (and described in considerable detail) by Robert Owen and Karl Marx, among others.

labor force grew by 123 percent.[20] Some foreign observers calculate that the decline is considerably greater.[21]

However, it is not the place of Western observers, living in societies whose modern economic development caused massive and wanton environmental destruction, to lecture Chinese on the dangers that industrialization poses to the world of nature. Indeed, it would be more than a bit hypocritical for an American to do so when the United States, with less than 6 percent of the world's population, consumes more than 40 percent of the world's natural resources. Chinese Communist leaders are painfully aware that they confront a dilemma in which the survival of the Chinese people demands both the exploitation *and* the survival of their natural surroundings. The Chinese will resolve the dilemma in their own fashion, without benefit of the advice of foreign moralizers.

The social dislocations wrought by market forces are largely responsible for the upsurge in crime so frequently lamented by officials of the Deng regime. Beyond such economic crimes as bribery and official profiteering, which are clearly market-generated and which have become so pervasive that they are now apathetically accepted as part of the normal functioning of a "socialist market economy," there has been an enormous increase in common crimes during the Deng era. Between 1978 and 1990, according to official figures, there was an elevenfold increase in serious crimes.[22] Although the most visible urban crimes—especially those involving drugs and unemployed youths—have received the most attention in the urban-based press, crime in the countryside seems more serious and of greater political import. Peasant criminal activity has been directed mainly against state property, particularly the theft of commodities from government warehouses and the pillaging of natural resources—coal and

[20] *Guangming ribao*, August 12, 1993. Cited in "Quarterly Chronicle and Documentation," *The China Quarterly*, No. 136 (December 1993), p. 1047. The ability of Chinese agriculture to increase production sufficiently to feed a population that more than doubled over this period, and at higher nutritional levels, was not the result of the growth of the rural workforce, which was largely redundant, but rather because of the massive use of chemical fertilizers beginning in the late 1950s, one of the major accomplishments of the Mao regime.

[21] Vaclav Smil, for example, estimates that farmland has declined by one-third since 1957. Smil, *China's Environmental Crisis*, pp. 57–58.

[22] *People's Daily*, (overseas edition), November 11, 1992. Since the 1985 urban economic reforms, serious crime has been increasing at an average annual rate of 40 percent.

especially oil. Such theft is commonplace in much of the countryside and has become the primary source of income for some peasant families. Armed attacks on railroads, long symbolic of state authority, are also common, sometimes carried out by semi-regular bands of peasants known as *chefei luba* (train and highway bandits), who rob not only trains but also riverboats, buses, and automobiles.[23] Peasant criminal activities have spilled over into the cities, where the miserable living conditions and nomadic mode of life of migrant wage laborers breed petty and sometimes serious crimes. The reappearance of widespread criminal activity in the rural areas is in part due to the commune system's demise, which took from the peasants a modest degree of security and gave them a great deal of freedom of movement in return.

A market society presupposes the dissolution of traditional (or pre-capitalist) values as well as traditional institutions. In particular, the functioning of a market society requires values that sanctify individual gain, the accumulation of private wealth, and above all the pursuit of profit—and, consequently, the subordination of customary notions of fairness, justice, and communality, or what is sometimes called "the moral economy of the crowd."[24] Classically, in England, the ideological battle was joined over the customary principle of "the right to live" (or the "right to subsistence"), to which were opposed the values of classical economic liberalism. Foremost among the latter was the pursuit of individual profit through the policy of laissez-faire, presumably in quest of the ultimate goal of "economic improvement."[25]

In China, the creation of a market economy required the destruction of *both* socialist and traditional values. While Maoist ideology had undermined much of what remained of the traditional value system, in some respects it also reinforced the surviving communitarian elements of traditional morality. The most powerful continuities re-

[23] For an informative account of rural criminal activity, see Liu Binyan, "Another 'Rural Encirclement of the Cities' Campaign," *China Focus*, Vol. 2, No. 1 (January 1, 1994).
[24] See, especially, E. P. Thompson, *The Making of the English Working Class* (New York: Pantheon, 1964).
[25] See Polanyi, *The Great Transformation*, esp. Chapters 12 and 13.

volved around the notion that the state had a moral responsibility to provide a basic livelihood for the people. In the cities of Mao's China, this ideally took the form of lifetime job security and comprehensive welfare benefits for state workers, the quasi-socialist system that Deng's reform ideologists disparaged as a "feudal" hangover. In the countryside it was the basic subsistence guarantees provided by the communes. Such was the Chinese version, in modern socialist dress, of the traditional and precapitalist English ethic of "the right to live." This, in brief, was the implicit social contract between the Maoist state and the Chinese people. In order for the Deng regime to establish a market economy, and especially a capitalist labor market that such an economy required, these Maoist institutions and values had to be discredited and eliminated.

Deng Xiaoping, once in power, made no serious effort to revitalize socialist values and institutions. After a brief and politically expedient flirtation with socialist democracy, he set about promoting values conducive to the creation of a market economy. The essentials of that process were quite simple, revolving around the popularization of several seemingly banal but socially and psychologically potent slogans. "To get rich is glorious" sanctified acquisitiveness and entrepreneurship. The injunction that "some must get rich first" sanctioned inequality. And the emphasis on "smashing the iron rice bowl" announced that the government no longer guaranteed the right of subsistence. As intended, the overall effect of these various slogans and injunctions was to ethically sanction the pursuit of profit. All of these themes were elaborated upon, in extenso, in Marxian theoretical terms in the official ideological literature of the 1980s.

The result of the replacement of Maoist values by the precepts of the market was to create an ideological vacuum and a moral desert. Both socialists and traditionalists mourn the moral condition of post-Mao China, and they do so from both "postcapitalist" and "precapitalist" perspectives. A writer who holds to the traditionalist belief that Chinese intellectuals are the carriers of an age-old code of ethics expressed the feelings of many when he wrote near the close of the Deng era:

> . . . the rapidity and severity of the decline in Chinese social morality and ethics is intolerable. The moral crisis in China is

more widespread and more serious than the similar crisis in the former socialist nations of Eastern Europe. . . .

The pendulum has swung from the extremism of the Maoist age to the extremism of the current period, from moral absolutism to nihilism, from radical collectivism to radical individualism, from the suppression of all desire to its indulgence. . . .

Some foreign observers of China pay attention only to the unprecedented growth in the economy, ignoring the fact that the current degree of social disorder, alienation, and moral degeneration is also without precedent. At no previous time in her history has China ever seen phenomena such as today's general lack of any feeling of social responsibility paired with the absence of any sense that this is a worrisome thing. Never before have so few citizens suffered pangs of conscience upon harming their fellows or the greater society. Never before have so many gazed upon the suffering of others with such utter indifference.[26]

These social costs and consequences of market reform are hardly unique to China. The commodification of land and labor, grotesque extremes in the distribution of wealth, the dominance of town over countryside, the proletarianization of the peasantry, the horrors of factory work, the lack of adequate social welfare, environmental destruction, and the subordination of traditional moral values and ethics ("drowned in the icy waters of egotistical calculation," as Marx put it) to an aggressive and vulgar materialism—these are among the universal features of capitalist development. Similar costs were exacted by the conquests of capitalism in Europe in the nineteenth century and they have been repeated—with national variations, of course—throughout the greater part of the world during the twentieth century. Save for the dizzying speed and the massive scale of the process, the social results of the workings of the market in the post-Mao era have rather few special "Chinese characteristics." Although the origins and the nature of China's capitalist system may be unusual, its social consequences are quite typical.

What is exceptional is that Chinese capitalism developed in a society and among a people that experienced several generations of

---

[26] Liu Zi'an, "China Calls for Morality," *China Focus*, Vol. 2, No. 4 (April 1, 1994), pp. 3, 5.

"socialism." What, then, are the social and political implications of this extraordinary reversal of what so many for so long assumed to be the normal historical sequence of "the transition from capitalism to socialism"? At the close of the Deng era, it is natural to pose that question and also to inquire into the dynamics of the socioeconomic system created in the name of "reform." What contradictions and conflicts are likely to be engendered by China's "socialist market economy"? And what does the the new system—and perhaps the remnants of the old—portend for the future of Chinese socialism?

It will be many decades before Chinese history yields answers to these questions. But I shall set forth a few brief thoughts here, by way of conclusion to this inquiry.

It is most unlikely that it was Deng Xiaoping's intention to establish a capitalist regime when he proposed his reform program in 1978. Faced with the very real threat of economic stagnation, Deng and his associates believed that the market and other capitalist devices could be selectively used to speed the pace and quality of China's economic development. That, in turn, it was assumed in rather orthodox Marxist fashion, would provide the necessary material basis for a fully socialist society to flower sometime in the future, while, in the meantime, strengthening the Chinese nation and raising the abysmally low living standards of its people. The ends of socialism, nationalism, and popular welfare would be equally well served.

The aims were laudable and the diagnosis of China's economic condition was percipient, as the rapid deterioration of the Soviet Union's economy during the 1980s would suggest. The belief that capitalist means and techniques could be used to further socialist ends was not without precedent in the Marxist tradition. Lenin, after all, had been a consistent advocate of borrowing the latest methods of the advanced capitalist countries (especially from Germany and the United States) to build Russian socialism. And Lenin's New Economic Policy of 1921 had, in its time, portended a longer and wider capitalist detour from the socialist road than the one Deng Xiaoping and the Chinese reformers seemed to have had in mind in the late 1970s.

There was also a Chinese historical precedent. In the late nineteenth century, in the waning decades of the imperial regime, conservative Chinese modernizers, the "self-strengtheners," had attempted to borrow Western technology and methods while preserving traditional culture and society. To this end, they had revived the famous *ti-yung* (essence and function) formula, and turned it into a Confucian rationalization for borrowing from the West: Western technology (*yung*) would be used to fortify the Chinese essence (*ti*). But the Confucian modernizers soon discovered that insofar as they were successful in importing Western material means they were undermining the Chinese ends they intended to preserve.

It is unlikely that Deng Xiaoping looked back to this celebrated but failed effort. Had he done so, he might have learned that the means and ends of capitalism are not easily separated. As it was, Deng repeated the mistake of his modernizing predecessors, although achieving much greater economic successes while doing so. The more the methods of capitalism were economically successful in Deng's China, the more they overwhelmed the socialist ends they originally were intended to serve. Chinese society in the age of market reform brings to mind Marx's depiction of the dynamic and unruly nature of capitalism—"a society that has conjured up such gigantic means of production and exchange is like the sorcerer who is no longer able to control the powers of the nether world whom he has called up by his spells."[27]

It is now clear that "the powers of the nether world" have triumphed in China and that the processes of capitalist development that were set in motion in 1978 are irreversible. However, one cannot prove that a capitalist economy (or mode of production) is dominant in China on the basis of one or another of the usual definitions of capitalism. Capitalism is notoriously defiant of definition, as Robert Heilbroner has pointed out,[28] and many of the most eminent students of the history of capitalism have taken great pains to avoid defining the subject of their inquiries.[29] Bolder observers who have ventured to set forth definitions have fallen short. Thus Robert Tucker's prop-

[27] "Communist Manifesto," in Marx and Engels, *Selected Works*, Vol. 1, p. 38.
[28] Robert L. Heilbroner, *The Nature and Logic of Capitalism* (New York: Norton, 1985), esp. Chapter 1.
[29] Including Fernand Braudel, as Heilbroner notes (p. 15), and Heilbroner himself in some dozen books preceding *The Nature and Logic of Capitalism*.

osition that capitalism, according to Marx, is a system of production based on "the exploitation of wage labor for the accumulation of capital"[30] seems eminently sound—but, as we have seen,[31] leads to the conclusion that an essentially capitalist mode of production prevailed throughout the Mao period, thus erasing the distinction between the Mao and Deng eras. Other definitions, most quite plausible, encounter similar difficulties when applied to concrete historical realities.

The phenomenon of capitalism is all-pervasive, but its essence remains elusive. In the brief discussion that follows, I will avoid an explicit definition and simply note four features of the Dengist reform program that have convinced me that an essentially capitalist mode of production became dominant in China in the Deng era, albeit a capitalism of the peculiar bureaucratic kind that has been discussed in Chapter 11.

The Deng Xiaoping regime inherited from its Maoist predecessor many of the necessary (but not sufficient) features of a capitalist economy. Among them was a relatively well-developed modern industrial and technological base; a hybrid mode of economic development that had separated the immediate producers from the means of production; the predominance of wage labor, formally in the cities, in disguised form in the countryside; and an efficient system for capital accumulation—through the state's extraction of surplus value, especially from the countryside.

The reformers added four crucial elements that a market economy required. First, China was partially integrated into the world economy through Deng Xiaoping's open-door policy, a powerful force for molding internal Chinese socioeconomic relations in accordance with international capitalist norms. Second, profit-making was universalized in the conduct of economic life and established as the main criterion for judging the success or failure of enterprises, state as well as private. While profit as such is by no means uniquely capitalist, it is essential to a capitalist regime, "the life blood of capitalism," as Heilbroner has said.[32] Third, and most important, a market economy both presupposes and reproduces the full commodification of labor-

---

[30] Tucker, *The Marxian Revolutionary Idea*, pp. 42–43.
[31] In Chapter 2.
[32] Heilbroner, *The Nature and Logic of Capitalism*, p. 76.

power—and that has largely been accomplished through the proletarianization of a good portion of the peasantry and the "smashing of the iron rice bowl" in the cities. Finally, the construction and functioning of a market economy presupposes an entrepreneurial class, and the Communist state which created the new market economy also set about to create a new Chinese bourgeoisie. With the basic social relationships demanded by the market thus fashioned over the 1980s, the Chinese mode of production was predominantly capitalist by the end of that most extraordinary and ultimately most tragic of decades.

China's capitalism is not fully developed, to be sure. Absent are the legal systems and norms of human behavior which accompanied and facilitated the development of capitalism in the Western countries, and which took many decades, indeed centuries, to evolve. More glaringly absent is a developed system of private property. The lack of private ownership of the major means of production and the still-predominant role of the state in the modern sector of the economy are the two major factors cited by those who maintain that China is still essentially "socialist," or at least not yet really capitalist.

These features are indeed important, but perhaps less so than might appear at first glance. For leased properties, especially in the countryside and increasingly so in the cities, are more and more treated as private property. And economic enterprises, whatever their formal ownership status, all fully act as capitalist entities in an essentially capitalist marketplace.[33] State and collective ownership, in many important respects, have become fictitious, although a still politically necessary fiction. Nonetheless, demands for de jure privatization will no doubt eventually be heard from farmers, managers, and bureaucrats who will want the properties and enterprises they now control and profit from to become fully alienable. They desire the legal as well as the de facto freedom to buy and sell property and, above all, the right to pass on accumulated wealth and productive property to their heirs. Thus far, however, the post-Mao regime has been successful in avoiding the politically explosive question of formal ownership without undermining the functionally capitalist character of the reformed economic system.

Ambiguity on the ownership question is perhaps a virtue. Or, at

---

[33] For example, state-owned firms raise capital by selling stock on the Shanghai and Shenzhen exchanges.

least, it is socially functional. Retaining the fiction of state and collective property gives some credence to the socialist claims of Communist leaders—at least to those who simplistically take the absence of private ownership of the means of production to be socialism. Ambiguity on the ownership of productive property also allows greater leeway for the operations of China's bureaucratic bourgeoisie. As we have observed, in a society where the bourgeoisie had been destroyed by a Communist state in the name of carrying out "the transition to socialism," the task of creating a new class of entrepreneurs necessary for the functioning of a capitalist market could only be performed by the Communist state itself, now in the name of creating a "socialist market economy." The bureaucrats of the Communist regime, high and low, were best positioned to take advantage of the new market mechanisms—and to heed Deng Xiaoping's injunction to get rich. After some initial hesitation, many did so, overcoming such ideological inhibitions as they may have had.

It is thus hardly surprising that the new Chinese bourgeoisie not only is the creature of the Communist state and its policies but is also largely composed of Party and state officials, ex-officials, their relatives, and their friends. While a significant portion of the bourgeoisie is private—not having sprung directly from the bureaucracy—they are nonetheless wholly dependent on bureaucratic patronage. Moreover, a major segment of the Chinese bourgeoisie is actually composed of bureaucratic organs of the Communist Party-state apparatus, the largest of which is the PLA, an increasingly important actor in the international world of capitalist trade, finance, and investment.

Given its strongly bureaucratic character, China's new capitalist class contributes not to "pluralism," as many Western observers reflexively assume, but rather to a further blurring of the line between state and society. The history of Chinese capitalism thus far provides little support for the recently faddish notion of an emergent "civil society" striving to free itself from the clutches of the state. Indeed, China's new capitalists are psychologically as well as economically dependent on the Communist state—and rely on the state's apparatus of repression for their political and economic well-being, not least of all to tame the working classes. A bourgeoisie whose economic fortunes are so closely bound up with the political fortunes of the Communist state is not a social class that holds great democratic potential.

It is possible that China's new capitalists eventually will shed their bureaucratic roots, evolve into a genuinely independent bourgeoisie, and assert their interests (which may or may not be favorable to democracy) against the power of the state. But that, should it occur, will involve a very lengthy process of historical evolution that will be counted in generations, not in years or even decades. In the meantime, the present bureaucratic capitalist regime (presided over by the Communist Party-state, or a future functional equivalent) is likely to remain dominant, as long as it is able to maintain a sufficiently vigorous pace of economic growth to satisfy its bureaucratic, entrepreneurial, and nationalistic constituents. That regime will continue to promote the most massive process of capitalist economic transformation in world history, with social and ecological devastations and psychological ravages occurring on a correspondingly massive scale.

In this frenzy of capitalist development, promoted by a nationalistic regime seeking the most rapid possible route to modernization regardless of social cost, little of Chinese socialism—or what once passed for socialism—survives. The rulers of the Deng era cannot fairly be accused of having destroyed a socialist society, for no socialism worthy of the name ever existed. But one can mourn the loss of any serious striving for socialism by the leaders of a party which still poses as Marxist—and deplore the suppression of democratic Marxists and other socialists, who are denounced either as "leftists" or as "bourgeois rightists" as political convenience dictates. One can also mourn the indiscriminate sweeping away of all quasi-socialist institutions and values inherited from the Mao era, which, according to the imperatives of the market, stand in the way of "development." And one might also grieve the abandonment of the hope held by Chinese intellectuals since the late nineteenth century that China could become modern and industrialized without its people suffering all the agonies of a capitalist regime.

Yet the leaders of the People's Republic still feel the need to claim a socialist lineage. They present themselves as the true descendants of both Marx and Mao, and as the guardians of the revolution of 1949. While the political and psychological significance of this claim to a socialist legitimacy may well be worth pondering, socialism itself has been ever more narrowly redefined to meet the political needs of the moment, with the definition eventually reduced to modern economic development, pure and simple. Such was the import of Deng Xiaoping's final commentary on socialism, set forth in 1992, perhaps a fitting summation of his ideological legacy: "Socialism's real nature is to liberate the productive forces, and the ultimate goal of socialism is to achieve common prosperity."[34]

While there remains a claim to a socialist legitimacy, however spurious, there clearly is no socialist vision. Visions of a socialist utopia have been displaced entirely by nationalist visions of China's wealth and power, and its future greatness, for which rapid economic development is, of course, the most essential prerequisite. Nationalism is hardly a new phenomenon in the history of Chinese Communism. The Chinese Communist Party was born in a highly nationalist milieu and the revolution it led was as much a war for national independence as it was a social class struggle for the liberation of the oppressed. In a country so long impinged upon by foreign imperialism, nationalism and social revolution were natural allies, and they reinforced each other during the long revolutionary struggle. But nationalism and socialism make for an unholy alliance, and the tension between them inevitably grew after 1949, one of the major contradictions of the Mao period. That nationalism, the principal ideological expression of the bourgeois side of the Chinese Communist Revolution, ultimately proved triumphant is more than apparent in the ideology and the social policies of the Deng era. It is a triumph that reflects itself in the striking contrast between the chauvinistic vigor of the regime's patriotic celebrations and its feeble, rote-like repetitions of stale Marxist-Leninist slogans. The triumph of nationalism asserts itself in a new historiography which portrays modern Chinese history almost exclusively as the history of modernization and great modernizers, from Zeng Guofan to Deng Xiaoping, while ignoring the social class conflicts that marked that history. Nationalism and class struggle, an uneasy marriage during Maoist times, finally have been divorced.

But the contemporary emphasis on nationalism is not simply a matter of ideological preference. Or it might better be said that na-

---

[34] "Central Document No. 2 (1992): On Transmitting and Studying Comrade Deng Xiaoping's Important Remarks," FBIS-CHI-91-063-S.

tionalism is a matter of ideological preference because it suits both the mentality and the material interests of China's ruling bureaucratic strata, while socialism does not. For postrevolutionary bureaucrats, the great majority of whom have no direct personal experience in the revolutionary struggle, nationalism supports the political status quo, fortifying their place and their privileges in a national political apparatus. By contrast, socialism, which presupposes democracy in any conceivable post-Mao reincarnation, threatens bureaucratic power and opportunities for wealth.

Nationalism also reinforces capitalism—at least insofar as the market is seen as the most efficient instrument to realize the eminently nationalist goal of wealth and power. But the social results of Chinese capitalism are not likely to please the nationalist. For the savage capitalism that operates under the cloak of a socialist market economy is bringing about enormous social transformations and upheavals—massive proletarianization, more intensive forms of exploitation, greater alienation, enormous gaps between rich and poor, and growing economic and social differences between town and countryside. In short, what Marx called capitalism's "uninterrupted disturbance of all social conditions"[35] is generating new and ever-sharper class conflicts that are proving incompatible with the nationalist denial of social divisions within the nation. Deng Xiaoping's insistence on unity and stability may have been a necessary condition to set a dynamic capitalism in motion, but social and political harmony is not likely to be the result of the process.

Yet there remains the hope that China is not inevitably doomed to endure what Karl Marx once called "all the fatal vicissitudes of the capitalist regime,"[36] the hope that something of socialism can be salvaged within the framework of the existing sociopolitical system and that Communism (or at least Chinese Communism) is reformable. Such were the convictions of most Chinese intellectuals in the early

---

[35] As Marx characterized the result of the bourgeoisie's need to revolutionize production constantly. "Communist Manifesto," p. 36.

[36] As Marx phrased it in holding out the faint possibility that Russia might "bypass" capitalism and proceed to a socialist reorganization of society on the basis of the traditional village commune. "Marx to the Editorial Board of the 'Otechestvenniye Zapiski,' " Karl Marx and Frederick Engels, *Selected Correspondence* (Moscow: Foreign Languages Publishing House, 1953), p. 378.

years of Deng Xiaoping's reign, based on a faith in the utility of the market, a faith shared by a good many sympathetic Western scholars who assured their readers that the market was a necessary instrument to bring about the long-sought "transition to socialism."[37] That belief, in turn, was inspired in part by a wildly optimistic assessment of market socialism in Eastern Europe, especially in Hungary and Yugoslavia.

In recent years the hope that the existing system can be reformed in a genuinely socialist fashion has focused on local rural industries and what is said to be their collectivist, communitarian, and democratic potential.[38] The importance of township and village enterprises (TVEs) is undeniable. They constitute by far the most dynamic sector of the Chinese economy, the value of their extraordinarily diverse output having increased at an astonishing annual rate of about 30 percent since 1980.[39] The TVEs employ well over 100 million workers and it is this rural industrial sector, not agriculture, that has been the main source of rural household income growth, especially since 1985.

Yet, however economically successful, there are numerous considerations which counsel skepticism about the socialist potential of rural industry. While rural enterprises are officially described as part of the collective sector of the economy, the meaning of "collective" is ambiguous and actual ownership and control of the TVEs is obscure. While a small number of rural industries are collectively owned and operated by their workers, and a substantial number are privately owned, the great majority are owned or controlled by local governments. A considerable number of the latter, however, are con-

---

[37] For example, the influential introductory essay by Mark Selden and Victor Lippit, editors of *The Transition to Socialism in China*, pp. 3–31.

[38] The intellectual origins of local rural industry in China can be traced to the writings of the famed anthropologist and sociologist Fei Xiaotong in the 1930s and 1940s. In English translation, see Fei Hsiao-tung, *China's Gentry*. The first to implement the concept was Mao Zedong during the Great Leap Forward. But rural industrialization only began to flourish on a large scale under Deng Xiaoping's reform regime, now with the assistance of Fei Xiaotong, who returned to public life in 1978 after having been silenced for twenty years as a "rightist." One of the most eloquent advocates today of the socialist potential of rural industry is Cui Zhiyuan. See his "China's Rural Industrialization: Flexible Specialization, Moebius-Strip Ownership and Proudhonian Socialism" (University of Chicago, research paper).

[39] As contrasted with the still very impressive rate of approximately 11 percent for industry as a whole.

tracted or leased to private capitalists, both foreign and domestic, and have become de facto privatized; others are operated under complex partnership and share-holding arrangements where ownership and control are particularly ambiguous. But the great majority of rural industries are owned and managed by local government organs. It is by no means clear who the real beneficiaries are. There is not yet sufficient evidence to judge if this is a successful form of "municipal socialism," as characterized by one observer,[40] or another manifestation of bureaucratic capitalism where the greatest profits go not to the local community but rather to the officials who govern the community.

In either case, rural enterprises operate in a larger market economy and must conform to the rules of the capitalist market, including the exploitation of wage labor. And it is precisely the commodification of labor-power, as Ellen Meiksins Wood has forcefully pointed out, that "places the strictest limits on the 'socialization' of the market and its capacity to assume a human face."[41] While there is considerably less naiveté today about the magic of the market than there was in the early 1980s, there is a strong reluctance among China's remaining socialist intellectuals to acknowledge fully the deleterious social consequences of market relationships. They would prefer to believe, now that the Dengist regime has gone so far in erecting a capitalist economy, that it is possible to utilize the economically beneficial aspects of the market without suffering its destructive social and ecological consequences.

It must also be noted that the belief in the socialist potentialities of rural industry, even supposing that the TVEs actually have all the collectivist virtues sometimes attributed to them, assumes the cooperation of a beneficent state. That, in turn, rests on the hope that the politics of the post-Deng era will bring sympathetic democratic socialists to power in the Chinese Communist Party. Or, alternatively, it rests on a faith, as one optimistic observer has put it, that "local

---

[40] Peter Nolan, "Politics, Planning and the Transition from Central Planning in China" (Cambridge University, unpublished paper), cited in Ajit Singh, "The Plan, the Market and Evolutionary Economic Reform in China," *UNCTAD Discussion Papers*, No. 76 (December 1993), p. 28.

[41] Ellen Meiksins Wood, "From Opportunity to Imperative: The History of the Market," *Monthly Review*, Vol. 46, No. 3 (July–August 1994), p. 39.

democracy can coexist with authoritarianism in high politics."[42] The realization of any of these political hopes seems improbable.

Finally, there is little historical evidence to encourage the belief that small collectivist communities implanted in a wider capitalist environment can, by force of moral or social example, transform the overall social and political structure. Such "utopian socialist" undertakings have been attempted since the mid-nineteenth century. And however noble Owenite, Fourierist, and other experiments have been, they have vanished, leaving few socialist traces.

But arguments for the socialist potential of China's rural industry cannot be dismissed on the basis of Western historical precedents, if only because the sheer human and economic size of the Chinese movement makes most comparisons meaningless. Not enough is known about the social relations of China's rural industrial enterprises to pass quick judgments on their social significance and future direction. In the wake of the failures of statist socialist projects, minds should be open to alternative socialist possibilities, however much they might clash with the dogmas of the past. The continuing Chinese experiment in rural industrialization deserves the most serious and sympathetic consideration, especially since its most ardent advocates represent one of the few genuinely democratic socialist currents in the contemporary politics of the People's Republic. At the very least, infusing village and township enterprises with some degree of socialist and democratic content might mitigate the social ravages of the market, even if it is unlikely to halt the frenzied forces of capitalist development unleashed by the Dengist state.

The township and village industries are a "socialist survival" of sorts. Although most of the extraordinary growth of this sector of the rural economy occurred during the Deng era, and while the TVEs might well appear to some as a form of proto-industrialization preceding the emergence of large-scale capitalist industry, it should be recalled that rural industrialization was originally a distinctively Maoist policy. It was introduced during the Great Leap Forward, and revived during the Cultural Revolution, with the announced aim of narrowing the differences between worker and peasant, and between

---

[42] Cui, "China's Rural Industrialization," p. 29.

town and countryside.[43] Whatever the ultimate social role and fate of the TVEs, it is inconceivable that rural industrialization could have taken place on the scale that it has in China, and in a partly collectivist mold, in the "normal" course of a capitalist economy developing out of a feudal (or other precapitalist) social formation.

There are other socialist survivals that need to be taken into account in considering the social future of China. Among these there must be mentioned the most heroic and massive of modern revolutionary traditions forged in the 1930s and 1940s, and still celebrated as "the Yan'an spirit." Another socialist legacy is the century-long effort by the Chinese intelligentsia to avoid the social evils of capitalism. Further, there is a Chinese population who until very recently was schooled in egalitarian and cooperative values, values that periodically have been recalled in the post-Mao era during times of socioeconomic distress and political upheaval. And more tangibly but perhaps more dubiously socialist, there remains a very sizable and crucial state industrial sector (which is by no means a "dinosaur," as the popular press habitually describes it),[44] along with a significant degree of central planning.

But these are remnants of a quasi-socialist past, not necessarily harbingers of a socialist future. They are remnants that float in what

---

[43] "Don't crowd into the cities. Vigorously develop industry in the countryside and turn peasants into workers on the spot," was Mao Zedong's 1961 dictum on rural industrialization. "Reading Notes on the Soviet Union's 'Political Economy,'" *Mao Zedong sixiang wansui* (Taipei, 1969), pp. 389–90. At the time, however, most of the rural industries that had been established during the Great Leap were being abolished by Liu Shaoqi's policies designed to revive and recentralize the economy to overcome the grave economic crisis into which the Great Leap had degenerated. Rural industry was revived and expanded in the late 1960s and early 1970s, with considerable success, according to most accounts. On the Great Leap Forward origins of China's rural industrialization, see Philip Huang's perceptive account in *The Peasant Family and Rural Development in the Yangzi Delta, 1350–1988* (Stanford: Stanford University Press, 1990). On the 1970s, see Perkins (ed.), *Rural Small-Scale Industry in the People's Republic of China.*

[44] State enterprises produced about 50 percent of industrial output in the early 1990s, having surrendered about 40 percent of the output to TVEs (the "collective" sector) and an additional 10 percent to private and foreign firms. However, the growth in the nonstate sector has come almost entirely at the expense of inefficient small-scale state enterprises. Large state enterprises, not TVEs, are at the forefront of technological innovation, and for the most part they operate efficiently. Virtually all of the "losses" in state industry come from deliberately set low prices in energy industries, such as oil and coal. Singh, "The Plan . . . ," pp. 25, 30. There is nothing particularly socialist about large state industries, most of which are now organized in huge conglomerates that operate in capitalist fashion.

has become a capitalist sea, into which the Beijing government enjoins citizens and even its own officials to plunge.[45] It is, to be sure, a capitalism with a strong bureaucratic character, and one that is state-promoted. Chinese capitalism is also an undeveloped capitalism, in the sense that new bourgeois social relationships have yet to be fully rooted in private property. But it is capitalism nonetheless, with all of its economic dynamism and its social destructiveness, tearing apart existing society through simultaneous processes of embourgeoisement and proletarianization, drowning all that was once sacred in "the icy water of egotistical calculation," and leaving no god save the worship of money. It now seems inevitable that China will have to experience all the vicissitudes of capitalism before the Chinese people can once again conceive a realistic vision of socialism.

That such a process of capitalist development could be presided over by a Communist Party seems incongruous. But behind that apparent incongruity there operates a certain political logic and social rationality. For it was the Communist Party-state whose "market adjustment" policies in the late 1970s, deemed necessary at the time for the modernization of the nation and the Party's own political survival, produced contemporary Chinese capitalism in the first place. It was the Communist state that created the rural and urban entrepreneurial elites required to operate a market economy. Perhaps most important, and least incongruous, is that Party-state bureaucracies and individual Communist bureaucrats have become directly involved in the workings of Chinese capitalism and derive the greatest benefits from it.

During the Mao period the Communist state stood as an obstacle to both socialism and capitalism, leaving China suspended as a "post-revolutionary society," in a misty realm that was neither socialist nor capitalist. In the Deng Xiaoping era the Communist state remained a formidable obstacle to socialism—but obviously no longer to capitalism.

Yet the Communist state has not become irrelevant because of the development of a capitalist economy, as is widely supposed. Rather, the Communist political structure is eminently functional,

---

[45] *Xiahai*, or "plunge into the sea" is a popular expression for going into private business.

logically serving as the protector of the capitalist system and the bourgeois classes it created. In China today, the coercion of the market is enforced by a repressive state apparatus, whose functions include the disciplining of the workforce and keeping social conflicts within bounds. Such is the typical role of the state in a capitalist economy. The only real incongruity is that Chinese state leaders still claim a socialist legitimacy in addition to their eminently well-deserved nationalist one.

China's socialist future, if there is to be one, will not evolve from the existing sociopolitical system but rather in popular resistance to it. It will come not as a result of the maturation of the reformed economy, as the regime still vaguely promises, but in a democratic struggle against the social consequences of capitalism. Socialism is the natural historic antagonist of capitalism, and it is likely that movements of resistance to the Chinese Communist dictatorship will assume both a socialist and a democratic character.

Any viable movement for democratic socialist change must ultimately be rooted in the proletariat. For China is now an industrialized country, no longer a predominantly agrarian land, with industrial production accounting for more than 80 percent of the value of total national output.

Such a socialist movement inevitably will involve conflict with the Communist state, for Chinese capitalism is inextricably bound up with the state and its repressive bureaucratic organs. The conflict, should it come, is not likely to be a peaceful one, for so many of the bureaucrats and the bureaucratic agencies of the Communist regime have a direct economic stake in the existing capitalist order of things. In China, in contrast to Russia and Eastern Europe, Communism and capitalism are irrevocably intertwined, and they will henceforth stand or fall together. This is the strange and paradoxical case because of the relative success of the post-Mao regime's market reforms, which fatally linked a capitalist market economy to a Stalinist bureaucratic apparatus.

BIBLIOGRAPHY

NEWSPAPERS AND PERIODICALS

Asian Survey
Australian Journal of Chinese Affairs
Beijing Review
Bulletin of Concerned Asian Scholars
Cheng Ming
Chicago Tribune
China Daily
China Focus
China Labour Bulletin
China News Digest
The China Quarterly
China Trade Report
Chinese Law and Government
Chinese Sociology and Anthropology
Contemporary China
Daily Report, People's Republic of China, Foreign Broadcast Information Service
    (FBIS)
Economic Research
Far Eastern Economic Review
Historical Research
Hongqi (Red Flag)
The Independent (London)
Index on Censorship
Inside China Mainland
International Herald Tribune

Issues and Studies
Joint Research Publication Service (JPRS)
Journal of Asian Studies
Journal of Contemporary Asia
Los Angeles Times
Ming Bao
Modern China
Monthly Review
National Review
New Left Review
The New York Review of Books
The New York Times
Pacific Affairs
Philosophic Research
Renmin Ribao (People's Daily)
Seventies Monthly (Hong Kong)
Theory and Society
The Wall Street Journal
The Washington Post
Wenhuibao
Wisconsin State Journal
World Development

BOOKS

Andors, Phyllis. *The Unfinished Liberation of Chinese Women*. Bloomington, Indiana: Indiana University Press, 1983.

Bahro, Rudolf. *The Alternative in Eastern Europe*. London: Verso, 1981.

Balazs, Etienne. *Chinese Civilization and Bureaucracy*. New Haven, Conn.: Yale University Press, 1964.

Banister, Judith. *China's Changing Population*. Stanford: Stanford University Press, 1987.

Barmé, Geremie and John Miniford, eds. *Seeds of Fire: Chinese Voices of Conscience*. New York: Hill and Wang, 1989.

Baum, Richard, ed. *China's Four Modernizations: The New Technological Revolution*. Boulder, Co.: Westview Press, 1980.

Bergère, Marie-Claire. *The Golden Age of the Chinese Bourgeoisie, 1911–1937*. Cambridge: Cambridge University Press, 1989.

Bialer, Seweryn. *Stalin's Successors: Leadership, Stability and Change in the Soviet Union*. New York: Cambridge University Press, 1980.

Bowie, Robert R. and John K. Fairbank, eds. *Communist China 1955–1959: Policy Documents*. Cambridge: Harvard University Press, 1962.

Brinton, Crane. *The Anatomy of Revolution*. New York: Vintage, 1965.

Brugger, Bill, ed. *China Since the Gang of Four*. New York: St. Martin's, 1980.

Butterfield, Fox. *China, Alive in the Bitter Sea*. New York: Times Books, 1982.

Chan, Anita, Richard Madsen and Jonathan Unger. *Chen Village: The Recent History of a Peasant Community in Mao's China.* Berkeley: University of California Press, 1984.

Chen Duxiu. *Shehui zhuyi taolun ji* (Collection of Discussions on Socialism). Canton, 1922.

————. *Zhongguo keming wendi lunwenji* (A Collection of Articles on Problems of the Chinese Revolution). Shanghai, 1927.

Chen, Jerome, ed. *Mao Papers: Anthology and Bibliography.* London: Oxford University Press, 1970.

Cheng, Chu-yuan. *China's Economic Development: Growth and Structural Change.* Boulder, Co.: Westview Press, 1982.

Chi Hsin. *The Case of the Gang of Four.* Hong Kong: Cosmos Books, 1977.

China's Statistical Yearbook, 1984. Beijing, 1984.

Ci, Jiwei. *Dialectic of the Chinese Revolution: From Utopianism to Hedonism.* Stanford: Stanford University Press, 1994.

Croll, Elisabeth. *Chinese Women Since Mao.* London: Zed Books, 1983.

————. *Feminism and Socialism in China.* London: Routledge & Kegan Paul, 1978.

Decision of the Central Committee of the Chinese Communist Party Concerning the Great Proletarian Cultural Revolution. Peking: Foreign Languages Press, 1966.

Deng Xiaoping. *Fundamental Issues in Present-Day China.* Beijing: Foreign Languages Press, 1987.

————. *Selected Works of Deng Xiaoping.* Beijing: Foreign Languages Press, 1984.

Deutscher, Isaac. *The Unfinished Revolution: Russia, 1917–1967.* London: Oxford University Press, 1967.

Dirlik, Arif. *The Origins of Chinese Communism.* New York: Oxford University Press, 1989.

———— and Maurice Meisner, eds. *Marxism and the Chinese Experience: Issues in Chinese Socialism.* Armonk, N.Y.: M. E. Sharpe, 1989.

Dittmer, Lowell. *Liu Shao-ch'i and the Chinese Cultural Revolution.* Berkeley: University of California Press, 1974.

Documents of the Thirteenth National Congress of the Communist Party of China (1987). Beijing: Foreign Languages Press, 1987.

Draper, Hal. *Karl Marx's Theory of Revolution.* Volume I, *State and Bureaucracy.* New York: Monthly Review Press, 1977.

Dugger, Ronnie. *On Reagan: The Man and His Presidency.* New York: McGraw-Hill, 1983.

Eighth National Congress of the Communist Party of China, Volumes I and II. Peking: Foreign Languages Press, 1956.

Evans, Peter. *Dependent Development: The Alliance of Multinational, State and Local Capital in Brazil.* Princeton: Princeton University Press, 1979.

Fang Lizhi. *Bringing Down the Great Wall.* New York: Norton, 1992.

Fei Hsiao-tung. *China's Gentry: Essays in Urban-Rural Relations.* Chicago: University of Chicago Press, 1953.

Feigon, Lee. *China Rising.* Chicago: Ivan R. Dee, 1990.

Feuerwerker, Albert. *China's Early Industrialization.* Cambridge: Harvard University Press, 1958.

Galbraith, John Kenneth. *The Culture of Contentment.* Boston: Houghton Mifflin, 1992.

Gargan, Edward A. *China's Fate: A People's Turbulent Struggle with Reform and Repression.* New York: Doubleday, 1991.

Garside, Roger. *Coming Alive: China After Mao.* New York: Mentor, 1982.

Gittings, John. *China Changes Face.* New York: Oxford University Press, 1990.

Goldman, Merle. *Sowing the Seeds of Democracy in China: Political Reform in the Deng Xiaoping Era.* Cambridge: Harvard University Press, 1994.

Han Minzhu, ed. *Cries for Democracy: Writings and Speeches from the 1989 Chinese Democracy Movement.* Princeton: Princeton University Press, 1990.

Harding, Harry. *China's Second Revolution: Reform After Mao.* Washington, D.C.: Brookings Institution, 1987.

Heilbroner, Robert L. *The Nature and Logic of Capitalism.* New York: Norton, 1985.

Hinton, William. *The Great Reversal.* New York: Monthly Review Press, 1990.

————. *Shenfan.* New York: Random House, 1983.

Hobsbawm, Eric. *The Age of Extremes: A History of the World, 1914–1991.* New York: Pantheon, 1994.

Hopkins, Terrence K. and Immanuel Wallerstein, eds. *Processes of the World-System.* Beverly Hills, Calif.: Sage Publications, 1980.

Huang, Philip C. *The Peasant Family and Rural Development in the Yangzi Delta, 1350–1988.* Stanford: Stanford University Press, 1990.

Isaacs, Harold. *The Tragedy of the Chinese Revolution.* New York: Atheneum, 1966.

Israel, John and Donald W. Klein. *Rebels and Bureaucrats: China's December 9ers.* Berkeley: University of California Press, 1976.

Joffe, Ellis. *The Chinese Army After Mao.* Cambridge: Harvard University Press, 1987.

Johnson, Chalmers. *Peasant Nationalism and Communist Power.* Stanford: Stanford University Press, 1962.

Johnson, Kay Ann. *Women, the Family, and Peasant Revolution in China.* Chicago: University of Chicago Press, 1983.

Joint Economic Committee of the United States Congress. *China: A Reassessment of the Economy.* Washington, D.C., 1975.

Joseph, William. *The Critique of Ultra-leftism in China, 1958–1981.* Stanford: Stanford University Press, 1984.

Kau, Michael Ying-Mao and Susan H. Marsh, eds. *China in the Era of Deng Xiaoping: A Decade of Reform.* Armonk, N.Y.: M. E. Sharpe, 1993.

Kautsky, Karl. *The Class Struggle.* Chicago: Kerr, 1910.

Kraus, Richard Curt. *Class Conflict in Chinese Socialism.* New York: Columbia University Press, 1981.

Kung, Chi-keung. "Intellectuals and Masses: The Case of Qu Qiubai," unpublished dissertation, University of Wisconsin–Madison, 1995.

Kuznets, Simon. *Economic Growth of Nations: Total Output and Production Structure.* Cambridge: Harvard University Press, 1971.

Lardy, Nicholas R. *Agriculture in China's Modern Economic Development.* Cambridge: Cambridge University Press, 1983.

————— and Kenneth Lieberthal, eds. *Chen Yun's Strategy for China's Development: A Non-Maoist Alternative*. Armonk, N.Y.: M. E. Sharpe, 1983.

Lee, Bennett and Geremie Barmé, eds. *The Wounded: New Stories of the Cultural Revolution*. Hong Kong: Joint Publishing Co., 1979.

Lee, Hong Yung. *From Revolutionary Cadres to Technocrats in Socialist China*. Berkeley: University of California Press, 1991.

—————. *The Politics of the Chinese Cultural Revolution*. Berkeley: University of California Press, 1978.

Lenin, V. I. *Collected Works*. 45 volumes. Moscow: Foreign Languages Publishing House, 1946–67.

—————. *Selected Works*, Volume 2. Moscow: Foreign Languages Publishing House, 1950.

Lewis, John W., ed. *The City in Communist China*. Stanford: Stanford University Press, 1971.

—————. *Party Leadership and Revolutionary Power in China*. London: Cambridge University Press, 1970.

Liang Heng and Judith Shapiro. *Son of the Revolution*. New York: Alfred A. Knopf, 1983.

The Limits of Reform in China. Washington, D.C.: East Asia Program, The Wilson Center, 1981.

Link, Perry, ed. *Roses and Thorns: The Second Blooming of a Hundred Flowers in Chinese Fiction, 1979–1980*. Berkeley: University of California Press, 1984.

Lippit, Victor D. *The Economic Development of China*. Armonk, N.Y.: M. E. Sharpe, 1987.

Liu Binyan. *China's Crisis, China's Hope*. Cambridge: Harvard University Press, 1990.

—————, with Ruan Ming and Xu Gang. *Tell the World*. New York: Pantheon, 1989.

Liu Shao-ch'i. *Collected Works of Liu Shao-ch'i*. Hong Kong: Union Research Institute, 1968.

Luxemburg, Rosa. *Rosa Luxemburg Speaks*. Mary-Alice Waters, ed. New York: Pathfinder Press, 1970.

—————. *The Russian Revolution and Leninism or Marxism?* Ann Arbor: University of Michigan Press, 1961.

Ma Hong and Sun Shangqing, eds. *Studies in the Problems of China's Economic Structure*. Beijing, 1981. JPRS-CEA-84-064-1.

Mandel, Ernest. *Power and Money: A Marxist Theory of Bureaucracy*. London: Verso, 1992.

Mao Zedong. *The Chinese Revolution and the Chinese Communist Party* (1939). Peking: Foreign Languages Press, 1954.

—————. *A Critique of Soviet Economics*. New York: Monthly Review Press, 1977.

—————. *Mao Zedong Sixiang Wansui* (Long Live the Thought of Mao Tse-tung), 2 volumes. Taipei, 1967, 1969.

—————. *On the Correct Handling of Contradictions Among the People*. Peking: Foreign Languages Press, 1957.

—————. *Selected Works of Mao Tse-tung*, Volume 1. London: Lawrence & Wishart, 1954.

————. *Selected Works of Mao Tse-tung*, Volumes I–V. Peking: Foreign Languages Press, 1961, 1967, 1977.

Marx, Karl. *Capital*, Volume I. Chicago: Kerr, 1906.

————. *Economic and Philosophic Manuscripts of 1844*. Moscow: Foreign Languages Publishing House, 1956.

————. *Grundisse*, translated by Martin Nicolaus. New York: Vintage, 1973.

————. *Selected Writings in Sociology and Social Philosophy*. T. B. Bottomore and Maximilien Rubel, eds. London: Watts, 1956.

———— and Frederick Engels. *Selected Works*. Moscow: Foreign Languages Publishing House, 1953.

Meek, Ronald. *Studies in the Labour Theory of Value*. London: Lawrence & Wishart, 1956.

Meisner, Maurice. *Mao's China and After*. New York: The Free Press, 1986.

————. *Marxism, Maoism, and Utopianism*. Madison: University of Wisconsin Press, 1982.

Moore, Barrington. *Social Origins of Dictatorship and Democracy*. Boston: Beacon Press, 1966.

Morse, Ronald A., ed. *The Limits of Reform in China*. Boulder, Co.: Westview Press, 1983.

Murphy, Rhoads. *The Fading of the Maoist Vision*. New York: Methuen, 1980.

Nathan, Andrew. *China's Crisis*. New York: Columbia University Press, 1990.

————. *Chinese Democracy*. Berkeley: University of California Press, 1985.

Nee, Victor and David Mozingo, eds. *State and Society in Contemporary China*. Ithaca: Cornell University Press, 1983.

Nee, Victor and James Peck, eds. *China's Uninterrupted Revolution: From 1840 to the Present*. New York: Pantheon, 1975.

On the Historical Experience of the Dictatorship of the Proletariat. Peking: Foreign Languages Press, 1961.

Pepper, Suzanne. *China's Universities: Post-Mao Enrollment Policies and Their Impact on the Structure of Secondary Education: A Research Report*. Ann Arbor: Center for Chinese Studies, University of Michigan, 1984.

Perkins, Dwight H., ed. *Rural Small-Scale Industry in the People's Republic of China*. Berkeley: University of California Press, 1977.

Perry, Elizabeth and Christine Wong, eds. *The Political Economy of Reform in Post-Mao China*. Cambridge: Harvard University Press, 1985.

Pickowicz, Paul. *Marxist Literary Thought in China: The Influence of Ch'u Chiu-pai*. Berkeley: University of California Press, 1981.

Piriyarangsan, Sungsidh. *Thai Bureaucratic Capitalism, 1932–1960*. Bangkok: Chulalongkorn University Social Research Institute, 1983.

Polanyi, Karl. *The Great Transformation*. Boston: Beacon Press, 1957.

Richman, Barry M. *Industrial Society in Communist China*. New York: Random House, 1969.

Riskin, Carl. *China's Political Economy: The Quest for Development Since 1949*. New York: Oxford University Press, 1987.

Rostow, W. W. *The Stages of Economic Growth: A Non-Communist Manifesto*. Cambridge: Cambridge University Press, 1960.

Rozman, Gilbert, ed. *The Modernization of China*. New York: The Free Press, 1981.

Saich, Tony, ed. *The Chinese People's Movement: Perspectives on Spring 1989*. Armonk, N.Y.: M. E. Sharpe, 1990.

Schell, Orville. *To Get Rich Is Glorious*. New York: Pantheon, 1985.

Schram, Stuart R. *Ideology and Policy in China Since the Third Plenum, 1978–1984*. London: Contemporary China Institute, School of Oriental and African Studies, University of London, 1984.

———. *The Political Thought of Mao Tse-tung*. New York: Praeger, 1969.

———, ed. *Mao Tse-tung Unrehearsed: Talks and Letters, 1956–71*. Middlesex, England: Penguin Books, 1974.

Schurmann, Franz. *Ideology and Organization in Communist China*. Berkeley: University of California Press, 1968.

Schwartz, Benjamin I. *Chinese Communism and the Rise of Mao*. Cambridge: Harvard University Press, 1951.

———. *Communism and China: Ideology in Flux*. Cambridge: Harvard University Press, 1968.

Selden, Mark. *The Political Economy of Chinese Development*. Armonk, N.Y.: M. E. Sharpe, 1993.

———. *The Yenan Way in Revolutionary China*. Cambridge: Harvard University Press, 1971.

———, ed. *The People's Republic of China: A Documentary History of Revolutionary Change*. New York: Monthly Review Press, 1979.

——— and Victor Lippit, eds. *The Transition to Socialism in China*. Armonk, N.Y.: M. E. Sharpe, 1982.

Seymour, James, ed. *The Fifth Modernization: China's Human Rights Movement, 1978–1979*. Stanfordville, N.Y.: Human Rights Publishing Group, 1980.

Shanin, Teodor, ed. *Late Marx and the Russian Road*. New York: Monthly Review Press, 1983.

Shue, Vivienne. *Peasant China in Transition*. Berkeley: University of California Press, 1980.

———. *The Reach of the State*. Stanford: Stanford University Press, 1988.

Sigurdson, Jon. *Rural Industrialization in China*. Cambridge: Harvard East Asian Monographs, 1977.

Singh, Ajit. "The Plan, the Market and Evolutionary Economic Reform in China," *UNCTAD Discussion Papers*, no. 76, December 1993.

Siu, Helen F. and Zelda Stern, eds. *Mao's Harvest*. New York: Oxford University Press, 1983.

Skocpol, Theda. *State and Social Revolutions: A Comparative Analysis of France, Russia, and China*. Cambridge: Cambridge University Press, 1979.

Smil, Vaclav. *China's Environmental Crisis*. Armonk, N.Y.: M. E. Sharpe, 1993.

Spence, Jonathan D. *The Gate of Heavenly Peace: The Chinese and Their Revolution, 1895–1980*. New York: Viking, 1981.

———. *The Search for Modern China*. New York: Norton, 1990.

Stalin, Joseph. *Economic Problems of Socialism in the U.S.S.R.* Moscow: Foreign Languages Publishing House, 1952.

Starr, John Bryan. *Continuing the Revolution: The Political Thought of Mao*. Princeton, N.J.: Princeton University Press, 1979.

State Statistical Bureau, People's Republic of China. *Main Indicators, Development of the National Economy of the People's Republic of China (1949–1978)*. Beijing, 1979.

———. *State Statistical Yearbook*.

Stavis, Benedict. *The Politics of Agricultural Mechanization in China*. Ithaca, N.Y.: Cornell University Press, 1978.

Su Shaozhi et. al. *Marxism in China*. Nottingham: Spokesman, 1983.

Sullivan, Michael. "Mao Zedong's Theory of Continuing the Revolution: Ideology and Policy Disputation During the Transition to the Post-Mao Era, 1974–78," unpublished dissertation, The Flinders University of South Australia, 1993, 3 volumes.

Sun, Yan. *The Chinese Reassessment of Socialism, 1976–1992*. Princeton: Princeton University Press, 1995.

Sweezy, Paul M. *Post-Revolutionary Society*. New York: Monthly Review Press, 1980.

Tang Tsou. *The Cultural Revolution and Post-Mao Reforms*. Chicago: University of Chicago Press, 1986.

Terrill, Ross. *The Future of China After Mao*. New York: Dell, 1978.

———. *The White-Boned Demon*. New York: Morrow, 1984.

Thompson, E. P. *The Making of the English Working Class*. New York: Pantheon, 1964.

Tucker, Robert C. *The Marxian Revolutionary Idea*. New York: Norton, 1969.

Twitchett, Denis and John K. Fairbank, eds. *The Cambridge History of China*. New York: Cambridge University Press, 1978-1991.

Ulam, Adam. *The Unfinished Revolution: An Essay on the Sources of Influence of Marxism and Communism*. New York: Vintage, 1964.

Unger, Jonathan. *Education Under Mao: Class and Competition in Canton Schools*. New York: Columbia University Press, 1982.

———, ed. *The Pro-Democracy Protests in China: Reports from the Provinces*. Armonk, N.Y.: M. E. Sharpe, 1991.

United States Central Intelligence Agency. *China: Economic Performance in 1987 and Outlook for 1988*. Washington, D.C.: Directorate of Intelligence, EA88-10018, May 1988.

———. *The Chinese Economy in 1988 and 1989*. Washington, D.C.: Directorate of Intelligence, August 1989.

———. *People's Republic of China: Handbook of Economic Indicators*. Washington, D.C., 1976.

United States Department of Commerce. *The Chinese Economy and Foreign Trade Perspectives*. Washington, D.C., 1977.

Vogel, Ezra. *Canton Under Communism*. Cambridge: Harvard University Press, 1969.

———. *One Step Ahead in China: Guangdong Under Reform*. Cambridge: Harvard University Press, 1989.

Wakeman, Frederic Jr. *The Fall of Imperial China*. New York: The Free Press, 1975.

Walder, Andrew. *Communist Neo-Traditionalism: Work and Authority in Chinese Industry*. Berkeley: University of California Press, 1986.

Walicki, A. *The Controversy Over Capitalism*. Oxford: Clarendon Press, 1969.

Wallerstein, Immanuel. *The Capitalist World-Economy*. Cambridge: Cambridge University Press, 1979.

Wang Xizhe. *Wang Xizhe Lunwen Ji* (Collected Essays of Wang Xizhe). Hong Kong: The Seventies Magazine Press, 1981.

White, Gordon. *Riding the Tiger: The Politics of Economic Reform in Post-Mao China*. Stanford: Stanford University Press, 1993.

Wolf, Eric. *Europe and the People Without History*. Berkeley: University of California Press, 1982.

Woo, Jung-en. *Race to the Swift: State and Finance in Korea's Industrialization*. New York: Columbia University Press, 1991.

Wood, Ellen Meiksins. *Democracy Against Capitalism*. Cambridge: Cambridge University Press, 1995.

Wright, Mary C., ed. *China in Revolution: The First Phase, 1900–1913*. New Haven, Conn.: Yale University Press, 1968.

Xu Dixin et. al. *China's Search for Economic Growth*. Beijing: New World Press, 1982.

Xue Muqiao, ed. *Almanac of China's Economy, 1981*. Hong Kong: Modern Cultural Co., 1982.

Young, Marilyn B. *The Vietnam Wars 1945–1990*. New York: HarperCollins, 1991.

Yu Guangyuan, ed. *China's Socialist Modernization*. Beijing: Foreign Languages Press, 1984.

Yu, Mok Chiu and J. Frank Harrison, eds. *Voices from Tiananmen Square*. Montreal: Black Rose Books, 1990.

INDEX